Third Workshop on Neural Generation and Translation (WNGT 2019)

Hong Kong, China
4 November 2019

ISBN: 978-1-7138-0072-9

Printed from e-media with permission by:

Curran Associates, Inc.
57 Morehouse Lane
Red Hook, NY 12571

Some format issues inherent in the e-media version may also appear in this print version.

Copyright© (2019) by the Association for Computational Linguistics
All rights reserved.

Printed with permission by Curran Associates, Inc. (2020)

For permission requests, please contact the Association for Computational Linguistics
at the address below.

Association for Computational Linguistics
209 N. Eighth Street
Stroudsburg, Pennsylvania 18360

Phone: 1-570-476-8006
Fax: 1-570-476-0860

acl@aclweb.org

Additional copies of this publication are available from:

Curran Associates, Inc.
57 Morehouse Lane
Red Hook, NY 12571 USA
Phone: 845-758-0400
Fax: 845-758-2633
Email: curran@proceedings.com
Web: www.proceedings.com

EMNLP-IJCNLP 2019

Neural Generation and Translation

Proceedings of the Third Workshop

November 4, 2019
Hong Kong, China

©2019 The Association for Computational Linguistics

Apple and the Apple logo are trademarks of Apple Inc., registered in the U.S. and other countries.

Introduction

Welcome to the Third Workshop on Neural Generation and Translation. This workshop aims to cultivate research on the leading edge in neural machine translation and other aspects of machine translation, generation, and multilinguality that utilize neural models. In this year's workshop we are extremely pleased to be able to host four invited talks from leading lights in the field, namely: Michael Auli, Mohit Bansal, Mirella Lapata and Jason Weston. In addition this year's workshop will feature a session devoted to a new shared task on efficient machine translation. We received a total of 68 submissions, from which we accepted 36. There were three crosssubmissions, seven long abstracts and 26 full papers. There were also seven system submission papers. All research papers were reviewed twice through a double blind review process, and avoiding conflicts of interest. The workshop had an acceptance rate of 53%. Due to the large number of invited talks, and to encourage discussion, only the two papers selected for best paper awards will be presented orally, and the remainder will be presented in a single poster session. We would like to thank all authors for their submissions, and the program committee members for their valuable efforts in reviewing the papers for the workshop. We would also like to thank Google and Apple for their generous sponsorship.

Organizers:

Alexandra Birch, (Edinburgh)
Andrew Finch, (Apple)
Hiroaki Hayashi (CMU)
Ioannis Konstas (Heriot Watt University)
Thang Luong, (Google)
Graham Neubig, (CMU)
Yusuke Oda, (Google)
Katsuhito Sudoh (NAIST)

Program Committee:

Roee Aharoni
Antonio Valerio Miceli Barone
Joost Bastings
Marine Carpuat
Daniel Cer
Boxing Chen
Eunah Cho
Li Dong
Nan Du
Kevin Duh
Ondřej Dušek
Markus Freitag
Claire Gardent
Ulrich Germann
Isao Goto
Edward Grefenstette
Roman Grundkiewicz
Jiatao Gu
Barry Haddow
Vu Cong Duy Hoang
Daphne Ippolito
Sébastien Jean
Hidetaka Kamigaito

Shumpei Kubosawa
Sneha Kudugunta
Lemao Liu
Shujie Liu
Hongyin Luo
Benjamin Marie
Sebastian J. Mielke
Hideya Mino
Makoto Morishita
Preslav Nakov
Vivek Natarajan
Laura Perez-Beltrachini
Vinay Rao
Alexander Rush
Chinnadhurai Sankar
Rico Sennrich
Raphael Shu
Akihiro Tamura
Rui Wang
Xiaolin Wang
Taro Watanabe
Sam Wiseman
Biao Zhang

Invited Speakers:

Michael Auli (Facebook AI Research)
Mohit Bansal (University of North Carolina)
Nanyun Peng (University of Southern California)
Jason Weston (Facebook AI Research)

Table of Contents

Workshop Program

Poster Session

Findings of the Third Workshop on
Neural Generation and Translation

Hiroaki Hayashi$^\diamond$, Yusuke Oda$^\clubsuit$, Alexandra Birch$^\spadesuit$, Ioannis Konstas$^\triangle$,
Andrew Finch$^\heartsuit$, Minh-Thang Luong$^\clubsuit$, Graham Neubig$^\diamond$, Katsuhito Sudoh*

$^\diamond$Carnegie Mellon University, $^\clubsuit$Google Brain, $^\spadesuit$University of Edinburgh
$^\triangle$Heriot-Watt University, $^\heartsuit$Apple, *Nara Institute of Science and Technology

Abstract

This document describes the findings of the Third Workshop on Neural Generation and Translation, held in concert with the annual conference of the Empirical Methods in Natural Language Processing (EMNLP 2019). First, we summarize the research trends of papers presented in the proceedings. Second, we describe the results of the two shared tasks 1) efficient neural machine translation (NMT) where participants were tasked with creating NMT systems that are both accurate and efficient, and 2) document generation and translation (DGT) where participants were tasked with developing systems that generate summaries from structured data, potentially with assistance from text in another language.

1 Introduction

Neural sequence to sequence models (Kalchbrenner and Blunsom, 2013; Sutskever et al., 2014; Bahdanau et al., 2015) are now a workhorse behind a wide variety of different natural language processing tasks such as machine translation, generation, summarization and simplification. The 3rd Workshop on Neural Machine Translation and Generation (WNGT 2019) provided a forum for research in applications of neural models to machine translation and other language generation tasks (including summarization (Rush et al., 2015), NLG from structured data (Wen et al., 2015), dialog response generation (Vinyals and Le, 2015), among others). Overall, the workshop was held with two goals.

First, it aimed to synthesize the current state of knowledge in neural machine translation and generation: this year we continued to encourage submissions that not only advance the state of the art through algorithmic advances, but also analyze and understand the current state of the art, pointing to future research directions. Towards this

goal, we received a number of high-quality research contributions on both workshop topics, as summarized in Section 2.

Second, the workshop aimed to expand the research horizons in NMT: we continued to organize the Efficient NMT task which encouraged participants to develop not only accurate but computationally efficient systems. In addition, we organized a new shared task on "Document-level Generation and Translation", which aims to push forward document-level generation technology and contrast the methods for different types of inputs. The results of the shared task are summarized in Sections 3 and 4.

2 Summary of Research Contributions

We published a call for long papers, extended abstracts for preliminary work, and cross-submissions of papers submitted to other venues. The goal was to encourage discussion and interaction with researchers from related areas.

We received a total of 68 submissions, from which we accepted 36. There were three cross-submissions, seven long abstracts and 26 full papers. There were also seven system submission papers. All research papers were reviewed twice through a double blind review process, and avoiding conflicts of interest.

There were 22 papers with an application to generation of some kind, and 14 for translation which is a switch from previous workshops where the focus was on machine translation. The caliber of the publications was very high and the number has more than doubled from last year (16 accepted papers from 25 submissions).

Proceedings of the 3rd Workshop on Neural Generation and Translation (WNGT 2019), pages 1–14
Hong Kong, China, November 4, 2019. ©2019 Association for Computational Linguistics
www.aclweb.org/anthology/D19-56%2d

3 Shared Task: Document-level Generation and Translation

The first shared task at the workshop focused on document-level generation and translation. Many recent attempts at NLG have focused on sentence-level generation (Lebret et al., 2016; Gardent et al., 2017). However, real world language generation applications tend to involve generation of much larger amount of text such as dialogues or multi-sentence summaries. The inputs to NLG systems also vary from structured data such as tables (Lebret et al., 2016) or graphs (Wang et al., 2018), to textual data (Nallapati et al., 2016). Because of such difference in data and domain, comparison between different methods has been non-trivial. This task aims to (1) push forward such document-level generation technology by providing a testbed, and (2) examine the differences between generation based on different types of inputs including both structured data and translations in another language.

In particular, we provided the following 6 tracks which focus on different input/output requirements:

- **NLG (Data → En, Data → De):** Generate document summaries in a target language given only structured data.

- **MT (De ↔ En):** Translate documents in the source language to the target language.

- **MT+NLG (Data+En → De, Data+De → En):** Generate document summaries given the structured data and the summaries in another language.

3.1 Evaluation Measures

We employ standard evaluation metrics for data-to-text NLG and MT along two axes:

Textual Accuracy Measures: We used BLEU (Papineni et al., 2002) and ROUGE (Lin, 2004) as measures for texual accuracy compared to reference summaries.

Content Accuracy Measures: We evaluate the fidelity of the generated content to the input data using relation generation (RG), content selection (CS), and content ordering (CO) metrics (Wiseman et al., 2017).

	Train	Valid	Test
# documents	242	240	241
Avg. # tokens (En)	323	328	329
Avg. # tokens (De)	320	324	325
Vocabulary size (En)	4163	-	-
Vocabulary size (De)	5425	-	-

Table 1: Data statistics of RotoWire English-German Dataset.

The content accuracy measures were calculated using information extraction models trained on respective target languages. We followed (Wiseman et al., 2017) and ensembled 6 information extraction models (3 CNN-based, 3 LSTM-based) with different random seeds for each language.

3.2 Data

Due to the lack of a document-level parallel corpus which provides structured data for each instance, we took an approach of translating an existing NLG dataset. Specifically, we used a subset of the RotoWire dataset (Wiseman et al., 2017) and obtained professional German translations, which are sentence-aligned to the original English articles. The obtained parallel dataset is called the RotoWire English-German dataset, and consists of box score tables, an English article, and its German translation for each instance. Table 1 shows the statistics of the obtained dataset. We used the test split from this dataset to calculate the evaluation measures for all the tracks.

We further allowed the following additional resources for each track:

- NLG: RotoWire, Monolingual

- MT: WMT19, Monolingual

- MT+NLG: RotoWire, WMT19, Monolingual

RotoWire refers to the RotoWire dataset (Wiseman et al., 2017) (train/valid), WMT19 refers to the set of parallel corpora allowable by the WMT 2019 English-German task, and Monolingual refers to monolingual data allowable by the same WMT 2019 task, pre-trained embeddings (*e.g.*, GloVe (Pennington et al., 2014)), pre-trained contextualized embeddings (*e.g.*, BERT (Devlin et al., 2019)), pre-trained language models (*e.g.*, GPT-2 (Radford et al., 2019)).

Systems which follow these resource constraints are marked constrained, otherwise unconstrained. Results are indicated by the initials (C/U).

3.3 Baseline Systems

Considering the difference in inputs for MT and NLG tracks, we prepared two baselines for respective tracks.

FairSeq-19 FairSeq (Ng et al., 2019) was used for MT and MT+NLG tracks for both directions of translations. We used the published WMT'19 single model and did not tune on in-domain data.

NCP+CC: A two-stage model from (Puduppully et al., 2019) was used for NLG tracks. We utilized the pretrained English model trained on RotoWire dataset for English article generation, while the German model was trained on RotoWire English-German dataset.

3.4 Submitted Systems

Four teams, Team EdiNLG, Team FIT-Monash, Team Microsoft, Team Naver Labs Europe, and Team SYSTRAN-AI participated in the shared task. We note the common trends across many teams and discuss the systems of individual teams below. On MT tracks, all the teams have adopted a variant of Transformer (Vaswani et al., 2017) as a sequence transduction model and trained on corpora with different data-augmentation methods. Trained systems were then fine-tuned on in-domain data including our RotoWire English-German dataset. The focus of data augmentation was two-fold: 1) acquiring in-domain data and 2) utilizing document boundaries from existing corpora. Most teams applied back-translation on various sources including NewsCrawl and the original RotoWire dataset for this purpose.

NLG tracks exhibited a similar trend for the sequence model selection, except for Team EdiNLG who employed LSTM.

3.4.1 Team EdiNLG

Team EdiNLG built their NLG system upon (Puduppully et al., 2019) by extending it to further allow copying from the table in addition to generating from vocabulary and the content plan. Additionally, they included features indicating the win/loss team records and team rank in terms of points for each player. They trained the NLG

model for both languages together, using a shared BPE vocabulary obtained from target game summaries and by prefixing the target text with the target language indicator.

For MT and MT+NLG tracks, they mined the in-domain data by extracting basketball-related texts from *Newscrawl* when one of the following conditions are met: 1) player names from the RotoWire English-German training set appear, 2) two NBA team names appear in the same document, or 3) "*NBA*" appears in titles. This resulted in 4.3 and 1.1 million monolingual sentences for English and German, respectively. The obtained sentences were then back-translated and added to the training corpora. They submitted their system **EdiNLG** in all six tracks.

3.4.2 Team FIT-Monash

Team FIT-Monash built a document-level NMT system (Maruf et al., 2019) and participated in MT tracks. The document-level model was initialized with a pre-trained sentence-level NMT model on news domain parallel corpora. Two strategies for composing document-level context were proposed: flat and hierarchical attention. Flat attention was applied on all the sentences, while hierarchical attention was computed at sentence and word-level in a hierarchical manner. Sparse attention was applied at sentence-level in order to identify key sentences that are important for translating the current sentence.

To train a document-level model, the team focused on corpora that have document boundaries, including News Commentary, Rapid, and the RotoWire dataset. Notably, greedy decoding was employed due to computational cost. The submitted system is an ensemble of three runs indicated as **FIT-Monash**.

3.4.3 Team Microsoft

Team Microsoft (MS) developed a Transformer-based NLG system which consists of two sequence-to-sequence models. The two step method was inspired by the approach from (Puduppully et al., 2019), where the first model is a recurrent pointer network that selects encoded records, and the second model takes the selected content representation as input and generates summaries. The proposed model (**MS-End-to-End**) learned both models at the same time with a combined loss function. Additionally, they have investigated the use of pre-trained language models for NLG track. Specifically, they fine-tuned GPT-2 (Radford et al., 2019) on concatenated pairs of (template, target) summaries, while constructing templates following (Wiseman et al., 2017). The two sequences are concatenated around a special token which indicates *"rewrite"*. At decoding time, they adopted nucleus sampling (Holtzman et al., 2019) to enhance the generation quality. Different thresholds for nucleus sampling were investigated, and two systems with different thresholds were submitted: **MS-GPT-50** and **MS-GPT-90**, where the numbers refer to Top-p thresholds.

The generated summaries in English using the following systems were then translated with the MT systems which is described below. Hence, this marks Team Microsoft's German NLG (Data $\rightarrow$ De) submission unconstrained, due to the usage of parallel data beyond the RotoWire English-German dataset.

As for the MT model, a pre-trained system from (Xia et al., 2019) was fine-tuned on the RotoWire English-German dataset, as well as back-translated sentences from the original RotoWire dataset for the English-to-German track. Back-translation of sentences obtained from *Newscrawl* according to the similarity to RotoWire data (Moore and Lewis, 2010) was attempted but did not lead to improvement. The resulting system is shown as **MS** on MT track reports.

3.4.4 Team Naver Labs Europe

Team Naver Labs Europe (NLE) took the approach of transferring the model from MT to NLG. They first trained a sentence-level MT model by iteratively extend the training set from the WMT19 parallel data and RotoWire English-German dataset to back-translated *Newscrawl* data. The best sentence-level model was then fine-tuned at document-level, followed by fine-tuning on the RotoWire English-German dataset (constrained **NLE**) and additionally on the back-translated original RotoWire dataset (unconstrained **NLE**).

To fully leverage the MT model, input record values prefixed with special tokens for record types were sequentially fed in a specific order. Combined with the target summary, the pair of record representations and the target summaries formed data for a sequence-to-sequence model. They fine-tuned their document-level MT model on these NLG data which included the original RotoWire and RotoWire English-German dataset.

The team tackled MT+NLG tracks by concatenating source language documents and the sequence of records as inputs. To encourage the model to use record information more, they randomly masked certain portion of tokens in the source language documents.

3.4.5 Team SYSTRAN-AI

Team SYSTRAN-AI developed their NLG system based on the Transformer (Vaswani et al., 2017). The model takes as input each record from the box score featurized into embeddings and decode the summary. In addition, they introduced a content selection objective where the model learns to predict whether or not each record is used in the summary, comprising a sequence of binary classfication decision.

Furthermore, they performed data augmentation by synthesizing records whose numeric values were randomly changed in a way that does not change the win / loss relation and remains within a sane range. The synthesized records were used to generate a summary to obtain new (record, summary) pairs and were included added the training data. To bias the model toward generating more records, they further fine-tuned their model on a subset of training examples which contain $N(=16)$ records in the summary. The submitted systems are **SYSTRAN-AI** and **SYSTRAN-AI-Detok**, which differ in tokenization.

3.5 Results

We show the results for each track in Table 2 through 7. In the NLG and MT+NLG tasks, we report BLEU, ROUGE (F1) for textual accuracy, RG (P), CS(P, R), and CO (DLD) for content accuracy. While for MT tasks, we only report BLEU. We summarize the shared task results for each track below.

In NLG (En) track, all the participants encouragingly submitted systems outperforming a strong baseline by (Puduppully et al., 2019). We observed an apparent difference between the constrained and unconstrained settings. Team NLE's approach showed that pre-training of the document-level generation model on news corpora is effective even if the source input differs (German text vs linearized records). Among constrained systems, it is worth noting that all the systems but Team EdiNLG used the Transformer, but the result did not show noticeable improvements compared to EdiNLG. It was also shown that the generation using pre-trained language models is sensitive to how the sampling is performed; the results of MS-GPT-90 and MS-GPT-50 differ only in the nucleus sampling hyperparameter, which led to significant differences in every evaluation measure.

The NLG (De) track imposed a greater challenge compared to its English counterpart due to the lack of training data. The scores has generally dropped compared to NLG (En) results. To alleviate the lack of German data, most teams developed systems under unconstrained setting by utilizing MT resources and models. Notably, Team NLE's has achieved similar performance to the constrained system results on NLG (En). However, Team EdiNLG achieved similar performance under the constrained setting by fully leveraging the original RotoWire using the sharing of vocabulary.

In MT tracks, we see the same trend that the system under unconstrained setting (NLE) outperformed all the systems under the constrained setting. The improvement observed in the unconstrained setting came from fine-tuning on the back-translated original RotoWire dataset, which offers purely in-domain parallel documents.

While the results are not directly comparable due to different hyperparameters used in systems, fine-tuning on in-domain parallel sentences was shown effective (FairSeq-19 vs others). When incorporating document-level data, it was shown that document-level models (NLE, FIT-Monash, MS) perform better than sentence-level models (EdiNLG, FairSeq-19), even if a sentence-level model is trained on document-aware corpora.

For MT+NLG tracks, interestingly, no teams found the input structured data useful, thus applying MT models for MT+NLG tracks. Compared to the baseline (FairSeq-19), fine-tuning on in-domain data resulted in better performance overall as seen in the results of Team MS and NLE. The key difference between Team MS and NLE is the existence of document-level fine-tuning, where Team NLE outperformed in terms of textual accuracy (BLEU and ROUGE) overall, in both target languages.

4 Shared Task: Efficient NMT

The second shared task at the workshop focused on efficient neural machine translation. Many MT shared tasks, such as the ones run by the Conference on Machine Translation (Bojar et al., 2017), aim to improve the state of the art for MT with respect to accuracy: finding the most accurate MT system regardless of computational cost. However, in production settings, the efficiency of the implementation is also extremely important. The efficiency shared task for WNGT (inspired by the "small NMT" task at the Workshop on Asian Translation (Nakazawa et al., 2017)) was focused on creating systems for NMT that are not only accurate, but also efficient. Efficiency can include a number of concepts, including memory efficiency and computational efficiency. This task concerns itself with both, and we cover the detail of the evaluation below.

4.1 Evaluation Measures

We used metrics to measure several different aspects connected to how good the system is. These were measured for systems that were run on CPU, and also systems that were run on GPU.

Accuracy Measures: As a measure of translation accuracy, we used BLEU (Papineni et al., 2002) and NIST (Doddington, 2002) scores.

Computational Efficiency Measures: We measured the amount of time it takes to translate the entirety of the test set on CPU or GPU. Time for loading models was measured by having the model translate an empty file, then subtracting this from the total time to translate the test set file.

Memory Efficiency Measures: We measured: (1) the size on disk of the model, (2) the number of parameters in the model, and (3) the peak consumption of the host memory and GPU memory.

These metrics were measured by having participants submit a container for the virtualization environment Docker[1], then measuring from outside the container the usage of computation time and memory. All evaluations were performed on dedicated instances on Amazon Web Services[2], specifically of type `m5.large` for CPU evaluation, and `p3.2xlarge` (with a NVIDIA Tesla V100 GPU).

---

[1]`https://www.docker.com/`
[2]`https://aws.amazon.com/`

System	BLEU	R-1	R-2	R-L	RG	CS (P/R)		CO	Type
EdiNLG	17.01	44.87	18.53	25.38	91.41	30.91	64.13	21.72	C
MS-GPT-90	13.03	45.25	15.17	21.34	88.70	32.84	50.58	17.36	C
MS-GPT-50	15.17	45.34	16.64	22.93	94.35	33.91	53.82	19.30	C
MS-End-to-End	15.03	43.84	17.49	23.86	93.38	32.40	58.02	18.54	C
NLE	20.52	49.38	22.36	27.29	94.08	41.13	54.20	25.64	U
SYSTRAN-AI	17.59	47.76	20.18	25.60	83.22	31.74	44.90	20.73	C
SYSTRAN-AI-Detok	18.32	47.80	20.19	25.61	84.16	34.88	43.29	22.72	C
NCP+CC	15.80	44.83	17.07	23.46	88.59	30.47	55.38	18.31	C

Table 2: Results on the NLG: (Data → **En**) track of DGT task.

System	BLEU	R-1	R-2	R-L	RG	CS (P/R)		CO	Type
EdiNLG	10.95	34.10	12.81	19.70	70.23	23.40	41.83	16.06	C
MS-GPT-90	10.43	41.35	12.59	18.43	75.05	31.23	41.32	16.32	U
MS-GPT-50	11.84	41.51	13.65	19.68	82.79	34.81	42.51	17.12	U
MS-End-to-End	11.66	40.02	14.36	20.67	80.30	28.33	49.13	16.54	U
NLE	16.13	44.27	17.50	23.09	79.47	29.40	54.31	20.62	U
NCP+CC	7.29	29.56	7.98	16.06	49.69	21.61	26.14	11.84	C

Table 3: Results on the NLG: (Data → **De**) track of DGT task.

System	BLEU	Type
FIT-Monash	47.39	C
EdiNLG	41.15	C
MS	57.99	C
NLE	62.16	U
NLE	58.22	C
FairSeq-19	42.91	C

Table 4: DGT results on the MT track (De → En).

System	BLEU	Type
FIT-Monash	41.46	C
EdiNLG	36.85	C
MS	47.90	C
NLE	48.02	C
FairSeq-19	36.26	C

Table 5: DGT results on the MT track (En → De)

4.2 Data

The data used was from the WMT 2014 English-German task (Bojar et al., 2014), using the pre-processed corpus provided by the Stanford NLP Group[3]. Use of other data was prohibited.

4.3 Baseline Systems

Two baseline systems were prepared:

Echo: Just send the input back to the output.

Base: A baseline system using attentional LSTM-based encoder-decoders with attention (Bahdanau et al., 2015).

4.4 Submitted Systems

Two teams, Team Marian and Team Notre Dame submitted to the shared task, and we will summarize each below.

4.4.1 Team Marian

Team Marian's submission (Kim et al., 2019) was based on their submission to the shared task the previous year, consisting of Transformer models optimized in a number of ways (Junczys-Dowmunt et al., 2018). This year, they made

---

[3]`https://nlp.stanford.edu/projects/nmt/`

System	BLEU	R-1	R-2	R-L	RG	CS (P/R)		CO	Type
EdiNLG	36.85	69.66	41.47	57.25	81.01	77.32	78.49	62.21	C
MS	47.90	75.95	51.75	65.61	80.98	76.88	84.57	67.84	C
NLE	48.24	75.89	51.80	65.90	80.65	75.10	88.72	69.17	C
FairSeq-19	36.26	68.22	40.31	56.38	81.64	77.67	75.82	60.83	C

Table 6: Results on the MT+NLG: (Data+En → **De**) track of DGT task.

System	BLEU	R-1	R-2	R-L	RG	CS (P/R)		CO	Type
EdiNLG	41.15	76.57	50.97	66.62	91.40	78.99	63.04	51.73	C
MS	57.99	83.03	63.03	75.44	95.77	92.49	91.62	84.70	C
NLE	62.24	84.38	66.11	77.17	95.63	91.71	92.69	85.05	C
FairSeq-19	42.91	77.57	52.66	68.66	93.53	83.33	84.22	70.47	C

Table 7: Results on the MT+NLG: (Data+De → **En**) track of DGT task.

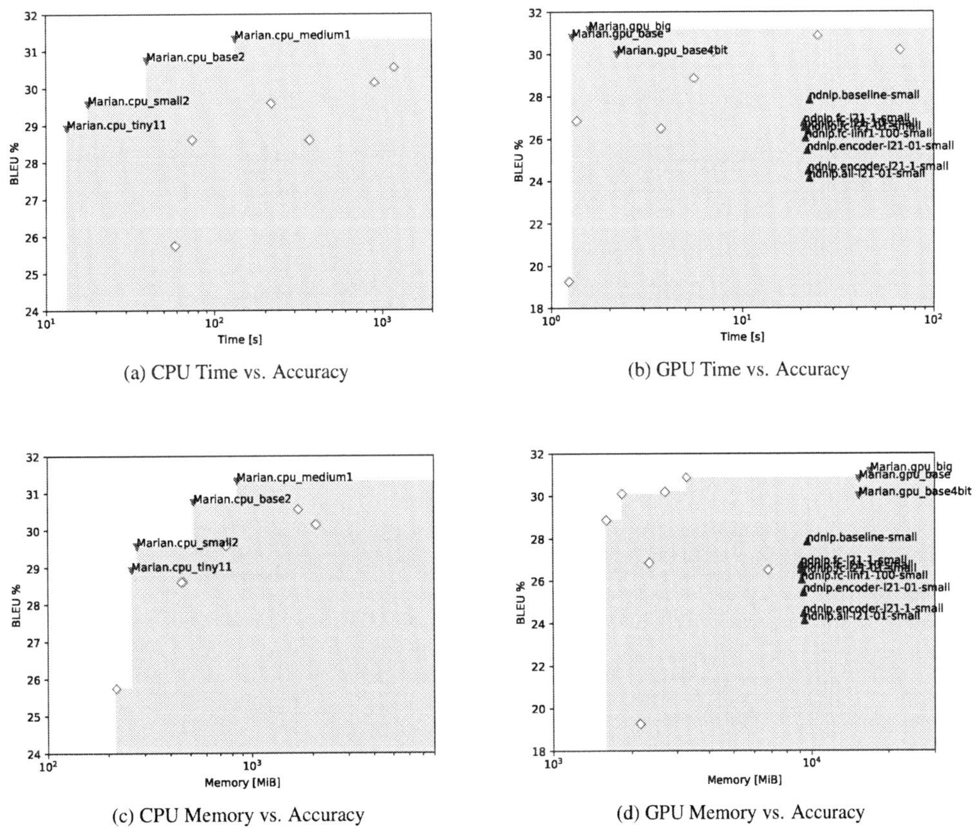

Figure 1: Time and memory vs. accuracy measured by BLEU on the newstest2015 set, calculated on both CPU and GPU. White diamonds (◇) represent the results in the previous campaign. Orange areas show regions dominated by some Pareto frontier systems.

a number of improvements. Improvements were made to teacher-student training by (1) creating more data for teacher-student training using backward, then forward translation, (2) using multiple teachers to generate better distilled data for training student models. In addition, there were modeling improvements made by (1) replacing simple averaging in the attention layer with an efficiently calculable "simple recurrent unit," (2) parameter tying between decoder layers, which reduces memory usage and improves cache locality on the CPU. Finally, a number of CPU-specific optimizations were performed, most notably including 8-bit matrix multiplication along with a flexible quantization scheme.

4.4.2 Team Notre Dame

Team Notre Dame's submission (Murray et al., 2019) focused mainly on memory efficiency. They did so by performing "Auto-sizing" of the transformer network, applying block-sparse regularization to remove columns and rows from the parameter matrices.

4.5 Results

A brief summary of the results of the shared task (for newstest2015) can be found in Figure 1, while full results tables for all of the systems can be found in Appendix A. From this figure we can glean a number of observations.

For the CPU systems, all submissions from the Marian team clearly push the Pareto frontier in terms of both time and memory. In addition, the Marian systems also demonstrated a good trade-off between time/memory and accuracy.

For the GPU systems, all systems from the Marian team also outperformed other systems in terms of the speed-accuracy trade-off. However, the Marian systems had larger memory consumption than both Notre Dame systems, which specifically optimized for memory efficiency, and all previous systems. Interestingly, each GPU system by the Marian team shares almost the same amount of GPU memory as shown in Table 12 and Figure 2(b). This may indicate that the internal framework of the Marian system tries to reserve enough amount of the GPU memory first, then use the acquired memory as needed by the translation processes.

On the other hand, we can see that the Notre Dame systems occupy only a minimal amount of GPU memory, as the systems use much smaller

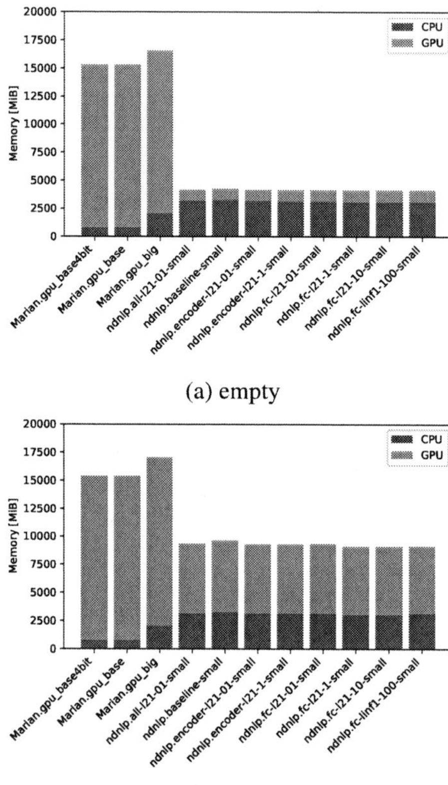

(a) empty

(b) newstest2015

Figure 2: Memory consumption for each GPU system.

amounts on the empty set (Figure 2(a)). These different approaches to constant or variable size memory consumption may be based on different underlying perspectives of "memory efficiency," and it may be difficult to determine which policy is better without knowing the actual environment in which a system will be used.

5 Conclusion

This paper summarized the results of the Third Workshop on Neural Generation and Translation, where we saw a number of research advances. Particularly, this year introduced a new document generation and translation task, that tested the efficacy of systems for both the purposes of translation and generation in a single testbed.

Acknowledgments

We thank Apple and Google for their monetary support of student travel awards for the workshop, and AWS for its gift of AWS credits (to Graham Neubig) that helped support the evaluation.

References

Dzmitry Bahdanau, Kyunghyun Cho, and Yoshua Bengio. 2015. Neural machine translation by jointly learning to align and translate. In *Proc. ICLR*.

Ondřej Bojar, Rajen Chatterjee, Christian Federmann, Yvette Graham, Barry Haddow, Shujian Huang, Matthias Huck, Philipp Koehn, Qun Liu, Varvara Logacheva, et al. 2017. Findings of the 2017 conference on machine translation (wmt17). In *Proc. WMT*, pages 169–214.

Ondrej Bojar et al. 2014. Findings of the 2014 workshop on statistical machine translation. In *Proc. WMT*, pages 12–58.

Jacob Devlin, Ming-Wei Chang, Kenton Lee, and Kristina Toutanova. 2019. BERT: Pre-training of Deep Bidirectional Transformers for Language Understanding. In *Proceedings of the 2019 Conference of the North American Chapter of the Association for Computational Linguistics: Human Language Technologies, Volume 1 (Long and Short Papers)*, pages 4171–4186, Minneapolis, Minnesota. Association for Computational Linguistics.

George Doddington. 2002. Automatic evaluation of machine translation quality using n-gram co-occurrence statistics. In *Proc. HLT*, pages 138–145.

Claire Gardent, Anastasia Shimorina, Shashi Narayan, and Laura Perez-Beltrachini. 2017. The WebNLG Challenge: Generating Text from RDF Data. In *Proceedings of the 10th International Conference on Natural Language Generation*, pages 124–133, Santiago de Compostela, Spain. Association for Computational Linguistics.

Ari Holtzman, Jan Buys, Maxwell Forbes, and Yejin Choi. 2019. The Curious Case of Neural Text Degeneration. *arXiv:1904.09751 [cs]*.

Marcin Junczys-Dowmunt, Kenneth Heafield, Hieu Hoang, Roman Grundkiewicz, and Anthony Aue. 2018. Marian: Cost-effective high-quality neural machine translation in C++. In *Proceedings of the 2nd Workshop on Neural Machine Translation and Generation*, pages 129–135, Melbourne, Australia. Association for Computational Linguistics.

Nal Kalchbrenner and Phil Blunsom. 2013. Recurrent continuous translation models. In *Proc. EMNLP*, pages 1700–1709.

Young Jin Kim, Marcin Junczys-Dowmunt, and Hany Hassan. 2019. From research to production and back: Fast and accurate neural machine translation. In *Proceedings of the 3rd Workshop on Neural Generation and Translation*.

Rémi Lebret, David Grangier, and Michael Auli. 2016. Neural Text Generation from Structured Data with Application to the Biography Domain. In *Proceedings of the 2016 Conference on Empirical Methods in Natural Language Processing*, pages 1203–1213, Austin, Texas. Association for Computational Linguistics.

Chin-Yew Lin. 2004. ROUGE: A Package for Automatic Evaluation of Summaries. In *Text Summarization Branches Out*, pages 74–81, Barcelona, Spain. Association for Computational Linguistics.

Sameen Maruf, André F. T. Martins, and Gholamreza Haffari. 2019. Selective Attention for Context-aware Neural Machine Translation. In *Proceedings of the 2019 Conference of the North American Chapter of the Association for Computational Linguistics: Human Language Technologies, Volume 1 (Long and Short Papers)*, pages 3092–3102, Minneapolis, Minnesota. Association for Computational Linguistics.

Robert C. Moore and William Lewis. 2010. Intelligent selection of language model training data. In *Proc. ACL*, pages 220–224.

Kenton Murray, Brian DuSell, and David Chiang. 2019. Auto-sizing the transformer network: Shrinking parameters for the wngt 2019 efficiency task. In *Proceedings of the 3rd Workshop on Neural Generation and Translation*.

Toshiaki Nakazawa, Shohei Higashiyama, Chenchen Ding, Hideya Mino, Isao Goto, Hideto Kazawa, Yusuke Oda, Graham Neubig, and Sadao Kurohashi. 2017. Overview of the 4th workshop on asian translation. In *Proc. WAT*, pages 1–54, Taipei, Taiwan. Asian Federation of Natural Language Processing.

Ramesh Nallapati, Bowen Zhou, Cicero dos Santos, Çağlar Gulçehre, and Bing Xiang. 2016. Abstractive Text Summarization using Sequence-to-sequence RNNs and Beyond. In *Proceedings of The 20th SIGNLL Conference on Computational Natural Language Learning*, pages 280–290, Berlin, Germany. Association for Computational Linguistics.

Nathan Ng, Kyra Yee, Alexei Baevski, Myle Ott, Michael Auli, and Sergey Edunov. 2019. Facebook FAIR's WMT19 news translation task submission. In *Proceedings of the Fourth Conference on Machine Translation (Volume 2: Shared Task Papers, Day 1)*, pages 314–319, Florence, Italy. Association for Computational Linguistics.

Kishore Papineni, Salim Roukos, Todd Ward, and Wei-Jing Zhu. 2002. BLEU: a method for automatic evaluation of machine translation. In *Proc. ACL*, pages 311–318.

Jeffrey Pennington, Richard Socher, and Christopher Manning. 2014. Glove: Global Vectors for Word Representation. In *Proceedings of the 2014 Conference on Empirical Methods in Natural Language Processing (EMNLP)*, pages 1532–1543, Doha, Qatar. Association for Computational Linguistics.

Ratish Puduppully, Li Dong, and Mirella Lapata. 2019. Data-to-text generation with content selection and planning. In *Proceedings of the AAAI Conference on Artificial Intelligence*, volume 33, pages 6908–6915.

Alec Radford, Jeffrey Wu, Rewon Child, David Luan, Dario Amodei, and Ilya Sutskever. 2019. Language Models are Unsupervised Multitask Learners.

Alexander M. Rush, Sumit Chopra, and Jason Weston. 2015. A neural attention model for abstractive sentence summarization. In *Proc. EMNLP*, pages 379–389.

Ilya Sutskever, Oriol Vinyals, and Quoc VV Le. 2014. Sequence to sequence learning with neural networks. In *Proc. NIPS*, pages 3104–3112.

Ashish Vaswani, Noam Shazeer, Niki Parmar, Jakob Uszkoreit, Llion Jones, Aidan N. Gomez, Lukasz Kaiser, and Illia Polosukhin. 2017. Attention is all you need. In *Proc. NIPS*.

Oriol Vinyals and Quoc Le. 2015. A neural conversational model. *arXiv preprint arXiv:1506.05869*.

Qingyun Wang, Xiaoman Pan, Lifu Huang, Boliang Zhang, Zhiying Jiang, Heng Ji, and Kevin Knight. 2018. Describing a Knowledge Base. In *Proceedings of the 11th International Conference on Natural Language Generation*, pages 10–21, Tilburg University, The Netherlands. Association for Computational Linguistics.

Tsung-Hsien Wen, Milica Gasic, Nikola Mrkšić, Pei-Hao Su, David Vandyke, and Steve Young. 2015. Semantically conditioned lstm-based natural language generation for spoken dialogue systems. In *Proc. EMNLP*, pages 1711–1721.

Sam Wiseman, Stuart Shieber, and Alexander Rush. 2017. Challenges in Data-to-Document Generation. In *Proceedings of the 2017 Conference on Empirical Methods in Natural Language Processing*, pages 2253–2263.

Yingce Xia, Xu Tan, Fei Tian, Fei Gao, Di He, Weicong Chen, Yang Fan, Linyuan Gong, Yichong Leng, Renqian Luo, Yiren Wang, Lijun Wu, Jinhua Zhu, Tao Qin, and Tie-Yan Liu. 2019. Microsoft Research Asia's Systems for WMT19. In *Proceedings of the Fourth Conference on Machine Translation (Volume 2: Shared Task Papers, Day 1)*, pages 424–433, Florence, Italy. Association for Computational Linguistics. WMT.

A Full Shared Task Results

For completeness, in this section we add tables of the full shared task results. These include the full size of the image file for the translation system (Table 8), the comparison between compute time and evaluation scores on CPU (Table 9) and GPU (Table 10), and the comparison between memory and evaluation scores on CPU (Table 11) and GPU (Table 12).

Table 8: Image file sizes of submitted systems.

Team	System	Size [MiB]
Marian	cpu_base2	135.10
	cpu_medium1	230.22
	cpu_small2	93.00
	cpu_tiny11	91.61
	gpu_base4bit	322.68
	gpu_base	452.59
	gpu_big	773.27
Notre Dame	all-l21-01-small	2816.63
	baseline-small	2845.04
	encoder-l21-01-small	2813.67
	encoder-l21-1-small	2779.60
	fc-l21-01-small	2798.94
	fc-l21-1-small	2755.80
	fc-l21-10-small	2755.76
	fc-linf1-100-small	2759.10

Table 9: Time consumption and MT evaluation metrics (CPU systems).

Dataset	Team	System	Time Consumption [s] Total	Diff	BLEU %	NIST
Empty	Marian	cpu_base2	4.97	—	—	—
		cpu_medium1	6.03	—	—	—
		cpu_small2	4.67	—	—	—
		cpu_tiny11	4.71	—	—	—
newstest2014	Marian	cpu_base2	57.52	52.55	28.04	7.458
		cpu_medium1	181.81	175.78	28.58	7.539
		cpu_small2	28.32	23.64	26.97	7.288
		cpu_tiny11	22.26	17.56	26.38	7.178
newstest2015	Marian	cpu_base2	45.01	40.04	30.74	7.607
		cpu_medium1	139.06	133.03	31.32	7.678
		cpu_small2	22.64	17.97	29.57	7.437
		cpu_tiny11	18.08	13.37	28.92	7.320

Table 10: Time consumption and MT evaluation metrics (GPU systems).

Dataset	Team	System	Time Consumption [s]		BLEU %	NIST
			Total	Diff		
Empty	Marian	gpu_base4bit	9.77	—	—	—
		gpu_base	2.69	—	—	—
		gpu_big	5.22	—	—	—
	Notre Dame	all-l21-01-small	7.92	—	—	—
		baseline-small	8.13	—	—	—
		encoder-l21-01-small	7.96	—	—	—
		encoder-l21-1-small	7.89	—	—	—
		fc-l21-01-small	7.85	—	—	—
		fc-l21-1-small	7.56	—	—	—
		fc-l21-10-small	7.57	—	—	—
		fc-linf1-100-small	7.61	—	—	—
newstest2014	Marian	gpu_base4bit	12.42	2.66	27.50	7.347
		gpu_base	4.22	1.53	28.00	7.449
		gpu_big	7.09	1.88	28.61	7.534
	Notre Dame	all-l21-01-small	36.80	28.89	21.60	6.482
		baseline-small	36.07	27.95	25.28	7.015
		encoder-l21-01-small	35.82	27.86	23.20	6.725
		encoder-l21-1-small	35.41	27.52	22.06	6.548
		fc-l21-01-small	35.76	27.91	24.07	6.869
		fc-l21-1-small	34.46	26.90	23.97	6.859
		fc-l21-10-small	34.00	26.43	23.87	6.852
		fc-linf1-100-small	34.46	26.84	23.80	6.791
newstest2015	Marian	gpu_base4bit	11.97	2.20	29.99	7.504
		gpu_base	3.98	1.29	30.79	7.595
		gpu_big	6.80	1.58	31.15	7.664
	Notre Dame	all-l21-01-small	30.21	22.29	24.13	6.670
		baseline-small	30.47	22.35	27.85	7.224
		encoder-l21-01-small	29.67	21.71	25.45	6.869
		encoder-l21-1-small	29.93	22.04	24.47	6.734
		fc-l21-01-small	29.80	21.95	26.39	7.053
		fc-l21-1-small	28.42	20.87	26.77	7.093
		fc-l21-10-small	28.63	21.06	26.54	7.051
		fc-linf1-100-small	28.91	21.29	26.04	6.971

Table 11: Peak memory consumption (CPU systems).

Dataset	Team	System	Memory [MiB]		
			Host	GPU	Both
Empty	Marian	cpu_base2	336.30	—	336.30
		cpu_medium1	850.76	—	850.76
		cpu_small2	229.53	—	229.53
		cpu_tiny11	227.73	—	227.73
newstest2014	Marian	cpu_base2	523.93	—	523.93
		cpu_medium1	850.98	—	850.98
		cpu_small2	276.30	—	276.30
		cpu_tiny11	260.86	—	260.86
newstest2015	Marian	cpu_base2	523.12	—	523.12
		cpu_medium1	850.95	—	850.95
		cpu_small2	275.76	—	275.76
		cpu_tiny11	260.09	—	260.09

Table 12: Peak memory consumption (GPU systems).

Dataset	Team	System	Memory [MiB]		
			Host	GPU	Both
Empty	Marian	gpu_base4bit	788.67	14489	15277.67
		gpu_base	791.82	14489	15280.82
		gpu_big	2077.75	14489	16566.75
	Notre Dame	all-l21-01-small	3198.89	991	4189.89
		baseline-small	3261.73	973	4234.73
		encoder-l21-01-small	3192.87	1003	4195.87
		encoder-l21-1-small	3164.45	1003	4167.45
		fc-l21-01-small	3160.32	999	4159.32
		fc-l21-1-small	3069.05	1049	4118.05
		fc-l21-10-small	3092.01	1057	4149.01
		fc-linf1-100-small	3116.35	1037	4153.35
newstest2014	Marian	gpu_base4bit	781.83	14641	15422.83
		gpu_base	793.07	14641	15434.07
		gpu_big	2078.78	14961	17039.78
	Notre Dame	all-l21-01-small	3199.95	9181	12380.95
		baseline-small	3285.20	9239	12524.20
		encoder-l21-01-small	3194.96	9169	12363.96
		encoder-l21-1-small	3164.86	9119	12283.86
		fc-l21-01-small	3160.80	9155	12315.80
		fc-l21-1-small	3070.67	9087	12157.67
		fc-l21-10-small	3068.12	9087	12155.12
		fc-linf1-100-small	3119.96	9087	12206.96
newstest2015	Marian	gpu_base4bit	783.05	14641	15424.05
		gpu_base	789.34	14641	15430.34
		gpu_big	2077.42	14961	17038.42
	Notre Dame	all-l21-01-small	3198.86	6171	9369.86
		baseline-small	3266.11	6359	9625.11
		encoder-l21-01-small	3193.13	6103	9296.13
		encoder-l21-1-small	3166.56	6135	9301.56
		fc-l21-01-small	3160.88	6159	9319.88
		fc-l21-1-small	3079.92	6017	9096.92
		fc-l21-10-small	3069.32	6015	9084.32
		fc-linf1-100-small	3130.95	6015	9145.95

Hello, It's GPT-2 - How Can I Help You?
Towards the Use of Pretrained Language Models
for Task-Oriented Dialogue Systems

Paweł Budzianowski[1,2,3] and **Ivan Vulić**[2,3]
[1]Engineering Department, Cambridge University, UK
[2]Language Technology Lab, Cambridge University, UK
[3]PolyAI Limited, London, UK
`pfb30@cam.ac.uk, iv250@cam.ac.uk`

Abstract

Data scarcity is a long-standing and crucial challenge that hinders quick development of task-oriented dialogue systems across multiple domains: task-oriented dialogue models are expected to learn grammar, syntax, dialogue reasoning, decision making, and language generation from absurdly small amounts of task-specific data. In this paper, we demonstrate that recent progress in language modeling pre-training and transfer learning shows promise to overcome this problem. We propose a task-oriented dialogue model that operates solely on text input: it effectively bypasses explicit policy and language generation modules. Building on top of the TransferTransfo framework (Wolf et al., 2019) and generative model pre-training (Radford et al., 2019), we validate the approach on complex multi-domain task-oriented dialogues from the MultiWOZ dataset. Our automatic and human evaluations show that the proposed model is on par with a strong task-specific neural baseline. In the long run, our approach holds promise to mitigate the data scarcity problem, and to support the construction of more engaging and more eloquent task-oriented conversational agents.

1 Introduction

Statistical conversational systems can be roughly clustered into two main categories: 1) task-oriented modular systems and 2) open-domain chit-chat neural models. The former typically consist of independently trained constituent modules such as language understanding, dialogue management, and response generation. The main goal of such systems is to provide meaningful system responses which are invaluable in building conversational agents of practical value for restricted domains and tasks. However, data collection and annotation for such systems is complex, time-intensive, expensive, and not easily transferable (Young et al., 2013). On the other hand, open-domain conversational bots (Li et al., 2017; Serban et al., 2017) can leverage large amounts of freely available unannotated data (Ritter et al., 2010; Henderson et al., 2019a). Large corpora allow for training end-to-end neural models, which typically rely on sequence-to-sequence architectures (Sutskever et al., 2014). Although highly data-driven, such systems are prone to producing unreliable and meaningless responses, which impedes their deployment in the actual conversational applications (Li et al., 2017).

Due to the unresolved issues with the end-to-end architectures, the focus has been extended to retrieval-based models. Here, the massive datasets can be leveraged to aid task-specific applications (Kannan et al., 2016; Henderson et al., 2017, 2019b). The retrieval systems allow for the full control over system responses, but the behaviour of the system is often highly predictable. It also depends on the pre-existing set of responses, and the coverage is typically insufficient for a multitude of domains and tasks. However, recent progress in training high-capacity language models (e.g., GPT, GPT-2) (Radford et al., 2018, 2019) on large datasets reopens the question of whether such generative models can support task-oriented dialogue applications. Recently, Wolf et al. (2019) and Golovanov et al. (2019) showed that the GPT model, once fine-tuned, can be useful in the domain of personal conversations. In short, their approach led to substantial improvements on the Persona-Chat dataset (Zhang et al., 2018), showcasing the potential of exploiting large pretrained generative models in the conversational domain.[1]

In this paper, we demonstrate that large generative models pretrained on large general-domain

---

[1]E.g., TransferTransfo (Wolf et al., 2019) yields gains in all crucial dialogue evaluation measures such as fluency, consistency and engagingness on the Persona-Chat dataset.

Proceedings of the 3rd Workshop on Neural Generation and Translation (WNGT 2019), pages 15–22
Hong Kong, China, November 4, 2019. ©2019 Association for Computational Linguistics
www.aclweb.org/anthology/D19-56%2d

Dialogue Context:
Visitor: Hi I need a help with finding a hotel
Belief state: hotel()
Database state: hotel(many)

        System: Hello, any requirements?

Visitor: I need to find a luxury hotel in the centre please.
Belief state: hotel(price-expensive;area-centre)
Database state: hotel(three)

Dialogue-Context-to-Text:
      System: <u><restaurant_name> should fit you.</u>

Figure 1: Dialogue-context-to-text task.

corpora can support *task-oriented dialogue applications*. We first discuss how to combine a set of diverse components such as word tokenization, multi-task learning, and probabilistic sampling to support task-oriented applications. We then show how to adapt the task-oriented dialogue framework to operate entirely on text input, effectively bypassing an explicit dialogue management module and a domain-specific natural language generation module. The proposed model operates entirely in the sequence-to-sequence fashion, consuming only simple text as input. The entire dialogue context, which includes the belief state, the database state and previous turns, is provided to the decoder as raw text. The proposed model follows the recently proposed TransferTransfo framework (Wolf et al., 2019), and relies on pretrained models from the GPT family (Radford et al., 2018, 2019).

Our results in the standard Dialogue-Context-to-Text task (see Figure 1) on the multi-domain Multi-WOZ dataset (Budzianowski et al., 2018b) suggest that our GPT-based task-oriented dialogue model learns to generate and understand domain-specific tokens, which in turn leads to a seamless adaptation to particular focused domains. While automatic evaluation indicates that our framework still falls slightly short of a strong task-specific neural baseline, it also hints at the main advantage of our framework: it is widely portable and easily adaptable to a large number of domains, bypassing the intricate modular design only at a small cost in performance. Furthermore, user-centered evaluations suggest that there is no significant difference between the two models.

2 From Unsupervised Pretraining to Dialogue Modeling

Task-oriented dialogue modeling requires substantial amounts of domain-specific manually labeled data. A natural question to ask is: Can we leverage transfer learning through generative pretraining on large unlabelled corpora to enable task-oriented dialogue modeling. In this work, we rely on the standard language modeling (LM) pretraining, where the task is to predict the next word given the preceding word sequence (Bengio et al., 2003). The objective maximizes the likelihood over the word sequence $S = \{w_1, ..., w_{|S|}\}$:

$$\mathcal{L}_1(S) = \sum_{i=1}^{|S|} \log P(w_i|w_0, w_1, ..., w_{i-1}). \quad (1)$$

Transfer learning based on such LM pretraining combined with the Transformer decoder model (Vaswani et al., 2017) resulted in significant progress across many downstream tasks (Rei, 2017; Howard and Ruder, 2018; Radford et al., 2018, 2019).

2.1 TransferTransfo Framework

Golovanov et al. (2019) and Wolf et al. (2019) achieved a first successful transfer of a generative pretrained GPT model to an open-domain dialogue task. The pretrained GPT model is fine-tuned in a multi-task learning fashion following the original work (Radford et al., 2018). The LM objective from Eq. (1) is combined with the next utterance classification task:

$$p(c, a) = \text{softmax}(h_l * W_h). \quad (2)$$

c and a represent the context of the conversation (c) and a proposed answer (a), h_l is the last hidden state of the transformer decoder, and W_h is learnt during the fine-tuning phase. The model significantly improves upon previous baselines over all automatic dialogue evaluation metrics as well as in evaluation with human subjects when evaluated on the Persona-Chat dataset (Zhang et al., 2018).

The GPT input consists of token embeddings and positional embeddings. In order to move from a single-speaker setting to a setting with two interlocutors, Wolf et al. (2019) introduced *dialogue-state* embeddings. These embeddings inform the model whether the current token comes from an utterance of the first speaker or an utterance of the second speaker. The dialogue-state embeddings are learned during the fine-tuning phase.

3 Domain Transfer for (Task-Oriented) Dialogue Modeling

We now briefly discuss several advances in modeling of natural language that facilitate applicability

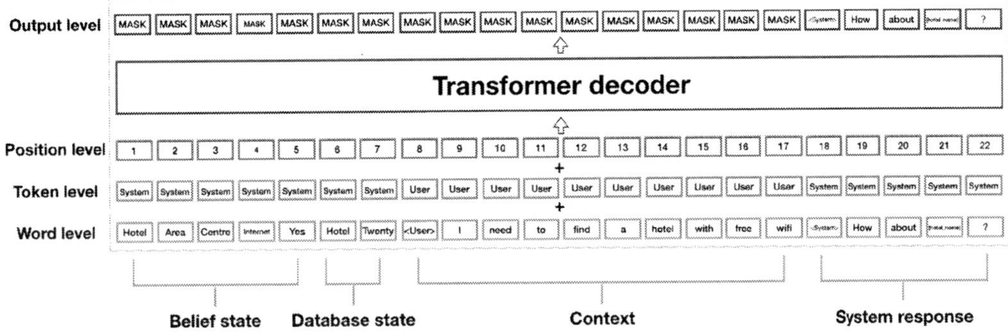

Figure 2: The framework for modeling task-oriented conversations based on a pretrained GPT model which uses only unstructured simple text as input. The context, belief state, and database state are joined together without explicit standalone dialogue policy and generation modules. The token-level (i.e., dialogue-state) embeddings are learned following Wolf et al. (2019).

of pretrained generative models in task-oriented dialogue modeling. To the best of our knowledge, this work is first to combine these existing components to enable task-oriented dialogue modeling.

3.1 Domain Adaptation and Delexicalization

Dealing with out-of-vocabulary (OOV) words has been a long-standing challenge in dialogue modeling, e.g., it is crucial for task-oriented generation where the generated output is often *delexicalized* (Wen et al., 2015). Delexicalization replaces slot values by their corresponding (generic) slot tokens and it allows learning value-independent parameters. Recently, owing to subword-level tokenisation (Sennrich et al., 2016), language models are now able to deal with OOVs and domain-specific vocabularies more effectively (Radford et al., 2018).

3.2 Simple Text-Only Input

There have been some empirical validations recently which suggest that posing NLP tasks in the form of simple text can yield improvements with unsupervised architectures (Wolf et al., 2019; Radford et al., 2019). For instance, in task-oriented dialogue modeling the Sequicity model (Lei et al., 2018) sees the classification over the belief state as a generation problem. That way, the entire dialogue model pipeline is based on the sequence-to-sequence architecture: the output from one model is the input to the subsequent recurrent model. We follow this approach by providing both the belief state and the knowledge base state in a simple text format to the generator. This significantly simplifies the paradigm of building task-oriented models: any new source of information can be simply

added to as another part of the text-only input provided in "natural language".

3.3 Transferring Language Generation Capabilities

Transformer architecture shows ability to learn new (i.e., domain-specific) token embeddings in the fine-tuning phase (Radford et al., 2018; Wolf et al., 2019). This means that the GPT models can adapt through special tokens to particular tasks. By providing the input representation as text with domain-specific tokens, we can use off-the-shelf architectures and adapt to the domain-specific input without the need of training new dialogue submodules. As mentioned in §2.1, the token level layer (Figure 2) informs the transformer decoder what part of the input comes from the system side or from the user side. In our framework, we create two task-oriented specific tokens (System and User tokens) that are learned during fine-tuning.

3.4 Generation Quality

Finally, the long-standing problem of dull and repetitive response generation (Li et al., 2017) has been in the focus of recent work (Kulikov et al., 2018; Holtzman et al., 2019). Owing to new sampling strategies, generative models are now able to create longer and more coherent sequence outputs. This has been validated also for open-domain dialogue modeling (Wolf et al., 2019; Golovanov et al., 2019). We experiment with standard decoding strategies as well as with the recently proposed *nucleus* sampling procedure (Holtzman et al., 2019). A standard *greedy sampling* strategy chooses the most probable word as :

$$\arg\max_{w_i} = \log P(w_i|w_0, w_1, ..., w_{i-1}).$$

On the other hand, nucleus sampling is restricted only to words from the p-th percentile of the distribution during generation. The probabilities of words for which the cumulative sum exceeds the percentile are rescaled and the sequence is sampled from this subset. We probe the ability of such large pretrained models to generate more varied and semantically richer responses relying on nucleus sampling in lieu of greedy sampling without hurting the actual performance.

4   Fine-Tuning GPT on MultiWOZ

To evaluate the ability of transferring the GPT generation capability to constrained/focused dialogue tasks and domains, we rely on the multi-domain MultiWOZ dataset (Budzianowski et al., 2018b). MultiWOZ consists of 7 domains and $10,438$ dialogues and it is substantially larger than previous available datasets (Wen et al., 2017; El Asri et al., 2017). The conversations are natural as they were gathered through human-human interactions. However, the dialogues are based on domain-specific vocabulary such as booking IDs or telephone numbers that need to be delexicalized as they are entirely database-dependent.

Natural Language as (the Only) Input. GPT operates solely on the text input. This is in opposition to the standard task-oriented dialogue architectures (Wen et al., 2017; Zhao et al., 2017) where the belief state and the database state are encoded in a numerical form. For example, the database state is typically defined as n-bin encodings representing a number of available entities at the current state of the conversation (Wen et al., 2017). Therefore, we transform the belief state and the knowledge base representation to a simple text representation. The belief state takes the following form:

```
Domain1 Slot1 Value1 Slot2 Value2
Domain2 Slot1 ...
```

and the database representation is provided as:

```
Domain1 # of entities
Domain2 # of entities ...
```

This is also similar in spirit to the Sequicity architecture (Lei et al., 2018) where the second recurrent model takes as input the belief state in the natural language (i.e., simple text-only) form. In this work, we also transform the knowledge base state to a similar natural language format. These two pieces of information are then concatenated with the history of the conversation forming the full dialogue context, see Figure 2. Following Wolf et al. (2019), we add new token embeddings for two parties involved in the conversation to inform the attention layers what part of the context comes from the user, and what part is related to the system. Figure 2 presents the final architecture.

Training Details. We use the open-source implementation of the GPT architecture that provides both GPT and GPT-2 fine-tunable checkpoints.[2] Following previous work (Radford et al., 2018; Wolf et al., 2019), we set the weight on the language model loss to be two times higher than the one for the response prediction. The parameters for the batch size (24), learning rate (1e-5) and the number of candidates per sequence (2) were chosen based on the grid search. [3]

5   Results and Analysis

Following prior work (Budzianowski et al., 2018b; Zhao et al., 2019; Chen et al., 2019), our evaluation task is the dialogue-context-to-text generation task (see Figure 1). Given a dialogue history, the oracle belief state and the database state, the model needs to output the adequate response. By relying on the oracle belief state, prior work has bypassed the possible errors originating from natural language understanding (Budzianowski et al., 2018b).

The main evaluation is based on the comparison between the following two models: 1) the baseline is a neural response generation model with an oracle belief state obtained from the wizard annotations as in (Budzianowski et al., 2018a); 2) the model proposed in §4 and shown in Figure 2 that works entirely with text-only format as input (see §4). We test all three available pretrained GPT models - the original GPT model (Radford et al., 2018). and two GPT-2 models referred to as small (GPT2) and medium (GPT2-M) (Radford et al., 2019).

---

[2] `https://github.com/huggingface/transfer-learning-conv-ai`

[3] We searched over the following values: learning rates $\in \{1\text{-e4}, 1\text{-e5}, 5\text{-e6}, 1\text{-e6}\}$, batch sizes $\in \{8, 12, 16, 20, 24\}$ and candidate set sizes $\in \{1, 2, 4, 6\}$.

	Baseline	GPT	GPT2-S	GPT2-M
Inform (%)	**76.7**	71.53	66.43	70.96
Success (%)	**64.63**	55.36	55.16	61.36
BLEU (%)	18.05	17.80	18.02	**19.05**

Table 1: Evaluation on MultiWOZ with the greedy sampling procedure.

	Baseline	GPT	GPT2-S	GPT2-M
Inform (%)	72.57	70.43	69.3	**73.96**
Success (%)	57.63	51.0	54.93	**61.20**
BLEU (%)	15.75	15.65	15.64	**16.55**

Table 2: Evaluation on MultiWOZ with the nucleus sampling procedure.

5.1 Evaluation with Automatic Measures

We report scores with three standard automatic evaluation measures. Two of them relate to the dialogue task completion: whether the system has provided an appropriate entity (*Inform*) and then answered all requested attributes (*Success* rate). Finally, fluency is measured by the BLEU score (Papineni et al., 2002).

First, three versions of GPT were fine-tuned on MultiWOZ and evaluated with greedy sampling. The results are summarized in Table 1). They show that the baseline obtains the highest score on task-related metrics while the highest BLUE score was achieved by GPT2-M. Although the results are lower for the GPT-based methods, we note the design simplicity of the GPT-based task-oriented dialogue models. Further, the gap in performance might be partially attributed to the chosen greedy sampling procedure which puts too much focus on the properties of the original pretraining phase (Holtzman et al., 2019).

Therefore, we also report the results with the nucleus sampling method in Table 2. The scores confirm the importance of choosing the correct sampling method. The GPT2 models improve the score on *Inform* and *Success* metrics. It is worth noting the consistent drop in BLUE scores across all models. This comes from the fact that nucleus sampling allows for increased variability: this might reduce the probability of generating domain-specific tokens.

We have also qualitatively analyzed a sample of successful dialogues. Only around 50% of dialogues are successful both with the baseline and with the GPT-based models. Moreover, there are no clearly observed distinct patterns between successful dialogues for the two model types. This

Model 1		vs	Model 2
GPT	59 %	41%	Baseline
GPT	46 %	54 %	Target
GPT2	46 %	54 %	Target
GPT2	45 %	55 %	Baseline
Baseline	43 %	57 %	Target
GPT2	51 %	49 %	GPT

Table 3: Human ranking of responses between all pairs of four analyzed models and the original responses.

suggests that they might be effectively ensembled using a ranking model to evaluate the score of each response (Henderson et al., 2019b). We will investigate the complementarity of the two approaches along with ensemble methods in future work.

5.2 Human Evaluation

In another, now user-centered experiment, the goal was to analyze the generation quality. Turkers, native speakers of English, were asked to rate their binary preference when presented with one-turn responses from the baseline, GPT, GPT2-M and the original dialogues (*Target*). The turkers were required to choose what response they prefer when presented with two responses from two different models, resulting in more than 300 scores per each model pair.

The results are summarized in Table 3, while some example dialogues with responses are provided in Figure 3. As expected, the original responses are ranked higher than all neural models with the largest difference observed between the oracle and the baseline model. Although the generated output from the GPT is strongly preferred against the neural baseline, interestingly the opposite is observed with the GPT2 model. These inconclusive results call for further analyses in future work, and also show that there are no substantial differences in the quality of generated responses when comparing the strong neural baseline and the GPT-based models.

6 Conclusion

In this paper, we have made a first step towards leveraging large pretrained generative models for modeling task-oriented dialogue in multiple domains. The simplicity of the fine-tuning procedure where all necessary information can be encoded as simple text enables a quick adaptation to constrained domains and domain-specific vocabularies. We hope that this framework will inform and guide future research in hope of simultaneously improving and simplifying the design of task-oriented conversational systems.

References

Yoshua Bengio, Réjean Ducharme, Pascal Vincent, and Christian Jauvin. 2003. A neural probabilistic language model. *Journal of machine learning research*, 3(Feb):1137–1155.

Paweł Budzianowski, Iñigo Casanueva, Bo-Hsiang Tseng, and Milica Gašić. 2018a. Towards end-to-end multi-domain dialogue modelling. *Tech. Rep. CUED/F-INFENG/TR.706, University of Cambridge, Engineering Department*.

Paweł Budzianowski, Tsung-Hsien Wen, Bo-Hsiang Tseng, Iñigo Casanueva, Stefan Ultes, Osman Ramadan, and Milica Gasic. 2018b. MultiWOZ-A Large-scale multi-domain wizard-of-oz dataset for task-oriented dialogue modelling. In *Proceedings of EMNLP*, pages 5016–5026.

Wenhu Chen, Jianshu Chen, Pengda Qin, Xifeng Yan, and William Yang Wang. 2019. Semantically conditioned dialog response generation via hierarchical disentangled self-attention. *arXiv preprint arXiv:1905.12866*.

Layla El Asri, Hannes Schulz, Shikhar Sharma, Jeremie Zumer, Justin Harris, Emery Fine, Rahul Mehrotra, and Kaheer Suleman. 2017. Frames: A corpus for adding memory to goal-oriented dialogue systems. In *Proceedings of SIGDIAL*, pages 207–219.

Sergey Golovanov, Rauf Kurbanov, Sergey Nikolenko, Kyryl Truskovskyi, Alexander Tselousov, and Thomas Wolf. 2019. Large-scale transfer learning for natural language generation. In *Proceedings of the 57th Annual Meeting of the Association for Computational Linguistics*, pages 6053–6058, Florence, Italy. Association for Computational Linguistics.

Matthew Henderson, Rami Al-Rfou, Brian Strope, Yunhsuan Sung, Laszlo Lukacs, Ruiqi Guo, Sanjiv Kumar, Balint Miklos, and Ray Kurzweil. 2017. Efficient natural language response suggestion for smart reply. *arXiv preprint arXiv:1705.00652*.

Matthew Henderson, Paweł Budzianowski, Iñigo Casanueva, Sam Coope, Daniela Gerz, Girish Kumar, Nikola Mrkšić, Georgios Spithourakis, Pei-Hao Su, Ivan Vulić, and Tsung-Hsien Wen. 2019a. A repository of conversational datasets. In *Proceedings of the Workshop on NLP for Conversational AI*. Data available at github.com/PolyAI-LDN/conversational-datasets.

Matthew Henderson, Ivan Vulić, Daniela Gerz, Iñigo Casanueva, Paweł Budzianowski, Sam Coope, Georgios Spithourakis, Tsung-Hsien Wen, Nikola Mrksi'c, and Pei-Hao Su. 2019b. Training neural response selection for task-oriented dialogue systems. In *Proceedings of ACL*.

Ari Holtzman, Jan Buys, Maxwell Forbes, and Yejin Choi. 2019. The curious case of neural text degeneration. *arXiv preprint arXiv:1904.09751*.

Jeremy Howard and Sebastian Ruder. 2018. Universal language model fine-tuning for text classification. In *Proceedings of the 56th Annual Meeting of the Association for Computational Linguistics (Volume 1: Long Papers)*, pages 328–339.

Anjuli Kannan, Karol Kurach, Sujith Ravi, Tobias Kaufmann, Andrew Tomkins, Balint Miklos, Greg Corrado, Laszlo Lukacs, Marina Ganea, Peter Young, et al. 2016. Smart reply: Automated response suggestion for email. In *Proceedings of the 22nd ACM SIGKDD International Conference on Knowledge Discovery and Data Mining*, pages 955–964. ACM.

Ilya Kulikov, Alexander H Miller, Kyunghyun Cho, and Jason Weston. 2018. Importance of a search strategy in neural dialogue modelling. *arXiv preprint arXiv:1811.00907*.

Wenqiang Lei, Xisen Jin, Min-Yen Kan, Zhaochun Ren, Xiangnan He, and Dawei Yin. 2018. Sequicity: Simplifying task-oriented dialogue systems with single sequence-to-sequence architectures. In *Proceedings of ACL*, pages 1437–1447.

Jiwei Li, Will Monroe, Tianlin Shi, Sébastien Jean, Alan Ritter, and Dan Jurafsky. 2017. Adversarial learning for neural dialogue generation. In *Proceedings of the 2017 Conference on Empirical Methods in Natural Language Processing*, pages 2157–2169.

Kishore Papineni, Salim Roukos, Todd Ward, and Wei-Jing Zhu. 2002. BLEU: A method for automatic evaluation of machine translation. In *Proceedings of ACL*, pages 311–318.

Alec Radford, Karthik Narasimhan, Tim Salimans, and Ilya Sutskever. 2018. Improving language understanding by generative pre-training.

Alec Radford, Jeffrey Wu, Rewon Child, David Luan, Dario Amodei, and Ilya Sutskever. 2019. Language models are unsupervised multitask learners. *OpenAI Blog*, 1(8).

Marek Rei. 2017. Semi-supervised multitask learning for sequence labeling. In *Proceedings of the 55th Annual Meeting of the Association for Computational Linguistics (Volume 1: Long Papers)*, pages 2121–2130.

Alan Ritter, Colin Cherry, and Bill Dolan. 2010. Unsupervised modeling of twitter conversations. In *Human Language Technologies: The 2010 Annual Conference of the North American Chapter of the Association for Computational Linguistics*, pages 172–180.

Rico Sennrich, Barry Haddow, and Alexandra Birch. 2016. Neural machine translation of rare words with subword units. In *Proceedings of the 54th Annual Meeting of the Association for Computational Linguistics (Volume 1: Long Papers)*, volume 1, pages 1715–1725.

Iulian Vlad Serban, Alessandro Sordoni, Ryan Lowe, Laurent Charlin, Joelle Pineau, Aaron Courville, and Yoshua Bengio. 2017. A hierarchical latent variable encoder-decoder model for generating dialogues. In *Proceedings of AAAI*, pages 3295–3301.

Ilya Sutskever, Oriol Vinyals, and Quoc V Le. 2014. Sequence to sequence learning with neural networks. In *Proceedings of NeurIPS*, pages 3104–3112.

Ashish Vaswani, Noam Shazeer, Niki Parmar, Jakob Uszkoreit, Llion Jones, Aidan N Gomez, Łukasz Kaiser, and Illia Polosukhin. 2017. Attention is all you need. In *Advances in neural information processing systems*, pages 5998–6008.

Tsung-Hsien Wen, Milica Gašić, Nikola Mrkšić, Pei-Hao Su, David Vandyke, and Steve Young. 2015. Semantically conditioned lstm-based natural language generation for spoken dialogue systems. In *Proceedings of the 2015 Conference on Empirical Methods in Natural Language Processing (EMNLP)*.

Tsung-Hsien Wen, David Vandyke, Nikola Mrkšić, Milica Gašić, Lina M Rojas-Barahona, Pei-Hao Su, Stefan Ultes, and Steve Young. 2017. A network-based end-to-end trainable task-oriented dialogue system. In *Proceedings of EACL*, pages 438–449.

Thomas Wolf, Victor Sanh, Julien Chaumond, and Clement Delangue. 2019. Transfertransfo: A transfer learning approach for neural network based conversational agents. *arXiv preprint arXiv:1901.08149*.

Steve Young, Milica Gašić, Blaise Thomson, and Jason D. Williams. 2013. POMDP-based statistical spoken dialog systems: A review. *Proceedings of the IEEE*, 101(5):1160–1179.

Saizheng Zhang, Emily Dinan, Jack Urbanek, Arthur Szlam, Douwe Kiela, and Jason Weston. 2018. Personalizing dialogue agents: I have a dog, do you have pets too? In *Proceedings of the 56th Annual Meeting of the Association for Computational Linguistics (Volume 1: Long Papers)*, pages 2204–2213.

Tiancheng Zhao, Kaige Xie, and Maxine Eskenazi. 2019. Rethinking action spaces for reinforcement learning in end-to-end dialog agents with latent variable models. In *Proceedings of the 2019 Conference of the North American Chapter of the Association for Computational Linguistics: Human Language Technologies, Volume 1 (Long and Short Papers)*, pages 1208–1218.

Tiancheng Zhao, Ran Zhao, and Maxine Eskenazi. 2017. Learning discourse-level diversity for neural dialog models using conditional variational autoencoders. In *Proceedings of ACL*, pages 654–664.

Dialogue 1:
Visitor: I need to book a taxi to arrive by [value_time] .

Baseline: Where will you be departing from ?
GPT: I would be happy to help with your request, first i'll need to know where you are going and what time you want to leave or arrive by.

Visitor: I need to be picked up from [restaurant_name] and i am headed to the [attraction_name] .

Baseline: Your taxi has been booked . the car will be a [taxi_type] and the contact number is [taxi_phone].
GPT: Your taxi is booked. You will be picked up at [restaurant_name] and the contact number is [taxi_phone]. Is there anything else i can help you with?

...

Dialogue 2:
Visitor: I am looking for some places to go, do you have any attractions in the [value_area] ?

Baseline: There are [value_count] attractions in the [value_area]. Do you have a particular type of attraction in mind?
GPT: Sure! There are many colleges and museums in the area. Do you have a preference for type or price range?

Visitor: i really do not have a preference . can you recommend a few ?

Baseline: I recommend [attraction_name] It is located in the [value_area].
GPT: How about the [attraction_name]?

Visitor: Sure. Also could you help me find a restaurant serving unusual food in the same part of town ?

Baseline: There are no restaurants in the [value_area] of town. Would you like to try a different type of food?
GPT: Unfortunately, there are no restaurants that match that description. Would you like to try a different area or type of food?

Figure 3: The comparison of generated responses from the baseline model and GPT2-M.

Recycling a Pre-trained BERT Encoder for Neural Machine Translation

Kenji Imamura and **Eiichiro Sumita**

National Institute of Information and Communications Technology

3-5 Hikaridai, Seika-cho, Soraku-gun, Kyoto 619-0289, Japan

`{kenji.imamura,eiichiro.sumita}@nict.go.jp`

Abstract

In this paper, a pre-trained Bidirectional Encoder Representations from Transformers (BERT) model is applied to Transformer-based neural machine translation (NMT).

In contrast to monolingual tasks, the number of unlearned model parameters in an NMT decoder is as huge as the number of learned parameters in the BERT model. To train all the models appropriately, we employ two-stage optimization, which first trains only the unlearned parameters by freezing the BERT model, and then fine-tunes all the sub-models.

In our experiments, stable two-stage optimization was achieved, in contrast the BLEU scores of direct fine-tuning were extremely low. Consequently, the BLEU scores of the proposed method were better than those of the Transformer base model and the same model without pre-training. Additionally, we confirmed that NMT with the BERT encoder is more effective in low-resource settings.

1 Introduction

Bidirectional Encoder Representations from Transformers (BERT) (Devlin et al., 2019) is a language representation model trained in advance on a very large monolingual dataset. We adapt this model to our own tasks after fine-tuning (Freitag and Al-Onaizan, 2016; Servan et al., 2016) using task-specific data. Systems using BERT have achieved high accuracy in various tasks, such as the General Language Understanding Evaluation (GLUE) benchmark (Wang et al., 2019) and the reading comprehension benchmark using the Stanford Question Answering Dataset (SQuAD) (Rajpurkar et al., 2018). However, most tasks using BERT are monolingual because it was originally developed for natural language understanding.

Recently, models in which the ideas of BERT are extended to multiple languages have been proposed (Lample and Conneau, 2019). These models, which are pre-trained using multilingual data, are called cross-lingual language models (XLMs). We can construct a machine translation system using two XLM models as the encoder and decoder.

In this paper, we apply a pre-trained BERT encoder to neural machine translation (NMT) based on the Transformer (Vaswani et al., 2017). Specifically, the encoder of the Transformer NMT is replaced with the BERT encoder. Generally, systems using BERT, including machine translation systems based on an XLM, are fine-tuned using task-specific data. However, stable training is difficult using simple fine-tuning because the number of unlearned parameters is huge in our system. Therefore, we employ two-stage training, which first trains only unlearned parameters and then applies fine-tuning.

Our experimental results demonstrated that two-stage optimization stabilized training, whereas direct fine-tuning made the BLEU scores quite low. As a result, the BLEU scores improved in comparison with the scores of the Transformer base model and models with the same structure but without pre-training. Our results indicate that we can reuse neural networks trained for one purpose (natural language understanding, in this case) for another purpose (machine translation, in this case) if we use two-stage optimization. From this viewpoint, this paper presents an example of network recycling.

The remainder of this paper is organized as follows. In Section 2, an overview of the BERT related models is provided. In Section 3, our proposal, that is, NMT using the BERT model and its training method, is described. In Section 4, the proposed method is evaluated through experiments. In Section 5, we discuss back-translation

Proceedings of the 3rd Workshop on Neural Generation and Translation (WNGT 2019), pages 23–31

Hong Kong, China, November 4, 2019. ©2019 Association for Computational Linguistics

www.aclweb.org/anthology/D19-56%2d

and model recycling, including related work. Finally, we conclude the paper in Section 6.

2 Pre-trained Language Models

2.1 BERT

The form of the BERT model (Devlin et al., 2019) is the same as that of a Transformer encoder, in which the input is a word sequence and the output consists of representations that correspond to the input words. The input contexts are encoded by multi-head self-attention mechanisms.

BERT models are distributed with pre-training. The distributed models have a depth of 12 or 24 layers, which is deeper than the Transformer base model (six layers). Users (or system developers) construct various systems by adding a small network to adapt BERT to their own tasks and fine-tune the system using task-specific data. For example, when the BERT model is used for a document classification task, a classifier is constructed by adding a generation layer for classification (which consists of linear and softmax sublayers) to the BERT model. Similarly, when a named entity recognizer is constructed, generation layers that convert word representations to named entity tags are added, and the entire model is finetuned. The numbers of additional parameters in these models are much smaller than the number of parameters in the BERT model.

The BERT model is pre-trained to perform two tasks: masked language modeling and next-sentence prediction. Both tasks train the model to improve its language prediction performance.

The masked language model is trained to restore the original word sequence from noisy input. In this task, some words are replaced with special tokens, [MASK], or other words. For instance, if the original sentence is "my dog is hairy" and "my dog is [MASK]" is given as the input word sequence, then the system predicts that the original word for [MASK] was hairy. During prediction, both forward and backward contexts in a sentence are used.

In the next-sentence prediction task, the system learns whether two given sentences are consecutive. To implement binary classification using the Transformer, a special token [CLS] is placed at the head of an input sentence, and classification is performed from the representation of [CLS]. Additionally, [SEP] is used as a sentence separator.

BERT has achieved high accuracy on various tasks, such as the GLUE benchmark (Wang et al., 2019) and the reading comprehension benchmark using SQuAD (Rajpurkar et al., 2018). However, the above tasks are monolingual.

2.2 XLMs

XLMs, in which the ideas of BERT are extended to multiple languages (Lample and Conneau, 2019) have been proposed. Although the form of the XLM model is also Transformer, it is trained from multilingual corpora. It also learns bilingual correspondences in a Transformer model by inputting a connected bilingual sentence.

Machine translation can be realized using XLMs by regarding two pre-trained models as an encoder and decoder. NMT using BERT described in this paper is fundamentally the same as XLM-based NMT. However, our aim is to connect different systems, and we regard our approach as model recycling (Ramachandran et al., 2016) using the BERT encoder and Transformer decoder.

Most pre-trained systems, including XLM-based machine translation, are trained only using fine-tuning (Devlin et al., 2019; Lample and Conneau, 2019). However, if the number of unlearned parameters is huge compared with the number of pre-trained parameters, then the pre-trained parameter values will be destroyed due to a phenomenon called *catastrophic forgetting* (Goodfellow et al., 2013), and consequently, training will diverge. We must suppress this problem to stably train the model.

3 NMT with BERT

In this section, we describe our proposal: NMT using the BERT encoder.

3.1 Model

The NMT system in this paper is an encoder-decoder based on the Transformer. The structure is shown in Figure 1. Because the BERT model is also the Transformer encoder, we adopt it as the encoder for NMT without modification. The outputs from the BERT encoder, which are representations of source words, are input to the context attention mechanism in the Transformer decoder to generate a translation. Note that we call the encoder of the conventional NMT the Transformer encoder to distinguish it from the BERT encoder. The number of layers in the Transformer decoder is fixed to six throughout the paper.

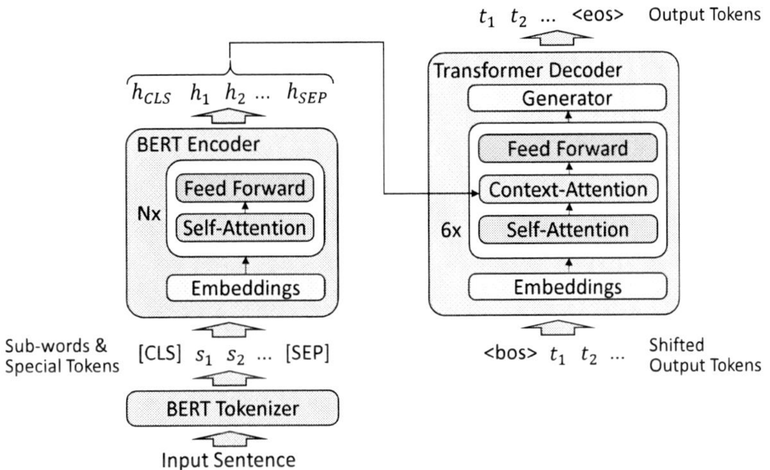

Figure 1: Structure of NMT using a BERT encoder.

Because the BERT encoder is pre-trained using a specific tokenizer, we must use the BERT tokenizer when we apply it to machine translation. The BERT tokenizer includes sub-word segmentation based on WordPiece (Wu et al., 2016). Additionally, the input to the encoder contains [CLS] and [SEP] tokens at the head and tail, respectively.

Although the Transformer decoder is used here, we assume that a recurrent neural network decoder (Sutskever et al., 2014; Bahdanau et al., 2014) can also be applied,.

3.2 Training

When we construct a system using pre-trained BERT models, we generally add a task-specific network and fine-tune the system using task-specific data. Because the additional network is small (i.e., the number of additional parameters is small), the models can be learned by fine-tuning.

In this paper, the additional network is the decoder, whose number of parameters is huge. Indeed, the number of model parameters of the BERT encoder (pre-trained) and Transformer decoder (unlearned) used in Section 4 were 110M and 80M, respectively. We cannot train such a large number of unlearned parameters only by fine-tuning. Thus, we employ two-stage optimization in this paper, that is decoder training and fine-tuning.

3.2.1 Decoder Training

In this stage, only the decoder parameters are updated while the encoder parameters are frozen.

Specifically, the model is trained using parallel corpora, as in conventional NMTs. During training, however, backpropagation is only applied to the decoder and is dropped before the encoder. This means that we do not need to compute the gradients and maintain the input/output values in the BERT encoder, and we can train the model using GPUs with a relatively small memory even though the model size is huge. Dropout is only applied to the Transformer decoder, that is, it is not applied to the BERT encoder.

Note that decoder training continues until the loss of the development set is minimized. We discuss the efficient number of epochs for the decoder training in Section 4.3 when we combine it with fine-tuning.

3.2.2 Fine-Tuning

In the fine-tuning stage, model parameters in the BERT encoder are also updated to optimize the entire model.

Although the model has already been trained until the loss of the development set is minimized during decoder training, both the encoder and decoder are further optimized in an end-to-end manner by updating the encoder parameters. Dropout is applied to both the BERT encoder and Transformer decoder. In the fine-tuning stage, backpropagation is applied to all layers, and a large amount of memory is consumed.

Task	Set	# Sentences	# Tokens (En)
WMT-2014	train	4,468,840	116M
En-De	newstest2013	3,000	66K
	newstest2014	2,737	63K
	newstest2015	2,169	68K
IWSLT-2015	train	133,317	2.7M
En-Vi	tst2012	1,553	34K
	tst2013	1,268	34K

Table 1: Sizes of the experimental datasets.

4 Experiments

4.1 Experimental Settings

Data: In this paper, we used data for shared tasks that were pre-processed by the Stanford NLP Group.[1] The sizes of the datasets are shown in Table 1.

The first task is the news translation task of English-to-German (En-De) from the Workshop on Statistical Machine Translation (WMT-2014) (Bojar et al., 2014). Four sets in total have been published. In this paper, we used `newstest2013` as the development set, and the other two sets (`newstest2014` and `2015`) were used as test sets.

Moreover, to contrast the results with those of a low-resource setting, we also used the English-to-Vietnamese (En-Vi) corpus used in the International Workshop on Spoken Language Translation (IWSLT-2015) (Cettolo et al., 2015). We used `tst2012` as the development set and `tst2013` as the test set.

The target sentences of the above data were further segmented into 16K sub-words using byte-pair encoding (Sennrich et al., 2016b). For the source sentences, we segmented 30K sub-words using the BERT tokenizer if the encoder model was BERT. If the encoder was the conventional Transformer, we segmented the source sentences into 16K sub-words using our byte-pair encoder.

BERT Model: We used a pre-trained model published in the BERT GitHub repository[2] called the BERT base model, whose features are uncased inputs, 12 layers, 768 hidden units, and 12 heads.[3] The number of parameters is about 110M. This

Type	Option	Value
Decoder training	Batch size	Approx. 500 sents.
	Optimizer	Adam
		$\beta_1 = 0.9$, $\beta_2 = 0.99$
	Learning rate	4.0×10^{-4}
	Warm-up	5 epochs
	Cool-down	Inverse square root
	Label smoothing	0.1
	Dropout	0.15
	Loss function	Label-smoothed cross entropy
	Initializer	Xavier uniform
Fine-tuning	Identical to decoder training except for the learning rate and warm-up	
Test	Beam size	10
	Length penalty	1.0 (fixed)

Table 2: Hyperparameter settings.

model was trained using BookCorpus (Zhu et al., 2015) and English Wikipedia (3.3G words in total).

Note that we converted the published model into a model that is compatible with the PyTorch library using a tool[4] because it was trained for the TensorFlow library.

Translation System: We used fairseq[5] as the basic translator. It is an NMT system constructed on the PyTorch library and includes Transformer models. We replaced its encoder with the BERT model and used the fairseq decoder without modification.

The decoder used here was six-layer Transformer. We set the numbers of hidden units and heads to be the same as those of the encoder (i.e., 768 units and 12 heads) to incorporate encoder outputs into the decoder using the context attention mechanism.

Hyperparameters: Table 2 summarizes the hyperparameter settings. The hyperparameters for fine-tuning were almost the same as those of decoder training, except for the learning rate (LR) and warm-up.

Evaluation: We used BLEU (Papineni et al., 2002) as the evaluation metric. The MultEval tool (Clark et al., 2011)[6] was used for statistical testing, which is based on the bootstrap resampling method. The significance level was 5% ($p < 0.05$).

---

[1] `https://nlp.stanford.edu/projects/nmt/`

[2] `https://github.com/google-research/bert`

[3] `https://storage.googleapis.com/bert_models/2018_10_18/uncased_L-12_H-768_A-12.zip`

[4] `https://github.com/huggingface/pytorch-pretrained-BERT`

[5] `https://github.com/pytorch/fairseq`

[6] `https://github.com/jhclark/multeval`

	System	LR	Dev. PPL $\downarrow$	BLEU $\uparrow$			Remark
				2013	2014	2015	
Baselines	Transformer base	4.0×10^{-4}	4.23	26.29	27.22	29.48	Stat. test baseline
	Transformer BERT size	4.0×10^{-4}	4.04	26.15	27.09	29.32	
NMT with BERT	Direct fine-tuning	8×10^{-5}	4.28	0.13 (-)	0.10 (-)	0.12 (-)	# Epochs = 33
		4.0×10^{-4}	4.09	0.48 (-)	0.42 (-)	0.54 (-)	# Epochs = 29
	Proposed: Decoder training only	4.0×10^{-4}	4.76	24.13 (-)	23.62 (-)	25.74 (-)	# Epochs = 65
	+ Fine-tuning	4×10^{-5}	3.93	**27.14** (+)	28.27 (+)	30.68 (+)	# Epochs = 21
		8×10^{-5}	**3.92**	27.05 (+)	**28.90** (+)	**30.89** (+)	# Epochs = 9
		1.2×10^{-4}	3.93	27.03 (+)	28.50 (+)	30.51 (+)	# Epochs = 11
		1.6×10^{-4}	3.94	26.64	28.59 (+)	30.51 (+)	# Epochs = 11
		2.0×10^{-4}	3.95	26.89 (+)	28.67 (+)	30.24 (+)	# Epochs = 12
		4.0×10^{-4}	N/A because training did not converge				

Table 3: Results of the system comparison.
The bold values indicate the best results. The (+) and (-) symbols indicate that the results significantly improved or degraded ($p < 0.05$) with respect to the Transformer base model, respectively.

4.2 System Comparison

In this section, we compare systems using WMT-2014 data.

We compare the proposed methods with Vaswani et al. (2017)'s Transformer base model (6 layers, 512 hidden units, and 8 heads) as the baseline. For reference, we also use another Transformer NMT called Transformer BERT size, in which the model structure of the encoder agrees with that of the BERT encoder (i.e., 12 layers, 768 hidden units, and 12 heads). This system is compared to determine whether the model capacity influences translation quality.

The decoders of the proposed systems were first trained until the loss of the development set was minimized (`newstest2013`), and then the systems were fine-tuned. The learning rates during fine-tuning were changed from 1/10 to 1 times those of the decoder training. The warm-up periods were also changed to be proportional to the learning rates. The results are shown in Table 3. In the table, Dev. PPL indicates the perplexity of the development set, and the years of the BLEU scores denote the results of `newstest2013, 2014,` and `2015`, respectively.

First, we compare the baselines. Transformer BERT size yielded a better model than that of Transformer base because its perplexity was lower. However, the BLEU scores were slightly degraded (but not significantly). Increasing the number of parameters did not lead to better translation quality.

Next, we compare the NMT system with BERT and the Transformer base. When the entire model was directly fine-tuned, training converged but the BLEU scores dramatically decreased even if we used different learning rates. This implies that the models were broken.[7] Unlike monolingual tasks using the BERT model, it was difficult to directly apply fine-tuning for NMT using the pre-trained BERT encoder.

By contrast, in the decoder training-only model, namely the model immediately after decoder training, training was successfully finished. However, the development perplexity was higher and the BLEU scores were lower than those of the baseline. The entire model was not learned completely because of the data mismatch, which was that the pre-training and our training data were different.

After fine-tuning, by contrast, the perplexity decreased and the BLEU score increased. Compared with those of Transformer base, the BLEU scores significantly improved in almost all cases. Because the development perplexity decreased with respect to Transformer BERT size, we can say that these improvements resulted from learning performance rather than the number of model parameters.

We changed the learning rates from 4×10^{-5} to 4.0×10^{-4} in the fine-tuning. When the learning rate was 4.0×10^{-4} (the decoder training learning rate), we could not tune the model because there was no convergence. For the other learning rates, there were no large differences in per-

---

[7] Indeed, very long translations were generated due to frequent repetition in the case of the low learning rate (8×10^{-5}). We suppose that the decoder was not learned sufficiently. In the case of the high learning rate (4.0×10^{-4}), long and completely wrong translations were generated. We suppose that the encoder was broken.

Decoder training		Fine-tuning		BLEU ↑			
# Epochs	Dev. PPL ↓	# Epochs	Dev. PPL ↓	2013	2014	2105	Remark
0	—	33	4.28	0.13 (-)	0.10 (-)	0.12 (-)	Direct fine-tuning
1	33.05	34	4.23	26.67	28.77	30.16 (-)	
2	11.47	20	4.20	26.80	28.58	30.82	
3	8.12	18	4.10	**27.41**	28.93	30.78	
5	6.69	18	4.02	27.20	28.43 (-)	30.80	
10	5.50	15	3.96	27.33	28.59	30.42	
20	5.08	18	**3.91**	27.00	28.87	**30.92**	
30	4.89	10	3.92	27.18	28.39 (-)	30.70	
40	4.86	12	**3.91**	27.01	**29.04**	30.70	
50	4.81	11	**3.91**	27.02	28.65	30.77	
65	4.76	9	3.92	27.05	28.90	30.89	Decoder training converged Baseline for statistical testing

Table 4: Changes in the perplexity of the development set (Dev. PPL) and BLEU scores with respect to the number of decoder training epochs.

plexity or BLEU scores. However, we confirmed that there were some differences in convergence time (# Epochs), and fine-tuning converged in nine epochs when the learning rate was 8×10^{-5}. Therefore, we fixed the learning rate for fine-tuning to 8×10^{-5} in our subsequent experiments.

4.3 Number of Epochs for Decoder Training

The proposed method first performs decoder training until convergence, and then applies fine-tuning. However, this approach may not be optimal because decoder training is slow. For instance, it took 65 epochs for decoder training in the experiment in the previous section. In this section, we investigate whether decoder training can be made more efficient by stopping it before convergence.

Table 4 shows the results after fine-tuning when decoder training was stopped after various numbers of epochs. Fine-tuning was conducted until convergence in all cases. The table shows the changes in development perplexity and the BLEU scores, whose baselines are shown on the bottom line. Note that zero epochs of decoder training (the top line) mean that fine-tuning was directly applied without decoder training (the same as in Table 3).

As the number of epochs of decoder training decreased, fine-tuning required more epochs and the final perplexity increased. However, the BLEU scores were almost stable. Indeed, only three scores significantly decreased with respect to the baseline.

Because we assume that the optimal settings of decoder training depend on the data and hyperparameters, we cannot provide explicit criteria values in this paper. At the very least, our experimental results show the following conclusions.

- To shorten the total training time, it is best to perform decoder training for three epochs ($3 + 18 = 21$ epochs in total).

- To obtain the best model (i.e., the model with the minimum development perplexity), 20 epochs are sufficient for decoder training (which yields a Dev. PPL of 3.91).

4.4 Experiment on a Low-resource Language Pair

In this section, the effect of the BERT encoder on a low-resource setting is explored using IWSLT-2015 En-Vi data (133K sentences). All experimental settings, except for the corpus, were same as those in Section 4.1. The results are shown in Table 5.

In the low-resource setting, the development perplexity decreased in comparison with the baseline when applying the BERT encoder and performing decoder training only. However, the BLEU score degraded, as in the large data setting (Section 4.2).

By contrast, when fine-tuning was applied, both the perplexity and BLEU scores largely improved with respect to the baseline. The BLEU score of `tst2013` improved by +3.45. Considering the score of `newstest2015` in the experiment in Table 3 was +1.41 for the same settings, these results show that the BERT encoder is more effective for improving translation quality in a low-resource setting.

5 Discussion and Related Work

5.1 Contrast with Back-Translation

Back-translation (Sennrich et al., 2016a) is a technique to improve translation quality using mono-

	System	LR	Dev. PPL $\downarrow$	BLEU $\uparrow$	
				2012	2013
Baseline	Transformer base	4.0×10^{-4}	11.54	24.03	26.12
NMT with BERT	Proposed: Decoder training only	4.0×10^{-4}	11.45	21.77 (-)	23.23 (-)
	+ Fine-tuning	8×10^{-5}	**8.98**	**26.77** (+)	**29.57** (+)

Table 5: Results of the IWSLT-2015 data.

lingual corpora. It translates monolingual corpora of the target language into the source language, generates pseudo-parallel sentences, and trains the source-to-target translator from a mixture of pseudo- and manually created parallel corpora. Because BERT encoders are trained using source monolingual corpora, they complement each other.

However, there are differences between BERT encoders and back-translation from the viewpoint of parallel corpus sizes. BERT encoders themselves do not need parallel corpora for training. They can be applied to low-resource language pairs for which large parallel corpora are difficult to obtain. However, huge monolingual corpora are necessary to train BERT encoders. Therefore, they are suitable for translation from resource-rich languages (e.g., English) to low-resource languages.

By contrast, back-translation requires a certain size of parallel corpora to translate back from the target to the source languages. This is because back-translated results are not confident if the parallel corpora are small (Edunov et al., 2018). Therefore, back-translation is suitable for translating middle-resource language pairs.

Note that unsupervised machine translation can be realized using the XLM described in Section 2.2 by connecting two autoencoders as an encoder-decoder. Those autoencoders are trained to encode source-target-source and target-source-target using monolingual corpora. Therefore, this approach can be regarded as including back-translation. Because back-translation was originally developed to enhance decoders, it is reasonable to incorporate it into pre-training.

5.2 NMT Using Source Monolingual Corpora

There are other methods that improve translation quality using source monolingual corpora.

Zhang and Zong (2016) proposed a multi-task learning method that learns a sentence reordering model from source language corpora and a translation model from parallel corpora. Cheng et al. (2016) proposed semi-supervised NMT that simultaneously trains a translation model and two autoencoders using parallel and source/target monolingual corpora. Both methods must use parallel and monolingual corpora during training.

Our method explicitly distinguishes training stages: 1) pre-training of a BERT encoder using monolingual corpora, 2) training of a decoder using parallel corpora, and 3) fine-tuning the entire model. This means that monolingual corpora are only necessary in the pre-training stage, and we can focus on this stage to obtain the advantages of large corpora.

5.3 Pre-Training versus Recycling

The BERT model used in this paper was designed and trained for natural language understanding, and machine translation is an unintended purpose. Therefore, we use the word "recycle."

We assume that pre-training and recycling are distinguished by the number of unlearned parameters. The numbers of model parameters in this paper were 110M for the BERT encoder and 80M for the Transformer decoder. We could not optimize them using fine-tuning alone. In this case, it is appropriate to call the model recycling, and two-stage optimization becomes effective. We believe that our study can be regarded as an example of model recycling.

6 Conclusions

In this paper, an NMT system that incorporates a BERT encoder was presented. We applied two-stage optimization, that is, decoder training and fine-tuning, because the number of unlearned parameters was as large as the number of pre-trained model parameters. Consequently, we constructed a higher quality NMT than that trained from given parallel data. Moreover, it was particularly effective in a low-resource setting. We also investigated the appropriate number of epochs for decoder training and confirmed that several to tens of epochs were sufficient.

There are some future directions for this study. First, various pre-trained models have been distributed, such as the BERT large model, multilingual BERT, and XLMs. Exploring the relationship between these models and translation quality is our future work. Applying the pre-trained models to various language pairs, from low- to high-resource language pairs, is also a curious direction. Regarding model recycling, we plan to combine heterogeneous models in future work.

Acknowledgments

This work was supported by the "Research and Development of Enhanced Multilingual and Multipurpose Speech Translation Systems" a program of the Ministry of Internal Affairs and Communications, Japan.

References

Dzmitry Bahdanau, Kyunghyun Cho, and Yoshua Bengio. 2014. Neural machine translation by jointly learning to align and translate. *CoRR*, abs/1409.0473.

Ondrej Bojar, Christian Buck, Christian Federmann, Barry Haddow, Philipp Koehn, Johannes Leveling, Christof Monz, Pavel Pecina, Matt Post, Herve Saint-Amand, Radu Soricut, Lucia Specia, and Aleš Tamchyna. 2014. Findings of the 2014 workshop on statistical machine translation. In *Proceedings of the Ninth Workshop on Statistical Machine Translation*, pages 12–58, Baltimore, Maryland, USA. Association for Computational Linguistics.

Mauro Cettolo, Kam Moejies amd Sebastian Stüker, Luisa Bentivogli, Roldano Cattoni, and Marcello Federico. 2015. The IWSLT 2015 evaluation campaign. In *Proceedings of the International Workshop on Spoken Language Translation*, Da Nang, Vietnam.

Yong Cheng, Wei Xu, Zhongjun He, Wei He, Hua Wu, Maosong Sun, and Yang Liu. 2016. Semi-supervised learning for neural machine translation. In *Proceedings of the 54th Annual Meeting of the Association for Computational Linguistics (Volume 1: Long Papers)*, pages 1965–1974, Berlin, Germany.

Jonathan H. Clark, Chris Dyer, Alon Lavie, and Noah A. Smith. 2011. Better hypothesis testing for statistical machine translation: Controlling for optimizer instability. In *Proceedings of the 49th Annual Meeting of the Association for Computational Linguistics: Human Language Technologies*, pages 176–181, Portland, Oregon, USA.

Jacob Devlin, Ming-Wei Chang, Kenton Lee, and Kristina Toutanova. 2019. BERT: Pre-training of deep bidirectional transformers for language understanding. In *Proceedings of the 2019 Conference of the North American Chapter of the Association for Computational Linguistics: Human Language Technologies, Volume 1 (Long and Short Papers)*, pages 4171–4186, Minneapolis, Minnesota.

Sergey Edunov, Myle Ott, Michael Auli, and David Grangier. 2018. Understanding back-translation at scale. In *Proceedings of the 2018 Conference on Empirical Methods in Natural Language Processing*, pages 489–500, Brussels, Belgium.

Markus Freitag and Yaser Al-Onaizan. 2016. Fast domain adaptation for neural machine translation. *CoRR*, abs/1612.06897.

Ian J. Goodfellow, Mehdi Mirza, Da Xiao, Aaron Courville, and Yoshua Bengio. 2013. An empirical investigation of catastrophic forgetting in gradient-based neural networks. *arXiv preprint*.

Guillaume Lample and Alexis Conneau. 2019. Cross-lingual language model pretraining. *CoRR*, abs/1901.07291.

Kishore Papineni, Salim Roukos, Todd Ward, and Wei-Jing Zhu. 2002. Bleu: a method for automatic evaluation of machine translation. In *Proceedings of the 40th Annual Meeting of the Association for Computational Linguistics (ACL)*, pages 311–318, Philadelphia, Pennsylvania, USA.

Pranav Rajpurkar, Robin Jia, and Percy Liang. 2018. Know what you don't know: Unanswerable questions for squad. *CoRR*, abs/1806.03822.

Prajit Ramachandran, Peter J. Liu, and Quoc V. Le. 2016. Unsupervised pretraining for sequence to sequence learning. *CoRR*, abs/1611.02683.

Rico Sennrich, Barry Haddow, and Alexandra Birch. 2016a. Improving neural machine translation models with monolingual data. In *Proceedings of the 54th Annual Meeting of the Association for Computational Linguistics (ACL-2016, Volume 1: Long Papers)*, pages 86–96, Berlin, Germany.

Rico Sennrich, Barry Haddow, and Alexandra Birch. 2016b. Neural machine translation of rare words with subword units. In *Proceedings of the 54th Annual Meeting of the Association for Computational Linguistics (Volume 1: Long Papers)*, pages 1715–1725, Berlin, Germany.

Christophe Servan, Josep Maria Crego, and Jean Senellart. 2016. Domain specialization: a post-training domain adaptation for neural machine translation. *CoRR*, abs/1612.06141.

Ilya Sutskever, Oriol Vinyals, and Quoc V. Le. 2014. Sequence to sequence learning with neural networks. In *Proceedings of Advances in Neural Information Processing Systems 27 (NIPS 2014)*, pages 3104–3112.

Ashish Vaswani, Noam Shazeer, Niki Parmar, Jakob Uszkoreit, Llion Jones, Aidan N. Gomez, Lukasz Kaiser, and Illia Polosukhin. 2017. Attention is all you need. *CoRR*, abs/1706.03762.

Alex Wang, Amanpreet Singh, Julian Michael, Felix Hill, Omer Levy, and Samuel R. Bowman. 2019. Glue: A multi-task benchmark and analysis platform for natural language understanding. In *International Conference on Learning Representations*.

Yonghui Wu, Mike Schuster, Zhifeng Chen, Quoc V. Le, Mohammad Norouzi, Wolfgang Macherey, Maxim Krikun, Yuan Cao, Qin Gao, Klaus Macherey, Jeff Klingner, Apurva Shah, Melvin Johnson, Xiaobing Liu, Lukasz Kaiser, Stephan Gouws, Yoshikiyo Kato, Taku Kudo, Hideto Kazawa, Keith Stevens, George Kurian, Nishant Patil, Wei Wang, Cliff Young, Jason Smith, Jason Riesa, Alex Rudnick, Oriol Vinyals, Greg Corrado, Macduff Hughes, and Jeffrey Dean. 2016. Google's neural machine translation system: Bridging the gap between human and machine translation. *CoRR*, abs/1609.08144.

Jiajun Zhang and Chengqing Zong. 2016. Exploiting source-side monolingual data in neural machine translation. In *Proceedings of the 2016 Conference on Empirical Methods in Natural Language Processing (EMNLP-2016)*, pages 1535–1545, Austin, Texas.

Yukun Zhu, Ryan Kiros, Richard S. Zemel, Ruslan Salakhutdinov, Raquel Urtasun, Antonio Torralba, and Sanja Fidler. 2015. Aligning books and movies: Towards story-like visual explanations by watching movies and reading books. In *2015 IEEE International Conference on Computer Vision (ICCV)*, pages 19–27.

Generating a Common Question from Multiple Documents using Multi-source Encoder-Decoder Models

Woon Sang Cho[◇] **Yizhe Zhang**[†] **Sudha Rao**[†] **Chris Brockett**[†] **Sungjin Lee**[§*]

[◇]Princeton University
[†]Microsoft Research AI
[§]Amazon Alexa AI

[◇]{woonsang}@princeton.edu, [§]{sungjinl}@amazon.com
[†]{yizzhang,sudhra,chrisbkt}@microsoft.com

Abstract

Ambiguous user queries in search engines result in the retrieval of documents that often span multiple topics. One potential solution is for the search engine to generate multiple refined queries, each of which relates to a subset of the documents spanning the same topic. A preliminary step towards this goal is to generate a question that captures common concepts of multiple documents. We propose a new task of generating common question from multiple documents and present simple variant of an existing multi-source encoder-decoder framework, called the Multi-Source Question Generator (MSQG). We first train an RNN-based single encoder-decoder generator from (single document, question) pairs. At test time, given multiple documents, the *Distribute* step of our MSQG model predicts target word distributions for each document using the trained model. The *Aggregate* step aggregates these distributions to generate a common question. This simple yet effective strategy significantly outperforms several existing baseline models applied to the new task when evaluated using automated metrics and human judgments on the MS-MARCO-QA dataset.

1 Introduction

Search engines return a list of results in response to a user query. In the case of ambiguous queries, retrieved results often span multiple topics and might benefit from further clarification from the user. One approach to disambiguate such queries is to first partition the retrieved results by topic and then ask the user to choose from queries refined for each partition.

For example, a query *'how good is apple?'* could retrieve documents some of which relate to apple the fruit, and some of which relate to Apple the company. In such a scenario, if the search engine generates two refinement queries *'how good is apple the fruit?'* and *'how good is the company apple?'*, the user could then choose one of it as a way to clarify her initial query.

In this work, we take a step towards this aim by proposing a model that generates a common question that is relevant to a set of documents. At training time, we train a standard sequence-to-sequence model (Sutskever et al., 2014) with a large number of (single document, question) pairs to generate a relevant question given a single document. At test time, given multiple (N) input documents, we use our model, called the Multi-Source Question Generator (MSQG), to allow document-specific decoders to collaboratively generate a common question. We first encode the N input documents separately using the trained encoder. Then, we perform an iterative procedure to i) (Distribute step) compute predictive word distributions from each document-specific decoder based on previous context and generation ii) (Aggregate step) aggregate predictive word distributions by voting and generate a single shared word for all decoders. These two steps are repeated until an end-of-sentence token is generated. We train and test our model on the MS-MARCO-QA dataset and evaluate it by assessing whether the original passages can be retrieved from the generated question, as well as human judgments for fluency, relevancy, and answerability. Our model significantly outperforms multiple baselines. Our main contributions are:

i) a new task of generating a common question from multiple documents, where a common question target is does *not* exist, unlike multilingual sources to common language translation tasks.

ii) an extensive evaluation of an existing multi-source encoder-decoder models including

---

* Work was done when affiliated with Microsoft Research AI

Proceedings of the 3rd Workshop on Neural Generation and Translation (WNGT 2019), pages 32–43
Hong Kong, China, November 4, 2019. ©2019 Association for Computational Linguistics
www.aclweb.org/anthology/D19-56%2d

our simple variant model for generating a common question.

iii) an empirical evaluation framework based on automated metrics and human judgments on *answerability*, *relevancy*, and *fluency* to extensively evaluate our proposed MSQG model against the baselines.

2   Related Work

The use of neural networks to generate natural language questions has mostly focused on question answering (Labutov et al., 2015; Serban et al., 2016; Rothe et al., 2016; Song et al., 2017; Duan et al., 2017; Du et al., 2017; Buck et al., 2017; Song et al., 2018; Harrison and Walker, 2018; Sun et al., 2018). A number of works process multiple passages by concatenating, adding, or attention-weight-summing among passage features into a single feature, and use it for downstream tasks (Zoph and Knight, 2016; Garmash and Monz, 2016; Libovický and Helcl, 2017; Wang et al., 2018; Yan et al., 2018; Lebanoff et al., 2018; Celikyilmaz et al., 2018; Nishimura et al., 2018; Libovický et al., 2018; Li et al., 2018b; Nishida et al., 2019). Our processing mechanisms are similar to Garmash and Monz (2016), Firat et al. (2016), and Dong and Smith (2018). The information retrieval literature is primarily concerned with reformulating queries, by either selecting expansion terms from candidates as in pseudo-relevance feedback (Salton, 1971; Zhai and Lafferty, 2001; Xu and Croft, 1996; Metzler and Croft, 2007; Cao et al., 2008; Bernhard, 2010; Nogueira and Cho, 2017; Li et al., 2018a). Our task differs because there is no *supervision* unlike multi-lingual translation tasks where a single target translation is available given sources from multiple languages.

3   Method

3.1   Multi-Source Question Generator

Our Multi-Source Question Generator (MSQG) model introduces a mechanism to generate a common question given multiple documents. At *training* time, it employs a standard sequence-to-sequence (S2S) model using a large number of (single document, question) pairs. At *test* time, it generates a common question given multiple documents, similar to Garmash and Monz (2016) and Firat et al. (2016). Specifically, our MSQG model iterates over two interleaved steps, until an end-of-sentence (EOS) token is generated:

Distribute Step   During the Distribute step, we take an instance of the trained S2S model, and perform inference with N different input documents. Each document is then encoded using one copy of the model to generate a unique target vocabulary distribution $\mathcal{P}_{i,t}^{\text{dec}}$ (for document i, at time t) for the next word. Note that source information comes from not only encoded latent representation from a source document, but also the cross-attention between source and generation.

Aggregate Step   During the Aggregate step, we aggregate the N different target distributions into one distribution by averaging them as below:

$$\tilde{\mathcal{P}}_t^{\text{dec}} = \frac{1}{N}(\beta_1 \mathcal{P}_{1,t}^{\text{dec}} + \beta_2 \mathcal{P}_{2,t}^{\text{dec}} + \cdots + \beta_N \mathcal{P}_{N,t}^{\text{dec}})$$

where $\tilde{\mathcal{P}}_t^{\text{dec}}$ is the final decoding distribution at time t, and $\Sigma_i^N \beta_i = N$. In our experiments, we weight all the decoding distributions equally ($\beta_i = 1$) to smooth out features that are distinct in each document i, where $i \in \{1, \ldots, N\}$.

Note that the *average* Aggregate can be perceived as a *majority voting* scheme, in that each document-specific decoder will vote over the vocabulary and the final decision is made in a collaborative manner. We also experimented with different Aggregate functions: (i) MSQG^{mult} multiplies the distributions, which is analogous to a *unanimous voting* scheme. However, it led to sub-optimal results since one unfavorable distribution can discourage decoding of certain common words. (ii) MSQG^{max} takes the maximum probability of each word across N distributions and normalizes them into a single distribution, but it could not generate sensible questions so we excluded from our pool of baselines.

3.2   Model Variants

Avoiding repetitive generation   We observed that naively averaging the target distributions at every decoding time continually emphasized the common topic, thereby decoding repetitive topic words. To increase the diversity of generated tokens, we mask those tokens that have already been decoded in subsequent decoding steps. This strategy is reasonable for our task since questions generally tend to be short and rarely have repeated words. This mechanism can be viewed as a hard counterpart of the coverage models developed in Tu et al. (2016) and See et al. (2017). We denote this feature by $rmrep$ in subscript.

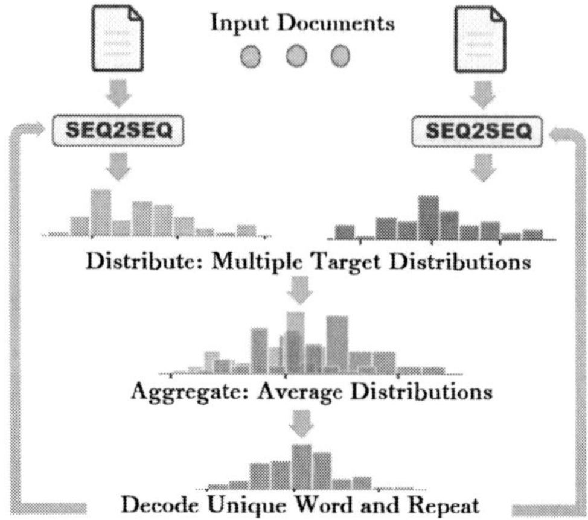

Figure 1: Multi-Source Question Generator (MSQG) model at test time. The simple architecture significantly outperforms the baselines for generating common questions, based on a number of metrics.

Shared encoder feature To initialize multiple decoders with the common meaning of the documents in a partition, we broadcast the *mean* of encoded latent representation to each decoder and denote this variant by the subscript $sharedh$. Note that the source document can affect the generated target vocabulary distribution $\mathcal{P}_{i,t}^{dec}$ at Distribute step through source-generation cross-attention.

4 Results

4.1 Experimental setup

Our training method uses the standard LSTM-based (Hochreiter and Schmidhuber, 1997) S2S with bi-linear attention (Luong et al., 2015). An input to our encoder is a concatenation of 100-dim GloVe (Pennington et al., 2014) vector, 100-dim predicate location vector, and 1024-dim ELMo (Peters et al., 2018) vector. Targets are embedded into 100-dim vectors. The S2S is bi-directional with a 256-dim bi-linear attention in each direction with ReLU (Nair and Hinton, 2010). Our encoder has two layers and we use an Adam (Kingma and Ba, 2014) with a learning rate of 2×10^{-5}.

4.2 Baselines

S2S We compare our model with a standard S2S baseline where we *concatenate* the N documents into a single document to generate a question. We provide detailed discussions about the effect of document order in supplementary material (SM). Two variants are considered (S2S and $S2S_{rmrep}$). Beam size is set to 5.

MESD We also compare our model with the multi-encoder single-decoder (MESD) baseline where documents are encoded individually into $\{v_i\}_{i=1}^{N}$. The single decoder's initial hidden state is initialized by the mean of $\{v_i\}_{i=1}^{N}$, following (Dong and Smith, 2018).

4.3 Dataset

We use the Microsoft MAchine Reading COmprehension Question-Answering Dataset (MS-MARCO-QA) (Nguyen et al., 2016), where a single data instance consists of an anonymized Bing search query q and top-10 retrieved passages. Among the 10 passages, a passage is labelled *is-selected:True* if annotators used it, if any, to construct answers, and most instances contain one or two selected passages. For training S2S, we use a single selected passage $p^* \in \{p_1, p_2, \ldots, p_{10}\}$ as input, and the query q as target output.

4.4 Constructing Evaluation Sets

For automatic evaluation, we follow the standard evaluation method from the MS-MARCO Re-Ranking task. For each generated question $\tilde{q}$, we construct an evaluation set that contains 100 passages in total.[1]

First, using the 10-passage sets from the MS-MARCO-QA development dataset as inputs, we generate common questions with the baselines and our MSQG models, decoded for a maximum length of 25 words. A sample generation is provided in the SM. Secondly, we evaluate the generations by using the pre-trained BERT-based MS-MARCO passage re-ranker $\mathcal{R}$, which is publicly available and state-of-the-art as of April 1, 2019 (Nogueira and Cho, 2019). We assess whether the 10-passage set used to generate the question ranks higher than 90 other passages drawn from a pool of ~8.8 million MS-MARCO passages using the generated question. These 90 passages are retrieved via a different criterion: BM25 (Robertson and Zaragoza, 2009) using Lucene[2]. Note that there are multiple 10-passage sets that generate the same question $\tilde{q}$. For each of these 10-passage sets, we construct a 100-passage evaluation set using the same 90 passages retrieved via the BM25 criterion.

---

[1] A small number of evaluation sets had less than 100 passages because of duplicates between the source 10-passage set and the 90 passages retrieved via BM25.

[2] https://lucene.apache.org/

Fluency				Relevancy				Answerability			
	MSQG	S2S	Human		MSQG	S2S	Human		MSQG	S2S	Human
Completely grammatical	81.37%	71.28%	**82.48%**	Completely relevant	84.00%	71.00%	**86.40%**	Completely answered	71.89%	48.45%	**72.79%**
Comprehensible	16.58%	21.81%	16.35%	Somewhat relevant	7.06%	7.56%	6.69%	Somewhat answered	7.28%	5.83%	6.83%
Not comprehensible	2.05%	6.91%	1.17%	Not relevant	8.94%	21.44%	6.91%	Not answered	20.83%	45.72%	20.38%

Human judges preferred:				*Human judges preferred:*				*Human judges preferred:*			
Our Method		Neutral	Comparison	Our Method		Neutral	Comparison	Our Method		Neutral	Comparison
MSQG	**75.77%**	9.74%	14.49%	S2S	MSQG	**79.22%**	8.06%	12.72%	S2S	MSQG	**78.50%**	9.09%	12.40%	S2S
MSQG	42.11%	10.66%	**47.24%**	Human	MSQG	40.81%	9.67%	**49.52%**	Human	MSQG	40.66%	10.26%	**49.08%**	Human

Table 1: Human evaluation of fluency, relevancy, and answerability. We used the top-ranked 30% of judges provided by a crowdsourcing service. Three judges performed each hit. Spammers were blocked at runtime. Agreement with most common was 81% overall. MSQG refers to $\text{MSQG}_{sharedh,rmrep}$. The upper table shows evaluations of individual models and the lower shows pairwise comparisons: ($Human \leftrightarrow \text{MSQG}_{sharedh,rmrep}$) and ($\text{MSQG}_{sharedh,rmrep} \leftrightarrow$ S2S). Comparison results are significant at $p < 0.00001$.

Model	Retrieval Statistics			Unique $\tilde{q}$
	MRR	nDCG	MRR@10	% dev.
S2S	0.0520	0.2147	0.0266	70.6
S2S_{rmrep}	0.0540	0.2152	0.0284	**80.4**
MESD	0.0509	0.2141	0.0248	68.6
MEMD^{mult}	0.0513	0.2142	0.0256	61.4
MEMD	0.0560	0.2209	0.0287	66.9
$\text{MSQG}_{sharedh}$	0.0569	0.2220	0.0298	67.0
$\text{MSQG}_{sharedh,rmrep}$	**0.0704**	**0.2337**	**0.0441**	70.3

Table 2: Our proposed model $\text{MSQG}_{sharedh,rmrep}$ significantly outperforms baselines, based on the automated retrieval statistics. Discussion of the proportion of unique questions is dealt in supplementary material.

4.5 Evaluation Metrics

MRR, MRR@10, nDCG An input to the re-ranker $\mathcal{R}$ is a concatenation of the generated question and one passage i.e. $[\tilde{q}, p]$. For each pair, it returns a score $\in (0, 1)$ where 1 denotes that the input passage is the most suitable for $\tilde{q}$. We score all 100 pairs in an evaluation set. For the source 10-passage set, we average the 10 scores into one score as one combined document and obtain the retrieval statistics MRR, MRR@10 (Voorhees, 2001; Radev et al., 2002), and nDCG (Järvelin and Kekäläinen, 2002) (see the SM for details).

Human Judgments We also conduct human evaluation where we compare questions generated by $\text{MSQG}_{sharedh,rmrep}$ and the S2S baseline, and the reference question using three criteria: *fluency*, *relevancy*, and *answerability* to the original 10 passages. We randomly select 200 (10-passage, reference question) sets from which we generate questions, yielding 2,000 (passage, question) evaluation pairs for our model, baseline, and reference, respectively (see the SM for details).

4.6 Results

Table 3 shows the mean retrieval statistics and their proportion of unique generated questions from 55,065 10-passage instances. Notice that our proposed MSQG models are more effective in terms of retrieving the source 10-passage sets. Particularly, $\text{MSQG}_{sharedh,rmrep}$ outperforms the baselines in all metrics, indicating that broadcasting the mean of the document vectors to initialize the decoders (*sharedh*), and increasing the coverage of vocabulary (*rmrep*) are effective mechanisms for generating common questions.

Overall, the retrieval statistics are relatively low. Most 100 passages in the evaluation sets have high pair-wise cosine similarities. We computed similarities of passage pairs for a significant portion of the dataset until convergence. A random set of 10 passages has an average pair-wise similarity of 0.80, whereas the top-10 re-ranked passages have an average of 0.85 based on BERT (Devlin et al., 2018) embeddings. Given the small similarity margin, the retrieval task is challenging. Despite of low statistics, we obtained statistical significance based on MRR with $p < 0.00001$ between *all* model pairs (see the SM for details).

Human evaluation results are shown in Table 1. In the comparison tasks, our proposed model significantly outperforms the strong baseline by a large margin. Nevertheless, judges preferred the reference over our model on all three aspects. The individual tasks corroborate our observations.

5 Conclusion

We present a new task of generating common questions based on shared concepts among documents, and extensively evaluated multi-source encoder-decoder framework models, including our variant model MSQG applied to this new task. We also provide an empirical evaluation framework based on automated metrics and human judgments to evaluated multi-source generation framework for generating common questions.

References

Mohammad Aliannejadi, Hamed Zamani, Fabio Crestani, and Bruce Croft. 2019. Asking clarifying questions in open-domain information-seeking conversations. In *SIGIR '19*.

Dzmitry Bahdanau, Kyunghyun Cho, and Yoshua Bengio. 2014. Neural machine translation by jointly learning to align and translate. *CoRR*, abs/1409.0473.

Delphine Bernhard. 2010. Query expansion based on pseudo relevance feedback from definition clusters. In *Coling 2010: Posters*, pages 54–62, Beijing, China. Coling 2010 Organizing Committee.

Christian Buck, Jannis Bulian, Massimiliano Ciaramita, Wojciech Gajewski, Andrea Gesmundo, Neil Houlsby, and Wei Wang. 2017. Ask the right questions: Active question reformulation with reinforcement learning.

Guihong Cao, Jian-Yun Nie, Jianfeng Gao, and Stephen Robertson. 2008. Selecting good expansion terms for pseudo-relevance feedback. In *Proceedings of the 31st Annual International ACM SIGIR Conference on Research and Development in Information Retrieval*, SIGIR '08, pages 243–250, New York, NY, USA. ACM.

Asli Celikyilmaz, Antoine Bosselut, Xiaodong He, and Yejin Choi. 2018. Deep communicating agents for abstractive summarization. In *Proceedings of the 2018 Conference of the North American Chapter of the Association for Computational Linguistics: Human Language Technologies, Volume 1 (Long Papers)*, pages 1662–1675, New Orleans, Louisiana. Association for Computational Linguistics.

Eric Chu and Peter J. Liu. 2018. Unsupervised neural multi-document abstractive summarization. *CoRR*, abs/1810.05739.

Jacob Devlin, Ming-Wei Chang, Kenton Lee, and Kristina Toutanova. 2018. BERT: pre-training of deep bidirectional transformers for language understanding. *CoRR*, abs/1810.04805.

Rui Dong and David Smith. 2018. Multi-input attention for unsupervised OCR correction. In *Proceedings of the 56th Annual Meeting of the Association for Computational Linguistics (Volume 1: Long Papers)*, pages 2363–2372, Melbourne, Australia. Association for Computational Linguistics.

Xinya Du, Junru Shao, and Claire Cardie. 2017. Learning to ask: Neural question generation for reading comprehension. In *Proceedings of the 55th Annual Meeting of the Association for Computational Linguistics (Volume 1: Long Papers)*, pages 1342–1352, Vancouver, Canada. Association for Computational Linguistics.

Nan Duan, Duyu Tang, Peng Chen, and Ming Zhou. 2017. Question generation for question answering. In *Proceedings of the 2017 Conference on Empirical Methods in Natural Language Processing*, pages 866–874, Copenhagen, Denmark. Association for Computational Linguistics.

Orhan Firat, Baskaran Sankaran, Yaser Al-Onaizan, Fatos T. Yarman-Vural, and Kyunghyun Cho. 2016. Zero-resource translation with multi-lingual neural machine translation. *CoRR*, abs/1606.04164.

Jianfeng Gao, Michel Galley, and Lihong Li. 2018. Neural approaches to conversational AI. *arXiv preprint arXiv:1809.08267*.

Ekaterina Garmash and Christof Monz. 2016. Ensemble learning for multi-source neural machine translation. In *Proceedings of COLING 2016, the 26th International Conference on Computational Linguistics: Technical Papers*, pages 1409–1418, Osaka, Japan. The COLING 2016 Organizing Committee.

Vrindavan Harrison and Marilyn Walker. 2018. Neural generation of diverse questions using answer focus, contextual and linguistic features.

Sepp Hochreiter and Jürgen Schmidhuber. 1997. Long short-term memory. *Neural Comput.*, 9(8):1735–1780.

Kalervo Järvelin and Jaana Kekäläinen. 2002. Cumulated gain-based evaluation of ir techniques. *ACM Trans. Inf. Syst.*, 20(4):422–446.

Diederik P. Kingma and Jimmy Ba. 2014. Adam: A method for stochastic optimization. *CoRR*, abs/1412.6980.

Igor Labutov, Sumit Basu, and Lucy Vanderwende. 2015. Deep questions without deep understanding. In *Proceedings of the 53rd Annual Meeting of the Association for Computational Linguistics and the 7th International Joint Conference on Natural Language Processing (Volume 1: Long Papers)*, pages 889–898, Beijing, China. Association for Computational Linguistics.

Logan Lebanoff, Kaiqiang Song, and Fei Liu. 2018. Adapting the neural encoder-decoder framework from single to multi-document summarization. In *Proceedings of the 2018 Conference on Empirical Methods in Natural Language Processing*, pages 4131–4141, Brussels, Belgium. Association for Computational Linguistics.

Canjia Li, Yingfei Sun, Ben He, Le Wang, Kai Hui, Andrew Yates, Le Sun, and Jungang Xu. 2018a. NPRF: A neural pseudo relevance feedback framework for ad-hoc information retrieval. In *Proceedings of the 2018 Conference on Empirical Methods in Natural Language Processing*, pages 4482–4491, Brussels, Belgium. Association for Computational Linguistics.

Ruizhi Li, Xiaofei Wang, Sri Harish Reddy Mallidi, Takaaki Hori, Shinji Watanabe, and Hynek Hermansky. 2018b. Multi-encoder multi-resolution framework for end-to-end speech recognition. *CoRR*, abs/1811.04897.

Jindřich Libovický and Jindřich Helcl. 2017. Attention strategies for multi-source sequence-to-sequence learning. In *Proceedings of the 55th Annual Meeting of the Association for Computational Linguistics (Volume 2: Short Papers)*, pages 196–202, Vancouver, Canada. Association for Computational Linguistics.

Jindřich Libovický, Jindřich Helcl, and David Mareček. 2018. Input combination strategies for multi-source transformer decoder. In *Proceedings of the Third Conference on Machine Translation: Research Papers*, pages 253–260, Belgium, Brussels. Association for Computational Linguistics.

Yi Luan, Yangfeng Ji, Hannaneh Hajishirzi, and Boyang Li. 2016. Multiplicative representations for unsupervised semantic role induction. In *ACL*.

Thang Luong, Hieu Pham, and Christopher D. Manning. 2015. Effective approaches to attention-based neural machine translation. In *Proceedings of the 2015 Conference on Empirical Methods in Natural Language Processing*, pages 1412–1421, Lisbon, Portugal. Association for Computational Linguistics.

Donald Metzler and W. Bruce Croft. 2007. Latent concept expansion using markov random fields. In *Proceedings of the 30th Annual International ACM SIGIR Conference on Research and Development in Information Retrieval*, SIGIR '07, pages 311–318, New York, NY, USA. ACM.

Nasrin Mostafazadeh, Chris Brockett, Bill Dolan, Michel Galley, Jianfeng Gao, Georgios Spithourakis, and Lucy Vanderwende. 2017. Image-grounded conversations: Multimodal context for natural question and response generation. In *Proceedings of the Eighth International Joint Conference on Natural Language Processing (Volume 1: Long Papers)*, pages 462–472, Taipei, Taiwan. Asian Federation of Natural Language Processing.

Vinod Nair and Geoffrey E. Hinton. 2010. Rectified linear units improve restricted boltzmann machines. In *Proceedings of the 27th International Conference on International Conference on Machine Learning*, ICML'10, pages 807–814, USA. Omnipress.

Tri Nguyen, Mir Rosenberg, Xia Song, Jianfeng Gao, Saurabh Tiwary, Rangan Majumder, and Li Deng. 2016. MS MARCO: A human generated machine reading comprehension dataset. In *Proceedings of the Workshop on Cognitive Computation: Integrating neural and symbolic approaches 2016 co-located with the 30th Annual Conference on Neural Information Processing Systems (NIPS 2016), Barcelona, Spain, December 9, 2016*.

Kyosuke Nishida, Itsumi Saito, Kosuke Nishida, Kazutoshi Shinoda, Atsushi Otsuka, Hisako Asano, and Junji Tomita. 2019. Multi-style generative reading comprehension. *CoRR*, abs/1901.02262.

Yuta Nishimura, Katsuhito Sudoh, Graham Neubig, and Satoshi Nakamura. 2018. Multi-source neural machine translation with missing data. In *Proceedings of the 2nd Workshop on Neural Machine Translation and Generation*, pages 92–99, Melbourne, Australia. Association for Computational Linguistics.

Rodrigo Nogueira and Kyunghyun Cho. 2017. Task-oriented query reformulation with reinforcement learning. In *Proceedings of the 2017 Conference on Empirical Methods in Natural Language Processing*, pages 574–583, Copenhagen, Denmark. Association for Computational Linguistics.

Rodrigo Nogueira and Kyunghyun Cho. 2019. Passage re-ranking with BERT. *CoRR*, abs/1901.04085.

Jeffrey Pennington, Richard Socher, and Christopher D. Manning. 2014. GloVe: Global vectors for word representation. In *Proceedings of the 2014 Conference on Empirical Methods in Natural Language Processing*, pages 1532–1543.

Matthew E. Peters, Mark Neumann, Mohit Iyyer, Matt Gardner, Christopher Clark, Kenton Lee, and Luke Zettlemoyer. 2018. Deep contextualized word representations. In *Proc. of NAACL*.

Dragomir R. Radev, Hong Qi, Harris Wu, and Weiguo Fan. 2002. Evaluating web-based question answering systems. In *Proceedings of the Third International Conference on Language Resources and Evaluation (LREC'02)*, Las Palmas, Canary Islands - Spain. European Language Resources Association (ELRA).

Stephen Robertson and Hugo Zaragoza. 2009. The probabilistic relevance framework: Bm25 and beyond. *Found. Trends Inf. Retr.*, 3(4):333–389.

A Rothe, Brenden Lake, and Todd Gureckis. 2016. Asking and evaluating natural language questions. In *Proceedings of the 38th Annual Conference of the Cognitive Science Society*.

G. Salton. 1971. *The SMART Retrieval System—Experiments in Automatic Document Processing*. Prentice-Hall, Inc., Upper Saddle River, NJ, USA.

Abigail See, Peter J. Liu, and Christopher D. Manning. 2017. Get to the point: Summarization with pointer-generator networks. In *Proceedings of the 55th Annual Meeting of the Association for Computational Linguistics (Volume 1: Long Papers)*, pages 1073–1083, Vancouver, Canada. Association for Computational Linguistics.

Iulian Vlad Serban, Alberto García-Durán, Caglar Gulcehre, Sungjin Ahn, Sarath Chandar, Aaron Courville, and Yoshua Bengio. 2016. Generating factoid questions with recurrent neural networks: The 30M factoid question-answer corpus. In *Proceedings of the 54th Annual Meeting of the Association for Computational Linguistics (Volume 1: Long Papers)*, pages 588–598, Berlin, Germany. Association for Computational Linguistics.

Linfeng Song, Zhiguo Wang, and Wael Hamza. 2017. A unified query-based generative model for question generation and question answering.

Linfeng Song, Zhiguo Wang, Wael Hamza, Yue Zhang, and Daniel Gildea. 2018. Leveraging context information for natural question generation. In *Proceedings of the 2018 Conference of the North American Chapter of the Association for Computational Linguistics: Human Language Technologies, Volume 2 (Short Papers)*, pages 569–574, New Orleans, Louisiana. Association for Computational Linguistics.

Xingwu Sun, Jing Liu, Yajuan Lyu, Wei He, Yanjun Ma, and Shi Wang. 2018. Answer-focused and position-aware neural question generation. In *Proceedings of the 2018 Conference on Empirical Methods in Natural Language Processing*, pages 3930–3939, Brussels, Belgium. Association for Computational Linguistics.

Ilya Sutskever, Oriol Vinyals, and Quoc V Le. 2014. Sequence to sequence learning with neural networks. In *NIPS*.

Zhaopeng Tu, Zhengdong Lu, Yang Liu, Xiaohua Liu, and Hang Li. 2016. Modeling coverage for neural machine translation. In *Proceedings of the 54th Annual Meeting of the Association for Computational Linguistics (Volume 1: Long Papers)*, pages 76–85, Berlin, Germany. Association for Computational Linguistics.

Ellen M. Voorhees. 2001. The trec question answering track. *Nat. Lang. Eng.*, 7(4):361–378.

Yizhong Wang, Kai Liu, Jing Liu, Wei He, Yajuan Lyu, Hua Wu, Sujian Li, and Haifeng Wang. 2018. Multi-passage machine reading comprehension with cross-passage answer verification. In *Proceedings of the 56th Annual Meeting of the Association for Computational Linguistics (Volume 1: Long Papers)*, pages 1918–1927, Melbourne, Australia. Association for Computational Linguistics.

Jinxi Xu and W. Bruce Croft. 1996. Query expansion using local and global document analysis. In *Proceedings of the 19th Annual International ACM SIGIR Conference on Research and Development in Information Retrieval*, SIGIR '96, pages 4–11, New York, NY, USA. ACM.

Ming Yan, Jiangnan Xia, Chen Wu, Bin Bi, Zhongzhou Zhao, Ji Zhang, Luo Si, Rui Wang, Wei Wang, and Haiqing Chen. 2018. A deep cascade model for multi-document reading comprehension. *CoRR*, abs/1811.11374.

Chengxiang Zhai and John Lafferty. 2001. Model-based feedback in the language modeling approach to information retrieval. In *Proceedings of the Tenth International Conference on Information and Knowledge Management*, CIKM '01, pages 403–410, New York, NY, USA. ACM.

Barret Zoph and Kevin Knight. 2016. Multi-source neural translation. In *Proceedings of the 2016 Conference of the North American Chapter of the Association for Computational Linguistics: Human Language Technologies*, pages 30–34, San Diego, California. Association for Computational Linguistics.

Model	Retrieval Statistics			Unique $\hat{q}$
	MRR	**nDCG**	**MRR@10**	**% dev.**
S2S-$\mathcal{M}_{256}$	0.0368	0.1943	0.0147	66.3
S2S-$\mathcal{M}_{512}$	0.0393	0.1980	0.0165	71.1
S2S	0.0520	0.2147	0.0266	70.6
S2S$_{rmrep}$	0.0540	0.2152	0.0284	**80.4**
MESD-$\mathcal{M}_{512}$	0.0367	0.1941	0.0147	72.6
MESD	0.0509	0.2141	0.0248	68.6
MSQG-$\mathcal{M}_{512}$	0.0450	0.2056	0.0210	72.0
MSQG^{mult}	0.0513	0.2142	0.0256	61.4
MSQG	0.0560	0.2209	0.0287	66.9
MSQG$_{sharedh}$	0.0569	0.2220	0.0298	67.0
MSQG$_{sharedh,rmrep}$	**0.0704**	**0.2337**	**0.0441**	70.3

Table 3: Full results, comparing models constructed with $\mathcal{M}_{256}$, $\mathcal{M}_{512}$, and $\mathcal{M}_{256}^{attn}$. $\mathcal{M}_{512}$ has the most number of parameters among the three considered.

Supplementary Material

A Full Experiment Results

Table 3 shows the retrieval results on a larger set of baselines and MSQG models. $\mathcal{M}_{256}^{attn}$ is an attention-based encoder-decoder with hidden size 256 for both encoder and decoder. $\mathcal{M}_{256}$ and $\mathcal{M}_{512}$ are non-attention encoder-decoders with hidden sizes 256 and 512. S2S denotes $\mathcal{M}_{256}^{attn}$, as in the main paper. It shows that models constructed using $\mathcal{M}_{256}^{attn}$ are more effective as opposed to models using $\mathcal{M}_{512}$ which has more parameters. Furthermore, we see that the averaging scheme in the *Reduction* step, broadcasting the same encoder mean, and increasing coverage of vocabulary tokens are important features to generating common questions using MSQG models.

B Effect of Document Order on S2S

To examine if the order of multiple input documents are critical for S2S, we obtain the attention weights at each decoding time, gathered across the development dataset. Next, we perform a simple ordinary least squares regression, where the predictors are indexed word positions in a concatenated input, and responses are assumed noisy attention weights over the development dataset for each word position.

The slope coefficient fell within the 95% confidence interval that includes the null: $\left[-2.75 \times 10^{-5}, 3.03 \times 10^{-5}\right]$ and a statistically significant intercept value of 0.0021. The result also validates that an average 10-passage string is approximately 476 ($\approx \frac{1}{0.0021}$) words long. Thus, we conclude that the attention weights are evenly distributed across multiple document at test time, and the document ordering is not critical to the

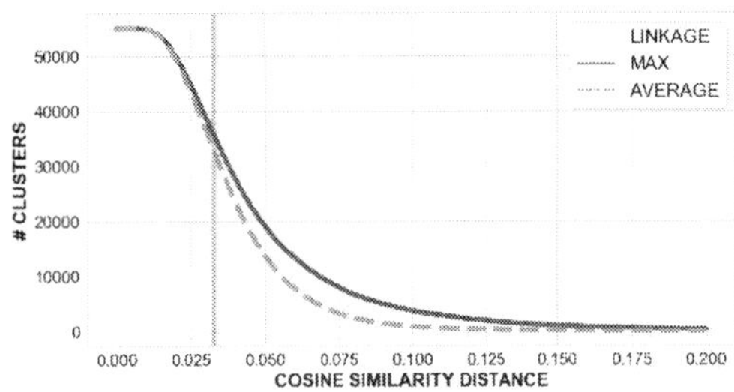

Figure 2: Agglomerative Clustering of 55,065 source 10-passage sets. Each set is represented by the mean of 10 BERT embeddings. Both max and average linkages yield the same inflection point at 0.0326, corresponding to 35,928 and 32,871 clusters. This method implies that the target proportion of unique generations should be at least 65% or 60%, which all models but MSQG^{mult} achieve.

performance of S2S.

C Clustering Duplicate 10-passage Sets

In the MS-MARCO-QA dataset, there are many highly similar 10-passage sets retrieved from semantically close MS-MARCO queries. Examples of semantically close MS-MARCO queries include [*"symptoms blood sugar is low"*, *"low blood sugar symptoms"*, *"symptoms of low blood sugar levels"* , *"signs and symptoms of low blood sugar"*, *"what symptoms from low blood sugar"*, ...], from which we expect duplicate generated questions, thus in sum, less than 55,065 different questions.

Therefore, to estimate the *target* proportion of unique generations, we examine the number of semantically similar 10-passage sets through agglomerative clustering. Figure 2 shows cluster results with varying degrees of affinity thresholds, and observe that the effective models should generate at least 65% unique questions from the development dataset. This, together with the low retrieval statistics of MSQG^{mult}, implies that multiplying the distributions is not an appropriate *Reduction* step.

On the other hand, generating the most number of unique questions does not imply that the model better generates common questions. In particular, S2S$_{rmrep}$ generates the most diverse questions, however, its retrieval statistics are significantly lower than its MSQG counterparts.

D   Statistical Significance Tests

Retrieval evaluation on ∼55K evaluation sets using the re-ranker $\mathcal{R}$ is compute-intensive. Thus, for each model, we randomly sample and obtain retrieval statistics for 15K evaluation sets which are enough to mimic the true evaluation set distribution.

Then, to assess statistical significance, we use a non-parametric two-sample test, such as Mann-Whitney (MW) or Kolmogorov-Smirnov statistic, and test whether any pair of 15K retrieval sets between two models come from the same distribution. In our task, both tests reached the same conclusion. MW two-sample tests on MRR results showed statistical significance at $p < 0.00001$ for *all* model pairs dealt in the main paper, in spite of the relatively low retrieval statistics.

E   Human Evaluation Templates

UHRS comparison and individual task instructions and shown in the next pages.

F   Generated Questions Sample

Passage 1: *cucumbers and zucchini look similar but have nutritional differences . photo credit martin poole / digital vision / getty images . do n't let the similarities between cucumbers and zucchini confuse you . even though both cylindrical vegetables are dark green with white flesh , they are distinctively different species . both cucumbers and zucchini belong to the curcurbit family , which also counts gourds , melons , pumpkins and squash among its members . cucumbers and zucchini differ both in how people commonly eat them and in their nutritional values . people almost always eat cukes raw , while zucchini is more often cooked .*

Passage 2: *cucumber and squash seedlings both have elongated foliage for the first set of leaves after they emerge from the soil . the second set of leaves on a seedling varies . cucumber leaves are in the shape of a triangle and are flat in the center and rough to the touch . squash plants vary in shape as to the particular variety , but have three to five lobes and are larger than cucumber leaves . zucchini squash has elongated serrated leaves .*

Passage 3: *zucchini vs cucumber . zucchini and cucumber are two vegetables that look mightily similar and hard to distinguish from each other . but in close inspection , they are actually very different . so read on . zucchini . zucchini is defined to be the kind of vegetable that is long , green colored and has many seeds .*

Passage 4: *as a general rule , we prefer cucumbers raw and zucchini cooked . while you ca n't replace one with the other , zucchinis and cucumbers do complement one another . slice two cucumbers , two zucchinis and one sweet onion , and soak them all in rice vinegar for at least an hour in the refrigerator .*

Passage 5: *cucumber and zucchini are popular vegetables that are similar in appearance and botanical classification . but they differ significantly in taste , texture and culinary application . zucchini and cucumber are both members of the botanical family cucurbitaceae , which includes melons , squashes and gourds .*

Passage 6: *melon vs. squash . the cucumber is not particularly sweet , but it shares a genus with the cantaloupe and is botanically classified as a melon . the zucchini is a variety of summer squash and is of the same species as crookneck squash .*

Passage 7: *cucumber vs. zucchini . side by side , they might fool you : cucumbers and zucchinis share the same dark green skin , pale seedy flesh , and long cylindrical shape . to the touch , however , these near - twins are not the same : cucumbers are cold and waxy , while zucchinis are rough and dry . the two vegetables also perform very differently when cooked .*

Passage 8: *the second set of squash leaves grow much quicker and larger than cucumber leaves in the same time . squash leaves may be up to four times as large as a cucumber leaf when they are the same age .*

Passage 9: *in reality , zucchini is really defined as a vegetable so when it comes to the preparation of it , it has different temperament . cucumber . cucumber is both classified as a fruit and a vegetable . it is long and is green in color , too . it is part of what they call the gourd family .*

Passage 10: *zucchini 's flowers are edible ; cucumber 's flowers are not . zucchini is generally considered as a vegetable ; cucumber is classified as both a fruit and a vegetable . yes , they can fool the eye because of their similar look but as you go deeper , they are very different in so many ways .*

Question generated by MSQG$_{sharedh,rmrep}$**:**
what are the difference between cucumber and zucchini

Question generated by S2S:
different types of zucchini

Reference question:
difference between cucumber and zucchini

Title: Compare two questions

Instructions

The goal of this task is to understand which of the two given questions is better when evaluated on the criteria of answerability, fluency and relevancy to the given passage.

You will be shown a passage and two questions (Q1 & Q2).

Your task is to answer the following:

Answerability: Which of the two questions is better answered in the passage?
(Note: Ignore minor errors and disfluencies in English here.)
Question A   No preference   Question B

Fluency: Which of the two questions is more fluent/grammatical English?
Question A   No preference   Question B

Relevance: Which of the two questions is more relevant to the passage?
(Note: a question can be relevant even if it is not answerable in the passage.)
Question A   No preference   Question B

Example 1

Passage:

egg prices soar across india nov 20 , 2017 , 19:29 ist . after vegetables , now it 's eggs that will burn a hole in your pocket . the prices of eggs have reached a record high across india . hit by tight supply in the many states , egg prices in the country have increased by up to 40 per cent . egg prices in retail markets in the national capital are ruling at rs 7 - 7.50 per piece , up from rs 4 - 5 last year , according to trade data .

Question A: *average price of egg in india*

Question B: *how much does it cost to raise a egg egg*

Answerability: Question A is much better answered than Question B

Reason: Question A is answered in the passage whereas Question B is only relevant to passage (but not answered in the passage).

Fluency: Question A is much more fluent than Question B

Reason: Because Question A is grammatical whereas Question B contains grammatical errors.

Relevancy: Question A is much more relevant than Question B

Reason: Because Question A is answered in the passage whereas the question Question B does not make sense.

Title: Rate how good is the question on basis of answerability, fluency and relevancy.

Instructions

The goal of this task is to how good is the question on basis of answerability, fluency and relevancy to a given passage.

You will be shown a passage and a question asked to answer the following:

a. How well is the question answered in the given passage?
   Choose from the following:
   - Question is completely answered in the passage
   - Question is somewhat answered in the passage
   - Question is not answered in the passage

b. How fluent is the question?
   Choose from the following:
   - Question is completely grammatical
   - Question is comprehensible but includes a few grammatical errors
   - Question is not comprehensible

c. How relevant is the question to the given passage?
   Choose from the following:
   - Question is completely relevant to the passage
   - Question is somewhat relevant to the passage
   - Question is not relevant to the passage

Example 1

Passage:

wells fargo center philadelphia parking lots location , transportation options , parking info , and seat maps available here . where is wells fargo center philadelphia parking lots in philadelphia ? find out at stubhub .

Question: *how much is parking by wells fargo Philadelphia*

Answerability: Question is somewhat answered in the passage

Reason: Although the passage does not directly include the parking cost, it points to a website that could contain this information. Hence the question is somewhat answered in the passage.

Fluency: Question is comprehensible but includes a few grammatical errors

Reason: A fluent version of the question would look something like *"how much would parking by wells fargo philadelphia cost"*

Relevancy: Question is completely relevant to the passage

Reason: Since the question is asking about parking by Wells Fargo and the passage is talking about the same.

Generating Diverse Story Continuations with Controllable Semantics

Lifu Tu[1]   **Xiaoan Ding**[2]   **Dong Yu**[3]   **Kevin Gimpel**[1]

[1]Toyota Technological Institute at Chicago, Chicago, IL, 60637, USA
[2]University of Chicago, Chicago, IL, 60637, USA
[3]Tencent AI Lab, Bellevue, WA, 98004, USA

{lifu, kgimpel}@ttic.edu, xiaoanding@uchicago.edu, dyu@tencent.com

Abstract

We propose a simple and effective modeling framework for controlled generation of multiple, diverse outputs. We focus on the setting of generating the next sentence of a story given its context. As controllable dimensions, we consider several sentence attributes, including sentiment, length, predicates, frames, and automatically-induced clusters. Our empirical results demonstrate: (1) our framework is accurate in terms of generating outputs that match the target control values; (2) our model yields increased maximum metric scores compared to standard n-best list generation via beam search; (3) controlling generation with semantic frames leads to a stronger combination of diversity and quality than other control variables as measured by automatic metrics. We also conduct a human evaluation to assess the utility of providing multiple suggestions for creative writing, demonstrating promising results for the potential of controllable, diverse generation in a collaborative writing system.

1 Introduction

We consider the problem of automatic story continuation generation, i.e., how to generate story continuations conditioned on the story context. Inspired by recent work in controllable generation (Hu et al., 2017; Ficler and Goldberg, 2017), we propose a simple and effective modeling framework for controlled generation of multiple, diverse outputs based on interpretable control variables. Each control variable corresponds to an attribute of a sentence. Compared to previous work that only seeks to control the values of sentiment (Hu et al., 2017) and length (Kikuchi et al., 2016), we further explore neural text generation with particular verbal predicates, semantic frames, and automatically-induced clusters.

We compare the diversity of story continuations controlled by different sentence attributes and find

Context:	
sandra needed a new phone . her old one had broken . she walked into the store and bought a new one . she was very excited .	
Control Attributes and Generated Continuations:	
Sentiment:	
positive	sandra was happy to have a new phone .
Predicates:	
loved	sandra loved the new one .
gave	sandra 's mom gave sandra a refund .
Frames:	
Calendric_unit	it was the perfect day of her life .
Cardinal_numbers	it was a perfect one .
Activity_ongoing	she kept it on the couch .

Table 1: Story continuations conditioned on various control attributes generated from our framework.

that using frames yields a stronger combination of diversity and quality than other control variables as measured by automatic metrics. Unlike certain other attributes, frames have hundreds of possible values. Some frame values can help to get a natural continuation, while others are not applicable when considering the story context.

We quantitatively evaluate both controllability and diversity. Our empirical results show that: (1) our framework is accurate in terms of generating outputs that match the target attribute values; (2) our framework increases maximum metrics scores compared to n-best list generation with beam search; (3) controlling generation with frames leads to a stronger combination of diversity and quality than other control variables as measured by automatic metrics.

We also explore methods to rerank continuations to choose attribute values automatically and obtain a small number of high-quality outputs. We consider two frame ranking methods: one reranks the generated continuations using a reverse scoring model (Li et al., 2016) and returns the k-best generations; the second first predicts the k most likely frames based on the context, and uses these

Proceedings of the 3rd Workshop on Neural Generation and Translation (WNGT 2019), pages 44–58
Hong Kong, China, November 4, 2019. ©2019 Association for Computational Linguistics
www.aclweb.org/anthology/D19-56%2d

frames to generate continuations. One potential use case of controllable, diverse story generation is collaborative writing applications (Clark et al., 2018b). We conduct a human evaluation to assess the utility of providing multiple suggestions from our models in this setting, demonstrating promising results for the potential of controllable generation for collaborative writing.

2 Task Description and Definitions

Given a story context and a control attribute value, our goal is to generate a story continuation that: (1) conforms to the given attribute value, (2) is relevant to the story context, and (3) is complementary to continuations with other control attribute values, thereby providing a diverse set of continuations when used with multiple attribute values.

We use $x = \langle x_1, x_2, ..., x_{|x|} \rangle$ to denote a story context and $y = \langle y_1, y_2, ..., y_{|y|} \rangle$ to denote a story continuation. The last token $y_{|y|}$ is assumed to be $\langle eos \rangle$. We develop a framework to model tuples (x, l, y), where l is a control attribute. The control attribute represents a characteristic of the continuation, such as its length, sentiment, automatically-induced cluster, verbal predicate, or set of semantic frames. Table 1 shows several examples of control attributes and generated continuations corresponding to them from our model.

3 Model

Our controllable generation framework is a variation of a sequence-to-sequence (seq2seq) model with attention (Sutskever et al., 2014; Bahdanau et al., 2015; Luong et al., 2015). To represent the control attribute values, we define an attribute embedding function R that maps a given attribute value l to a vector z: $z = R(l)$. Here l can be a single discrete number or a set of discrete numbers, depending on what attributes are being used. The control variable z contains two parts: $z = [z_{\text{enc}}; z_{\text{dec}}]$ where semicolon (;) denotes vertical concatenation and z_{enc} and z_{dec} are additional inputs for the encoder and decoder respectively.

Encoder. For our encoder, we use a standard bidirectional recurrent neural network (RNN):

$$\overrightarrow{s_i} = f_{e1}([v_i; z_{\text{enc}}], \overrightarrow{s_{i-1}})$$
$$\overleftarrow{s_i} = f_{e2}([v_i; z_{\text{enc}}], \overleftarrow{s_{i+1}})$$
$$s_i = [\overrightarrow{s_i}; \overleftarrow{s_i}]$$

where v_i is the vector representation of word x_i, $s_i \in \mathbb{R}^d$ is the hidden state at time i, and f_{e1} and f_{e2} are the forward and backward RNN functions.

Decoder. Our decoder uses an RNN with the general global attention scheme from Luong et al. (2015). An additional input z_{dec} is fed to the decoder at each time step to reflect the characteristics of the control variable:

$$h_j = f_d([y_{j-1}; z_{\text{dec}}], h_{j-1})$$

where h_j is the decoder RNN hidden vector at time step j and f_d is the decoder RNN function. Then, the conditional probability with controllable generation can be decomposed as follows:

$$\log p_\Theta(y \mid x, l) = \sum_{j=1}^{|y|} \log p_\Theta(y_j \mid y_{<j}, s, l)$$

Here s represents the hidden states of the source sequence and Θ are the parameters of the seq2seq attention model.

Training. Our training objective is:

$$\min_{\Theta, R} \sum_{\langle x, l, y \rangle \in \mathcal{D}} -\log p_\Theta(y \mid x, l) \qquad (1)$$

where $\mathcal{D}$ is the training data, i.e., we assume attribute values l are provided during training. In practice, these will be predicted automatically using a linguistic analyzer. With certain attributes, we do not update the attribute value embeddings R, i.e., we fix z_{enc} and z_{dec} to one-hot vectors.

Inference. We can specify the value of the control variable and generate specific outputs. By changing the variable values, we obtain multiple continuations for the same context. Beam search is used for decoding.

4 Control Attributes

In this section, we describe the control attributes we explored using our framework. Table 2 shows examples of generated continuations for a single story context with several values for the control attributes described below. Given our simple modeling framework, it would be natural to experiment with combining control attributes via summation or averaging of the attribute representations, but we leave an investigation of this to future work, focusing here on using one attribute at a time.

Context:	i bought a pair of earbuds at target . i spent ten dollars . someone told me they were cheaper at the dollar store . they were only a dollar .
Gold Continuation:	i wish i had known that before .

Sentiment	
negative	**i was disappointed .**
neutral	i decided to keep them .
positive	i was able to get a new pair .

Length	
4	i was shocked .
5	i was rather disappointed .
6	i bought a new pair .
7	i was able to buy them .
8	**i was glad i bought them .**
9	i was able to buy a new pair .
10	i was able to buy a new pair .
11	i was able to buy a new pair of shoes .
12	i was able to buy a new pair of new ones .
13	i was able to buy a new pair of rubber flavored items .
14	i was able to buy a new pair and i was very happy .

Verbal Predicates	
wish, known	**i wish i will always recognize them .**
got	i got a new one .
decided	i never decided on the new restaurants .
went	i went home with a new friend .
is	it is a great price .
get	now i have to get a new one .
felt	i felt very disappointed .
go	i will go to the grocery store .
took	i took them to the store .
left	i left the store with a new tip .
realized	after many years , i realized that .
loved	i loved them .
ran	i ran back to the store .

Frame Semantics	
gold frame set*	**i wanted to be a professional photographer .**
Arriving	i got the earbuds .
Quantity	it was a lot of fun .
Becoming	it ended up being a target .
Cardinal_numbers	i paid for $ 50 dollars .
Being_obligated	i guess i had a similar card .
Kinship	my parents were proud .
Statement	i told them i would not be a target .
Causation	they sent me to the seller 's desk .
Opinion	i think i was a millionaire .
Perception_experience	it was a hit .

Clusters	
0	i ended up buying a new one .
1	i bought a new pair of shoes .
2	**i was a good price .**
3	i bought a new pair of shoes for free .
4	i decided to buy a new pair of headphones .

Oracle BOW	
-	i then wish that i had no time .

Table 2: Generated continuations from our framework with different control attribute values. Boldface indicates attribute values of the human-written continuation. * = the frame set in the human-written continuation contains the following frames: *Desiring*, *Experiencer*, *Event*, *Being_named*, and *Entity*.

Sentiment. Stories may express sentiment regarding their characters or circumstances. We acquire sentiment labels by running the pretrained analyzer from Socher et al. (2013) on the continuations in the training data. The analyzer produces three labels: "negative", "neutral", or "positive". During training, z_{enc} and z_{dec} are fixed one-hot vectors for each value.

Length. Some prior work has generated summaries with a desired length (Kikuchi et al., 2016; Fan et al., 2018a). We similarly use length of the continuation as a control attribute. Instead of using an embedding for each integer length value, we group the lengths into a small number of bins (details are provided below). z_{enc} and z_{dec} are fixed one-hot vectors for each bin.

Verbal Predicates. Semantic role labeling (SRL) is a form of shallow semantic parsing that annotates predicates and their arguments in sentences. We consider predicates from a semantic role labeling as control attributes. We use the SRL system from AllenNLP (Gardner et al., 2018) to automatically obtain predicates for the continuations in our training set. Then, a predicate vector is obtained by first summing up 100-dimensional GloVe embeddings (Pennington et al., 2014) of the predicted predicates (if there is more than one), then reducing the dimension to 64 using principal component analysis.[1] We wish to clarify that we do not use the argument structure from the SRL system. We restrict our focus to simply the set of verbal predicates in the SRL structure; this would presumably be simpler to use in interactive settings where users would specify attribute values for generating continuations.

Frame Semantics. A story is composed of a sequence of meaningful events (Chatman, 1980), often following particular patterns described in various terms such as scripts (Schank and Abelson, 1977) and frames. FrameNet (Baker et al., 1998) is an inventory of semantic frames, which are semantic abstractions describing universal categories of events, concepts, and relationships.

We consider frame semantics as another control attribute in our framework. In order to get a frame semantic representation for a continuation, we use SEMAFOR (Das et al., 2014). SEMAFOR automatically produces a frame-semantic parse for a sentence, which consists of spans that evoke particular frames in FrameNet as well as annotations

---

[1]The reason we use PCA here is to make all attribute embeddings have comparable embedding size, though we did not systematically evaluate the effect of this choice.

of textual spans that correspond to frame-specific arguments. For our purposes, we drop the arguments and only use the set containing all frames that are evoked in the sentence. A sentence may contain multiple frames. For example, in the sentence "Roa's advice made Emma a lot happier in her life!", "a lot" evokes the *Quantity* frame while "Emma a lot happier" evokes the *Effect* frame.

The frame set variable z is computed by summing embeddings for the frames in the set:

$$z = R(l) = \sum_{j \in l} R_j \qquad (2)$$

where l is the frame set and R_j is the representation of frame j. The frame embeddings are learned during training.[2] For modeling purposes, we restrict our attention to the 100 most frequent frames in the training data. The rest of the frames are pooled together to form a single additional "catch-all" frame.

Automatically-Induced Clusters. We also experiment with running k-means clustering on the bag-of-words sentence representations of the continuations in the training set. We treat these automatically-induced cluster labels as control attribute values. Below we describe experiments with different cluster labels and analyze the characteristics of the generated outputs.

Oracle Bag-of-Words Sentence Representations. We also consider the use of a bag-of-words (BOW) sentence representation as a control attribute. Naturally, the sentence representation of the continuation is not available before generating the continuation in practice. However, we can use this attribute to verify the capability of our model to reconstruct the continuation from its bag-of-words representation.

5 Experimental Setup

5.1 Datasets

We experiment with the publicly available ROC story corpus developed by Mostafazadeh et al. (2016). It consists of approximately 100K five-sentence stories of everyday events. We sample 2000 stories as a development set and 2000 as our test set. The remaining stories form our training set. Our goal is to generate the fifth sentence (the

"continuation") given the previous four sentences. We use the 10k most frequent words in the training set as our vocabulary. A special token $\langle unk \rangle$ is introduced for unknown words.

5.2 Evaluation

Previous work evaluates generation tasks with automatic metrics, such as perplexity (**PPL**), **BLEU** (Papineni et al., 2002),[3] and **ROUGE** (Lin, 2004). We adopt these in our evaluation and add three more metrics using the pretrained story scorer from Sagarkar et al. (2018). The scorer rates a generated continuation given its context along three dimensions: **relevance (R)**, **interestingness (I)**, and **overall quality (O)**. The story scorer does not use a gold standard continuation.

In addition, to evaluate the diversity of the generation, we use **Max-BLEU**[4] and **Max-ROUGE**. First, we compute BLEU and ROUGE scores over a set of outputs $(y_1, y_2, ..., y_n)$ with different attribute values given the same story context, then we compute the max scores:

$$\text{Max-BLEU} = \max_i \text{BLEU}(y_i, r)$$
$$\text{Max-ROUGE} = \max_i \text{ROUGE}(y_i, r)$$

where r is the gold standard continuation.

We also use **Self-BLEU** (Zhu et al., 2018) to evaluate the diversity of a set of outputs. It is calculated by averaging the BLEU scores computed between all pairs of generated continuations for a given context, then averaging this quantity over all contexts. The smaller the Self-BLEU score is, the more diverse are the generated outputs.

5.3 Training Details

Our seq2seq model has a 2-layer biLSTM (Hochreiter and Schmidhuber, 1997) encoder and a 1-layer LSTM decoder. The hidden dimension of all layers is 512. The word embedding dimension is also 512. For optimization, we use Adam (Kingma and Ba, 2014) with learning rate 0.001. We use early stopping based on perplexity on the development set.

---

[2]The dimension of the frame vector is 64 in our experiments.

[3]In this paper, all BLEU scores are BLEU-2 scores (i.e., using unigrams and bigrams).

[4]While max metric scores are not solely measuring diversity, they do provide a sense of the potential of the list. If all entries on the list are the same, the max metric scores would equal the average metric scores. The difference between the max and average metric scores therefore can be viewed as providing a bound on the diversity.

Target Sentiment	Generated Continuations		
	negative	neutral	positive
negative	**68.5**	19.6	12.0
neutral	7.0	**73.9**	19.2
positive	0.8	3.1	**96.2**

Table 3: Sentiment match percentages of generated continuations and target sentiment values.

	dif $= 0$	dif ≤ 1	dif ≤ 2	dif ≤ 3
3 bins	95.8	100	-	-
30 bins	70.35	94.8	99.25	99.9

Table 4: Frequency (%) of the generated continuations in the range of dif $= |l - l_p|$ where l is the continuation length and l_p is the desired length.

Predicate	M%	Predicate	M%
was	100	got	100
had	100	decided	94.4
went	99.9	is	100
made	99.25	were	100
found	100	get	99.95
felt	99.55	go	100
took	99.2	ended	98.25
be	99.95	told	99.9
gave	99.95	left	99.85
said	100	bought	100

Table 5: Match percentages (M%) showing fraction of stories for which generated continuations contain the desired predicate. The 20 most frequent predicates are shown; additional results are in the Appendix.

6 Results

We now present our experimental results. Section 6.1 includes results related to how well our generated output matches the desired attribute values. Section 6.2 presents results when generating continuations with oracle attribute values. In Section 6.3 we use our set-level metrics to evaluate sets of outputs with various attribute values. In Section 6.4 we report results when attempting to automatically infer attribute values to generate a small set of high-quality outputs.

6.1 Controllability Evaluation

In this section, we evaluate the controllability accuracy of our framework by automatically measuring the match between the attribute values of the generated continuations and the desired values. For certain control variables, like sentiment and frames, this automatic evaluation is prone to errors in the associated analyzers. That is, the metrics that rely on automatic analyzers could become artificially high if our generation models learn to produce outputs that match the biases of the analyzers. We could instead consider manual evaluation of control accuracy. However, we were more interested in devoting our manual evaluation to the question of whether users would find the system outputs useful for a particular goal.

Sentiment. We generate three continuations for each story in the development set, one for each sentiment label. Using the same sentiment analyzer from Socher et al. (2013) as above, we obtain predicted sentiment labels for the continuations. Table 3 shows the sentiment distribution for each label. We see that the vast majority of the time, the continuations match the desired values. Matching positive sentiment is easiest for our model, followed by neutral.

Length. We quantize the generation lengths into bins, each representing a size range. Below are the two settings we consider:

- 3 bins: We use three bins with the following length ranges: [1,7], [8,13], and [14, ∞).

- 30 bins: We use a bin for each length. No sentence is longer than 30.

During training, we do not update the representations of the length control variable. After training, we treat the length of the continuation in the development set as the target control variable and generate continuations for each length. The results are shown in Table 4 and demonstrate that our model can generate continuations with the desired length with only small differences.

Verbal Predicates. We select the top 100 most frequent verbal predicates in the training data. Then for all the stories in the development set, we generate a continuation for each of the 100 predicates. We check whether the predicate appears in the generated continuations. As the results in Table 5 show, the framework can nearly always generate outputs with the desired predicates.

Frame Semantics. In order to check how frequently the generated output matches the desired frames, we generate continuations for the top 100 frames (one frame for each continuation) for all stories in the development set. We check whether the frame appears in the specific continuation using SEMAFOR. The results are shown in Table 6. Most frames have very high match accuracies, but there are a few frames with much

Frame	M%	Frame	M%
Calendric_unit	99.5	Locative_relation	87.4
Arriving	98.9	Quantity	92.5
Temporal_collocation	99.9	Becoming	99.6
Cardinal_numbers	89.1	Being_obligated	97.7
Kinship	94.4	Intentionally_act	99.7
Statement	98.0	Causation	98.6
Emotion_directed	98.7	Buildings	93.0
Personal_relationship	92.7	Food	79.2
Self_motion	86.4	Capability	99.9
Desirability	98.1	Observable_body_parts	74.2

Table 6: Match percentages (M%) showing fraction of stories for which generated continuations contain the desired frame. Additional results are in the Appendix.

	Generated Continuations				
Target Value	0	1	2	3	4
0	**79.9**	2.8	3.1	0.9	13.4
1	5.1	**63.1**	26.4	1.4	4.2
2	2.6	2.0	**90.6**	0.3	4.7
3	20.9	20.1	24.6	**31.0**	3.5
4	0.9	0.3	0.5	0.1	**98.3**

Table 7: Cluster match percentages (%) for each value of the cluster control variable.

lower accuracy, such as "Food" and "Observable_body_parts". These are more concrete frames that may be difficult to reasonably incorporate in certain story contexts.

Automatically-Induced Clusters. Given the cluster, the model generates a continuation. Then, we represent the continuation as a bag-of-words sentence embedding (using the same method as when performing the initial clustering) and find the cluster that has the nearest cluster embedding. Then we check whether the two clusters match.

In analyzing the clusters, we observed that cluster 0 corresponds to simple but reasonable continuations. Cluster 2 corresponds to continuations with positive sentiment. Cluster 4 contains continuations with more actions. Some of the generated outputs are shown in Table 2. From the results in Table 7, we still see controllability for most clusters; however, for target cluster 3, which is rather generic based on our observations, the generated output seems flat.

6.2 Evaluation with Oracle Attributes

Table 8 shows automatic metric scores with oracle attribute values, i.e., using the attribute values of the gold standard continuations. Unsurprisingly, compared with the seq2seq baseline, the perplexity decreases and the ROUGE and BLEU scores increase with oracle attributes. We also find that

the scores from the story scorer, which does not use the gold standard while scoring, also show improvements over the baseline. We note that frame semantics form one of the most useful control attributes, aside from those that use words directly.

The oracle BOW representation of the gold standard continuation yields the lowest perplexity and highest ROUGE and BLEU scores. It is not surprising that using this attribute would be useful according to metrics that favor matching the gold standard. However, these results do show that our simple modeling framework can make use of the information in the control variable with a high degree of effectiveness. In addition, while the scores from the story scorer are generally higher than for other control attributes, they are roughly on par with those when using predicates and frames.

6.3 Evaluating Sets of Continuations

We now evaluate *sets* of continuations using our set-level metrics. Standard methods to generate sets of outputs include beam search (BS) and temperature-based sampling (TS), which we use as baselines. TS with temperature τ corresponds to transforming probabilities p_i as follows: $\hat{p}_i \propto p_i^{\frac{1}{\tau}}$. A high temperature τ leads to high variety in generated samples, but also more noise, while lower temperatures lead to samples with less noise but also less diversity.

For each attribute, we generate continuations for each of its values, and compare to BS and TS systems with the same number of outputs. For example, for sentiment, we generate continuations for each of the 3 sentiment values and compare to BS and TS with 3 continuations.

Results are shown in Table 9. BS shows the least diversity (as evidenced by its high self-BLEU scores). However, it generally yields high average ROUGE and BLEU scores. TS does very well in terms of diversity, and this diversity enables it to produce higher max scores than BS, but it has lower averages when using small numbers of continuations (3 or 5).

Our sentiment- and cluster-controlled systems outperform TS in max metric scores and BS in diversity (self-BLEU). They also have the highest average BLEU scores, though the differences are small. With 30 continuations, TS with $\tau = 0.5$ performs best across all metrics; this number of continuations appears to be well-suited for temperature 0.5. As we move to 100 continuations, we

	PPL (↓)	ROUGE		BLEU (↑)	Story Scorer		
		ROUGE-1 (↑)	ROUGE-L (↑)		O (↑)	R (↑)	I (↑)
seq2seq	25.8	27.0	23.5	17.7	5.5	5.5	4.8
sentiment	25.0	26.7	23.5	17.7	5.5	5.6	4.8
length	23.1	27.3	24.6	20.3	5.7	5.8	5.0
predicates	17.1	42.9	35.1	26.4	6.0	6.2	5.2
frames	15.0	41.1	35.0	27.2	5.9	6.1	5.2
clusters	24.3	28.6	25.0	18.4	5.5	6.1	5.1
BOW	5.7	64.5	54.5	45.4	6.2	6.2	5.2
gold standard	-	-	-	-	6.5	6.7	5.7

Table 8: Automatic metrics for baseline system and when using oracle values for control attributes. For the gold standard continuation, we report only the story scorer results because they do not require a gold standard (unlike the other metrics).

		ROUGE				BLEU (↑)		Self-BLEU (↓)
		ROUGE-1 (↑)		ROUGE-L (↑)				
		Max	(Avg)	Max	(Avg)	Max	(Avg)	
3 continuations:	BS, beam = 3	31.8	**(26.7)**	27.3	**(22.6)**	19.7	(17.0)	50.5
	TS, $\tau = 0.5$	32.5	(25.5)	27.8	(21.6)	20.3	(16.3)	27.0
	TS, $\tau = 0.6$	30.5	(22.2)	25.9	(18.8)	19.0	(14.8)	**23.8**
	sentiment	**32.8**	(25.6)	**28.9**	(22.5)	**21.1**	**(17.1)**	30.7
	predicted frames	30.8	(22.5)	27.0	(19.9)	19.7	(15.7)	30.3
	frames + reranking	30.7	(21.9)	26.3	(18.9)	18.8	(14.7)	25.8
5 continuations:	BS, beam = 5	33.9	**(26.3)**	29.4	**(22.3)**	21.3	(16.2)	68.1
	TS, $\tau = 0.5$	35.0	(25.3)	30.0	(21.5)	21.7	(16.2)	**40.8**
	clusters	**36.1**	(24.5)	**31.7**	(21.4)	**22.9**	**(16.4)**	43.8
30 continuations:	BS, beam = 30	40.0	**(25.4)**	34.3	(20.8)	25.6	(16.0)	92.5
	TS, $\tau = 0.5$	**43.0**	**(25.4)**	**37.5**	**(21.6)**	**28.1**	**(16.3)**	**74.0**
	length	42.1	(24.7)	35.9	(20.0)	26.2	(14.8)	82.2
100 continuations:	BS, beam = 100	44.4	(25.0)	38.6	(20.6)	29.2	(15.9)	96.2
	TS, $\tau = 0.5$	47.8	**(25.4)**	42.3	**(21.6)**	**32.1**	**(16.3)**	85.6
	frames (individual)	47.0	(24.0)	41.2	(20.8)	29.8	(15.5)	**72.1**
	frames (sets)	**48.3**	(23.1)	**42.7**	(20.1)	31.2	(15.1)	75.5

Table 9: Metric scores to evaluate the potential of a list of continuations. We report the maximum and average metric scores over the continuations in each list to evaluate the quality of the lists, and self-BLEU to evaluate diversity. Best results for each metric and each number of outputs are in bold.

find that using our frame control variable leads to better diversity than TS, suggesting that the move to 100 samples has introduced some amount of repetition. By contrast, the 100 distinct frames and frame sets yield better diversity.

6.4 Automatically Choosing Attribute Values

Using our framework, we can generate continuations with any attribute values. However, if we are interested in generating a single continuation, we do not know the ideal attribute values to use. So, we propose two methods to automatically select a small set of values for the frame attribute.

Frames + Reranking: Following Li et al. (2016), we rerank the outputs from the 100 most frequent frame sets by linearly combining the forward score $p(y \mid x)$ and the "reverse score" $\lambda p(x \mid y)$, where the latter comes from a separately-trained seq2seq model. The forward score $p(y \mid x)$ is adjusted by dividing by the length of y in order to not favor shorter outputs.

Predicted Frames: We also build a model to automatically predict the frames in the continuation. Given the frames in a sentence x, we compute a binary frame vector f_x where entry j is 1 if frame j appears in x. We train a model that predicts the frame vector of the continuation given the frame vectors of the previous 4 sentences. The model is an LSTM followed by averaging of hidden states. Mean squared error is minimized during training. After training, the k continuations are selected based on the k frames with the highest predicted score under this frame prediction model.

We use these two methods to produce 3 continuations for each story and report results in Table 9. They both achieve a similar balance of quality and diversity as TS with $\tau = 0.6$, with reranking leading to greater diversity than frame prediction and the latter showing higher ROUGE/BLEU scores.

7 Human Evaluation

Our previous results demonstrate that our frame control system has strong controllability and diversity in generation. In this section, we conduct a human evaluation to assess the utility of providing multiple suggestions from our models in a creative writing setting. We consider four different systems: **BS** with beam size 3; **TS** with 3 continuations using $\tau = 0.6$, which we found to produce outputs with more diversity than 0.5; **reranking** the 100 most frequent frame sets and using the top 3; and using continuations from the top-3 **predicted** frames under our frame prediction model.[5]

To assess which set of generations from these four systems are most helpful in a collaborative writing setting, we collect annotations using Amazon Mechanical Turk. We randomly select 100 stories. For each story, we generate three outputs as a set of suggestions for each system, so there are 600 comparision pairs in total. We show workers two sets of outputs from different systems and ask them to select which suggestion is more helpful for writing the next line in the story. We also provide a choice of "neither one is helpful at all". We ask them explicitly to imagine they are writing the next line of the given story (see the appendix for more details).

Table 10 shows the results.[6] We observe that workers prefer the BS baseline over TS, although TS yields higher diversity. This could be because the continuations from BS are shorter, simpler, and more fluent. In addition, we observe that workers prefer the outputs from the reranking system over BS more often than not. Although the predicted frame system yields more diverse outputs, workers still prefer BS, likely due to the difficulty in predicting frames. The reranking and predicted frame systems are both preferred to TS, though the gap is smaller with the predicted system. We also see that generating helpful suggestions is a difficult task: in many cases workers thought neither system was helpful, especially when given the outputs from BS/TS or TS/predicted.

One may ask why workers do not show a stronger preference for the more diverse sets of outputs. From our own preliminary annotations, we believe this is because diverse outputs tend to be longer and harder to understand, and also because greater diversity increases the chance of producing disfluent or nonsensical outputs. The BS outputs, by comparison, are sensical and mostly on-topic. Even if the suggestions are not creative, they may still help a worker to think about a new direction for the story to take. Nonsensical or disfluent suggestions, however, are rarely helpful.

| | | Human Preference | | |
system 1	system 2	1	2	neither
BS	TS	43	16	29
BS	reranking	18	30	15
BS	predicted	38	29	19
TS	reranking	18	38	16
TS	predicted	18	27	34
reranking	predicted	27	24	21

Table 10: Human preferences when given three continuations from each pair of systems.

8 Related Work

Automatic story generation has a long history, with early work based primarily on hand-written rules (Klein et al., 1973; Meehan, 1977; Dehn, 1981; Turner, 1993). Subsequent methods were based on planning from artificial intelligence (Theune et al., 2003; Oinonen et al., 2006; Riedl and Young, 2010) and, more recently, data-driven methods have been developed (McIntyre and Lapata, 2010; Elson, 2012; Daza et al., 2016; Roemmele and Gordon, 2015; Clark et al., 2018a; Martin et al., 2018; Fan et al., 2018b; Yao et al., 2019; Fan et al., 2019). In concurrent work, Gupta et al. (2019) also propose methods to generate more diverse and interesting story endings, albeit without control variables.

In stronger relevance to our work, Clark et al. (2018b) explore a creative writing setting with a machine in the loop, albeit with mixed results in terms of the quality of system suggestions. Predicting and controlling with frame values suggests a new way of interacting with collaborative writing systems, as long as frames can be communicated to users in ways they can easily understand. Recently, Clark et al. (2018a) proposed a neural text generation method that explicitly represents and tracks entities. In addition, event sequences (Chaturvedi et al., 2017; Liu et al., 2018) are important elements in narrative texts but under-explored for story generation.

---

[5]The BS and TS baselines do not use control variables.

[6]We remove results from 10-question sets where more than half of the questions were answered with the "neither" option, as we were concerned that these annotators did not fully understand the task or did not spend enough time studying the continuations. This occurred in roughly one third of question sets.

These and related characteristics of creative writing could be incorporated into our framework as control attributes in future work.

The broader neural text generation community has also recently been interested in controllable text generation, i.e., generating text with specified characteristics reflected by control variables. In some previous work, the variables to be controlled are embedded into vectors which are then fed into models to reflect the characteristics of the variables. Kikuchi et al. (2016) and Fan et al. (2018a) developed methods for controllable summarization, for example permitting users to control the length of the generated summary. Related work has controlled style, topic, and sentiment polarity (Hu et al., 2017; Wang et al., 2017; Shen et al., 2017; Yang et al., 2018).

Despite the widespread usage of beam search for neural text generation, it has long been observed that its outputs are lacking in diversity. Several efforts have been made to provide diverse outputs for generation tasks, such as dialogue (Li et al., 2016) and machine translation (Devlin and Matsoukas, 2012; Gimpel et al., 2013; Li and Jurafsky, 2016). Diverse beam search (Vijayakumar et al., 2018) produces a list of outputs with a diversity-augmented objective. Ippolito et al. (2019) compare several methods for producing a set of diverse outputs from conditional language models. We leave a careful comparison to such algorithms to future work.

9 Conclusion and Future Work

We proposed a controllable framework that generates the next sentence of a story given its context. We experimented with a broad range of control attributes and demonstrated that our framework can accurately generate outputs that match the target values. Sets of outputs from our method show high diversity and high oracle metric scores. The human evaluation shows that the multiple suggestions from our model show promise for integration in a collaborative writing system. Future work could explore other control attributes as well as a compositional framework to control multiple attributes jointly.

Acknowledgments

We would like to thank TTIC SL@TTIC researchers who participated in a preliminary annotation study.

References

Dzmitry Bahdanau, Kyunghyun Cho, and Yoshua Bengio. 2015. Neural machine translation by jointly learning to align and translate. In *Proceedings of International Conference on Learning Representations*.

Collin F. Baker, Charles J. Fillmore, and John B. Lowe. 1998. The Berkeley FrameNet project. In *COLING-ACL '98: Proceedings of the Conference*, pages 86–90, Montreal, Canada.

Seymour Benjamin Chatman. 1980. *Story and discourse: Narrative structure in fiction and film*. Cornell University Press.

Snigdha Chaturvedi, Haoruo Peng, and Dan Roth. 2017. Story comprehension for predicting what happens next. In *Proceedings of the 2017 Conference on Empirical Methods in Natural Language Processing*, pages 1603–1614. Association for Computational Linguistics.

Elizabeth Clark, Yangfeng Ji, and Noah A. Smith. 2018a. Neural text generation in stories using entity representations as context. In *Proceedings of the 2018 Conference of the North American Chapter of the Association for Computational Linguistics: Human Language Technologies, Volume 1 (Long Papers)*, pages 2250–2260. Association for Computational Linguistics.

Elizabeth Clark, Anne Spencer Ross, Chenhao Tan, Yangfeng Ji, and Noah A. Smith. 2018b. Creative writing with a machine in the loop: Case studies on slogans and stories. In *IUI*, pages 329–340. ACM.

Dipanjan Das, Desai Chen, Andr F. T. Martins, Nathan Schneider, and Noah A. Smith. 2014. Frame-semantic parsing. *Computational Linguistics*, 40:1:9–56.

Angel Daza, Hiram Calvo, and Jesús Figueroa-Nazuno. 2016. Automatic text generation by learning from literary structures. In *Proceedings of the Fifth Workshop on Computational Linguistics for Literature*, pages 9–19.

Natalie Dehn. 1981. Story generation after TALE-SPIN. In *IJCAI*, pages 16–18.

Jacob Devlin and Spyros Matsoukas. 2012. Trait-based hypothesis selection for machine translation. In *Proceedings of the 2012 Conference of the North American Chapter of the Association for Computational Linguistics: Human Language Technologies*, pages 528–532. Association for Computational Linguistics.

David K. Elson. 2012. *Modeling Narrative Discourse*. Ph.D. thesis, Columbia University.

Angela Fan, David Grangier, and Michael Auli. 2018a. Controllable abstractive summarization. In *Proceedings of the 2nd Workshop on Neural Machine*

Translation and Generation, pages 45–54. Association for Computational Linguistics.

Angela Fan, Mike Lewis, and Yann Dauphin. 2018b. Hierarchical neural story generation. In *Proceedings of the 56th Annual Meeting of the Association for Computational Linguistics (Volume 1: Long Papers)*, pages 889–898, Melbourne, Australia. Association for Computational Linguistics.

Angela Fan, Mike Lewis, and Yann Dauphin. 2019. Strategies for structuring story generation. In *Proceedings of the 57th Annual Meeting of the Association for Computational Linguistics*, pages 2650–2660, Florence, Italy. Association for Computational Linguistics.

Jessica Ficler and Yoav Goldberg. 2017. Controlling linguistic style aspects in neural language generation. In *Proceedings of the Workshop on Stylistic Variation*, pages 94–104, Copenhagen, Denmark. Association for Computational Linguistics.

Matt Gardner, Joel Grus, Mark Neumann, Oyvind Tafjord, Pradeep Dasigi, Nelson F. Liu, Matthew Peters, Michael Schmitz, and Luke Zettlemoyer. 2018. Allennlp: A deep semantic natural language processing platform. In *Proceedings of Workshop for NLP Open Source Software (NLP-OSS)*, pages 1–6. Association for Computational Linguistics.

Kevin Gimpel, Dhruv Batra, Chris Dyer, and Gregory Shakhnarovich. 2013. A systematic exploration of diversity in machine translation. In *Proceedings of the 2013 Conference on Empirical Methods in Natural Language Processing*, pages 1100–1111, Seattle, Washington, USA. Association for Computational Linguistics.

Prakhar Gupta, Vinayshekhar Bannihatti Kumar, Mukul Bhutani, and Alan W Black. 2019. Writer-Forcing: Generating more interesting story endings. In *Proceedings of the Second Workshop on Storytelling*, Florence, Italy. Association for Computational Linguistics.

Sepp Hochreiter and Jürgen Schmidhuber. 1997. Long short-term memory. *Neural Computation*.

Zhiting Hu, Zichao Yang, Xiaodan Liang, Ruslan Salakhutdinov, and Eric P. Xing. 2017. Toward controlled generation of text. In *Proc. of ICML*.

Daphne Ippolito, Reno Kriz, Joao Sedoc, Maria Kustikova, and Chris Callison-Burch. 2019. Comparison of diverse decoding methods from conditional language models. In *Proceedings of the 57th Annual Meeting of the Association for Computational Linguistics*, pages 3752–3762, Florence, Italy. Association for Computational Linguistics.

Yuta Kikuchi, Graham Neubig, Ryohei Sasano, Hiroya Takamura, and Manabu Okumura. 2016. Controlling output length in neural encoder-decoders. In *Proceedings of the 2016 Conference on Empirical Methods in Natural Language Processing*, pages 1328–1338, Austin, Texas. Association for Computational Linguistics.

Diederik Kingma and Jimmy Ba. 2014. Adam: A method for stochastic optimization. *CoRR*, abs/1412.6980.

Sheldon Klein, John F. Aeschlimann, David F. Balsiger, Steven L. Converse, Claudine Court, Mark Foster, Robin Lao, John D. Oakley, and Joel Smith. 1973. Automatic novel writing: A status report. Technical Report 186, University of Wisconsin-Madison.

Jiwei Li, Michel Galley, Chris Brockett, Jianfeng Gao, and Bill Dolan. 2016. A diversity-promoting objective function for neural conversation models. In *Proceedings of the 2016 Conference of the North American Chapter of the Association for Computational Linguistics: Human Language Technologies*, pages 110–119, San Diego, California. Association for Computational Linguistics.

Jiwei Li and Daniel Jurafsky. 2016. Mutual information and diverse decoding improve neural machine translation. *CoRR*, abs/1601.00372.

Chin-Yew Lin. 2004. Rouge: A package for automatic evaluation of summaries. In *Text Summarization Branches Out: Proceedings of the ACL-04 Workshop*, pages 74–81, Barcelona, Spain. Association for Computational Linguistics.

Fei Liu, Trevor Cohn, and Timothy Baldwin. 2018. Narrative modeling with memory chains and semantic supervision. *CoRR*, abs/1805.06122.

Thang Luong, Hieu Pham, and Christopher D. Manning. 2015. Effective approaches to attention-based neural machine translation. In *Proceedings of the 2015 Conference on Empirical Methods in Natural Language Processing*, pages 1412–1421, Lisbon, Portugal. Association for Computational Linguistics.

Lara J Martin, Prithviraj Ammanabrolu, Xinyu Wang, William Hancock, Shruti Singh, Brent Harrison, and Mark O Riedl. 2018. Event representations for automated story generation with deep neural nets. In *Thirty-Second AAAI Conference on Artificial Intelligence*.

Neil McIntyre and Mirella Lapata. 2010. Plot induction and evolutionary search for story generation. In *Proceedings of the 48th Annual Meeting of the Association for Computational Linguistics*, pages 1562–1572.

James R. Meehan. 1977. TALE-SPIN, an interactive program that writes stories. In *Proceedings of the 5th International Joint Conference on Artificial Intelligence (IJCAI)*, pages 91–98.

Nasrin Mostafazadeh, Nathanael Chambers, Xiaodong He, Devi Parikh, Dhruv Batra, Lucy Vanderwende,

Pushmeet Kohli, and James Allen. 2016. A corpus and cloze evaluation for deeper understanding of commonsense stories. In *Proceedings of the 2016 Conference of the North American Chapter of the Association for Computational Linguistics: Human Language Technologies*, pages 839–849, San Diego, California. Association for Computational Linguistics.

K.M. Oinonen, Mariet Theune, Antinus Nijholt, and J.R.R. Uijlings. 2006. *Designing a story database for use in automatic story generation*, Lecture Notes in Computer Science, pages 298–301. Springer Verlag.

Kishore Papineni, Salim Roukos, Todd Ward, and Wei-Jing Zhu. 2002. Bleu: a method for automatic evaluation of machine translation. In *Proceedings of the 40th Annual Meeting of the Association for Computational Linguistics*, pages 311–318, Philadelphia, Pennsylvania, USA. Association for Computational Linguistics.

Jeffrey Pennington, Richard Socher, and Christopher Manning. 2014. Glove: Global vectors for word representation. In *Proceedings of the 2014 Conference on Empirical Methods in Natural Language Processing (EMNLP)*, pages 1532–1543, Doha, Qatar. Association for Computational Linguistics.

Mark O. Riedl and Robert Michael Young. 2010. Narrative planning: Balancing plot and character. *Journal of Artificial Intelligence Research*, 39:217–268.

Melissa Roemmele and Andrew S. Gordon. 2015. Creative help: a story writing assistant. In *International Conference on Interactive Digital Storytelling*, pages 81–92. Springer.

Manasvi Sagarkar, John Wieting, Lifu Tu, and Kevin Gimpel. 2018. Quality signals in generated stories. In *Proceedings of the Seventh Joint Conference on Lexical and Computational Semantics (*SEM 2018)*, New Orleans, Louisiana.

Roger C. Schank and Robert P. Abelson. 1977. *Scripts, Plans, Goals and Understanding: an Inquiry into Human Knowledge Structures*. L. Erlbaum, Hillsdale, NJ.

Tianxiao Shen, Tao Lei, Regina Barzilay, and Tommi Jaakkola. 2017. Style transfer from non-parallel text by cross-alignment. In *Advances in Neural Information Processing Systems 30*, pages 6833–6844. Curran Associates, Inc.

Richard Socher, Alex Perelygin, Jean Wu, Jason Chuang, Christopher D. Manning, Andrew Ng, and Christopher Potts. 2013. Recursive deep models for semantic compositionality over a sentiment treebank. In *Proceedings of the 2013 Conference on Empirical Methods in Natural Language Processing*, pages 1631–1642. Association for Computational Linguistics.

Ilya Sutskever, Oriol Vinyals, and Quoc V Le. 2014. Sequence to sequence learning with neural networks. In Z. Ghahramani, M. Welling, C. Cortes, N. D. Lawrence, and K. Q. Weinberger, editors, *Advances in Neural Information Processing Systems 27*, pages 3104–3112. Curran Associates, Inc.

Mariët Theune, Sander Faas, Anton Nijholt, and Dirk Heylen. 2003. The virtual storyteller: story creation by intelligent agents. In *Proceedings of the 1st International Conference on Technologies for Interactive Digital Storytelling and Entertainment*, pages 204–215. Springer.

Scott R. Turner. 1993. *Minstrel: a computer model of creativity and storytelling*. Ph.D. thesis, University of California at Los Angeles.

Ashwin K. Vijayakumar, Michael Cogswell, Ramprasaath R. Selvaraju, Qing Sun, Stefan Lee, David J. Crandall, and Dhruv Batra. 2018. Diverse beam search: Decoding diverse solutions from neural sequence models. In *Proc. of AAAI*.

Di Wang, Nebojsa Jojic, Chris Brockett, and Eric Nyberg. 2017. Steering output style and topic in neural response generation. In *Proceedings of the 2017 Conference on Empirical Methods in Natural Language Processing*, pages 2140–2150, Copenhagen, Denmark. Association for Computational Linguistics.

Zichao Yang, Zhiting Hu, Chris Dyer, Eric P Xing, and Taylor Berg-Kirkpatrick. 2018. Unsupervised text style transfer using language models as discriminators. In S. Bengio, H. Wallach, H. Larochelle, K. Grauman, N. Cesa-Bianchi, and R. Garnett, editors, *Advances in Neural Information Processing Systems 31*, pages 7287–7298. Curran Associates, Inc.

Lili Yao, Nanyun Peng, Weischedel Ralph, Kevin Knight, Dongyan Zhao, and Rui Yan. 2019. Plan-and-write: Towards better automatic storytelling. In *Thirty-Third AAAI Conference on Artificial Intelligence*.

Yaoming Zhu, Sidi Lu, Lei Zheng, Jiaxian Guo, Weinan Zhang, Jun Wang, and Yong Yu. 2018. Texygen: A benchmarking platform for text generation models. *SIGIR*.

A Appendix

Model. Figure 1 shows our modeling framework.

Additional Experimental Results. Figure 2 shows the length distribution of the continuations in the training data. Figure 3, Table 11, and Table 12 show the frequency (%) of matching the target control variable for length, predicates, and frames, respectively.

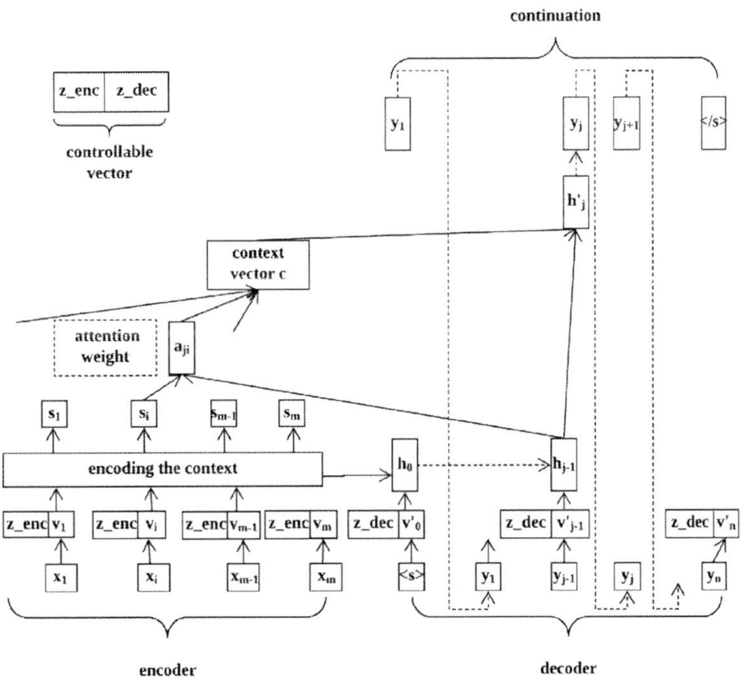

Figure 1: Our modeling framework for controllable generation.

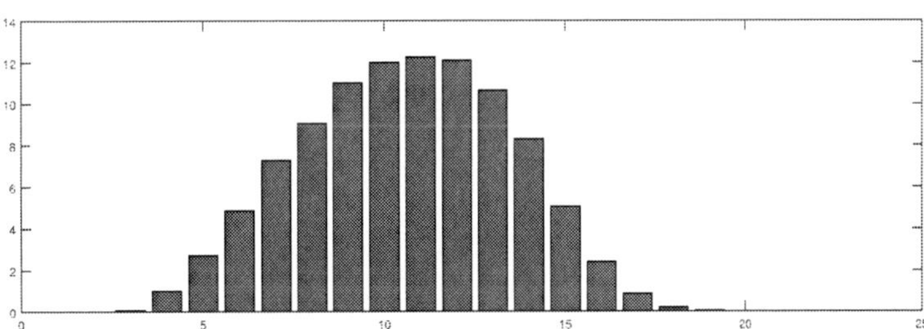

Figure 2: The length distribution of the continuations in the training data. The horizontal axis shows continuation lengths and the vertical axis shows the frequency (%) of the length.

Human Evaluation Setup. The form used on Amazon Mechanical Turk is shown in Figure 4.

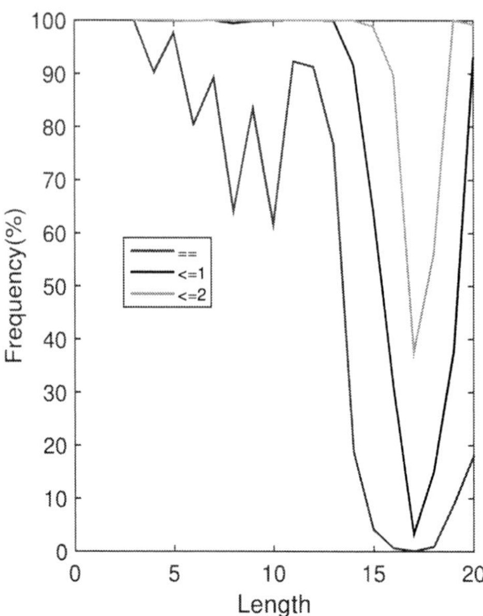

Figure 3: Frequency (%) of the generated continuations for different ranges of $\text{dif} = |l - l_p|$. The horizontal axis is the desired length. The vertical axis is the percentage of generated outputs with the given values of dif. Here l is the story continuation length and l_p is generated sentence length as the target control variable. "==" refers to $l = l_p$, "<= i" refers to $|l - l_p| <= i$.

predicate	acc	predicate	acc	predicate	acc	predicate	acc	predicate	acc
was	100	got	100	had	100	decided	94.4	went	99.9
is	100	made	99.25	were	100	found	100	get	99.95
felt	99.55	go	100	took	99.2	ended	98.25	be	99.95
told	99.9	gave	99.95	left	99.85	said	100	bought	100
came	98.7	realized	79.75	loved	99.8	have	99.1	won	100
became	99.75	put	83.6	ran	100	see	99.9	saw	98.75
started	99.85	buy	100	make	97.3	knew	99.6	looked	98.65
lost	99.05	enjoyed	99.95	called	98.5	learned	99.8	ate	95.35
turned	93.05	do	100	wait	99.85	take	99.8	fell	99.35
wanted	90.25	find	100	thought	80.05	stopped	98.65	play	100
has	98.15	eat	100	let	100	walked	99.9	did	96.55
being	99.05	done	94.05	returned	99.6	laughed	86.6	tried	99.6
's	99.25	asked	99.9	began	93.75	helped	97.65	caught	99.6
broke	99.9	getting	99.95	keep	97.15	paid	97.1	been	97
finished	99.9	threw	99.4	spent	99.85	passed	99.95	help	98.85
are	99.65	drove	99.25	work	81.25	going	35.9	leave	99.85
brought	98.4	feel	99.75	picked	73.65	agreed	98.35	needed	24.2
worded	100	used	98.75	pay	100	kept	98.8	liked	98.65
arrived	99.2	played	99.95	come	98.7	thanked	98.3	relieved	97.35
stop	99.15	playing	98.75	cried	100	died	97.75	know	89.05

Table 11: Frequency (%) of the generated continuations containing the desired predicate.

frame	acc	frame	acc	frame	acc	frame	acc
Calendric_unit	99.5	Locative_relation	87.4	Arriving	98.85	Quantity	92.5
Temporal_collocation	99.9	Becoming	99.6	Cardinal_numbers	89.05	Being_obligated	97.65
Kinship	94.35	Intentionally_act	99.65	Statement	98	Causation	98.55
Emotion_directed	98.65	Buildings	93	Personal_relationship	92.7	Food	79.2
Self_motion	86.4	Capability	99.95	Desirability	98.1	Observable_body_parts	74.15
Experiencer_focus	91.75	Time_vector	99	Request	99.35	Deciding	99.6
Relational_quantity	95.7	Measure_duration	96.7	Frequency	99.75	People	90.8
Ingestion	86.25	Vehicle	86.45	Age	98.55	Increment	98.6
Leadership	80.6	Desiring	90.7	Stimulus_focus	93.4	Activity_start	95.95
Education_teaching	96.5	Degree	100	Grasp	92.7	Commerce_buy	98.7
Scrutiny	93.5	Locale_by_use	65.15	Conquering	95.3	Giving	99.3
Clothing	49.05	Attempt	98.95	Becoming_aware	90.25	Building_subparts	73.7
Motion	96.55	Placing	73.15	Natural_features	26.7	Getting	85.05
Locating	76.55	Sufficiency	97.75	Feeling	98.7	Awareness	95.7
Experiencer_obj	87.4	Working_on	67.65	Aggregate	70.3	Performers_and_roles	87.95
Change_position_on_a_scale	72.45	Roadways	71.9	Containers	44.1	Coming_to_believe	92.4
Assistance	99.4	Ordinal_numbers	96.5	Relative_time	92.6	Choosing	96.55
Existence	88.15	Dimension	69.65	Cause_harm	89.75	Perception_active	87.1
Text	63.6	Cause_motion	81.2	Possession	76.85	Type	78.2
Body_movement	66	Opinion	87.7	Removing	74	Money	97.5
Have_as_requirement	25.4	Using	93.1	Storing	71.4	People_by_age	57.25
Contacting	73.35	Make_noise	97.9	Substance	50.4	Required_event	91.7
Political_locales	85.3	Difficulty	89.8	Activity_ongoing	94	Direction	98.6
Perception_experience	35	Impact	95.6	Locale	87.25	Waiting	96.65
Concessive	95.15	Partitive	63.65	Operate_vehicle	61.55	Size	98.3

Table 12: Frequency (%) of the generated continuations containing the desired frame.

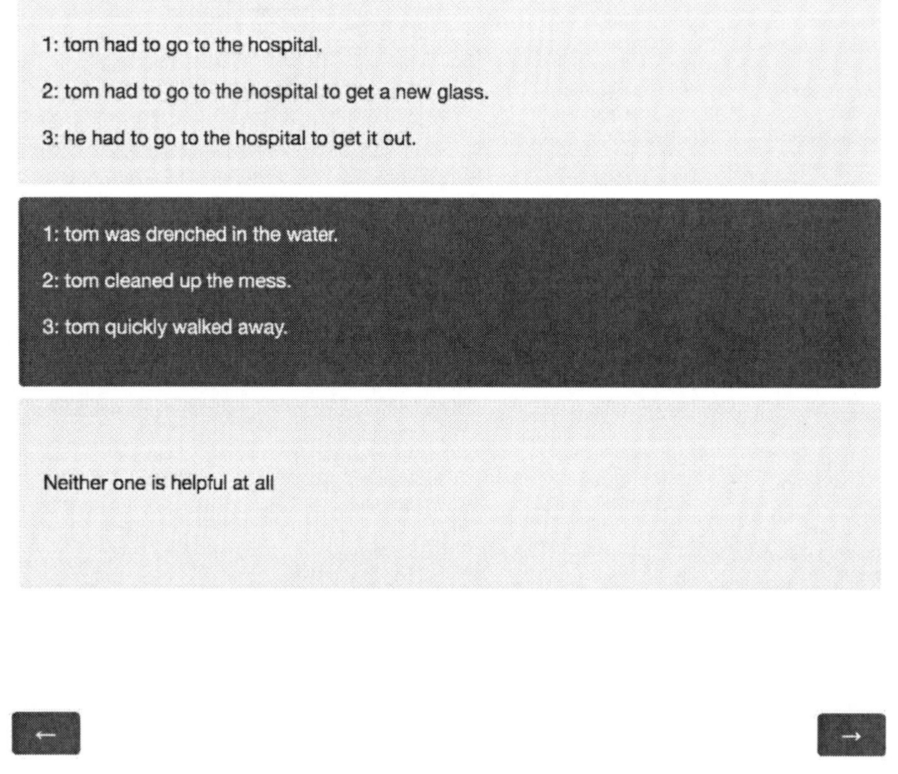

Figure 4: The form for human evaluation of the generation systems for their potential in a collaborative writing setting.

Domain Differential Adaptation for Neural Machine Translation

Zi-Yi Dou, Xinyi Wang, Junjie Hu, Graham Neubig
Language Technologies Institute, Carnegie Mellon University
{zdou, xinyiw1, junjieh, gneubig}@cs.cmu.edu

Abstract

Neural networks are known to be data hungry and domain sensitive, but it is nearly impossible to obtain large quantities of labeled data for every domain we are interested in. This necessitates the use of domain adaptation strategies. One common strategy encourages generalization by aligning the global distribution statistics between source and target domains, but one drawback is that the statistics of different domains or tasks are inherently divergent, and smoothing over these differences can lead to sub-optimal performance. In this paper, we propose the framework of *Domain Differential Adaptation (DDA)*, where instead of smoothing over these differences we embrace them, directly modeling the difference between domains using models in a related task. We then use these learned domain differentials to adapt models for the target task accordingly. Experimental results on domain adaptation for neural machine translation demonstrate the effectiveness of this strategy, achieving consistent improvements over other alternative adaptation strategies in multiple experimental settings.[1]

1 Introduction

Most recent success of deep neural networks rely on the availability of high quality and labeled training data (He et al., 2017; Vaswani et al., 2017; Povey et al., 2018; Devlin et al., 2019). In particular, neural machine translation (NMT) models tend to perform poorly if they are not trained with enough parallel data from the test domain (Koehn and Knowles, 2017). However, it is not realistic to collect large amounts of parallel data in all possible domains due to the high cost of data collection. Moreover, certain domains by nature have far less data than others. For example, there is much more news produced and publicly available than

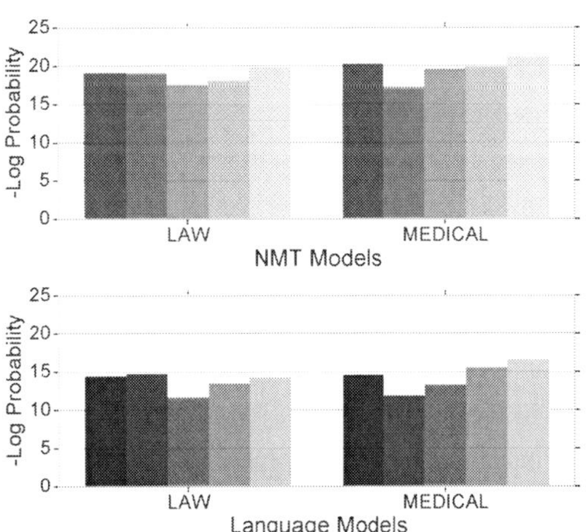

Figure 1: Mean log probabilities of NMT models and LMs trained on law and medical domains for the words ("needle", "hepatic", "complete", "justify", "suspend"). LM and NMT probabilities are correlated for each domain. (More examples in Section 5.1.)

more sensitive medical records. Therefore, it is essential to explore effective methods for utilizing out-of-domain data to train models that generalize well to in-domain data.

There is a rich literature in domain adaptation for neural networks (Luong and Manning, 2015; Tan et al., 2017; Chu et al., 2017; Ying et al., 2018). In particular, we focus on two lines of work that are conducive to *unsupervised* adaptation, where there is no training data available in the target domain. The first line of work focuses on aligning representations of data from different domains with the goal of improving data sharing across the two domains using techniques such as mean maximum discrepancy (Long et al., 2015) or adversarial training (Ganin et al., 2016; Sankaranarayanan and Balaji, 2017). However, these methods attempt to smooth over the differences in the domains by learning domain-invariant

---

[1]Code is available at https://github.com/zdou0830/DDA.

Proceedings of the 3rd Workshop on Neural Generation and Translation (WNGT 2019), pages 59–69
Hong Kong, China, November 4, 2019. ©2019 Association for Computational Linguistics
www.aclweb.org/anthology/D19-56%2d

features, and in the case when these differences are actually necessary for correctly predicting the output, this can lead to sub-optimal performance (Xie et al., 2017). Another line of research tries to directly integrate in-domain models of other tasks to adapt models in the target task. For example, Gulcehre et al. (2015) use pre-trained in-domain LMs with out-of-domain NMT models by directly using a weighted sum of probability distributions from both models, or fusing the hidden states of both models and fine-tuning. These LMs can potentially capture features of the in-domain data, but models of different tasks are inherently different and thus coming up with an optimal method for combining them is non-trivial.

The main intuition behind our method is that models with different data requirements, namely LMs and NMT models, exhibit similar behavior when trained on the same domain, but there is little correlation between models trained on data from different domains (as demonstrated empirically in Figure 1). Because of this, directly adapting an out-of-domain NMT model by integrating an in-domain LM (i.e. with methods in Gulcehre et al. (2015)) may be sub-optimal, as the in-domain and out-of-domain NMT may not be highly correlated. However, the *difference* between LMs from two different domains will likely be similar to the *difference* between the NMT models. Based on these observations, we propose a new unsupervised adaptation framework, Domain Differential Adaptation (DDA), that utilizes models of a related task to capture *domain differences*. Specifically, we use LMs trained with in-domain and out-of-domain data, which gives us hints about how to compensate for domain differences and adapt an NMT model trained on out-of-domain parallel data. Although we mainly examine NMT in this paper, the general idea can be applied to other tasks as well.

We evaluate DDA in two different unsupervised domain adaptation settings on four language pairs. DDA demonstrates consistent improvements of up to 4 BLEU points over an unadapted NMT baseline, and up to 2 BLEU over an NMT baseline adapted using existing methods. An analysis reveals that DDA significantly improves the NMT model's ability to generate words more frequently seen in in-domain data, indicating that DDA is a promising approach to domain adaptation of NMT and neural models in general.

2 Background

2.1 Neural Language Models

Given a sequence of tokens $\mathbf{y} = (y_1, y_2, \cdots, y_N)$, LMs compute a probability of the sequence $p(\mathbf{y})$ by decomposing it into the probability of each token y_t given the history $(y_1, y_2, \cdots, y_{t-1})$. Formally, the probability of the sequence $\mathbf{y}$ is calculated as:

$$p(\mathbf{y}) = \prod_{t=1}^{N} p(y_t|y_1, y_2, \cdots, y_{t-1}).$$

LMs are comonly modeled using some variety of recurrent neural networks (RNN; (Hochreiter and Schmidhuber, 1997; Cho et al., 2014)), where at each timestep t, the network first outputs a context-dependent representation s_t^{LM}, which is then used to compute the conditional distribution $p(y_t|y_{<t})$ using a softmax layer. During training, gradient descent is used to maximize the log-likelihood of the monolingual corpus Y:

$$\max_{\theta_{LM}} \sum_{\mathbf{y}^i \in Y} \log p(\mathbf{y}^i; \theta_{LM}).$$

2.2 Neural Machine Translation Models

Current neural machine translation models are generally implemented in the encoder-decoder framework (Sutskever et al., 2014; Cho et al., 2014), where the encoder generates a context vector for each source sentence $\mathbf{x}$ and the decoder then outputs the translation $\mathbf{y}$, one target word at a time.

Similarly to LMs, NMT models would also generate hidden representation s_t^{NMT} at each timestep t, and then compute the conditional distribution $p(y_t|y_{<t}, \mathbf{x})$ using a softmax layer. Both encoder and decoder are jointly trained to maximize the log-likelihood of the parallel training corpus (X, Y):

$$\max_{\theta_{NMT}} \sum_{(\mathbf{x}^i, \mathbf{y}^i) \in (X,Y)} \log p(\mathbf{y}^i|\mathbf{x}^i; \theta_{NMT}).$$

During decoding, NMT models generate words one by one. Specifically, at each time step t, the NMT model calculates the probability of next word $p_{\text{NMT}}(y_t|y_{<t}, \mathbf{x})$ for each of all previous hypotheses $\{y_{\leq t-1}^{(i)}\}$. After appending the new word to the previous hypothesis, new scores would be calculated and top K ones are selected as new hypotheses $\{y_{\leq t}^{(i)}\}$.

3 Domain Differential Adaptation

In this section, we propose two approaches under the overall umbrella of the DDA framework: Shallow Adaptation (DDA-Shallow) and Deep Adaptation (DDA-Deep). At a high level, both methods capture the domain difference by two LMs, trained on in-domain (LM-in) and out-of-domain (LM-out) monolingual data respectively. Without access to in-domain parallel data, we want to adapt the NMT model trained on out-of-domain parallel data (NMT-out) to approximate the NMT model trained on in-domain parallel data (NMT-in).

In the following sections, we assume that LM-in, LM-out as well as the NMT-out model have been pretrained separately before being integrated.

3.1 Shallow Adaptation

Given LM-in, LM-out, and NMT-out, our first method, *i.e. shallow adaptation* (DDA-Shallow), combines the three models only at *decoding* time. As we have stated above, at each time step t, NMT-out would generate the probability of the next word $p_{\text{NMT-out}}(y_t|y_{<t}, \mathbf{x})$ for each of all previous hypotheses $\{y_{<t}^{(i)}\}$. Similarly, language models LM-in and LM-out would output probabilities of the next word $p_{\text{LM-in}}(y_t|y_{<t})$ and $p_{\text{LM-out}}(y_t|y_{<t})$, respectively.

For DDA-Shallow, the candidates proposed by NMT-out are rescored considering scores given by LM-in and LM-out. Specifically, at each decoding timestep t, the probability of the next generated word y_t, is obtained by an interpolation of log-probabilities from LM-in, LM-out into NMT-out.

Formally, the log probability of y_t is

$$\log\left(p(y_t)\right) \propto \log\left(p_{\text{NMT-out}}(y_t|y_{<t}, \mathbf{x})\right)$$
$$+ \beta\left[\log\left(p_{\text{LM-in}}(y_t|y_{<t})\right) - \log\left(p_{\text{LM-out}}(y_t|y_{<t})\right)\right],$$
$$(1)$$

where β is a hyper-parameter.[2]

Intuitively, Equation 1 encourages the model to generate more words in the target domain as well as reduce the probability of generating words in the source domain.

3.2 Deep Adaptation

DDA-Shallow only functions during decoding time so there is almost no learning involved. In addition, hyper-parameter β is the same for all

---

words, which limits the model's flexibility. Our second more expressive *deep adaptation* (DDA-Deep) method enables the model to learn how to make predictions based on the hidden states of LM-in, LM-out, and NMT-out. We freeze the parameters of the LMs and only fine-tune the fusion strategy and NMT parameters.

Formally, at each time step t, we have three hidden states $s_{\text{LM-out}}^{(t)}$, $s_{\text{LM-in}}^{(t)}$, and $s_{\text{NMT-out}}^{(t)}$. We then concatenate them and use a gating strategy to combine the three hidden states:

$$s_{\text{concat}}^{(t)} = \left[s_{\text{LM-out}}^{(t)}; s_{\text{LM-in}}^{(t)}; s_{\text{NMT-out}}^{(t)}\right], \quad (2.1)$$

$$g_{\text{LM-out}}^{(t)}, g_{\text{LM-in}}^{(t)}, g_{\text{NMT-out}}^{(t)} = F\left(s_{\text{concat}}^{(t)}\right), \quad (2.2)$$

$$s_{\text{DA}}^{(t)} = g_{\text{LM-out}}^{(t)} \odot s_{\text{LM-out}}^{(t)} + g_{\text{LM-in}}^{(t)} \odot s_{\text{LM-in}}^{(t)}$$
$$+ g_{\text{NMT-out}}^{(t)} \odot s_{\text{NMT-out}}^{(t)}. \quad (2.3)$$

Here F is a linear transformation and $\odot$ stands for elementwise multiplication. As the three gating values g, we use matrices of the same dimension as the hidden states. This design gives the model more flexibility in combining the states.

One potential problem of training with only out-of-domain parallel corpora is that our method cannot learn a reasonable strategy to predict in-domain words, since it would never come across them during training or fine-tuning. In order to solve this problem, we copy some in-domain monolingual data from target side to source side as in Currey et al. (2017) to form pseudo in-domain parallel corpora. The pseudo in-domain data is concatenated with the original dataset when training the models.

4 Experiments

4.1 Setup

Datasets. We test both DDA-Shallow and DDA-Deep in two different data settings. In the first setting we use the dataset of Koehn and Knowles (2017), training on the law, medical and IT datasets of the German-English OPUS corpus[3] (Tiedemann, 2012). The standard splits contain 2K development and test sentences in each domain, and about 715K, 1M and 337K training sentences respectively. In the second setting, we train our models on the WMT-14 datasets[4] (Bojar

---

[2]Note that this quantity is simply proportional to the log probability, so it is important to re-normalize the probability after interpolation to ensure $\sum_k p(y_t = k) = 1$.

[3]http://opus.nlpl.eu

[4]https://www.statmt.org/wmt14/translation-task.html

| Method | De-En | | | | | | Cs-En | De-En |
| | LAW | | MED | | IT | | WMT | |
	MED	IT	LAW	IT	LAW	MED	TED	TED
w/o copying monolingual data								
Koehn and Knowles (2017)	12.1	3.5	3.9	2.0	1.9	6.5	-	-
Baseline	13.60	4.34	4.57	3.29	4.30	8.56	24.25	24.00
LM-Shallow	13.74	4.41	4.54	3.41	4.29	8.15	24.29	24.03
DDA-Shallow	16.39*	5.49*	5.89*	4.51*	5.87*	10.29*	26.52*	25.53*
w/ copying monolingual data								
Baseline	17.14	6.14	5.09	4.59	5.09	10.65	25.60	24.54
LM-Deep	17.74	6.01	5.16	4.87	5.01	11.88	25.98	25.12
DDA-Deep	18.02†	6.51*	5.85*	5.39*	5.52†	12.48*	26.44*	25.46†
w/ back-translated data								
Baseline	22.89	13.36	9.96	8.03	8.68	13.71	30.12	28.88
LM-Deep	23.58	14.04	10.02	9.05	8.48	15.08	30.34	28.72
DDA-Deep	23.74	13.96	10.74*	8.85	9.28*	16.40*	30.69	28.85

Table 1: Translation accuracy (BLEU; Papineni et al. (2002)) under different settings. The first three rows list the language pair, the source domain, and the target domain. "LAW", "MED" and "IT" represent law, medical and IT domains, respectively. We use compare-mt (Neubig et al., 2019) to perform significance tests (Koehn, 2004) and statistical significance compared with the best baseline is indicated with $*$ ($p < 0.005$) and $\dagger$ ($p < 0.05$).

et al., 2014) which contain data from several domains and test on the multilingual TED test sets of Duh (2018).[5] We consider two language pairs for this setting, namely Czech and German to English. The Czech-English and German-English datasets consist of about 1M and 4.5M sentences respectively and the development and test sets contain about 2K sentences. Byte-pair encoding (Sennrich et al., 2016b) is employed to process training data into subwords with a vocabulary size of 50K for both settings.

Models. NMT-out is a 500 dimensional 2-layer attentional LSTM encoder-decoder model (Bahdanau et al., 2015) implemented on top of OpenNMT (Klein et al., 2017). LM-in and LM-out are also 2-layer LSTMs with hidden sizes of 500. Here we mainly test on RNN-based models, but there is nothing architecture-specific in our methods preventing them from being easily adapted to other architectures such as the Transformer model (Vaswani et al., 2017).

Baselines. We compare our methods with three baseline models: 1) Shallow fusion and deep fusion (Gulcehre et al., 2015): they directly combine LM-in with NMT-out[6]. Shallow fusion combines LM-in and NMT-out during decoding while deep fusion learns to combine hidden states of LM-in and NMT-out. We denote shallow fusion and deep fusion as "LM-Shallow" and "LM-Deep". 2) The copied monolingual data model (Currey et al., 2017) which copies target in-domain monolingual data to the source side to form synthetic in-domain data. 3) Back-translation (Sennrich et al., 2016a) which enriches the training data by generating synthetic in-domain parallel data via a target-to-source NMT model which is trained on a out-of-domain corpus.

4.2 Main Results

4.2.1 Adapting Between Domains

The first 6 result columns of Table 1 show the experimental results on the OPUS dataset. We can see the LM-Shallow model can only marginally improve and sometimes even harms the performance of baseline models. On the other hand, our proposed DDA-Shallow model can outperform the baseline significantly by over 2 BLEU points. This reinforces the merit of our main idea of explicitly modeling the *difference* between domains, instead of simply modeling the target domain itself.

Under the setting where additional copied in-domain data is added into the training set, both LM-Deep and DDA-Deep perform better than the baseline model, with DDA-Deep consistently outperforming the LM-Deep method, indicating the presence of an out-of-domain LM is helpful. We also compare with back-translation, a

---

[5]http://www.cs.jhu.edu/ kevinduh/a/multitarget-tedtalks

[6]To ensure the fairness of comparison, we use our gating formula (Equation (2.2)) and fine-tune all parts of NMT-out for deep fusion.

strong baseline for domain adaptation. We obtain back-translated data via a target-to-source NMT model and concatenate the back-translated data with the original training data to train models. Again, DDA generally brings improvements over the baseline and LM-Deep with back-translated data.

4.2.2 Adapting from a General Domain to a Specific Domain

The last two result columns of Table 1 show the experimental results in the WMT-TED setting. As we can see, in this data setting our baseline performance is much stronger than the first setting. Similarly to the previous setting, DDA-Shallow can significantly improve the baseline model by over 2 BLEU points. However, the DDA-Deep model cannot outperform baselines by a large margin, probably because the baseline models are strong when adapting from a general domain to a specific domain and thus additional adaptation strategies can only lead to incremental improvements.

5 Analysis

5.1 Domain Differences between NMT Models and LMs

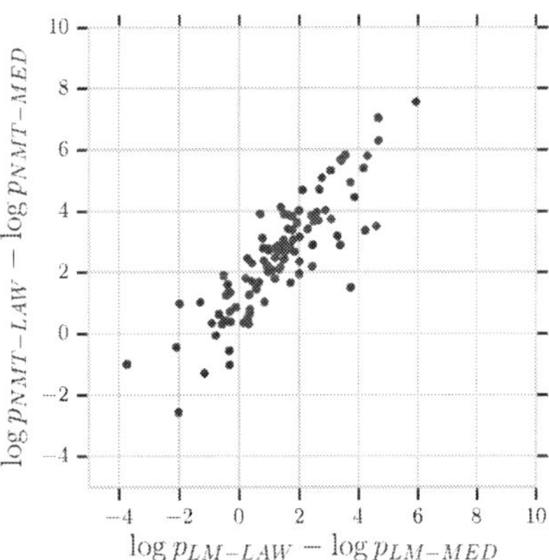

Figure 2: Correlation between $\log p_{\text{NMT-LAW}} - \log p_{\text{NMT-MED}}$ and $\log p_{\text{LM-LAW}} - \log p_{\text{LM-MED}}$. We decode each model on the medical set by feeding in the gold labels and calculate the mean of total log probabilities. We plot 100 words that appear frequently in both domains.

In this section, we visualize the correlation between $\log p_{\text{NMT-in}} - \log p_{\text{NMT-out}}$ and $\log p_{\text{LM-in}} - \log p_{\text{LM-out}}$. We treat the law domain as the target domain and the medical domain as the source domain. Specifically, we train four models NMT-LAW, NMT-MED, LM-LAW, LM-MED with law and medical data and decode each model on the medical set by feeding in the gold labels and calculate the mean of total log probabilities, then plot the correlation of 100 words that appear most frequently in both domains. Figure 2 shows that the difference between NMT models and LMs are roughly correlated, which supports the main motivation of the DDA framework.

5.2 Fusing Different Parts of the Models

In this section, we try to fuse different parts of LMs and NMT models. Prior works have tried different strategies such as fusing the hidden states of LMs with NMT models (Gulcehre et al., 2015) or combining multiple layers of a deep network (Peters et al., 2018). Therefore, it would be interesting to find out which combination of hidden vectors in our DDA-Deep method would be more helpful. Specifically, we try to fuse word embeddings, hidden states and output probabilities.

Components	LAW-MED	MED-LAW
Word-Embed	17.43	5.26
Hidden States	18.02	5.85
Word-Embed & Hidden States	18.00	5.79

Table 2: Performance of DDA-Deep when fusing different parts of models on the law and medical datasets.

We conduct experiments on the law and medical datasets in OPUS, and experimental results are shown in Table 2. We find that generally fusing hidden states is better than fusing word embeddings, and fusing hidden states together with word embeddings does not show any improvements over simply fusing hidden states alone. These results indicate that combining the higher-level information captured by the encoder states is more advantageous for domain adaptation. Also, we found that directly using DDA-Deep to fuse output probabilities was unstable even after trying several normalization techniques, possibly because of the sensitivity of output probabilities.

5.3 Analysis of the Adaptation Effect

In this section, we quantitatively and qualitatively analyze the effect of our proposed DDA framework on adapting the NMT model to in-domain

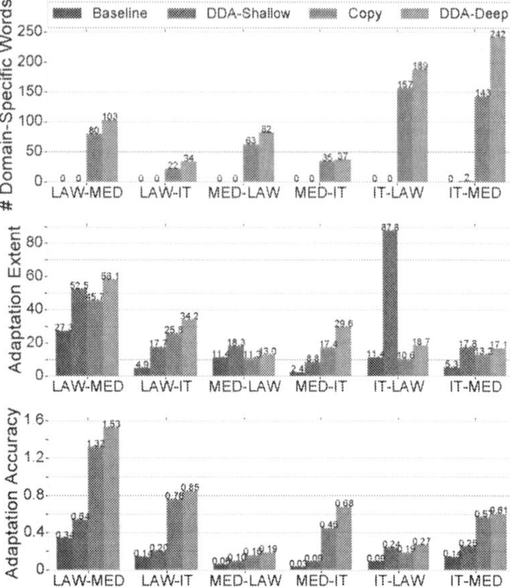

Figure 3: Number of generated domain-specific subwords, scores of adaptation extent and adaptation accuracy for each method. *Top*: count of words only exist in in-domain data produced by different models; *Middle*: adaptation extent of different models; *Bottom*: adaptation accuracy of different models.

Source	warum wurde Ab- ili- fy zugelassen ?
Reference	why has Ab- ili- fy been approved ?
Baseline	reasons was received why a reminder was accepted ?
DDA-Shallow	why has been approved?
Copy	why ,
DDA-Deep	why was Ab- ili- fy authorised ?

Table 3: Translation examples under the law to medical adaptation setting.

data. We conduct analysis on the level of the subwords that were used in the MT system, and study whether our methods can generate in-domain subwords that have never appeared or appeared less frequently in the out-of-domain dataset as well as whether our methods can generate these in-domain subwords accurately.

First, we focus on domain-specific subwords, *i.e.* subwords that appear *exclusively* in the in-domain data. The counts of these subwords are shown in Figure 3. In general, both the baseline and DDA-Shallow struggle at generating subwords that never appear in the out-of-domain parallel data. On the other hand, copying monolingual data performs better in this facet, because it exposes the model to subwords that appear only in the in-domain data. DDA-Deep generates the largest number of in-domain subwords among the four models, indicating the effectiveness of our method.

Second, we propose two subword-level evaluation metrics that study whether the models can generate in-domain subwords and if the generated in-domain subwords are correct. We first define

metric "Adaptation Extent" (AE) as follows:

$$\text{AE} = \frac{1}{|V|} \sum_{w \in V} \frac{\text{freq\_in}(w)}{\text{freq\_out}(w)} \text{count}(w), \qquad (3)$$

where V is the whole vocabulary, $\text{freq\_in}(w)$ and $\text{freq\_out}(w)$ represent the frequency of subword w in both in-domain and out-of-domain corpora, and $\text{count}(w)$ measures how many times subword w appears in the translation result.

We define "Adaptation Accuracy" (AA) in a similar way:

$$\text{AA} = \frac{1}{|V|} \sum_{w \in V} \frac{\text{freq\_in}(w)}{\text{freq\_out}(w)} F1(w), \qquad (4)$$

where $F1$ denotes the F1-score of subword w. In order to avoid dividing by zero, we use add-one smoothing when calculating $\text{freq\_out}(w)$. While AE measures the *quantity* of in-domain subwords the models can generate, AA tells us the *quality* of these subwords, namely whether the in-domain subwords form meaningful translations.

We plot the AE and AA scores of our methods as well as the baselines in Figure 3. The AE scores demonstrate that both DDA-Shallow and DDA-Deep adapt the model to a larger extent compared to other baselines even though DDA-Shallow fails to generate domain-specific subwords. In addition, the AA scores reveal that DDA-Deep outperforms other methods in terms of adaptation accuracy while DDA-Shallow is relatively weak in this respect. However, it should be noted that there is still large gap between deep adaptation method and the upper bound where the gold reference is used as a "translation"; the upper bound is about 10 for each setting.

We also we sample some translation results and show them in Table 3 to qualitatively demonstrate the differences between the methods. We could

Strategy	LAW-MED	MED-LAW
LM-in + LM-out	18.02	6.51
two LMs-in	17.60	6.06
two LMs-out	17.42	6.03
two LMs-general	17.64	6.22

Table 4: Performance of ensembling different LMs on the law and medical datasets. LMs-general are trained with both in-domain and out-of-domain datasets.

see that by modifying the output probabilities, the DDA-Shallow strategy has the ability to adjust tokens translated by the baseline model to some extent, but it is not capable of generating the domain-specific subwords "Ab- i li- fy". However, the DDA-Deep strategy can encourage the model to generate domain-specific tokens and make the translation more correct.

All of the above quantitative and qualitative results indicate that our strategies indeed help the model adapt from the source to target domains.

5.4 Necessity of Integrating both LMs

In this section, we further examine the necessity of integrating both in-domain and out-of-domain LMs. Although previous experimental results partially support the statement, we perform more detailed analysis to ensure the gain in BLEU points is because of the joint contribution of LM-in and LM-out.

Ensembling LMs. Ensembling multiple models is a common and broadly effective technique for machine learning, and one possible explanation for our success is that we are simply adding more models into the mix. To this end, we compare DDA-Deep with three models: the first one integrates NMT-out with two LMs-in trained with different random seeds and the second one integrates NMT-out with two LMs-out; we also integrate two general-domain LMs which are trained on both the in-domain and out-of-domain data and compare the performance. The experimental results are shown in Table 4.

We can see that DDA-Deep achieves the best performance compared with the three other models, demonstrating the gain in BLEU is not simply because of using more models.

Continued Training. In this section, we attempt to gain more insights about the contribution of

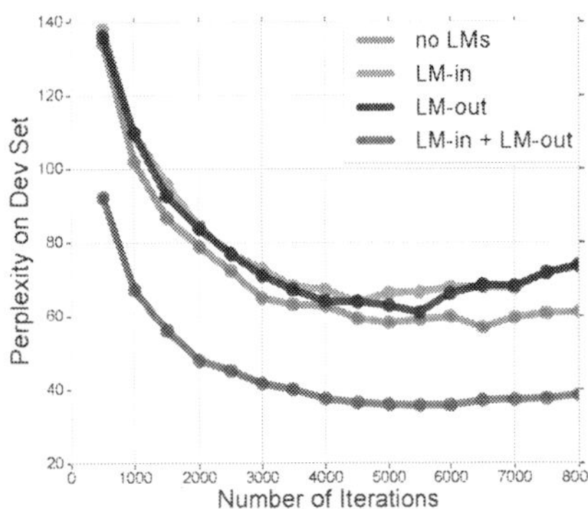

Figure 4: Perplexity on the development set for each method under the continued training setting. "no LMS", "LM-in", "LM-out" and "LM-in + LM-out" denote the baseline model, LM-Deep with LM-in, LM-Deep with LM-out and DDA-Deep respectively.

LM-in and LM-out by investigating how DDA-Deep behaves under a continued training setting, where a small number of in-domain parallel sentences are available. We first train the NMT-out model until convergence on the out-of-domain corpus, and then fine-tune it with DDA-Deep on the in-domain corpus. Here we use the medical and IT datasets as our out-of-domain and in-domain corpora respectively, mainly because the baseline model performs poorly under this setting. We randomly select $10,000$ parallel sentences in the in-domain dataset for continued training.

We freeze LM-in and LM-out as before and fine-tune the NMT-out model. The results are shown in Figure 4. We find that the perplexity of deep adaptation method on the development set drops more dramatically compared to baseline models. Figure 4 shows that integrating only LM-in or LM-out with the NMT model does not help, and sometimes even hurts the performance. This finding indicates that there indeed exists some correlation between LMs trained on different domains. Using both LM-in and LM-out together is essential for the NMT model to utilize the domain difference to adapt more effectively.

However, if we look at the BLEU points on the development set, DDA-deep with continued training performs much worse than the baseline model (13.36 vs. 15.61), as shown in Table 5 ($\beta = 0$). This sheds light on some limitations of our proposed method, which we will discuss in the next section.

Coverage penalty β	0.00	0.05	0.10	0.15	0.20	0.25	0.30
Baseline (no LMs)	15.61	16.28	17.26	**17.59**	17.21	16.39	15.96
LM-Deep (LM-out)	13.56	14.61	15.52	15.92	**15.98**	15.76	15.24
LM-Deep (LM-in)	12.00	13.36	14.56	15.10	15.62	**15.98**	15.57
DDA-Deep (LM-in + LM-out)	13.36	15.18	17.52	18.46	**18.62**	18.03	17.17

Table 5: BLEU points of models after continued training on the IT development dataset with different values of coverage penalty β.

5.5 Limitations of Current DDA Methods

Although our two proposed methods under the DDA framework achieve impressive results on unsupervised domain adaptation for NMT, the translation results still fall behind the gold reference by a large margin and the DDA-Deep performs much worse than the baseline model under a continued training setting as demonstrated in previous sections. In this section, we specify some limitations with our proposed methods and list a few future directions.

The objectives of LMs and NMT models are inherently different: LMs care more about the fluency whereas NMT models also need to consider translation adequacy, that is, the translations should faithfully reflect the source sentence (Tu et al., 2016). Therefore, directly integrating LMs with NMT models might have a negative impact on adequacy.

To verify this hypothesis, under the continued training setting we adopt a decoding-time coverage penalty (Wu et al., 2016), which is a simple yet effective strategy to reduce the number of dropped tokens. As shown in Table 5, the coverage penalty can improve the deep adaptation method by more than 5 BLEU points while the baseline model can only be improved by 2 BLEU points. The best DDA-Deep method outperforms the baseline by 1.03 BLEU points.

These results suggest some promising future directions for designing models under the DDA framework. Although current DDA methods can extract domain differences from two LMs, they cannot fully reduce the negative effect of LM objective on the NMT model. Therefore, it may be useful to add domain related priors that encourage the in-domain annd out-of-domain LMs to be more distinct, so that they can capture more domain-specific information. Another possible option is to add extra objectives to LM pretraining so that it can be fused with the NMT model more seamlessly.

6 Related Work

Finally, we overview related works in the general field of unsupervised domain adaptation, and then list some specific domain adaptation strategies for neural machine translation.

6.1 Unsupervised Domain Adaptation

Prior unsupervised domain adaptation methods for neural models mainly address the problem by aligning source domain and target domain by minimizing certain distribution statistics. For instance, Long et al. (2015) propose deep adaptation networks that minimize a multiple kernel maximum mean discrepancy (MK-MMD) between source and target domains. Sankaranarayanan and Balaji (2017) on the other hand utilize adversarial training to match different domains. Researchers have also tried to use language models for unsupervised domain adaptation. For example, Siddhant et al. (2019) propose to apply Embeddings from Language Models (ELMo) (Peters et al., 2018) and its variants in unsupervised transfer learning.

6.2 Domain Adaptation for NMT

Domain adaptation is an active research topic in NMT (Chu and Wang, 2018). Many previous works focus on the setting where a small amount of in-domain data is available. For instance, continued training (Luong and Manning, 2015; Freitag and Al-Onaizan, 2016) is one of the most popular methods, whose basic idea is to first train an NMT model on out-of-domain data and then finetune it on the in-domain data. Also, Wang et al. (2017) propose instance weighting methods for NMT domain adaptation problem, the main goal of which is to assign higher weights to in-domain data than out-of-domain data.

Using LMs or monolingual data to address domain adaptation has been investigated by several researchers (Sennrich et al., 2016a; Currey et al., 2017; Hu et al., 2019). Moore and Lewis (2010);

Axelrod et al. (2011) use LMs to score the out-of-domain data and then select data that are similar to in-domain text based on the resulting scores, a paradigm adapted by Duh et al. (2013) to neural models. Gulcehre et al. (2015) propose two fusion techniques, namely shallow fusion and deep fusion, to integrate LM and NMT model. Shallow fusion mainly combines LM and NMT model during decoding while deep fusion integrates the two models during training. Researchers have also proposed to perform adaptation for NMT by retrieving sentences or n-grams in the training data similar to the test set (Farajian et al., 2017; Bapna and Firat, 2019). However, it can be difficult to find similar parallel sentences in domain adaptation settings.

7 Conclusion

We propose a novel framework of domain differential adaptation (DDA) that models the differences between domains with the help of models in a related task, based on which we adapt models for the target task. Two simple strategies under the proposed framework for neural machine translation are presented and are demonstrated to achieve good performance. Moreover, we introduce two subword-level evaluation metrics for domain adaptation in machine translation and analyses reveal that our methods can adapt models to a larger extent and with a higher accuracy compared with several alternative adaptation strategies.

However, as shown in our analysis, there are certain limitations for our current methods. Future directions include adding more prior knowledge into our methods as well as considering more sophisticated combining strategies. We will also validate our framework on other pairs of tasks, such as text summarization and language modeling.

Acknowledgements

We are grateful to anonymous reviewers for their helpful suggestions and insightful comments. We also thank Junxian He, Austin Matthews, Paul Michel for proofreading the paper.

This material is based upon work generously supported partly by the National Science Foundation under grant 1761548 and the Defense Advanced Research Projects Agency Information Innovation Office (I2O) Low Resource Languages for Emergent Incidents (LORELEI) program under Contract No. HR0011-15-C0114. The views and conclusions contained in this document are those of the authors and should not be interpreted as representing the official policies, either expressed or implied, of the U.S. Government. The U.S. Government is authorized to reproduce and distribute reprints for Government purposes notwithstanding any copyright notation here on.

References

Amittai Axelrod, Xiaodong He, and Jianfeng Gao. 2011. Domain adaptation via pseudo in-domain data selection. In *Conference on Empirical Methods in Natural Language Processing (EMNLP)*.

Dzmitry Bahdanau, Kyunghyun Cho, and Yoshua Bengio. 2015. Neural machine translation by jointly learning to align and translate. In *International Conference on Learning Representations (ICLR)*.

Ankur Bapna and Orhan Firat. 2019. Non-parametric adaptation for neural machine translation. In *Conference of the North American Chapter of the Association for Computational Linguistics (NAACL)*.

Ondrej Bojar, Christian Buck, Christian Federmann, Barry Haddow, Philipp Koehn, Johannes Leveling, Christof Monz, Pavel Pecina, Matt Post, Herve Saint-Amand, et al. 2014. Findings of the 2014 workshop on statistical machine translation. In *Workshop on Machine Translation (WMT)*.

Kyunghyun Cho, Bart van Merrienboer, Caglar Gulcehre, Dzmitry Bahdanau, Fethi Bougares, Holger Schwenk, and Yoshua Bengio. 2014. Learning phrase representations using rnn encoder–decoder for statistical machine translation. In *Conference on Empirical Methods in Natural Language Processing (EMNLP)*.

Chenhui Chu, Raj Dabre, and Sadao Kurohashi. 2017. An empirical comparison of domain adaptation methods for neural machine translation. In *Annual Meeting of the Association for Computational Linguistics (ACL)*.

Chenhui Chu and Rui Wang. 2018. A survey of domain adaptation for neural machine translation. In *International Conference on Computational Linguistics (COLING)*.

Anna Currey, Antonio Valerio Miceli Barone, and Kenneth Heafield. 2017. Copied monolingual data improves low-resource neural machine translation. In *Conference on Machine Translation (WMT)*.

Jacob Devlin, Ming-Wei Chang, Kenton Lee, and Kristina Toutanova. 2019. Bert: Pre-training of deep bidirectional transformers for language understanding. In *Conference of the North American Chapter of the Association for Computational Linguistics (NAACL)*.

Kevin Duh. 2018. The multitarget ted talks task. http://www.cs.jhu.edu/~kevinduh/a/multitarget-tedtalks/.

Kevin Duh, Graham Neubig, Katsuhito Sudoh, and Hajime Tsukada. 2013. Adaptation data selection using neural language models: Experiments in machine translation. In *Annual Meeting of the Association for Computational Linguistics (ACL)*.

M Amin Farajian, Marco Turchi, Matteo Negri, and Marcello Federico. 2017. Multi-domain neural machine translation through unsupervised adaptation. In *Conference on Machine Translation (WMT)*.

Markus Freitag and Yaser Al-Onaizan. 2016. Fast domain adaptation for neural machine translation. *arXiv preprint arXiv:1612.06897*.

Yaroslav Ganin, Evgeniya Ustinova, Hana Ajakan, Pascal Germain, Hugo Larochelle, François Laviolette, Mario Marchand, and Victor Lempitsky. 2016. Domain-adversarial training of neural networks. *The Journal of Machine Learning Research*, 17(1):2096–2030.

Caglar Gulcehre, Orhan Firat, Kelvin Xu, Kyunghyun Cho, Loic Barrault, Huei-Chi Lin, Fethi Bougares, Holger Schwenk, and Yoshua Bengio. 2015. On using monolingual corpora in neural machine translation. *arXiv preprint arXiv:1503.03535*.

Kaiming He, Georgia Gkioxari, Piotr Dollár, and Ross Girshick. 2017. Mask r-cnn. In *International Conference on Computer Vision (ICCV)*.

Sepp Hochreiter and Jürgen Schmidhuber. 1997. Long short-term memory. *Neural computation*, 9(8):1735–1780.

Junjie Hu, Mengzhou Xia, Graham Neubig, and Jaime Carbonell. 2019. Domain adaptation of neural machine translation by lexicon induction. In *Annual Meeting of the Association for Computational Linguistics (ACL)*.

Guillaume Klein, Yoon Kim, Yuntian Deng, Jean Senellart, and Alexander M Rush. 2017. Opennmt: Open-source toolkit for neural machine translation. *arXiv preprint arXiv:1701.02810*.

Philipp Koehn. 2004. Statistical significance tests for machine translation evaluation. In *Conference on Empirical Methods in Natural Language Processing (EMNLP)*.

Philipp Koehn and Rebecca Knowles. 2017. Six challenges for neural machine translation. In *Workshop on Neural Machine Translation (WMT)*.

Mingsheng Long, Yue Cao, Jianmin Wang, and Michael I Jordan. 2015. Learning transferable features with deep adaptation networks. In *International Conference on Machine Learning (ICML)*.

Minh-Thang Luong and Christopher D Manning. 2015. Stanford neural machine translation systems for spoken language domains. In *International Workshop on Spoken Language Translation (IWSLT)*.

Robert C. Moore and William Lewis. 2010. Intelligent selection of language model training data. In *Annual Meeting of the Association for Computational Linguistics (ACL)*.

Graham Neubig, Zi-Yi Dou, Junjie Hu, Paul Michel, Danish Pruthi, and Xinyi Wang. 2019. compare-mt: A tool for holistic comparison of language generation systems. In *Conference of the North American Chapter of the Association for Computational Linguistics (NAACL) Demo Track*.

Kishore Papineni, Salim Roukos, Todd Ward, and Wei-Jing Zhu. 2002. Bleu: a method for automatic evaluation of machine translation. In *Annual Meeting of the Association for Computational Linguistics (ACL)*.

Matthew Peters, Mark Neumann, Mohit Iyyer, Matt Gardner, Christopher Clark, Kenton Lee, and Luke Zettlemoyer. 2018. Deep contextualized word representations. In *Conference of the North American Chapter of the Association for Computational Linguistics (NAACL)*.

Daniel Povey, Gaofeng Cheng, Yiming Wang, Ke Li, Hainan Xu, Mahsa Yarmohamadi, and Sanjeev Khudanpur. 2018. Semi-orthogonal low-rank matrix factorization for deep neural networks. In *Annual Conference of the International Speech Communication Association (INTERSPEECH)*.

Swami Sankaranarayanan and Yogesh Balaji. 2017. Generate to adapt: Aligning domains using generative adversarial networks. In *Conference on Computer Vision and Pattern Recognition (CVPR)*.

Rico Sennrich, Barry Haddow, and Alexandra Birch. 2016a. Improving neural machine translation models with monolingual data. In *Annual Meeting of the Association for Computational Linguistics (ACL)*.

Rico Sennrich, Barry Haddow, and Alexandra Birch. 2016b. Neural machine translation of rare words with subword units. In *Annual Meeting of the Association for Computational Linguistics (ACL)*.

Aditya Siddhant, Anuj Goyal, and Angeliki Metallinou. 2019. Unsupervised transfer learning for spoken language understanding in intelligent agents. In *AAAI Conference on Artificial Intelligence (AAAI)*.

Ilya Sutskever, Oriol Vinyals, and Quoc V. Le. 2014. Sequence to sequence learning with neural networks. In *Advances in Neural Information Processing Systems (NeurIPS)*.

Ben Tan, Yu Zhang, Sinno Jialin Pan, and Qiang Yang. 2017. Distant domain transfer learning. In *AAAI Conference on Artificial Intelligence (AAAI)*.

Jörg Tiedemann. 2012. Parallel data, tools and interfaces in opus. In *International Conference on Language Resources and Evaluation (LREC)*.

Zhaopeng Tu, Zhengdong Lu, Yang Liu, Xiaohua Liu, and Hang Li. 2016. Modeling coverage for neural machine translation. In *Annual Meeting of the Association for Computational Linguistics (ACL)*.

Ashish Vaswani, Noam Shazeer, Niki Parmar, Jakob Uszkoreit, Llion Jones, Aidan N Gomez, Łukasz Kaiser, and Illia Polosukhin. 2017. Attention is all you need. In *Advances in Neural Information Processing Systems (NeurIPS)*.

Rui Wang, Masao Utiyama, Lemao Liu, Kehai Chen, and Eiichiro Sumita. 2017. Instance weighting for neural machine translation domain adaptation. In *Conference on Empirical Methods in Natural Language Processing (EMNLP)*.

Yonghui Wu, Mike Schuster, Zhifeng Chen, Quoc V Le, Mohammad Norouzi, Wolfgang Macherey, Maxim Krikun, Yuan Cao, Qin Gao, Klaus Macherey, et al. 2016. Google's neural machine translation system: Bridging the gap between human and machine translation. *arXiv preprint arXiv:1609.08144*.

Qizhe Xie, Zihang Dai, Yulun Du, Eduard Hovy, and Graham Neubig. 2017. Controllable invariance through adversarial feature learning. In *Advances in Neural Information Processing Systems (NeurIPS)*.

Wei Ying, Yu Zhang, Junzhou Huang, and Qiang Yang. 2018. Transfer learning via learning to transfer. In *International Conference on Machine Learning (ICML)*.

Transformer-based Model for Single Documents Neural Summarization

Elozino Egonmwan and **Yllias Chali**
University of Lethbridge
Lethbridge, AB, Canada
{elozino.egonmwan, yllias.chali}@uleth.ca

Abstract

We propose a system that improves performance on single document summarization task using the CNN/DailyMail and Newsroom datasets. It follows the popular encoder-decoder paradigm, but with an extra focus on the encoder. The intuition is that the probability of correctly decoding an information significantly lies in the pattern and correctness of the encoder. Hence we introduce, encode – encode – decode. A framework that encodes the source text first with a transformer, then a sequence-to-sequence (`seq2seq`) model. We find that the transformer and seq2seq model complement themselves adequately, making for a richer encoded vector representation. We also find that paying more attention to the vocabulary of target words during abstraction improves performance. We experiment our hypothesis and framework on the task of extractive and abstractive single document summarization and evaluate using the standard CNN/DailyMail dataset and the recently released Newsroom dataset.

1 Introduction

Document summarization has been an active area of research, especially on the CNN/DailyMail dataset. Even with recent progress (Gehrmann et al., 2018; Chen and Bansal, 2018), there is still some work to be done in the field. Although `extractive summarization` seem to be less challenging because new words are not generated, identifying salient parts of the document without any guide in the form of a query, is a substantial problem to tackle.

Earlier approaches for extractive summarization use manual-feature engineering implemented with graphs (Parveen and Strube, 2015; Erkan and Radev, 2004), integer linear programming (ILP) (Boudin et al., 2015; Nayeem and Chali, 2017).

More recent approaches are data-driven and implement a variety of neural networks (Jadhav and Rajan, 2018; Narayan et al., 2017) majorly with an encoder-decoder framework (Narayan et al., 2018; Cheng and Lapata, 2016).

Similar to the work of Nallapati et al. (2017), we consider the extractive summarization task as a sequence classification problem. A major challenge with this approach, is the fact that the training data is not sequentially labelled. Hence creating one from the abstractive ground-truth summary, is crucial. We improve on Nallapati et al. (2017)'s approach to generate this labelled data, and evaluation shows that our extractive labels are more accurate. Another hurdle in this task, is the imbalance in the created data, that is, most of the document's sentences are labelled 0 (excluded from the summary) than 1, because just a few sentences actually make up a summary. Hence the neural extractor tends to be biased and suffer from a lot of false-negative labels. We also present a simple approach to reduce this bias. Most importantly, our neural extractor uses the recent bidirectional transformer encoder (Vaswani et al., 2017) with details provided in Section 3.1.

More interesting than extractive summaries, abstractive summaries correlate better with summaries that a human would present. `Abstractive summarization` does not simply reproduce salient parts of the document verbatim, but rewrites them in a concise form, usually introducing novel words along the way by utilizing some key abstraction techniques such as paraphrasing (Gupta et al., 2018), compression (Filippova et al., 2015) or sentence fusion (Barzilay and McKeown, 2005). However, it is met with major challenges like grammatical correctness and repetition of words especially when generating long-worded sentences. Nonetheless remarkable progress have been achieved with the

Proceedings of the 3rd Workshop on Neural Generation and Translation (WNGT 2019), pages 70–79
Hong Kong, China, November 4, 2019. ©2019 Association for Computational Linguistics
www.aclweb.org/anthology/D19-56%2d

use of seq2seq models (Gehrmann et al., 2018; See et al., 2017; Chopra et al., 2016; Rush et al., 2015) and a reward instead of loss function via deep-reinforcement learning (Chen and Bansal, 2018; Paulus et al., 2017; Ranzato et al., 2015).

We see abstractive summarization in same light as several other authors (Chen and Bansal, 2018; Hsu et al., 2018; Liu et al., 2018) – extract salient sentences and then abstract; thus sharing similar advantages as the popular divide-and-conquer algorithm. More-so, it mitigates the problem of information redundancy, since the mini-source, ie extracted document, contains distinct salient sentences. Our abstractive model is a blend of the transformer and seq2seq model. We notice improvements using this framework in the abstractive setting. This is because, to generate coherent and grammatically correct sentences, we need to be able to learn long-term dependency relations. The transformer complements the seq2seq model in this regard with its multi-head self attention. Also the individual attention heads in the transformer model mimics behavior related to the syntactic and semantic structure of the sentence (Vaswani et al., 2017, 2018). Hence, the transformer produces a richer meaningful vector representation of the input, from which we can encode a fixed state vector for decoding.

The main contributions of this work are:

- We present a simple algorithm for building a sentence-labelled corpus for extractive summarization training that produces more accurate results.

- We propose a novel framework for the task of extractive single document summarization that improves the current state-of-the-art on two specific datasets.

- We introduce the encode - encode - decode paradigm using two complementary models, transformer and seq2seq for generating abstractive summaries that improves current top performance on two specific datasets.

2 Task Definition

Given a document $D = (S_1, ..., S_n)$ with n sentences comprising of a set of words $D_W = \{d_1, ..., d_w\}$, the task is to produce an *extractive* (S_E) or *abstractive* (S_A) summary that contains salient information in D, where $S_E \subseteq D_W$ and $S_A = \{w_1, ..., w_s\} \mid \exists w_i \notin D_W$.

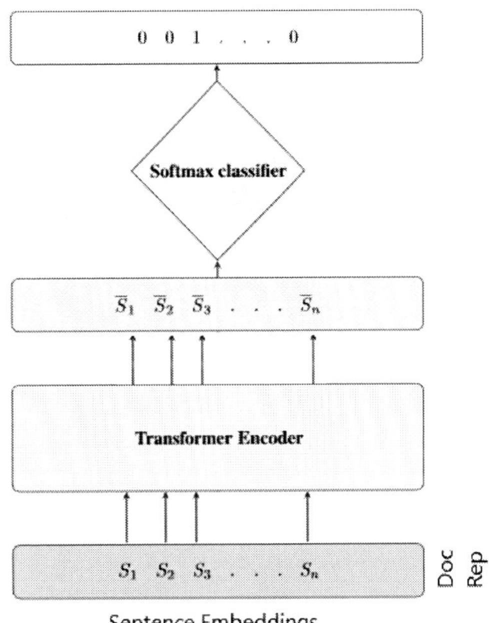

Figure 1: Extractive Model Architecture

3 Method

We describe our summarization model in two modules – *Extraction* and *Abstraction*. The abstraction module simply learns to paraphrase and compress the output of the extracted document sentences.

3.1 Extraction

As illustrated in Figure 1, our model classifies each sentence in a document as being summary-worthy or not. However, in order to enhance this sequence classification process, we encode the input document with a TRANSFORMER. A logistic classifier then learns to label each sentence in the transformed document.

3.1.1 TRANSFORMER Encoder

The input to the Transformer is the document representation, which is a concatenation of the vector representation of its sentences. Each sentence representation is obtained by averaging the vector representation of its constituent words.

$$S_i = 1/m \sum_{i=1}^{m} w_i \tag{1}$$

$$D_j = S_1 \| S_2 \| \ldots \| S_n \tag{2}$$

The transformer encoder is composed of 6 stacked identical layers. Each layer contains 2 sub-layers with multi-head self attention and position-wise fully connected feed-forward network respectively. Full details with implementation are provided in (Vaswani et al., 2017, 2018). The bidirectional Transformer often referred to as the Transformer encoder learns a rich representation of the document that captures long-range syntactic and semantic dependency between the sentences.

3.1.2 Sentence Extraction

The final layer of our extraction model is a softmax layer which performs the classification. We learn the probability of including a sentence in the summary,

$$y_p^i = softmax(WS_i^i + b) \quad (3)$$

where W and b are trainable parameters and S_i^i is the transformed representation of the ith sentence in document D_j, by minimizing the cross-entropy loss

$$L = -(y_t log(y_p) + (1 - y_t) log(1 - y_p)) \quad (4)$$

between the predicted probabilities, y_p and true sentence-labels, y_t during training.

3.1.3 Extractive Training

Filtering Currently, no extractive summarization dataset exists. Hence it is customary to create one from the abstractive ground-truth summaries (Chen and Bansal, 2018; Nallapati et al., 2017). We observe however, that some summaries are more abstractive than others. Since the extractive labels are usually gotten by doing some n-gram overlap matching, the greater the abstractiveness of the ground-truth the more inaccurate the tuned extractive labels are. We filter out such samples [1] as illustrated in Table 1. In our work, we consider a reference summary R_j as *overly abstractive* if it has zero bigram overlap with the corresponding document D_j, excluding stop words.

$$\#bigram(D_j, R_j) == 0 \quad (5)$$

See et al. (2017) and Paulus et al. (2017) truncate source documents to 400 tokens and target

---

[1]Filtering is used only for the training set, to ensure that evaluation comparisons on the test set with existing models are fair

summaries to 100 tokens. We totally exclude documents with more than 30 sentences and truncate or pad as necessary to 20 sentences per document. From the over 280,000 and 1.3M training pairs in the CNN/DM and Newsroom training dataset respectively, our filtering yields approximately 150,000 and 250,000 abstractive summarization sub-dataset. We report evaluation scores using the training sets as-is versus our filtered training sets, to show that filtering the training samples does improve results.

Document: world-renowned chef, author and emmy winning television personality anthony bourdain visits quebec in the next episode of " anthony bourdain : parts unknown, " airing sunday, may 5, at 9 p.m. et. follow the show on twitter and facebook.
Summary: 11 things to know about quebec. o canada! our home and delicious land.'

Table 1: Example of an *overly abstractive* summary with zero bigram overlap with the document from a CNN/DM training sample.

Tuning We use a very simple approach to create extractive labels for our neural extractor. We hypothesize that each reference summary sentence originates from at least one document sentence. The goal is to identify the most-likely document sentence. Different from Nallapati et al. (2017)'s approach to greedily add sentences to the summary that maximizes the ROUGE score, our approach is more similar to Chen and Bansal (2018)'s model that calculates the individual reference sentence-level score as per its similarity with each sentence in the corresponding document. However, our sentence-level similarity score is based on its bigram overlap:

$$score(R_j^t) = amax_i(bigram(D_j^i, R_j^t)) \quad (6)$$

for each tth sentence in the reference summary, R_j, per i^{th} sentence in document D_j, in contrast to Chen and Bansal (2018)'s that uses ROUGE-L_{recall} score. Additionally, for every time both words in the set of bigrams-overlap are stopwords, we decrement the similarity score by 1, for example, *(on, the)* is an invalid bigram-overlap while *(the, President)* is valid. We do this, to capture more important similarities instead of trivial ones.

For statistical purposes, we evaluate our extractive trainer for tuning the document's sentences to

0's and 1's against (Nallapati et al., 2017)'s which is our foundation.

Extractive Trainer	R-1	R-2	R-L
Ours	49.5	27.8	45.8
Ours + filter	**51.4**	**31.7**	**50.3**
(Nallapati et al., 2017)	48.4	27.5	44.4

Table 2: **ROUGE-F1** (%) scores of manually crafted extractive trainers for producing sentence-level extractive labels for CNN/DM.

We apply our tuned dataset to the neural extractive summarizer explained in Sections 3.1.1 and 3.1.2 and report results in Tables 3 and 4.

Imbalanced Extractive Labels   Because a summary is a snippet of the document, the majority of the labels are rightly 0 (excluded from the summary). Hence a high classification accuracy does not necessarily translate to a highly salient summary. Therefore, we consider the F1_score, which is a weighted average of the precision and recall, and apply an early stopping criteria when minimizing the loss, if the F1_score does not increase after a set number of training epochs. Additionally during training, we synthetically balance the labels, by forcing some random sentences to be labelled as 1 and subsequently masking their weights.

Number of sentences to extract   The number of extracted sentences is not trivial, as this significantly affects the summary length and hence evaluation scores. Chen and Bansal (2018) introduced a stop criterion in their reinforcement learning process. We implemented a basic subjective approach based on the dataset. Since the gold summaries are typically 3 or 4 sentences long, we extract the top 3 sentences by default, but proceed to additionally extract a 4th sentence if the confidence score from the softmax function is greater than 0.55.

3.2 Abstraction

The input to our abstraction module is a subset of the document's sentences which comprises of the output of the extraction phase from Section 3.1.2. For each document D_j, initially comprising of n sentences, we abstract its extracted sentences,

$$S_j^E = \{S_j^1, S_j^2, ..., S_j^m\} \qquad (7)$$

where $m < n$ and $S_j^E \subseteq D_j$, by learning to jointly paraphrase (Gupta et al., 2018) and compress (Filippova et al., 2015). We add one more encoding layer to the standard encoder-aligner-decoder (Bahdanau et al., 2014; Luong et al., 2015), ie, encode-encode-align-decode. The intuition is to seemingly improve the performance of the decoder by providing an interpretable and richly encoded sequence. For this, we interleave two efficient models – transformer (Vaswani et al., 2017) and sequence-to-sequence (Sutskever et al., 2014), specifically GRU-RNN (Chung et al., 2014; Cho et al., 2014). Details are presented in subsequent subsections.

3.2.1   Encoder – TRANSFORMER

The transformer encoder has same implementation from Vaswani et al. (2017) as explained in Section 3.1.1, except the inputs are sentence-level vector representations not document. Also, the sentence representations in this module are not averaged constituent word representations as in the extraction module but concatenated. That is, for each ith sentence in equation 7, its vector representation, is the concatenation of its constituent word embeddings

$$S_j^i = w_1 \| w_2 \| \ldots \| w_n \qquad (8)$$

The output of equation 8 serves as the input vector representation to the transformer encoder. We use the transformer-encoder during abstraction as sort of a pre-training module of the input sentence.

3.2.2   Encoder – GRU-RNN

We use a single layer uni-directional GRU-RNN whose input is the output of the transformer. The GRU-RNN encoder (Chung et al., 2014; Cho et al., 2014) produces fixed-state vector representation of the transformed input sequence using the following equations:

$$z = \sigma(s_t U^z + x_{t-1} W^z) \qquad (9)$$

$$r = \sigma(s_t U^r + x_{t-1} W^r) \qquad (10)$$

$$h = tanh(s_t U^h + (x_{t-1} \odot r) W^h) \qquad (11)$$

$$x_t = (1 - z) \odot h + z \odot x_{t-1} \qquad (12)$$

where r and z are the reset and update gates respectively, W and U are the network's parameters, x_t is the hidden state vector at timestep t, s_t is the input vector and $\odot$ represents the Hadamard product.

Extractive Model	R-1	R-2	R-L
LEAD (See et al., 2017)	40.3	17.7	36.5
LEAD (Narayan et al., 2018)	39.6	17.7	36.2
LEAD (ours)	40.1	17.6	36.0
(Nallapati et al., 2017)	39.6	16.2	35.3
REFRESH (Narayan et al., 2018)	40.0	18.2	36.6
FAST (Chen and Bansal, 2018)	41.4	18.7	37.7
NEUSUM (Zhou et al., 2018)	41.6	19.0	37.0
Content Selector (Gehrmann et al., 2018)	42.0	15.9	37.3
TRANS-ext	41.0	18.4	36.9
TRANS-ext + filter	**42.8**	**21.1**	**38.4**

Table 3: **ROUGE-F1** (%) scores (with 95% confidence interval) of various extractive models on the **CNN/DM** test set. The first section shows LEAD-3 model scores. The second section shows scores for baseline models. The third section shows our model's scores

Extractive Model	R-1	R-2	R-L
LEAD* (Grusky et al., 2018)	30.49	21.27	28.42
TextRank* (Barrios et al., 2016)	22.77	9.79	18.98
TRANS-ext	37.21	25.17	32.41
TRANS-ext + filter	**41.52**	**30.62**	**36.96**

Table 4: **ROUGE-F1** (%) scores (with 95% confidence interval) of various extractive models on the **Newsroom** released test set. * marks results taken from Grusky et al. (2018)

3.3 Decoder – GRU-RNN

The fixed-state vector representation produced by the GRU-RNN encoder is used as initial state for the decoder. At each time step, the decoder receives the previously generated word, y_{t-1} and hidden state s_{t-1} at time step t_{-1}. The output word, y_t at each time step, is a softmax probability of the vector in equation 11 over the set of vocabulary words, V.

4 Experiments

We used pre-trained 300-dimensional $gloVe$[2] word-embeddings (Pennington et al., 2014). The transformer encoder was setup with the $transformer\_base$ hyperparameter setting from the tensor2tensor library (Vaswani et al., 2018)[3], but the hidden size and dropout were reset to 300 and 0.0 respectively. We also use 300 hidden units for the GRU-RNN encoder. The tensor2tensor library comes with pre-processed/tokenized versions of the dataset, we however perform these operations independently. For abstraction, our target vocabulary is a set of approximately 50,000 and 80,000 words for CNN/DM and Newsroom

corpus respectively. It contains words in our target training and test sets that occur at least twice. Experiments showed that using this subset of vocabulary words as opposed to over 320,000 vocabulary words contained in $gloVe$ improves both training time and performance of the model. During the abstractive training, we match summary sentence with its corresponding extracted document sentence using equation 6 and learn to minimize the seq2seq loss implemented in `tensorflow` API[4] with `AdamOptimizer` (Kingma and Ba, 2014). We employ early stopping when the validation loss does not decrease after 5 epochs. We apply gradient clipping at 5.0 (Pascanu et al., 2013). We use greedy-decoding during training and validation and set the maximum number of iterations to 5 times the target sentence length. Beam-search decoding is used during inference.

4.1 Datasets

We evaluate our models on the non-anonymized version of the **CNN-DM** corpus (Hermann et al., 2015; Nallapati et al., 2016) and the recent **Newsroom** dataset (Grusky et al., 2018) released by Connected Experiences Lab[5]. The Newsroom

---

[2] https://nlp.stanford.edu/projects/glove/

[3] https://github.com/tensorflow/tensor2tensor

[4] https://www.tensorflow.org/api_docs/python/tf/contrib/seq2seq/sequence_loss

[5] https://summari.es

Abstractive Model	R-1	R-2	R-L
RL+Intra-Att (Paulus et al., 2017)	41.16	15.75	**39.08**
KIGN+Pred (Li et al., 2018)	38.95	17.12	35.68
FAST (Chen and Bansal, 2018)	40.88	17.80	38.54
Bottom-Up (Gehrmann et al., 2018)	41.22	18.68	38.34
TRANS-ext + abs	41.05	17.87	36.73
TRANS-ext + filter +abs	**41.89**	**18.90**	38.92

Table 5: **ROUGE-F1** (%) scores (with 95% confidence interval) of various abstractive models on the **CNN/DM** test set.

Abstractive Model	R-1	R-2	R-L
Abs-N* (Rush et al., 2015)	5.88	0.39	5.32
Pointer* (See et al., 2017)	26.02	13.25	22.43
TRANS-ext + abs	33.81	15.37	28.92
TRANS-ext + filter + abs	**35.74**	**16.52**	**30.17**

Table 6: **ROUGE-F1** (%) scores (with 95% confidence interval) of various abstractive models on the **Newsroom** released test set. * marks results taken from Grusky et al. (2018)

corpus contains over 1.3M news articles together with various metadata information such as the title, summary, coverage and compression ratio. CNN/DM summaries are twice as long as Newsroom summaries with average word lengths of 66 and 26 respectively.

4.2 Evaluation

Following previous works (See et al., 2017; Nallapati et al., 2017; Chen and Bansal, 2018), we evaluate both datasets on standard ROUGE-1, ROUGE-2 and ROUGE-L (Lin, 2004). It calculates the appropriate n-gram word-overlap between the reference and system summaries.

4.3 Results Analysis

We used the official `pyrouge` script[6] with option[7]. Table 3 and 5 presents extractive and abstractive results on the CNN/DM dataset respectively, while Tables 4 and 6 for the Newsroom dataset. For clarity, we present results separately for each model and dataset.

Our baseline non-filtered extractive (TRANS-ext) model is highly competitive with top models. Our TRANS-ext + filter produces an average of about +1 and +9 points across reported ROUGE variants on the CNN/DM and Newsroom datasets respectively, showing that our model does a better job at identifying the most salient parts of the document than existing state-of-the-art extractive

models. We observe the large margin in the Newsroom dataset results, as existing baselines are just the LEAD-3 and TEXTRANK of (Barrios et al., 2016). The Newsroom dataset was recently released and is yet to be thoroughly explored, however it is a larger dataset and contains more diverse summaries as analyzed by Grusky et al. (2018).

We also experimented with the empirical outcome of using imbalanced extractive labels which usually leads to bias towards the majority class. Interestingly, our extractive model has +20% F_Score increase when trained with balanced labels. Switching the transformer encoder with a seq2seq encoder, resulted in a drop of about 2 ROUGE points, showing that the transformer encoder does learn features that adds meaning to the vector representation of our input sequence.

Our baseline non-filtered abstractive (TRANS-ext + abs) model is also highly competitive with top models, with a drop of -0.81 ROUGE-2 points against Gehrmann et al. (2018)'s model which is the current state-of-the art. Our TRANS-ext + filter + abs produces an average of about +0.5 and +7 points across reported ROUGE variants on the CNN/DM and Newsroom datasets respectively, showing empirically that our model is an improvement of existing abstractive summarization models.

On the abstractiveness of our summaries, after aligning with the ground-truth as explained in Section 3.2 about 60% of our extracted document sentences were paraphrased and compressed.

[6]`https://github.com/andersjo/pyrouge/tree/master/tools/ROUGE-1.5.5`
[7]-n 2 -w 1.2 -m -a -c 95

O: the two clubs, who occupy the top two spots in spain's top flight, are set to face each other at the nou camp on sunday. **G:** real madrid face barcelona in the nou camp **R:** real madrid will travel to the nou camp to face barcelona on sunday.
O: dangelo conner, from new york, filmed himself messing around with the powerful weapon in a friend's apartment, first waving it around, then sending volts coursing through a coke can . **G:** dangelo conner from new york was fooling around with his gun **R:** dangelo conner, from new york ,was fooling around with stun gun.
O: jamie peacock broke his try drought with a double for leeds in their win over salford on sunday. **G:** jamie adam scored to win over salford for leeds **R:** jamie peacock scored two tries for leeds in their win over salford.
O: britain's lewis hamilton made the perfect start to his world title defense by winning the opening race of the f1 season in australia sunday to lead a mercedes one-two in melbourne . **G:** lewis hamilton wins first race of season in australia **R:** lewis hamilton wins opening race of 2015 f1 season in australia .

Table 7: Examples of some of our generated paraphrases from the CNN/DM dataset, where **O**, **G**, **R** represents Originating document sentence, our model's Generated paraphrase and Reference sentences from the ground-truth summary respectively.

We highlight examples of some of the generated paraphrases in Table 7. Table 7 show that our paraphrases are well formed, abstractive (*e.g powerful weapon – gun, messing around – fooling around*), capable of performing syntactic manipulations (*e.g for leeds in their win over sadford – win over salford for leeds*) and compression as seen in all the examples.

5 Related Work

Summarization has remained an interesting and important NLP task for years due to its diverse applications - news headline generation, weather forecasting, emails filtering, medical cases, recommendation systems, machine reading compre-

hension MRC and so forth (Khargharia et al., 2018).

Early summarization models were mostly extractive and manual-feature engineered (Knight and Marcu, 2000; Jing and McKeown, 2000; Dorr et al., 2003; Berg-Kirkpatrick et al., 2011). With the introduction of neural networks (Sutskever et al., 2014) and availability of large training data, deep learning became a viable approach (Rush et al., 2015; Chopra et al., 2016).

Extraction has been handled on different levels of granularity – word (Cheng and Lapata, 2016), phrases (Bui et al., 2016; Gehrmann et al., 2018), sentence (Cheng and Lapata, 2016; Nallapati et al., 2016, 2017) each with its challenges. Word and phrase level extraction although more concise usually suffers from grammatical incorrectness, while sentence-level extraction are too lengthy and sometimes contain redundant information. Hence Berg-Kirkpatrick et al. (2011); Filippova et al. (2015); Durrett et al. (2016) learn to extract and compress at sentence-level.

Identifying the likely most salient part of the text as summary-worthy is very crucial. Some authors have employed integer linear programming (Martins and Smith, 2009; Gillick and Favre, 2009; Boudin et al., 2015), graph concepts (Erkan and Radev, 2004; Parveen et al., 2015; Parveen and Strube, 2015), ranking with reinforcement learning (Narayan et al., 2018) and mostly related to our work – binary classification (Shen et al., 2007; Nallapati et al., 2017; Chen and Bansal, 2018)

Our binary classification architecture differs significantly from existing models because it uses a transformer as the building block instead of a bidirectional GRU-RNN (Nallapati et al., 2017), or bidirectional LSTM-RNN (Chen and Bansal, 2018). To the best of our knowledge, our utilization of the transformer encoder model as a building block for binary classification is novel, although the transformer has been successfully used for language understanding (Devlin et al., 2018), machine translation (MT) (Vaswani et al., 2017) and paraphrase generation (Zhao et al., 2018).

For generation of abstractive summaries, before the ubiquitous use of neural nets, manually crafted rules and graph techniques were utilized with considerable success. Barzilay and McKeown (2005); Cheung and Penn (2014) fused two sentences into one using their dependency parsed trees. Recently, sequence-to-sequence models (Sutskever et al., 2014) with attention (Bahdanau et al., 2014; Chopra et al., 2016), copy mechanism (Vinyals et al., 2015; Gu et al., 2016), pointer-generator (See et al., 2017), graph-based attention (Tan et al., 2017) have been explored. Since the system generated summaries are usually evaluated on ROUGE, its been beneficial to directly optimize this metric during training via a suitable policy using reinforcement learning (Paulus et al., 2017; Celikyilmaz et al., 2018).

Similar to Rush et al. (2015); Chen and Bansal (2018) we abstract by simplifying our extracted sentences. We jointly learn to paraphrase and compress, but different from existing models purely based on RNN, we implement a blend of two proven efficient models – transformer encoder and GRU-RNN. Zhao et al. (2018) paraphrased with a transformer-decoder, we find that using the GRU-RNN decoder but with a two-level stack of hybrid encoders (transformer and GRU-RNN) gives better performance. To the best of our knowledge, this architectural blend is novel.

6 Conclusion

We proposed two frameworks for extractive and abstractive summarization and demonstrated that they each improve results over existing state-of-the art. Our models are simple to train, and the intuition/hypothesis behind the formulation are straightforward and logical. The scientific correctness is provable, as parts of our model architecture have been used in other NLG-related tasks such as MT with state-of-the art results.

Acknowledgments

We would like to thank the anonymous reviewers for their useful comments. The research reported in this paper was conducted at the University of Lethbridge and supported by Alberta Innovates and Alberta Education.

References

Dzmitry Bahdanau, Kyunghyun Cho, and Yoshua Bengio. 2014. Neural machine translation by jointly learning to align and translate. *arXiv preprint arXiv:1409.0473*.

Federico Barrios, Federico López, Luis Argerich, and Rosa Wachenchauzer. 2016. Variations of the similarity function of textrank for automated summarization. *CoRR*.

Regina Barzilay and Kathleen R McKeown. 2005. Sentence fusion for multidocument news summarization. *Computational Linguistics*, 31(3):297–328.

Taylor Berg-Kirkpatrick, Dan Gillick, and Dan Klein. 2011. Jointly learning to extract and compress. In *Proceedings of the 49th Annual Meeting of the Association for Computational Linguistics: Human Language Technologies-Volume 1*, pages 481–490. Association for Computational Linguistics.

Florian Boudin, Hugo Mougard, and Benoit Favre. 2015. Concept-based summarization using integer linear programming: From concept pruning to multiple optimal solutions. In *Conference on Empirical Methods in Natural Language Processing (EMNLP) 2015*.

Duy Duc An Bui, Guilherme Del Fiol, John F Hurdle, and Siddhartha Jonnalagadda. 2016. Extractive text summarization system to aid data extraction from full text in systematic review development. *Journal of biomedical informatics*, 64:265–272.

Asli Celikyilmaz, Antoine Bosselut, Xiaodong He, and Yejin Choi. 2018. Deep communicating agents for abstractive summarization. In *Proceedings of the 2018 Conference of the North American Chapter of the Association for Computational Linguistics: Human Language Technologies, Volume 1 (Long Papers)*, pages 1662–1675.

Yen-Chun Chen and Mohit Bansal. 2018. Fast abstractive summarization with reinforce-selected sentence rewriting. In *Proceedings of the 56th Annual Meeting of the Association for Computational Linguistics (Volume 1: Long Papers)*, pages 675–686.

Jianpeng Cheng and Mirella Lapata. 2016. Neural summarization by extracting sentences and words. In *Proceedings of the 54th Annual Meeting of the Association for Computational Linguistics (Volume 1: Long Papers)*, volume 1, pages 484–494.

Jackie Chi Kit Cheung and Gerald Penn. 2014. Unsupervised sentence enhancement for automatic summarization. In *Proceedings of the 2014 Conference on Empirical Methods in Natural Language Processing (EMNLP)*, pages 775–786.

Kyunghyun Cho, Bart Van Merriënboer, Caglar Gulcehre, Dzmitry Bahdanau, Fethi Bougares, Holger Schwenk, and Yoshua Bengio. 2014. Learning phrase representations using rnn encoder-decoder for statistical machine translation. *arXiv preprint arXiv:1406.1078*.

Sumit Chopra, Michael Auli, and Alexander M Rush. 2016. Abstractive sentence summarization with attentive recurrent neural networks. In *Proceedings of the 2016 Conference of the North American Chapter of the Association for Computational Linguistics: Human Language Technologies*, pages 93–98.

Junyoung Chung, Caglar Gulcehre, KyungHyun Cho, and Yoshua Bengio. 2014. Empirical evaluation of gated recurrent neural networks on sequence modeling. *arXiv preprint arXiv:1412.3555*.

Jacob Devlin, Ming-Wei Chang, Kenton Lee, and Kristina Toutanova. 2018. Bert: Pre-training of deep bidirectional transformers for language understanding. *arXiv preprint arXiv:1810.04805*.

Bonnie Dorr, David Zajic, and Richard Schwartz. 2003. Hedge trimmer: A parse-and-trim approach to headline generation. In *Proceedings of the HLT-NAACL 03 on Text summarization workshop-Volume 5*, pages 1–8. Association for Computational Linguistics.

Greg Durrett, Taylor Berg-Kirkpatrick, and Dan Klein. 2016. Learning-based single-document summarization with compression and anaphoricity constraints. In *Proceedings of the 54th Annual Meeting of the Association for Computational Linguistics (Volume 1: Long Papers)*, volume 1, pages 1998–2008.

Günes Erkan and Dragomir R Radev. 2004. Lexrank: Graph-based lexical centrality as salience in text summarization. *Journal of artificial intelligence research*, 22:457–479.

Katja Filippova, Enrique Alfonseca, Carlos A Colmenares, Lukasz Kaiser, and Oriol Vinyals. 2015. Sentence compression by deletion with lstms. In *Proceedings of the 2015 Conference on Empirical Methods in Natural Language Processing*, pages 360–368.

Sebastian Gehrmann, Yuntian Deng, and Alexander Rush. 2018. Bottom-up abstractive summarization. In *Proceedings of the 2018 Conference on Empirical Methods in Natural Language Processing*, pages 4098–4109.

Dan Gillick and Benoit Favre. 2009. A scalable global model for summarization. In *Proceedings of the Workshop on Integer Linear Programming for Natural Langauge Processing*, pages 10–18. Association for Computational Linguistics.

Max Grusky, Mor Naaman, and Yoav Artzi. 2018. Newsroom: A dataset of 1.3 million summaries with diverse extractive strategies. In *Proceedings of the 2018 Conference of the North American Chapter of the Association for Computational Linguistics: Human Language Technologies, Volume 1 (Long Papers)*, pages 708–719.

Jiatao Gu, Zhengdong Lu, Hang Li, and Victor OK Li. 2016. Incorporating copying mechanism in sequence-to-sequence learning. In *Proceedings of the 54th Annual Meeting of the Association for Computational Linguistics (Volume 1: Long Papers)*, volume 1, pages 1631–1640.

Ankush Gupta, Arvind Agarwal, Prawaan Singh, and Piyush Rai. 2018. A deep generative framework for paraphrase generation. In *Thirty-Second AAAI Conference on Artificial Intelligence*.

Karl Moritz Hermann, Tomas Kocisky, Edward Grefenstette, Lasse Espeholt, Will Kay, Mustafa Suleyman, and Phil Blunsom. 2015. Teaching machines to read and comprehend. In *Advances in neural information processing systems*, pages 1693–1701.

Wan-Ting Hsu, Chieh-Kai Lin, Ming-Ying Lee, Kerui Min, Jing Tang, and Min Sun. 2018. A unified model for extractive and abstractive summarization using inconsistency loss. In *Proceedings of the 56th Annual Meeting of the Association for Computational Linguistics (Volume 1: Long Papers)*, pages 132–141.

Aishwarya Jadhav and Vaibhav Rajan. 2018. Extractive summarization with swap-net: Sentences and words from alternating pointer networks. In *Proceedings of the 56th Annual Meeting of the Association for Computational Linguistics (Volume 1: Long Papers)*, volume 1, pages 142–151.

Hongyan Jing and Kathleen R McKeown. 2000. Cut and paste based text summarization. In *Proceedings of the 1st North American chapter of the Association for Computational Linguistics conference*, pages 178–185. Association for Computational Linguistics.

Debabrata Khargharia, Nabajit Newar, and Nomi Baruah. 2018. Applications of text summarization. *International Journal of Advanced Research in Computer Science*, 9(3).

Diederik P Kingma and Jimmy Ba. 2014. Adam: A method for stochastic optimization. *arXiv preprint arXiv:1412.6980*.

Kevin Knight and Daniel Marcu. 2000. Statistics-based summarization-step one: Sentence compression. *AAAI/IAAI*, 2000:703–710.

Chenliang Li, Weiran Xu, Si Li, and Sheng Gao. 2018. Guiding generation for abstractive text summarization based on key information guide network. In *Proceedings of the 2018 Conference of the North American Chapter of the Association for Computational Linguistics: Human Language Technologies, Volume 2 (Short Papers)*, pages 55–60.

Chin-Yew Lin. 2004. Rouge: A package for automatic evaluation of summaries. *Text Summarization Branches Out*.

Peter J Liu, Mohammad Saleh, Etienne Pot, Ben Goodrich, Ryan Sepassi, Lukasz Kaiser, and Noam Shazeer. 2018. Generating wikipedia by summarizing long sequences. *arXiv preprint arXiv:1801.10198*.

Thang Luong, Hieu Pham, and Christopher D Manning. 2015. Effective approaches to attention-based neural machine translation. In *Proceedings of the 2015 Conference on Empirical Methods in Natural Language Processing*, pages 1412–1421.

André FT Martins and Noah A Smith. 2009. Summarization with a joint model for sentence extraction and compression. In *Proceedings of the Workshop on Integer Linear Programming for Natural Langauge Processing*, pages 1–9. Association for Computational Linguistics.

Ramesh Nallapati, Feifei Zhai, and Bowen Zhou. 2017. Summarunner: A recurrent neural network based sequence model for extractive summarization of documents. In *AAAI*, pages 3075–3081.

Ramesh Nallapati, Bowen Zhou, Cicero dos Santos, Ça glar Gulçehre, and Bing Xiang. 2016. Abstractive text summarization using sequence-to-sequence rnns and beyond. *CoNLL 2016*, page 280.

Shashi Narayan, Shay B Cohen, and Mirella Lapata. 2018. Ranking sentences for extractive summarization with reinforcement learning. In *Proceedings of the 2018 Conference of the North American Chapter of the Association for Computational Linguistics: Human Language Technologies, Volume 1 (Long Papers)*, volume 1, pages 1747–1759.

Shashi Narayan, Nikos Papasarantopoulos, Shay B Cohen, and Mirella Lapata. 2017. Neural extractive summarization with side information. *arXiv preprint arXiv:1704.04530*.

Mir Tafseer Nayeem and Yllias Chali. 2017. Extract with order for coherent multi-document summarization. In *Proceedings of TextGraphs-11: the Workshop on Graph-based Methods for Natural Language Processing*, pages 51–56.

Daraksha Parveen, Hans-Martin Ramsl, and Michael Strube. 2015. Topical coherence for graph-based extractive summarization. In *Proceedings of the 2015 Conference on Empirical Methods in Natural Language Processing*, pages 1949–1954.

Daraksha Parveen and Michael Strube. 2015. Integrating importance, non-redundancy and coherence in graph-based extractive summarization. In *IJCAI*, pages 1298–1304.

Razvan Pascanu, Tomas Mikolov, and Yoshua Bengio. 2013. On the difficulty of training recurrent neural networks. In *International conference on machine learning*, pages 1310–1318.

Romain Paulus, Caiming Xiong, and Richard Socher. 2017. A deep reinforced model for abstractive summarization. *arXiv preprint arXiv:1705.04304*.

Jeffrey Pennington, Richard Socher, and Christopher Manning. 2014. Glove: Global vectors for word representation. In *Proceedings of the 2014 conference on empirical methods in natural language processing (EMNLP)*, pages 1532–1543.

Marc'Aurelio Ranzato, Sumit Chopra, Michael Auli, and Wojciech Zaremba. 2015. Sequence level training with recurrent neural networks. *arXiv preprint arXiv:1511.06732*.

Alexander M Rush, Sumit Chopra, and Jason Weston. 2015. A neural attention model for abstractive sentence summarization. In *Proceedings of the 2015 Conference on Empirical Methods in Natural Language Processing*, pages 379–389.

Abigail See, Peter J Liu, and Christopher D Manning. 2017. Get to the point: Summarization with pointer-generator networks. *arXiv preprint arXiv:1704.04368*.

Dou Shen, Jian-Tao Sun, Hua Li, Qiang Yang, and Zheng Chen. 2007. Document summarization using conditional random fields. In *IJCAI*, volume 7, pages 2862–2867.

Ilya Sutskever, Oriol Vinyals, and Quoc V Le. 2014. Sequence to sequence learning with neural networks. In *Advances in neural information processing systems*, pages 3104–3112.

Jiwei Tan, Xiaojun Wan, and Jianguo Xiao. 2017. Abstractive document summarization with a graph-based attentional neural model. In *Proceedings of the 55th Annual Meeting of the Association for Computational Linguistics (Volume 1: Long Papers)*, pages 1171–1181.

Ashish Vaswani, Samy Bengio, Eugene Brevdo, Francois Chollet, Aidan Gomez, Stephan Gouws, Llion Jones, Łukasz Kaiser, Nal Kalchbrenner, Niki Parmar, et al. 2018. Tensor2tensor for neural machine translation. In *Proceedings of the 13th Conference of the Association for Machine Translation in the Americas (Volume 1: Research Papers)*, volume 1, pages 193–199.

Ashish Vaswani, Noam Shazeer, Niki Parmar, Jakob Uszkoreit, Llion Jones, Aidan N Gomez, Łukasz Kaiser, and Illia Polosukhin. 2017. Attention is all you need. In *Advances in neural information processing systems*, pages 5998–6008.

Oriol Vinyals, Meire Fortunato, and Navdeep Jaitly. 2015. Pointer networks. In *Proceedings of the 28th International Conference on Neural Information Processing Systems-Volume 2*, pages 2692–2700. MIT Press.

Sanqiang Zhao, Rui Meng, Daqing He, Andi Saptono, and Bambang Parmanto. 2018. Integrating transformer and paraphrase rules for sentence simplification. In *Proceedings of the 2018 Conference on Empirical Methods in Natural Language Processing*, pages 3164–3173, Brussels, Belgium. Association for Computational Linguistics.

Qingyu Zhou, Nan Yang, Furu Wei, Shaohan Huang, Ming Zhou, and Tiejun Zhao. 2018. Neural document summarization by jointly learning to score and select sentences. In *Proceedings of the 56th Annual Meeting of the Association for Computational Linguistics (Volume 1: Long Papers)*, pages 654–663.

Making Asynchronous Stochastic Gradient Descent Work for Transformers

Alham Fikri Aji and **Kenneth Heafield**
School of Informatics, University of Edinburgh
10 Crichton Street
Edinburgh EH8 9AB
Scotland, European Union
`a.fikri@ed.ac.uk, kheafiel@inf.ed.ac.uk`

Abstract

Asynchronous stochastic gradient descent (SGD) converges poorly for Transformer models, so synchronous SGD has become the norm for Transformer training. This is unfortunate because asynchronous SGD is faster at raw training speed since it avoids waiting for synchronization. Moreover, the Transformer model is the basis for state-of-the-art models for several tasks, including machine translation, so training speed matters. To understand why asynchronous SGD under-performs, we blur the lines between asynchronous and synchronous methods. We find that summing several asynchronous updates, rather than applying them immediately, restores convergence behavior. With this method, the Transformer attains the same BLEU score 1.36 times as fast.

1 Introduction

Models based on Transformers (Vaswani et al., 2017) achieve state-of-the-art results on various machine translation tasks (Bojar et al., 2018). Distributed training is crucial to training these models in a reasonable amount of time, with the dominant paradigms being asynchronous or synchronous stochastic gradient descent (SGD). Prior work (Chen et al., 2016, 2018; Ott et al., 2018) commented that asynchronous SGD yields low quality models without elaborating further; we confirm this experimentally in Section 2.1. Rather than abandon asynchronous SGD, we aim to repair convergence.

Asynchronous SGD and synchronous SGD have two key differences: batch size and staleness. Synchronous SGD increases the batch size in proportion to the number of processors because gradients are summed before applying one update. Asynchronous SGD updates with each gradient as it arises, so the batch size is the same as on a single processor. Asynchronous SGD also has stale gradients because parameters may update several times while a gradient is being computed.

To tease apart the impact of batch size and stale gradients, we perform a series of experiments on both recurrent neural networks (RNNs) and Transformers manipulating batch size and injecting staleness. Out experiments show that small batch sizes slightly degrade quality while stale gradients substantially degrade quality.

To restore convergence, we propose a hybrid method that computes gradients asynchronously, sums gradients as they arise, and updates less often. Gradient summing has been applied to increase batch size or reduce communication (Dean et al., 2012; Lian et al., 2015; Ott et al., 2018; Bogoychev et al., 2018); we find it also reduces harmful staleness. In a sense, updating less often increases staleness because gradients are computed with respect to parameters that could have been updated. However, if staleness is measured by the number of intervening updates to the model, then staleness is reduced because updates happen less often. Empirically, our hybrid method converges comparably to synchronous SGD, preserves final model quality, and runs faster because processors are not idle.

2 Exploring Asynchronous SGD

2.1 Baseline: The Problem

To motivate this paper and set baselines, we first measure how poorly Transformers perform when trained with baseline asynchronous SGD (Chen et al., 2016, 2018; Ott et al., 2018). We train a Transformer model under both synchronous and asynchronous SGD, contrasting the results with an RNN model. Moreover, we sweep learning rates to verify this effect is not an artifact of choosing

Proceedings of the 3rd Workshop on Neural Generation and Translation (WNGT 2019), pages 80–89
Hong Kong, China, November 4, 2019. ©2019 Association for Computational Linguistics
www.aclweb.org/anthology/D19-56%2d

	Trans. BLEU		RNN BLEU	
Learn Rate	Sync.	Async.	Sync.	Async.
0.0002	35.08	13.27	34.11	33.77
0.0003	35.66	30.72	33.79	33.95
0.00045	35.59	5.21	33.68	33.68
0.0006	35.42	0.00	34.30	33.76
0.0009	34.79	0.00	34.28	33.47
0.0012	33.96	0.00	34.37	33.23
0.0024	29.35	0.00	33.98	32.83
0.00375	25.25	0.00	33.80	31.89

Table 1: Performance of the Transformer and RNN model trained synchronously and asynchronously, across different learning rates.

hyperparameters that favor one scenario. Further experimental setup appears in Section 4.1.

Results in Table 1 confirm that asynchronous SGD generally yields lower-quality systems than synchronous SGD. For Transformers, the asynchronous results are catastrophic, often yielding 0 BLEU. We can also see that Transformers and asynchronous SGD are more sensitive to learning rates compared to RNNs and synchronous SGD.

To understand why asynchronous SGD underperforms, we run series of ablation experiments based on the differences between synchronous and asynchronous SGD. We focus on two main aspects: batch size and stale gradient updates.

2.2 Batch Size

In asynchronous SGD, each update uses a gradient from one processor. Synchronous SGD sums gradients from all processors, which is mathematically equivalent running a larger batch on one processor (though it might not fit in RAM). Therefore, the effective batch size in N-workers synchronous training is N times larger compared to its asynchronous counterparts.

Using a larger batch size reduces noise in estimating the overall gradient (Wang et al., 2013), and has been shown to slightly improve performance (Smith et al., 2017; Popel and Bojar, 2018). To investigate whether small batch sizes are the main issue with asynchronous Transformer training, we sweep batch sizes and compare with synchronous training.

2.3 Gradient Staleness

In asynchronous training, a computed gradient update is applied immediately to the model, without having to wait for other processors to finish. This approach may cause a stale gradient, where parameters have updated while a processor was computing its gradient. Staleness can be defined as the number of updates that occurred between the processor pulling parameters and pushing its gradient. Under the ideal case where every processor spends equal time to process a batch, asynchronous SGD with N processors produces gradients with staleness $N - 1$. Empirically, we can also expect an average staleness of $N - 1$ with normally distributed computation time (Zhang et al., 2016).

An alternative way to interpret staleness is the distance between the parameters with which the gradient was computed and the parameters being updated by the gradient. Therefore, higher learning rate contributes to the staleness, as the parameters move faster.

Prior work has shown that neural models can still be trained on stale gradients, albeit with potentially slower convergence or a lower quality. Furthermore, Zhang et al. (2016); Srinivasan et al. (2018) report that model performance degrades in proportion to the gradient staleness. We introduce artificial staleness to confirm the significance of gradient staleness towards the Transformer performance.

3 Incremental Updates in Adam

Investigating the effect of batch size and staleness further, we analyze why it makes a difference that gradients computed from the same parameters are applied one at a time (incurring staleness) instead of summed then applied once (as in synchronous SGD). As seen in Section 4.3, our artificial staleness was damaging to convergence even though gradients were synchronously computed with respect to the same parameters. In standard stochastic gradient descent there is no difference: gradients are multiplied by the learning rate then substracted from the parameters in either case. The Adam optimizer handles incremental updates and sums differently.

Adam is scale invariant. For example, suppose that two processors generate gradients 0.5 and 0.5 with respect to the same parameter in the first iteration. Incrementally updating with 0.5 and 0.5 is the same as updating with 1 and 1 due to scale invariance. Updating with the summed gradient, 1, will only move parameters half as far. This is the theory underlying the rule of thumb that learning rate should scale with batch size (Ott et al., 2018).

Time (t)		0	1	2	3	4	5	6
Constant	g_t		1	1	1	1	1	1
	m_t	0	0.1	0.19	0.271	0.344	0.41	0.469
	v_t	0	0.02	0.04	0.059	0.078	0.096	0.114
	$\hat{m}_t$	0	1	1	1	1	1	1
	$\hat{v}_t$	0	1	1	1	1	1	1
	θ	0	-0.001	-0.002	-0.003	-0.004	-0.005	-0.006
Scaled	g_t		0.5	1.5	0.5	1.5	0.5	1.5
	m_t	0	0.05	0.195	0.226	0.353	0.368	0.481
	v_t	0	0.005	0.05	0.054	0.098	0.101	0.144
	$\hat{m}_t$	0	0.5	1.026	0.832	1.026	0.898	1.026
	$\hat{v}_t$	0	0.25	1.26	0.917	1.26	1.05	1.26
	θ	0	-0.001	-0.002	-0.003	-0.004	-0.005	-0.005
Different sign	g_t		-1	2	-1	2	-1	2
	m_t	0	-0.1	0.11	-0.001	0.199	0.079	0.271
	v_t	0	0.02	0.1	0.118	0.195	0.211	0.287
	$\hat{m}_t$	0	-1	0.579	-0.004	0.579	0.193	0.579
	$\hat{v}_t$	0	1	2.515	2	2.515	2.2	2.515
	θ	0	0.001	0.001	0.001	0.000	0.000	-0.000

Table 2: The Adam optimizer slows down when gradients have larger variance even if they have the same average, in this case 1. When alternating between -1 and 2, Adam takes 6 steps before the parameter has the correct sign. Updates can even slow down if gradients point in the same direction but have different scales. The learning rate is $\alpha = 0.001$.

In practice, gradients reported by different processors are usually not the same: they are noisy estimates of the true gradient. In Table 2, we show examples where noise causes Adam to slow down. Summing gradients smooths out some of the noise. Next, we examine the formal basis for this effect.

Formally, Adam estimates the full gradient with an exponentially decaying average m_t of gradients g_t.

$$m_t \leftarrow \beta_1 m_{t-1} + (1 - \beta_1) g_t$$

where β_1 is a decay hyperparameter. It also computes a decaying average v_t of second moments

$$v_t \leftarrow \beta_2 v_{t-1} + (1 - \beta_2) g_t^2$$

where β_2 is a separate decay hyperparameter. The squaring g_t^2 is taken element-wise. These estimates are biased because the decaying averages were initialized to zero. Adam corrects for the bias to obtain unbiased estimates $\hat{m}_t$ and $\hat{v}_t$.

$$\hat{m}_t \leftarrow m_t/(1 - \beta_1^t)$$

$$\hat{v}_t \leftarrow v_t/(1 - \beta_2^t)$$

These estimates are used to update parameters θ

$$\theta_t \leftarrow \theta_{t-1} - \alpha \frac{\hat{m}_t}{\sqrt{\hat{v}_t} + \epsilon}$$

where α is the learning rate hyperparameter and ϵ prevents element-wise division by zero.

Replacing estimators in the update rule with statistics they estimate and ignoring the usually-minor ϵ

$$\frac{\hat{m}_t}{\sqrt{\hat{v}_t} + \epsilon} \approx \frac{E g_t}{\sqrt{E(g_t^2)}}$$

which expands following the variance identity

$$\frac{E g_t}{\sqrt{E(g_t^2)}} = \frac{E g_t}{\sqrt{Var(g_t) + (E g_t)^2}}$$

Dividing both the numerator and denominator by $|E g_t|$, we obtain

$$= \frac{\text{sign}(E g_t)}{\sqrt{Var(g_t)/(E g_t)^2 + 1}}$$

The term $Var(g_t)/(E g_t)^2$ is statistical efficiency, the square of coefficient of variation. In other words, Adam gives higher weight to gradients if historical samples have a lower coefficient of variation. The coefficient of variation of a sum of N independent[1] samples decreases as $1/\sqrt{N}$. Hence sums (despite having less frequent updates) may

---

[1] Batch selection takes compute time into account, so technically noise is not independent.

actually cause Adam to move faster because they have smaller coefficient of variation. An example appears in Table 2: updating with 1 moves faster than individually applying -1 and 2.

4 Ablation Study

We conduct ablation experiments to investigate the poor performance in asynchronous Transformer training for the neural machine translation task.

4.1 Experiment Setup

Our experiments use systems for the WMT 2017 English to German news translation task. The Transformer is standard with six encoder and six decoder layers. The RNN model (Barone et al., 2017) is based on the winning WMT17 submission (Sennrich et al., 2017) with 8 layers. Both models use back-translated monolingual corpora (Sennrich et al., 2016a) and byte-pair encoding (Sennrich et al., 2016b).

We follow the rest of the hyperparameter settings on both Transformer and RNN models as suggested in the papers (Vaswani et al., 2017; Sennrich et al., 2017). Both models were trained on four GPUs with a dynamic batch size of 10 GB per GPU using the Marian toolkit (Junczys-Dowmunt et al., 2018). Both models are trained for 8 epochs or until reaching five continuous validations without loss improvement. Quality is measured on newstest2016 using sacreBLEU (Post, 2018), preserving newstest2017 as test for later experiments. The Transformer's learning rate is linearly warmed up for 16k updates. We apply an inverse square root learning rate decay following Vaswani et al. (2017) for both models. All of these experiments use the Adam optimizer, which has shown to perform well on a variety of tasks (Kingma and Ba, 2014) and was used in the original Transformer paper (Vaswani et al., 2017).

For subsequent experiments, we will use a learning rate of 0.0003 for Transformers and 0.0006 for RNNs. These were near the top in both asynchronous and synchronous settings (Table 1).

4.2 Batch Size

We first explore the effect of batch size towards the model's quality. We use dynamic batching, in which the toolkit fits as many sentences as it can into a fixed amount of memory (so e.g. more sentences will be in a batch if all of them are short). Hence batch sizes are denominated in memory

sizes. Our GPUs each have 10 GB available for batches which, on average, corresponds to 250 sentences.

With 4 GPUs, baseline synchronous SGD has an effective batch size of 40 GB, compared to 10 GB in asynchronous. We fill in the two missing scenarios: synchronous SGD with a total effective batch size of 10 GB and asynchronous SGD with a batch size of 40 GB. Because GPU memory is limited, we simulate a larger batch size in asynchronous SGD by locally accumulating gradients in each processor four times before sending the summed gradient to the parameter server (Ott et al., 2018; Bogoychev et al., 2018).

Models with a batch size of 40GB achieve better BLEU *per update*, compared with its 10GB variant as shown in Figure 1. However, synchronous SGD training still outperforms asynchronous SGD training, even with smaller batch size. From this experiment, we conclude that batch size is not the primary driver of poor performance of asynchronously trained Transformers, though it does have some lingering impact on final model quality. For RNNs, batch size and distributed training algorithm had little impact beyond the early stages of training, continuing the theme that Transformers are more sensitive to noisy gradients.

4.3 Gradient Staleness

To study the impact of gradient staleness, we introduce staleness into synchronous SGD. Workers only pull the latest parameter once every U updates, yielding an average staleness of $\frac{(U-1)}{2}$. Since asynchronous SGD has average staleness 3 with $N = 4$ GPUs, we set $U = 7$ to achieve the same average staleness of 3. Additionally, we also tried a lower average staleness of 2 by setting $U = 5$. We also see the effect of doubling the learning rate so the parameter moves twice as far, hence introduces staleness in terms of model distance.

In order to focus on the impact of the staleness, we set the batch size to 40 GB total RAM consumption, be they 4 GPUs with 10 GB each in synchronous SGD or emulated 40 GB batches on each GPU in asynchronous SGD.

Results are shown in Figure 2. Staleness 3 substantially degrades Transformer convergence and final quality (Figure 2a). However, the impact of staleness 2 is relatively minor. We also continue to see that Transformers are more sensitive than

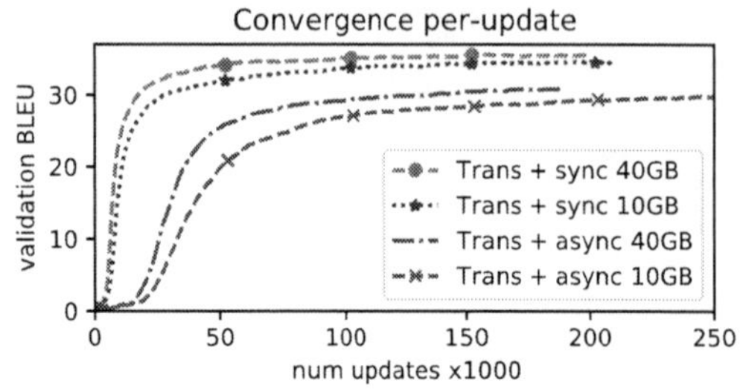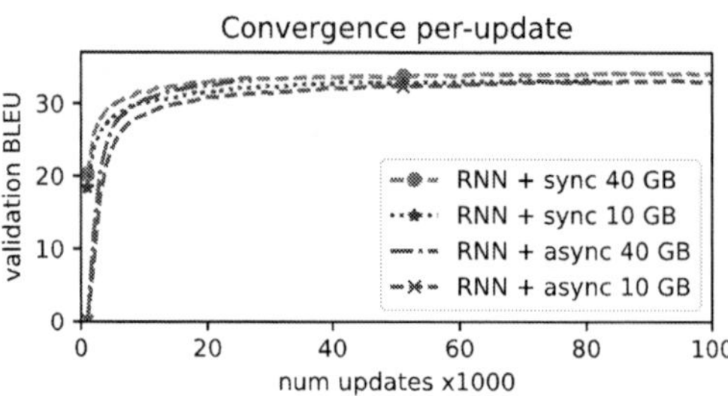

(a) Convergence over updates in Transformer model with various batch sizes

(b) Convergence over updates in RNN model with various batch sizes

Figure 1: The effect of batch sizes on convergence of Transformer and RNN models.

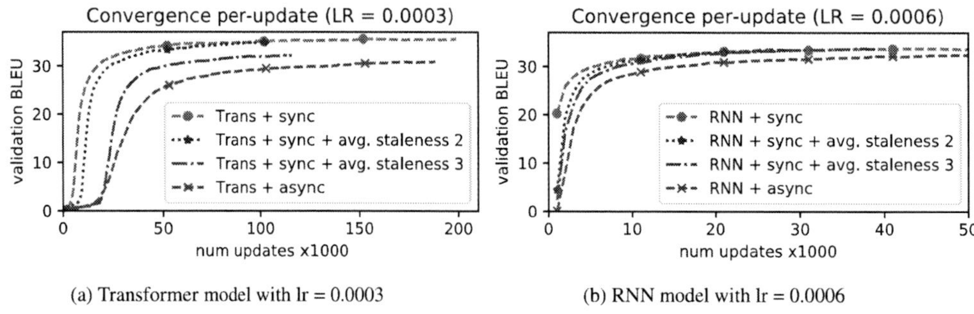

(a) Transformer model with lr = 0.0003

(b) RNN model with lr = 0.0006

Figure 2: Artificial staleness in synchronous SGD compared to synchronous and asynchronous baselines, all with our usual learning rate for each model.

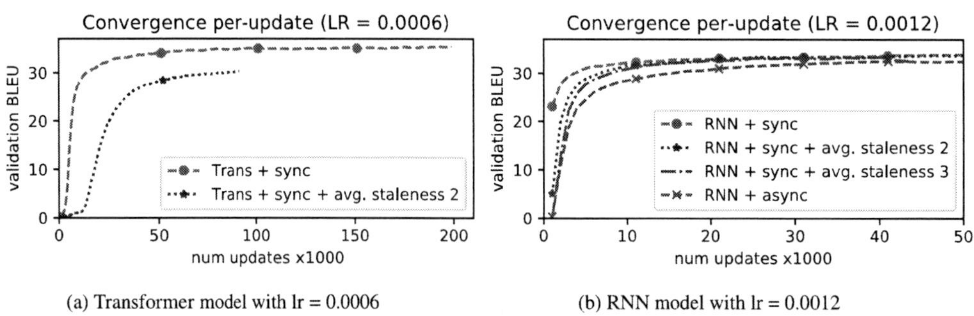

(a) Transformer model with lr = 0.0006

(b) RNN model with lr = 0.0012

Figure 3: Artificial staleness in synchronous SGD with doubled learning rates. Transformers with learning rate 0.0006 and staleness 3 (synchronous and asynchronous) did not rise above 0.

RNNs to training conditions.

Results for Transformer worsen when we double the learning rate (Figure 3). With staleness 3, the model stayed at 0 BLEU for both synchronous or asynchronous SGD, consistent with our earlier result (Table 1).

We conclude that staleness is primary, but not wholly, responsible for the poor performance of asynchronous SGD in training Transformers. However, asynchronous SGD still underperforms synchronous SGD with artificial staleness of 3 and

the same batch size (40 GB). Our synchronous SGD training has consistent parameters across processors, whereas processors might have different parameters in asynchronous training. The staleness distribution might also play a role because staleness in asynchronous SGD follows a normal distribution (Zhang et al., 2016) while our synthetic staleness in synchronous SGD follows a uniform distribution.

5 Asynchronous Transformer Training

5.1 Accumulated Asynchronous SGD

Previous experiments have shown that increasing the batch size and reducing staleness improves the final quality of asynchronous training. Increasing the batch size can be achieved by accumulating gradients before updating. We experiment with variations on three ways to accumulate gradients:

Local Accumulation: Gradients can be accumulated locally in each processor before sending it to the parameter server (Ott et al., 2018; Bogoychev et al., 2018). This approach scales the effective batch size and reduces communication costs as the workers communicate less often. However, this approach does not reduce staleness as the parameter server updates immediately after receiving a gradient. We experiment with accumulating four gradients locally, resulting in 40 GB effective batch size.

Global Accumulation: Each processor sends the computed gradient to the parameter server normally. However, the parameter server holds the gradient and only updates the model after it receives multiple gradients (Dean et al., 2012; Lian et al., 2015). This approach scales the effective batch size. On top of that, it decreases staleness as the parameter server updates less often. However, it does not reduce communication costs. We experiment with accumulating four gradients globally, resulting in 40 GB effective batch size and 0.75 average staleness.

Combined Accumulation: Local and global accumulation can be combined to gain the benefits of both: reduced communication cost and reduced average staleness. In this approach, gradients are accumulated locally in each processor before being sent. The parameter server also waits and accumulates gradients before running an optimizer. We accumulate two gradients both locally and globally. This yields in 40 GB effective batch size and 1.5 average staleness.

We tested the three gradient accumulation flavors on the English-to-German task with both Transformer and RNN models. Synchronous SGD also appears as a baseline. To compare results, we report best BLEU, raw training speed, and time needed to reach several BLEU checkpoints. Results are shown in Table 3.

Asynchronous SGD with global accumulation actually improves the final quality of the model over synchronous SGD, albeit not meaningfully.

This one change, accumulating every 4 gradients (the number of GPUs), restores quality in asynchronous methods. It also achieves the fastest time to reach near-convergence BLEU in both Transformer and RNN.

While using local accumulation provides even faster raw speed, the model produces the worst quality among the other accumulation techniques. Asynchronous SGD with 4x local accumulation is essentially just ordinary asynchronous SGD with 4x larger batch size and 4x less update frequency. In particular, gradient staleness is still the same, therefore this does not help the convergence per-update.

Combined accumulation performs somewhat in the middle. It does not converge as fast as asynchronous SGD with full global accumulation but not as poor as asynchronous SGD with full local accumulation. Its speed is also in between, reflecting communication costs.

5.2 Generalization Across Learning Rates

Earlier in Table 1 we show that asynchronous Transformer learning is very sensitive towards the learning rate. In this experiment, we use an asynchronous SGD with global gradient accumulation to train English-to-German on different learning rates. We compare our result with vanilla synchronous and vanilla asynchronous SGD.

Our finding empirically show that asynchronous Transformer training while globally accumulating the gradients is significantly more robust. As shown in Table 5, the model is now capable to learn on higher learning rate and yield comparable results compared to its synchronous variant.

5.3 Generalization Across Languages

To test whether our findings on English-to-German generalize, we train two more translation systems using globally accumulated gradients. Specifically, we train English to Finnish (EN $\rightarrow$ FI) and English to Russian (EN $\rightarrow$ RU) models for the WMT 2018 task (Bojar et al., 2018). We validate our model on newstest2015 for EN $\rightarrow$ FI and newstest2017 for EN $\rightarrow$ RU. Then, we test our model on newstest2017 for EN $\rightarrow$ DE and newstest2018 for both EN $\rightarrow$ FI and EN $\rightarrow$ RU. The same network structures and hyperparameters are used as before.

The results shown in Table 4 empirically confirm that accumulating the gradient to obtain a

Transformer

Communication	accumulation		batch	avg.	speed	best	hours to X BLEU		
	local	global	size	staleness	(wps)	BLEU	33	34	35
synchronous	1	4	40 GB	0	36029	35.66	5.3	7.6	15.6
asynchronous	1	1	10 GB	3	39883	30.72	-	-	-
asynchronous	4	1	40 GB	3	45177	30.98	-	-	-
asynchronous	2	2	40 GB	1.5	43115	35.68	4.9	6.8	15.4
asynchronous	1	4	40 GB	0.75	39514	35.84	4.6	6.7	11.4

RNN

Communication	accumulation		batch	avg.	speed	best	hours to X BLEU		
	local	global	size	staleness	(wps)	BLEU	32	33	34
synchronous	1	4	40 GB	0	23054	34.30	3.6	6.2	18.8
asynchronous	1	1	10 GB	3	24683	33.76	2.7	5.1	-
asynchronous	4	1	40 GB	3	27090	33.83	4.1	6.1	-
asynchronous	2	2	40 GB	1.5	25578	34.20	3.2	5.9	13.7
asynchronous	1	4	40 GB	0.75	24312	34.48	3.1	5.4	14.5

Table 3: Quality and convergence of asynchronous SGD with accumulated gradients on English to German dataset. Dashes indicate that model never reach the target BLEU.

Model	EN $\rightarrow$ DE		EN $\rightarrow$ FI		EN $\rightarrow$ RU	
newstest	2016	2017	2017	2018	2015	2018
Trans. + synchronous SGD	35.66	28.81	18.47	14.03	29.31	25.49
Trans. + asynchronous SGD	30.72	24.68	11.63	8.73	21.12	17.78
Trans. + asynchronous SGD + 4x global accum.	35.84	28.66	18.47	13.78	29.12	25.25
RNN + synchronous SGD	34.30	27.43	16.94	12.75	26.96	23.11
RNN + asynchronous SGD	33.76	26.84	14.94	10.96	26.39	22.48
RNN. + asynchronous SGD + 4x global accum.	34.48	27.56	17.05	12.76	27.15	23.41

Table 4: The effect of global accumulation on translation quality for different language pairs on development and test set, measured with BLEU score.

	Communication		
	Sync.	Async.	Async
Learn Rate			+ 4x GA
0.0003	35.66	30.72	35.84
0.0006	35.42	0.00	35.81
0.0012	33.96	0.00	33.62
0.0024	29.35	0.00	1.20

Table 5: Performance of the asynchronous Transformer on English to German with 4x Global accumulations (GA) across different learning rates on development set measured with BLEU score.

larger batch size and a lower staleness in Transformer massively improves the result, compared to basic asynchronous SGD (+6 BLEU on average). The improvement is smaller in RNN experiment, but still substantial (+1 BLEU on average). We also have further confirmation that training a Transformer model with normal asynchronous SGD is impractical.

6 Related Work

6.1 Gradient Summing

Several papers wait and sum P gradients from different workers as a way to reduce staleness. In Chen et al. (2016), gradients are accumulated from different processors, and whenever the P gradients have been pushed, other processors cancel their process and restart from the beginning. This is relatively wasteful since some computation is thrown out and $P-1$ processors still idle for synchronization. Gupta et al. (2016) suggest that restarting is not necessary but processors still idle waiting for P to finish. Our proposed method follows Lian et al. (2015) in which an update happens every time P gradients have arrived and processors continually generate gradients without synchronization.

Another direction to overcome stale gradient is to reduce its effect towards the model update. McMahan and Streeter (2014) dynamically adjust the learning rate depending on the staleness. Dutta et al. (2018) suggests completely ignoring stale gradient pushes.

6.2 Increasing Staleness

In the opposite direction, some work has added noise to gradients or increased staleness, typically to cut computational costs. Recht et al. (2011) propose a lock-free asynchronous gradient update. Lossy gradient compression by bit quantization (Seide et al., 2014; Alistarh et al., 2017) or threshold based sparsification (Aji and Heafield, 2017; Lin et al., 2017) also introduce noisy gradient updates. On top of that, these techniques store unsent gradients to be added into the next gradient, increasing staleness for small gradients.

Dean et al. (2012) mention that communication overload can be reduced by reducing gradient pushes and parameter synchronization frequency. In McMahan et al. (2017), each processor independently updates its own local model and periodically synchronize the parameter by averaging across other processors. Ott et al. (2018) accumulates gradients locally, before sending it to the parameter server. Bogoychev et al. (2018) also locally accumulates the gradient, but also updates local parameters in between.

7   Conclusion

We evaluated the behavior of Transformer and RNN models under asynchronous training. We divide our analysis based on two main different aspects in asynchronous training: batch size and stale gradient. Our experimental results show that:

- In general, asynchronous training damages the final BLEU of the NMT model. However, we found that the damage with the Transformer is significantly more severe. In addition, asynchronous training also requires a smaller learning rate to perform well.

- With the same number of processors, asynchronous SGD has a smaller effective batch size. We empirically show that training under a larger batch size setting can slightly improves the convergence. However, the im-

provement is very minimal. The result in asynchronous Transformer model is subpar, even with a larger batch size.

- Stale gradients play a bigger role in the training performance of asynchronous Transformer. We have shown that the Transformer model's performed poorly by adding a synthetic stale gradient.

Based on these findings, we suggest applying a modification in asynchronous training by accumulating a few gradients (for example for the number of processors) in the server before applying an update. This approach increases the batch size while also reducing the average staleness. We empirically show that this approach combine the high quality training of synchronous SGD and high training speed of asynchronous SGD.

Future works should extend those experiments to different hyper-parameter configurations. One direction is to investigate wether vanilla asynchronous Trasnformer can be trained under different optimizers. Another direction is to experiment with more workers where gradients in asynchronous SGD are more stale.

8   Acknowledgements

Alham Fikri Aji is funded by the Indonesia Endowment Fund for Education scholarship scheme. This work was performed using resources provided by the Cambridge Service for Data Driven Discovery (CSD3) operated by the University of Cambridge Research Computing Service (http://www.csd3.cam.ac.uk/), provided by Dell EMC and Intel using Tier-2 funding from the Engineering and Physical Sciences Research Council (capital grant EP/P020259/1), and DiRAC funding from the Science and Technology Facilities Council (www.dirac.ac.uk).

References

Alham Fikri Aji and Kenneth Heafield. 2017. Sparse communication for distributed gradient descent. In *Proceedings of the 2017 Conference on Empirical Methods in Natural Language Processing*, pages 440–445.

Dan Alistarh, Demjan Grubic, Jerry Li, Ryota Tomioka, and Milan Vojnovic. 2017. Qsgd: Communication-efficient sgd via gradient quantization and encoding. In *Advances in Neural Information Processing Systems*, pages 1709–1720.

Antonio Valerio Miceli Barone, Jindřich Helcl, Rico Sennrich, Barry Haddow, and Alexandra Birch. 2017. Deep architectures for neural machine translation. In *Proceedings of the Second Conference on Machine Translation*, pages 99–107.

Nikolay Bogoychev, Kenneth Heafield, Alham Fikri Aji, and Marcin Junczys-Dowmunt. 2018. Accelerating asynchronous stochastic gradient descent for neural machine translation. In *Proceedings of the 2018 Conference on Empirical Methods in Natural Language Processing*, pages 2991–2996.

Ondej Bojar, Christian Federmann, Mark Fishel, Yvette Graham, Barry Haddow, Matthias Huck, Philipp Koehn, and Christof Monz. 2018. Findings of the 2018 conference on machine translation (wmt18). In *Proceedings of the Third Conference on Machine Translation (WMT), Volume 2: Shared Task Papers*, pages 272–307. Association for Computational Linguistics.

Jianmin Chen, Xinghao Pan, Rajat Monga, Samy Bengio, and Rafal Jozefowicz. 2016. Revisiting distributed synchronous sgd. *arXiv preprint arXiv:1604.00981*.

Mia Xu Chen, Orhan Firat, Ankur Bapna, Melvin Johnson, Wolfgang Macherey, George Foster, Llion Jones, Niki Parmar, Mike Schuster, Zhifeng Chen, et al. 2018. The best of both worlds: Combining recent advances in neural machine translation. *arXiv preprint arXiv:1804.09849*.

Jeffrey Dean, Greg Corrado, Rajat Monga, Kai Chen, Matthieu Devin, Mark Mao, Andrew Senior, Paul Tucker, Ke Yang, Quoc V Le, et al. 2012. Large scale distributed deep networks. In *Advances in neural information processing systems*, pages 1223–1231.

Sanghamitra Dutta, Gauri Joshi, Soumyadip Ghosh, Parijat Dube, and Priya Nagpurkar. 2018. Slow and stale gradients can win the race: Error-runtime trade-offs in distributed sgd. *arXiv preprint arXiv:1803.01113*.

Suyog Gupta, Wei Zhang, and Fei Wang. 2016. Model accuracy and runtime tradeoff in distributed deep learning: A systematic study. In *2016 IEEE 16th International Conference on Data Mining (ICDM)*, pages 171–180. IEEE.

Marcin Junczys-Dowmunt, Roman Grundkiewicz, Tomasz Dwojak, Hieu Hoang, Kenneth Heafield, Tom Neckermann, Frank Seide, Ulrich Germann, Alham Fikri Aji, Nikolay Bogoychev, André F. T. Martins, and Alexandra Birch. 2018. Marian: Fast neural machine translation in C++. In *Proceedings of ACL 2018, System Demonstrations*, pages 116–121, Melbourne, Australia. Association for Computational Linguistics.

Diederik P Kingma and Jimmy Ba. 2014. Adam: A method for stochastic optimization. *arXiv preprint arXiv:1412.6980*.

Xiangru Lian, Yijun Huang, Yuncheng Li, and Ji Liu. 2015. Asynchronous parallel stochastic gradient for nonconvex optimization. In *Advances in Neural Information Processing Systems*, pages 2737–2745.

Yujun Lin, Song Han, Huizi Mao, Yu Wang, and William J Dally. 2017. Deep gradient compression: Reducing the communication bandwidth for distributed training. *arXiv preprint arXiv:1712.01887*.

Brendan McMahan, Eider Moore, Daniel Ramage, Seth Hampson, and Blaise Aguera y Arcas. 2017. Communication-efficient learning of deep networks from decentralized data. In *Artificial Intelligence and Statistics*, pages 1273–1282.

Brendan McMahan and Matthew Streeter. 2014. Delay-tolerant algorithms for asynchronous distributed online learning. In *Advances in Neural Information Processing Systems*, pages 2915–2923.

Myle Ott, Sergey Edunov, David Grangier, and Michael Auli. 2018. Scaling neural machine translation. In *Proceedings of the Third Conference on Machine Translation: Research Papers*, pages 1–9.

Martin Popel and Ondřej Bojar. 2018. Training tips for the transformer model. *The Prague Bulletin of Mathematical Linguistics*, 110(1):43–70.

Matt Post. 2018. A call for clarity in reporting bleu scores. In *Proceedings of the Third Conference on Machine Translation: Research Papers*, pages 186–191.

Benjamin Recht, Christopher Re, Stephen Wright, and Feng Niu. 2011. Hogwild: A lock-free approach to parallelizing stochastic gradient descent. In *Advances in neural information processing systems*, pages 693–701.

Frank Seide, Hao Fu, Jasha Droppo, Gang Li, and Dong Yu. 2014. 1-bit stochastic gradient descent and its application to data-parallel distributed training of speech dnns. In *Fifteenth Annual Conference of the International Speech Communication Association*.

Rico Sennrich, Alexandra Birch, Anna Currey, Ulrich Germann, Barry Haddow, Kenneth Heafield, Antonio Valerio Miceli Barone, and Philip Williams. 2017. The University of Edinburgh's neural mt systems for WMT17. In *Proceedings of the Second Conference on Machine Translation*, pages 389–399.

Rico Sennrich, Barry Haddow, and Alexandra Birch. 2016a. Improving neural machine translation models with monolingual data. In *Proceedings of the 54th Annual Meeting of the Association for Computational Linguistics (Volume 1: Long Papers)*, pages 86–96, Berlin, Germany. Association for Computational Linguistics.

Rico Sennrich, Barry Haddow, and Alexandra Birch. 2016b. Neural machine translation of rare words with subword units. In *Proceedings of the 54th Annual Meeting of the Association for Computational Linguistics*, pages 1715–1725.

Samuel L Smith, Pieter-Jan Kindermans, Chris Ying, and Quoc V Le. 2017. Don't decay the learning rate, increase the batch size. *arXiv preprint arXiv:1711.00489*.

Anand Srinivasan, Ajay Jain, and Parnian Barekatain. 2018. An analysis of the delayed gradients problem in asynchronous SGD.

Ashish Vaswani, Noam Shazeer, Niki Parmar, Jakob Uszkoreit, Llion Jones, Aidan N Gomez, Łukasz Kaiser, and Illia Polosukhin. 2017. Attention is all you need. In *Advances in Neural Information Processing Systems*, pages 5998–6008.

Chong Wang, Xi Chen, Alexander J Smola, and Eric P Xing. 2013. Variance reduction for stochastic gradient optimization. In *Advances in Neural Information Processing Systems*, pages 181–189.

Wei Zhang, Suyog Gupta, Xiangru Lian, and Ji Liu. 2016. Staleness-aware async-sgd for distributed deep learning. In *IJCAI*.

Controlled Text Generation for Data Augmentation in Intelligent Artificial Agents

Nikolaos Malandrakis[1], Minmin Shen[2], Anuj Goyal[2],
Shuyang Gao[2], Abhishek Sethi[2], Angeliki Metallinou[2]
[1] Signal Analysis and Interpretation Laboratory (SAIL), USC, Los Angeles, CA 90089
[2] Amazon Alexa AI
`malandra@usc.edu,`
`{shenm,anujgoya,shuyag,abhsethi,ametalli}@amazon.com`

Abstract

Data availability is a bottleneck during early stages of development of new capabilities for intelligent artificial agents. We investigate the use of text generation techniques to augment the training data of a popular commercial artificial agent across categories of functionality, with the goal of faster development of new functionality. We explore a variety of encoder-decoder generative models for synthetic training data generation and propose using conditional variational auto-encoders. Our approach requires only direct optimization, works well with limited data and significantly outperforms the previous controlled text generation techniques. Further, the generated data are used as additional training samples in an extrinsic intent classification task, leading to improved performance by up to 5% absolute f-score in low-resource cases, validating the usefulness of our approach.

1 Introduction

Voice-powered artificial agents have seen widespread commercial use in recent years, with agents like Google's Assistant, Apple's Siri and Amazon's Alexa rising in popularity. These agents are expected to be highly accurate in understanding the users' requests and to be capable of handling a variety of continuously expanding functionality. New capabilities are initially defined via a few phrase templates. Those are expanded, typically through larger scale data collection, to create datasets for building the machine learning algorithms required to create a serviceable Natural Language Understanding (NLU) system. This is a lengthy and expensive process that is repeated for new functionality expansion and can significantly slow down development time.

We investigate the use of neural generative encoder-decoder models for text data generation.

Given a small set of phrase templates for some new functionality, our goal is to generate new *semantically similar* phrases and augment our training data. This data augmentation is not necessarily meant as a replacement for large-scale data collection, but rather as a way to accelerate the early stages of new functionality development. This task shares similarities with paraphrasing. Therefore, inspired by work in paraphrasing (Prakash et al., 2016) and controlled text generation (Hu et al., 2018), we investigate the use of variational autoencoder models and methods to condition neural generators.

For controlled text generation, (Hu et al., 2018) used a variational autoencoder with an additional discriminator and trained the model in a wake-sleep way. (Zhou and Wang, 2018) used reinforcement via an emoji classifier to generate emotional responses. However, we found that when the number of samples is relatively small compared to the number of categories, such an approach might be counter-productive, because the required classifier components can not perform well. Inspired by recent advantages of connecting information theory with variational auto-encoders and invariant feature learning (Moyer et al., 2018), we instead use this approach to our controlled text generation task, without a discriminator.

Furthermore, our task differs from typical paraphrasing in that semantic similarity between the output text and the NLU functionality is not the only objective. The synthetic data should be evaluated in terms of its lexical diversity and novelty, which are important properties of a high quality training set.

Our key contributions are as follows:

- We thoroughly investigate text generation techniques for NLU data augmentation with sequence to sequence model and variational auto-encoders, in an atypically low-resource

Proceedings of the 3rd Workshop on Neural Generation and Translation (WNGT 2019), pages 90–98
Hong Kong, China, November 4, 2019. ©2019 Association for Computational Linguistics
www.aclweb.org/anthology/D19-56%2d

setting.

- We validate our method in an extrinsic intent classification task, showing that the generated data brings considerable accuracy gains in low resource settings.

2 Related Work

Neural networks have revolutionized the field of text generation, in machine translation (Sutskever et al., 2014), summarization (See et al., 2017) and image captioning (You et al., 2016). However, conditional text generation has been relatively less studied as compared to conditional image generation and poses some unique problems. One of the issues is the non-differentiability of the sampled text that limits the applicability of a global discriminator in end-to-end training. The problem has been relatively addressed by using CNNs for generation (Rajeswar et al., 2017), policy gradient reinforcement learning methods including SeqGAN (Yu et al., 2017), LeakGAN (Guo et al., 2018), or using latent representation like Gumbel softmax ((Jang et al., 2016)). Many of these approaches suffer from high training variance, mode collapse or cannot be evaluated beyond a qualitative analysis.

Many models have been proposed for text generation. Seq2seq models are standard encoder-decoder models widely used in text applications like machine translation (Luong et al., 2015) and paraphrasing (Prakash et al., 2016). Variational Auto-Encoder (VAE) models are another important family (Kingma and Welling, 2013) and they consist of an encoder that maps each sample to a latent representation and a decoder that generates samples from the latent space. The advantage of these models is the variational component and its potential to add diversity to the generated data. They have been shown to work well for text generation (Bowman et al., 2016). Conditional VAE (CVAE) (Kingma et al., 2014) was proposed to improve over seq2seq models for generating more diverse and relevant text. CVAE based models (Serban et al., 2017; Zhao et al., 2017; Shen et al., 2017; Zhou and Wang, 2018) incorporate stochastic latent variables that represents the generated text, and append the output of VAE as an additional input to decoder.

Paraphrasing can be performed using neural networks with an encoder-decoder configuration, including sequence to sequence (S2S) (Luong et al., 2015) and generative models (Bowman et al., 2016) and various modifications have been proposed to

| domain: Movies |
| intent: MovieRating |
| slots: **movie_title** |
| can children watch the movie **movie_title** |
| can i watch the movie **movie_title** with my son |
| is **movie_title** p. g. thirteen |
| is **movie_title** suitable for children |

| domain: Movies |
| intent: GetActorMovies |
| slots: **genre**, **person_name** |
| give me **genre** movies starring **person_name** |
| suggest **genre** movies starring **person_name** |
| what **genre** movies is **person_name** in |
| what are **genre** movies with **person_name** |

Figure 1: Example of template carrier phrases for two signatures s.

allow for control of the output distribution of the data generation (Yan et al., 2015; Hu et al., 2018).

Unlike the typical paraphrasing task we care about the lexical diversity and novelty of the generated output. This has been a concern in paraphrase generation: a generator that only produces trivial outputs can still perform fairly well in terms of typical paraphrasing evaluation metrics, despite the output being of little use. Alternative metrics have been proposed to encourage more diverse outputs (Shima and Mitamura, 2011). Typically evaluation of paraphrasing or text generation tasks is performed by using a similarity metric (usually some variant of BLEU (Papineni et al., 2002)) calculated against a held-out set (Prakash et al., 2016; Rajeswar et al., 2017; Yu et al., 2017).

3 Methodology

3.1 Problem Definition

New capabilities for virtual agents are typically defined by a few phrases templates, also called *carrier phrases*, as seen in Fig. 1. In carrier phrases the entity values, like the movie title 'Batman', are replaced with their entity types, like **movie_title**. These are also called *slot values* and *slot types*, respectively, in the NLU literature. For our generation task, these phrases define a category: all carrier phrases that share the same domain, intent and slot types are equivalent, in the sense that they prompt the same agent response. For the remainder of this paper we will refer to the combination of domain, intent and slot types as the *signature* of a phrase. Given a small amount of example carrier phrases for a given signature of a new capability (typically under 5 phrases), our goal is to generate additional semantically similar carrier phrases for the target signature.

The core challenge lies in the very limited data we can work with. The low number of phrases per category is, as we will show, highly problematic when training some adversarial or reinforcement structures. Additionally the high number of categories makes getting an output of the desired signature harder, because many similar signatures will be very close in latent space.

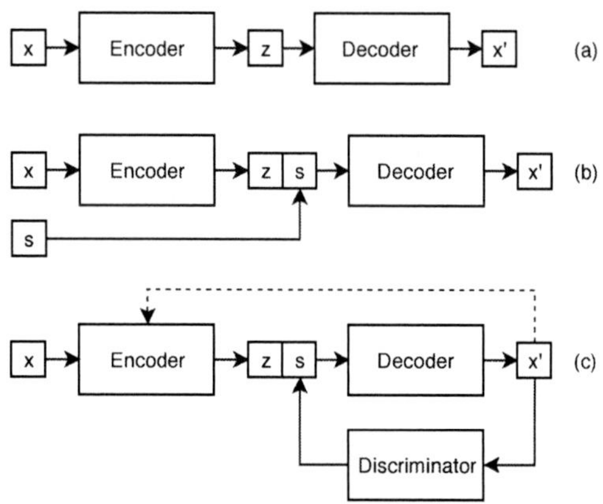

Figure 2: The variants of VAE we used: (a) VAE, (b) Conditional VAE (CVAE) and (c) VAE with discriminator

3.2 Generation models

Following is a short description of the models we evaluated for data generation. For all models we assume we have training carrier phrases $c_i \in D_{tr}^s$ across signatures s, and we pool together the data from all the signatures for training. The variational auto-encoders we used can be seen in Fig 2.

Sequence to Sequence with Attention Here, we use the seq2seq with global attention proposed in (Luong et al., 2015) as our baseline generation model. The model is trained on all input-output pairs of carrier phrases belonging to the same signature s, e.g., $c_1, c_2 \in D_{tr}^s$. At generation, we aim to control the output by using an input carrier of the target signature s.

Variational Auto-Encoders (VAEs) The VAE model can be trained with a paraphrasing objective, e.g., on pairs of carrier phrases $c_1, c_2 \in D_{tr}^s$, similarly to the seq2seq model. Alternatively, the

VAE model can be trained with a reconstruction objective e.g., $c_1 \in D_{tr}$ can be both the input and the output. However, if we train with a reconstruction objective, during generation, we ignore the encoder and randomly sample the VAE prior z (typically from a normal distribution). As a result, we have no control over the output signature distribution, and we may generate any of the signatures s in our training data. This disadvantage motivates the investigation of two controlled VAE models.

VAE with discriminator is a modification of a VAE proposed by (Hu et al., 2018) for a similar task of controlled text generation. In this case, adversarial type of training is used by training a discriminator, i.e., a classifier for the category (signature **s**), to explicitly enforce control over the generated output. The network is trained in steps, with the VAE trained first, then the discriminator is attached and the entire network re-trained using a sleep-wake process. We tried two variations of this, one training a VAE, another training a CVAE, before adding the discriminator. Note that control over the output depends on the discriminator performance. While this model worked well for controlling between a small number of output categories as in (Hu et al., 2018), our setup includes hundreds of signatures s, which posed challenges in achieving accurate control over the output phrases (Sec. 5.2).

Conditional VAE (CVAE) Inspired by (Moyer et al., 2018) for invariant feature learning, we propose to use a CVAE based controlled model structure. Such structure is a modification on the VAE, where we append the desired category label, here signature **s**, in 1-hot encoding, to each step of the decoder without an additional discriminator as shown in (Hu et al., 2018). Note that the original conditional VAE has already been applied to controlled visual settings (Yan et al., 2015). It has been shown that by direct optimizing the loss, this model automatically learns a invariant representation **z** that is independent of the category (signature s (Moyer et al., 2018)) although no explicit constraint is forced. We propose to use this model in our task, because it is easy to train (no wake-sleep or adversarial training), requires less data, and provides us a way to control the desired VAE output signature, by setting the desired signature encoding to **s**. Like the standard VAE, the CVAE can be trained either with a paraphrasing or with a reconstruction objective. If training with reconstruction, during generation we randomly sample from z but can control the output signature by setting s.

All model encoders and decoders are GRUs. For the discriminator we tried CNN and LSTM with no significant performance differences.

4 Datasets

We experiment on two datasets collected for Alexa, a commercial artificial agent.

Movie dataset It contains carrier phrases that are created as part of developing new movie-related functionality. It is composed of 179 signatures defined with an average of eight carrier phrases each. This data represents a typical new capability that starts out with few template carriers phrases, and we use it to examine if this low resource dataset can benefit from synthetic data generation.

Live entertainment dataset It contains live customer data from deployed entertainment related capabilities (music, books, etc), selected for their semantic relevance to movies. These utterances were de-lexicalized by replacing slot values with their respective slot types. We used a frequency threshold to filter out rare carrier phrases, and ensure a minimum number of three carrier phrases per signature.

Table 1 shows the data splits for the movie, live entertainment and 'all' datasets, the latter containing both movies and live entertainment data, including the number of signatures, slot types and unique non-slot words in each set. While the data splits were stratified, signatures with fewer than four carriers were placed only in the train set, leading to the discrepancy in signature numbers across partitions.

5 Experiments

5.1 Experimental setup

At the core of our data augmentation task lies the question "what defines a good training data set?". We can evaluate aspects of the generated data via synthetic metrics, but the most reliable method is to generate data for an extrinsic task and evaluate any improvements in performance. In this paper we employ both methods are reporting results for intrinsic and extrinsic evaluation metrics.

For the intrinsic evaluation, we train the data generator either only on movie data or on 'all' data (movies and entertainment combined), using the respective dev sets for hyper-parameter tuning. Dur-

ing generation, we similarly consider either the movies test set, or the 'all' test set, and aim to generate *ten synthetic phrases* per test set phrase. VAE type generators can be trained for paraphrasing ($c1 \rightarrow c2$) or reconstruction ($c1 \rightarrow c1$). During generation, sampling can be performed either from the prior, e.g., by ignoring the encoder and sampling $z \sim \mathcal{N}(0, I)$ to generate an output, or from the posterior e.g., using c_1 as input to the encoder and producing the output $c2$. Note that not all combinations are applicable to all models. Those applicable are shown in Table 3, where 'para', 'recon', 'prior' and 'post' denote paraphrasing, reconstruction, prior and posterior respectively. Special handling was required for a VAE with reconstruction training and prior sampling, where we have no control over the output signature. To solve this, we compared each output phrase to every signature in the train set (via BLEU4 (Papineni et al., 2002)) and assigned it to the highest scoring signature. Some sample output phrases can be seen in Fig. 3.

To examine the usefulness of the generated data for an extrinsic ask, we perform intent classification, a standard task in NLU. Our classifier is a BiLSTM model. We use the same data as for the data generation experiments (see Table 1), and group our class labels into intents (as opposed to signatures), which leads to classifying 136 intents in the combined movies and entertainment data ('all'). Our setup follows two steps: First, the data generators are trained on 'all' train sets, and used to generate phrases for the dev sets ('all' and movies). Second, the intent classifier is trained on the 'all' train and dev sets (baseline), vs the combination of 'all' train, dev and generated synthetic data, which is our proposed approach. We evaluate on the 'all' and movies test sets, and use macro-averaged F-score across all intents as our metric.

5.2 Intrinsic evaluation

To evaluate the generated data we use an ensemble of evaluation metrics attempting to quantify three important aspects of the data: (1) how accurate or relevant the data is to the task, (2) how diverse the set of generated phrases is and (3) how novel these synthetic phrases are. Intuitively, a NLG system can be very accurate - generate valid phrases of the correct signature - while only generating phrases from the train set or while generating the same phrase multiple times for the same signature; either of these scenarios would not lead to useful data. To

domain	subset	carriers	signatures	slots	words
	train	1,382	179	21	353
Movies	dev	622	109	15	292
	test	520	69	10	254
	train	4269	588	120	332
Live Entertainment	dev	1236	244	77	194
	test	1335	271	74	217
	train	5,651	767	141	685
All	dev	1,858	353	92	486
	test	1,855	340	84	471

Table 1: Data distribution and splits. 'All' contains the combined Movie and Entertainment live datasets

domain	subset	carriers	intents
	train	5651	136
	dev	1858	101
All	train+dev	7509	136
	test	1855	94
Movies	test	520	37

Table 2: Data distribution and splits for the extrinsic task.

evaluate accuracy we compare the generated data to a held out *test set* using BLEU4 (Papineni et al., 2002) and the slot carry-over rate, the probability that a generated phrase contains the exact same slot types as the target signature s. To evaluate novelty we compare the generated data to the train set of the generator, using 1-BLEU4 (where higher is better) and 1-Match rate, where the match rate is the chance that a perfect match to a generated phrase exists in the train set. These scores tell us how different, at the lexical level, the generated phrases are to the phrases that already exist in the train set. Finally, to evaluate diversity we compare the phrases in the generated data to each other, using again 1-BLEU4 and the unique rate, the number of unique phrase produced over the total number of phrases produced. These scores indicate how lexically different the generated phrases are to each other. Figure 4 shows the set comparisons made to generate the intrinsic evaluation metrics. Note that these metrics mostly evaluate surface forms; we expect phrases generated for the same signature to be *semantically* similar to phrases with the same signature in the train set and to each other, however we would like them to be *lexically* novel and diverse.

Table 3 presents the intrinsic evaluation results, where generators are trained and tested on 'all' data,

for the best performing model per case, tuned on the dev set. First, note the slot carry over (slot c.o.), which can be used as a sanity check measuring the chance of getting a phrase with the desired slot types. Most models reach 0.8 or higher slot c.o. as expected, but some fall short, indicating failure to produce the desired signature. The failure for VAE and CVAE models with discriminators is most notable, and can be explained by the fact that we have a large number of train signatures ($\sim$800) and too few samples per signature (mean 8, median 4), to accurately train the discriminator. We verified that the discriminator overall accuracy does not exceed 0.35. The poor discriminator performance leads to the decoder not learning how to use signature **s**. The failure of VAE with posterior sampling is similarly explained by the large number of signatures: the signatures are so tightly packed in the latent space, that the variance of sampling **z** is likely to result in phrases from similar but different signatures.

This sanity check leaves us with five reasonably performing models: S2S, VAE trained for reconstruction and sampled from the prior and CVAE with multiple training and sampling strategies. Overall, these models achieve high accuracy with respect to the slot c.o. and BLEU4 metrics, assisted by the rather limited vocabulary of the data. To examine the trade-offs between the models, in Fig. 5, we show the accuracy BLEU4 as a function of diversity unique rate, i.e., how many different phrases we generated. Each point is a model trained with different hyper-parameter settings, across relevant hyper-parameters, network component dimensionalities etc. As expected, diversity is negatively correlated with accuracy. We make similar observations for novelty metrics (plots omitted for brevity), i.e., diversity and novelty are negatively correlated

	Model: S2S
	Input: i **negation** feel like watching a movie with **person_name**
outputs	i **negation** like movies by **person_name**
	i **negation** feel like watching movies by **person_name**
	i **negation** feel like watching a movie by **person_name**
	i **negation** like **person_name**
	i **negation** feel like watching a movie
	i **negation** want to talk about **person_name**
	no i **negation** like **person_name** movies

	Model: VAE, sampling from prior distribution
	Input: GetMovieAwards (intent) - **award_title**, **movie_title** (slots)
outputs	did **movie_title** win an **award_title**
	any **award_title** won by **movie_title**
	tell me any **award_title** which **movie_title** won
	was **movie_title** nominated for an **award_title** the movie **movie_title**
	any **award_title** for **movie_title**
	what are the **award_title** which **movie_title** won
	give me any **award_title** the movie was nominated for

	Model: CVAE, sampling from prior distribution
	Input: GetActorMovies (intent) - **genre**, **person_name** (slots)
outputs	give me **genre** movies starring **person_name**
	show me other **genre** movies with **person_name** in it
	what are the **genre** movies that **person_name** starred in
	tell me **genre** movies starring **person_name**
	what are **genre** movies with **person_name**
	genre movies starring **person_name**
	suggest **genre** movies starring **person_name**

Figure 3: Sample output phrases. The S2S model and all posterior sampling models use a phrase as an input. For prior sampling the desired signature is the model input.

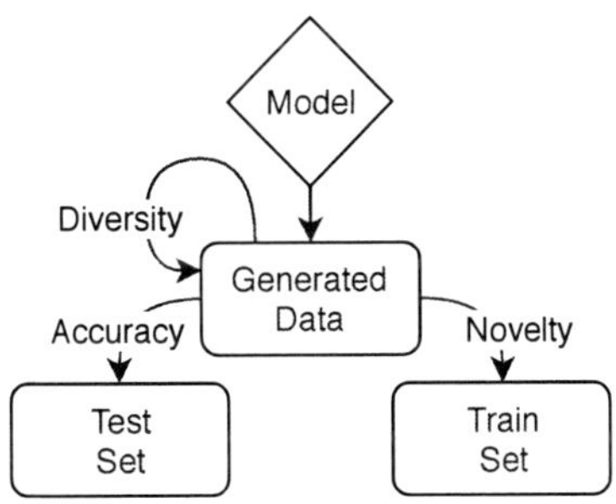

Figure 4: Intrinsic evaluation overview

to accuracy within the hyper-parameter constraints of each model. However the trade-off is not equally steep for all models. Across our experiments the VAE and CVAE models with reconstruction training and prior sampling provided the most favorable trade-offs with CVAE being the best option for very

high accuracy, as seen in Fig. 5.

In Table 4, we show intrinsic results on the movies test set. For brevity, we show the mean relative change for the best performing models for each metric, computed between using only movie data to train the generators vs using the combined 'all' data. In the latter case, the live entertainment data is added to train a more robust generator for movies. As expected, we notice a small loss in accuracy (-1.9 % rel. change on average for BLEU4) when using the 'all' data for generator training, but also a significant gain in diversity and novelty of the movie generated data (121 % and 153 % rel. change on average respectively for 1-BLEU4). Overall, the reconstruction VAE and CVAE models achieve the best results and have favorable performance trade-offs when using 'all' data to enrich movie data generation.

		S2S	VAE		VAE+DISC	CVAE			CVAE+DISC
training		para	recon	para	recon	recon	recon	para	recon
sampling		post	prior	post	prior	prior	post	post	prior
accuracy	BLEU4	0.86	0.91	0.24	0.42	0.91	0.88	0.90	0.11
	slot c.o.	0.84	0.95	0.02	0.12	0.98	0.93	0.95	0.01
diversity	1-BLEU4	0.06	0.19	0.83	0.84	0.14	0.23	0.33	0.19
	uniq. rate	0.58	0.68	0.98	0.76	0.44	0.56	0.68	0.97
novelty	1-BLEU4	0.25	0.07	0.75	0.98	0.04	0.12	0.21	0.99
	1-match rate	0.89	0.76	0.99	1.00	0.32	0.50	0.59	1.00

Table 3: Best performance per metric for each model when applied to 'all' domains.

metric	% change			
	CVAE prior	CVAE posterior	CVAE s2s	VAE prior
accuracy				
BLEU4	-0.7%	-0.7%	-4.3%	-2.0%
slot c.o.	-2.7%	-3.1%	-9.5%	-5.9%
diversity				
1-BLEU4	112.1%	103.6%	133.7%	134.6%
uniq. rate	19.6%	19.7%	32.7%	37.1%
novelty				
1-BLEU4	147.1%	40.7%	222.1%	201.2%
1-match rate	113.5%	36.7%	145.4%	90.1%

Table 4: Relative change when adding more training data for generator training (movies only vs 'all') across evaluation metrics on the movies test set

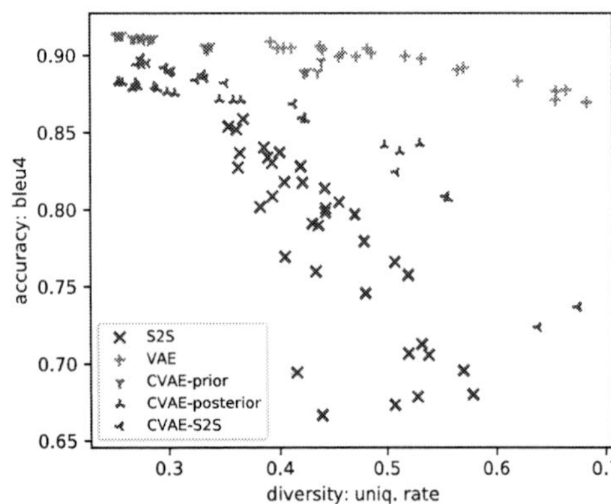

Figure 5: Intrinsic accuracy BLEU4 as a function of intrinsic diversity for the 'all' test set for multiple hyper-parameter combinations of each model.

5.3 Extrinsic Evaluation

In Figure 6 we present the change in the F1 score for intent classification when adding the generated data into the classifier training (compared to the baseline classifier with no generated data) as a function of the intrinsic BLEU4 accuracy metric. The plot presents results on the movies test set. Each point is a model trained with different hyper-parameters and the line $y = 0$ represents zero change from baseline, while models over this line represent improvement. Some hyper-parameter choices clearly lead to sub-optimal results, but they are included to show the relationship between intrinsic and extrinsic performance across a wider range of conditions. We notice that many generators produce useful synthetic data that lead to improvement in intent classification, with the best performing ones being the CVAE models with around 5% absolute improvement in F-score on the movie test set ($p < 0.01$). This is an encouraging results, as it verifies the usefulness of the generated data for improving the extrinsic low resource task. For the 'all' test set experiments, the improvement is less pronounced, with maximum gain from synthetic data being around 2%, again for the CVAE models. This smaller improvement could be because this test set is not as low resource (roughly twice as many train carriers phrases per

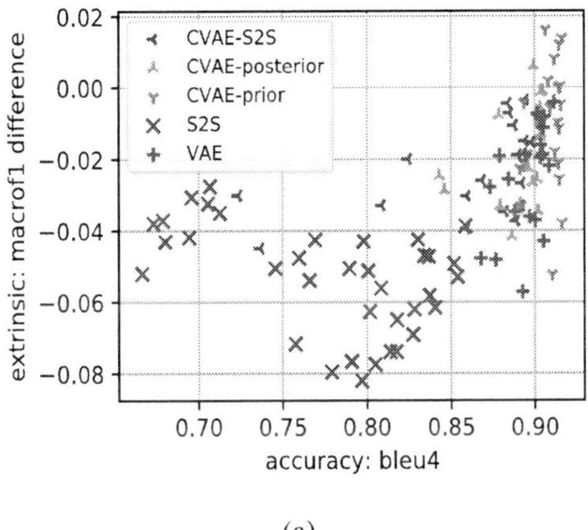 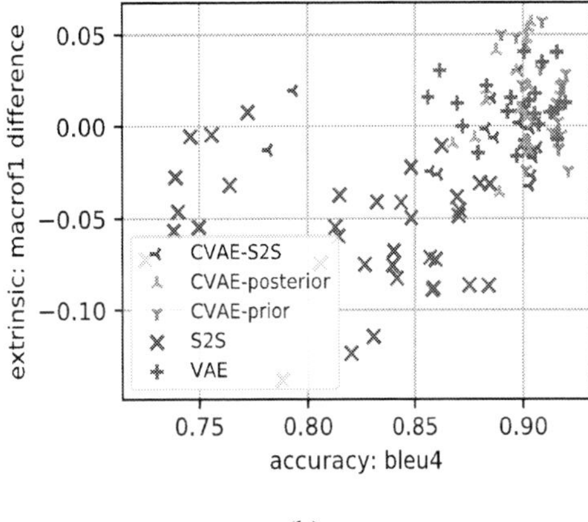

Figure 6: Extrinsic task performance change as a function of intrinsic accuracy BLEU4 for (a) all domains and (b) the movies domain. The y axis represents how much performance improved or deteriorated after adding synthetic data to the train set.

intent on average, 41.55 instead of 24.25), therefore harder to improve using synthetic data. Note that the baseline F1 scores (no synthetic data) are 0.58 for movies and 0.60 for the 'all' test set.

We investigate the correlation between the intrinsic metrics and the extrinsic F score by performing Ordinary Least Squares (OLS) regression between the two types of metrics, computed on the 'all' test set. We find that intrinsic accuracy metrics like BLEU4 and slot c.o. have significant positive correlation with macro F (R^2 of 0.31 and 0.40 respectively, $p \approx 0$) across all experiments/models, though perhaps not as high as one might expect. We also computed via OLS the combined predictive power of all intrinsic metrics for predicting extrinsic F, and estimated an R^2 coefficient of 0.53 ($p \approx 0$). The diversity and novelty metrics add a lot of predictive power to the OLS model when combined with accuracy metrics, raising R^2 from 0.40 to 0.53, validating the need to take these aspects of NLG performance into account. However, intrinsic diversity and novelty are only good predictors of extrinsic performance when combined with accuracy, so they only become significant when comparing models of similar intrinsic accuracy.

6 Conclusions

We described a framework for controlled text generation for enriching training data for new NLU functionality. Our challenging text generation setup required control of the output phrases over a large number of low resource signatures of NLU func-

tionality. We used intrinsic metrics to evaluate the quality of the generated synthetic data in terms of accuracy, diversity and novelty. We empirically investigated variational encoder-decoder type models and proposed to use a CVAE based model, which yielded the best results, being able to generate phrases with favorable accuracy, diversity and novelty trade-offs. We also demonstrated the usefulness of our proposed methods by showing that the synthetic data can improve the accuracy of an extrinsic low resource classification task.

7 Acknowledgments

This work was performed while Nikolaos Malandrakis was at Amazon Alexa AI, Sunnyvale.

References

Samuel R. Bowman, Luke Vilnis, Oriol Vinyals, Andrew M. Dai, Rafal Jozefowicz, and Samy Bengio. 2016. Generating sentences from a continuous space. In *Proceedings of the SIGNLL Conference on Computational Natural Language Learning (CONLL)*, pages 10–21.

Jiaxian Guo, Weinan Zhang Yong Yu Sidi Lu, Han Cai, and Jun Wang. 2018. Long text generation via adversarial training with leaked information. In *Proceedings of AAAI*, pages 5141–5148.

Zhiting Hu, Zichao Yang, Xiaodan Liang, Ruslan Salakhutdinov, and Eric P. Xing. 2018. Toward controlled generation of text. arXiv:1703.00955.

Eric Jang, Shixiang Gu, and Ben Poole. 2016. Categorical reparameterization with gumbel-softmax. arXiv:1611.01144.

Diederik P Kingma, Shakir Mohamed, Danilo Jimenez Rezende, and Max Welling. 2014. Semi-supervised learning with deep generative models. In *Advances in Neural Information Processing Systems*, pages 3581–3589.

Diederik P Kingma and Max Welling. 2013. Auto-encoding variational bayes. arXiv:1312.6114.

Minh-Thang Luong, Hieu Pham, and Christopher D. Manning. 2015. Effective approaches to attention-based neural machine translation. arXiv:1508.04025.

Daniel Moyer, Shuyang Gao, Rob Brekelmans, Aram Galstyan, and Greg Ver Steeg. 2018. Invariant representations without adversarial training. In *Advances in Neural Information Processing Systems 31*, pages 9101–9110.

Kishore Papineni, Salim Roukos, Todd Ward, and Wei-Jing Zhu. 2002. Bleu: A method for automatic evaluation of machine translation. In *Proceedings of the 40th Annual Meeting on Association for Computational Linguistics*, pages 311–318.

Aaditya Prakash, Sadid A. Hasan, Kathy Lee, Vivek Datla, Ashequl Qadir, Joey Liu, and Oladimeji Farri. 2016. Neural paraphrase generation with stacked residual lstm networks. arXiv:1610.03098.

Rajeswar, Subramanian S., Dutil F., Pal C., and A. Courville. 2017. Adversarial generation of natural language. arXiv:1705.10929.

Abigail See, Peter J. Liu, and Christopher D. Manning. 2017. Get to the point: Summarization with pointer generator networks. In *Proceedings of ACL*, pages 1073–1083.

Iulian Vlad Serban, Alessandro Sordoni, Ryan Lowe, Laurent Charlin, Joelle Pineau, Aaron C Courville, and Yoshua Bengio. 2017. A hierarchical latent variable encoder-decoder model for generating dialogues. In *AAAI*, pages 3295–3301.

Xiaoyu Shen, Hui Su, Yanran Li, Wenjie Li, Shuzi Niu, Yang Zhao, Akiko Aizawa, and Guoping Long. 2017. A conditional variational framework for dialog generation. arXiv:1705.00316.

Hideki Shima and Teruko Mitamura. 2011. Diversity-aware evaluation for paraphrase patterns. In *Proceedings of the TextInfer 2011 Workshop on Textual Entailment*, pages 35–39.

Ilya Sutskever, Oriol Vinyals, and Quoc V Le. 2014. Sequence to sequence learning with neural networks. *Advances in neural information processing systems*, pages 3104–3112.

Xinchen Yan, Jimei Yang, Kihyuk Sohn, and Honglak Lee. 2015. Attribute2image: Conditional image generation from visual attributes. arXiv:1512.00570.

Quanzeng You, Chen Fang Hailin Jin, Zhaowen Wang, and Jiebo Luo. 2016. Image captioning with semantic attention. In *Proceedings of the IEEE conference on computer vision and pattern recognition*, pages 4651–4659.

Lantao Yu, Jun Wang Weinan Zhang, and Yong Yu. 2017. Seqgan: Sequence generative adversarial nets with policy gradient. In *Proceedings of AAAI*, pages 2852–2858.

Tiancheng Zhao, Ran Zhao, and Maxine Eskenazi. 2017. Learning discourse-level diversity for neural dialog models using conditional variational autoencoders. arXiv:1703.10960.

Xianda Zhou and William Yang Wang. 2018. MojiTalk: Generating emotional responses at scale. In *Proceedings of ACL)*, pages 1128–1137.

Zero-Resource Neural Machine Translation with Monolingual Pivot Data

Anna Currey
University of Edinburgh
`a.currey@sms.ed.ac.uk`

Kenneth Heafield
University of Edinburgh
`kheafiel@ed.ac.uk`

Abstract

Zero-shot neural machine translation (NMT) is a framework that uses source-pivot and target-pivot parallel data to train a source-target NMT system. An extension to zero-shot NMT is zero-resource NMT, which generates pseudo-parallel corpora using a zero-shot system and further trains the zero-shot system on that data. In this paper, we expand on zero-resource NMT by incorporating monolingual data in the pivot language into training; since the pivot language is usually the highest-resource language of the three, we expect monolingual pivot-language data to be most abundant. We propose methods for generating pseudo-parallel corpora using pivot-language monolingual data and for leveraging the pseudo-parallel corpora to improve the zero-shot NMT system. We evaluate these methods for a high-resource language pair (German-Russian) using English as the pivot. We show that our proposed methods yield consistent improvements over strong zero-shot and zero-resource baselines and even catch up to pivot-based models in BLEU (while not requiring the two-pass inference that pivot models require).

1 Introduction

Neural machine translation (NMT) has achieved impressive results on several high-resource translation tasks (Hassan et al., 2018; Wu et al., 2016). However, these systems have relied on large amounts of parallel training data between the source and the target language; for many language pairs, such data may not be available. Even two high-resource languages, such as German and Russian, may not have sufficient parallel data between them.

Recently, unsupervised NMT systems that learn to translate using only monolingual corpora have been proposed as a solution to this problem (Artetxe et al., 2018; Lample et al., 2018). However, such systems do not make full use of available parallel corpora between the source and target languages and a potential pivot language.

Although most language pairs may have little in-domain parallel data available, it is often possible to find parallel corpora with a third *pivot* language. For example, while German↔Russian parallel data is relatively scarce, German↔English and Russian↔English data is abundant. Pivot-based and zero-shot NMT systems have been proposed as a means of taking advantage of this data to translate between e.g. German and Russian.

In pivot-based machine translation, text is first translated from the source language into the pivot language, and then from the pivot language into the target language. Although such methods can result in strong translation performance (Johnson et al., 2017), they have a few disadvantages. The two-step pivoting translation process doubles the latency during inference and has the potential to propagate errors from the source→pivot translation into the final target output. Additionally, there is a risk that relevant information in the source sentence can be lost in the pivot translation (e.g. case distinctions if pivoting through English) and not represented in the target sentence. Zero-shot methods that take advantage of multilingual NMT systems to perform direct source→target translation have become a popular method for addressing this problem, and zero-resource methods build off of zero-shot methods by fine-tuning on pseudo-parallel data to improve direct translation (see section 2.1 for a review of zero-shot and zero-resource methods). Zero-resource methods are beneficial because they can potentially take advantage of all available training data, including parallel and monolingual corpora.

The goal of this paper is to augment zero-resource NMT with monolingual data from the

Proceedings of the 3rd Workshop on Neural Generation and Translation (WNGT 2019), pages 99–107
Hong Kong, China, November 4, 2019. ©2019 Association for Computational Linguistics
www.aclweb.org/anthology/D19-56%2d

pivot language. Although there have been several explorations into using parallel corpora through a pivot language to improve NMT (Firat et al., 2016; Lakew et al., 2017; Park et al., 2017) and using monolingual source and target corpora in NMT (Edunov et al., 2018; Gulcehre et al., 2015; Hoang et al., 2018; Niu et al., 2018; Sennrich et al., 2016a; Zhang and Zong, 2016), this is to our knowledge the first attempt at using monolingual pivot-language data to augment NMT training. Leveraging monolingual pivot-language data is worthwhile because the pivot language is often the highest-resource language of the three (e.g. it is often English), so we expect there to be more high-quality monolingual pivot data than monolingual source or target data in many cases. Thus, we make use of parallel source↔pivot data, parallel target↔pivot data, and monolingual pivot-language data to build a zero-resource NMT system. Although we use a basic multilingual NMT system as the basis, the methods proposed here could easily be applied to any zero-shot NMT architecture.

2 Related Work

2.1 Zero-Shot and Zero-Resource NMT

Zero-shot neural machine translation, i.e. NMT between two languages for which no parallel data was used at training time, is often done by leveraging multilingual NMT systems. Firat et al. (2016) first attempted zero-shot NMT with a multilingual model consisting of several encoders and decoders, but found that without fine-tuning, the model was not able to translate between the zero-shot language pairs. On the other hand, multilingual NMT with shared encoders and decoders (Ha et al., 2016; Johnson et al., 2017) is more successful at zero-shot NMT, although its performance still lags behind pivoting.

Several modifications to the multilingual NMT architecture have been proposed with the goal of improving zero-shot NMT performance; here, we review some such modifications. Lu et al. (2018) added an interlingua layer to the multilingual NMT model; this layer transforms language-specific encoder outputs into language-independent decoder inputs. Platanios et al. (2018) updated the shared encoder/decoder multilingual NMT model by adding a contextual parameter generator. This generator generates the encoder and decoder parameters for a given source

and target language, taking only source and target language as input. Arivazhagan et al. (2019) augmented the NMT loss function with a term that promotes the creation of an interlingua.

In this paper, we concentrate on the task of zero-resource translation, which starts from a multilingual NMT system and improves the zero-shot direction using pseudo-parallel corpora. Firat et al. (2016) found that zero-shot NMT performance could be strongly improved by fine-tuning on a pseudo-parallel corpus created by back-translating from the pivot language into each zero-shot language. Similarly, Lakew et al. (2017) improved low-resource zero-shot NMT by back-translating directly between the two zero-shot languages and fine-tuning on the resulting corpus. Park et al. (2017) combined both of these methods and also included NMT-generated sentences on the target side of the pseudo-parallel corpora.

2.2 NMT with Monolingual Data

This paper builds off the idea of back-translation in order to incorporate pivot-language monolingual data into NMT. Back-translation was introduced for NMT by Sennrich et al. (2016a). This technique consists of first training a target→source NMT system and using that to translate the target monolingual data into the source language. The resulting pseudo-parallel source→target corpus is used to augment the training of the final system.

Several methods for improving back-translation have also been proposed. Zhang and Zong (2016) extended back-translation to monolingual source-language data by using the initial system to translate the source data to the target and re-training on the resulting pseudo-parallel corpus. Niu et al. (2018) augmented multilingual NMT with back-translation. They trained a single model for source→target and target→source translation, used that model to back-translate source and target monolingual data, and fine-tuned the model on the back-translated corpora.

3 Zero-Resource NMT with Pivot Monolingual Data

In this paper, we concentrate on zero-resource NMT between two languages X and Y given a pivot language Z. We assume access to X↔Z and Y↔Z parallel corpora, but no direct X↔Y parallel corpus. Our goal is to use additional monolingual data in the pivot language Z to improve both

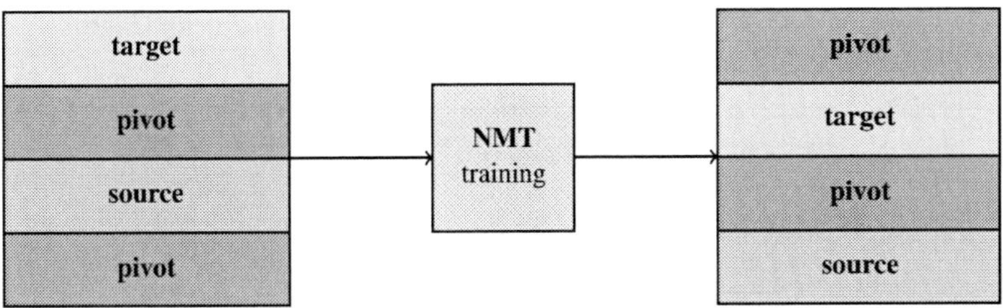

(a) An initial multilingual NMT model is trained on source↔pivot and target↔pivot parallel data (section 3.1).

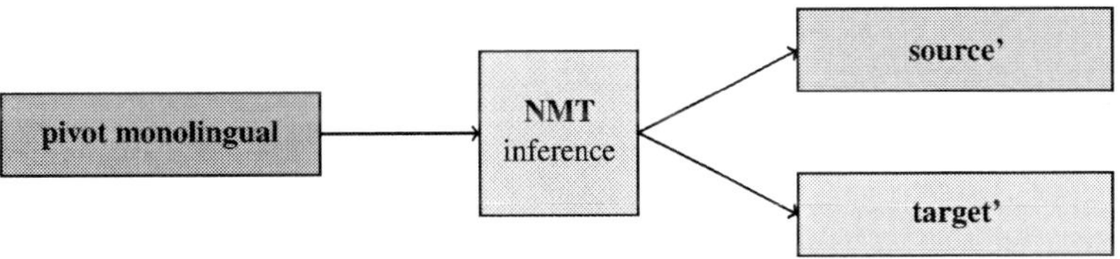

(b) The pivot monolingual corpus is back-translated into the source and target languages using the trained NMT model (section 3.2).

(c) The source'→target' and target'→source' pseudo-parallel corpora are used to train the final NMT system from scratch or fine-tune the initial model (section 3.3). In practice, we concatenate this data with a subset of the original parallel data (not shown here).

Figure 1: Illustration of the basic steps in our zero-resource NMT model using pivot-language monolingual data.

X→Y and Y→X translation simultaneously. Figure 1 gives an overview of our proposed method.

3.1 Initial Multilingual Models

We start by giving an overview of the multilingual NMT models that are used as the basis for our experiments. Here, we do not consider single-directional bilingual NMT models, only multilingual NMT models. This is because we would like to translate directly between language X and language Y at inference time without using the pivot language; translating through the pivot language would double the amount of time it takes to translate and potentially lead to information loss or error propagation. In this work, we also do not consider the case of adding monolingual data from the main languages of interest (X and Y), although such data would likely further improve translation quality.

Our initial multilingual NMT model is based on the model introduced by Johnson et al. (2017), although here we use the transformer architecture (Vaswani et al., 2017). We train the initial model on mixed X→Z, Z→X, Y→Z, and Z→Y parallel data and use tags at the beginning and end of each source sentence to indicate the desired target language. We shuffle all of the data together randomly, regardless of source and target language. We do not employ any extensions to the zero-shot architecture (Arivazhagan et al., 2019; Lu et al., 2018; Platanios et al., 2018), although the methods described here could easily be applied to such extensions as well.

3.2 Back-Translation of Pivot Monolingual Data

We turn now to the task of leveraging the monolingual corpus in the pivot language Z to improve the multilingual NMT models. We aim to improve only X→Y and Y→X translation, without regard to performance on the other language pairs that are included in the multilingual system (X↔Z and Y↔Z).

First, we use the initial multilingual model described in section 3.1 to back-translate the monolingual pivot data into both languages of interest (X and Y). Since the initial multilingual model was trained on both these directions (Z→X and

Method	Back-Translated Data	Training Regime
pivot from scratch	BT-pivot	train from scratch
pivot fine-tune	BT-pivot	fine-tune initial model
pivot-parallel combined	BT-pivot + BT-parallel	fine-tune initial model

Table 1: Summary of the proposed methods for zero-shot NMT using pivot-language monolingual data.

Z→Y), we expect it to do reasonably well at back-translation. Thus, for each sentence in the Z monolingual corpus, we have its translation in both X and Y, so we can create a pseudo-parallel corpus X'↔Y' (where the prime symbol indicates machine-translated text). We concatenate both directions (X'→Y' and Y'→X') together to create our back-translated pivot (*BT-pivot*) corpus. This resulting corpus contains synthetic data on both the source and the target side.

3.3 Using the BT-Pivot Corpus

The BT-pivot corpus uses the monolingual corpus from the pivot language Z to create a direct pseudo-parallel corpus between the two languages of interest, X and Y. In this section, we introduce three methods for using this BT-pivot data to create a zero-resource NMT system for X↔Y translation. In all cases, we concatenate the BT-pivot corpus with a subset of the original training data to train the zero-resource models; in preliminary experiments, we found that using some original training data yielded slightly higher BLEU scores than training on back-translated data alone. We take only a subset of the original parallel training data rather than the entire corpus in order to cut down on training time.

We dub our first method *pivot from scratch*. In this method, we discard the initial NMT model and train a new NMT model from scratch using the BT-pivot data (concatenated with the subset of the original parallel corpora). We use the same model hyperparameters as for the initial NMT model.

Our second method, *pivot fine-tune*, is similar to the first: both methods use the BT-pivot data (along with the subset of the original parallel data). However, for pivot fine-tune, we use the BT-pivot data and the subset of the parallel data to fine-tune the original multilingual model described in section 3.1, rather than training a new model from scratch.

Finally, we propose a *pivot-parallel combined* method. This method also fine-tunes the original multilingual model, but uses an augmented fine-tuning dataset. In addition to the BT-pivot corpus and the subset of the original training data, we add a back-translated parallel (*BT-parallel*) corpus generated following Firat et al. (2016) as follows:

1. Use the initial multilingual model to translate the Z side of the subsetted X↔Z parallel corpus into language Y.

2. Combine the resulting Y' data with the X side of the subsetted X↔Z parallel corpus to create a Y'→X parallel corpus.

3. Use the initial multilingual model to translate the Z side of the subsetted Y↔Z parallel corpus into language X.

4. Combine the resulting X' data with the Y side of the subsetted Y↔Z parallel corpus to create a X'→Y parallel corpus.

5. Concatenate the two back-translated corpora (X'→Y and Y'→X) to create the BT-parallel corpus.

The BT-parallel corpus is then combined with the BT-pivot corpus and the subset of the original parallel data and used to fine-tune the initial multilingual model.

Table 1 summarizes the three proposed methods for zero-shot NMT. The three methods vary in the back-translated data used (BT-pivot only vs. BT-pivot and BT-parallel) and in the training regime (training a new model from scratch vs. fine-tuning the initial multilingual model). In initial experiments, we also tried a version of the pivot-parallel combined method that trained a new model from scratch, although this did not do as well as the pivot-parallel combined method with fine-tuning.

4 Experimental Setup

4.1 Data

We run our experiments on a high-resource setting: translation between German (DE) and Russian (RU) using English (EN) as the pivot. The data comes from the WMT16 news translation

Corpus	Sentences
EN↔DE	4 497 878
EN↔RU	2 500 502
EN monolingual	1 000 000

Table 2: Number of sentences in each training corpus for the DE↔RU experiments.

task (Bojar et al., 2016). We use all available parallel corpora for EN↔DE (Europarl v7, Common Crawl, and News Commentary v11) and for EN↔RU (Common Crawl, News Commentary v11, Yandex Corpus, and Wiki Headlines) to train the initial multilingual system, but no direct DE↔RU parallel data. When the parallel data is used alongside the back-translated corpora for fine-tuning or re-training from scratch (as described in section 3.1), we randomly sample one million sentences from each parallel corpus.

For pivot (EN) monolingual data, we take a random subset of one million sentences from the News Crawl 2015 corpus. Since the goal of this paper is to study the effectiveness of using pivot-language monolingual data, we do not use any DE or RU monolingual data; however, we expect that such data would also be beneficial. Table 2 shows the size of each training corpus after preprocessing. We use the overlapping DE and RU sentences from newstest2014 as the validation set (1505 sentences), newstest2015 as the test set (1433 sentences), and newstest2016 as the held-out set (1500 sentences). The overlapping sentences were originally written in English and were translated by human translators into German and Russian (Bojar et al., 2016).

All data is tokenized and truecased using the Moses scripts (Koehn et al., 2007). We use a joint byte pair encoding (Sennrich et al., 2016b) vocabulary for all three languages (DE, EN, and RU) trained on all parallel data with 50k merge operations. Similarly to Johnson et al. (2017), we use tags at the beginning and end of the source sentence to indicate the desired target language.

4.2 Models

All models in our experiments are based on the transformer architecture (Vaswani et al., 2017). We use the Sockeye toolkit (Hieber et al., 2017) to run all experiments. We find that the default Sockeye hyperparameters work well, so we stick with those throughout. We use beam search with

beam size 5 both when back-translating and during inference.

4.3 Baselines

Initial Models Without Monolingual Data

We compare our models to three baselines that are trained without any monolingual data. We refer to these baselines as *initial models* because they are used as the basis for our proposed models: we use them to generate the BT-pivot data and we fine-tune them using the generated data to create our proposed models.

The first baseline is a multilingual model based on Johnson et al. (2017), but we use the transformer architecture and add target language tags at both the beginning and end of the source sentences. This multilingual model is trained on the English↔German and English↔Russian parallel data. We evaluate this model both with direct (zero-shot) translation (German→Russian and Russian→German) and with pivot translation through English.

Secondly, we consider the zero-resource NMT method proposed by Lakew et al. (2017). This method consists of selecting sentences from the DE↔EN parallel corpus and back-translating them from DE into RU, resulting in a RU'→DE pseudo-parallel corpus. The same is also done with the RU↔EN parallel corpus to create a DE'→RU pseudo-parallel corpus. These corpora are then concatenated with the original parallel data and used to fine-tune the multilingual model. This zero-resource method is only evaluated on direct DE→RU and RU→DE translation (not on pivoting through EN).

We also compare our models to a zero-resource baseline based on the technique introduced by Firat et al. (2016). This method fine-tunes the initial multilingual model with the BT-parallel corpus described in section 3.3 (concatenated with the origial data). Like the other zero-resource baseline, this baseline is only evaluated on direct translation (not on pivot translation).

Baselines with Monolingual Data

In addition to the initial models, we compare our proposed zero-resource NMT methods to two baselines trained with monolingual EN data. For both of these baselines, we evaluate both direct zero-shot translation and pivot translation through EN.

	BLEU	RU→DE		DE→RU	
		test	held-out	test	held-out
initial models	multilingual direct	15.2	14.5	3.4	2.7
	multilingual pivot	21.7	20.2	21.3	19.3
	Lakew et al., 2017	14.4	13.2	19.4	17.0
	Firat et al., 2016	21.0	18.3	22.6	20.7
baselines	copied corpus direct	10.2	9.5	3.7	3.1
	copied corpus pivot	21.1	19.9	20.9	18.9
	back-translation direct	14.8	14.1	3.7	2.9
	back-translation pivot	22.4	20.9	22.3	20.4
proposed models	pivot from scratch	22.3	21.5	23.0	20.6
	pivot fine-tune	22.4	21.5	23.0	20.3
	pivot-parallel combined	**22.5**	**21.6**	**23.6**	**21.1**

Table 3: BLEU scores for the initial multilingual models and zero-resource models without monolingual data, for the baselines with pivot monolingual data, and for our proposed zero-resource models with pivot monolingual data. We report results on the test set (newstest2015) and the held-out set (newstest2016). For the baselines and the initial multilingual models, we use consider both direct (zero-shot) and pivot translation.

The first is based on the copied corpus method of Currey et al. (2017). We train an identical model to the initial multilingual model, but with additional EN→EN pseudo-parallel training data from the EN monolingual corpus. Thus, this model is trained on DE↔EN, RU↔EN, and EN→EN data. We do not fine-tune this model with any pseudo-parallel data.

The second baseline we consider is back-translation (Sennrich et al., 2016a). Starting from the trained multilingual model, we back-translate the EN monolingual data into both DE and RU, then fine-tune the multilingual model on the original training data, plus the DE'→EN and RU'→EN pseudo-parallel corpora.

5 Results

Table 3 shows translation performance (as estimated by BLEU score) for our main experiments. We display results for initial multilingual models without any monolingual data (rows 1–4), for copied corpus and back-translation baselines using the monolingual data (rows 5–8), and for our proposed zero-resource models (rows 9–11). For the initial multilingual model and for the copied corpus and back-translation baselines, we consider both direct source→target translation and translation through the pivot language (source→EN→target).

5.1 Initial Models Without Monolingual Data

For the multilingual baseline, direct source→target translation does very poorly for DE→RU. Although the performance is somewhat more reasonable for RU→DE, direct translation still lags far behind pivot (source→EN→target) translation for this model. Our results differ from those of Johnson et al. (2017), who showed reasonable performance in both directions for zero-shot translation. However, they tested their zero-shot systems only on closely related languages or very large-scale multilingual systems, whereas we use somewhat smaller training sets and distantly related languages. This might be an explanation for the discrepancy in results.

Both zero-resource models (Lakew et al., 2017 and Firat et al., 2016) outperform the multilingual baseline overall for direct translation. In addition, the latter closes the gap with the pivot translation baseline for DE→RU and almost closes it for RU→DE. Thus, fine-tuning on back-translated parallel data is very helpful in improving zero-resource NMT. In the next sections, we evaluate methods for further improving zero-resource NMT using EN monolingual data.

5.2 Baselines with Monolingual Data

The results for the copied corpus and back-translation baselines (using both direct and pivot translation) are shown in rows 5–8 of Table 3. Both models are unable to translate well using only direct translation, but when pivot translation is used, their performance improves. In particular, the back-translation pivot baseline achieves slightly higher BLEU scores overall than any of the initial models trained without monolingual data.

Currey et al. (2017) showed that the copied corpus method was useful for adding target-language monolingual data to NMT training. Here, we see that the same method is not beneficial (and in fact is slightly harmful compared to the baseline) for adding pivot-language monolingual data to NMT. This could be because the copied corpus is used here to improve translation directions that are not of interest (i.e. translation into and out of English, rather than DE↔RU translation).

5.3 Proposed Models with Monolingual Data

We display the results for our three proposed models in the last three rows of Table 3. Compared to the best pivot-based model (back-translation), the pivot from scratch and pivot fine-tune models perform slightly better overall in both translation directions (DE→RU and RU→DE). Additionally, the pivot-parallel combined model improves over the best pivot-based model by about 1 BLEU for DE→RU and also does slightly better for RU→DE. This BLEU gain is especially interesting since the proposed models do not require two-step inference, unlike the back-translation pivot-based model.

Comparing to the best direct translation model (the zero-resource model based on Firat et al., 2016) leads to similar conclusions. The pivot from scratch and pivot fine-tune methods do similarly to this baseline for DE→RU translation and improve over it by 1.3–3.2 BLEU for RU→DE translation. For the pivot-parallel combined model, the gains over the baseline for DE→RU are stronger than for the other two methods, and the gains for RU→DE are similar. Thus, we have shown that adding pivot-language monolingual data through these methods can strongly improve zero-resource NMT performance.

All three of our proposed models improve over a strong direct translation baseline and perform similarly to or better than a pivot-based translation baseline that uses EN monolingual data without requiring the two-step inference process necessary for pivot-based translation. The pivot from scratch and pivot fine-tune models give similar results, while the pivot-parallel combined method, which

| | DE→RU | | RU→DE | |
BLEU	iter 1	iter 2	iter 1	iter 2
from scratch	**23.0**	**23.0**	22.3	**22.7**
fine-tune	23.0	**23.3**	22.4	**22.8**
combined	**23.6**	22.7	**22.5**	21.2

Table 4: BLEU scores for the proposed models on the test set (newstest2015). We show BLEU scores for one and two iterations (iter 1 and iter 2).

adds in the back-translated parallel corpus, yields the best BLEU scores out of all models across the board.

6 Iterating the Proposed Models

Inspired by Hoang et al. (2018) and Niu et al. (2018), we study whether iterating the proposed models can improve translation performance. Starting from the trained models from section 5.3, we run a second iteration as follows:

1. Back-translate the same EN data using the new model to create a new BT-pivot corpus (as described in section 3.2).

2. For the pivot-parallel combined method, back-translate the EN side of the parallel data as well (following Firat et al., 2016).

3. Fine-tune the model or train the model from scratch using the new data concatenated with the subset of the original parallel data (as described in section 3.3).

Table 4 shows the performance on the test dataset (newstest2015) when a second iteration of back-translation and training is performed. For the pivot from scratch and pivot fine-tune methods, we see small gains (up to 0.4 BLEU) from running a second iteration. These small improvements help the pivot from scratch and pivot fine-tune methods catch up to the single-iteration version of the pivot-parallel combined method. On the other hand, running a second iteration is very costly in terms of training time, since it requires another back-translation step and another training step. For the pivot-parallel combined model, which was the best-performing model with one iteration, adding a second iteration damages performance in terms of BLEU score. This seems to match the results of Hoang et al. (2018) that indicate that there are diminishing returns as more iterations are added.

7 Conclusions

This paper introduced the task of zero-resource neural machine translation using pivot-language monolingual data. We introduced a way of generating a pseudo-parallel source↔target training corpus using the monolingual pivot-language corpus, and we showed three ways of leveraging this corpus to train a final source↔target NMT system. All three methods improved over strong baselines that used both direct source→target translation and pivot translation through EN; the pivot-parallel combined method was the most successful.

Our proposed paradigm has several benefits. First, it shows that monolingual data from a language other than the source and target languages can aid NMT performance, complementing literature on using source- and target-language monolingual data in NMT. Second, this paradigm is architecture-agnostic, so it would be easy to apply to architectures that improve upon the basic zero-shot and zero-resource models (e.g. Arivazhagan et al., 2019; Lu et al., 2018; Platanios et al., 2018). However, the methods we have proposed are not without limitations. First, using the pivot-language monolingual data might not work as well when the source and target languages are closely related; this might be a case where source and target monolingual data is more useful than pivot monolingual data. These models also tune a multilingual NMT system for translation in two directions only (source→target and target→source), so they would not be applicable in cases where a single massively multilingual NMT system (Aharoni et al., 2019) is required.

In the future, we hope to additionally study the use of source-language and target-language monolingual data in zero-resource NMT. We would also like to test our proposed zero-resource methods on other zero-shot NMT architectures and on other language pairs. We also think that data selection methods on the back-translated data (Niu et al., 2018) could be helpful, since zero-shot multilingual NMT models often generate translations in the wrong target language (Arivazhagan et al., 2019).

References

Roee Aharoni, Melvin Johnson, and Orhan Firat. 2019. Massively multilingual neural machine translation. *arXiv preprint arXiv:1903.00089.*

Naveen Arivazhagan, Ankur Bapna, Orhan Firat, Roee Aharoni, Melvin Johnson, and Wolfgang Macherey. 2019. The missing ingredient in zero-shot neural machine translation. *arXiv preprint arXiv:1903.07091.*

Mikel Artetxe, Gorka Labaka, Eneko Agirre, and Kyunghyun Cho. 2018. Unsupervised neural machine translation. In *6th International Conference on Learning Representations.*

Ondřej Bojar, Rajen Chatterjee, Christian Federmann, Yvette Graham, Barry Haddow, Matthias Huck, Antonio Jimeno Yepes, Philipp Koehn, Varvara Logacheva, Christof Monz, Matteo Negri, Aurélie Névéol, Mariana Neves, Martin Popel, Matt Post, Raphael Rubino, Carolina Scarton, Lucia Specia, Marco Turchi, Karin Verspoor, and Marcos Zampieri. 2016. Findings of the 2016 Conference on Machine Translation. In *Proceedings of the First Conference on Machine Translation*, pages 131–198. Association for Computational Linguistics.

Anna Currey, Antonio Valerio Miceli Barone, and Kenneth Heafield. 2017. Copied monolingual data improves low-resource neural machine translation. In *Proceedings of the Second Conference on Machine Translation*, pages 148–156. Association for Computational Linguistics.

Sergey Edunov, Myle Ott, Michael Auli, and David Grangier. 2018. Understanding back-translation at scale. In *Proceedings of the 2018 Conference on Empirical Methods in Natural Language Processing*, pages 489–500. Association for Computational Linguistics.

Orhan Firat, Baskaran Sankaran, Yaser Al-Onaizan, Fatos T Yarman Vural, and Kyunghyun Cho. 2016. Zero-resource translation with multi-lingual neural machine translation. In *Proceedings of the 2016 Conference on Empirical Methods in Natural Language Processing*, pages 268–277. Association for Computational Linguistics.

Caglar Gulcehre, Orhan Firat, Kelvin Xu, Kyunghyun Cho, Loïc Barrault, Huei-Chi Lin, Fethi Bougares, Holger Schwenk, and Yoshua Bengio. 2015. On using monolingual corpora in neural machine translation. *arXiv preprint arXiv:1503.03535.*

Thanh-Le Ha, Jan Niehues, and Alexander Waibel. 2016. Toward multilingual neural machine translation with universal encoder and decoder. In *Proceedings of the 13th International Workshop on Spoken Language Translation.*

Hany Hassan, Anthony Aue, Chang Chen, Vishal Chowdhary, Jonathan Clark, Christian Federmann, Xuedong Huang, Marcin Junczys-Dowmunt, William Lewis, Mu Li, Shujie Liu, Tie-Yan Liu, Renqian Luo, Arul Menezes, Tao Qin, Frank Seide, Xu Tan, Fei Tian, Lijun Wu, Shuangzhi Wu, Yingce

Xia, Dongdong Zhang, Zhirui Zhang, and Ming Zhou. 2018. Achieving human parity on automatic Chinese to English news translation. *arXiv preprint arXiv:1803.05567.*

Felix Hieber, Tobias Domhan, Michael Denkowski, David Vilar, Artem Sokolov, Ann Clifton, and Matt Post. 2017. Sockeye: A toolkit for neural machine translation. *arXiv preprint arXiv:1712.05690.*

Vu Cong Duy Hoang, Philipp Koehn, Gholamreza Haffari, and Trevor Cohn. 2018. Iterative back-translation for neural machine translation. In *Proceedings of the Second Workshop on Neural Machine Translation and Generation*, pages 18–24. Association for Computational Linguistics.

Melvin Johnson, Mike Schuster, Quoc V Le, Maxim Krikun, Yonghui Wu, Zhifeng Chen, Nikhil Thorat, Fernanda Viégas, Martin Wattenberg, Greg Corrado, Macduff Hughes, and Jeffrey Dean. 2017. Google's multilingual neural machine translation system: Enabling zero-shot translation. *Transactions of the Association for Computational Linguistics*, 5:339–351.

Philipp Koehn, Hieu Hoang, Alexandra Birch, Chris Callison-Burch, Marcello Federico, Nicola Bertoldi, Brooke Cowan, Wade Shen, Christine Moran, Richard Zens, Chris Dyer, Ondřej Bojar, Alexandra Constantin, and Evan Herbst. 2007. Moses: Open source toolkit for statistical machine translation. In *Proceedings of the 45th Annual Meeting of the ACL*, pages 177–180. Association for Computational Linguistics.

Surafel M Lakew, Quintino F Lotito, Matteo Negri, Marco Turchi, and Marcello Federico. 2017. Improving zero-shot translation of low-resource languages. In *Proceedings of the 14th International Workshop on Spoken Language Translation*.

Guillaume Lample, Ludovic Denoyer, and Marc'Aurelio Ranzato. 2018. Unsupervised machine translation using monolingual corpora only. In *6th International Conference on Learning Representations*.

Yichao Lu, Phillip Keung, Faisal Ladhak, Vikas Bhardwaj, Shaonan Zhang, and Jason Sun. 2018. A neural interlingua for multilingual machine translation. In *Proceedings of the Third Conference on Machine Translation*, pages 84–92. Association for Computational Linguistics.

Xing Niu, Michael Denkowski, and Marine Carpuat. 2018. Bi-directional neural machine translation with synthetic parallel data. In *Proceedings of the Second Workshop on Neural Machine Translation and Generation*, pages 84–91. Association for Computational Linguistics.

Jaehong Park, Jongyoon Song, and Sungroh Yoon. 2017. Building a neural machine translation system using only synthetic parallel data. *arXiv preprint arXiv:1704.00253.*

Emmanouil Antonios Platanios, Mrinmaya Sachan, Graham Neubig, and Tom Mitchell. 2018. Contextual parameter generation for universal neural machine translation. In *Proceedings of the 2018 Conference on Empirical Methods in Natural Language Processing*, pages 425–435. Association for Computational Linguistics.

Rico Sennrich, Barry Haddow, and Alexandra Birch. 2016a. Improving neural machine translation models with monolingual data. In *Proceedings of the 54th Annual Meeting of the ACL*, pages 86–96. Association for Computational Linguistics.

Rico Sennrich, Barry Haddow, and Alexandra Birch. 2016b. Neural machine translation of rare words with subword units. In *Proceedings of the 54th Annual Meeting of the ACL*, pages 1715–1725. Association for Computational Linguistics.

Ashish Vaswani, Noam Shazeer, Niki Parmar, Jakob Uszkoreit, Llion Jones, Aidan N Gomez, Łukasz Kaiser, and Illia Polosukhin. 2017. Attention is all you need. In *Advances in Neural Information Processing Systems 30*, pages 5998–6008.

Yonghui Wu, Mike Schuster, Zhifeng Chen, Quoc V. Le, Mohammad Norouzi, Wolfgang Macherey, Maxim Krikun, Yuan Cao, Qin Gao, Klaus Macherey, Jeff Klingner, Apurva Shah, Melvin Johnson, Xiaobing Liu, ukasz Kaiser, Stephan Gouws, Yoshikiyo Kato, Taku Kudo, Hideto Kazawa, Keith Stevens, George Kurian, Nishant Patil, Wei Wang, Cliff Young, Jason Smith, Jason Riesa, Alex Rudnick, Oriol Vinyals, Greg Corrado, Macduff Hughes, and Jeffrey Dean. 2016. Google's neural machine translation system: Bridging the gap between human and machine translation. *arXiv preprint arXiv:1609.08144.*

Jiajun Zhang and Chengqing Zong. 2016. Exploiting source-side monolingual data in neural machine translation. In *Proceedings of the 2016 Conference on Empirical Methods in Natural Language Processing*, pages 1535–1545. Association for Computational Linguistics.

On the use of BERT for Neural Machine Translation

Stéphane Clinchant
NAVER LABS Europe, France
stephane.clinchant@naverlabs.com

Kweon Woo Jung
NAVER Corp.,
South Korea
kweonwoo.jung@navercorp.com

Vassilina Nikoulina
NAVER LABS Europe, France
vassilina.nikoulina@naverlabs.com

Abstract

Exploiting large pretrained models for various NMT tasks have gained a lot of visibility recently. In this work we study how BERT pretrained models could be exploited for supervised Neural Machine Translation. We compare various ways to integrate pretrained BERT model with NMT model and study the impact of the monolingual data used for BERT training on the final translation quality. We use WMT-14 English-German, IWSLT15 English-German and IWSLT14 English-Russian datasets for these experiments. In addition to standard task test set evaluation, we perform evaluation on out-of-domain test sets and noise injected test sets, in order to assess how BERT pretrained representations affect model robustness.

1 Introduction

Pretrained Language Models (LM) such as ELMO and BERT (Peters et al., 2018; Devlin et al., 2018) have turned out to significantly improve the quality of several Natural Language Processing (NLP) tasks by transferring the prior knowledge learned from data-rich monolingual corpora to data-poor NLP tasks such as question answering, bio-medical information extraction and standard benchmarks (Wang et al., 2018; Lee et al., 2019). In addition, it was shown that these representations contain syntactic and semantic information in different layers of the network (Tenney et al., 2019). Therefore, using such pretrained LMs for Neural Machine Translation (NMT) is appealing, and has been recently tried by several people (Lample and Conneau, 2019; Edunov et al., 2019; Song et al., 2019).

Unfortunately, the results of the above-mentioned works are not directly comparable to each other as they used different methods, datasets and tasks. Furthermore, pretrained LMs have mostly shown improvements in low-resource or unsupervised NMT settings, and has been little studied in standard supervised scenario with reasonable amount of data available.

Current state of the art NMT models rely on the Transformer model (Vaswani et al., 2017), a feed-forward network relying on attention mechanism, which has surpassed prior state of the art architecture based on recurrent neural nets (Bahdanau et al., 2014; Sutskever et al., 2014). Beyond machine translation, the transformer models have been reused to learn bi-directional language models on large text corpora. The BERT model (Devlin et al., 2018) consists in a transformer model aiming at solving a masked language modelling task, namely correctly predicting a masked word from its context, and a next sentence prediction task to decide whether two sentences are consecutive or not. In this work, we study how pretrained BERT models can be exploited for *transformer-based* NMT, thus exploiting the fact that they rely on the same architecture.

The objective of this work is twofold. On one hand, we wish to perform systematic comparisons of different BERT+NMT architectures for standard supervised NMT. In addition, we argue that the benefits of using pretrained representations has been overlooked in previous studies and should be assessed beyond BLEU scores on in-domain datasets. In fact, LMs trained on huge datasets have the potentials of being more robust in general and improve the performance for domain adaptation in MT.

In this study, we compare different ways to train and reuse BERT for NMT. For instance, we show that BERT can be trained only with a masked LM task on the NMT source corpora and yield significant improvement over the baseline. In addition, the models robustness is analyzed thanks to synthetic noise.

Proceedings of the 3rd Workshop on Neural Generation and Translation (WNGT 2019), pages 108–117
Hong Kong, China, November 4, 2019. ©2019 Association for Computational Linguistics
www.aclweb.org/anthology/D19-56%2d

The paper is organized as follows. In section 2, we review relevant state of the art. Section 3 enumerates different models we experiment with. Finally section 4 and 5 present our results before discussing the main contributions of this work in section 6.

2 Related Works

The seminal work of (Bengio et al., 2003; Collobert and Weston, 2008) were one of the first to show that neural nets could learn word representations useful in a variety of NLP tasks, paving the way for the word embedding era thanks to *word2vec* (Mikolov et al., 2013) and its variants (Pennington et al., 2014; Levy and Goldberg, 2014).

With the recent advances and boost in performance of neural nets, ELMO (Peters et al., 2018) employed a Bi-LSTM network for language modelling and proposed to combine the different network layers to obtain effective word representations. Shortly after the publication of ELMO, the BERT model (Devlin et al., 2018) was shown to have outstanding performance in various NLP tasks. Furthermore, the BERT model was refined in (Baevski et al., 2019) where the transformer self-attention mechanism is replaced by two directional self-attention blocks: a left-to-right and right-to-left blocks are combined to predict the masked tokens.

With respect to NMT, backtranslation (Sennrich et al., 2016a) is up to now one of the most effective ways to exploit large monolingual data. However, backtranslation has the drawback of being only applicable for target language data augmentation, while pretrained LMs can be used both for source and target language (independently (Edunov et al., 2019) or jointly (Lample and Conneau, 2019; Song et al., 2019)).

Lample and Conneau (2019) initializes the entire encoder and decoder with a pretrained MaskLM or Crosslingual MaskLM language models trained on multilingual corpora. Such initialization proved to be beneficial for unsupervised machine translation, but also for English-Romanian supervised MT, bringing additional improvements over standard backtranslation with MLM initialization.

Edunov et al. (2019) uses ELMO (Peters et al., 2018) language model to set the word embeddings layer in NMT model. In addition, the ELMO embedding are compared with the cloze-style BERT (Baevski et al., 2019) ones. The embedding network parameters are then either fixed, or fine-tuned. This work shows improvements on English-German and English-Turkish translation tasks when using pretrained language model for source word embedding initialization. However, the results are less clear when reusing embedding on the target language side.

Futhermore, Song et al. (2019) goes one step further and proposes Masked Sequence-to-Sequence pretraining method. Rather than masking a single token, it masks a sequence of token in the encoder and recovers them in the decoder. This model has shown new state of the art for unsupervised machine translation.

Our work is an attempt to perform systematic comparison on some of the aforementioned architectures that incorporate pretrained LM in NMT model, concentrating on BERT pretrained LM representations applied on supervised machine translation. However, we restrict ourselves to encoder part only, and leave the decoder initialization for future work.

Regarding robustness, several recent studies (Karpukhin et al., 2019; Vaibhav et al., 2019) have tackled robustness issues with data augmentation. In this work, we study whether the robustness problem can be addressed at the model level rather than at data level. Michel et al. (2019) address robustness problem with generative adversarial networks. This method, as well as data augmentation methods are complementary to our work and we believe that they address different issues of robustness.

3 Methods

Typical NMT model adopts the encoder-decoder architecture where the encoder forms contextualized word embedding from a source sentence and the decoder generates a target translation from left to right.

Pretrained LM, namely BERT, can inject prior knowledge on the encoder part of NMT, providing rich contextualized word embedding learned from large monolingual corpus. Moreover, pretrained LMs can be trained once, and reused for different language pairs[1].

---

[1] As opposed to backtranslation techniques which requires full NMT model retraining

In this study, we focus on reusing BERT models for the NMT encoder[2]. We will compare the following models:

- **Baseline:**. A *transformer-big* model with shared decoder input-output embedding parameters.

- **Embedding (Emb):** The baseline model where the embedding layer is replaced by the BERT parameters (thus having $6 + 6$ encoder layers). The model is then fine tuned similar to the ELMO setting from (Edunov et al., 2019)

- **Fine-Tuning (FT):** The baseline model with the encoder initialized by the BERT parameters as in Lample and Conneau (2019)

- **Freeze:** The baseline model with the encoder initialized by the BERT parameters and frozen. This means that the whole encoder has been trained in purely monolingual settings, and only parameters responsible for the translation belong to the attention and decoder models.

We exploit the fact that BERT uses the same architecture as NMT encoder which allows us to initialize NMT encoder with BERT pretrained parameters. BERT pretraining has two advantages over NMT training:

- it solves a simpler (monolingual) task of 'source sentence encoding', compared to NMT (bilingual task) which has to 'encode source sentence information', and 'translate into a target language'.

- it has a possibility to exploit much larger data, while NMT encoder is limited to source side of parallel corpus only.

Even though the role of NMT encoder may go beyond source sentence encoding (nothing prevents the model from encoding 'translation related' information at the encoder level), better initialization of encoder with BERT pretrained LM allows for faster NMT learning. Comparing settings where we freeze BERT parameters against fine-tuning BERT allows to shed some light on the capacity of the encoder/decoder model to learn 'translation-related' information.

Moreover, since the BERT models are trained to predict missing tokens from their context, their representations may also be more robust to missing tokens or noisy inputs. We perform extensive robustness study at section 4 verifying this hypothesis.

Finally, language models trained on huge datasets have the potentials of being more robust in general and improve the performance for domain adaptation in MT. We therefore compare BERT models trained on different datasets, and perform evaluation on related test sets in order to assess the capacity of pretrained LMs on domain adaptation.

4 WMT experiments

4.1 Preprocessing

We learn BPE (Sennrich et al., 2016b) model with 32K split operations on the concatenation of Wiki and News corpus. This model is used both for Pretrained LM subwords splitting and NMT source (English) side subwords splitting. German side of NMT has been processed with 32K BPE model learnt on target part of parallel corpus only. Please note, that this is different from standard settings for WMT En-De experiments, which usually uses joint BPE learning and shared source-target embeddings. We do not adopt standard settings since it contradicts our original motivation for using pretrained LM: English LM is learnt once and reused for different language pairs.

4.2 Training

BERT For pretraining BERT models, we use three different monolingual corpora of different sizes and different domains. Table 1 summarizes the statistics of these three monolingual corpora.

- *NMT-src*: source part of our parallel corpus that is used for NMT model training.

- *Wiki*: English wikipedia dump

- *News*: concatenation of 70M samples from "News Discussion", "News Crawl" and "Common Crawl" English monolingual datasets distributed by WMT-2019 shared task[3]. This resulted in total 210M samples.

The motivation of using NMT-src is to test whether the resulting NMT model is more robust

---

[2]Similar approach can be applied on the target language but we leave it for future work.

[3]http://www.statmt.org/wmt19/translation-task.html

	Lines	Tokens
NMT-src	4.5M	104M
Wiki	72M	2086M
News	210M	3657M

Table 1: Monolingual (English) training data

	Lines	Tok/line (en/de)
news14	3003	19.7/18.3
news18	2997	19.5/18.3
iwslt15	2385	16.4/15.4
OpenSub	5000	6.3/5.5
KDE	5000	8/7.7
wiki	5000	17.7/15.5

Table 2: In/Out of Domain test sets. news14 and news18 are test sets from WMT-14 and WMT-18 news translation shared task. iwslt: test set from IWSLT-15 MT Track[4]. Wiki is randomly 5K sampled from parallel Wikipedia distributed by OPUS[5], OpenSub, KDE and Wiki are randomly 5K sampled from parallel Wikipedia, Open Subtitles and KDE corpora distributed by OPUS[6]

after having being trained on the source corpora. The Wiki corpora is bigger than the NMT-src but could be classified as out-of-domain compared to news dataset. Finally, the news dataset is the biggest one and consists mostly of in-domain data.

In all of our experiments, we only consider using the masked LM task for BERT as the next sentence prediction tasks put restrictions on possible data to use. We closely follow the masked LM task described in (Devlin et al., 2018) with few adjustments optimized for downstream NMT training. We use frequency based sampling (Lample and Conneau, 2019) in choosing 15% of tokens to mask, instead of uniformly sampling. Instead of MASK token we used UNK token hoping that thus trained model will learn certain representation for unknowns that could be exploited by NMT model. Warm-up learning scheme described in (Vaswani et al., 2017) results in faster convergence than linear decaying learning rate. The batch size of 64000 tokens per batch is used, with maximum token length of 250, half the original value, as we input single sentence only. We do not use [CLS] token in the encoder side, as attention mechanism in NMT task can extract necessary information from token-level representations. The BERT model is equivalent to the encoder side of Transformer Big model. We train BERT model up to 200k iterations until the accuracy for masked LM on development saturates.

NMT For NMT system training, we use WMT-14 English-German dataset.

We use *Transformer-Big* as our baseline model. We share input embedding and output embedding parameters just before softmax on the decoder side. Warm up learning scheme is used with warm-up steps of 4000. We use batch size of 32000 tokens per batch. Dropout of 0.3 is applied to residual connections, and no dropout is applied in attention layers. We decode with beam size 4 with length penalty described in Wu et al. (2016). We conduct model selection with perplexity on development set. We average 5 checkpoints around lowest perplexity.

4.3 Evaluation

We believe that the impact of pretrained LM in NMT model can not be measured by BLEU performance on in-domain test set only. Therefore we introduce additional evaluation that allows to measure the impact of LM pretraining on different out-of-domain tests. We also propose an evaluation procedure to evaluate the robustness to various types of noise for our models.

Domain Besides standard WMT-14 news test set, models are evaluated on additional test sets given by Table 2. We include two in-domain (news) test sets, as well as additional out-of-domain test sets described in Table 2.

Noise robustness. For robustness evaluation, we introduce different type of noise to the standard *news14* test set:

Typos: Similar to Karpukhin et al. (2019), we add synthetic noise to the test set by randomly (1) swapping characters (chswap), (2) randomly inserting or deleting characters (chrand), (3) uppercasing words (*up*). These test sets translations are evaluated against the golden *news14* reference.

Unk: An unknown character is introduced at the beginning (noted *UNK.S*) or at the end of the sentence (noted *UNK.E*) before a punctuation symbol if any (this unknown character could be thought as as an unknown emoji, a character in different script, a rare unicode character). This token is introduced both for source and target sentence, and the evaluation is performed with the augmented-reference.

Intuitively, we expect the model to simply copy UNK token and proceed to the remaining tokens.

Interestingly, this simple test seems to produce poor translations, therefore puzzling the attention and decoding process a lot. Table 3 gives an example of such translations for baseline model[7].

Since the tasks are correlated, a better model might be better on noisy test sets as it behaves better in general. If we want to test that some models are indeed better, we need to disentangle this effect and show that the gain in performance is not just a random effect. A proper way would be to compute the BLEU correlation between the original test set and the noisy versions but it would require a larger set of models for an accurate correlation estimation.

Δ(chrF) : We propose to look at the *distribution of the difference of sentence charf between the noisy test set and the original test set.* Indeed, looking at BLEU delta may not provide enough information since it is corpus-level metric. Ideally, we would like to measure a number of sentences or a margin for which we observe an 'important decrease' in translation quality. According to Ma et al. (2018); Bojar et al. (2017), sentence level chrF achieves good correlation with human judgements for En-De news translations.

More formally, let s be a sentence from the standard news14 test set, n a noise operation, m a translation model and r the reference sentence[8]:

$$\Delta(\text{chrF})(m, n, s) = \text{chrF}(m(n(s)), r) - \text{chrF}(m(s), r) \quad (1)$$

In the analysis, we will report the distribution of **Δ(chrF)** and its mean value as a summary. If a model is good at dealing with noise, then the produced sentence will be similar to the one produced by the noise-free input sentence. Therefore, the Δ(chrF) will be closer to zero.

4.4 Results

Table 4 presents the results of our experiments. As expected, freezing the encoder with BERT parameters lead to a significant decrease in translation quality. However, other BERT+NMT architectures mostly improve over the baseline both on in-domain and out-of-domain test sets. We conclude, that the information encoded by BERT is useful but not sufficient to perform the translation

task. We believe, that the role of the NMT encoder is to encode both information specific to source sentence, but also information specific to the target sentence (which is missing in BERT training).

Next, we observe that even NMTSrc.FT (NMT encoder is initialized with BERT trained on source part of parallel corpus) improves over the baseline. Note that this model uses the same amount of data as the baseline. BERT task is simpler compared to the task of the NMT encoder, but it is still related, thus BERT pretraining allows for a better initialization point for NMT model.

When using more data for BERT training (Wiki.FT and News.FT), we gain even more improvements over the baseline.

Finally, we observe comparable results for News.Emb and News.FT (the difference in BLEU doesn't exceed 0.3 points, being higher for News.FT on in-domain tests, and News.Emb for out-of-domain tests). Although News.FT configuration keeps the size of the model same as standard NMT system, News.Emb adds BERT parameters to NMT parameters which doubles the size of NMT encoder. Additional encoder layers introduced in News.Emb does not add significant value.

4.5 Robustness analysis

Table 5 reports BLEU scores for the noisy test sets (described in section 4.3). As expected, we observe an important drop in BLEU scores due to the introduced noise. We observe that most pretrained BERT models have better BLEU scores compared to baseline for all type of noise (except NMTSrc.FT which suffers more from unknown token introduction in the end of the sentence compared to the Baseline). However, these results are not enough to conclude, whether higher BLEU scores of BERT-augmented models are due to better robustness, or simply because these models are slightly better than the baseline in general.

This is why figure 1 reports the mean Δ(chrF) for several models. Δ(chrF) scores for UNK tests show that BERT models are not better than expected. However, for chswap, chrand, upper, the BERT models have a slightly lower Δ(chrF). Based on these results, we conclude that pretraining the encoder with a masked LM task does not really bring improvement in terms of robustness to unknowns. It seems that BERT does yield improvement for NMT as a better initialization for

---

[7]Output for (UNK.S+src) input is not an error, the model does produces an English sentence!

[8]In the case of UNK transformation, the reference is changed but we omit that to simplify the notation.

source sentence	"In home cooking, there is much to be discovered - with a few minor tweaks you can achieve good, if not sometimes better results," said Proctor.
translation(src)	"Beim Kochen zu Hause gibt es viel zu entdecken - mit ein paar kleinen nderungen kann man gute, wenn nicht sogar manchmal bessere Ergebnisse erzielen", sagte Proktor.
translation(UNK.S + src)	• "In home cooking, there is much to be discovered - with a few minor tweaks you can achieve good, if not sometimes better results", sagte Proktor.

Table 3: Example of a poor translation when adding unknown token to source sentences (translation done with a baseline transformer model)

	news14	news18	iwslt15	wiki	kde	OpenSub
Baseline	27.3	39.5	28.9	17.6	18.1	15.3
NMTsrc.FT	27.7	40.1	28.7	18.3	18.4	15.3
Wiki.FT	27.7	**40.6**	28.7	18.4	**19.0**	15.4
News.FT	**27.9**	40.2	29.1	18.8	17.9	15.7
News.Emb	27.7	39.9	**29.3**	**18.9**	18.2	**16.0**
News.Freeze	23.6	35.5	26.5	15.0	15.1	13.8

Table 4: FT: initialize NMT encoder with BERT and finetune; Freeze: fix NMT encoder parameters to BERT parameters; Emb: fix encoder embeddding layer with BERT contextual word embeddings.

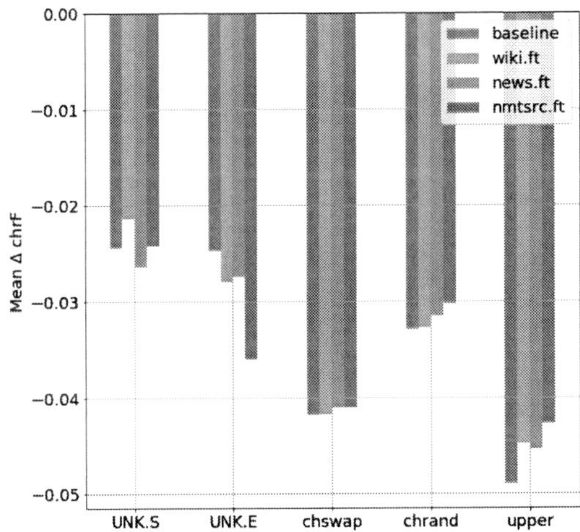

Figure 1: Mean Δ(**chrF**) for several noisy test set and models. For the UNK test, the BERT models are similar or worst than the basline. For the chrand, chswap, upper, the BERT models are slightly better.

NMT encoders but the full potential of masked LM task is not fully exploited for NMT.

5 IWSLT experiments

In order to explore the potential of masked LM encoder pretraining for NMT in lower resource settings, we train NMT models on English-German IWSLT 2015[9] and English-Russian IWSLT 2014[10] MT track datasets. These are pretty small datasets (compared to previous experiments) which contain around 200K parallel sentences each.

5.1 Experimental settings

In these experiments we (1) reuse pretrained BERT models from previous experiments or (2) train IWSLT BERT model. IWSLT BERT model is trained on the concatenation of all the data available at IWSLT 2014-2018 campaigns. After filtering out all the duplicates it contains around 780K sentences and 13.8M tokens.

We considered various settings for IWSLT baseline. First, for source side of the dataset, we took 10K BPE merge operations, where BPE model was trained (1) either on the source side of NMT data only, or (2) on all monolingual English IWSLT data. Target side BPE uses 10K merge operations trained on the target side of the NMT dataset in all the IWSLST experiments. In our first set of experiments, BPE model learnt on source data only lead to similar translation performance as BPE model learnt on all IWSLT English data. Therefore, in what follows we report results only

[9]https://sites.google.com/site/iwsltevaluation2015/mt-track
[10]https://sites.google.com/site/iwsltevaluation2014/mt-track

Models	news14	+UNK.S	+UNK.E	+chswap	+chrand	+up
Baseline	27.3	24.8	24.4	24.2	24.7	23.5
NMTsrc.FT	27.7	24.9	22.9	24.4	25.2	**24.5**
Wiki.FT	27.7	**25.8**	**24.9**	24.4	24.9	24.4
News.FT	**27.9**	24.9	**24.9**	24.5	**25.3**	**24.5**
News.Emb	27.7	24.7	24.8	**24.6**	**25.3**	24.2

Table 5: Robustness tests. BLEU scores for clean and 'noisified' (with different noise type) *news14* testset.

for the latter (referred as $bpe10k$).

NMT model training on IWSLT datasets with Transformer Big architecture on IWSLT data has diverged both for en-de and en-ru dataset. Therefore we use Transformer Base (*tbase*) architecture as a baseline model for these experiments. IWSLT BERT model is also based on *tbase* architecture described in Vaswani et al. (2017) and for the rest follows same training procedure as described in the section 4.

In order to explore the potential of single pretrained model for all language pairs/datasets we try to reuse Wiki and News pretrained BERT models from previous experiments for encoder initialization of NMT model. However, in the previous experiments, our pretrained BERT models used 32K BPE vocabulary and Transformer Big (*tbig*) architecture which means that we have to reuse the same settings for the encoder trained on IWSLT dataset. It has been shown by Ding et al. (2019), these are not optimal settings for IWSLT training because it leads to too many parameters for the amount of data available. Therefore, in order to reduce the amount of the parameters of the model, we also consider the case where we reduce the amount of the decoder layers from 6 to 3 (*tbig.dec3*).

5.2 Results

Table 6 reports the results of different sets of the experiments on IWSLT data. First, we observe that BERT pretrained model improves over the baseline, in any settings (BPE vocabulary, model architecture, dataset used for pretraining). In particular, it is interesting to mention that without pretraining, both *tbig.bpe32k* and *tbig.bpe10k* models diverge when trained on IWSLT. However, BERT pretraining gives a better initialization point, and allows to achieve very good performance both for en-de and en-ru. Thus, such pretraining can be an interesting technique in low-resource scenarios.

	en-de	en-ru
	Baseline	
tbase.bpe10k	25.9	9.6
tbase.dec3.bpe10k	26.4	16.3
	BERT+NMT	
IWSLT.FT.*tbase.bpe10k*	27.4	17.6
IWSLT.FT.*tbase.dec3.bpe10k*	27.2	**18.1**
Wiki.FT.*tbig.bpe32k*	26.9	17.6
Wiki.FT.*tbig.dec3.bpe32k*	**27.7**	17.8
News.FT.*tbig.bpe32k*	27.1	17.9
News.FT.*tbig.dec3.bpe32k*	27.6	17.9

Table 6: IWSLT dataset results. IWSLT.FT: encoder is initialised with BERT model trained on IWSLT data; *tbase/tbig*: transformer base/big architecture for NMT model; *dec3*: decoder layers reduced for 6 to 3; *bpe10k/bpe32k* : amount of BPE merge operations used for source language, learnt on the same dataset as BERT model (IWSLT or Wiki+News).

We do not observe big difference between IWSLT pretrained model and News/Wiki pretrained model. We therefore may assume that News/Wiki BERT model can be considered as "general" English pretrained encoder, and be used as a good starting point in any new model translating from English (no matter target language or domain).

6 Discussion

BERT pretraining has been very successful in NLP. With respect to MT, it was shown to provide better performance in Lample and Conneau (2019); Edunov et al. (2019) and allows to integrate large source monolingual data in NMT model as opposed to target monolingual data usually used for backtranslation.

In this experimental study, we have shown that:

- The next sentence prediction task in BERT is not necessary to improve performance - a *masked LM task* already is beneficial.

- It is beneficial to train BERT on the **source**

corpora, therefore supporting the claim that pretraining the encoder provide a better intialization for NMT encoders.

- Similar to Edunov et al. (2019), we observe that the impact of BERT pretraining is more important as the size of the training data decreases (WMT vs IWSLT).

- Information encoded by BERT is not sufficient to perform the translation: NMT encoder encodes both information specific to source sentence, and to the target sentence as well (cf the low performance of BERT frozen encoder).

- Pretraining the encoder enables us to train bigger models. In IWSLT, the transformer big models were diverging, but when the encoder is initialized with pretrained BERT the training became possible. For WMT14, training a 12 layer encoder from scratch was problematic, but News.Emb model (which contains 12 encoder layers) was trained and gave one of the best performances on WMT14.

- Finetuning BERT pretrained encoder is more convenient : it leads to similar performance compared to reusing BERT as embedding layers, with faster decoding speed.

- BERT pretrained models seem to be generally better on different noise and domain test sets. However, we didn't manage to obtain clear evidence that these models are more robust.

This experimental study was limited to a particular dataset, language pair and model architecture. However, many other combinations are possible. First, similar type of study needs to be performed with BERT pretrained model for NMT decoder. Also, the model can be extended to other scenarios with BERT models such as Baevski et al. (2019). In addition, the comparison with ELMO embeddings is also interesting as in Edunov et al. (2019). Using embedding mostly influenced by neighboring words seems to echo the recent results of convolutional self attention network (Yang et al., 2019). Using convolutional self attention network in BERT could bring additional benefit for the pretrained representations. Another direction could look at the impact of the number of layers in BERT for NMT.

Besides, one key question in this study was about the role of encoder in NMT as the roles of encoders and decoders are not clearly understood in current neural architectures. In the transformer architecture, the encoder probably computes some interlingual representations. In fact, nothing constraints the model in reconstructing or predicting anything about the source sentences. If that is the case, why would a monolingual encoder help for the NMT task?

One hypothesis is that encoders have a role of self encoding the sentences but also a translation effect by producing interlingual representations. In this case, a monolingual encoder could be a better starting point and could be seen as a regularizer of the whole encoders. Another hypothesis is that the regularization of transformers models is not really effective and simply using BERT models achieve this effect.

7 Conclusion

In this paper, we have compared different ways to use BERT language models for machine translation. In particular, we have argued that the benefit of using pretrained representations should not only be assessed in terms of BLEU score for the in-domain data but also in terms of generalization to new domains and in terms of robustness.

Our experiments show that fine-tuning the encoder leads to comparable results as reusing the encoder as an additional embedding layers. However, the former has an advantage of keeping the same model size as in standard NMT settings, while the latter adds additional parameters to the NMT model which increases significantly the model size and might be critical in certain scenarios.

For MT practioners, using BERT has also several practical advantages beyond BLEU score. BERT can be trained for one source language and further reused for several translation pairs, thus providing a better initialization point for the models and allowing for better performance.

With respect to robustness tests, the conclusion are less clear. Even if pretrained BERT models obtained better performance on noisy test sets, it seems that they are not more robust than expected and that the potential of masked LM tasks is not fully exploited for machine translation. An interesting future work will be to assess the robustness of models from Song et al. (2019).

References

Alexei Baevski, Sergey Edunov, Yinhan Liu, Luke Zettlemoyer, and Michael Auli. 2019. Cloze-driven pretraining of self-attention networks. *CoRR*, abs/1903.07785.

Dzmitry Bahdanau, Kyunghyun Cho, and Yoshua Bengio. 2014. Neural machine translation by jointly learning to align and translate. *arXiv e-prints*, abs/1409.0473.

Yoshua Bengio, Réjean Ducharme, Pascal Vincent, and Christian Janvin. 2003. A neural probabilistic language model. *J. Mach. Learn. Res.*, 3:1137–1155.

Ondřej Bojar, Yvette Graham, and Amir Kamran. 2017. Results of the wmt17 metrics shared task. In *Proceedings of the Second Conference on Machine Translation, Volume 2: Shared Task Papers*, pages 489–513, Copenhagen, Denmark. Association for Computational Linguistics.

Ronan Collobert and Jason Weston. 2008. A unified architecture for natural language processing: Deep neural networks with multitask learning. In *Proceedings of the 25th International Conference on Machine Learning*, ICML '08, pages 160–167, New York, NY, USA. ACM.

Jacob Devlin, Ming-Wei Chang, Kenton Lee, and Kristina Toutanova. 2018. BERT: pre-training of deep bidirectional transformers for language understanding. *CoRR*, abs/1810.04805.

Shuoyang Ding, Adithya Renduchintala, and Kevin Duh. 2019. A call for prudent choice of subword merge operations. *CoRR*, abs/1905.10453.

Sergey Edunov, Alexei Baevski, and Michael Auli. 2019. Pre-trained language model representations for language generation. *CoRR*, abs/1903.09722.

Vladimir Karpukhin, Omer Levy, Jacob Eisenstein, and Marjan Ghazvininejad. 2019. Training on synthetic noise improves robustness to natural noise in machine translation. *CoRR*, abs/1902.01509.

Guillaume Lample and Alexis Conneau. 2019. Cross-lingual language model pretraining. *CoRR*, abs/1901.07291.

Jinhyuk Lee, Wonjin Yoon, Sungdong Kim, Donghyeon Kim, Sunkyu Kim, Chan Ho So, and Jaewoo Kang. 2019. Biobert: a pre-trained biomedical language representation model for biomedical text mining. *CoRR*, abs/1901.08746.

Omer Levy and Yoav Goldberg. 2014. Neural word embedding as implicit matrix factorization. In *Proceedings of the 27th International Conference on Neural Information Processing Systems - Volume 2*, NIPS'14, pages 2177–2185, Cambridge, MA, USA. MIT Press.

Qingsong Ma, Ondej Bojar, and Yvette Graham. 2018. Results of the wmt18 metrics shared task: Both characters and embeddings achieve good performance. In *Proceedings of the Third Conference on Machine Translation, Volume 2: Shared Task Papers*, pages 682–701, Belgium, Brussels. Association for Computational Linguistics.

Paul Michel, Xian Li, Graham Neubig, and Juan Miguel Pino. 2019. On evaluation of adversarial perturbations for sequence-to-sequence models. *CoRR*, abs/1903.06620.

Tomas Mikolov, Ilya Sutskever, Kai Chen, Greg Corrado, and Jeffrey Dean. 2013. Distributed representations of words and phrases and their compositionality. In *Proceedings of the 26th International Conference on Neural Information Processing Systems - Volume 2*, NIPS'13, pages 3111–3119, USA. Curran Associates Inc.

Jeffrey Pennington, Richard Socher, and Christopher Manning. 2014. Glove: Global vectors for word representation. In *Proceedings of the 2014 Conference on Empirical Methods in Natural Language Processing (EMNLP)*, pages 1532–1543, Doha, Qatar. Association for Computational Linguistics.

Matthew E. Peters, Mark Neumann, Mohit Iyyer, Matt Gardner, Christopher Clark, Kenton Lee, and Luke Zettlemoyer. 2018. Deep contextualized word representations. *CoRR*, abs/1802.05365.

Rico Sennrich, Barry Haddow, and Alexandra Birch. 2016a. Improving neural machine translation models with monolingual data. In *Proceedings of the 54th Annual Meeting of the Association for Computational Linguistics (Volume 1: Long Papers)*, pages 86–96, Berlin, Germany. Association for Computational Linguistics.

Rico Sennrich, Barry Haddow, and Alexandra Birch. 2016b. Neural machine translation of rare words with subword units. In *Proceedings of the 54th Annual Meeting of the Association for Computational Linguistics (Volume 1: Long Papers)*, pages 1715–1725, Berlin, Germany. Association for Computational Linguistics.

Kaitao Song, Xu Tan, Tao Qin, Jianfeng Lu, and Tie-Yan Liu. 2019. Mass: Masked sequence to sequence pre-training for language generation.

Ilya Sutskever, Oriol Vinyals, and Quoc V. Le. 2014. Sequence to sequence learning with neural networks. In *Proceedings of the 27th International Conference on Neural Information Processing Systems - Volume 2*, NIPS'14, pages 3104–3112, Cambridge, MA, USA. MIT Press.

Ian Tenney, Dipanjan Das, and Ellie Pavlick. 2019. Bert rediscovers the classical nlp pipeline.

Vaibhav, Sumeet Singh, Craig Stewart, and Graham Neubig. 2019. Improving robustness of machine translation with synthetic noise. *CoRR*, abs/1902.09508.

Ashish Vaswani, Noam Shazeer, Niki Parmar, Jakob Uszkoreit, Llion Jones, Aidan N Gomez, Ł ukasz Kaiser, and Illia Polosukhin. 2017. Attention is all you need. In I. Guyon, U. V. Luxburg, S. Bengio, H. Wallach, R. Fergus, S. Vishwanathan, and R. Garnett, editors, *Advances in Neural Information Processing Systems 30*, pages 5998–6008. Curran Associates, Inc.

Alex Wang, Amanpreet Singh, Julian Michael, Felix Hill, Omer Levy, and Samuel Bowman. 2018. GLUE: A multi-task benchmark and analysis platform for natural language understanding. In *Proceedings of the 2018 EMNLP Workshop BlackboxNLP: Analyzing and Interpreting Neural Networks for NLP*, pages 353–355, Brussels, Belgium. Association for Computational Linguistics.

Yonghui Wu, Mike Schuster, Zhifeng Chen, Quoc V. Le, Mohammad Norouzi, Wolfgang Macherey, Maxim Krikun, Yuan Cao, Qin Gao, Klaus Macherey, Jeff Klingner, Apurva Shah, Melvin Johnson, Xiaobing Liu, Lukasz Kaiser, Stephan Gouws, Yoshikiyo Kato, Taku Kudo, Hideto Kazawa, Keith Stevens, George Kurian, Nishant Patil, Wei Wang, Cliff Young, Jason Smith, Jason Riesa, Alex Rudnick, Oriol Vinyals, Greg Corrado, Macduff Hughes, and Jeffrey Dean. 2016. Google's neural machine translation system: Bridging the gap between human and machine translation. *CoRR*, abs/1609.08144.

Baosong Yang, Longyue Wang, Derek F. Wong, Lidia S. Chao, and Zhaopeng Tu. 2019. Convolutional self-attention networks. *CoRR*, abs/1904.03107.

On the Importance of the Kullback-Leibler Divergence Term in Variational Autoencoders for Text Generation

Victor Prokhorov♣, Ehsan Shareghi♣, Yingzhen Li♠
Mohammad Taher Pilehvar♣◇, Nigel Collier♣
♣ Language Technology Lab, DTAL, University of Cambridge
♠Microsoft Research Cambridge ,◇Tehran Institute for Advanced Studies
♣{vp361, es776, mp792, nhc30}@cam.ac.uk
♠Yingzhen.Li@microsoft.com

Abstract

Variational Autoencoders (VAEs) are known to suffer from learning uninformative latent representation of the input due to issues such as approximated posterior collapse, or entanglement of the latent space. We impose an explicit constraint on the Kullback-Leibler (KL) divergence term inside the VAE objective function. While the explicit constraint naturally avoids posterior collapse, we use it to further understand the significance of the KL term in controlling the information transmitted through the VAE channel. Within this framework, we explore different properties of the estimated posterior distribution, and highlight the trade-off between the amount of information encoded in a latent code during training, and the generative capacity of the model. [1]

1 Introduction

Despite the recent success of deep generative models such as Variational Autoencoders (VAEs) (Kingma and Welling, 2014) and Generative Adversarial Networks (GANs) (Goodfellow et al., 2014) in different areas of Machine Learning, they have failed to produce similar generative quality in NLP. In this paper we focus on VAEs and their mathematical underpinning to explain their behaviors in the context of text generation.

The vanilla VAE applied to text (Bowman et al., 2016) consists of an encoder (inference) and decoder (generative) networks: Given an input x, the encoder network parameterizes $q_\phi(z|x)$ and infers about latent continuous representations of x, while the decoder network parameterizes $p_\theta(x|z)$ and generates x from the continuous code z. The two models are jointly trained by maximizing the Evidence Lower Bound (ELBO), $\mathcal{L}(\theta, \phi; x, z)$:

$$\langle \log p_\theta(x|z) \rangle_{q_\phi(z|x)} - D_{KL}(q_\phi(z|x)\|p(z)) \quad (1)$$

where the first term is the reconstruction term, and the second term is the Kullback-Leibler (KL) divergence between the posterior distribution of latent variable z and its prior $p(z)$ (i.e., $\mathcal{N}(0, I)$). The KL term can be interpreted as a regularizer which prevents the inference network from copying x into z, and for the case of a Gaussian prior and posterior has a closed-form solution.

With powerful autoregressive decoders, such as LSTMs, the internal decoder's cells are likely to suffice for representing the sentence, leading to a sub-optimal solution where the decoder ignores the inferred latent code z. This allows the encoder to become independent of x, an issue known as posterior collapse ($q_\phi(z|x) \approx p(z)$) where the inference network produces uninformative latent variables. Several solutions have been proposed to address the posterior collapse issue: (i) Modifying the architecture of the model by weakening decoders (Bowman et al., 2016; Miao et al., 2015; Yang et al., 2017; Semeniuta et al., 2017), or introducing additional connections between the encoder and decoder to enforce the dependence between x and z (Zhao et al., 2017; Goyal et al., 2017; Dieng et al., 2018); (ii) Using more flexible or multimodal priors (Tomczak and Welling, 2017; Xu and Durrett, 2018); (iii) Alternating the training by focusing on the inference network in the earlier stages (He et al., 2019), or augmenting amortized optimization of VAEs with instance-based optimization of stochastic variational inference (Kim et al., 2018; Marino et al., 2018).

All of the aforementioned approaches impose one or more of the following limitations: restraining the choice of decoder, modifying the training algorithm, or requiring a substantial alternation of the objective function. As exceptions to these, δ-VAE (Razavi et al., 2019) and β-VAE (Higgins et al., 2017) aim to avoid the posterior collapse by explicitly controlling the regularizer term

---

[1] The code is available on https://github.com/VictorProkhorov/KL_Text_VAE

Proceedings of the 3rd Workshop on Neural Generation and Translation (WNGT 2019), pages 118–127
Hong Kong, China, November 4, 2019. ©2019 Association for Computational Linguistics
www.aclweb.org/anthology/D19-56%2d

in eqn. 1. While δ-VAE aims to impose a lower bound on the divergence term, β-VAE (§2.2) controls the impact of regularization via an additional hyperparameter (i.e., $\beta D_{KL}\big(q_\phi(z|x)||p(z)\big)$). A special case of β-VAE is annealing (Bowman et al., 2016), where β increases from 0 to 1 during training.

In this study, we propose to use an extension of β-VAE (Burgess et al., 2018) which permits us to explicitly control the magnitude of the KL term while avoiding the posterior collapse issue even in the existence of a powerful decoder. We use this framework to examine different properties of the estimated posterior and the generative behaviour of VAEs and discuss them in the context of text generation via various qualitative and quantitative experiments.

2 Kullback-Leibler Divergence in VAE

We take the encoder-decoder of VAEs as the sender-receiver in a communication network. Given an input message x, a sender generates a compressed encoding of x denoted by z, while the receiver aims to fully decode z back into x. The quality of this communication can be explained in terms of *rate* (R) which measures the compression level of z as compared to the original message x, and *distortion* (D) which quantities the overall performance of the communication in encoding a message at sender and successfully decoding it at the receiver. Additionally, the capacity of the encoder channel can be measured in terms of the amount of mutual information between x and z, denoted by $\mathrm{I}(x; z)$ (Cover and Thomas, 2012).

2.1 Reconstruction vs. KL

The reconstruction loss can naturally measure distortion ($D := -\langle \log p_\theta(x|z) \rangle$), while the KL term quantifies the amount of compression (rate; $R := D_{KL}[q_\phi(z|x)||p(z)]$) by measuring the divergence between a channel that transmits zero bit of information about x, denoted by $p(z)$, and the encoder channel of VAEs, $q_\phi(z|x)$. Alemi et al. (2018) introduced the $H - D \leq \mathrm{I}(x; z) \leq R$ bounds[2], where H is the empirical data entropy (a constant). These bounds on mutual information allow us to analyze the trade-off between the reconstruction and KL terms in eqn. (1). For instance,

since $\mathrm{I}(x; z)$ is non-negative (using Jensen's inequality), the posterior collapse can be explained as the situation where $\mathrm{I}(x; z) = 0$, where encoder transmits no information about x, causing $R = 0, D = H$. Increasing $\mathrm{I}(x; z)$ can be encouraged by increasing both bounds: increasing the upper-bound (KL term) can be seen as the mean to control the maximum capacity of the encoder channel, while reducing the distortion (reconstruction loss) will tighten the bound by pushing the lower bound to its limits ($H - D \to H$). A similar effect on the lower-bound can be encouraged by using stronger decoders which could potentially decrease the reconstruction loss. Hence, having a framework that permits the use of strong decoders while avoiding the posterior collapse is desirable. Similarly, channel capacity can be decreased.

2.2 Explicit KL Control via β-VAE

Given the above interpretation, we now turn to a slightly different formulation of ELBO based on β-VAE (Higgins et al., 2017). This allows control of the trade-off between the reconstruction and KL terms, as well as to set explicit KL value. While β-VAE offers regularizing the ELBO via an additional coefficient $\beta \in \mathbb{R}^+$, a simple extension (Burgess et al., 2018) of its objective function incorporates an additional hyperparameter C to explicitly control the magnitude of the KL term,

$$\big\langle \log p_\theta(x|z) \big\rangle_{q_\phi(z|x)} - \beta | D_{KL}\big(q_\phi(z|x)||p(z)\big) - C | \quad (2)$$

where $C \in \mathbb{R}^+$ and $|.|$ denotes the absolute value. While we could apply constraint optimization to impose the explicit constraint of KL=C, we found that the above objective function satisfies the constraint (§3). Alternatively, it has been shown (Pelsmaeker and Aziz, 2019) the similar effect could be reached by replacing the second term in eqn. 2 with $\max\big(C, D_{KL}\big(q_\phi(z|x)||p(z)\big)\big)$ at the risk of breaking the ELBO when KL$<C$ (Kingma et al., 2016).

3 Experiments

We conduct various experiments to illustrate the properties that are encouraged via different KL magnitudes. In particular, we revisit the interdependence between rate and distortion, and shed light on the impact of KL on the sharpness of the approximated posteriors. Then, through a set of qualitative and quantitative experiments for text generation, we demonstrate how certain genera-

---

[2]This is dependent on the choice of encoder. For other bounds on mutual information see Poole et al. (2018); Hoffman and Johnson (2016).

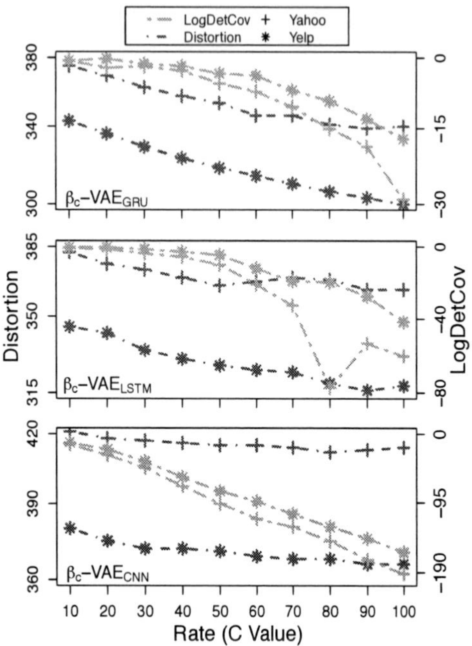

Figure 1: Rate-Distortion and *LogDetCov* for $C = \{10, 20, ..., 100\}$ on Yahoo and Yelp corpora.

tive behaviours could be imposed on VAEs via a range of maximum channel capacities. Finally, we run some experiments to find if any form of syntactic information is encoded in the latent space. For all experiments, we use the objective function of eqn. 2 with $\beta = 1$. We do not use larger βs because the constraint KL = C is always satisfied. [3]

Corpora We use 5 different corpora covering different domains and size through this section: Yelp and Yahoo Yang et al. (2017) both have ($100k$,$10k$,$10k$) sentences in (train, dev, test) sets and $20k$ words in vocabulary, Children's Book Test (CBT; Weston et al. (2016)) has ($192k$,$10k$,$12k$) sentences and $12k$ vocab, Wikipedia (WIKI; Marvin and Linzen (2018)) has ($2m$,$270k$,$270k$) sentences and $20k$ vocab, and WebText (Radford et al., 2019) has ($1m$,$23k$,$24k$) sentences and $22k$ vocab. [4]

Models We examine three VAE architectures, covering a range of decoding strengths to examine if the objective function in eqn. 2 is immune to posterior collapse regardless of the choice of

encoder-decoder architectures: β_C-VAE$_{\text{LSTM}}$ with (LSTM encoder, LSTM decoder), β_C-VAE$_{\text{GRU}}$ with (GRU encoder, GRU decoder) (Cho et al., 2014), and β_C-VAE$_{\text{CNN}}$ with (LSTM encoder, CNN decoder) (Dauphin et al., 2016). The dimension of word embeddings is 256 and the dimension of the latent variable is 64. The encoder and the decoder, for both VAE$_{\text{LSTM}}$ and VAE$_{\text{GRU}}$, have hidden size of 512 dimensions. VAE$_{\text{CNN}}$ has exactly the same encoder as VAE$_{\text{LSTM}}$, while the decoder follows similar architecture to GLU with a bottleneck structure (with two blocks) (Dauphin et al., 2016) and has 512 channels externally and 128 internally for the convolutions with the filter size of 20. All models were trained for 10 epochs and optimised the objective function (eqn. 2) with Adam (Kingma and Ba, 2015) with following learning rates: $10^{-5} \times 85$ for VAE$_{\text{GRU}}$ and VAE$_{\text{LSTM}}$, and 10^{-4} for VAE$_{\text{CNN}}$. To couple the encoder with the decoder we concatenate the latent variable to word embeddings at each time step without initialisation of hidden state.

3.1 Rate and Distortion

To analyse the dependence between the values of explicit rate (C) and distortion, we trained our models with different values of C, ranging from 10 to 100. Figure 1 reports the results for β_C-VAE$_{\text{GRU}}$, β_C-VAE$_{\text{LSTM}}$, and β_C-VAE$_{\text{CNN}}$ models on Yahoo and Yelp corpora. In all our experiments we found that $C-1 \leq KL \leq C+1$, demonstrating that the objective function effectively imposed the desired constraint on KL term. Hence, setting any $C > 0$ can in practice avoid the collapse issue.

The general trend is that by increasing the value of C one can get a better reconstruction (lower distortion) while the amount of gain varies depending on the VAE's architecture and corpus. [5] Additionally, we measured rate and distortion on CBT, WIKI, and WebText corpora using β_C-VAE$_{\text{LSTM}}$ and observed the same trend with the increase of C, see Table 1. This observation is consistent with the bound on I$(x; z)$ we discussed earlier (§2.1) such that with an increase of KL we increase an upper bound on I$(x; z)$ which in turn allows to have smaller values of reconstruction loss. Additionally, as reported in Table 1, encouraging higher rates (via larger C) encourages more active units

---

[3] β can be seen as a Lagrange multiplier and any β value that allows for constraint satisfaction ($R = C$) is fine.

[4] Corpora and preprocessing scripts will be released.

[5] We attribute the difference in performance across our models to the non-optimal selection of training hyperparameters, and corpus specific factors such as sentence length.

	C	D	R	LogDetCov	$\|\mu\|_2^2$	AU	Bucket 1		Bucket 2		Bucket 3		All	
							BL2/RG2	BL4/RG4	BL2/RG2	BL4/RG4	BL2/RG2	BL4/RG4	BL2/RG2	BL4/RG4
CBT	3	62	3	-0.39	0.05	8	7.49/2.63	1.28/0.13	8.95/3.48	1.49/0.10	10.37/4.81	1.68/0.12	9.46/3.54	1.57/0.12
	15	53	15	-0.38	0.05	29	21.68/12.92	8.99/3.07	14.82/7.01	4.25/0.81	14.68/6.73	3.31/0.36	15.87/8.86	4.60/1.43
	100	32	99	-43.82	1.27	64	50.00/43.23	38.74/30.16	26.78/18.49	15.99/9.23	19.24/9.90	7.65/2.24	27.65/24.33	16.09/14.24
WIKI	3	81	3	-0.35	0.00	5	4.61/3.64	1.47/1.03	5.93/2.67	1.09/0.19	7.39/3.00	1.17/0.12	6.78/3.08	1.33/0.42
	15	70	15	-0.57	0.01	12	13.73/8.46	7.12/3.86	10.07/4.45	3.93/1.32	9.93/3.27	1.95/0.29	10.08/5.35	3.42/1.79
	100	17	100	-4.97	0.15	64	65.67/63.17	60.02/55.92	37.25/32.76	30.88/26.33	18.73/11.41	11.22/6.20	31.84/35.37	24.17/29.08
WebText	3	77	3	-0.21	0.01	4	9.51/5.27	2.96/1.14	9.59/4.59	1.68/0.22	12.59/6.37	3.96/1.01	11.88/5.54	3.35/0.70
	15	67	15	-0.51	0.01	16	21.69/12.41	9.86/3.69	15.48/7.44	5.35/1.51	15.63/7.29	5.59/1.59	15.84/7.85	5.69/1.76
	100	22	100	-7.85	0.41	64	84.85/82.48	81.89/78.79	61.65/58.33	56.35/53.05	35.07/27.33	27.31/20.99	45.84/45.30	38.71/39.66

Table 1: β_C-VAE$_\text{LSTM}$ performance with $C = \{3, 15, 100\}$ on the test sets of CBT, WIKI, and WebText. Each bucket groups sentences of certain length. Bucket 1: length ≤ 10; Bucket 2: $10 <$ length ≤ 20; Bucket 3: $20 <$ length ≤ 30, and **All** contains all sentences. BL2/RG2 denotes BLEU-2/ROUGE-2, BL4/RG4 denotes BLEU-2/ROUGE-2 BLEU-4/ROUGE-4, AU denotes active units, D denotes distortion, and R denotes rate.

(AU; Burda et al. (2015)) in the latent code z. [6]

As an additional verification, we also group the test sentences into buckets based on their length and report BLEU-2/4 and ROUGE-2/4 metrics to measure the quality of reconstruction step in Table 1. As expected, we observe that increasing rate has a consistently positive impact on improving BLEU and ROUGE scores.

3.2 Aggregated Posterior

To understand how the approximated posteriors are being affected by the magnitude of the KL, we adopted an approach from Zhao et al. (2017) and looked at the divergence between the aggregated posterior, $q_\phi(z) = \sum_{x \sim q(x)} q_\phi(z|x)$, and prior $p(z)$. Since during generation we generate samples from the prior, ideally we would like the aggregated posterior to be as close as possible to the prior.

We obtained unbiased samples of z first by sampling an x from data and then $z \sim q_\phi(z|x)$, and measured the log determinant of covariance of the samples $(\log \det(\text{Cov}[q_\phi(z)]))$. As reported in Figure 1, we observed that $\log \det(\text{Cov}[q_\phi(z)])$ degrades as C grows, indicating sharper approximate posteriors. We then consider the difference of $p(z)$ and $q(z)$ in their means and variances, by computing the KL divergence from the moment-matching Gaussian fit of $q(z)$ to $p(z)$: This returns smaller values for $\beta_{C=5}$-VAE$_\text{GRU}$ (Yelp: 0, Yahoo: 0), and larger values for $\beta_{C=100}$-VAE$_\text{GRU}$ (Yelp: 8, Yahoo: 5), which illustrates that the overlap between $q_\phi(z)$ and $p(z)$ shrinks further as C grows.

The above observation is better pronounced in Table 1, where we also report the mean $(\|\mu\|_2^2)$ of unbiased samples of z, highlighting the divergence from the mean of the prior distribution as rate increases. Therefore, for the case of lower C, the latent variables observed during training are closer to the generated sample from the prior which makes the decoder more suitable for generation purpose. We will examine this hypothesis in the following section.

3.3 Text Generation

To empirically examine how channel capacity translates into generative capacity of the model, we experimented with the β_C-VAE$_\text{LSTM}$ models from Table 1. To generate a novel sentence, after a model was trained, a latent variable z is sampled from the prior distribution and then transformed into a sequence of words by the decoder $p(x|z)$.

During decoding for generation we try three decoding schemes: (i) Greedy: which selects the most probable word at each step, (ii) Top-k (Fan et al., 2018): which at each step samples from the K most probable words, and (iii) Nucleus Sampling (NS) (Holtzman et al., 2019): which at each step samples from a flexible subset of most probable words chosen based on their cumulative mass (set by a threshold p, where $p = 1$ means sampling from the full distribution). While similar to Top-k, the benefit of NS scheme is that the vocabulary size at each time step of decoding varies, a property that encourages diversity and avoids degenerate text patterns of greedy or beam search decoding (Holtzman et al., 2019). We experiment with NS ($p = \{0.5, 0.9\}$) and Top-k ($k = \{5, 15\}$).

---

[6]To see if the conclusions hold with different number of parameters, we doubled the number of parameters in β_C-VAE$_\text{GRU}$ and β_C-VAE$_\text{LSTM}$ and observed the similar pattern with a slight change in performance.

	Greedy	Top-15	NS(p=0.9)
C=3	1: oh, i m not going to be a good man. 2: oh, it s a good thing, said the story girl. 3: oh, how can you do it, dear? 4: oh, how can you do it, dear? 5: oh, how can you do it, miss? 6: and what is the matter with you? 7: and what is the matter with you?	1: come - look on my mind, said he. 2: how could i tell you, that it s a great deal? 3: said i. my sister, what a fool! 4: and how was the way, you? 5: said the other little breezes, but i do n t . 6: and where s the news of the world? 7: ⟨unk⟩ of ⟨unk⟩, said i. ay, ⟨unk⟩!	1: and what is one of those trees creatures? 2: here s a nice heart among those waters! 3: good-bye, said reddy fox, hardly frightened was out of his life. 4: now, for a neighbor, who knows him. 5: oh, prince ivan, dear me! 6: cried her mother, who is hidden or power. 7: but this was his plight, and the smith knew.
C=15	1: old mother west wind and her eyes were in the same place, but she had never seen her. 2: old mother west wind and his wife had gone and went to bed to the palace. 3: little joe otter and there were a ⟨unk⟩ of them to be seen. 4: little joe otter s eyes are just as big as her. 5: a few minutes did not answer the ⟨unk⟩. 6: a little while they went on. 7: a little while they went.	1: eric found out this little while, but there in which the old man did not see it so. 2: old mother west wind and his wife gave her to take a great ⟨unk⟩, she said. 3: little joe otter got back to school all the ⟨unk⟩ together. 4: little joyce s eyes grew well at once, there. 5: pretty a woman, but there had vanished. 6: from the third day, she went. 7: three months were as usual.	1: aunt tommy took a sudden notion of relief and yellow-dog between him sharply until he tried to go to. 2: his lord marquis of laughter expressed that soft hope and miss cornelia was not comforted. 3: meanwhile the hounds were both around and then by a thing was not yet. 4: in a tone, he began to enter after dinner. 5: once a word became, just got his way. 6: for a few moments, began to find. 7: meantime the thrushes were ⟨unk⟩.
C=100	1: it will it, all her ⟨unk⟩, not even her with her? 2: it will get him to mrs. matilda and nothing to eat her long clothes. 3: the thing she put to his love, when it were ⟨unk⟩ and too. 4: one day, to the green forest now and a long time ago, sighed. 5: one and it became clear of him on that direction by the night ago. 6: every word of his horse was and the rest as the others were ready for him. 7: a time and was half the ⟨unk⟩ as before the first ⟨unk⟩ things were ready as.	1: it will her you, at last, bad and never in her eyes. 2: other time, i went into a moment – she went in home and. 3: going quite well to his mother, and remember it the night in night! 4: one and it rained for his feet, for she was their eyes like ever. 5: the thing knew the tracks of ⟨unk⟩ and he never got an ⟨unk⟩ before him. 6: of course he heard a sound of her as much over the ⟨unk⟩ that night can. 7: every, who had an interest in that till his legs got splendid tongue than himself.	1: it s; they liked the red, but i kept her and growing. 2: it ⟨unk⟩ not to her, in school, and never his bitter now. 3: was it now of the beginning, and dr. hamilton was her away and. 4: of course she flew for a long distance; and they came a longing now. 5: one door what made the pain called for her first ear for losing up. 6: one and he got by looking quite like her part till the marriage know ended. 7: without the thought that danced in the ground which made these delicate child s teeth so.

Table 2: Homotopy (CBT corpus) - The three blocks correspond to $C = \{3, 15, 100\}$ values used for training β_C-VAE$_{\text{LSTM}}$. The columns correspond to the three decoding schemes: greedy, top-k (with k=15), and the nucleus sampling (NS; with p=0.9). Initial two latent variables z were sampled from a the prior distribution i.e. $z \sim p(z)$ and the other five latent variables were obtained by interpolation. The sequences that highlighted in gray are the one that decoded into the same sentences condition on different latent variable. **Note**: Even though the learned latent representation should be quite different for different models (trained with different C) in order to be consistent all the generated sequences presented in the table were decoded from the same seven latent variables.

3.3.1 Qualitative Analysis

We follow the settings of homotopy experiment (Bowman et al., 2016) where first a set of latent variables was obtained by performing a linear interpolation between $z_1 \sim p(z)$ and $z_2 \sim p(z)$. Then each z in the set was converted into a sequence of words by the decoder $p(x|z)$. Besides the initial motivation of Bowman et al. (2016) to examine how neighbouring latent codes look like, our additional incentive is to analyse how sensitive the decoder is to small variations in the latent variable when trained with different channel capacities, $C = \{3, 15, 100\}$.

Table 2 shows the generated sentences via different decoding schemes for each channel capacity. For space reason, we only report the generated sentences for greedy, Top-k = 15, and NS $p = 0.9$. To make the generated sequences comparable across different decoding schemes or C values, we use the same samples of z for decoding.

Sensitivity of Decoder To examine the sensitivity[7] of the decoder to variations of the latent variable, we consider the sentences generate with the greedy decoding scheme (the first column in Table 2). The other two schemes are not suitable for this analysis as they include sampling proce-

---

[7]Note: we vary z in one (randomly selected) direction (interpolating between z_1 and z_2). Alternatively, the sensitivity analysis can be done by varying z along the gradient direction of $\log p(x|z)$.

	C		$\lvert V\rvert$	Greedy FCE	%unk	len.	SB	$\lvert V\rvert$	NS(p=0.9) FCE	%unk	len.	SB
CBT	3		335	86.6(0.4)	9.7	15.3	4.2	9.8k	70.4(0.0)	2.1	15.6	0.0
	15		335	52.3(0.3)	12.7	15.2	0.3	9.8k	70.7(0.2)	2.4	15.4	0.0
	100		335	47.3(0.1)	21.3	17.5	0.0	9.8k	75.1(0.1)	2.2	17.6	0.0
Test			328	-	30.7	15.3	-	6.1k	-	3.6	15.3	-
WIKI	3		1.5k	134.6(0.8)	27.3	19.9	7.6	20k	89.8(0.1)	5.8	19.4	0.0
	15		1.5k	69.2(0.1)	18.9	19.8	0.2	20k	89.3(0.1)	5.6	19.8	0.0
	100		1.5k	58.9(0.1)	34.8	20.7	0.0	20k	96.5(0.1)	4.5	20.7	0.0
Test			1.5k	-	32.7	19.6	-	20k	-	5.2	19.6	-
WebText	3		2.3k	115.8(0.7)	18.8	17.5	2.0	21.9k	86.4(0.1)	7.1	15.6	0.0
	15		2.3k	74.4(0.1)	15.5	15.8	0.1	21.9k	85.8(0.1)	6.9	15.9	0.0
	100		2.3k	62.5(0.1)	27.3	18.0	0.0	21.9k	93.7(0.1)	4.8	18.0	0.0
Test			2.2k	-	30.1	16.1	-	17.1k	-	6.8	16.1	-

Table 3: Forward Cross Entropy (FCE). Columns represent stats for Greedy and NS decoding schemes for β_C-VAE$_{\text{LSTM}}$ models trained with $C = \{3, 15, 100\}$ on CBT, WIKI or WebText. Each entry in the table is a mean of negative log likelihood of an LM. The values in the brackets are the standard deviations. $\lvert V\rvert$ is the vocabulary size; Test stands for test set; %unk is the percentage of ⟨unk⟩ symbols in a corpora; len. is the average length of a sentence in the generated corpus; SB is the self-BLEU:4 score calculated on the 10K sentences in the generated corpus.

dure. This means that if we decode the same latent variable twice we will get two different sentences. We observed that with lower channel capacity ($C = 3$) the decoder tends to generate identical sentences for the interpolated latent variables (we highlight these sentences in gray), exhibiting decoder's lower sensitivity to z's variations. However, with the increase of channel capacity ($C = 15, 100$) the decoder becomes more sensitive. This observation is further supported by the increasing pattern of active units in Table 1: Given that AU increases with increase of C one would expect that activation pattern of a latent variable becomes more complex as it comprises more information. Therefore small change in the pattern would have a greater effect on the decoder.

Coherence of Sequences We observe that the model trained with large values of C compromises sequences' coherence during the sampling. This is especially evident when we compare $C = 3$ with $C = 100$. Analysis of Top-15 and NS (p=0.9) generated samples reveals that the lack of coherence is not due to the greedy decoding scheme per se, and can be attributed to the model in general. To understand this behavior further, we need two additional results from Table 1: LogDetCov and $\lVert\mu\rVert_2^2$. One can notice that as C increases LogDetCov decreases and $\lVert\mu\rVert_2^2$ increases. This indicates that the aggregated posterior becomes further apart from the prior, hence the latent codes seen during

the training diverge more from the codes sampled from the prior during generation. We speculate this contributes to the coherence of the generated samples, as the decoder is not equipped to decode prior samples properly at higher Cs.

3.3.2 Quantitative Analysis

Quantitative analysis of generated text without gold reference sequences (e.g. in Machine Translation or Summarization) has been a long-standing challenge. Recently, there have been efforts towards this direction, with proposal such as self-BLEU (Zhu et al.), forward cross entropy (Cífka et al., 2018, FCE) and Fréchet InferSent Distance (Cífka et al., 2018, FID). We opted for FCE as a complementary metric to our qualitative analysis. To calculate FCE, first a collection of synthetic sentences are generated by sampling $z \sim p(z)$ and decoding the samples into sentences. The synthetic sequences are then used to train a language model (an LSTM with the parametrisation of our decoder). The FCE score is estimated by reporting the negative log likelihood (NLL) of the trained LM on the set of human generated sentences.

We generated synthetic corpora using trained models from Table 1 with different C and decoding schemes and using the same exact z samples for all corpora. Since the generated corpora using different C values would have different coverage of words in the test set (i.e., Out-of-Vocabulary ratios), we used a fixed vocabulary to minimize the effect of different vocabularies in our analysis. Our dictionary contains words that are common in all of the three corpora, while the rest of the words that don't exist in this dictionary are replaced with $\langle unk \rangle$ symbol. Similarly, we used this fixed dictionary to preprocess the test sets. Also, to reduce bias to a particular set of sampled z's we measure the FCE score three times, each time we sampled a new training corpus from a β_C-VAE$_{\text{LSTM}}$ decoder and trained an LM from scratch. In Table 3 we report the average FCE (NLL) for the generated corpora.

In the qualitative analysis we observed that the text generated by the β_C-VAE$_{\text{LSTM}}$ trained with large values of $C = 100$ exhibits lower quality (i.e., in terms of coherence). This observation is supported by the FCE score of NS(p=0.9) decoding scheme (3), since the performance drops when the LM is trained on the corpus generated with $C = 100$. The generated corpora with $C = 3$ and $C = 15$ achieve similar FCE score. However, these patterns are reversed for Greedy decoding scheme[8], where the general tendency of FCE scores suggests that for larger values of C the β_C-VAE$_{\text{LSTM}}$ seems to generate text which better approximates the natural sentences in the test set. To understand this further, we report additional statistics in Table 3: percentage of $\langle unk \rangle$ symbols, self-BLEU and average sentence length in the corpus.

The average sentence length, in the generated corpora is very similar for both decoding schemes, removing the possibility that the pathological pattern on FCE scores was caused by difference in sentence length. However, we observe that for Greedy decoding more than 30% of the test set consists of $\langle unk \rangle$. Intuitively, seeing more evidence of this symbol during training would improve our estimate for the $\langle unk \rangle$. As reported in the table, the %unk increases on almost all corpora as C grows, which is then translated into getting a better FCE score at test. Therefore, we believe that FCE at high %unk is not a reliable quantitative metric to assess the quality of the generated syntactic corpora. Furthermore, for Greedy decoding, self-BLEU decreases when C increases. This suggests that generated sentences for higher value of C are more diverse. Hence, the LM trained on more diverse corpora can generalise better, which in turn affects the FCE.

In contrast, the effect the $\langle unk \rangle$ symbol has on the corpora generated with the NS(p=0.9) decoding scheme is minimal for two reasons: First, the vocabulary size for the generated corpora, for all values of C is close to the original corpus (the corpus we used to train the β_C-VAE$_{\text{LSTM}}$). Second, the vocabularies of the corpora generated with three values of C is very close to each other. As a result, minimum replacement of the words with the $\langle unk \rangle$ symbol is required, making the experiment to be more reflective of the quality of the generated text. Similarly, self-BLEU for the NS(p=0.9) is the same for all values of C. This suggests that the diversity of sentences has minimal, if any, effect on the FCE.

3.4 Syntactic Test

In this section, we explore if any form of syntactic information is captured by the encoder and represented in the latent codes despite the lack of any explicit syntactic signal during the training of the β_C-VAE$_{\text{LSTM}}$. To train the models we used the same WIKI data set as in Marvin and Linzen (2018), but we filtered out all the sentences that are longer than 50 space-separated tokens.[9]

We use the data set of Marvin and Linzen (2018) which consists of pairs of grammatical and ungrammatical sentences to test various syntactic phenomenon. For example, a pair in subject-verb agreement category would be: (*The author laughs, The author laugh*). We encode both the grammatical and ungrammatical sentences into the latent codes z^+ and z^-, respectively. Then we condition the decoder on the z^+ and try to determine whether the decoder assigns higher probability to the grammatical sentence (denoted by x^+): $p(x^-|z^+) < p(x^+|z^+)$ (denoted by p_1 in Table 4). We repeat the same experiment but this time try to determine whether the decoder, when conditioned on the ungrammatical code (z^-), still prefers to assign higher probability to the grammatical sentence: $p(x^-|z^-) < p(x^+|z^-)$ (denoted by p_2 in Table 4). Table 4 shows the p_1 and p_2 for the β_C-VAE$_{\text{LSTM}}$ model trained with $C = \{3, 100\}$. Both the p_1 and p_2 are similar to the accuracy and correspond to how many times a grammatical sentence was assigned a higher probability.

As reported for C=3, p_1 and p_2 match in almost all cases. This is to some degree expected

---

⁸For the other decoding schemes: Top-{5,15} and NS(p=0.5) the pattern is the same as for the Greedy. For space reason we only report the FCE for Greedy.

⁹We applied the filtering to decrease the training time of our models.

	$C = 3$		$C = 100$			
Syntactic Categories	p_1	p_2	p_1	p_2	$\bar{p}_1$	$\bar{p}_2$
SUBJECT-VERB AGREEMENT						
Simple	0.81	0.81	1.0	0.23	0.68	0.47
In a sentential complement	0.79	0.79	0.98	0.14	0.69	0.48
Short VP coordination	0.74	0.73	0.96	0.08	0.78	0.43
Long VP coordination	0.61	0.61	0.97	0.06	0.55	0.47
Across a prepositional phrase	0.78	0.78	0.97	0.07	0.62	0.49
Across a subject relative clause	0.77	0.77	0.93	0.08	0.68	0.41
Across an object relative clause	0.69	0.69	0.92	0.11	0.61	0.45
Across an object relative (no that)	0.58	0.58	0.94	0.09	0.61	0.44
In an object relative clause	0.74	0.74	0.99	0.01	0.60	0.45
In an object relative (no that)	0.74	0.74	0.99	0.02	0.61	0.46
REFLEXIVE ANAPHORA						
Simple	0.79	0.78	0.99	0.07	0.70	0.39
In a sentential complement	0.74	0.73	1.00	0.00	0.70	0.38
Across a relative clause	0.63	0.62	0.99	0.03	0.69	0.35
NEGATIVE POLARITY ITEMS						
Simple	0.42	0.33	1.00	0.00	0.76	0.20
Across a relative clause	0.37	0.36	1.00	0.00	0.98	0.02

Table 4: p_1: $p(x^-|z^+) < p(x^+|z^+)$ and p_2: $p(x^-|z^-) < p(x^+|z^-)$; $\bar{p}_1$: $p(x^-|\bar{z}^+) < p(x^+|\bar{z}^+)$ and $\bar{p}_2$: $p(x^-|\bar{z}^-) < p(x^+|\bar{z}^-)$; $\beta_{C=3}$-VAE$_{\text{LSTM}}$ (D:103, R:3); $\beta_{C=100}$-VAE$_{\text{LSTM}}$ (D:39, R:101).

since lower channel capacity encourages a more dominating decoder which in our case was trained on grammatical sentences from the WIKI. On the other hand, this illustrates that despite avoiding the KL-collapse issue, the dependence of the decoder on the latent code is so negligible that the decoder hardly distinguishes the grammatical and ungrammatical inputs. This changes for $C = 100$, as in almost all the cases the decoder becomes strongly dependent on the latent code and can differentiate between what it has seen as input and the closely similar sentence it hasn't received as the input: The decoder assigns larger probability to the ungrammatical sentence when conditioned on the z^- and, similarly, larger probability to the grammatical sentence when conditioned on the z^+.

However, the above observations neither confirm nor reject existence of grammar signal in the latent codes. We run a second set of experiments where we aim to discard sentence specific information from the latent codes by averaging the codes[10] inside each syntactic category. The averaged codes are denoted by $\bar{z}^+$ and $\bar{z}^-$, and the corresponding accuracies are reported by $\bar{p}_1$ and $\bar{p}_2$ in Table 4. Our hypothesis is that the only invariant factor during averaging the codes inside a category is the grammatical property of its corresponding sentences.

As expected, due to the weak dependence of decoder on latent code, the performance of the model under $C = 3$ is almost identical (not included for space limits) when comparing p_1 vs. $\bar{p}_1$, and p_2 vs. $\bar{p}_2$. However, for $C = 100$ the performance of the model deteriorates. While we leave further exploration of this behavior to our future work, we speculate this could be an indication of two things: the increase of complexity in the latent code which encourages a higher variance around the mean, or the absence of syntactic signal in the latent codes.

4 Discussion and Conclusion

In this paper we analysed the interdependence of the KL term in Evidence Lower Bound (ELBO) and the properties of the approximated posterior for text generation. To perform the analysis we used an information theoretic framework based on a variant of β-VAE objective, which permits explicit control of the KL term, and treats KL as a mechanism to control the amount of information transmitted between the encoder and decoder.

The immediate impact of the explicit constraint is avoiding the collapse issue ($D_{KL} = 0$) by setting a non-zero positive constraint ($C \geq 0$) on the KL term ($|D_{KL}(q_\phi(z|x)||p(z)) - C|$). We experimented with a range of constraints (C) on the KL term and various powerful and weak decoder architectures (LSTM, GRU, and CNN), and empiri-

---

[10]Each syntactic category is further divided into sub-categories, for instance *simple subject-verb agreement* We average z's within each sub-categories.

cally confirmed that in all cases the constraint was satisfied.

We showed that the higher value of KL encourages not only divergence from the prior distribution, but also a sharper and more concentrated approximated posteriors. It encourages the decoder to be more sensitive to the variations on the latent code, and makes the model with higher KL less suitable for generation as the latent variables observed during training are farther away from the prior samples used during generation. To analyse its impact on generation we conducted a set of qualitative and quantitative experiments.

In the qualitative analysis we showed that small and large values of KL term impose different properties on the generated text: the decoder trained under smaller KL term tends to generate repetitive but mainly plausible sentences, while for larger KL the generated sentences were diverse but incoherent. This behaviour was observed across three different decoding schemes and complemented by a quantitative analysis where we measured the performance of an LSTM LM trained on different VAE-generated synthetic corpora via different KL magnitudes, and tested on human generated sentences.

Finally, in an attempt to understand the ability of the latent code in VAEs to represent some form of syntactic information, we tested the ability of the model to distinguish between grammatical and ungrammatical sentences. We verified that at lower (and still non-zero) KL the decoder tends to pay less attention to the latent code, but our findings regarding the presence of a syntactic signal in the latent code were inconclusive. We leave it as a possible avenue to explore in our future work. Also, we plan to develop practical algorithms for the automatic selection of the C's value, and verify our findings under multi-modal priors and complex posteriors.

Acknowledgments

The authors would like to thank the anonymous reviewers for their helpful suggestions. This research was supported by an EPSRC Experienced Researcher Fellowship (N. Collier: EP/M005089/1), an MRC grant (M.T. Pilehvar: MR/M025160/1) and E. Shareghi is supported by the ERC Consolidator Grant LEXICAL (648909). We gratefully acknowledge the donation of a GPU from the NVIDIA.

References

Alexander Alemi, Ben Poole, Ian Fischer, Joshua Dillon, Rif A. Saurous, and Kevin Murphy. 2018. Fixing a broken ELBO. In *ICML*.

Samuel R. Bowman, Luke Vilnis, Oriol Vinyals, Andrew M. Dai, Rafal Józefowicz, and Samy Bengio. 2016. Generating sentences from a continuous space. In *CoNLL*.

Yuri Burda, Roger B. Grosse, and Ruslan Salakhutdinov. 2015. Importance weighted autoencoders. *CoRR*, abs/1509.00519.

Christopher P. Burgess, Irina Higgins, Arka Pal, Loïc Matthey, Nick Watters, Guillaume Desjardins, and Alexander Lerchner. 2018. Understanding disentangling in β-vae. *CoRR*, abs/1804.03599.

Kyunghyun Cho, Bart van Merrienboer, Çaglar Gülçehre, Fethi Bougares, Holger Schwenk, and Yoshua Bengio. 2014. Learning phrase representations using RNN encoder-decoder for statistical machine translation. *CoRR*, abs/1406.1078.

Ondrej Cífka, Aliaksei Severyn, Enrique Alfonseca, and Katja Filippova. 2018. Eval all, trust a few, do wrong to none: Comparing sentence generation models. *CoRR*, abs/1804.07972.

Thomas M Cover and Joy A Thomas. 2012. *Elements of information theory*. John Wiley & Sons.

Yann N. Dauphin, Angela Fan, Michael Auli, and David Grangier. 2016. Language modeling with gated convolutional networks. *CoRR*, abs/1612.08083.

Adji B. Dieng, Yoon Kim, Alexander M. Rush, and David M. Blei. 2018. Avoiding latent variable collapse with generative skip models. *CoRR*, abs/1807.04863.

Angela Fan, Mike Lewis, and Yann N. Dauphin. 2018. Hierarchical neural story generation. *CoRR*, abs/1805.04833.

Ian J. Goodfellow, Jean Pouget-Abadie, Mehdi Mirza, Bing Xu, David Warde-Farley, Sherjil Ozair, Aaron C. Courville, and Yoshua Bengio. 2014. Generative adversarial nets. In *NIPS*.

Anirudh Goyal, Alessandro Sordoni, Marc-Alexandre Côté, Nan Rosemary Ke, and Yoshua Bengio. 2017. Z-forcing: Training stochastic recurrent networks. In *NIPS*.

Junxian He, Daniel Spokoyny, Graham Neubig, and Taylor Berg-Kirkpatrick. 2019. Lagging inference networks and posterior collapse in variational autoencoders. In *ICLR*.

Irina Higgins, Loïc Matthey, Arka Pal, Christopher Burgess, Xavier Glorot, Matthew Botvinick, Shakir Mohamed, and Alexander Lerchner. 2017. beta-vae: Learning basic visual concepts with a constrained variational framework. In *ICLR*.

Matthew D. Hoffman and Matthew J. Johnson. 2016. ELBO surgery: yet another way to carve up the variational evidence lower bound. *NIPS: Workshop on Advances in Approximate Bayesian Inference*.

Ari Holtzman, Jan Buys, Maxwell Forbes, and Yejin Choi. 2019. The curious case of neural text degeneration. *CoRR*, abs/1904.09751.

Yoon Kim, Sam Wiseman, Andrew C. Miller, David Sontag, and Alexander M. Rush. 2018. Semi-amortized variational autoencoders. In *ICML*.

Diederik P. Kingma and Jimmy Ba. 2015. Adam: A method for stochastic optimization.

Diederik P. Kingma, Tim Salimans, and Max Welling. 2016. Improving variational inference with inverse autoregressive flow. *CoRR*, abs/1606.04934.

Diederik P. Kingma and Max Welling. 2014. Auto-encoding variational bayes. In *ICLR*.

Joseph Marino, Yisong Yue, and Stephan Mandt. 2018. Iterative amortized inference. In *ICML*.

Rebecca Marvin and Tal Linzen. 2018. Targeted syntactic evaluation of language models. *CoRR*, abs/1808.09031.

Yishu Miao, Lei Yu, and Phil Blunsom. 2015. Neural variational inference for text processing. *CoRR*, abs/1511.06038.

Tom Pelsmaeker and Wilker Aziz. 2019. Effective estimation of deep generative language models. *CoRR*, abs/1904.08194.

Ben Poole, Sherjil Ozair, Aäron van den Oord, Alexander A Alemi, and George Tucker. 2018. On variational lower bounds of mutual information. In *NeurIPS Workshop on Bayesian Deep Learning*.

Alec Radford, Jeff Wu, Rewon Child, David Luan, Dario Amodei, and Ilya Sutskever. 2019. Language models are unsupervised multitask learners. *OpenAI Blog*.

Ali Razavi, Aaron van den Oord, Ben Poole, and Oriol Vinyals. 2019. Preventing posterior collapse with delta-VAEs. In *ICLR*.

Stanislau Semeniuta, Aliaksei Severyn, and Erhardt Barth. 2017. A hybrid convolutional variational autoencoder for text generation. In *EMNLP*.

Jakub M. Tomczak and Max Welling. 2017. VAE with a vampprior. *CoRR*, abs/1705.07120.

Jason Weston, Antoine Bordes, Sumit Chopra, and Tomas Mikolov. 2016. Towards ai-complete question answering: A set of prerequisite toy tasks. In *ICLR*.

Jiacheng Xu and Greg Durrett. 2018. Spherical latent spaces for stable variational autoencoders. *CoRR*, abs/1808.10805.

Zichao Yang, Zhiting Hu, Ruslan Salakhutdinov, and Taylor Berg-Kirkpatrick. 2017. Improved variational autoencoders for text modeling using dilated convolutions. *CoRR*, abs/1702.08139.

Shengjia Zhao, Jiaming Song, and Stefano Ermon. 2017. Infovae: Information maximizing variational autoencoders. *CoRR*, abs/1706.02262.

Yaoming Zhu, Sidi Lu, Lei Zheng, Jiaxian Guo, Weinan Zhang, Jun Wang, and Yong Yu. Texygen: A benchmarking platform for text generation models. In *SIGIR*.

Decomposing Textual Information For Style Transfer

Ivan P. Yamshchikov[*]
Max Planck Institute
for Mathematics in the Sciences
Leipzig, Germany
`ivan@yamshchikov.info`

Viacheslav Shibaev
Ural Federal University
Ekaterinburg, Russia

Aleksander Nagaev
Ural Federal University
Ekaterinburg, Russia

Jürgen Jost
Max Planck Institute
for Mathematics in the Sciences
Leipzig, Germany

Alexey Tikhonov[*]
Yandex
Berlin, Germany
`altsoph@gmail.com`

Abstract

This paper focuses on latent representations that could effectively decompose different aspects of textual information. Using a framework of style transfer for texts, we propose several empirical methods to assess information decomposition quality. We validate these methods with several state-of-the-art textual style transfer methods. Higher quality of information decomposition corresponds to higher performance in terms of bilingual evaluation understudy (BLEU) between output and human-written reformulations.

1 Introduction

The arrival of deep learning seems transformative for many areas of information processing and is especially interesting for generative models (Hu et al., 2017b). However, natural language generation is still a challenging task due to a number of factors that include the absence of local information continuity and non-smooth disentangled representations (Bowman et al., 2015), and discrete nature of textual information (Hu et al., 2017a). If information needed for different natural language processing (NLP) tasks could be encapsulated in independent components of the obtained latent representations, one could have worked with different aspects of text independently. This could also naturally simplify learning transfer for NLP models and potentially make them more interpretable.

Despite the fact that content and style are deeply fused in natural language, style transfer for texts is often addressed in the context of disentangled latent representations (Hu et al., 2017a; Shen et al., 2017; Fu et al., 2018; John et al., 2018; Romanov et al., 2018; Tian et al., 2018). A majority of these works use an encoder-decoder architecture with one or

---

Equal contribution

multiple style discriminators to improve latent representations. An encoder takes a given sentence as an input and generates a style-independent content representation. The decoder then uses this content representation and a target style representation to generate a new sentence in the needed style. This approach seems intuitive and appealing but has certain difficulties. For example, Subramanian et al. (2018) question the quality and usability of the disentangled representations for texts with an elegant experiment. The authors train a state of the art architecture that relies on disentangled representations and show that an external artificial neural network can predict the style of the input using a semantic component of an obtained latent representation (that supposedly did not incorporate stylistic information).

In this work, we demonstrate that the decomposition of latent representations is, indeed, attainable with encoder-decoder based methods but depends on the used architecture. Moreover, architectures with higher quality of information decomposition perform better in terms of the style transfer task.

The contribution of this paper is threefold: (1) we propose several ways to quantify the quality of the obtained latent semantic representations; (2) we show that the quality of such representation can significantly differ depending on the used architecture; (3) finally we demonstrate that architectures with higher quality of information decomposition perform better in terms of BLEU (Papineni et al., 2002) between output of a model and a human written reformulations.

2 Related Work

It is hard to define style transfer rigorously (Xu, 2017). Therefore recent contributions in the field are mostly motivated by several empirical results and rather address specific narrow aspects of style

Proceedings of the 3rd Workshop on Neural Generation and Translation (WNGT 2019), pages 128–137
Hong Kong, China, November 4, 2019. ©2019 Association for Computational Linguistics
www.aclweb.org/anthology/D19-56%2d

that could be empirically measured. Stylistic attributes of text include author-specific attributes (see (Xu et al., 2012) or (Jhamtani et al., 2017) on 'shakespearization'), politeness (Sennrich et al., 2016), the *'style of the time'* (Hughes et al., 2012), gender or political slant (Prabhumoye et al., 2018), and formality of speech (Rao and Tetreault, 2018). All these attributes are defined with varying degrees of rigor. Meanwhile, the general notion of literally style is only addressed in a very broad context. For example, Hughes et al. (2012) shows that the style of a text can be characterized quantitively and not only with an expert opinion; Potash et al. (2015) demonstrate that stylized texts could be generated if a system is trained on a dataset of stylistically similar texts; and literary styles of the authors could be learned end-to-end (Tikhonov and Yamshchikov, 2018a,b; Vechtomova et al., 2018).

In this particular submission we focus on a very narrow framework of sentiment transfer. There is certain controversy whether sentiment of a text could be regarded as its stylistic attribute, see (Tikhonov and Yamshchikov, 2018c). However, there seems to be certain agreement in the field that sentiment could be regarded as a viable attribute to be changed by the style transfer system. Addressing the problem of sentiment transfer Kabbara and Cheung (2016); Li et al. (2018); Xu et al. (2018) estimate the quality of the style transfer with a pre-trained binary sentiment classifier. Fu et al. (2018) and Ficler and Goldberg (2017) generalize this ad-hoc approach and in principle enable the information decomposition approach. They define a style as a set of arbitrary quantitatively measurable categorical or continuous parameters that could be automatically estimated with an external classifier. In this submission we stay within this empirical paradigm of literary style.

Generally speaking, a solution that works for one aspect of a style could not be applied for a different aspect of it. For example, a retrieve-edit approach by (Guu et al., 2018) works for sentiment transfer. A delete-retrieve model shows good results for sentiment transfer in (Li et al., 2018). However, these retrieval approaches could hardly be used for the style of the time or formality or any other case when the system is expected to paraphrase a given sentence to achieve the target style. To address this challenge Hu et al. (2017a) propose a more general approach to the controlled text generation combining variational autoencoder (VAE) with an extended wake-sleep mechanism in which the sleep procedure updates both the generator and external discriminator that assesses generated samples and feedbacks learning signals to the generator. Labels for style were concatenated with the text representation of the encoder and used with "hard-coded" information about the sentiment of the output as the input of the decoder. This approach is promising and is used in many recent contributions. Shen et al. (2017) use an adversarial loss to decompose information about the form of a sentence and apply a GAN to align hidden representations of sentences from two corpora. Fu et al. (2018) use an adversarial network to make sure that the output of the encoder does not include stylistic information. Hu et al. (2017a) also use an adversarial component to ensure there is no stylistic information within the representation. A dedicated component that controls semantic component of the latent representation is proposed by John et al. (2018) who demonstrate that decomposition of style and content could be improved with an auxiliary multi-task for label prediction and adversarial objective for a bag-of-words prediction. Romanov et al. (2018) also introduce a dedicated component to control semantic aspects of latent representations and an adversarial-motivational training that includes a special motivational loss to encourage a better decomposition.

The framework of information decomposition within latent representations is challenged by an alternative family of neural machine translation approaches. These are works on style transfer with (Carlson et al., 2018) and without parallel corpora (Zhang et al., 2018) in line with (Lample et al., 2017) and (Artetxe et al., 2017). In particular, Subramanian et al. (2018) state that learning a latent representation, which is independent of the attributes specifying its style is rarely attainable. They experiment with the model developed in (Fu et al., 2018) where by design the discriminator, which was trained adversarially and jointly with the model, gets worse at predicting the sentiment of the input when the coefficient of the adversarial loss increases. Authors show that a classifier that is separately trained on the resulting encoder representations easily recovers the sentiment of a latent representation produced by the encoder.

In this paper, we show that contrary to (Subramanian et al., 2018) decomposition of the stylistic and semantic information is attainable with autoencoder-type models and could be quantified. However, the quality of such decomposition severely depends on the particular architecture. We propose three different measures for information decomposition quality and using four different architectures show that models with better information decomposition outperform the state-of-the-art models in terms of BLEU between output and human-written reformulations.

3 Style transfer

In this work we experiment with extensions of a model, described in (Hu et al., 2017a), using Texar (Hu et al., 2018) framework. To generate plausible sentences with specific semantic and stylistic features every sentence is conditioned on a representation vector z which is concatenated with a particular code c that specifies desired attribute, see Figure 1. Under notation introduced in (Hu et al., 2017a) the base autoencoder (AE) includes a conditional probabilistic encoder E defined with parameters θ_E to infer the latent representation z given input x

$$z \sim E(x) = q_E(z, c|x).$$

Generator G defined with parameters θ_G is a GRU-RNN for generating and output $\hat{x}$ defined as a sequence of tokens $\hat{x} = \hat{x}_1, ..., \hat{x}_T$ conditioned on the latent representation z and a stylistic component c that are concatenated and give rise to a generative distribution

$$\hat{x} \sim G(z, c) = p_G(\hat{x}|z, c).$$

These encoder and generator form an AE with the following loss

$$\mathcal{L}_{ae}(\theta_G, \theta_E; x, c) = -\mathbb{E}_{q_E(z,c|x)}\left[\log q_G(x|z, c)\right].$$
(1)

This standard reconstruction loss that drives the generator to produce realistic sentences is combined with two additional losses. The first discriminator provides extra learning signals which enforce the generator to produce coherent attributes that match the structured code in c. Since it is impossible to propagate gradients from the discriminator through the discrete sample $\hat{x}$, we use a deterministic continuous approximation a "soft" generated sentence, denoted as $\tilde{G} = \tilde{G}_\tau(z, c)$ with "temperature" τ set to $\tau \to 0$ as training proceeds. The resulting soft generated sentence is fed into the

discriminator to measure the fitness to the target attribute, leading to the following loss

$$\mathcal{L}_c(\theta_G, \theta_E; x) = -\mathbb{E}_{q_E(z,c|x)}\left[\log q_D(c|\tilde{G})\right].$$
(2)

Finally, under the assumption that each structured attribute of generated sentences is controlled through the corresponding code in c and is independent from z one would like to control that other not explicitly modelled attributes do not entangle with c. This is addressed by the dedicated loss

$$\mathcal{L}_z(\theta_G; x) = -\mathbb{E}_{q_E(z,c|x)q_D(c|x)}\left[\log q_E(z|\tilde{G})\right].$$
(3)

The training objective for the baseline, shown in Figure 1, is therefore a sum of the losses from Equations (1) – (3) defined as

$$min_{\theta_G}\mathcal{L}_{baseline} = \mathcal{L}_{ae} + \lambda_c\mathcal{L}_c + \lambda_z\mathcal{L}_z, \quad (4)$$

where λ_c and λ_z are balancing parameters.

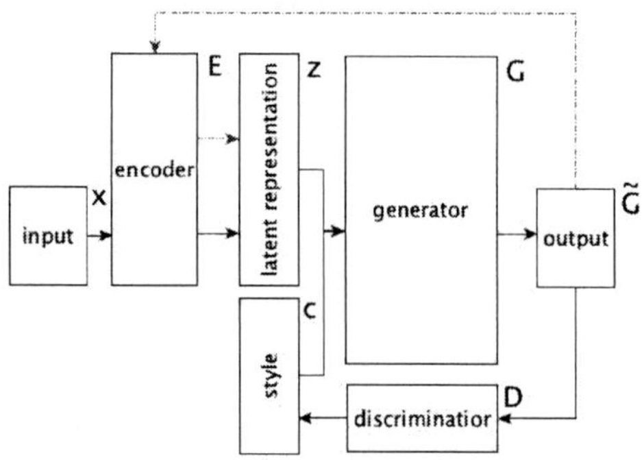

Figure 1: The generative model, where style is a structured code targeting sentence attributes to control. Blue dashed arrows denote the proposed independence constraint of latent representation and controlled attribute, see (Hu et al., 2017a) for the details.

Let us propose two further extensions of this baseline architecture. To improve reproducibility of the research the code of the studied models is open[1]. Both extensions aim to improve the quality of information decomposition within the latent representation. In the first one, shown in Figure 2, a special dedicated discriminator is added to the model to control that the latent representation does not contain stylistic information. The loss of this discriminator is defined as

$$\mathcal{L}_{D_z}(\theta_G; x, c) = -\mathbb{E}_{q_E(z|x)}\left[\log q_{D_z}(c|z)\right]. \quad (5)$$

[1]https://github.com/VAShibaev/textstyletransfer

Here a discriminator denoted as D_z is trying to predict code c using representation z. Combining the loss defined by Equation (4) with the adversarial component defined in Equation (5) the following learning objective is formed

$$min_{\theta_G} \mathcal{L} = \mathcal{L}_{baseline} - \lambda_{D_z} \mathcal{L}_{Dz},\qquad (6)$$

where $\mathcal{L}_{baseline}$ is a sum defined in Equation (4), λ_{D_z} is a balancing parameter.

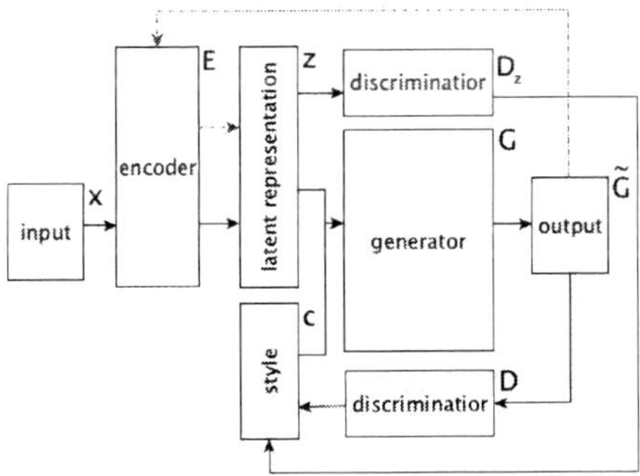

Figure 2: The generative model with dedicated discriminator introduced to ensure that semantic part of the latent representation does not have information on the style of the text.

The second extension of the baseline architecture does not use an adversarial component D_z that is trying to eradicate information on c from component z. Instead, the system, shown in Figure 3 feeds the "soft" generated sentence $\tilde{G}$ into encoder E and checks how close is the representation $E(\tilde{G})$ to the original representation $z = E(x)$ in terms of the cosine distance. We further refer to it as *shifted autoencoder* or SAE. Ideally, both $E(\tilde{G}(E(x), c))$ and $E(\tilde{G}(E(x), \bar{c}))$, where $\bar{c}$ denotes an inverse style code, should be both equal to $E(x)^2$. The loss of the shifted autoencoder is

$$min_{\theta_G} \mathcal{L} = \mathcal{L}_{baseline} + \lambda_{cos} \mathcal{L}_{cos} + \lambda_{cos-} \mathcal{L}_{cos-},\qquad (7)$$

where λ_{cos} and λ_{cos-} are two balancing parameters, with two additional terms in the loss, namely, cosine distances between the softened output processed by the encoder and the encoded original input, defined as

$$\mathcal{L}_{cos}(x, c) = \cos\left(E(\tilde{G}(E(x), c)), E(x) \right),$$

$$\mathcal{L}_{cos-}(x, c) = \cos\left(E(\tilde{G}(E(x), \bar{c})), E(x) \right).\qquad (8)$$

---

[2]This notation is valid under the assumption that every stylistic attribute is a binary feature

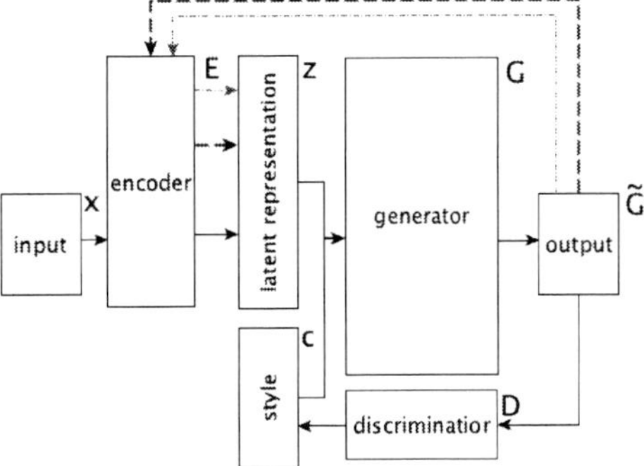

Figure 3: The generative model with a dedicated loss added to control that semantic representation of the output, when processed by the encoder, is close to the semantic representation of the input.

We also study a combination of both approaches described above, shown on Figure 4.

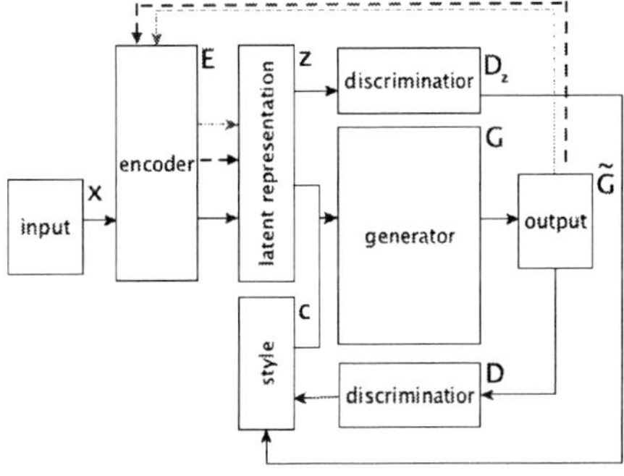

Figure 4: A combination of an additional discriminator used in Figure 2 with a shifted autoencoder shown in Figure 3

Tikhonov et al. (2019) carry out a series of experiments for these architectures. In this contribution, we work with the same data set of human-labeled positive and negative reviews but focus solely on the quality of information decomposition.

4 Information decomposition for texts

As we have mentioned earlier, several recent contributions rely on the idea that decomposing different aspects of textual information into various components of a latent representation might be helpful for a task of style transfer. To our knowledge, this is a supposition that is rarely addressed rigorously. The majority of the arguments in favor of information decomposition based architectures is of an intuitive and qualitative rather than quantitative nature. Moreover, there are specific arguments against this idea.

In particular, Subramanian et al. (2018) show that information decomposition does not necessarily occur in autoencoder-based systems using a method developed in (Fu et al., 2018). Subramanian et al. (2018) demonstrate that as training proceeds, the internal discriminator, which was trained adversarially and jointly with the model, gets worse at predicting the sentiment of the input. However, an external classifier that is separately trained on the resulting latent representations easily recovers the sentiment. This is a strong argument in favor of the idea that actual disentanglement does not happen. Instead of decomposing the semantic and stylistic aspects of information, the encoder merely 'tricks' internal classifier and 'hides' stylistic information in the semantic component ending up in some local optimum.

4.1 Empirical measure of information decomposition quality

Yelp![3] reviews dataset that was lately enhanced with human written reformulations by (Tian et al., 2018) is one of the most frequently used baselines for textual style transfer at the moment. It consists of restaurant reviews split into two categories, namely, positive and negative. There is a human written reformulation of every review in which the sentiment is changed that is commonly used as a ground truth for the task performance estimation.

We applied an empirical method to estimate the quality of information decomposition to the architectures described in Section 3 as well as architectures developed by (Tian et al., 2018). An external classifier was trained from scratch to predict a style of a message using component z of a latent representation produced by an encoder. If information decomposition does not happen, one would expect that accuracy of an external classifier would be close to 1. This would mean that despite intuitive expectations, information about the style of a message is present in z. If decomposition were effective, the accuracy of an external classifier would be close to 0.5; in (Tikhonov et al., 2019) it is shown that style transfer methods show varying results in terms of accuracy and BLEU for different retrains, so in this paper the accuracy of an external classifier and BLEU between the system's output and

<hr>

[3]https://www.yelp.com/dataset

human-written reformulations was measured after four independent retrains. On Figure 5, one can see the results of these experiments.

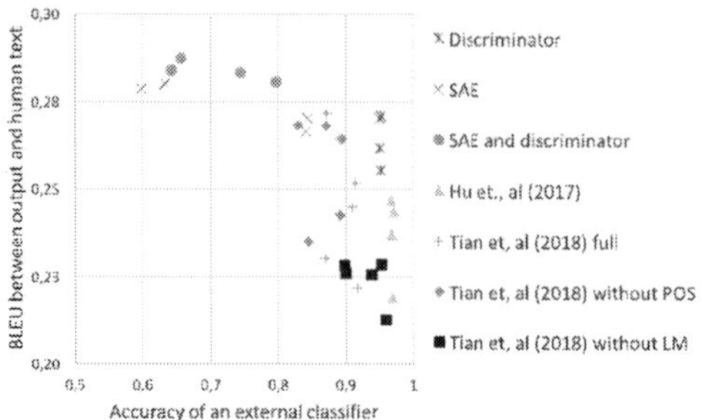

Figure 5: BLEU between system's output and human-written reformulations seems to be higher if accuracy of an external classifier is closer to one half. Systems that decompose information better tend to show higher BLEU.

The fact that the external classifier always predicts style with the probability that is above one half could be partially attributed to the fact that full information decomposition of sentiment and semantics is hardly attainable. For example, such adjectives as "delicious" or "yummy" incorporate positive sentiment with the semantics of taste, whereas "polite" or "friendly" in Yelp! reviews are combining positive sentiment with the semantics of service. This internal entanglement of sentiment and semantics is discussed in detail in (Tikhonov and Yamshchikov, 2018c). It is essential to mention that the very fact that semantics and stylistics are entangled on the level of words does not deny a theoretical possibility to build a latent representation where they are fully disentangled. Anyway, Figure 5 demonstrates that the quality of the disentanglement is much better for SAE-type architectures. Since the shifted autoencoder controls the cosine distance between soft output and input, the encoder has to disentangle the semantic component, rather than "hide" the sentiment information from the discriminator.

On Figure 6 one can see how state of the art approaches compare to each other in terms of BLEU between output and human-written reformulations. All systems were retrained five times from scratch to report error margins of the methods since the results are noisy. BLEU between output and human-written reformulations is higher for lower values of external classifier accuracy. Systems that perform better in terms of information decomposition outperform system with lower quality of information decomposition. Moreover, the system that does not rely on an idea of disentangled latent representations at all shows weaker results than systems with high information disentanglement. It is important to note that there is a variety of methods to assess the quality of style transfer such as PINC (Paraphrase In N-gram Changes) score (Carlson et al., 2018), POS distance (Tian et al., 2018), language fluency (John et al., 2018), etc. The methodology of style transfer quality assessment is addressed in detail in (Tikhonov et al., 2019), but BLEU between output and input is a very natural all-purpose metric for the task of such type that is common in the style transfer literature.

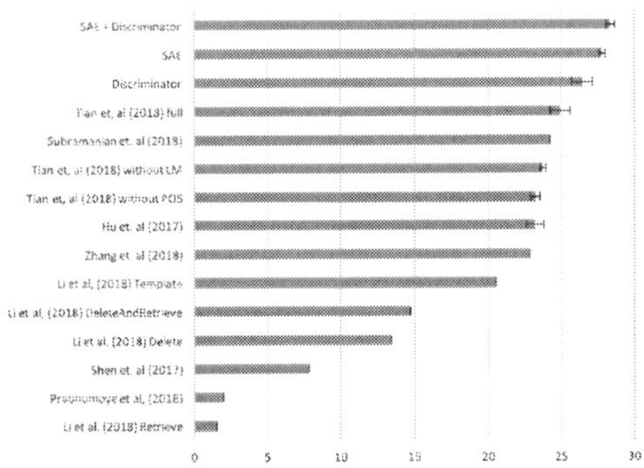

Figure 6: Overview of the BLEU between output and human-written reformulations of Yelp! reviews. Architecture with additional discriminator, shifted autoencoder (SAE) with additional cosine losses, and a combination of these two architectures measured after five re-runs outperform the baseline by (Hu et al., 2017a) as well as other state of the art models. Results of (Romanov et al., 2018) are not displayed due to the absence of self-reported BLEU scores

Tables 1 - 2 allow to compare random examples for different architectures. Generally, baseline and discriminator perform poorly once the syntax of a review is irregular or if there are some omissions in the text. SAE-based architectures tend to preserve the semantic component better. They also add sentimentally charged words at random not as often as the baseline and the discriminator-based architecture.

4.2 Preservation of semantic component

Another way to quantify the quality of latent representations is to calculate cosine distance and KL-divergence between semantic components of latent representations for the inputs and corresponding outputs. If we believe that the latent representation captures the semantics of the input that should be preserved in the output, the ideal behavior of the system is to produce equal latent representation for both the input and the output phrase. Indeed, on Figure 7 one can see that SAE manages to learn a space of latent representations in which semantic components of inputs and outputs are always equal to each other. Architecture with additional stylistic discriminator shows lower cosine distances and lower KL-divergences then the baseline yet. This results are in line with the measurements discussed above in Section 4.1.

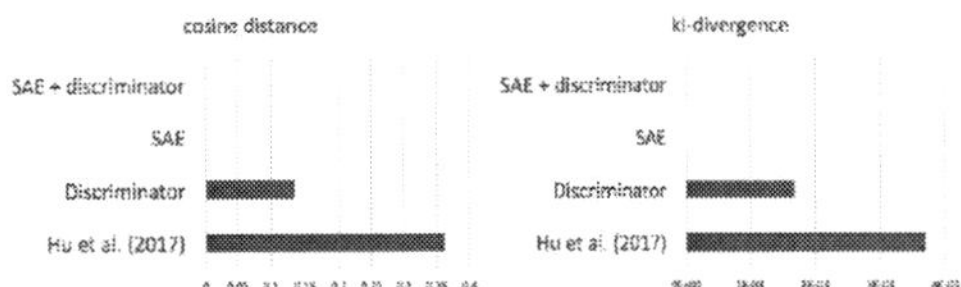

Figure 7: Comparison of cosine distances and KL-divergences between semantic components of latent representation for inputs and outputs. After 12 epochs of training SAE makes semantic component z for every output equal to the semantic component for a corresponding input. Discriminator corresponds to lower values of KL-divergence and cosine distance then baseline (Hu et al., 2017a)

To get an intuition on how the resulting latent space differs for different architectures, one can look at the t-SNE visualizations (Maaten and Hinton, 2008) for the resulting latent representations of the data that different systems produce. In Figure 8, one can see that the baseline latent representations easily allow recovering the sentiment.

In contrast with the baseline, the architecture with additional discriminator obtains better disentanglement. Figure 9 shows that in this case one has a harder time recovering the sentiment of the sentence based on its latent representation.

SAE does not only show a higher level of disentanglement but also produces equal semantic components for the input and the corresponding output. Judging by Figure 10 this makes SAE representations denser in certain areas of the semantic space and sparser in the others.

input	Human	baseline
the carne asada burrito is awesome!	the carne asada burrito is awful!	the worst asada burrito is gross!
the rooms are not that nice and the food is not that good either.	the rooms were spacious and food was very well cooked	the rooms are excellent that nice and the food is not that good either.
it was so delicious; i've never had anything like it!	everything tasted bad, nothing i liked	it was so rude; i've never had anything like it!
so, that was my one and only time ordering the benedict there.	i will be ordering the benedict again very good meal!	so, that was my one and best time ordering the perfect there.
you'll see why once you get there.	you'll see why i don't like it once you get there.	you'll see why once you get there.
i wanted to like this place but it just became a big disappointment.	a place like this is a great value	i helped to like this place it just became a big hidden.
and i had my sugar bowl favorite, the top hat sundae!	my sugar bowl favorite was not in stock.	and i had my sugar bowl worst, the lackluster hat gross!
um... we just told him that we didn't want to finance.	um... we just told him, sure we'd go ahead and finance!	amazing... we just told him that we did definitely want to open.
definitely a place to keep in mind.	not a place i would recommend	disappointing a place to keep in mind.
firstly, their fees are generally higher than other places.	the fees are comparable to other places.	best, their fees are generally higher than other places.
love the afternoon - tea at the phoenician.	hate the aternoon tea at the phoenician	absurd the inappropriate - tea at the insult.

Table 1: Several random input lines alongside with human written reformulation and the reformulation generated by the baseline.

Discriminator	SAE	SAE + Discriminator
the carne asada burrito is absurd!	the carne asada burrito is worst!	the carne asada burrito is sub-par!
the rooms are delicious that nice and the food is delicious that good either.	the rooms are definitely that nice and the food is definitely that good either.	the rooms are consistantly that nice and the food is consistantly that good either.
it was so not; i've never had anything like it!	it was so disgusting; i've never had anything like it!	it was so angry ; i've never had anything like it!
so, that was my one and fam time solid the benedict perfectly.	so, that was my one and kids time ordering the benedict there.	so, that was my one and always time ordering the benedict there.
you'll trash why once you get there.	you'll avoid why once you get there.	you'll see why once you get there.
i wanted to like this place but it just delightful a big genius.	i wanted to like this place but it just became a big midwest.	i wanted to like this place but it just mildly a big stocked.
and i had my sugar bowl favorite, the absurd hurts ache!	and i had my sugar bowl broken, the garage hat holes!	and i had my sugar bowl misleading, the top quesadilla sundae!
expertly... we just delightful him that we did magical want adds marvelous.	um... we just loved him that we did definatly want to finance.	um... we just entertained him that we did perfected want to incredible.
ridiculous a place to keep in mind.	would a place to keep in mind.	wont a place to keep in mind.
firstly, their project are generally higher than other places.	firstly, their draw are generally higher than other places.	sheila, their round are generally higher than other places.
horrific the trap - tea at the gut.	dumb the afternoon - tea at the rabbit.	wtf the afternoon - tea at the slim.

Table 2: Reformulations generated by the baseline with additional discriminator, shifted autoencoder and shifted autoencoder with additional discriminator corresponding to the inputs in Table 1.

Aligning results shown on Figures 5 - 10 one can clearly see several crucial things: (1) architectures based on the idea of disentangled latent representations show varying performance in terms of BLEU between output and human written reformulations; (2) architectures with higher quality of information decomposition in terms of correlation or KL-divergence between representations for input and output, show higher performance; (3) architectures that produce equal semantic components for a given input and corresponding output show the highest performance; (4) these results are aligned with empirical estimation of decomposition quality with external classifiers; it shows that architectures that are more successfully disentangling semantics of the input from its stylistics tend to perform better.

5 Conclusion

This paper addresses the questions of information decomposition for the task of textual style transfer. We propose three new architectures that use latent representations to decompose stylistic and semantics information of input. Two different methods to assess the quality of such decomposition are proposed. It is shown that architectures that produce an equal semantic component of latent representations for input and corresponding output

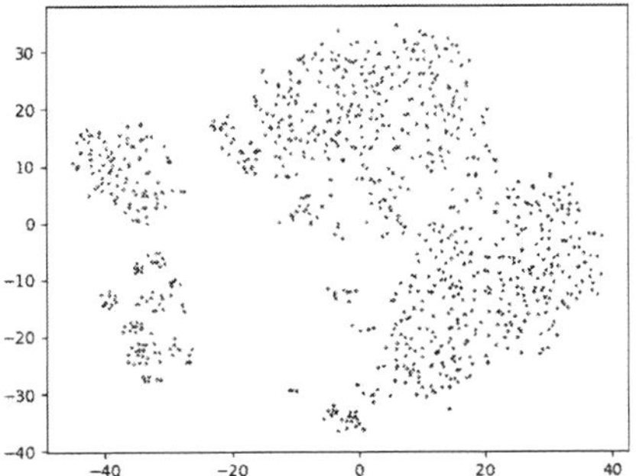

Figure 8: t-SNE visualisation of the obtained latent representations for the baseline architecture proposed in (Hu et al., 2017a). Red dots represent positive reviews. Blue dots represent negative reviews. One can clearly see that stylistic information can be recovered from the representation.

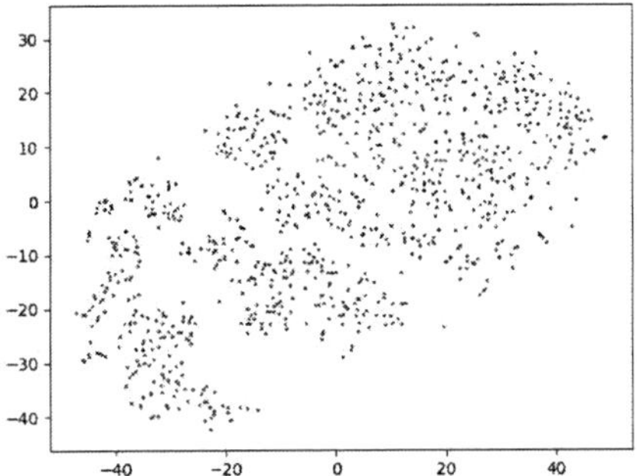

Figure 9: t-SNE visualisation of the obtained latent representations for the architecture with an additional discriminator. Red dots represent positive reviews. Blue dots represent negative reviews. One can see that it is harder to recover stylistic information from the representation.

outperform state of the art architectures in terms of BLEU between output and human written reformulations. An empirical method to assess the quality of information decomposition is proposed. There is a correspondence between higher BLEU between output and human written reformulations and better quality of information decomposition.

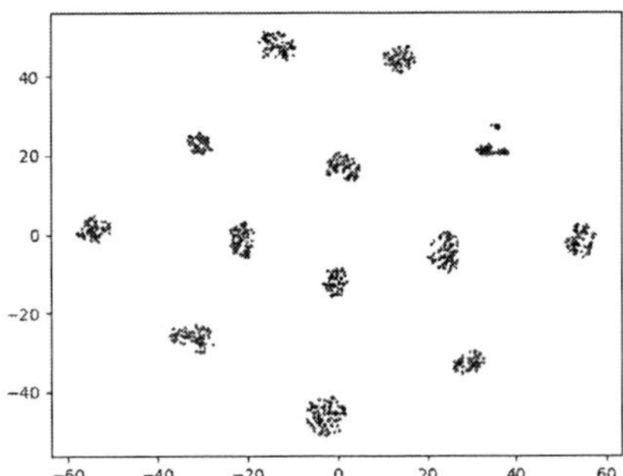

Figure 10: t-SNE visualisation of the obtained latent representations for the shifted autoencoder. Red dots represent positive reviews. Blue dots represent negative reviews. One can see that it is harder to recover stylistic information from the representation and the structure of the differs significantly from the latent representation space obtained by the baseline.

References

Mikel Artetxe, Gorka Labaka, Eneko Agirre, and Kyunghyun Cho. 2017. Unsupervised neural machine translation. In *arXiv preprint*.

Samuel R. Bowman, Gabor Angeli, Christopher Potts, and Christopher D. Manning. 2015. A large annotated corpus for learning natural language inference. In *Proceedings of the 2015 Conference on Empirical Methods in Natural Language Processing*, pages 632–642.

Keith Carlson, Allen Riddell, and Daniel Rockmore. 2018. Evaluating prose style transfer with the bible. *Royal Society open science*, 5(10):171920.

Jessica Ficler and Yoav Goldberg. 2017. Controlling linguistic style aspects in neural language generation. In *Proceedings of the Workshop on Stylistic Variation*, volume 94-104.

Zhenxin Fu, Xiaoye Tan, Nanyun Peng, Dongyan Zhao, and Rui Yan. 2018. Style transfer in text: Exploration and evaluation. *AAAI*.

Kelvin Guu, Tatsunori B. Hashimoto, Yonatan Oren, and Percy Liang. 2018. Generating sentences by editing prototypes. *Transactions of the Association of Computational Linguistics*, 6:437–450.

Zhiting Hu, Haoran Shi, Zichao Yang, Bowen Tan, Tiancheng Zhao, Junxian He, Wentao Wang, Xingjiang Yu, Lianhui Qin, Di Wang, Xuezhe Ma, Hector Liu, Xiaodan Liang, Wanrong Zhu, Devendra Singh Sachan, and Eric P. Xing. 2018. Texar: A modularized, versatile, and extensible toolkit for text generation. In *arXiv preprint*.

Zhiting Hu, Zichao Yang, Xiaodan Liang, Ruslan Salakhutdinov, and Eric P. Xing. 2017a. Toward controlled generation of text. In *International Conference on Machine Learning*, pages 1587–1596.

Zhiting Hu, Zichao Yang, Ruslan Salakhutdinov, and Eric Xing. 2017b. On unifying deep generative models. In *arXiv preprint*.

James M. Hughes, Nicholas J. Foti, David C. Krakauer, and Daniel N. Rockmore. 2012. Quantitative patterns of stylistic influence in the evolution of literature. *Proceedings of the National Academy of Sciences*, 109(20):7682–7686.

Harsh Jhamtani, Varun Gangal, Eduard Hovy, and Eric Nyberg. 2017. Shakespearizing modern language using copy-enriched sequence-to-sequence models. In *Proceedings of the Workshop on Stylistic Variation*, pages 10–19.

Vineet John, Lili Mou, Hareesh Bahuleyan, and Olga Vechtomova. 2018. Disentangled representation learning for text style transfer. In *arXiv preprint*.

Jad Kabbara and Jackie Chi Kit Cheung. 2016. Stylistic transfer in natural language generation systems using recurrent neural networks. *Proceedings of the Workshop on Uphill Battles in Language Processing: Scaling Early Achievements to Robust Methods*, pages 43–47.

Guillaume Lample, Alexis Conneau, Ludovic Denoyer, and Marc'Aurelio Ranzato. 2017. Unsupervised machine translation using monolingual corpora only. In *arXiv preprint*.

Juncen Li, Robin Jia, He He, and Percy Liang. 2018. Delete, retrieve, generate: A simple approach to sentiment and style transfer. In *Proceedings of the 2018 Conference of the North American Chapter of the Association for Computational Linguistics: Human Language Technologies*, volume 1, pages 865–1874.

Laurens van der Maaten and Geoffrey Hinton. 2008. Visualizing data using t-sne. *Journal of machine learning research*, 9:2579–2605.

Kishore Papineni, Salim Roukos, Todd Ward, and Wei-Jing Zhu. 2002. Gbleu: a method for automatic evaluation of machine translation. In *Proceedings of the 40th Annual Meeting of the Association for Computational Linguistics (ACL)*, pages 311–318.

Peter Potash, Alexey Romanov, and Anna Rumshisky. 2015. Ghostwriter: Using an lstm for automatic rap lyric generation. In *Proceedings of the 2015 Conference on Empirical Methods in Natural Language Processing*, pages 1919–1924. Association for Computational Linguistics.

Shrimai Prabhumoye, Yulia Tsvetkov, Alan W. Black, and Ruslan Salakhutdinov. 2018. Style transfer through back-translation. In *arXiv preprint*.

Sudha Rao and Joel Tetreault. 2018. Dear sir or madam, may i introduce the gyafc dataset: Corpus, benchmarks and metrics for formality style transfer. In *Proceedings of the Conference of the North American Chapter of the Association for Computational Linguistics: Human Language Technologies*, volume 1, pages 129–140.

Alexey Romanov, Anna Rumshisky, Anna Rogers, and David Donahue. 2018. Adversarial decomposition of text representation. In *arXiv preprint*.

Rico Sennrich, Barry Haddow, and Alexandra Birch. 2016. Controlling politeness in neural machine translation via side constraints. *In Proceedings of the 2016 Conference of the North American Chapter of the Association for Computational Linguistics: Human Language Technologies*, pages 35–40.

Tianxiao Shen, Tao Lei, Regina Barzilay, and Tommi Jaakkola. 2017. Style transfer from non-parallel text by cross-alignment. *31st Conference on Neural Information Processing Systems*, pages 6833–6844.

Sandeep Subramanian, Guillaume Lample, Eric M. Smith, Ludovic Denoyer, Marc Aurelio Ranzato, and Y-Lan Boureau. 2018. Multiple-attribute text style transfer. In *arXiv preprint*.

Youzhi Tian, Zhiting Hu, and Zhou Yu. 2018. Structured content preservation for unsupervised text style transfer. In *arXiv preprint*.

Alexey Tikhonov, Viacheslav Shibaev, Aleksander Nagaev, Aigul Nugmanova, and Ivan Yamshchikov. 2019. Style transfer for texts: to err is human, but error margins matter. In *EMNLP*.

Alexey Tikhonov and Ivan P. Yamshchikov. 2018a. Guess who? Multilingual approach for the automated generation of author-stylized poetry. In *IEEE Spoken Language Technology Workshop (SLT)*, pages 787–794.

Alexey Tikhonov and Ivan P. Yamshchikov. 2018b. Sounds Wilde. Phonetically extended embeddings for author-stylized poetry generation. In *Proceedings of the Fifteenth Workshop on Computational Research in Phonetics, Phonology, and Morphology*, pages 117–124.

Alexey Tikhonov and Ivan P. Yamshchikov. 2018c. What is wrong with style transfer for texts? In *arXiv preprint*.

Olga Vechtomova, Hareesh Bahuleyan, Amirpasha Ghabussi, and Vineet John. 2018. Generating lyrics with variational autoencoder and multi-modal artist embeddings. In *arXiv preprint*.

Jingjing Xu, Xu Sun, Qi Zeng, Xuancheng Ren, Xiaodong Zhang, Houfeng Wang, and Wenjie Li. 2018. Unpaired sentiment-to-sentiment translation: A cycled reinforcement learning approach. In *arXiv preprint*.

Wei Xu. 2017. From shakespeare to twitter: What are language styles all about? *Proceedings of the Workshop on Stylistic Variation*, pages 1–9.

Wei Xu, Alan Ritter, William B. Dolan, Ralph Grishman, and Colin Cherry. 2012. Paraphrasing for style. *Proceedings of COLING*, pages 2899–2914.

Zhirui Zhang, Shuo Ren, Shujie Liu, Jianyong Wang, Peng Chen, Mu Li, Ming Zhou, and Enhong Chen. 2018. Style transfer as unsupervised machine translation. In *arXiv preprint*.

Unsupervised Evaluation Metrics and Learning Criteria
for Non-Parallel Textual Transfer

Richard Yuanzhe Pang[1][§]   **Kevin Gimpel**[2]
[1]New York University, New York, NY 10011, USA
[2]Toyota Technological Institute at Chicago, Chicago, IL 60637, USA
`yzpang@nyu.edu, kgimpel@ttic.edu`

Abstract

We consider the problem of automatically generating textual paraphrases with modified attributes or properties, focusing on the setting without parallel data (Hu et al., 2017; Shen et al., 2017). This setting poses challenges for evaluation. We show that the metric of post-transfer classification accuracy is insufficient on its own, and propose additional metrics based on semantic preservation and fluency as well as a way to combine them into a single overall score. We contribute new loss functions and training strategies to address the different metrics. Semantic preservation is addressed by adding a cyclic consistency loss and a loss based on paraphrase pairs, while fluency is improved by integrating losses based on style-specific language models. We experiment with a Yelp sentiment dataset and a new literature dataset that we propose, using multiple models that extend prior work (Shen et al., 2017). We demonstrate that our metrics correlate well with human judgments, at both the sentence-level and system-level. Automatic and manual evaluation also show large improvements over the baseline method of Shen et al. (2017). We hope that our proposed metrics can speed up system development for new textual transfer tasks while also encouraging the community to address our three complementary aspects of transfer quality.

1   Introduction

We consider **textual transfer**, which we define as the capability of generating textual paraphrases with modified attributes or stylistic properties, such as politeness (Sennrich et al., 2016a), sentiment (Hu et al., 2017; Shen et al., 2017), and formality (Rao and Tetreault, 2018). An effective transfer system could benefit a range of user-facing text generation applications such as dialogue (Ritter et al., 2011) and writing assistance (Heidorn, 2000). It can also improve NLP systems via data augmentation and domain adaptation.

However, one factor that makes textual transfer difficult is the lack of parallel corpora. Advances have been made in developing transfer methods that do not require parallel corpora (see Section 2), but issues remain with automatic evaluation metrics. Li et al. (2018) used crowdsourcing to obtain manually-written references and used BLEU (Papineni et al., 2002) to evaluate sentiment transfer. However, this approach is costly and difficult to scale for arbitrary textual transfer tasks.

Researchers have thus turned to *unsupervised* evaluation metrics that do not require references. The most widely-used unsupervised evaluation uses a pretrained style classifier and computes the fraction of times the classifier was convinced of transferred style (Shen et al., 2017). However, relying solely on this metric leads to models that completely distort the semantic content of the input sentence. Table 1 illustrates this tendency.

We address this deficiency by identifying two competing goals: preserving semantic content and producing fluent output. We contribute two corresponding metrics. Since the metrics are unsupervised, they can be used directly for tuning and model selection, even on test data. The three metric categories are complementary and help us avoid degenerate behavior in model selection. For particular applications, practitioners can choose the appropriate combination of our metrics to achieve the desired balance among transfer, semantic preservation, and fluency. It is often useful to summarize the three metrics into one number, which we discuss in Section 3.3.

We also add learning criteria to the framework of Shen et al. (2017) to accord with our new metrics. We encourage semantic preserva-

---

§ Work completed while the author was a student at the University of Chicago and a visiting student at Toyota Technological Institute at Chicago.

Proceedings of the 3rd Workshop on Neural Generation and Translation (WNGT 2019), pages 138–147
Hong Kong, China, November 4, 2019. ©2019 Association for Computational Linguistics
www.aclweb.org/anthology/D19-56%2d

tion by adding a "cyclic consistency" loss (to ensure that transfer is reversible) and a loss based on paraphrase pairs (to show the model examples of content-preserving transformations). To encourage fluent outputs, we add losses based on pretrained corpus-specific language models. We also experiment with multiple, complementary discriminators and find that they improve the trade-off between post-transfer accuracy and semantic preservation.

To demonstrate the effectiveness of our metrics, we experiment with textual transfer models discussed above, using both their Yelp polarity dataset and a new literature dataset that we propose. Across model variants, our metrics correlate well with human judgments, at both the sentence-level and system-level.

2 Related Work

Textual Transfer Evaluation Recent work has included human evaluation of the three categories (post-transfer style accuracy, semantic preservation, fluency), but does not propose automatic evaluation metrics for all three (Li et al., 2018; Prabhumoye et al., 2018; Chen et al., 2018; Zhang et al., 2018). There have been recent proposals for supervised evaluation metrics (Li et al., 2018), but these require annotation and are therefore unavailable for new textual transfer tasks. There is a great deal of recent work in textual transfer (Yang et al., 2018b; Santos et al., 2018; Zhang et al., 2018; Logeswaran et al., 2018; Nikolov and Hahnloser, 2018), but all either lack certain categories of unsupervised metric or lack human validation of them, which we contribute. Moreover, the textual transfer community lacks discussion of early stopping criteria and methods of holistic model comparison. We propose a one-number summary for transfer quality, which can be used to select and compare models.

In contemporaneous work, Mir et al. (2019) similarly proposed three types of metrics for style transfer tasks. There are two main differences compared to our work: (1) They use a style-keyword masking procedure before evaluating semantic similarity, which works on the Yelp dataset (the only dataset Mir et al. (2019) test on) but does not work on our Literature dataset or similarly complicated tasks, because the masking procedure goes against preserving content-specific non-style-related words. (2) They do not provide a

way of aggregating three metrics for the purpose of model selection and overall comparison. We address these two problems, and we also propose metrics that are simple in addition to being effective, which is beneficial for ease of use and widespread adoption.

Textual Transfer Models In terms of generating the transferred sentences, to address the lack of parallel data, Hu et al. (2017) used variational autoencoders to generate content representations devoid of style, which can be converted to sentences with a specific style. Ficler and Goldberg (2017) used conditional language models to generate sentences where the desired content and style are conditioning contexts. Li et al. (2018) used a feature-based approach that deletes characteristic words from the original sentence, retrieves similar sentences in the target corpus, and generates based on the original sentence and the characteristic words from the retrieved sentences. Xu et al. (2018) integrated reinforcement learning into the textual transfer problem. Another way to address the lack of parallel data is to use learning frameworks based on adversarial objectives (Goodfellow et al., 2014); several have done so for textual transfer (Yu et al., 2017; Li et al., 2017; Yang et al., 2018a; Shen et al., 2017; Fu et al., 2018). Recent work uses target-domain language models as discriminators to provide more stable feedback in learning (Yang et al., 2018b).

To preserve semantics more explicitly, Fu et al. (2018) use a multi-decoder model to learn content representations that do not reflect styles. Shetty et al. (2017) use a cycle constraint that penalizes L_1 distance between input and round-trip transfer reconstruction. Our cycle consistency loss is inspired by Shetty et al. (2017), together with the idea of back translation in unsupervised neural machine translation (Artetxe et al., 2017; Lample et al., 2017), and the idea of cycle constraints in image generation by Zhu et al. (2017).

3 Evaluation

3.1 Issues with Most Existing Methods

Prior work in automatic evaluation of textual transfer has focused on post-transfer classification accuracy ("Acc"), computed by using a pretrained classifier to measure classification accuracy of transferred texts (Hu et al., 2017; Shen et al., 2017). However, there is a problem with

#ep	Acc	Sim	Sentence
original input			the host that walked us to the table and left without a word .
0.5	0.87	0.65	the food is the best and the food is the .
3.3	0.72	0.75	the owner that went to to the table and made a smile .
7.5	0.58	0.81	the host that walked through to the table and are quite perfect !

Table 1: Examples showing why Acc is insufficient. The original sentence has negative sentiment, and the goal is to transfer to positive. #ep is number of epochs trained when generating the sentence and Sim (described below) is the semantic similarity to the original sentence. High Acc is associated with low Sim.

relying solely on this metric. Table 1 shows examples of transferred sentences at several points in training the model of Shen et al. (2017). Acc is highest very early in training and decreases over time as the outputs become a stronger semantic match to the input, a trend we show in more detail in Section 6. Thus transfer quality is inversely proportional to semantic similarity to the input sentence, meaning that these metrics are complementary and difficult to optimize simultaneously.

We also identify a third category of metric, namely fluency of the transferred sentence, and similarly find it to be complementary to the first two. These three metrics can be used to evaluate textual transfer systems and to do hyperparameter tuning and early stopping. In our experiments, we found that training typically converges to a point that gives poor Acc. Intermediate results are much better under a combination of all three unsupervised metrics. Stopping criteria are rarely discussed in prior work on textual transfer.

3.2 Unsupervised Evaluation Metrics

We now describe our proposals. We validate the metrics with human judgments in Section 6.3.

Post-transfer classification accuracy ("Acc"): This metric was mentioned above. We use a CNN (Kim, 2014) trained to classify a sentence as being from $\mathbf{X}_0$ or $\mathbf{X}_1$ (two corpora corresponding to different styles or attributes). Then Acc is the percentage of transferred sentences that are classified as belonging to the transferred class.

Semantic Similarity ("Sim"): We compute semantic similarity between the input and transferred sentences. We embed sentences by averaging their word embeddings weighted by idf scores,

where $\mathrm{idf}(q) = \log(|C| \cdot |\{s \in C : q \in s\}|^{-1})$ (q is a word, s is a sentence, $C = \mathbf{X}_0 \cup \mathbf{X}_1$). We use 300-dimensional GloVe word embeddings (Pennington et al., 2014). Then, Sim is the average of the cosine similarities over all original/transferred sentence pairs. Though this metric is quite simple, we show empirically that it is effective in capturing semantic similarity. Simplicity in evaluation metrics is beneficial for computational efficiency and widespread adoption. The quality of transfer evaluations will be significantly boosted with even such a simple metric. We also experimented with METEOR (Denkowski and Lavie, 2014). However, given that we found it to be strongly correlated with Sim (shown in supplemental materials), we adopt Sim due to its computational efficiency and simplicity.

Different textual transfer tasks may require different degrees of semantic preservation. Our summary metric, described in Section 3.3, can be tailored by practitioners for various datasets and tasks which may require more or less weight on semantic preservation.

Fluency ("PP"): Transferred sentences can exhibit high Acc and Sim while still being ungrammatical. So we add a third unsupervised metric to target fluency. We compute perplexity ("PP") of the transferred corpus, using a language model pretrained on the concatenation of $\mathbf{X}_0$ and $\mathbf{X}_1$. We note that perplexity is distinct from fluency. However, certain measures based on perplexity have been shown to correlate with sentence-level human fluency judgments (Gamon et al., 2005; Kann et al., 2018). Furthermore, as discussed in Section 3.3, we punish abnormally small perplexities, as transferred texts with such perplexities typically consist entirely of words and phrases that do not result in meaningful sentences. Our summary metric, described in Section 3.3, can be tailored by practitioners for various datasets and tasks which may require more or less weight on semantic preservation.

3.3 Summarizing Metrics into One Score

It is often useful to summarize multiple metrics into one number, for ease of tuning and model selection. To do so, we propose an adjusted geometric mean (GM) of a generated sentence q:

$$\mathrm{GM}_{\mathbf{t}}(q) = \left([100 \cdot \mathrm{Acc} - t_1]_+ \cdot [100 \cdot \mathrm{Sim} - t_2]_+ \right.$$
$$\left. \cdot \min\{[t_3 - \mathrm{PP}]_+, [\mathrm{PP} - t_4]_+\}\right)^{\frac{1}{3}} \qquad (1)$$

where $\mathbf{t} = (t_i)_{i\in[4]}$, and $[\cdot]_+ = \max(\cdot, 0)$. Note that as discussed above, we punish abnormally small perplexities by setting t_4.

When choosing models, different practitioners may prefer different trade-offs of Acc, Sim, and PP. As one example, we provide a set of parameters based on *our* experiments: $\mathbf{t} = (63, 71, 97, -37)$. We sampled 300 pairs of transferred sentences from a range of models from our two different tasks (Yelp and literature) and asked annotators which of the two sentences is better. We denote a pair of sentences by (y^+, y^-) where y^+ is preferred. We train the parameters $\mathbf{t}$ using the following loss:

$$L_{\mathrm{GM}}(\mathbf{t}) = \max(0, -\mathrm{GM}_\mathbf{t}(y^+) + \mathrm{GM}_\mathbf{t}(y^-) + 1)$$

In future work, a richer function $f(\mathrm{Acc}, \mathrm{Sim}, \mathrm{PP})$ could be learned from additional annotated data, and more diverse textual transfer tasks can be integrated into the parameter training.

4   Textual Transfer Models

The textual transfer systems introduced below are designed to target the metrics. These system variants are also used for metric evaluation. Note that each variant of the textual transfer system uses different components described below.

Our model is based on Shen et al. (2017). We define $\mathbf{y} \in \mathbb{R}^{200}$ and $\mathbf{z} \in \mathbb{R}^{500}$ to be latent style and content variables, respectively. $\mathbf{X}_0$ and $\mathbf{X}_1$ are two corpora containing sentences $\mathbf{x}_0^{(i)}$ and $\mathbf{x}_1^{(i)}$ respectively, where the word embeddings are in $\mathbb{R}^{100}$. We transfer using an encoder-decoder framework. The encoder $E : \mathcal{X} \times \mathcal{Y} \to \mathcal{Z}$ (where $\mathcal{X}, \mathcal{Y}, \mathcal{Z}$ are sentence domain, style space, and content space, respectively) is defined using an RNN with gated recurrent unit (GRU; Chung et al., 2014) cells. The decoder/generator $G : \mathcal{Y} \times \mathcal{Z} \to \mathcal{X}$ is defined also using a GRU RNN. We use $\widetilde{\mathbf{x}}$ to denote the style-transferred version of $\mathbf{x}$. We want $\widetilde{\mathbf{x}}_t^{(i)} = G(\mathbf{y}_{1-t}, E(\mathbf{x}_t^{(i)}, \mathbf{y}_t))$ for $t \in \{0, 1\}$.

4.1   Reconstruction and Adversarial Losses

Shen et al. (2017) used two families of losses for training: reconstruction and adversarial losses. The reconstruction loss solely helps the encoder and decoder work well at encoding and generating natural language, without any attempt at transfer:

$$L_{rec}(\theta_E, \theta_G)$$
$$= \sum_{t=0}^1 \mathbb{E}_{\mathbf{x}_t}\big[-\log p_G(\mathbf{x}_t \mid \mathbf{y}_t, E(\mathbf{x}_t, \mathbf{y}_t))\big] \quad (2)$$

The loss seeks to ensure that when a sentence $\mathbf{x}_t$ is encoded to its content vector and then decoded to generate a sentence, the generated sentence should match $\mathbf{x}_t$. For their adversarial loss, Shen et al. (2017) used a pair of discriminators: D_0 tries to distinguish between $\mathbf{x}_0$ and $\widetilde{\mathbf{x}}_1$, and D_1 between $\mathbf{x}_1$ and $\widetilde{\mathbf{x}}_0$. In particular, decoder G's hidden states are aligned instead of output words.

$$L_{adv_t}(\theta_E, \theta_G, \theta_{D_t}) = -\tfrac{1}{k}\sum_{i=1}^k \log D_t(\mathbf{h}_t^{(i)})$$
$$-\tfrac{1}{k}\sum_{i=1}^k \log(1 - D_t(\widetilde{\mathbf{h}}_{1-t}^{(i)})) \quad (3)$$

where k is the size of a mini-batch. D_t outputs the probability that its input is from style t where the classifiers are based on the convolutional neural network from Kim (2014). The CNNs use filter n-gram sizes of 3, 4, and 5, with 128 filters each. We obtain hidden states $\mathbf{h}$ by unfolding G from the initial state $(\mathbf{y}_t, \mathbf{z}_t^{(i)})$ and feeding in $\mathbf{x}_t^{(i)}$. We obtain hidden states $\widetilde{\mathbf{h}}$ by unfolding G from $(\mathbf{y}_{1-t}, \mathbf{z}_t^{(i)})$ and feeding in the previous output probability distributions.

4.2   Cyclic Consistency Loss

We use a "cyclic consistency" loss (Zhu et al., 2017) to encourage already-transferred sentences to be able to be recovered by transferring back again. This loss is similar to L_{rec} except we now transfer style twice in the loss. Recall that we seek to transfer $\mathbf{x}_t$ to $\widetilde{\mathbf{x}}_t$. After successful transfer, we expect $\widetilde{\mathbf{x}}_t$ to have style $\mathbf{y}_{1-t}$, and $\widetilde{\widetilde{\mathbf{x}}}_t$ (transferred back from $\widetilde{\mathbf{x}}_t$) to have style $\mathbf{y}_t$. We want $\widetilde{\widetilde{\mathbf{x}}}_t$ to be very close to the original untransferred $\mathbf{x}_t$. The loss is defined as

$$L_{cyc}(\theta_E, \theta_G) = \sum_{t=0}^1 \mathbb{E}_{\mathbf{x}_t}\big[-\log p_G(\mathbf{x}_t \mid \mathbf{y}_t, \widetilde{\mathbf{z}}_t)\big] \quad (4)$$

where $\widetilde{\mathbf{z}}_t = E(G(\mathbf{y}_{1-t}, E(\mathbf{x}_t, \mathbf{y}_t)), \mathbf{y}_{1-t})$ or, more concisely, $\widetilde{\mathbf{z}}_t = E(\widetilde{\mathbf{x}}_t, \mathbf{y}_{1-t})$.

To use this loss, the first step is to transfer sentences $\mathbf{x}_t$ from style t to $1 - t$ to get $\widetilde{\mathbf{x}}_t$. The second step is to transfer $\widetilde{\mathbf{x}}_t$ of style $1 - t$ back to t so that we can compute the loss of the words in $\mathbf{x}_t$ using probability distributions computed by the decoder. Backpropagation on the embedding, encoder, and decoder parameters will only be based on the second step, because the first step involves argmax operations which prevent backpropagation. Still, we find that the cyclic loss greatly improves semantic preservation during transfer.

4.3 Paraphrase Loss

While L_{rec} provides the model with one way to preserve style (i.e., simply reproduce the input), the model does not see any examples of style-preserving paraphrases. To address this, we add a paraphrase loss very similar to losses used in neural machine translation. We define the loss on a sentential paraphrase pair $\langle \mathbf{u}, \mathbf{v} \rangle$ and assume that $\mathbf{u}$ and $\mathbf{v}$ have the same style and content. The loss is the sum of token-level log losses for generating each word in $\mathbf{v}$ conditioned on the encoding of $\mathbf{u}$:

$$L_{para}(\theta_E, \theta_G)$$
$$= \sum_{t=0}^{1} \mathbb{E}_{\langle \mathbf{u}, \mathbf{v} \rangle} \left[-\log p_G(\mathbf{v} \mid \mathbf{y}_t, E(\mathbf{u}, \mathbf{y}_t)) \right] \quad (5)$$

For paraphrase pairs, we use the ParaNMT-50M dataset (Wieting and Gimpel, 2018).[1]

4.4 Language Modeling Loss

We attempt to improve fluency (our third metric) and assist transfer with a loss based on matching a pretrained language model for the target style. The loss is the cross entropy (CE) between the probability distribution from this language model and the distribution from the decoder:

$$L_{lang}(\theta_E, \theta_G) = \sum_{t=0}^{1} \mathbb{E}_{\mathbf{x}_t} \left[\sum_i \mathrm{CE}(\mathbf{l}_{t,i}, \mathbf{g}_{t,i}) \right] \quad (6)$$

where $\mathbf{l}_{t,i}$ and $\mathbf{g}_{t,i}$ are distributions over the vocabulary defined as follows:

$$\mathbf{l}_{t,i} = p_{LM_{1-t}}(\cdot \mid \widetilde{\mathbf{x}}_{t_{1:(i-1)}})$$
$$\mathbf{g}_{t,i} = p_G(\cdot \mid \widetilde{\mathbf{x}}_{t_{1:(i-1)}}, \mathbf{y}_{1-t}, E(\mathbf{x}_t, \mathbf{y}_t))$$

where $\cdot$ stands for all words in the vocabulary built from the corpora. When transferring from style t to $1 - t$, $\mathbf{l}_{t,i}$ is the distribution under the language model $p_{LM_{1-t}}$ pretrained on sentences from style $1 - t$ and $\mathbf{g}_{t,i}$ is the distribution under the decoder G. The two distributions $\mathbf{l}_{t,i}$ and $\mathbf{g}_{t,i}$ are over words at position i given the $i - 1$ words already predicted by the decoder. The two style-specific language models are pretrained on the corpora corresponding to the two styles. They are GRU RNNs with a dropout probability of 0.5, and they are kept fixed during the training of the transfer network.

4.5 Multiple Discriminators

Note that each of the textual transfer system variants uses different losses or components described

in this section. To create more variants, we add a second pair of discriminators, D_0' and D_1', to the adversarial loss to address the possible mode collapse problem (Nguyen et al., 2017). In particular, we use CNNs with n-gram filter sizes of 3, 4, and 5 for D_0 and D_1, and we use CNNs with n-gram sizes of 1, 2, and 3 for D_0' and D_1'. Also, for D_0' and D_1', we use the Wasserstein GAN (WGAN) framework (Arjovsky et al., 2017). The adversarial loss takes the following form:

$$L_{adv_t'}(\theta_E, \theta_G, \theta_{D_t'}) = \frac{1}{k} \sum_{i=1}^{k} \left[D_t'(\widetilde{\mathbf{h}}_t^{(i)}) \right.$$
$$\left. - D_t'(\mathbf{h}_t^{(i)}) + \xi(\| \nabla_{\mathring{\mathbf{h}}_t^{(i)}} D_t'(\mathring{\mathbf{h}}_t^{(i)}) \|_2 - 1)^2 \right] \quad (7)$$

where $\mathring{\mathbf{h}}_t^{(i)} = \epsilon_i \mathbf{h}_t^{(i)} + (1 - \epsilon_i) \widetilde{\mathbf{h}}_t^{(i)}$ where $\epsilon_i \sim$ Uniform$([0, 1])$ is sampled for each training instance. The adversarial loss is based on Arjovsky et al. (2017),[2] with the exception that we use the hidden states of the decoder instead of word distributions as inputs to D_t', similar to Eq. (3).

We choose WGAN in the hope that its differentiability properties can help avoid vanishing gradient and mode collapse problems. We expect the generator to receive helpful gradients even if the discriminators perform well. This approach leads to much better outputs, as shown below.

4.6 Summary

We iteratively update (1) θ_{D_0}, θ_{D_1}, $\theta_{D_0'}$, and $\theta_{D_1'}$ by gradient descent on L_{adv_0}, L_{adv_1}, $L_{adv_0'}$, and $L_{adv_1'}$, respectively, and (2) θ_E, θ_G by gradient descent on $L_{total} = \lambda_1 L_{rec} + \lambda_2 L_{para} + \lambda_3 L_{cyc} + \lambda_4 L_{lang} - \lambda_5 (L_{adv_0} + L_{adv_1}) - \lambda_6 (L_{adv_0'} + L_{adv_1'})$. Depending on which model is being trained (see Table 2), the λ_i's for the unused losses will be zero. More details are shown in Section 5. The appendix shows the full algorithm.

5 Experimental Setup

5.1 Datasets

Yelp sentiment. We use the same Yelp dataset as Shen et al. (2017), which uses corpora of positive and negative Yelp reviews. The goal of the transfer task is to generate rewritten sentences with similar content but inverted sentiment. We use the same train/development/test split as Shen et al. (2017). The dataset has 268K, 38K, 76K positive training, development, and test sentences, respectively, and 179K/25K/51K negative sentences. Like Shen

---

[1] We first filter out sentence pairs where one sentence is the substring of another, and then randomly select 90K pairs.

[2] We use a default value of $\xi = 10$.

et al. (2017), we only use sentences with 15 or fewer words.

Literature. We consider two corpora of literature. The first corpus contains works of Charles Dickens collected from Project Gutenberg. The second corpus is comprised of modern literature from the Toronto Books Corpus (Zhu et al., 2015). Sentences longer than 25 words are removed. Unlike the Yelp dataset, the two corpora have very different vocabularies. This dataset poses challenges for the textual transfer task, and it provides diverse data for assessing quality of our evaluation system. Given the different and sizable vocabulary, we preprocess by using the named entity recognizer in Stanford CoreNLP (Manning et al., 2014) to replace names and locations with -PERSON- and -LOCATION- tags, respectively. We also use byte-pair encoding (BPE), commonly used in generation tasks (Sennrich et al., 2016b). We only use sentences with lengths between 6 and 25. The resulting dataset has 156K, 5K, 5K Dickens training, development, and testing sentences, respectively, and 165K/5K/5K modern literature sentences.

5.2 Hyperparameter Settings

Section 4.6 requires setting the λ weights for each component. Depending on which model is being trained (see Table 2), the λ_i's for the unused losses will be zero. Otherwise, we set $\lambda_1 = 1$, $\lambda_2 = 0.2$, $\lambda_3 = 5$, $\lambda_4 = 10^{-3}$, $\lambda_5 = 1$, $\lambda_6 = 2^{-ep}$ where ep is the number of epochs. For optimization we use Adam (Kingma and Ba, 2014) with a learning rate of 10^{-4}. We implement our models using TensorFlow (et al., 2015).[3] Code is available via the first author's webpage yzpang.me.

5.3 Pretrained Evaluation Models

For the pretrained classifiers, the accuracies on the Yelp and Literature development sets are 0.974 and 0.933, respectively. For language models, the perplexities on the Yelp and Literature development sets are 27.4 and 40.8, respectively.

6 Results and Analysis

6.1 Analyzing Metric Relationships

Table 2 shows results for the Yelp dataset and Figure 1 plots learning trajectories of those models.

---

[3]Our implementation is based on code from Shen et al. (2017).

	Acc	Sim	PP	GM
M0: Shen et al. (2017)	0.818	0.719	37.3	10.0
M1: M0+*para*	0.819	0.734	26.3	14.2
M2: M0+*cyc*	0.813	0.770	36.4	18.8
M3: M0+*cyc+lang*	0.807	0.796	28.4	21.5
M4: M0+*cyc+para*	0.798	0.783	39.7	19.2
M5: M0+*cyc+para+lang*	0.804	0.785	27.1	20.3
M6: M0+*cyc+2d*	0.805	**0.817**	43.3	21.6
M7: M6+*para+lang*	0.818	0.805	**29.0**	**22.8**

Table 2: Yelp results with various systems and automatic metrics at a nearly-fixed Acc, with best scores in boldface. We use M0 to denote Shen et al. (2017).

	Acc	Sim	PP	GM
M0: Shen et al. (2017)	0.694	0.728	**22.3**	8.81
M1: M0+*para*	0.702	0.747	23.6	11.7
M2: M0+*cyc*	0.692	0.781	49.9	**12.8**
M3: M0+*cyc+lang*	0.698	0.754	39.2	12.0
M4: M0+*cyc+para*	0.702	0.757	33.9	**12.8**
M5: M0+*cyc+para+lang*	0.688	0.753	28.6	11.8
M6: M0+*cyc+2d*	0.704	**0.794**	63.2	**12.8**
M7: M6+*para+lang*	0.706	0.768	49.0	**12.8**

Table 3: Literature results with various systems and automatic metrics at a nearly-fixed Acc, with best scores in boldface. We use M0 to denote Shen et al. (2017).

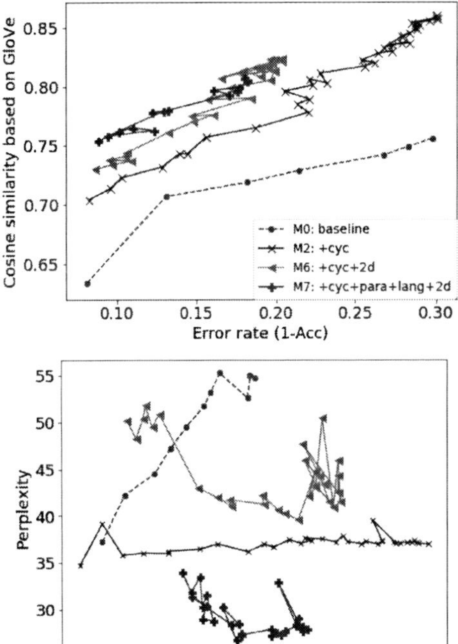

Figure 1: Learning trajectories with models from Table 2. Metrics are computed on the dev sets. Figures for Literature (with similar trends) are in supplementary.

Table 3 shows results for the Literature dataset. Models for the Literature dataset show similar

Dataset	Models		Transfer quality			Semantic preservation				Fluency			
	A	B	A>B	B>A	Tie	A>B	B>A	Tie	Δ_{Sim}	A>B	B>A	Tie	Δ_{PP}
Yelp	M0	M2	9.0	6.0	85.1	1.5	**25.4**	73.1	-0.05	10.4	**23.9**	65.7	0.9
	M0	M7	9.6	14.7	75.8	2.5	**54.5**	42.9	-0.09	4.6	**39.4**	56.1	8.3
	M6	M7	13.7	11.6	74.7	16.0	16.7	67.4	0.01	10.3	20.0	69.7	14.3
	M2	M7	5.8	9.3	84.9	8.1	**25.6**	66.3	-0.04	14.0	**26.7**	59.3	7.4
Literature	M2	M6	4.2	6.7	89.2	16.7	20.8	62.5	0.01	**40.8**	13.3	45.8	-13.3
	M6	M7	15.8	13.3	70.8	**25.0**	9.2	65.8	0.03	14.2	20.8	65.0	14.2

Table 4: Manual evaluation results (%) using models from Table 2 (i.e., with roughly fixed Acc). > means "better than". $\Delta_{\text{Sim}} = \text{Sim}(A) - \text{Sim}(B)$, and $\Delta_{\text{PP}} = \text{PP}(A) - \text{PP}(B)$ (note that lower PP generally means better fluency). Each row uses at least 120 sentence pairs. A cell is bold if it represents a model win of at least 10%.

trends. The figures show trajectories of statistics on corpora transferred/generated from the dev set during learning. Each two consecutive markers deviate by half an epoch of training. Lower-left markers generally precede upper-right ones. In Figure 1(a), the plots of Sim by error rate $(1 - \text{Acc})$ exhibit positive slopes, meaning that error rate is positively correlated with Sim. Curves to the upper-left corner represent better trade-off between error rate and Sim. In the plots of PP by Sim in Figure 1(b), the M0 curve exhibits large positive slope but the curves for other models do not, which indicates that M0 sacrifices PP for Sim. Other models maintain consistent PP as Sim increases during training.

6.2 System-Level Validation

Annotators were shown the untransferred sentence, as well as sentences produced by two models (which we refer to as A and B). They were asked to judge which better reflects the target style (A, B, or tie), which has better semantic preservation of the original (A, B, or tie), and which is more fluent (A, B, or tie). Results are shown in Table 4.

Overall, the results show the same trends as our automatic metrics. For example, on Yelp, large differences in human judgments of semantic preservation (M2>M0, M7>M0, M7>M2) also show the largest differences in Sim, while M6 and M7 have very similar human judgments and very similar Sim scores.

6.3 Sentence-Level Validation of Metrics

We describe a human sentence-level validation of our metrics in Table 5.

To validate Acc, human annotators were asked to judge the style of 100 transferred sentences (sampled equally from M0, M2, M6, M7). Note that it is a binary choice question (style 0 or style 1

Metric	Method of validation	Yelp	Lit.
Acc	% of machine and human judgments that match	94	84
Sim	Spearman's ρ b/w Sim and human ratings of semantic preservation	0.79	0.75
PP	Spearman's ρ b/w negative PP and human ratings of fluency	0.81	0.67

Table 5: Human sentence-level validation of metrics; 100 examples for each dataset for validating Acc; 150 each for Sim and PP; see text for validation of GM.

without "tie" option) so that human annotators had to make a choice. We then compute the percentage of machine and human judgments that match.

We validate Sim and PP by computing sentence-level Spearman's ρ between the metric and human judgments (an integer score from 1 to 4) on 150 generated sentences (sampled equally from M0, M2, M6, M7). We presented pairs of original sentences and transferred sentences to human annotators. They were asked to rate the level of semantic similarity (and similarly for fluency) where 1 means "extremely bad", 2 means "bad/ok/needs improvement", 3 means "good", and 4 means "very good." They were also given 5 examples for each rating (i.e., a total of 20 for four levels) before annotating. From Table 5, all validations show strong correlations on the Yelp dataset and reasonable correlations on Literature.

We validate GM by obtaining human pairwise preferences (without the "tie" option) of overall transfer quality and measuring the fraction of pairs in which the GM score agrees with the human preference. Out of 300 pairs (150 from each dataset), 258 (86%) match.

The transferred sentences used in the evaluation are sampled from the development sets produced by models M0, M2, M6, and M7, at the accuracy levels used in Table 2. In the data preparation for the manual annotation, there is sufficient randomization regarding model and textual transfer direction.

6.4 Comparing Losses

Cyclic Consistency Loss. We compare the trajectories of the baseline model (M0) and the +*cyc* model (M2). Table 2 and Figure 1 show that under similar Acc, M2 has much better semantic similarity for both Yelp and Literature. In fact, cyclic consistency loss proves to be the strongest driver of semantic preservation across all of our model configurations. The other losses do not constrain the semantic relationship across style transfer, so we include the cyclic loss in M3 to M7.

Paraphrase Loss. Table 2 shows that the model with paraphrase loss (M1) slightly improves Sim over M0 on both datasets under similar Acc. For Yelp, M1 has better Acc and PP than M0 at comparable semantic similarity. So, when used alone, the paraphrase loss helps. However, when combined with other losses (e.g., compare M2 to M4), its benefits are mixed. For Yelp, M4 is slightly better in preserving semantics and producing fluent output, but for Literature, M4 is slightly worse. A challenge in introducing an additional paraphrase dataset is that its notions of similarity may clash with those of content preservation in the transfer task. For Yelp, both corpora share a great deal of semantic content, but Literature shows systematic semantic differences even after preprocessing.

Language Modeling Loss. When comparing between M2 and M3, between M4 and M5, and between M6 and M7, we find that the addition of the language modeling loss reduces PP, sometimes at a slight cost of semantic preservation.

6.5 Results based on Supervised Evaluation

If we want to compare the models using one single number, GM is our unsupervised approach. We can also compute BLEU scores between our generated outputs and human-written gold standard outputs using the 1000 Yelp references from Li et al. (2018). For BLEU scores reported for the methods of Li et al. (2018), we use the values reported by Yang et al. (2018b). We use the same BLEU implementation as used by Yang et al. (2018b), i.e., `multi-bleu.perl`. We compare three models selected during training from each of our M6 and M7 settings. We also report post-transfer accuracies reported by prior work, as well

Model	BLEU	Acc*
Fu et al. (2018)		
Multi-decoder	7.6	0.792
Style embed.	15.4	0.095
Li et al. (2018)		
Template	18.0	0.867
Delete/Retrieve	12.6	0.909
Yang et al. (2018b)		
LM	13.4	0.854
LM + classifier	**22.3**	0.900
Untransferred	**31.4**	0.024

M.	BLEU	Acc
M0	4.9	0.818
M6	22.3	0.804
M6	**22.5**	0.843
M6	16.3	0.897
M7	17.0	0.814
M7	16.3	0.839
M7	12.9	0.901

Table 6: Results on Yelp sentiment transfer, where BLEU is between 1000 transferred sentences and human references, and Acc is restricted to the same 1000 sentences. Our best models (right table) achieve higher BLEU than prior work at similar levels of Acc, but untransferred sentences achieve the highest BLEU. Acc*: the definition of Acc varies by row because of different classifiers in use. Other results from Li et al. (2018) are not included as they are worse.

our own computed Acc scores for M0, M6, M7, and the untransferred sentences. Though the classifiers differ across models, their accuracy tends to be very high (> 0.97), making it possible to make rough comparisons of Acc across them.

BLEU scores and post-transfer accuracies are shown in Table 6. The most striking result is that *untransferred* sentences have the highest BLEU score by a large margin, suggesting that prior work for this task has not yet eclipsed the trivial baseline of returning the input sentence. However, at similar levels of Acc, our models have higher BLEU scores than prior work. We additionally find that supervised BLEU shows a trade-off with Acc: for a single model type, higher Acc generally corresponds to lower BLEU.

7 Conclusion

We proposed three kinds of metrics for non-parallel textual transfer, studied their relationships, and developed learning criteria to address them. We emphasize that all three metrics are needed to make meaningful comparisons among models. We expect our components to be applicable to a broad range of generation tasks.

Acknowledgments

We thank Karl Stratos and Zewei Chu for helpful discussions, the annotators for performing manual evaluations, and the anonymous reviewers for useful comments. We also thank Google for a faculty research award to K. Gimpel that partially supported this research.

References

Martín Abadi et al. 2015. TensorFlow: Large-scale machine learning on heterogeneous systems. Software available from tensorflow.org.

Martin Arjovsky, Soumith Chintala, and Léon Bottou. 2017. Wasserstein GAN. *arXiv preprint arXiv:1701.07875*.

Mikel Artetxe, Gorka Labaka, Eneko Agirre, and Kyunghyun Cho. 2017. Unsupervised neural machine translation. *arXiv preprint arXiv:1710.11041*.

Liqun Chen, Shuyang Dai, Chenyang Tao, Haichao Zhang, Zhe Gan, Dinghan Shen, Yizhe Zhang, Guoyin Wang, Ruiyi Zhang, and Lawrence Carin. 2018. Adversarial text generation via feature-mover's distance. In *Advances in Neural Information Processing Systems*, pages 4671–4682.

Junyoung Chung, Caglar Gulcehre, KyungHyun Cho, and Yoshua Bengio. 2014. Empirical evaluation of gated recurrent neural networks on sequence modeling. *arXiv preprint arXiv:1412.3555*.

Michael Denkowski and Alon Lavie. 2014. Meteor universal: Language specific translation evaluation for any target language. In *Proceedings of the EACL 2014 Workshop on Statistical Machine Translation*.

Jessica Ficler and Yoav Goldberg. 2017. Controlling linguistic style aspects in neural language generation. In *Proceedings of the Workshop on Stylistic Variation*, pages 94–104, Copenhagen, Denmark. Association for Computational Linguistics.

Zhenxin Fu, Xiaoye Tan, Nanyun Peng, Dongyan Zhao, and Rui Yan. 2018. Style transfer in text: exploration and evaluation. In *32nd AAAI Conference on Artificial Intelligence (AAAI-18)*.

Michael Gamon, Anthony Aue, and Martine Smets. 2005. Sentence-level MT evaluation without reference translations: Beyond language modeling. In *Proceedings of EAMT*, pages 103–111.

Ian Goodfellow, Jean Pouget-Abadie, Mehdi Mirza, Bing Xu, David Warde-Farley, Sherjil Ozair, Aaron Courville, and Yoshua Bengio. 2014. Generative adversarial nets. In *Advances in Neural Information Processing Systems*, pages 2672–2680.

George Heidorn. 2000. Intelligent writing assistance. *Handbook of natural language processing*, pages 181–207.

Zhiting Hu, Zichao Yang, Xiaodan Liang, Ruslan Salakhutdinov, and Eric P. Xing. 2017. Toward controlled generation of text. In *Proceedings of the 34th International Conference on Machine Learning*, volume 70 of *Proceedings of Machine Learning Research*, pages 1587–1596.

Katharina Kann, Sascha Rothe, and Katja Filippova. 2018. Sentence-level fluency evaluation: References help, but can be spared! In *Proceedings of the 22nd Conference on Computational Natural Language Learning, CoNLL 2018, Brussels, Belgium, October 31 - November 1, 2018*, pages 313–323.

Yoon Kim. 2014. Convolutional neural networks for sentence classification. *arXiv preprint arXiv:1408.5882*.

Diederik P. Kingma and Jimmy Ba. 2014. Adam: A method for stochastic optimization. *arXiv preprint arXiv:1412.6980*.

Guillaume Lample, Ludovic Denoyer, and Marc'Aurelio Ranzato. 2017. Unsupervised machine translation using monolingual corpora only. *arXiv preprint arXiv:1711.00043*.

Jiwei Li, Will Monroe, Tianlin Shi, Sébastien Jean, Alan Ritter, and Dan Jurafsky. 2017. Adversarial learning for neural dialogue generation. In *Proceedings of the Conference on Empirical Methods in Natural Language Processing*, pages 2147–2159. Association for Computational Linguistics.

Juncen Li, Robin Jia, He He, and Percy Liang. 2018. Delete, retrieve, generate: a simple approach to sentiment and style transfer. In *Proceedings of the 2018 Conference of the North American Chapter of the Association for Computational Linguistics: Human Language Technologies, Volume 1 (Long Papers)*, pages 1865–1874. Association for Computational Linguistics.

Lajanugen Logeswaran, Honglak Lee, and Samy Bengio. 2018. Content preserving text generation with attribute controls. In *Advances in Neural Information Processing Systems*, pages 5103–5113.

Christopher Manning, Mihai Surdeanu, John Bauer, Jenny Finkel, Steven Bethard, and David McClosky. 2014. The Stanford CoreNLP natural language processing toolkit. In *Proceedings of 52nd Annual Meeting of the Association for Computational Linguistics: System Demonstrations*, pages 55–60, Baltimore, Maryland. Association for Computational Linguistics.

Remi Mir, Bjarke Felbo, Nick Obradovich, and Iyad Rahwan. 2019. Evaluating style transfer for text. In *Proceedings of the 2019 Conference of the North American Chapter of the Association for Computational Linguistics: Human Language Technologies, Volume 1 (Long and Short Papers)*, pages 495–504, Minneapolis, Minnesota. Association for Computational Linguistics.

Tu Nguyen, Trung Le, Hung Vu, and Dinh Phung. 2017. Dual discriminator generative adversarial nets. In *Advances in Neural Information Processing Systems*, pages 2667–2677.

Nikola I Nikolov and Richard HR Hahnloser. 2018. Large-scale hierarchical alignment for author style transfer. *arXiv preprint arXiv:1810.08237*.

Kishore Papineni, Salim Roukos, Todd Ward, and Wei-Jing Zhu. 2002. Bleu: a method for automatic evaluation of machine translation. In *Proceedings of the 40th Annual Meeting of the Association for Computational Linguistics*.

Jeffrey Pennington, Richard Socher, and Christopher Manning. 2014. Glove: Global vectors for word representation. In *Proceedings of the 2014 Conference on Empirical Methods in Natural Language Processing*. Association for Computational Linguistics.

Shrimai Prabhumoye, Yulia Tsvetkov, Ruslan Salakhutdinov, and Alan W Black. 2018. Style transfer through back-translation. In *Proceedings of the 56th Annual Meeting of the Association for Computational Linguistics (Volume 1: Long Papers)*, pages 866–876, Melbourne, Australia. Association for Computational Linguistics.

Sudha Rao and Joel Tetreault. 2018. Dear sir or madam, may i introduce the gyafc dataset: Corpus, benchmarks and metrics for formality style transfer. *arXiv preprint arXiv:1803.06535*.

Alan Ritter, Colin Cherry, and William B Dolan. 2011. Data-driven response generation in social media. In *Proceedings of the conference on empirical methods in natural language processing*, pages 583–593. Association for Computational Linguistics.

Cicero Nogueira dos Santos, Igor Melnyk, and Inkit Padhi. 2018. Fighting offensive language on social media with unsupervised text style transfer. *arXiv preprint arXiv:1805.07685*.

Rico Sennrich, Barry Haddow, and Alexandra Birch. 2016a. Controlling politeness in neural machine translation via side constraints. In *Proceedings of the 2016 Conference of the North American Chapter of the Association for Computational Linguistics: Human Language Technologies*, pages 35–40. Association for Computational Linguistics.

Rico Sennrich, Barry Haddow, and Alexandra Birch. 2016b. Neural machine translation of rare words with subword units. In *Proceedings of the 54th Annual Meeting of the Association for Computational Linguistics (Volume 1: Long Papers)*, pages 1715–1725. Association for Computational Linguistics.

Tianxiao Shen, Tao Lei, Regina Barzilay, and Tommi Jaakkola. 2017. Style transfer from non-parallel text by cross-alignment. In *Advances in Neural Information Processing Systems 30*, pages 6833–6844. Curran Associates, Inc.

Rakshith Shetty, Bernt Schiele, and Mario Fritz. 2017. Author attribute anonymity by adversarial training of neural machine translation. *arXiv preprint arXiv:1711.01921*.

John Wieting and Kevin Gimpel. 2018. ParaNMT-50M: Pushing the limits of paraphrastic sentence embeddings with millions of machine translations.

In *Proceedings of the 56th Annual Meeting of the Association for Computational Linguistics*. Association for Computational Linguistics.

Jingjing Xu, Xu Sun, Qi Zeng, Xiaodong Zhang, Xuancheng Ren, Houfeng Wang, and Wenjie Li. 2018. Unpaired sentiment-to-sentiment translation: A cycled reinforcement learning approach. In *Proceedings of the 56th Annual Meeting of the Association for Computational Linguistics (Volume 1: Long Papers)*, pages 979–988, Melbourne, Australia. Association for Computational Linguistics.

Zhen Yang, Wei Chen, Feng Wang, and Bo Xu. 2018a. Improving neural machine translation with conditional sequence generative adversarial nets. In *Proceedings of the 2018 Conference of the North American Chapter of the Association for Computational Linguistics: Human Language Technologies, Volume 1 (Long Papers)*, pages 1346–1355, New Orleans, Louisiana. Association for Computational Linguistics.

Zichao Yang, Zhiting Hu, Chris Dyer, Eric P Xing, and Taylor Berg-Kirkpatrick. 2018b. Unsupervised text style transfer using language models as discriminators. *arXiv preprint arXiv:1805.11749*.

Lantao Yu, Weinan Zhang, Jun Wang, and Yong Yu. 2017. Seqgan: Sequence generative adversarial nets with policy gradient. In *Thirty-First AAAI Conference on Artificial Intelligence*.

Yi Zhang, Jingjing Xu, Pengcheng Yang, and Xu Sun. 2018. Learning sentiment memories for sentiment modification without parallel data. In *Proceedings of the 2018 Conference on Empirical Methods in Natural Language Processing*, pages 1103–1108, Brussels, Belgium. Association for Computational Linguistics.

Jun-Yan Zhu, Taesung Park, Phillip Isola, and Alexei A Efros. 2017. Unpaired image-to-image translation using cycle-consistent adversarial networks. *arXiv preprint arXiv:1703.10593*.

Yukun Zhu, Ryan Kiros, Rich Zemel, Ruslan Salakhutdinov, Raquel Urtasun, Antonio Torralba, and Sanja Fidler. 2015. Aligning books and movies: Towards story-like visual explanations by watching movies and reading books. In *Proceedings of the IEEE International Conference on Computer Vision*, pages 19–27.

Enhanced Transformer Model for Data-to-Text Generation

Li Gong, Josep Crego, Jean Senellart
SYSTRAN / 5 rue Feydeau, 75002 Paris, France
`firstname.lastname@systrangroup.com`

Abstract

Neural models have recently shown significant progress on data-to-text generation tasks in which descriptive texts are generated conditioned on database records. In this work, we present a new Transformer-based data-to-text generation model which learns content selection and summary generation in an end-to-end fashion. We introduce two extensions to the baseline transformer model: First, we modify the latent representation of the input, which helps to significantly improve the content correctness of the output summary; Second, we include an additional learning objective that accounts for content selection modelling. In addition, we propose two data augmentation methods that succeed to further improve performance of the resulting generation models. Evaluation experiments show that our final model outperforms current state-of-the-art systems as measured by different metrics: BLEU, content selection precision and content ordering. We made publicly available the transformer extension presented in this paper[1].

1 Introduction

Data-to-text generation is an important task in natural language generation (NLG). It refers to the task of automatically producing a descriptive text from non-linguistic structured data (tables, database records, spreadsheets, *etc.*). Table 1 illustrates an example of data-to-text NLG, with statistics of a NBA basketball game (top) and the corresponding game summary (bottom).

Traditional approaches perform the summary generation in two separate steps: content selection ("what to say") (Duboue and McKeown, 2001, 2003) and surface realization ("how to say it") (Stent et al., 2004; Reiter et al., 2005). After the emergence of sequence-to-sequence (S2S)

learning, a variety of data-to-text generation models are proposed (Lebret et al., 2016; Mei et al., 2015; Wiseman et al., 2017) and trained in an end-to-end fashion. These models are actually conditional language models which generate summaries conditioned on the latent representation of input tables. Despite producing overall fluent text, Wiseman et al. (2017) show that NLG models perform poorly on content-oriented measures.

Different from other NLG tasks (e.g., machine translation), data-to-text generation faces several additional challenges. First, data-to-text generation models have to select the content before generating text. In machine translation, the source and target sentences are semantically equivalent to each other, whereas in data-to-text generation, the model initially selects appropriate content from the input data to secondly generate fluent sentences that incorporate the selected content. Second, the training data in data-to-text generation task is often very limited. Unlike machine translation, where training data consist of translated sentence pairs, data-to-text generation models are trained from examples composed of structured data and its corresponding descriptive summary, which are much harder to produce.

In this paper, we tackle both challenges previously discussed. We introduce a new data-to-text generation model which jointly learns content selection and text generation, and we present two data augmentation methods. More precisely, we make the following contributions:

1. We adapt the Transformer (Vaswani et al., 2017) architecture by modifying the input table representation (record embedding) and introducing an additional objective function (content selection modelling).

2. We create synthetic data following two data augmentation techniques and investigate

---

[1] `https://github.com/gongliym/data2text-transformer`

Proceedings of the 3rd Workshop on Neural Generation and Translation (WNGT 2019), pages 148–156
Hong Kong, China, November 4, 2019. ©2019 Association for Computational Linguistics
www.aclweb.org/anthology/D19-56%2d

their impacts on different evaluation metrics.

We show that our model outperforms current state-of-the-art systems on BLEU, content selection precision and content ordering metrics.

2 Related Work

Automatic summary generation has been a topic of interest for a long time (Reiter and Dale, 1997; Tanaka-Ishii et al., 1998). It has interesting applications in many different domains, such as sport game summary generation (Barzilay and Lapata, 2005; Liang et al., 2009), weather-forecast generation (Reiter et al., 2005) and recipe generation (Yang et al., 2016).

Traditional data-to-text generation approaches perform the summary generation in two separate steps: content selection and surface realization. For content selection, a number of approaches were proposed to automatically select the elements of content and extract ordering constraints from an aligned corpus of input data and output summaries (Duboue and McKeown, 2001, 2003). In (Barzilay and Lapata, 2005), the content selection is treated as a collective classification problem which allows the system to capture contextual dependencies between input data items. For surface realization, Stent et al. (2004) proposed to transform the input data into an intermediary structure and then to generate natural language text from it; Reiter et al. (2005) presented a method to generate text using consistent data-to-word rules. Angeli et al. (2010) broke up the two steps into a sequence of local decisions where they used two classifiers to select content form database and another classifier to choose a suitable template to render the content.

More recently, work on this topic has focused on end-to-end generation models. Konstas and Lapata (2012) described an end-to-end generation model which jointly models content selection and surface realization. Mei et al. (2015) proposed a neural encoder-aligner-decoder model which first encodes the entire input record dataset then the aligner module performs the content selection for the decoder to generate output summary. Some other work extends the encoder-decoder model to be able to copy words directly from the input (Yang et al., 2016; Gu et al., 2016; Gulcehre et al., 2016). Wiseman et al. (2017) investigates different data-to-text generation approaches and introduces a new corpus (ROTOWIRE, see Table 1)

for the data-to-text generation task along with a series of automatic measures for the content-oriented evaluation. Based on (Wiseman et al., 2017), Puduppully et al. (2019) incorporates content selection and planing mechanisms into the encoder-decoder system and improves the state-of-the-art on the ROTOWIRE dataset.

3 Data-to-Text Generation Model

In this section, we first formulate the data-to-text generation problem and introduce our data-to-text generation baseline model. Next, we detail the extensions introduced to our baseline network, namely *Record Embedding* and *Content Selection Modelling*.

Problem Statement

The objective of data-to-text generation is to generate a descriptive summary given structured data. Input of the model consists of a table of records (see Table 1, top and middle). Let $\mathbf{s} = \{r_i\}_{i=1}^{I}$ be a set of records, each record r_i consists of four features:

- *Entity*: the name of player or team (e.g., Celtics, LeBron James)

- *Type*: the table header (e.g., WIN, PTS)

- *Value*: the value in the table (e.g., 14, Boston)

- *Info*: game information (e.g., H/W, V/L) which represents the team or player is Home- or Vis-team and Win- or Loss-team.

Note that there is no order relationship in s.

The output $\mathbf{t}$ (see Table 1, bottom) is a text document which is a descriptive summary for the record set s. Note $\mathbf{t} = t_1 \ldots t_J$ with J as the document length. Pairs (s, t) constitute the training data for data-to-text generation systems. Data-to-text generation probability is given by:

$$P(\mathbf{t}|\mathbf{s}, \theta) = \prod_{j=1}^{J} P(t_j|\mathbf{s}, \mathbf{t}_{<j}; \theta) \qquad (1)$$

where $\mathbf{t}_{<j} = t_1 \ldots t_{j-1}$ is the generated partial document and θ is the model parameters.

Data-to-Text Transformer Model

In this section, we present how we adapt the Transformer model for the data-to-text generation tasks. First, the input embedding of Transformer encoder is replaced by our record embedding to better incorporate the record information. Second, a new learning objective is added into our model to improve its content-oriented performance.

3.1 Record Embedding

The input of data-to-text model encoder is a sequence of records. Each record is a tuple of four features (*Entity, Type, Value, Info*). Inspired by previous work (Yang et al., 2016; Wiseman et al., 2017; Puduppully et al., 2019), we embed features into vectors, and use the concatenation of feature embeddings as the embedding of record.

$$\mathbf{r}_i = [\mathbf{r}_{i,1}; \mathbf{r}_{i,2}; \mathbf{r}_{i,3}; \mathbf{r}_{i,4}] \tag{2}$$

where $\mathbf{r}_i \in \mathbb{R}^{dim}$ is the ith record embedding in the input sequence and $\mathbf{r}_{i,j} \in \mathbb{R}^{\frac{dim}{4}}$ is the jth feature embedding in $\mathbf{r}_i$.

Since there is no order relationship within the records, the positional embedding of the Transformer encoder is removed.

3.2 Content Selection Modeling

Besides record embedding, we also add a new learning objective into the Transformer model.

As presented before, we need to select the content from the input records before generating the output summary. Some records are generally important no mater the game context, such as the team name record and team score record, whereas the importance of some other records depend on the game context. For example, a player having the highest points in the game is more likely to be mentioned in the game summary. Within the Transformer architecture, the self-attention mechanism can generate the latent representation for each record by jointly conditioning on all other records in the input dataset. A binary prediction layer is added on top of the Transformer encoder output (as shown in Figure 1) to predict whether or not one record will be mentioned in the target summary.

The architecture of our data-to-text Transformer model is shown in Figure 1. As presented before, the encoder takes the record embedding as input and generates the latent representation for each record in the input sequence. The output of encoder is then used to predict the importance of each record and also serves as the context of the decoder. The decoder of our model is the same as the original Transformer model in machine translation. It predicts the next word conditioned on

the encoder output and the previous tokens in the summary sequence.

In content selection modeling, the input record sequences together with its label sequences are used to optimize the encoder by minimizing the cross-entropy loss. In language generation training, the encoder and decoder are trained together to maximize the log-likelihood of the training data. The two learning objectives are trained alternatively[2].

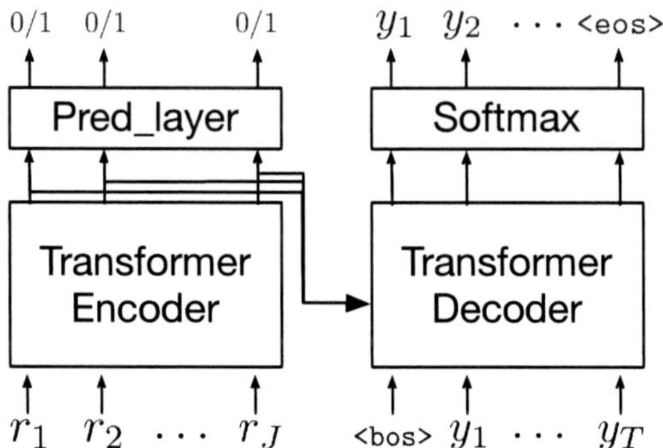

Figure 1: Model Architecture

4 Data Augmentation Methods

In data-to-text generation task, the model needs to not only generate fluent text, but also generate text which is coherent with the input records. Several content-oriented evaluation metrics are proposed in (Wiseman et al., 2017) to evaluate such cohesion, including the precision of record generation and the recall rate with respect to the records in gold summary.

In this section, we present two data augmentation methods: *synthetic data generation* and *training data selection*. Each of them has different impacts on the content-oriented evaluation results.

4.1 Synthetic Data Generation

In order to improve the cohesion between the input records and output summary, we need more data to enhance the encoder-decoder attention of the decoder. Here we introduce a method to generate synthetic training data.

We first randomly change the values of records and the changed record set ($\mathbf{s}'$) is then used to generate automatic summary ($\mathbf{t}'$) by a trained data-to-text system. The synthetic data pairs ($\mathbf{s}'$, $\mathbf{t}'$) are then used to improve such system.

---

[2]An alternative approach is joint training that achieves comparable results.

This idea is inspired by the *back-translation* technique widely used in neural machine translation, with two important differences:

First, *back-translation*, typically employs monolingual human texts, which are easy found. In our case, since it is difficult to find additional structured (table) data for the same kind of game matches, we use the existing data sets and introduce variations in the values of the table records. In order to keep the data cohesion in the table, the change is constrained with the following rules:

- only numeric values are changed. Non-numeric values such as the position of a player or the city name of a team are kept the same.

- after the change, the team scores should not violate the win/loss relation

- the changed values should stay in the normal range of its value type. It should not bigger than its maximum value or smaller than its minimum value through all games.

Our data generation technique doubles the amount of training data available for learning.

Second, another difference with the *back-translation* technique is the "translation direction". In machine translation, the additional monolingual text used is found in target language, and back-translated into the source language. Thus, ensuring that the target side of the synthetic data follows the same distribution as real human texts. In our case, the target side of synthetic data is also automatically generated which is known to introduce noise in the resulting network.

4.2 Training Data Selection

A deficiency of data-to-text NLG systems is the poor coverage of relations produced in the generated summaries. In order to increase the coverage, a simple solution consists of learning to produce a larger number of relations. Here, we present a straightforward method to bias our model to output more relations by means of fine-tuning on the training examples containing a greater number of relations.

We use an information extraction (IE) system to extract the number of relations of each training summary. Then, we select for fine-tuning our baseline model the subset of training data in which

each summary contains at least N relations. In this work, we take advantage of the IE system[3] provided by (Puduppully et al., 2019), and the distribution of the number of relations in the training summary is illustrated in Figure 2.

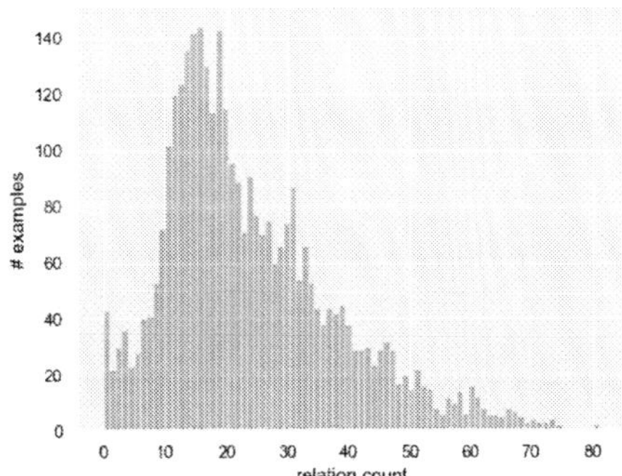

Figure 2: relation count distribution in training data.

5 Experimental Setup

5.1 Data and Preprocessing

We run the experiments with the ROTOWIRE dataset (Wiseman et al., 2017), a dataset of NBA basketball game summaries, paired with their corresponding box- and line-score tables. Table 1 illustrates an example of the dataset. In the box-score table, each team has at most 13 players and each player is described by 23 types of values. In the line-score table, each team has 15 different types of values. In addition, the date of each game is converted into the day of the week (such as "*Saturday*") as an additional record. In the preprocessing step, the input box- and line-score tables are converted into a fix-length sequence of records. Each sequence contains 629 records.[4] As for the associate summaries, the average length is 337 tokens, and the vocabulary size is 11.3K. The ROTOWIRE dataset contains 4853 summaries in total, in which 3398 summaries are for training, 727 for validation and 728 for test.

In content selection modelling, we need the labels of input records to indicate which records in the input will be mentioned in the output summary. Here we use a very simple method to gener-

---

[3] The model is publicly available at `https://github.com/ratishsp/data2text-plan-py`

[4] In the 629 records, 598 records are for players, 30 records for teams and 1 record for the date.

NAME	POS	MIN	PTS	FGM	FGA	FG_PCT	FG3M	FG3A	FG3_PCT	FTM	FTA	FT_PCT	OREB	DREB	REB	AST	TO	STL	BLK	PF
Matt Barnes	F	26	0	0	3	0	0	3	0	0	0	0	1	4	5	4	1	0	0	0
Blake Griffin	F	34	24	10	17	59	0	0	0	4	5	80	4	2	6	8	4	1	0	3
DeAndre Jordan	C	34	9	4	8	50	0	0	0	1	4	25	5	11	16	0	1	1	2	4
JJ Redick	G	34	23	9	15	60	5	8	63	0	0	0	0	3	3	2	1	1	0	2
Chris Paul	G	36	27	6	16	38	4	6	67	11	12	92	1	2	3	9	2	2	1	3
Glen Davis	N/A	13	2	1	2	50	0	0	0	0	0	0	0	4	4	1	0	3	0	0
Jamal Crawford	N/A	29	17	5	16	31	3	8	38	4	6	67	0	2	2	2	1	2	1	2
Hedo Turkoglu	N/A	6	0	0	0	0	0	0	0	0	0	0	0	2	2	0	1	0	0	1
Reggie Bullock	N/A	14	2	1	1	100	0	0	0	0	0	0	0	0	0	1	0	0	0	0
Jordan Farmar	N/A	12	2	1	3	33	0	1	0	0	0	0	0	0	0	2	1	0	0	3
Jared Cunningha	N/A	N/A	N/A	N/A	N/A	N/A	N/A	N/A	N/A	N/A	N/A	N/A	N/A	N/A	N/A	N/A	N/A	N/A	N/A	N/A
Chris Douglas-R	N/A	N/A	N/A	N/A	N/A	N/A	N/A	N/A	N/A	N/A	N/A	N/A	N/A	N/A	N/A	N/A	N/A	N/A	N/A	N/A
Ekpe Udoh	N/A	N/A	N/A	N/A	N/A	N/A	N/A	N/A	N/A	N/A	N/A	N/A	N/A	N/A	N/A	N/A	N/A	N/A	N/A	N/A
Giannis Antetok	F	38	18	8	12	67	0	1	0	2	3	67	1	8	9	6	3	2	0	3
Johnny O'Bryant	F	6	4	2	3	67	0	0	0	0	0	0	0	0	0	0	0	0	0	2
Larry Sanders	C	26	10	5	6	83	0	0	0	0	2	0	2	5	7	3	0	1	1	5
O.J. Mayo	G	23	3	1	6	17	0	2	0	1	3	33	0	1	1	3	2	0	0	4
Brandon Knight	G	27	8	3	10	30	2	6	33	0	0	0	1	4	5	5	4	0	0	3
Jared Dudley	N/A	30	16	7	12	58	2	4	50	0	0	0	2	6	8	3	3	2	0	1
Zaza Pachulia	N/A	20	5	1	3	33	0	0	0	3	4	75	2	5	7	2	2	0	0	1
Jerryd Bayless	N/A	28	16	7	13	54	2	3	67	0	0	0	1	3	4	2	1	0	0	4
Khris Middleton	N/A	24	12	5	10	50	1	5	20	1	1	100	1	3	4	2	0	1	0	2
Kendall Marshal	N/A	18	10	4	6	67	1	3	33	1	2	50	0	1	1	3	3	0	0	0
Damien Inglis	N/A	N/A	N/A	N/A	N/A	N/A	N/A	N/A	N/A	N/A	N/A	N/A	N/A	N/A	N/A	N/A	N/A	N/A	N/A	N/A
Jabari Parker	N/A	N/A	N/A	N/A	N/A	N/A	N/A	N/A	N/A	N/A	N/A	N/A	N/A	N/A	N/A	N/A	N/A	N/A	N/A	N/A
Nate Wolters	N/A	N/A	N/A	N/A	N/A	N/A	N/A	N/A	N/A	N/A	N/A	N/A	N/A	N/A	N/A	N/A	N/A	N/A	N/A	N/A

TEAM-NAME	CITY	P_QTR1	P_QTR2	P_QTR3	P_QTR4	PTS	FG_PCT	FG3_PCT	FT_PCT	REB	AST	TOV	WINS	LOSSES
Clippers	Los Angeles	28	22	32	24	106	46	46	74	41	29	12	19	8
Bucks	Milwaukee	24	28	31	19	102	53	33	53	46	29	18	14	14

The Los Angeles Clippers (19-8) defeated the Milwaukee Bucks (14-14) 106-102 on Saturday. Los Angeles has won three of their last four games. Chris Paul paced the team with a game-high 27 points and nine assists. DeAndre Jordan continued his impressive work on the boards, pulling down 16 rebounds, and Blake Griffin and J.J. Redick joined Paul in scoring over 20 points. The Clippers have a tough stretch of their schedule coming up with the Spurs, Hawks, Warriors and Raptors all on this week's docket. Even with the loss, Milwaukee finished their four-game Western Conference road trip 2-2, a job well done by the developing squad. In the three games since Jabari Parker went down with a season-ending ACL injury, coach Jason Kidd has cut the umbilical cord they had on Giannis Antetokounmpo. He played over 37 minutes for the second straight game Saturday, which is ten more minutes than his season average of 27 minutes per game. Larry Sanders returned to the starting lineup after sitting out Thursday's game on a league mandated one-game suspension. Ersan Ilyasova (concussion) and John Henson (foot) remain out, and it seems Ilyasova may be closer to returning than Henson.

Table 1: An example of box-score (top), line-score (middle) and the corresponding summary (bottom) from ROTOWIRE dataset. The definition of table header could be found at `https://github.com/harvardnlp/boxscore-data`

ate such labels. First, we label the entity records[5]. An entity record is labeled as 1 if its value is mentioned in the associated summary, otherwise it is labeled as 0. Second, for each player or team mentioned in the summary, the rest of its values in the table are labeled as 1 if they occur in the same sentence in the summary.

5.2 Evaluation metrics

The model output is evaluated with BLEU (Papineni et al., 2002) as well as several content-oriented metrics proposed by (Wiseman et al., 2017) including three following aspects:

- Relation Generation (RG) evaluates the number of extracted relations in automatic summaries and their correctness (precision) w.r.t the input record dataset;

- Content Selection (CS) evaluates the precision and recall rate of extracted relations in automatic summaries w.r.t that in the gold summaries;

- Content Ordering (CO) evaluates the normalized Damerau-Levenshtein Distance (Brill and Moore, 2000) between the sequence of extracted relations in automatic summaries and that in the gold summaries.

All these content-oriented metrics are based on an IE system which extracts record relations from

---

[5]Record whose *Value* feature is an entity (see Section 3), for example: "LeBron_James|NAME|LeBron_James|H/W". The labeling is according to the *Value* feature

Model	RG		CS		CO	BLEU
	#	P%	P%	R%	DLD%	
GOLD	23.32	94.77	100	100	100	100
TEMPL	54.29	99.92	26.61	59.16	14.42	8.51
WS-2017	23.95	75.10	28.11	35.86	15.33	14.57
NCP-2019	33.88	87.51	33.52	51.21	18.57	16.19
DATA-TRANS	23.31	79.81	36.90	43.06	22.75	20.60
+DATA_GEN	22.59	**82.49**	**39.48**	42.84	23.32	19.76
+DATA_SEL	**26.94**	79.54	35.27	**47.49**	22.22	19.97
+BOTH	24.24	80.52	37.33	44.66	23.04	20.22

Table 2: Automatic evaluation on ROTOWIRE development set using relation generation (RG) count (#) and precision (P%), content selection (CS) precision (P%) and recall (R%), content ordering (CO) in normalized Damerau-Levenshtein distance (DLD%), and BLEU.

summaries. For the purpose of comparison, we directly use the publicly available IE system of (Puduppully et al., 2019) to evaluate our models.

5.3 Training Details

In all experiments, we use our model with 1 encoder layer and 6 decoder layers, 512 hidden units (hence, the record feature embedding size is 128, see Section 3), 8 heads, GELU activations (Hendrycks and Gimpel, 2016), a dropout rate of 0.1 and learned positional embedding for the decoder. The model is trained with the Adam optimizer (Kingma and Ba, 2014), learning rate is fixed to 10^{-4} and batch size is 6. As for inference, we use beam size 4 for all experiments, and the maximum decoding length is 600.

We implement all our models in Pytorch, and train them on 1 GTX 1080 GPU.

6 Results

The results of our model on the development set are summarized in Table 2. GOLD represents the evaluation result on the gold summary. The RG precision rate is 94.77%, indicating that the IE system for evaluation is not perfect but has very high precision. After that, results of three contrast systems are reported, where TEMPL and WS-2017 are the updated results[6] of Wiseman et al. (2017) models. TEMPL is template-based generator model which generates a summary consisting of 8 sentences: a general description sentence about the teams playing in the game, 6 player-specific sentences and a conclusion sentence. WS-2017 reports an encoder-decoder

---

[6]Here we all use the IE system of (Puduppully et al., 2019) which is improved from the original IE system of (Wiseman et al., 2017)

model with conditional copy mechanism. NCP-2019 is the best system configuration (NCP+CC) reported in (Puduppully et al., 2019) which is a neural content planning model enhanced with conditional copy mechanism. As for our model, results with four configurations are reported.

DATA-TRANS represents our data-to-text Transformer model (as illustrated in Figure 1) without any data augmentation. Comparing to NCP-2019, our model performs 3.4% higher on content selection precision, 4.2% higher on content ordering metric and 4.4 points higher on BLEU. Our model performs better on the CO metric, we attribute this improvement to that our model generates nearly the same number of relations as the gold summary which reduces the edit distance between the two sequences of relations. However, our model is 7.7% lower on RG precision. And on the CS recall rate, our model is 8.2% lower than NCP-2019. This is probably due to the fact that NCP-2019 generates much more records than our model (33.88 vs. 23.31) which could result higher coverage on the relations in gold summary.

Comparing to TEMPL and WS-2017, our model is much better on BLEU and CS precision. Our model generates nearly the same number of relations as WS-2017, but with 7.2% higher on recall rate and 7.4% higher on CO metric.

By synthetic data generation (+DATA_GEN), we generate synthetic table records as described in secion 4.1. These synthetic table records are then used as input to the DATA-TRANS model to generate summaries. All training table records are used to generate synthetic data. The synthetic data is then combined with the original training data to fine-tune the DATA-TRANS model. From Table 2, we can see that the RG and CS precisions are both improved by 2.7% and 2.6% respectively. There is no significant change on others metrics. The CO metric is slightly improved due to higher RG and CS precisions. The CS recall rate is slightly degraded with the number of extracted relations.

By training data selection (+DATA_SEL), we select the data whose summary contains the number of relations $N >= 16$ as the new training data. The result training data size is 2242 (original size: 3398). It is then used to fine-tune the DATA-TRANS model. As shown in Table 2, as expected, the model after fine-tuning generates more relations in the output summaries. The average num-

Model	RG		CS		CO	BLEU
	#	P%	P%	R%	DLD%	
TEMPL	54.23	99.94	26.99	58.16	14.92	8.46
WS-2017	23.72	74.80	29.49	36.18	15.42	14.19
NCP-2019	34.28	87.47	34.18	51.22	18.58	16.50
DATA-TRANS	24.12	79.17	36.48	42.74	22.40	20.16
+DATA_GEN	24.01	**83.89**	**38.98**	42.85	23.02	19.48
+DATA_SEL	**27.47**	80.70	35.33	**46.25**	21.87	20.03
+BOTH	24.80	81.08	37.10	43.78	22.51	20.14

Table 3: Automatic evaluation on ROTOWIRE test set.

Model	RG		CS		CO	BLEU
	#	P%	P%	R%	DLD%	
DATA-TRANS	23.31	79.81	36.90	43.06	22.75	20.60
-CS_OBJ	23.37	72.70	32.67	41.99	21.14	20.28
-REC_EMB	18.00	63.14	32.94	37.71	21.15	20.24

Table 4: Ablation results on ROTOWIRE dev set.

ber of relations in the output summaries increases from 23.31 to 26.94. Respectively, the CS recall is increased from 43.06% to 47.49%. However, the CS precision is slightly degraded by 1.6%.

Finally, we combine both of the data augmentation methods (+BOTH). Synthetic data generation improves the RG and CS precisions. Training data selection improves the CS recall rate by making the model generate more relations. To combine the two methods, we choose to fine-tune the +DATA_GEN model with the selected training data of +DATA_SEL (so this configuration is actually +DATA_GEN+DATA_SEL). As shown in Table 2, all content-oriented evaluation metrics are improved compared to DATA-TRANS but not as much as each single of the data augmentation method. This configuration is like a trade-off between the two data augmentation configurations.

Results on the test set are reported in Table 3. They follow the same pattern as those found on the development set. Our DATA-TRANS model outperforms all other contrast systems on BLEU, CS precision and content ordering metrics. The synthetic data generation method helps to improve the RG and CS precisions. The training data selection method improves the CS recall by making the model generate more relations. Combining these two data augmentation methods, all content-oriented evaluation results are improved compared to DATA-TRANS. However, there is no significant change on BLEU.

7 Ablation Experiments

Next we evaluate the extensions introduced in our data-to-text Transformer model (DATA-TRANS) by means of ablation experiments. This is:

- The concatenation of feature embeddings as input of the encoder presented in Section 3.1 in order to generate a better representation of the input records.

- The secondary learning objective presented in Sectioin 3.2 aiming at improving the content-oriented results.

Removing the content selection additional objective function In this configuration, we keep the same data embedding and the model architecture as the DATA-TRANS, but the model is trained without the content selection objective. The evaluation results are shown in Table 4 (-CS_OBJ). We can see that the CS precision and CS recall are degraded by 4.2% and 1% respectively. The model extracts nearly the same number of records as the baseline system, but with much lower precision. The content ordering metric is also degraded by 1.6%. Surprisingly, there is no significant change on BLEU.

Removing Record Encoding In this configuration, the record encoding is removed from the DATA-TRANS model. Instead, we directly use the *Value* feature (see Section 3) sequence as the input. To keep model size unchanged, the dimension of embedding for the *Value* feature sequence is four times bigger than the original feature embedding size (see Equation 2). In addition, we also add back the positional embedding for the input sequence. Since the record sequence has a fixed length of 629, the positional embedding could help to build a 1-to-1 mapping from the position in record sequence and the position in the real table.

The model is trained with the same data and the same configuration as DATA-TRANS. From the results in Table 4 (-REC_EMB), we can see that without record embedding all content-oriented evaluation results are degraded, especially the RG precision and CS recall. And again, the model still achieves comparable BLEU score with DATA-TRANS which demonstrates the effectiveness of Transformer model on language modeling.

An example output of -REC_EMB system is shown in Table 5 (left). The generation has high precision at the beginning, and many erroneous relations are generated after several sentences. Our DATA-TRANS performs much better, but we can also observe such problem. The generation has high precision at the beginning and the quality degraded after several sentences. We believe this is

The Los Angeles Clippers (19-8) defeated the Milwaukee Bucks (14-14) 106-102 on Saturday. Milwaukee has won four straight games. They were paced by J.J. Redick's game with 23 points, five assists and five rebounds. Chris Paul had a nice game with 27 points and nine assists to go along with a double-double with nine points and nine assists. The Clippers shot 53 percent from the field and 46 percent from beyond the arc. Milwaukee will wrap up their two-game road trip in Houston against the Grizzlies on Tuesday. Milwaukee has lost four straight games. They've lost five of their last five games. Chris Paul (ankle) and Blake Griffin (knee) sat out Saturday's game. The Clippers missed their last two games with a hamstring strain. Jordan had to leave the lead the team with a foot injury but were able to return for the Clippers to action on Friday.

The Los Angeles Clippers (19-8) defeated the Milwaukee Bucks (14-14) 106-102 on Saturday. Los Angeles stopped their two-game losing streak with the win. Jamal Crawford paced the team with a game-high 17 points in 29 minutes off the bench. Crawford shot 9-of-16 from the field and 3-of-8 from downtown. He had nine assists, two rebounds and two steals in 29 minutes. Blake Griffin had 24 points, eight assists, six rebounds and one steal in 34 minutes. The Clippers will go on the road to face the Denver Nuggets on Monday. Milwaukee has lost two straight, and are now 9-2 in their last 10 games. Jabari Parker (ankle) didn't play Saturday as he recorded a double-double with 18 points and nine rebounds. Giannis Antetokounmpo (8-12 FG, 2-1 3Pt, 2-3 FT) and nine rebounds in 38 minutes off the bench. The Clippers will stay home and host the Brooklyn Nets on Monday.

Table 5: Example output from DATA-TRANS (right) and ablation model -REC_EMB (left). The corresponding box- and line-table are given in Table 1. Text that accurately reflects a record in the associated table data is in blue, erroneous text is in red. Text in black is not contradictory to the table records and text in orange is self-contradictory within the summary.

caused by the error accumulation effect in autoregressive decoding.

Another problem we have observed, not only in Table 5 but also in other output summaries, is repetition and self-contradictory. In the left example of Table 5, it contains two sentences (in orange color) which are completely contradictory with each other. And in the right example, the sentence in orange color contains contradictory information within the sentence.

8 Conclusions

We presented a Transformer-based data-to-text generation model. Experimental results have shown that our two modifications on the Transformer model significantly improve the content-oriented evaluation metrics. In addition, we proposed two data augmentation methods, each of them improves different aspects of the model. Our final model outperforms current state-of-the-art system on BLEU, content selection precision and content ordering metics. And we believe it has great potential for the future work. In the next step, we would like to apply some experimental techniques of machine translation such as right-to-left decoding and system ensemble to the data-to-text generation task.

References

Gabor Angeli, Percy Liang, and Dan Klein. 2010. A simple domain-independent probabilistic approach to generation. In *Proceedings of the 2010 Conference on Empirical Methods in Natural Language Processing*, pages 502–512. Association for Computational Linguistics.

Regina Barzilay and Mirella Lapata. 2005. Collective content selection for concept-to-text generation. In *Proceedings of the conference on Human Language Technology and Empirical Methods in Natural Language Processing*, pages 331–338. Association for Computational Linguistics.

Eric Brill and Robert C Moore. 2000. An improved error model for noisy channel spelling correction. In *Proceedings of the 38th Annual Meeting on Association for Computational Linguistics*, pages 286–293. Association for Computational Linguistics.

Pablo A Duboue and Kathleen R McKeown. 2001. Empirically estimating order constraints for content planning in generation. In *Proceedings of the 39th Annual Meeting on Association for Computational Linguistics*, pages 172–179. Association for Computational Linguistics.

Pablo A Duboue and Kathleen R McKeown. 2003. Statistical acquisition of content selection rules for natural language generation. In *Proceedings of the 2003 conference on Empirical methods in natural language processing*, pages 121–128. Association for Computational Linguistics.

Jiatao Gu, Zhengdong Lu, Hang Li, and Victor OK Li. 2016. Incorporating copying mechanism in sequence-to-sequence learning. *arXiv preprint arXiv:1603.06393*.

Caglar Gulcehre, Sungjin Ahn, Ramesh Nallapati, Bowen Zhou, and Yoshua Bengio. 2016. Pointing the unknown words. *arXiv preprint arXiv:1603.08148*.

Dan Hendrycks and Kevin Gimpel. 2016. Bridging nonlinearities and stochastic regularizers with gaussian error linear units.

Diederik P Kingma and Jimmy Ba. 2014. Adam: A method for stochastic optimization. *arXiv preprint arXiv:1412.6980*.

Ioannis Konstas and Mirella Lapata. 2012. Unsupervised concept-to-text generation with hypergraphs. In *Proceedings of the 2012 Conference of the North American Chapter of the Association for Computational Linguistics: Human Language Technologies*, pages 752–761. Association for Computational Linguistics.

Rémi Lebret, David Grangier, and Michael Auli. 2016. Neural text generation from structured data with application to the biography domain. *arXiv preprint arXiv:1603.07771*.

Percy Liang, Michael I Jordan, and Dan Klein. 2009. Learning semantic correspondences with less supervision. In *Proceedings of the Joint Conference of the 47th Annual Meeting of the ACL and the 4th International Joint Conference on Natural Language Processing of the AFNLP: Volume 1-Volume 1*, pages 91–99. Association for Computational Linguistics.

Hongyuan Mei, Mohit Bansal, and Matthew R Walter. 2015. What to talk about and how? selective generation using lstms with coarse-to-fine alignment. *arXiv preprint arXiv:1509.00838*.

Kishore Papineni, Salim Roukos, Todd Ward, and Wei-Jing Zhu. 2002. Bleu: a method for automatic evaluation of machine translation. In *Proceedings of the 40th annual meeting on association for computational linguistics*, pages 311–318. Association for Computational Linguistics.

Ratish Puduppully, Li Dong, and Mirella Lapata. 2019. Data-to-text generation with content selection and planning. In *Proceedings of the AAAI Conference on Artificial Intelligence*, volume 33, pages 6908–6915.

Ehud Reiter and Robert Dale. 1997. Building applied natural language generation systems. *Natural Language Engineering*, 3(1):57–87.

Ehud Reiter, Somayajulu Sripada, Jim Hunter, Jin Yu, and Ian Davy. 2005. Choosing words in computer-generated weather forecasts. *Artificial Intelligence*, 167(1-2):137–169.

Amanda Stent, Rashmi Prasad, and Marilyn Walker. 2004. Trainable sentence planning for complex information presentation in spoken dialog systems. In *Proceedings of the 42nd annual meeting on association for computational linguistics*, page 79. Association for Computational Linguistics.

Kumiko Tanaka-Ishii, Kôiti Hasida, and Itsuki Noda. 1998. Reactive content selection in the generation of real-time soccer commentary. In *Proceedings of the 17th international conference on Computational linguistics-Volume 2*, pages 1282–1288. Association for Computational Linguistics.

Ashish Vaswani, Noam Shazeer, Niki Parmar, Jakob Uszkoreit, Llion Jones, Aidan N Gomez, Łukasz Kaiser, and Illia Polosukhin. 2017. Attention is all you need. In *Advances in neural information processing systems*, pages 5998–6008.

Sam Wiseman, Stuart M Shieber, and Alexander M Rush. 2017. Challenges in data-to-document generation. *arXiv preprint arXiv:1707.08052*.

Zichao Yang, Phil Blunsom, Chris Dyer, and Wang Ling. 2016. Reference-aware language models. *arXiv preprint arXiv:1611.01628*.

Generalization in Generation: A closer look at Exposure Bias

Florian Schmidt
Department of Computer Science
ETH Zürich
`florian.schmidt@inf.ethz.ch`

Abstract

Exposure bias refers to the train-test discrepancy that seemingly arises when an autoregressive generative model uses only ground-truth contexts at training time but generated ones at test time. We separate the contributions of the model and the learning framework to clarify the debate on consequences and review proposed counter-measures.

In this light, we argue that generalization is the underlying property to address and propose unconditional generation as its fundamental benchmark. Finally, we combine latent variable modeling with a recent formulation of exploration in reinforcement learning to obtain a rigorous handling of true and generated contexts. Results on language modeling and variational sentence auto-encoding confirm the model's generalization capability.

1 Introduction

Autoregressive models span from n-gram models to recurrent neural networks to transformers and have formed the backbone of state-of-the-art machine learning models over the last decade on virtually any generative task in Natural Language Processing. Applications include machine translation (Bahdanau et al., 2015; Vaswani et al., 2017), summarization (Rush et al., 2015; Khandelwal et al., 2019), dialogue (Serban et al., 2016) and sentence compression (Filippova et al., 2015).

The training methodology of such models is rooted in the language modeling task, which is to predict a single word given a context of previous words. It has often been criticized that this setting is not suited for multi-step generation where – at test time – we are interested in generating words given a *generated* context that was potentially not seen during training. The consequences of this train-test discrepancy are summarized as *exposure bias*. Measures to mitigate the prob-

lem typically rely on replacing, masking or pertubing ground-truth contexts (Bengio et al., 2015; Bowman et al., 2016; Norouzi et al., 2016; Ranzato et al., 2016). Unfortunately, exposure bias has never been succesfully separated from general test-time log-likelihood assessment and minor improvements on the latter are used as the only signifier of reduced bias. Whenever explicit effects are investigated, no significant findings are made (He et al., 2019).

In this work we argue that the standard training procedure, despite all criticism, is an immediate consequence of combining autoregressive modeling and maximum-likelihood training. As such, the paramount consideration for improving test-time performance is simply regularization for better generalization. In fact, many proposed measures against exposure bias can be seen as exactly that, yet with respect to an usually implicit metric that is not maximum-likelihood.

With this in mind, we discuss regularization for conditional and unconditional generation. We note that in conditional tasks, such as translation, it is usually sufficient to regularize the *mapping* task – here translation – rather than the generative process itself. For unconditional generation, where tradeoffs between accuracy and coverage are key, generalization becomes much more tangible.

The debate on the right training procedure for autoregressive models has recently been amplified by the advent of *latent* generative models (Rezende et al., 2014; Kingma and Welling, 2013). Here, the practice of decoding with true contexts during training conflicts with the hope of obtaining a latent representation that encodes significant information about the sequence (Bowman et al., 2016). Interestingly, the ad hoc tricks to reduce the problem are similar to those proposed to ad-

Proceedings of the 3rd Workshop on Neural Generation and Translation (WNGT 2019), pages 157–167
Hong Kong, China, November 4, 2019. ©2019 Association for Computational Linguistics
www.aclweb.org/anthology/D19-56%2d

dress exposure bias in deterministic models.

Very recently, Tan et al. (2017) have presented a reinforcement learning formulation of exploration that allows following the intuition that an autoregressive model should not only be trained on ground-truth contexts. We combine their framework with latent variable modeling and a reward function that leverages modern word-embeddings. The result is a single learning regime for unconditional generation in a deterministic setting (language modeling) and in a latent variable setting (variational sentence autoencoding). Empirical results show that our formulation allows for better generalization than existing methods proposed to address exposure bias. Even more, we find the resulting regularization to also improve generalization under log-likelihood.

We conclude that it is worthwhile exploring reinforcement learning to elegantly extend maximum-likelihood learning where our desired notion of generalization cannot be expressed without violating the underlying principles. As a result, we hope to provide a more unified view on the training methodologies of autoregressive models and exposure bias in particular.

2 Autoregressive Modeling

Modern text generation methods are rooted in models trained on the language modeling task. In essence, a *language model* p is trained to predict a word given its left-side context

$$p(w_t|w_{1:t-1}) \,. \tag{1}$$

With a trained language model at hand, a simple recurrent procedure allows to generate text of arbitrary length. Starting from an initial special symbol $\hat{w}_0$, we iterate $t = 1 \ldots$ and alternate between sampling $\hat{w}_t \sim p(w_t|\hat{w}_{1:t-1})$ and appending $\hat{w}_t$ to the context $\hat{w}_{1:t-1}$. Models of this form are called *autoregressive* as they condition new predictions on old predictions.

Neural Sequence Models   Although a large corpus provides an abundance of word-context pairs to train on, the cardinality of the context space makes explicit estimates of (1) infeasible. Therefore, traditional n-gram language models rely on a truncated context and smoothing techniques to generalize well to unseen contexts.

Neural language models lift the context restriction and instead use neural context representations. This can be a hidden state as found in recurrent neural networks (RNNs), i.e. an LSTM (Hochreiter and Schmidhuber, 1997) state, or a set of attention weights, as in a transformer architecture (Vaswani et al., 2017). While the considerations in this work apply to all autoregressive models, we focus on recurrent networks which encode the context in a fixed-sized continuous representation $\mathbf{h}(w_{1:t-1})$. In contrast to transformers, RNNs can be generalized easily to variational autoencoders with a single latent bottleneck (Bowman et al., 2016), a particularly interesting special case of generative models .

2.1 Evaluation and Generalization

Conditional vs. Unconditional

Conditional generation tasks, such as translation or summarization, are attractive from an application perspective. However, for the purpose of studying exposure bias, we argue that unconditional generation is the task of choice for the following reasons.

First, exposure bias addresses conditioning on past words *generated* which becomes less essential when words in a source sentence are available, in particular when attention is used.

Second, the difficulty of the underlying mapping task, say translation, is of no concern for the mechanics of generation. This casts sentence autoencoding as a less demanding, yet more economic task.

Finally, generalization of conditional models is only studied with respect to the underlying mapping and not with respect to the conditional distribution itself. A test-set in translation usually does not contain a source sentence seen during training with a *different* target[1]. Instead, it contains unseen source-target pairs that evaluate the generalization of the mapping. Even more, at test-time most conditional models resort to an arg-max decoding strategy. As a consequence, the entropy of the generative model is zero (given the source) and there is no generalization at all with respect to generation. For these reasons, we address unconditional generation and sentence auto-encoding for the rest of this work.

The big picture   Let us briefly characterize output we should expect from a generative model with respect to generalization. Figure 1 shows

---

[1] Some datasets do provide several targets for a single source. However, those are typically only used for BLEU computation, which is the standard test metric reported.

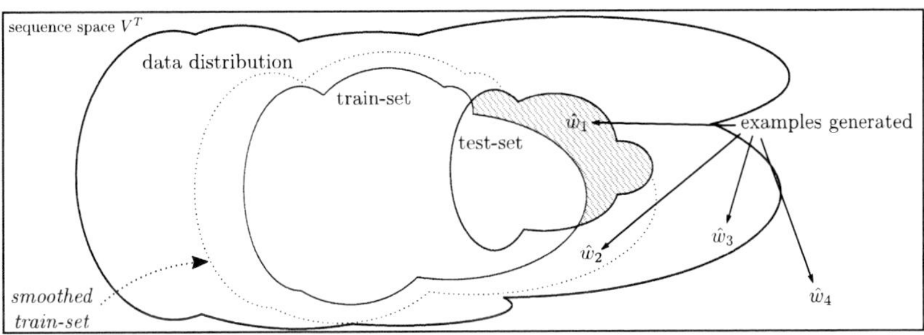

Figure 1: Generalization

an idealized two-dimensional dataspace of (fixed-length) sentences $w \in V^T$. We sketch the support of the unknown underlying generating distribution, the train set and the test set.[2] Let us look at some hypothetical examples $\hat{w}_1, \hat{w}_2, \hat{w}_3, \hat{w}_4$ generated from some well trained model. Samples like $\hat{w}_1$ certify that the model did not overfit to the training data as can be certified by test log-likelihood. In contrast, the remaining samples are indistinguishable under test log-likelihood in the sense that they identically decrease the metric (assuming equal model probability) even though $\hat{w}_2, \hat{w}_3$ have non-zero probability under the true data distribution. Consequently, we cannot identify $\hat{w}_4$ as a malformed example. Holtzman et al. (2019) show that neural generative models – despite their expressiveness – put significant probability on clearly unreasonable repetitive phrases, such as *I dont know. I dont know. I dont know.*[3]

Evaluation under smoothed data distribution
The most common approach to evaluating an unconditional probabilistic generative model is training and test log-likelihood. For a latent variable model, the exact log-likelihood (2) is intractable and a lowerbound must be used instead. However, at this point it should be noted that one can always estimate the log-likelihood from an empirical distribution across output generated. That is, one generates a large set of sequences S and sets $\hat{p}(w)$ to the normalized count of w in S. However, the variance of this estimate is impractical for all but the smallest datasets. Also, even a large test-set cannot capture the flexibility and compositionality found in natural language.

With aforementioned shortcomings of test log-likelihood in mind, it is worthwhile discussing a recently proposed evaluation technique. Fedus et al. (2018) propose to use n-gram statistics of the underlying data to asses generated output. For example, one can estimate an n-gram language model and report perplexity of the generated data under the n-gram model. Just as BLEU and ROUGE break the sequence reward assignment problem into smaller sub-problems, n-gram language models effectively *smooth* the sequence likelihood assignment which is usually done with respect to the empirical data distribution. Under this metric, some sequences such as $\hat{w}_2$ which are close to sequences in the dataset at hand might receive positive probability.

This raises two questions. First, can we break sequence-level evaluation into local statistics by using modern word embeddings instead of n-grams (as BLEU does)? Second, can we incorporate these measures already during training to obtain better generative models. These considerations will be key when defining a reward function in Section 4.5.

3   Teacher Forcing and Exposure Bias

A concern often expressed in the context of autoregressive models is that the recursive sampling procedure for generation presented in Section 1 is never used at training time; hence the model cannot learn to digest its own predictions. The resulting potential train-test discrepancy is referred to as *exposure bias* and is associated with compounding errors that arise when mistakes made early accumulate (Bengio et al., 2015; Ranzato et al., 2016; Goyal et al., 2016; Leblond et al., 2018). In this context, *teacher-forcing* refers to the fact that – seen from the test-time perspective – ground-truth contexts are substituted for model predictions. Although formally teacher forcing and exposure bias

---

[2]Here we do not discuss *generalization error*, the discrepancy between empirical test error and expected test error. It should also be noted that cross-validation provides another complementary technique to more robust model estimation, which we omit to keep the picture simple.

[3]They report that this also holds for non-grammatical repetitive phrase, which is what we would expect for $\hat{w}_4$.

should be seen as cause (if any) and symptom, they are often used exchangeably.

As is sometimes but rarely mentioned, the presence of the ground-truth context is simply a consequence of maximum-likelihood training and the chain rule applied to (1) as in $p(w_{1:T}) = \prod p(w_t | w_{1:t-1})$ (Goodfellow et al., 2016). As such, it is out of question whether generated contexts should be used as long as log-likelihood is the sole criterion we care about. In this work we will furthermore argue the following:

Proposition 1 *Exposure bias describes a lack of generalization with respect to an – usually implicit and potentially task and domain dependent – measure other than maximum-likelihood.*

The fact that we are dealing with generalization is obvious, as one can train a model – assuming sufficient capacity – under the criticized methodology to match the training distribution. Approaches that address exposure bias do not make the above notion of generalization explicit, but follow the intuition that training on other contexts than (only) ground-truth contexts should regularize the model and result in – subjectively – better results. Of course, these forms of regularization might still implement some form of log-likelihood regularization, hence improve log-likelihood generalization. Indeed, all of the following methods do report test log-likelihood improvements.

Proposed methods against exposure bias *Scheduled sampling* (Bengio et al., 2015) proposed for conditional generation randomly mixes in predictions form the model, which violates the underlying learning framework (Husz'ar, 2015). *RAML* (Norouzi et al., 2016) proposes to effectively perturbs the ground-truth context according to the exponentated payoff distribution implied by a reward function. Alternatively, adversarial approaches (Goyal et al., 2016) and learning-to-search (Leblond et al., 2018) have been proposed.

VAE Collapse In Section 4.1 we will take a look at *latent* generative models. In that context, the standard maximum-likelihood approach to autoregressive models has been criticized from a second perspective that is worth mentioning. Bowman et al. (2016) show empirically that autoregressive decoders $p(w|\mathbf{z})$ do not rely on the latent code $\mathbf{z}$, but

collapse to a language model as in (1).

While some work argues that the problem is rooted in autoregressive decoders being "too powerful" (Shen et al., 2018), the proposed measures often address the autoregressive training regime rather than the models (Bowman et al., 2016) and, in fact, replace ground-truth contexts just as the above methods to mitigate exposure bias.

In addition, a whole body of work has discussed the implications of optimizing only a bound to the log-likelihood (Alemi et al., 2017) and the implications of re-weighting the information-theoretic quantities inside the bound (Higgins et al., 2017; Rainforth et al., 2018).

4 Latent Generation with ERPO

We have discussed exposure bias and how it has been handled by either implicitly or explicitly leaving the maximum-likelihood framework. In this section, we present our reinforcement learning framework for unconditional sequence generation models. The generative story is the same as in a latent variable model:

1. Sample a latent code $\mathbf{z} \sim \mathbb{R}^d$

2. Sample a sequence from a code-conditioned policy $p_\theta(w|\mathbf{z})$.

However, we will rely on reinforcement learning to train the decoder $p(w|\mathbf{z})$. Note that for a constant code $\mathbf{z} = \mathbf{0}$ we obtain a language model as a special case. Let us now briefly review latent sequential models.

4.1 Latent sequential models

Formally, a latent model of sequences $w = w_{1:T}$ is written as a marginal over latent codes

$$p(w) = \int p(w, \mathbf{z}) d\mathbf{z} = \int p(w|\mathbf{z}) p_0(\mathbf{z}) d\mathbf{z} \ . \quad (2)$$

The precise form of $p(w|\mathbf{z})$ and whether $\mathbf{z}$ refers to a single factor or a sequence of factors $\mathbf{z}_{1:T}$ depends on the model of choice.

The main motivation of enhancing p with a latent factor is usually the hope to obtain a meaningful structure in the space of latent codes. How such a structure should be organized has been discussed in the *disentanglement* literature in great detail, for example in Chen et al. (2018), Hu et al. (2017) or Tschannen et al. (2018).

In our context, latent generative models are interesting for two reasons. First, explicitly introducing uncertainty inside the model is often motivated as a regularizing technique in Bayseian machine learning (Murphy, 2012) and has been applied extensively to latent sequence models (M. Ziegler and M. Rush, 2019; Schmidt and Hofmann, 2018; Goyal et al., 2017; Bayer and Osendorfer, 2014). Second, as mentioned in Section 3 (VAE collapse) conditioning on ground-truth contexts has been identified as detrimental to obtaining meaningful latent codes (Bowman et al., 2016) – hence a methodology to training decoders that relaxes this requirement might be of value.

Training via Variational Inference Variational inference (Zhang et al., 2018) allows to optimize a lower-bound instead of the intractable marginal likelihood and has become the standard methodology to training latent variable models. Introducing an inference model q and applying Jensen's inequality to (2), we obtain

$$\log p(w) = \mathbb{E}_{q(\mathbf{z}|w)}\left[\log \frac{p_0(\mathbf{z})}{q(\mathbf{z}|w)} + \log P(w|\mathbf{z})\right]$$
$$\geq D^{\text{KL}}(q(\mathbf{z}|w)||p_0(\mathbf{z})) + \mathbb{E}_{q(\mathbf{z}|w)}\left[\log P(w|\mathbf{z})\right] \quad (3)$$

Neural inference networks (Rezende et al., 2014; Kingma and Welling, 2013) have proven as effective amortized approximate inference models.

Let us now discuss how reinforcement learning can help training our model.

4.2 Generation as Reinforcement Learning

Text generation can easily be formulated as a reinforcement learning (RL) problem if words are taken as actions (Bahdanau et al., 2016). Formally, p_θ is a parameterized policy that factorizes autoregressively $p_\theta(w) = \prod p_\theta(w_t|\mathbf{h}(w_{1:t-1}))$ and $\mathbf{h}$ is is a deterministic mapping from past predictions to a continuous state, typically a recurrent neural network (RNN). The goal is then to find policy parameters θ that maximize the expected reward

$$J(\theta) = \mathbb{E}_{p_\theta(w)}[R(w, w^\star)] \quad (4)$$

where $R(w, w^\star)$ is a task-specific, not necessarily differentiable metric.

Policy gradient optimization The REINFORCE (Williams, 1992) training algorithm is a common strategy to optimize (4) using a gradient estimate via the log-derivative

$$\nabla_\theta J(\theta) = \mathbb{E}_{p_\theta(w)}[R(w, w^\star) \log p_\theta(w)] \quad (5)$$

Since samples from the policy $\hat{w} \sim p_\theta$ often yield low or zeros reward, the estimator (5) is known for its notorious variance and much of the literature is focused on reducing this variance via baselines or control-derivative (Rennie et al., 2016).

4.3 Reinforcement Learning as Inference

Recently, a new family of policy gradient methods has been proposed that draws inspiration from inference problems in probablistic models. The underlying idea is to pull the reward in (5) into a new *implicit* distribution $\tilde{p}$ that allows to draw samples $\hat{w}$ with much lower variance as it is informed about reward.

We follow Tan et al. (2017) who optimize an entropy-regularized version of (4), a common strategy to foster exploration. They cast the reinforcement learning problem as

$$\begin{aligned} J(\theta, \tilde{p}) = {} & \mathbb{E}_{\tilde{p}}[R(w, w^\star)] \\ & + \alpha D^{\text{KL}}(\tilde{p}(w)||p_\theta(w)) \\ & + \beta H(\tilde{p}) \end{aligned} \quad (6)$$

where α, β are hyper-parameters and $\tilde{p}$ is the new non-parametric, *variational* distribution[4] across sequences. They show that (6) can be optimized using the following EM updates

$$\text{E-step: } \tilde{p}^{n+1} \propto \exp\left(\frac{\alpha p_\theta{}^n(w) + R(w, w^\star)}{\alpha + \beta}\right) \quad (7)$$

$$\text{M-step: } \theta^{n+1} = \arg\max_\theta \mathbb{E}_{\tilde{p}^{n+1}}[\log p_\theta(w)] \quad (8)$$

As Tan et al. 2018 have shown, for $\alpha \to 0$, $\beta = 1$ and a specific reward, the framework recovers maximum-likelihood training.[5] It is explicitly not our goal to claim text generation with end-to-end reinforcement learning but to show that it is beneficial to operate in an RL regime relatively close to maximum-likelihood.

4.4 Optimization with Variational Inference

In conditional generation, a policy is conditioned on a source sentence, which guides generation towards sequences that obtain significant reward. Often, several epochs of MLE pretraining (Rennie et al., 2016; Bahdanau et al., 2016) are necessary to make this guidance effective.

---

[4]In (Tan et al., 2018) $\tilde{p}$ is written as q, which resembles variational distributions in approximate Bayesian inference. However, here $\tilde{p}$ is not defined over variables but datapoints.

[5]Refer to their work for more special cases, including MIXER (Ranzato et al., 2016)

In our unconditional setting, where a source is not available, we employ the latent code $\mathbf{z}$ to provide guidance. We cast the policy p_θ as a code-conditioned policy $p_\theta(w|\mathbf{z})$ which is trained to maximize a marginal version of the reward (6):

$$J(\theta) = \mathbb{E}_{p_0(\mathbf{z})}\mathbb{E}_{p_\theta(w|\mathbf{z})}[R(w, w^\star)]] . \quad (9)$$

Similar formulations of expected reward have recently been proposed as *goal-conditioned* policies (Ghosh et al., 2018). However, here it is our explicit goal to also learn the representation of the goal, our latent code. We follow Equation (3) and optimize a lower-bound instead of the intractable marginalization (9). Following (Bowman et al., 2015; Fraccaro et al., 2016) we use a deep RNN inference network for q to optimize the bound. The reparametrization-trick (Kingma and Welling, 2013) allows us to compute gradients with respect to q. Algorithm 1 shows the outline of the training procedure.

Algorithm 1 Latent ERPO Training

---

  for do $w^\star \in$ DATASET
    Sample a latent code $\mathbf{z} \sim q(\mathbf{z}|w^\star)$
    Sample a datapoint $\tilde{w} \sim \tilde{p}(w|\mathbf{z})$
    Perform a gradient step $\nabla_\theta \log p_\theta(\tilde{w}|\mathbf{z})$

Note that exploration (sampling $\tilde{w}$) and the gradient step are both conditioned on the latent code, hence stochasticity due to sampling a single $\mathbf{z}$ is coupled in both. Also, no gradient needs to be propagated into $\tilde{p}$.

So far, we have not discussed how to efficiently sample from the implicit distribution $\tilde{p}$. In the remainder of this section we present our reward function and discuss implications on the tractability of sampling.

4.5 Reward

Defining a meaningful reward function is central to the success of reinforcement learning. The usual RL forumlations in NLP require a measure of sentence-sentence similarity as reward. Common choices include BLEU (Papineni et al., 2002), ROUGE (Lin, 2004), CIDEr (Banerjee and Lavie, 2005) or SPICE (Anderson et al., 2016). These are essentially n-gram metrics, partly augmented with synonym resolution or re-weighting schemes.

Word-movers distance (WMD) (Kusner et al., 2015) provides an interesting alternative based on the optimal-transport problem. In essence, WMD computes the minimum accumulated distance that the word vectors of one sentence need to "travel" to coincide with the word vectors of the other sentence. In contrast to n-gram metrics, WMD can leverage powerful neural word representations. Unfortunately, the complexity of computing WMD is roughly $\mathcal{O}(T^3 \log T)$.

4.6 A Reward for Tractable Sampling

Tan et al. (2018) show that thanks to the factorization of p_θ the globally-normalized inference distribution $\tilde{p}$ in (7) can be written as a locally-normalized distribution at the word-level

$$\tilde{p}(w_t|w_{1:t-1}) \propto$$
$$\exp\left(\frac{\alpha p_\theta(w_t|w_{1:t-1}) + R_t(w, w^\star)}{\alpha + \beta}\right) \quad (10)$$

when the reward is written as incremental reward R_t defined via $R_t(w, w^\star) = R(w_{1:t}, w^\star) - R(w_{1:t-1}, w^\star)$. Sampling form (10) is still hard, if R_t hides dynamic programming routines or other complex time-dependencies. With this in mind, we choose a particularly simple reward

$$R(w, w^\star) = \sum_{t=1}^{T} \phi(w_t)^\top \phi(w_t^\star) \quad (11)$$

where ϕ is a lookup into a length-normalized pre-trained but fixed word2vec (Mikolov et al., 2013) embedding. This casts our reward as an efficient, yet drastic approximation to WMD, which assumes identical length and one-to-one word correspondences. Putting (10) and (11) together, we sample sequentially from

$$\tilde{p}(w_t|w_{1:t-1}) \propto$$
$$\exp\left(\frac{\alpha p_\theta(w_t|w_{1:t-1}) + \phi(w_t)^\top \phi(w_t^\star)}{\alpha + \beta}\right) \quad (12)$$

with the complexity $\mathcal{O}(dV)$ of a standard softmax. Compared to standard VAE training, Algorithm 1 only needs one additional forward pass (with identical complexity) to sample $\tilde{w}$ form $\tilde{p}$.

Equation (12) gives a simple interpretation of our proposed training methodology. We locally correct predictions made by the model proportionally to the distance to the ground-truth in the embeddings space. Hence, we consider the ground-truth and the model prediction for exploration.

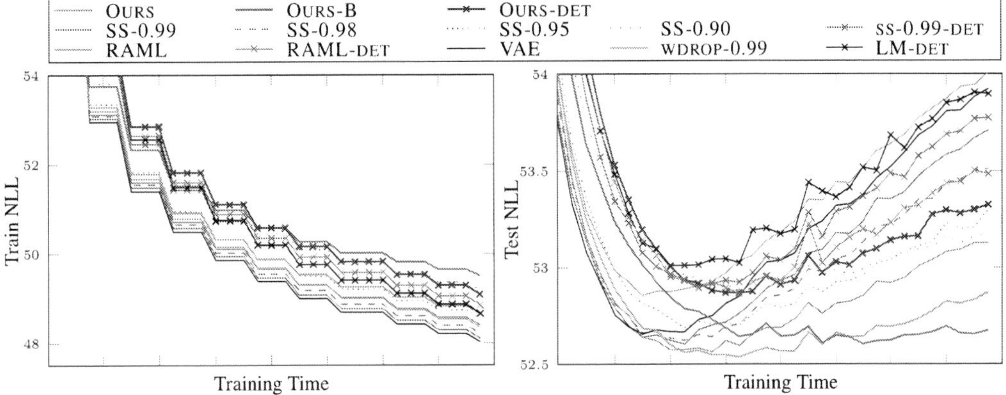

Figure 2: Generalization performance in terms of sequence NLL across latent and deterministic methods

5 Related Work

Our discussion of exposure bias complements recent work that summarizes modern generative models, for example Caccia et al. (2018) and Lu et al. (2018). Shortcomings of maximum-likelihood training for sequence generation have often been discussed (Ding and Soricut, 2017; Leblond et al., 2018; Ranzato et al., 2016), but without pointing to generalization as the key aspect. An overview of recent deep reinforcement learning methods for conditional generation can be found in (Keneshloo et al., 2018).

Our proposed approach follows work by Ding et al. (2017) and Tan et al. (2018) by employing both, policy and reward for exploration. In contrast to them, we do not use n-gram based reward. Compared to RAML (Norouzi et al., 2016), we do not perturb the ground-truth context, but correct the policy predictions. Scheduled sampling (Bengio et al., 2015) and word-dropout (Bowman et al., 2016) also apply a correction, yet one that only affects the probability of the ground-truth. Chen et al. (2017) propose Bridge modules that similarly to Ding et al. (2017) can incorporate arbitrary ground-truth perturbations, yet in an objective motivated by an auxiliary KL-divergence.

Merity et al. (2017) have shown that generalization is crucial to language modeling, but their focus is regularizing parameters and activations. Word-embeddings to measure deviations from the ground-truth have also been used by Inan et al. (2016), yet under log-likelihood. Concurrently to our work, Li et al. (2019) employ embeddings to design reward functions in abstractive summarization.

6 Experiments

Parametrization The policies of all our models and all baselines use the same RNN. We use a 256 dimensional GRU (Cho et al., 2014) and 100-dimensional pre-trained word2vec input embeddings. Optimization is preformed by Adam (Kingma and Ba, 2014) with an initial learning rate of 0.001 for all models. For all methods, including scheduled sampling, we do not anneal hyper-parameters such as the keep-probability for the following reasons. First, in an unconditional setting, using *only* the model's prediction is not a promising setting, so it is unclear what value to anneal to. Second, the continous search-space of schedules makes it sufficiently harder to compare different methods. For the same reason, we do not investigate annealing the KL term or the α, β-parametrization of the models. We use the inference network parametrization of (Bowman et al., 2016) which employs a diagonal Gaussian for q.

We found the training regime to be very sensitive to the α, β-parametrization. In particular, it is easy to pick a set of parameters that does not truly incorporate exploration, but reduces to maximum likelihood training with only ground truth contexts (see also the discussion of Figure 3 in Section 6.2). After performing a grid-search (as done also for RAML) we choose[6] $\alpha = 0.006, \beta = 0.067$ for OURS, the method proposed. In addition, we report for an alternative model OURS-B with $\alpha = 0.01, \beta = 0.07$.

---

[6]The scale of α is relatively small as the log-probabilities in (12) have significantly larger magnitude than the inner products, which are in $[0, 1]$ due to the normalization.

Data For our experiments, we use a one million sentences subset of the BooksCorpus (Kiros et al., 2015; Zhu et al., 2015) with a 90-10 train-test split and a 40K words vocabulary. The corpus size is chosen to challenge the above policy with both scenarios, overfitting and underfitting.

6.1 Baselines

As baselines we use a standard VAE and a VAE with RAML decoding that uses identical reward as our method (see Tan et al.(2018) for details on RAML as a special case). Furthermore, we use two regularizations of the standard VAE, scheduled sampling SS-P and word-dropout WDROP-P as proposed by Bowman et al. (2016), both with fixed probability p of using the ground-truth.

In addition, we report as special cases with $\mathbf{z} = \mathbf{0}$ results for our model (OURS-DET), RAML (RAML-DET), scheduled sampling (SS-P-DET), and the VAE (LM, a language model).

6.2 Results

Figure 2 shows training and test negative sequence log-likelihood evaluated during training and Table 1 shows the best performance obtained. All figures and tables are averaged across three runs.

Model	Train NLL	Test NLL
OURS	48.52	**52.54**
OURS-B	49.51	52.61
OURS-DET	48.06	52.87
SS-0.99	48.11	52.60
SS-0.98	48.21	52.62
SS-0.95	48.38	52.69
SS-0.90	49.02	52.89
SS-0.99-DET	48.08	52.90
RAML	48.26	52.56
RAML-DET	48.26	52.86
WDROP-0.99	48.19	52.86
LM	**47.65**	53.01
VAE	47.86	52.66
WDROP-0.9	50.86	54.65

Table 1: Training and test performance

We observe that all latent models outperform their deterministic counterparts (crossed curves) in terms of both, generalization and overall test performance. This is not surprising as regularization is one of the benefits of modeling uncertainty through latent variables. Scheduled sampling does improve generalization for $p \approx 1$ with diminishing returns at $p = 0.95$ and in general performed better than word dropout. Our proposed models outperform all others in terms of generalization and

test performance. Note that the performance difference over RAML, the second best method, is solely due to incorporating also model-predicted contexts during training.

Despite some slightly improved performance, all latent models except for OURS-B have a KL-term relatively close to zero. OURS-B is α-β-parametrized to incorporte slightly more model predictions at higher temperatur and manages to achieve a KL-term of about 1 to 1.5 bits. These findings are similar to what (Bowman et al., 2016) report *with* annealing but still significantly behind work that addresses this specific problem (Yang et al., 2017; Shen et al., 2018). Appendix A illustrates how our models can obtain larger KL-terms – yet at degraded performance – by controlling exploration. We conclude that improved autoregressive modeling inside the ERPO framework cannot alone overcome VAE-collapse.

We have discussed many approaches that deviate from training exclusively on ground-truth contexts. Therefore, an interesting quantity to monitor across methods is the fraction of words that correspond to the ground-truth. Figure 3 shows these fractions during training for the configurations that gave the best results. Interestingly, in the latent setting our method relies by far the least on ground-truth contexts whereas in the deterministic setting the difference is small.

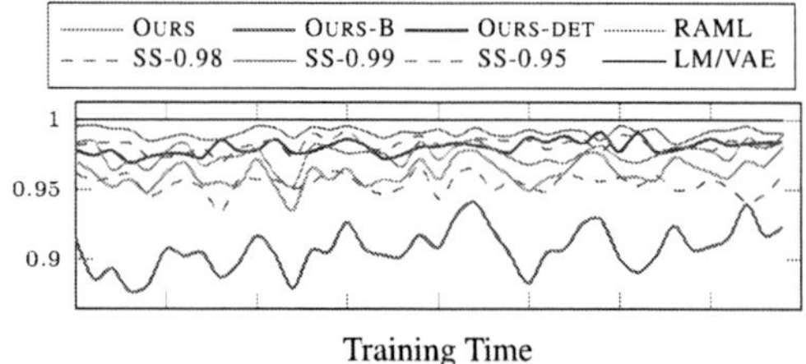

Figure 3: Fraction of correct words during training. Numbers include *forced* and *correctly predicted* words.

7 Conclusion

We have argued that exposure bias does not point to a problem with the standard methodology of training autoregressive sequence model. Instead, it refers to a notion of generalization to unseen sequences that does not manifest in log-likelihood training and testing, yet might be desirable in order to capture the flexibility of natural language.

To rigorously incorporate the desired generalization behavior, we have proposed to follow the reinforcement learning formulation of Tan et al. (2018). Combined with an embedding-based reward function, we have shown excellent generalization performance compared to the unregularized model and better generalization than existing techniques on language modeling and sentence autoencoding.

Future work We have shown that the simple reward function proposed here leads to a form of regularization that fosters generalization when evaluated inside the maximum-likelihood framework. In the future, we hope to conduct a human evaluation to assess the generalization capabilities of models trained under maximum-likelihood and reinforcement learning more rigorously. Only such a framework-independent evaluation can reveal the true gains of carefully designing reward functions compared to simply performing maximum-likelihood training.

References

Alexander A. Alemi, Ben Poole, Ian Fischer, Joshua V. Dillon, Rif A. Saurous, and Kevin Murphy. 2017. An information-theoretic analysis of deep latent-variable models. *CoRR*, abs/1711.00464.

Peter Anderson, Basura Fernando, Mark Johnson, and Stephen Gould. 2016. SPICE: semantic propositional image caption evaluation. *CoRR*, abs/1607.08822.

Dzmitry Bahdanau, Philemon Brakel, Kelvin Xu, Anirudh Goyal, Ryan Lowe, Joelle Pineau, Aaron C. Courville, and Yoshua Bengio. 2016. An actor-critic algorithm for sequence prediction. *CoRR*, abs/1607.07086.

Dzmitry Bahdanau, Kyunghyun Cho, and Yoshua Bengio. 2015. Neural machine translation by jointly learning to align and translate. In *ICLR*.

Satanjeev Banerjee and Alon Lavie. 2005. METEOR: An automatic metric for MT evaluation with improved correlation with human judgments. In *ACL Workshop on Intrinsic and Extrinsic Evaluation Measures for Machine Translation and/or Summarization*, pages 65–72, Ann Arbor, Michigan. Association for Computational Linguistics.

Justin Bayer and Christian Osendorfer. 2014. Learning stochastic recurrent networks. *arXiv preprint arXiv:1411.7610*. ArXiv.

Samy Bengio, Oriol Vinyals, Navdeep Jaitly, and Noam Shazeer. 2015. Scheduled sampling for sequence prediction with recurrent neural networks. In *NIPS*.

Samuel R. Bowman, Gabor Angeli, Christopher Potts, and Christopher D. Manning. 2015. A large annotated corpus for learning natural language inference. In *EMNLP*.

Samuel R. Bowman, Luke Vilnis, Oriol Vinyals, Andrew M. Dai, Rafal Józefowicz, and Samy Bengio. 2016. Generating sentences from a continuous space. In *ACL*.

Massimo Caccia, Lucas Caccia, William Fedus, Hugo Larochelle, Joelle Pineau, and Laurent Charlin. 2018. Language gans falling short. *CoRR*, abs/1811.02549.

Tian Qi Chen, Xuechen Li, Roger B. Grosse, and David Duvenaud. 2018. Isolating sources of disentanglement in variational autoencoders. *CoRR*, abs/1802.04942.

Wenhu Chen, Guanlin Li, Shujie Liu, Zhirui Zhang, Mu Li, and Ming Zhou. 2017. Neural sequence prediction by coaching. *CoRR*, abs/1706.09152.

Kyunghyun Cho, Bart van Merriënboer, Caglar Gulcehre, Dzmitry Bahdanau, Fethi Bougares, Holger Schwenk, and Yoshua Bengio. 2014. Learning phrase representations using RNN encoder–decoder for statistical machine translation. In *EMNLP*, pages 1724–1734.

Nan Ding and Radu Soricut. 2017. Cold-start reinforcement learning with softmax policy gradients. *CoRR*, abs/1709.09346.

William Fedus, Ian J. Goodfellow, and Andrew M. Dai. 2018. Maskgan: Better text generation via filling in the _______. In *ICLR*.

Katja Filippova, Enrique Alfonseca, Carlos A Colmenares, Lukasz Kaiser, and Oriol Vinyals. 2015. Sentence compression by deletion with lstms. In *EMNLP 2015*, pages 360–368.

Marco Fraccaro, Søren Kaae Sønderby, Ulrich Paquet, and Ole Winther. 2016. Sequential neural models with stochastic layers. pages 2199–2207. NIPS.

Dibya Ghosh, Abhishek Gupta, and Sergey Levine. 2018. Learning actionable representations with goal-conditioned policies. *CoRR*, abs/1811.07819.

Ian Goodfellow, Yoshua Bengio, and Aaron Courville. 2016. *Deep Learning*. MIT Press.

Anirudh Goyal, Alex Lamb, Ying Zhang, Saizheng Zhang, Aaron C. Courville, and Yoshua Bengio. 2016. Professor forcing: A new algorithm for training recurrent networks. In *NIPS*.

Anirudh Goyal, Alessandro Sordoni, Marc-Alexandre Côté, Nan Rosemary Ke, and Yoshua Bengio. 2017. Z-forcing: Training stochastic recurrent networks. In *NIPS*.

Tianxing He, Jingzhao Zhang, Zhiming Zhou, and James R. Glass. 2019. Quantifying exposure bias for neural language generation. *CoRR*, abs/1905.10617.

Irina Higgins, Loïc Matthey, Arka Pal, Christopher Burgess, Xavier Glorot, Matthew M Botvinick, Shakir Mohamed, and Alexander Lerchner. 2017. beta-vae: Learning basic visual concepts with a constrained variational framework. In *ICLR*.

Sepp Hochreiter and Jürgen Schmidhuber. 1997. Long short-term memory. *Neural Comput.*, 9(8):1735–1780.

Ari Holtzman, Jan Buys, Maxwell Forbes, and Yejin Choi. 2019. The curious case of neural text degeneration. *CoRR*, abs/1904.09751.

Z. Hu, Z. Yang, Liang X., R. Salakhutdinov, and E. R. Xing. 2017. Toward controlled generation of text. In *International Conference on Machine Learning (ICML)*.

Ferenc Husz'ar. 2015. How (not) to train your generative model: Scheduled sampling, likelihood, adversary?

Hakan Inan, Khashayar Khosravi, and Richard Socher. 2016. Tying word vectors and word classifiers: A loss framework for language modeling. *ArXiv*, abs/1611.01462.

Yaser Keneshloo, Tian Shi, Naren Ramakrishnan, and Chandan K. Reddy. 2018. Deep reinforcement learning for sequence to sequence models. *CoRR*, abs/1805.09461.

Urvashi Khandelwal, Kevin Clark, Dan Jurafsky, and Lukasz Kaiser. 2019. Sample efficient text summarization using a single pre-trained transformer. *CoRR*, abs/1905.08836.

Diederik P. Kingma and Jimmy Ba. 2014. Adam: A method for stochastic optimization. In *ICLR*.

Diederik P Kingma and Max Welling. 2013. Auto-encoding variational bayes. *arXiv preprint arXiv:1312.6114*.

Ryan Kiros, Yukun Zhu, Ruslan Salakhutdinov, Richard S Zemel, Antonio Torralba, Raquel Urtasun, and Sanja Fidler. 2015. Skip-thought vectors. *arXiv preprint arXiv:1506.06726*.

Matt J. Kusner, Yu Sun, Nicholas I. Kolkin, and Kilian Q. Weinberger. 2015. From word embeddings to document distances. In *ICML*, ICML'15, pages 957–966. JMLR.org.

Rémi Leblond, Jean-Baptiste Alayrac, Anton Osokin, and Simon Lacoste-Julien. 2018. SEARNN: training rnns with global-local losses. In *ICLR*.

Siyao Li, Deren Lei, Pengda Qin, and William Wang. 2019. Deep reinforcement learning with distributional semantic rewards for abstractive summarization.

Chin-Yew Lin. 2004. Rouge: A package for automatic evaluation of summaries. page 10.

Sidi Lu, Yaoming Zhu, Weinan Zhang, Jun Wang, and Yong Yu. 2018. Neural text generation: Past, present and beyond. *CoRR*, abs/1803.07133.

Zachary M. Ziegler and Alexander M. Rush. 2019. Latent normalizing flows for discrete sequences. *arXiv preprint arXiv:1901.10548*.

Stephen Merity, Nitish Shirish Keskar, and Richard Socher. 2017. Regularizing and optimizing LSTM language models. *CoRR*, abs/1708.02182.

Tomas Mikolov, Ilya Sutskever, Kai Chen, Greg S Corrado, and Jeff Dean. 2013. Distributed representations of words and phrases and their compositionality. In *NIPS*.

Kevin P. Murphy. 2012. *Machine Learning: A Probabilistic Perspective*. The MIT Press.

Mohammad Norouzi, Samy Bengio, Zhifeng Chen, Navdeep Jaitly, Mike Schuster, Yonghui Wu, and Dale Schuurmans. 2016. Reward augmented maximum likelihood for neural structured prediction. *CoRR*, abs/1609.00150.

Kishore Papineni, Salim Roukos, Todd Ward, and Wei Jing Zhu. 2002. Bleu: a method for automatic evaluation of machine translation.

Tom Rainforth, Adam R. Kosiorek, Tuan Anh Le, Chris J. Maddison, Maximilian Igl, Frank Wood, and Yee Whye Teh. 2018. Tighter variational bounds are not necessarily better. In *ICML*.

Marc'Aurelio Ranzato, Sumit Chopra, Michael Auli, and Wojciech Zaremba. 2016. Sequence level training with recurrent neural networks. In *ICLR*.

Steven J. Rennie, Etienne Marcheret, Youssef Mroueh, Jerret Ross, and Vaibhava Goel. 2016. Self-critical sequence training for image captioning. *CoRR*, abs/1612.00563.

Danilo Jimenez Rezende, Shakir Mohamed, and Daan Wierstra. 2014. Stochastic back-propagation and variational inference in deep latent gaussian models. In *ICML*.

Alexander M. Rush, Sumit Chopra, and Jason Weston. 2015. A neural attention model for abstractive sentence summarization. In *EMNLP*.

Florian Schmidt and Thomas Hofmann. 2018. Deep state space models for unconditional word generation. In *NeurIPS*.

Iulian Vlad Serban, Alessandro Sordoni, Yoshua Bengio, Aaron C Courville, and Joelle Pineau. 2016. Building end-to-end dialogue systems using generative hierarchical neural network models. In *AAAI*.

Xiaoyu Shen, Hui Su, Shuzi Niu, and Vera Demberg. 2018. Improving variational encoder-decoders in dialogue generation. *CoRR*, abs/1802.02032.

Bowen Tan, Zhiting Hu, Zichao Yang, Ruslan Salakhutdinov, and Eric P. Xing. 2018. Connecting the dots between MLE and RL for sequence generation. *CoRR*, abs/1811.09740.

Michael Tschannen, Olivier Bachem, and Mario Lucic. 2018. Recent advances in autoencoder-based representation learning. *CoRR*, abs/1812.05069.

Ashish Vaswani, Noam Shazeer, Niki Parmar, Jakob Uszkoreit, Llion Jones, Aidan N. Gomez, Lukasz Kaiser, and Illia Polosukhin. 2017. Attention is all you need. In *NIPS*.

Ronald J. Williams. 1992. Simple statistical gradient-following algorithms for connectionist reinforcement learning. *Mach. Learn.*, 8(3-4):229–256.

Zichao Yang, Zhiting Hu, Ruslan Salakhutdinov, and Taylor Berg-Kirkpatrick. 2017. Improved variational autoencoders for text modeling using dilated convolutions. *CoRR*, abs/1702.08139.

Cheng Zhang, Judith Butepage, Hedvig Kjellstrom, and Stephan Mandt. 2018. Advances in variational inference. *IEEE transactions on pattern analysis and machine intelligence*.

Yukun Zhu, Ryan Kiros, Richard Zemel, Ruslan Salakhutdinov, Raquel Urtasun, Antonio Torralba, and Sanja Fidler. 2015. Aligning books and movies: Towards story-like visual explanations by watching movies and reading books. *arXiv preprint arXiv:1506.06724*.

Machine Translation of Restaurant Reviews:
New Corpus for Domain Adaptation and Robustness

Alexandre Bérard   **Ioan Calapodescu**   **Marc Dymetman**

Claude Roux   **Jean-Luc Meunier**   **Vassilina Nikoulina**

Naver Labs Europe

`firstname.lastname@naverlabs.com`

Abstract

We share a French-English parallel corpus of Foursquare restaurant reviews, and define a new task to encourage research on Neural Machine Translation robustness and domain adaptation, in a real-world scenario where better-quality MT would be greatly beneficial. We discuss the challenges of such user-generated content, and train good baseline models that build upon the latest techniques for MT robustness. We also perform an extensive evaluation (automatic and human) that shows significant improvements over existing online systems. Finally, we propose task-specific metrics based on sentiment analysis or translation accuracy of domain-specific polysemous words.

1 Introduction

Very detailed information about social venues such as restaurants is available from user-generated reviews in applications like Google Maps, TripAdvisor or Foursquare[1] (4SQ). Most of these reviews are written in the local language and are not directly exploitable by foreign visitors: an analysis of the 4SQ database shows that, in Paris, only 49% of the restaurants have at least one review in English, and the situation can be much worse for other cities and languages (e.g., only 1% of Seoul restaurants for a French-only speaker).

Machine Translation of such user-generated content can improve the situation and make the data available for direct display or for downstream NLP tasks (e.g., cross-lingual information retrieval, sentiment analysis, spam or fake review detection), provided its quality is sufficient.

We asked professionals to translate 11.5k French 4SQ reviews (18k sentences) to English. We believe that this resource[2] will be valuable to the

---

[1] `https://foursquare.com/`

[2] `https://europe.naverlabs.com/`
`research/natural-language-processing/`
`machine-translation-of-restaurant-reviews/`

community for training and evaluating MT systems addressing challenges posed by user-generated content, which we discuss in detail in this paper.

We conduct extensive experiments and combine techniques that address these challenges (e.g., factored case, noise generation, domain adaptation with tags) on top of a strong Transformer baseline. In addition to BLEU evaluation and human evaluation, we use targeted metrics that measure how well polysemous words are translated, or how well sentiments expressed in the original review can still be recovered from its translation.

2 Related work

Translating restaurant reviews written by casual customers presents several challenges for NMT, in particular robustness to non-standard language and adaptation to a specific style or domain (see Section 3.2 for details).

Concerning robustness to noisy user generated content, Michel and Neubig (2018) stress differences with traditional domain adaptation problems, and propose a typology of errors, many of which we also detected in the 4SQ data. They also released a dataset (MTNT), whose sources were selected from a social media (Reddit) on the basis of being especially noisy (see Appendix for a comparison with 4SQ). These sources were then translated by humans to produce a parallel corpus that can be used to engineer more robust NMT systems and to evaluate them. This corpus was the basis of the WMT 2019 MT Robustness Task (Li et al., 2019), in which Berard et al. (2019) ranked first. We use the same set of robustness and domain adaptation techniques, which we study more in depth and apply to our review translation task.

Sperber et al. (2017), Belinkov and Bisk (2018) and Karpukhin et al. (2019) propose to improve robustness by training models on data-augmented

Proceedings of the 3rd Workshop on Neural Generation and Translation (WNGT 2019), pages 168–176
Hong Kong, China, November 4, 2019. ©2019 Association for Computational Linguistics
www.aclweb.org/anthology/D19-56%2d

corpora, containing noisy sources obtained by random word or character deletions, insertions, substitutions or swaps. Recently, Vaibhav et al. (2019) proposed to use a similar technique along with noise generation through replacement of a clean source by one obtained by back-translation.

We employ several well-known domain adaptation techniques: back-translation of large monolingual corpora close to the domain (Sennrich et al., 2016b; Edunov et al., 2018), fine-tuning with in-domain parallel data (Luong and Manning, 2015; Freitag and Al-Onaizan, 2016; Servan et al., 2016), domain tags for knowledge transfer between domains (Kobus et al., 2017; Berard et al., 2019).

Addressing the technical issues of robustness and adaptation of an NMT system is decisive for real-world deployment, but evaluation is also critical. This aspect is stressed by Levin et al. (2017) (NMT of curated hotel descriptions), who point out that automatic metrics like BLEU tend to neglect semantic differences that have a small textual footprint, but may be seriously misleading in practice, for instance by interpreting *available parking* as if it meant *free parking*. To mitigate this, we conduct additional evaluations of our models: human evaluation, translation accuracy of polysemous words, and indirect evaluation with sentiment analysis.

3 Task description

We present a new task of restaurant review translation, which combines domain adaptation and robustness challenges.

3.1 Corpus description

We sampled 11.5k French reviews from 4SQ, mostly in the *food* category,[3] split them into sentences (18k), and grouped them into train, valid and test sets (see Table 1). The French reviews contain on average 1.5 sentences and 17.9 words. Then, we hired eight professional translators to translate them to English. Two of them created the training set by post-editing (PE) the outputs of baseline NMT systems.[4] The other six translated the valid and test sets from scratch. They were asked to translate (or post-edit) the reviews sentence-by-sentence (to avoid any alignment problem), but they could see the full con-

---

[3]https://developer.foursquare.com/docs/
resources/categories

[4]ConvS2S or Transformer Big trained on the "UGC" corpus described in Section 6, without domain adaptation or robustness tricks.

Corpus	Sentences	Reviews	Words (FR)
4SQ-PE	12 080	8 004	141 958
4SQ-HT	2 784	1 625	29 075
4SQ-valid	1 243	765	13 976
4SQ-test	1 838	1 157	21 525

Table 1: 4SQ corpora. 4SQ-PE is the training set. 4SQ-HT is not used in this work.

text. We manually filtered the test set to remove translations that were not satisfactory. The full reviews and additional metadata (e.g., location and type of the restaurant) are also available as part of this resource, to encourage research on contextual machine translation. 4SQ-HT was translated from scratch by the same translators who post-edited 4SQ-PE. While we did not use it in this work, it can be used as extra training or development data. We also release a human translation of the French-language test set (668 sentences) of the Aspect-Based Sentiment Analysis task at SemEval 2016 (Pontiki et al., 2016).

3.2 Challenges

Translating restaurant reviews presents two main challenges compared to common tasks in MT. First, the reviews are written in a casual style, close to spoken language. Some liberty is taken w.r.t. spelling, grammar, and punctuation. Slang is also very frequent. MT should be robust to these variations. Second, they generally are reactions, by clients of a restaurant, about its food quality, service or atmosphere, with specific words relating to these aspects or sentiments. These require some degree of domain adaptation. The following table illustrates these issues, with outputs from an online MT system. Examples of full reviews from 4SQ-PE along with metadata are shown in Appendix.

(1)	é qd g vu sa ... and when I saw that ... é qd g seen his ...	(source) (reference) (online MT)
(2)	c'est trooop bon ! it's toooo good! it's good trooop!	
(3)	le cadre est nul the setting is lousy the frame is null	
(4)	le garçon a pété un cable the waiter went crazy the boy farted a cable	
(5)	pizza nickel, tres bonnes pattes great pizza, very good pasta nickel pizza, very good legs	

Examples 1 and 2 fall into the robustness category: 1 is an extreme form of SMS-like, quasi-phonetic, language (*et quand j'ai vu ça*); 2 is a literal transcription of a long-vowel phonetic stress (*trop → trooop*). Example 3 falls into the domain category: in a restaurant context, *cadre* typically refers to the *setting*. Examples 4 and 5 involve both robustness and domain adaptation: *pété un cable* is a non-compositional slang expression and *garçon* is not a *boy* in this domain; *nickel* is slang for *great*, *très* is missing an accent, and *pâtes* is misspelled as *pattes*, which is another French word.

Regarding robustness, we found many of the same errors listed by Michel and Neubig (2018) as noise in social media text: SMS language (*é qd g vu sa*), typos and phonetic spelling (*pattes*), repeated letters (*trooop, merciiii*), slang (*nickel, bof, mdr*), missing or wrong accents (*tres*), emoticons (':-)') and emojis (☺), missing punctuation, wrong or non-standard capitalization (lowercase proper names, capitalized words for emphasis). Regarding domain aspects, there are polysemous words with typical specific meaning *carte → map, menu*; *cadre → frame, executive, setting*), idiomatic expressions (*à tomber par terre → to die for*), and venue-related named entities (*La Boîte à Sardines*).

4 Robustness to noise

We propose solutions for dealing with non-standard case, emoticons, emojis and other issues.

4.1 Rare character placeholder

We segment our training data into subwords with BPE (Sennrich et al., 2016c), implemented in SentencePiece (Kudo and Richardson, 2018). BPE can deal with rare or unseen words by splitting them into more frequent subwords but cannot deal with unseen characters.[5] While this is not a problem in most tasks, 4SQ contains a lot of emojis, and sometimes symbols in other scripts (e.g., Arabic). Unicode now defines around 3k emojis, most of which are likely to be out-of-vocabulary.

We replace rare characters on both sides of the training corpus by a placeholder (<x>); a model trained on this data is typically able to copy the placeholder at the correct position. Then, at inference time, we replace the output tokens <x> by the rare source-side characters, in the same or-

	Uppercase	Lowercase
Input	UNE HONTE !	une honte !
Pre-proc	UN E _H ON TE _!	une _honte _!
MT output	A _H ON E Y !	A _dis gra ce !
Post-proc	A HONEY!	A disgrace!

Table 2: Capital letters break NMT. BPE segmentation and translation of capitalized or lowercase input.

der. This approach is similar to that of Jean et al. (2015), who used the attention mechanism to replace output UNK symbols with the aligned word in the source. Berard et al. (2019) used the same technique to deal with emojis in the WMT robustness task.

4.2 Capital letters

As shown in Table 2, capital letters are another source of confusion. *HONTE* and *honte* are considered as two different words. The former is out-of-vocabulary and is split very aggressively by BPE. This causes the MT model to hallucinate.

Lowercasing A solution is to lowercase the input, both at training and at test time. However, when doing so, some information may be lost (e.g., named entities, acronyms, emphasis) which may result in lower translation quality.

Factored translation Levin et al. (2017) do factored machine translation (Sennrich and Haddow, 2016; Garcia-Martinez et al., 2016) where a word and its case are split in two different features. For instance, *HONTE* becomes *honte + upper*.

We implement this with two embedding matrices, one for words and one for case, and represent a token as the sum of the embeddings of its factors. For the target side, we follow Garcia-Martinez et al. (2016) and have two softmax operations. We first predict the word in its lowercase form and then predict its case.[6] The embeddings of the case and word are then summed and used as input for the next decoder step.

Inline casing Berard et al. (2019) propose another approach, *inline casing*, which does not require any change in the model. We insert the case as a regular token into the sequence right after the word. Special tokens <U>, <L> and <T> (upper, lower and title) are used for this purpose and appended to the vocabulary. Contrary to the previous

---

[5]Unless actually doing BPE at the *byte* level, as suggested by Radford et al. (2019).

[6]Like the "dependency model" of Garcia-Martinez et al. (2016), we use the current state of the decoder and the embedding of the output word to predict its case.

solution, there is only one embedding matrix and one softmax.

In practice, words are assumed to be lowercase by default and the <L> tokens are dropped to keep the factored sequences as short as possible. *"Best fries EVER"* becomes *"best <T> _f ries _ever <U>"*. Like Berard et al. (2019), we force SentencePiece to split mixed-case words like *MacDonalds* into single-case subwords (*Mac* and *Donalds*).

Synthetic case noise   Another solution that we experiment with (see Section 6) is to inject noise on the source side of the training data by changing random source words to upper (5% chance), title (10%) or lower case (20%).

4.3   Natural noise

One way to make an NMT system more robust is to train it with some of the most common errors that can be found in the in-domain data. Like Berard et al. (2019), we detect the errors that occur naturally in the in-domain data and then apply them to our training corpus, while respecting their natural distribution. We call this "natural noise generation" in opposition to what is done in (Sperber et al., 2017; Belinkov and Bisk, 2018; Vaibhav et al., 2019) or in Section 4.2, where the noise is more synthetic.

Detecting errors   We compile a general-purpose French lexicon as a transducer,[7] implemented to be traversed with extended edit distance flags, similar to Mihov and Schulz (2004). Whenever a word is not found in the lexicon (which means that it is a potential spelling mistake), we look for a French word in the lexicon within a maximum edit distance of 2, with the following set of edit operations:

(1)	deletion (e.g., *apelle* instead of *appelle*)
(2)	insertion (e.g., *appercevoir* instead of *apercevoir*)
(3)	constrained substitution on diacritics (e.g., *mangè* instead of *mangé*)
(4)	swap counted as one operation: (e.g., *mnager* instead of *manger*)
(5)	substitution (e.g., *menger* instead of *manger*)
(6)	repetitions (e.g., *Merciiiii* with a threshold of max 10 repetitions)

We apply the transducer to the French monolingual Foursquare data (close to 1M sentences) to detect and count noisy variants of known French words. This step produces a dictionary mapping

the correct spelling to the list of observed errors and their respective frequencies.

In addition to automatically extracted spelling errors, we extract a set of common abbreviations from (Seddah et al., 2012) and we manually identify a list of common errors in French:

(7)	Wrong verb endings (e.g., *il a manger* instead of *il a mangé*)
(8)	Wrong spacing around punctuation symbols (e.g., *Les.plats ...* instead of *Les plats...*)
(9)	Upper case/mixed case words (e.g., *manQue de place* instead of *manque de place*)
(10)	SMS language (e.g., *bcp* instead of *beaucoup*)
(11)	Phonetic spelling (e.g., *sa* instead of *ça*)

Generating errors   With this dictionary, describing the real error distribution in 4SQ text, we take our large out-of-domain training corpus, and randomly replace source-side words with one of their variants (rules 1 to 6), while respecting the frequency of this variant in the real data. We also manually define regular expressions to randomly apply rules 7 to 11 (e.g., `"er "`→`"é "`).

We obtain a noisy parallel corpus (which we use instead of the "clean" training data), where about 30% of all source sentences have been modified, as shown below:

Error type	Examples of sentences with injected noise
(1) (6) (9)	L'Union **eU**ropée**ne** espere que la réunion de suiv**iii** entre le Président [...]
(2) (3) (10)	Le Comité **notte** avec **bcp** d'interet **k** les projets d'articles [...]
(4) (7) (8)	Réun**oin sur.la** comptabilit**er** nationale [...]

5   Domain Adaptation

To adapt our models to the restaurant review domain we apply the following types of techniques: back-translation of in-domain English data, fine-tuning with small amounts of in-domain parallel data, and domain tags.

5.1   Back-translation

Back-translation (BT) is a popular technique for domain adaptation when large amounts of in-domain monolingual data are available (Sennrich et al., 2016b; Edunov et al., 2018). While our in-domain parallel corpus is small (12k pairs), Foursquare contains millions of English-language reviews. Thus, we train an NMT model[8] in the reverse direction (EN→FR) and translate all the 4SQ

---

[7] In Tamgu: `https://github.com/naver/tamgu`

[8] Like the "UGC" model with rare character handling and inline case described in Section 6.3.

English reviews to French.[9] This gives a large synthetic parallel corpus.

This *in-domain* data is concatenated to the out-of-domain parallel data and used for training.

Edunov et al. (2018) show that doing back-translation with sampling instead of beam search brings large improvements due to increased diversity. Following this work, we test several settings:

Name	Description
BT-B	Back-translation with beam search.
BT-S	Back-translation with sampling.
BT-S × 3	Three different FR samplings for each EN sentence. This brings the size of the back-translated 4SQ closer to the out-of-domain corpus.
BT	No oversampling, but we sample a new version of the corpus for each training epoch.

We use a temperature[10] of $T = \frac{1}{0.9}$ to avoid the extremely noisy output obtained with $T = 1$ and strike a balance between quality and diversity.

5.2 Fine-tuning

When small amounts of in-domain parallel data are available, fine-tuning (FT) is often the preferred solution for domain adaptation (Luong and Manning, 2015; Freitag and Al-Onaizan, 2016). It consists in training a model on out-of-domain data, and then continuing its training for a few epochs on the in-domain data only.

5.3 Corpus tags

Kobus et al. (2017) propose a technique for multi-domain NMT, which consists in inserting a token in each source sequence specifying its domain. The system can learn the particularities of multiple domains (e.g., polysemous words that have a different meaning depending on the domain), which we can control at test time by manually setting the tag. Sennrich et al. (2016a) also use tags to control politeness in the model's output.

As our corpus (see Section 6.1) is not clearly divided into domains, we apply the same technique as Kobus et al. (2017) but use *corpus* tags (each sub-corpus has its own tag: TED, Paracrawl, etc.) which we add to each source sequence. Like in (Berard et al., 2019), the 4SQ post-edited and back-translated data also get their own tags (PE and BT).

Corpus tag	SRC: La **carte** est trop petite.
TED	The map is too small.
Multi-UN	The card is too small.
PE	The **menu** is too small.

Figure 1: Example of ambiguous source sentence, where using corpus tags help the model pick a more adequate translation.

Corpus	Lines	Words (FR)	Words (EN)
WMT	29.47M	1 003M	883.5M
UGC	51.39M	1 125M	1 041M

Table 3: Size of the WMT and UGC training corpora (after filtering).

Figure 1 gives an example where using the PE corpus tag at test time helps the model pick a more adequate translation.

6 Experiments

6.1 Training data

After some initial work with the WMT 2014 data, we built a new training corpus named UGC (User Generated Content), closer to our domain, by combining: Multi UN, OpenSubtitles, Wikipedia, Books, Tatoeba, TED talks, ParaCrawl[11] and Gourmet[12] (See Table 3). Notably, UGC does not include Common Crawl (which contains a lot of misaligned sentences and caused hallucinations), but it includes OpenSubtitles (Lison and Tiedemann, 2016) (spoken-language, possibly closer to 4SQ). We observed an improvement of more than 1 BLEU on news-test 2014 when switching to UGC, and almost 6 BLEU on 4SQ-valid.

6.2 Pre-processing

We use `langid.py` (Lui and Baldwin, 2012) to filter sentence pairs from UGC. We also remove duplicate sentence pairs, and lines longer than 175 words or with a length ratio greater than 1.5 (see Table 3). Then we apply SentencePiece and our rare character handling strategy (Section 4.1). We use a joined BPE model of size 32k, trained on the concatenation of both sides of the corpus, and set SentencePiece's vocabulary threshold to 100. Finally, unless stated otherwise, we always use the *inline casing* approach (see Section 4.2).

---

[9]This represents ≈15M sentences. This corpus is not available publicly, but the Yelp dataset (`https://www.yelp.com/dataset`) could be used instead.

[10]with $p(w_i) = \frac{exp(z_i/T)}{\sum_{k=1}^{|V|} exp(z_k/T)}$

[11]Corpora available at `http://opus.nlpl.eu/`

[12]3k translations of dishes and other food terminology `http://www.gourmetpedia.eu/`

6.3 Model and settings

For all experiments, we use the Transformer Big (Vaswani et al., 2017) as implemented in Fairseq, with the hyperparameters of Ott et al. (2018). Training is done on 8 GPUs, with accumulated gradients over 10 batches (Ott et al., 2018), and a max batch size of 3500 tokens (per GPU). We train for 20 epochs, while saving a checkpoint every 2500 updates ($\approx \frac{2}{5}$ epoch on UGC) and average the 5 best checkpoints according to their perplexity on a validation set (a held-out subset of UGC).

For fine-tuning, we use a fixed learning rate, and a total batch size of 3500 tokens (training on a single GPU without delayed updates). To avoid overfitting on 4SQ-PE, we do early stopping according to perplexity on 4SQ-valid.[13] For each fine-tuned model we test all 16 combinations of dropout in $\{0.1, 0.2, 0.3, 0.4\}$ and learning rate in $\{1, 2, 5, 10\} \times 10^{-5}$. We keep the model with the best perplexity on 4SQ-valid.[14]

6.4 Evaluation methodology

During our work, we used BLEU (Papineni et al., 2002) on *news-valid* (concatenation of news-test 2012 and 2013) to ensure that our models stayed good on a more general domain, and on *4SQ-valid* to measure performance on the 4SQ domain.

For sake of brevity, we only give the final BLEU scores on *news-test 2014* and *4SQ-test*. Scores on 4SQ-valid, and MTNT-test (for comparison with Michel and Neubig, 2018; Berard et al., 2019) are given in Appendix. We evaluate "detokenized" MT outputs[15] against raw (non-tokenized) references using SacreBLEU (Post, 2018).[16]

In addition to BLEU, we do an indirect evaluation on an Aspect-Based Sentiment Analysis (ABSA) task, a human evaluation, and a task-related evaluation based on polysemous words.

6.5 BLEU evaluation

Capital letters Table 4 compares the case handling techniques presented in Section 4.2. To better evaluate the robustness of our models to changes of case, we built 3 synthetic test sets from 4SQ-test, with the same target, but all source words in upper, lower or title case.

---

[13]The best perplexity was achieved after 1 to 3 epochs.

[14]The best dropout rate was always 0.1, and the best learning rate was either 2×10^{-5} or 5×10^{-5}.

[15]Outputs of our models are provided with the 4SQ corpus.

[16]SacreBLEU signature: BLEU+case.mixed+numrefs.1 +smooth.exp+tok.13a+version.1.2.10

Model	BLEU 4SQ	Case insensitive BLEU		
		Upper	Lower	Title
Cased	31.78	16.02	32.42	26.67
LC to cased	30.91	**33.09**	33.09	33.09
Factored case	31.62	32.31	32.96	29.86
Inline case	31.55	31.08	32.63	29.61
Noised case	**31.99**	32.64	**33.73**	**33.63**

Table 4: Robustness to capital letters (see Section 4.2). 4SQ's source side has been set to upper, lower or title case. The first column is case sensitive BLEU. "LC to cased" always gets the same scores because it is invariant to source case.

Model	news	noised news	4SQ
UGC (Inline case)	**40.68**	35.59	31.55
+ natural noise	40.43	**40.35**	**31.69**

Table 5: Baseline model with or without natural noise (see Section 4.3). *Noised news* is the same type of noise, artificially applied to news-test.

Inline and factored case perform equally well, significantly better than the default (cased) model, especially on all-uppercase inputs. Lowercasing the source is a good option, but gives a slightly lower score on regular 4SQ-test.[17] Finally, synthetic case noise added to the source gives surprisingly good results. It could also be combined with factored or inline case.

Natural noise Table 5 compares the baseline "inline case" model with the same model augmented with natural noise (Section 4.3). Performance is the same on 4SQ-test, but significantly better on news-test artificially augmented with 4SQ-like noise.

Domain adaptation Table 6 shows the results of the back-translation (BT) techniques. Surprisingly, BT with beam search (BT-B) deteriorates BLEU scores on 4SQ-test, while BT with sampling gives a consistent improvement. BLEU scores on news-test are not significantly impacted, suggesting that BT can be used for domain adaptation without hurting quality on other domains.

Table 7 compares the domain adaptation techniques presented in Section 5. We observe that:

1. Concatenating the small 4SQ-PE corpus to the 50M general domain corpus does not help much, unless using tags.

---

[17]The "LC to cased" and "Noised case" models are not able to preserve capital letters for emphasis (as in Table 2), and the "Cased" model often breaks on such examples.

Model	news	4SQ
UGC (Inline case)	40.68	31.55
UGC ⊕ BT-B	40.56	30.17
UGC ⊕ BT-S	40.64	32.64
UGC ⊕ BT	**40.84**	32.69
UGC ⊕ BT-S × 3	40.63	**32.84**

Table 6: Comparison of different back-translation schemes (see Section 5.1). ⊕ denotes the concatenation of several training corpora.

Model	Tag	news	4SQ
UGC (Inline case)	–	40.68	31.55
UGC ⊕ 4SQ-PE	–	40.80	32.05
UGC + FT	–	39.78	**35.02**
UGC ⊕ 4SQ-PE + tags	–	40.71	32.12
	PE	38.97	34.36
UGC ⊕ BT + tags	–	40.67	33.47
	BT	39.02	33.00

Table 7: Domain adaptation with 4SQ-PE fine-tuning (FT) or corpus tags. The "tag" column represents the corpus tag used at test time (if any).

Model	news	4SQ
WMT	39.37	26.26
UGC (Inline case)	40.68	31.55
Google Translate (Feb 2019)	36.31	29.63
DeepL (Feb 2019)	?	32.82
UGC ⊕ BT + FT	39.55	35.95
UGC ⊕ BT ⊕ PE + tags	**40.99**	35.72
Nat noise ⊕ BT + FT	39.91	**36.35**
Nat noise ⊕ BT ⊕ PE + tags	40.72	35.60

Table 8: Combination of several robustness or domain adaptation techniques. At test time, we don't use any tag on news, and use the PE tag on 4SQ (when applicable). BT: back-translation. PE: 4SQ-PE. FT: fine-tuning with 4SQ-PE. ⊕: concatenation.

French word	Meanings
Cadre	setting, frame, executive
Cuisine	<u>food</u>, kitchen
Carte	<u>menu</u>, <u>card</u>, map

Table 9: French polysemous words found in 4SQ, and translation candidates in English. The most frequent meanings in 4SQ are underlined.

2. *4SQ-PE + tags* is not as good as fine-tuning with 4SQ-PE. However, fine-tuned models get slightly worse results on news.

3. Back-translation combined with tags gives a large boost.[18] The BT tag should not be used at test time, as it degrades results.

4. Surprisingly, using no tag at test time works fine, even though all training sentences had tags.[19]

As shown in Table 8, these techniques can be combined to achieve the best results. The natural noise does not have a significant effect on BLEU scores. Back-translation combined with fine-tuning gives the best performance on 4SQ (+4.5 BLEU vs UGC). However, using tags instead of fine-tuning strikes a better balance between general domain and in-domain performance.

6.6 Targeted evaluation

In this section we propose two metrics that target specific aspects of translation adequacy: translation accuracy of domain-specific polysemous words and Aspect-Based Sentiment Analysis performance on MT outputs.

Translation of polysemous words We propose to count polysemous words specific to our domain, similarly to (Lala and Specia, 2018), to measure the degree of domain adaptation. TER between the translation hypotheses and the post-edited references in 4SQ-PE reveals the most common substitutions (e.g., "card" is often replaced with "menu", suggesting that "card" is a common mistranslation of the polysemous word "carte"). We filter this list manually to only keep words that are polysemous and that have a high frequency in the test set. Table 9 gives the 3 most frequent ones.[20]

Table 10 shows the accuracy of our models when translating these words. We see that the domain-adapted model is better at translating domain-specific polysemous words.

Indirect evaluation with sentiment analysis We also measure adequacy by how well the translation preserves the polarity of the sentence regarding various aspects. To evaluate this, we perform an indirect evaluation on the SemEval 2016 Aspect-Based Sentiment Analysis (ABSA) task (Pontiki et al., 2016). We use our internal ABSA systems trained on English or French SemEval

---

[18]Caswell et al. (2019); Berard et al. (2019) observed the same thing.

[19]We tried keeping a small percentage of UGC with no tag, or with an ANY tag, but this made no difference.

[20]Rarer ones are: *adresse* (place, address), *café* (coffee, café), *entrée* (starter, entrance), *formule* (menu, formula), *long* (slow, long), *moyen* (average, medium), *correct* (decent, right), *brasserie* (brasserie, brewery) and *coin* (local, corner).

Model	cadre	cuisine	carte	Total
Total (source)	23	32	29	100%
WMT	13	17	14	52%
UGC (Inline case)	22	27	18	80%
UGC $\oplus$ PE + tags	**23**	31	**29**	99%

Table 10: Number of correct translations for difficult polysemous words in 4SQ-test by different models. The first row is the number of source sentences that contain this word. Other domain-adapted models (e.g., "UGC + FT" or "UGC $\oplus$ BT") also get $\approx$ 99% accuracy.

ABSA Model	Aspect	Polarity
ABSA French	**64.7**	**83.2**
ABSA English	59.5	72.1
ABSA English on MT outputs		
WMT	54.5	66.1
UGC (Inline case)	58.1	70.7
UGC $\oplus$ BT $\oplus$ PE + tags	60.2	72.0
Nat noise $\oplus$ BT $\oplus$ PE + tags	60.8	73.3

Table 11: Indirect evaluation with Aspect-Based Sentiment Analysis (accuracy in %). *ABSA French*: ABSA model trained on French data and applied to the SemEval 2016 French test set; *ABSA English*: trained on English data and applied to human translations of the test set; *ABSA English* on MT outputs: applied to MT outputs instead of human translations.

2016 data. The evaluation is done on the SemEval 2016 French test set: either the original version (ABSA French), or its translation (ABSA English). As shown in Table 11, translations obtained with domain-adapted models lead to significantly better scores on the ABSA task than the generic models.

6.7 Human Evaluation

We conduct a human evaluation to confirm the observations with BLEU and to overcome some of the limitations of this metric.

We select 4 MT models for evaluation (see Table 12) and show their 4 outputs at once, sentence-by-sentence, to human judges, who are asked to rank them given the French source sentence in context (with the full review). For each pair of models, we count the number of wins, ties and losses, and apply the Wilcoxon signed-rank test.

We took the first 300 test sentences to create 6 tasks of 50 sentences each. Then we asked bilingual colleagues to rank the output of 4 models by their translation quality. They were asked to do one or more of these tasks. The judge did not know about the list of models, nor the model that produced any given translation. We got 12 an-

Pairs	Win	Tie	Loss
Tags $\approx$ Tags + noise	82	453	63
Tags $\gg$ Baseline	187	337	74
Tags $\gg$ GT	226	302	70
Tags + noise $\gg$ Baseline	178	232	97
Tags + noise $\gg$ GT	218	315	65
Baseline $\gg$ GT	173	302	123

Table 12: In-house human evaluation ("$\gg$" means better with $p \leq 0.05$). The 4 models *Baseline*, *GT*, *Tags* and *Tags + noise* correspond respectively to rows 2 (UGC with inline case), 3 (Google Translate), 6 (Combination of BT, PE and tags) and 8 (Same as 6 with natural noise) in Table 8.

swers. The inter-judge Kappa coefficient ranged from 0.29 to 0.63, with an average of 0.47, which is a good value given the difficulty of the task. Table 12 gives the results of the evaluation, which confirm our observations with BLEU.

We also did a larger-scale monolingual evaluation using Amazon Mechanical Turk (see Appendix), which lead to similar conclusions.

7 Conclusion

We presented a new parallel corpus of user reviews of restaurants, which we think will be valuable to the community. We proposed combinations of multiple techniques for robustness and domain adaptation, which address particular challenges of this new task. We also performed an extensive evaluation to measure the improvements brought by these techniques.

According to BLEU, the best single technique for domain adaptation is fine-tuning. Corpus tags also achieve good results, without degrading performance on a general domain. Back-translation helps, but only with sampling or tags. The robustness techniques (natural noise, factored case, rare character placeholder) do not improve BLEU.

While our models are promising, they still show serious errors when applied to user-generated content: missing negations, hallucinations, unrecognized named entities, insensitivity to context.[21] This suggests that this task is far from solved.

We hope that this corpus, our natural noise dictionary, model outputs and human rankings will help better understand and address these problems. We also plan to investigate these problems on lower resource languages, where we expect the task to be even harder.

---

[21]See additional examples in Appendix.

References

Yonatan Belinkov and Yonatan Bisk. 2018. Synthetic and Natural Noise Both Break Neural Machine Translation. In *ICLR*.

Alexandre Berard, Calapodescu Ioan, and Claude Roux. 2019. NAVER LABS Europe's Systems for the WMT19 Machine Translation Robustness Task. In *WMT*.

Isaac Caswell, Ciprian Chelba, and David Grangier. 2019. Tagged Back-Translation. In *WMT*.

Sergey Edunov, Myle Ott, Michael Auli, and David Grangier. 2018. Understanding Back-Translation at Scale. In *EMNLP*.

Markus Freitag and Yaser Al-Onaizan. 2016. Fast Domain Adaptation for Neural Machine Translation. *arXiv*.

Mercedes Garcia-Martinez, Loic Barrault, and Fethi Bougares. 2016. Factored Neural Machine Translation. *arXiv*.

Sébastien Jean, Kyunghyun Cho, Roland Memisevic, and Yoshua Bengio. 2015. On Using Very Large Target Vocabulary for Neural Machine Translation. *NAACL-HLT*.

Vladimir Karpukhin, Omer Levy, Jacob Eisenstein, and Marjan Ghazvininejad. 2019. Training on Synthetic Noise Improves Robustness to Natural Noise in Machine Translation. *arXiv*.

Catherine Kobus, Josep Crego, and Jean Senellart. 2017. Domain Control for Neural Machine Translation. In *RANLP*.

Taku Kudo and John Richardson. 2018. SentencePiece: A simple and language independent subword tokenizer and detokenizer for Neural Text Processing. In *EMNLP*.

Chiraag Lala and Lucia Specia. 2018. Multimodal lexical translation. In *LREC*.

Pavel Levin, Nishikant Dhanuka, Talaat Khalil, Fedor Kovalev, and Maxim Khalilov. 2017. Toward a full-scale neural machine translation in production: the Booking.com use case. In *MT Summit XVI*.

Xian Li, Paul Michel, Antonios Anastasopoulos, Yonatan Belinkov, Nadir K. Durrani, Orhan Firat, Philipp Koehn, Graham Neubig, Juan M. Pino, and Hassan Sajjad. 2019. Findings of the First Shared Task on Machine Translation Robustness. In *WMT*.

Pierre Lison and Jörg Tiedemann. 2016. OpenSubtitles2016: Extracting Large Parallel Corpora from Movie and TV Subtitles. In *LREC*.

Marco Lui and Timothy Baldwin. 2012. langid.py: An Off-the-shelf Language Identification Tool. In *Proceedings of the ACL 2012 System Demonstrations*, ACL.

Minh-Thang Luong and Christopher D. Manning. 2015. Stanford Neural Machine Translation Systems for Spoken Language Domain. In *IWSLT*.

Paul Michel and Graham Neubig. 2018. MTNT: A Testbed for Machine Translation of Noisy Text. In *EMNLP*.

Stoyan Mihov and Klaus U. Schulz. 2004. Fast Approximate Search in Large Dictionaries. *Computational Linguistics*.

Myle Ott, Sergey Edunov, David Grangier, and Michael Auli. 2018. Scaling Neural Machine Translation. In *WMT*.

Kishore Papineni, Salim Roukos, Todd Ward, and Wj Zhu. 2002. BLEU: a Method for Automatic Evaluation of Machine Translation. In *ACL*.

Maria Pontiki, Dimitris Galanis, Haris Papageorgiou, Ion Androutsopoulos, Suresh Manandhar, Mohammed AL-Smadi, Mahmoud Al-Ayyoub, Yanyan Zhao, Bing Qin, Orphée De Clercq, Veronique Hoste, Marianna Apidianaki, Xavier Tannier, Natalia Loukachevitch, Evgeniy Kotelnikov, Núria Bel, Salud Maria Jiménez-Zafra, and Gülşen Eryiğit. 2016. SemEval-2016 Task 5: Aspect Based Sentiment Analysis. In *Proceedings of the 10th International Workshop on Semantic Evaluation (SemEval)*.

Matt Post. 2018. A Call for Clarity in Reporting BLEU Scores. In *WMT*.

Alec Radford, Jeffrey Wu, Rewon Child, David Luan, Dario Amodei, and Ilya Sutskever. 2019. Language Models are Unsupervised Multitask Learners.

Djamé Seddah, Benoît Sagot, Marie Candito, Virginie Mouilleron, and Vanessa Combet. 2012. Building a treebank of noisy user-generated content: The French Social Media Bank. In *The 11th International Workshop on Treebanks and Linguistic Theories (TLT)*.

Rico Sennrich and Barry Haddow. 2016. Linguistic Input Features Improve Neural Machine Translation. In *WMT*.

Rico Sennrich, Barry Haddow, and Alexandra Birch. 2016a. Controlling Politeness in Neural Machine Translation via Side Constraints. In *NAACL-HLT*.

Rico Sennrich, Barry Haddow, and Alexandra Birch. 2016b. Improving Neural Machine Translation Models with Monolingual Data. In *ACL*.

Rico Sennrich, Barry Haddow, and Alexandra Birch. 2016c. Neural Machine Translation of Rare Words with Subword Units. In *ACL*.

Christophe Servan, Josep Crego, and Jean Senellart. 2016. Domain specialization: a post-training domain adaptation for neural machine translation. *arXiv*.

Matthias Sperber, Jan Niehues, and Alex Waibel. 2017. Toward Robust Neural Machine Translation for Noisy Input Sequences. In *IWSLT*.

Vaibhav, Sumeet Singh, Craig Stewart, and Graham Neubig. 2019. Improving Robustness of Machine Translation with Synthetic Noise. In *NAACL*.

Ashish Vaswani, Noam Shazeer, Niki Parmar, Jakob Uszkoreit, Llion Jones, Aidan N. Gomez, Łukasz Kaiser, and Illia Polosukhin. 2017. Attention Is All You Need. In *NIPS*.

Adaptively Scheduled Multitask Learning:
The Case of Low-Resource Neural Machine Translation

Poorya Zaremoodi[1,2]   **Gholamreza Haffari**[1]

[1]Monash University, Melbourne, Australia

[2]CSIRO Data61, Sydney, Australia

`first.last@monash.edu`

Abstract

Neural Machine Translation (NMT), a data-hungry technology, suffers from the lack of bilingual data in low-resource scenarios. Multitask learning (MTL) can alleviate this issue by injecting inductive biases into NMT, using auxiliary syntactic and semantic tasks. However, an effective *training schedule* is required to balance the importance of tasks to get the best use of the training signal. The role of training schedule becomes even more crucial in *biased-MTL* where the goal is to improve one (or a subset) of tasks the most, e.g. translation quality. Current approaches for biased-MTL are based on brittle *hand-engineered* heuristics that require trial and error, and should be (re-)designed for each learning scenario. To the best of our knowledge, ours is the first work on *adaptively* and *dynamically* changing the training schedule in biased-MTL. We propose a rigorous approach for automatically reweighing the training data of the main and auxiliary tasks throughout the training process based on their contributions to the generalisability of the main NMT task. Our experiments on translating from English to Vietnamese/Turkish/Spanish show improvements of up to +1.2 BLEU points, compared to strong baselines. Additionally, our analyses shed light on the dynamic of needs throughout the training of NMT: from syntax to semantic.

1 Introduction

While Neural Machine Translation (NMT) is known for its ability to learn end-to-end without any need for many brittle design choices and hand-engineered features, it is notorious for its demand for large amounts of bilingual data to achieve reasonable translation quality (Koehn and Knowles, 2017). Recent work has investigated multitask learning (MTL) for injecting inductive biases from auxiliary syntactic and/or se-

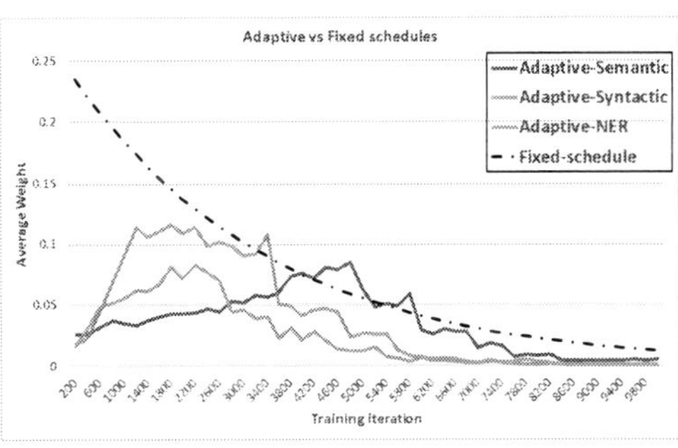

Figure 1: The dynamic in the relative importance of named entity recognition, syntactic parsing, and semantic parsing as the auxiliary tasks for the main machine translation task (based on our experiments in §3). The plot shows our proposed adaptive scheduling vs fixed scheduling (Kiperwasser and Ballesteros, 2018) (scaled down for better illustration).

mantic tasks into NMT to improve its generalisation (Zaremoodi and Haffari, 2018; Zaremoodi et al., 2018; Kiperwasser and Ballesteros, 2018).

The majority of the MTL literature has focused on investigating how to share common knowledge among the tasks through tying their parameters and joint training using standard algorithms. However, a big challenge of MTL is how to get the best signal from the tasks by changing their importance in the training process aka *training schedule*; see Figure 1.

Crucially, a proper training schedule would encourage positive transfer and prevent negative transfer, as the inductive biases of the auxiliary tasks may interfere with those of the main task leading to degradation of generalisation capabilities. Most of the works on training schedule focus on *general* MTL where the goal is to improve the performance of *all* tasks. They are based on addressing the imbalance in task difficulties and co-evolve easy and difficult tasks uniformly (performance-wise). These methods

Proceedings of the 3rd Workshop on Neural Generation and Translation (WNGT 2019), pages 177–186

Hong Kong, China, November 4, 2019. ©2019 Association for Computational Linguistics

www.aclweb.org/anthology/D19-56%2d

achieve competitive performance with existing single-task models of each task, and not necessarily much better performance (Chen et al., 2018; Guo et al., 2018b). On the other hand, *biased-MTL* focuses on the *main* task to achieve higher improvements on it. (Zaremoodi and Haffari, 2018) has proposed a fixed training schedule to balance out the importance of the main NMT task vs auxiliary task to improve NMT the most. (Kiperwasser and Ballesteros, 2018) has shown the effectiveness of a changing training schedule through the MTL process. However, their approach is based on *hand-engineered* heuristics, and should be (re-)designed and fine-tuned for every change in tasks or even training data.

In this paper, for the first time to the best of our knowledge, we propose a method to *adaptively* and *dynamically* set the importance weights of tasks for *biased-MTL*. By using *influence functions* from robust statistics (Cook and Weisberg, 1980; Koh and Liang, 2017), we adaptively examine the influence of training instances inside minibatches of the tasks on the generalisation capabilities on the main task. The generalisation is measured as the performance of the main task on a validation set, separated from the training set, in each parameter update step *dynamically*. In this paper, we consider translation as the main task along with syntactic and semantic auxiliary tasks, and re-weight instances in such a way to maximise the performance of the translation task. As our method is general and does not rely on hand-engineered heuristics, it can be used for effective learning of multitask architectures beyond NMT.

We evaluate our method on translating from English to Vietnamese/Turkish/Spanish, with auxiliary tasks including syntactic parsing, semantic parsing, and named entity recognition. Compared to strong training schedule baselines, our method achieves considerable improvements in terms of BLEU score. Additionally, our analyses on the weights assigned by the proposed training schedule show that although the dynamic of weights are different for different language pairs, the underlying pattern is gradually altering tasks importance from syntactic to semantic-related tasks.

In summary, our main contributions to MTL and low-resource NMT are as follows:

- We propose an effective training schedule for biased-MTL that adaptively and dynamically set the importance of tasks throughout the training to improve the main task the most.

- We extensively evaluate on three language pairs, and experimental results show that our model outperforms the hand-engineered heuristics.

- We present an analysis to better understand and shed light on the dynamic of needs of an NMT model during training: from syntax to semantic.

2 Learning to Reweigh Mini-Batches

Suppose we are given a set of a main task along with $K - 1$ auxiliary tasks, each of which with its own training set $\{(\boldsymbol{x}_i^{(k)}, \boldsymbol{y}_i^{(k)})\}_{i=1}^{N_k}$. In multitask formulation, parameters are learned by maximising the log-likelihood objective:

$$\arg \max_{\boldsymbol{\Theta}_{mtl}} \sum_{k=1}^{K} \sum_{i=1}^{N_k} w_i^{(k)} \log P_{\boldsymbol{\Theta}_{mtl}}(\boldsymbol{y}_i^{(k)}|\boldsymbol{x}_i^{(k)}).$$

Without loss of generality, let us assume we use minibatch-based stochastic gradient descent (SGD) to train the parameters of the multitask architecture. In standard multitask learning $w_i^{(k)}$ is set to 1, assuming all of the tasks and their training instances have the same importance. Conceptually, these weights provide a mechanism to control the influence of the data instances from auxiliary tasks in order to maximise the benefit in the generalisation capabilities of the main task. Recently, (Zaremoodi and Haffari, 2018; Kiperwasser and Ballesteros, 2018) have proposed *hand-engineered* heuristics to set the importance weights and change them dynamically throughout the training process, e.g., iterations of the stochastic gradient descent (SGD). However, there is no guarantee that these fixed schedules give rise to learning the best inductive biases from the auxiliary tasks for the main task.

Our main idea is to determine the importance weights $w_i^{(k)}$ for *each* training instance based on its contribution to the generalisation capabilities of the MTL architecture for machine translation, measured on a validation set D^{val} separated from the training set. As shown in Figure 2, at each parameter update iteration for the MTL architecture, the MTL training mini-batch is the concatenation of single mini-batches from all MTL tasks. We then assign an Adaptive Importance Weight

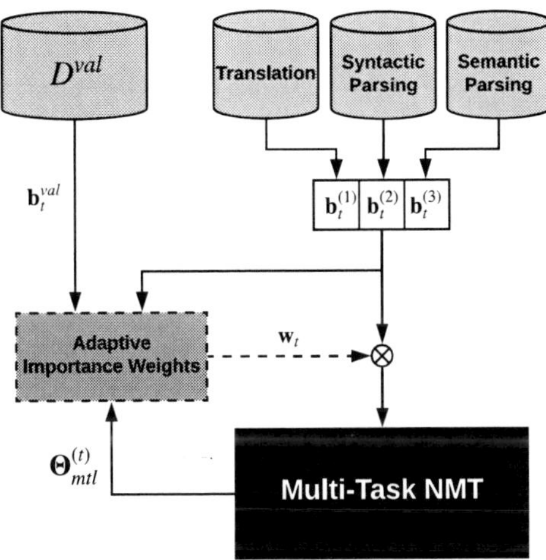

Figure 2: High-level idea for training an MTL architecture using adaptive importance weights (AIWs). Here, translation is the main task along with syntactic and semantic parsing as auxiliary linguistic tasks.

(AIW) to *each* training instance in the MTL minibatch, regardless from the task which they come from. In the experiments of §3, we will see that our proposed method *automatically* finds interesting patterns in how to best make use of the data from the auxiliary and main tasks, e.g. it starts by assigning higher weights (on average) to syntactic parsing which is then shifted to semantic parsing.

More specifically, we learn the AIWs based on the following optimisation problem:

$$\arg\min_{\hat{\boldsymbol{w}}} \; - \sum_{(\boldsymbol{x},\boldsymbol{y}) \in D^{val}} \log P_{\hat{\Theta}_{mtl}(\hat{\boldsymbol{w}})}(\boldsymbol{x}|\boldsymbol{y}) \tag{1}$$

$$\hat{\Theta}_{mtl}(\hat{\boldsymbol{w}}) := \Theta_{mtl}^{(t)} + \tag{2}$$
$$\eta \sum_{k=1}^{K} \sum_{i=1}^{|\boldsymbol{b}^{(k)}|} \hat{w}_i^{(k)} \nabla \log P_{\Theta_{mtl}^{(t)}}(\boldsymbol{y}_i^{(k)}|\boldsymbol{x}_i^{(k)})$$

where $\hat{w}_i^{(k)}$ is the *raw* weight of the ith training instance in the mini-batch $\boldsymbol{b}^{(k)}$ of the kth task, $\hat{\Theta}_{mtl}$ is the resulting parameter in case SGD update rule is applied on the current parameters $\Theta_{mtl}^{(t)}$ using instances weighted by $\hat{\boldsymbol{w}}$. Following (Ren et al., 2018), we zero out negative raw weights, and then normalise them with respect to the other instances in the MTL training mini-batch to obtain the AIWs: $w_i^{(k)} = \frac{\tilde{w}_i^{(k)}}{\sum_{k'} \sum_{i'} \tilde{w}_{i'}^{(k')}}$ where $\tilde{w}_i^{(k)} =$ ReLU$(\hat{w}_i^{(k)})$.

In the preliminary experiments, we observed that using $w_i^{(k)}$ as AIW does not perform well. We

Algorithm 1 Adaptively Scheduled Multitask Learning

1: **while** t=0 ... T-1 **do**
2:     $\boldsymbol{b}^{(1)}, .., \boldsymbol{b}^{(K)} \leftarrow$ SampleMB$(\boldsymbol{D}^{(1)}, .., \boldsymbol{D}^{(K)})$
3:     $\boldsymbol{b}^{(val)} \leftarrow$ SampleMB$(\boldsymbol{D}^{(val)})$
    ▷ Step 1: Update model with initialised weights
4:     $\ell_i^{(k)} \leftarrow - \log P_{\Theta_{mtl}^t}(\boldsymbol{y}_i^{(k)}|\boldsymbol{x}_i^{(k)})$ ▷ Forward
5:     $\hat{w}_{i,0}^{(k)} \leftarrow 0$ ▷ Initialise weights
6:     $\mathcal{L}_{trn} \leftarrow \sum_{k=1}^{K} \sum_{i=1}^{|\boldsymbol{b}^{(k)}|} \hat{w}_{i,0}^{(k)} \ell_i^{(k)}$
7:     $g_{trn} \leftarrow$ Backward$(\mathcal{L}_{trn}, \Theta_{mtl}^t)$
8:     $\hat{\Theta}_{mtl}^t = \Theta_{mtl}^t + \eta g_{trn}$
    ▷ Step 2: Calculate loss of the updated model on validation MB
9:     $\mathcal{L}_{val} = - \sum_{i=1}^{|\boldsymbol{b}^{val}|} \log P_{\hat{\Theta}_{mtl}^t}(\boldsymbol{y}_i|\boldsymbol{x}_i)$
    ▷ Step 3: Calculate raw weights.
10:    $g_{val} \leftarrow$ Backward$(\mathcal{L}_{val}, \hat{w}_0^{(k)})$
11:    $\hat{w}^{(k)} = g_{val}$
    ▷ Step 4: Normalise weights to get AIWs
12:    $\tilde{w}_i^{(k)} =$ ReLU$(\hat{w}_i^{(k)})$
13:    $w_i^{(k)} = \frac{\tilde{w}_i^{(k)}}{\sum_{k'} \sum_{i'} \tilde{w}_{i'}^{(k')}} + 1$
    ▷ Step 5: Update MTL with AIWs
14:    $\hat{\mathcal{L}}_{trn} \leftarrow \sum_{k=1}^{K} \sum_{i=1}^{|\boldsymbol{b}^{(k)}|} w_i^{(k)} \ell_i^{(k)}$
15:    $\hat{g}_{trn} \leftarrow$ Backward$(\hat{\mathcal{L}}_{trn}, \Theta_{mtl}^t)$
16:    $\Theta_{mtl}^{t+1} = \Theta_{mtl}^t + \eta \hat{g}_{trn}$
17: **end while**

speculate that a small validation set does not provide a good estimation of the generalisation, hence influence of the training instances. This is exacerbated as we approximate the validation set by only one of its mini-batches for the computational efficiency. Therefore, we hypothesise that the computed weights should not be regarded as the final verdict for the usefulness of the training instances. Instead, we regarded them as *rewards* for enhancing the training signals of instances that lead to a lower loss on the validation set. Hence, we use $1 + w_i^{(k)}$ as our AIWs in the experiments. The full algorithm is in Algorithm 1.

Implementation Details. As exactly solving the optimisation problem in Eq. (1) is challenging, we resort to an approximation and consider the raw weights as the gradient of the validation loss

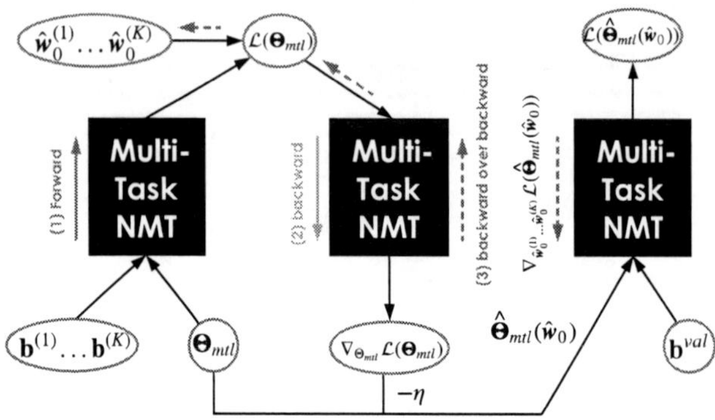

Figure 3: Computation graph of the proposed method for adaptively determining weights.

wrt the training instances' weights around zero. This is a notion called *influence* in robust statistics (Cook and Weisberg, 1980; Koh and Liang, 2017).

More concretely, let us define the loss function $\mathcal{L}(\hat{\Theta}_{mtl}) := -\sum_{i=1}^{|b^{val}|} \log P_{\hat{\Theta}_{mtl}}(y_i|x_i)$, where b^{val} is a minibatch from the validation set. The training instances' raw weights, i.e. influences, are then calculated using the chain rule:

$$\hat{w} = \nabla_{\hat{w}_0} \mathcal{L}(\hat{\Theta}_{mtl}(\hat{w}_0))\Big|_{\hat{w}_0=0}$$
$$= \nabla_{\hat{\Theta}_{mtl}} \mathcal{L}(\hat{\Theta}_{mtl})\Big|_{\hat{\Theta}_{mtl}=\Theta_{mtl}^{(t)}} \cdot \nabla_{\hat{w}_0} \hat{\Theta}_{mtl}(\hat{w}_0)\Big|_{\hat{w}_0=0}$$

The last term $\nabla_{\hat{w}_0} \hat{\Theta}_{mtl}$ involves backpropagation through $\hat{\Theta}_{mtl}$ wrt $\hat{w}_0$, which according to Eq. (2), involves an inner backpropagation wrt Θ_{mtl}. The computation graph is depicted in Figure 3.

3 Experiments

3.1 Bilingual Corpora

We use three language-pairs, translating from English to Vietnamese (Vi), Turkish (Tr) and Spanish (Es). We have chosen them to analyse the effect of adaptive mini-batch weighting on languages with different underlying linguistic structures. The structure of Vietnamese and Spanish is generally subject-verb-object (SVO) while Turkish follows subject-object-verb (SOV) structure. Although Spanish is not a low-resource language we have chosen it because of available accurate POS taggers and Named-Entity recognisers required for some of the analyses. For each pair, we use BPE (Sennrich et al., 2016) with 40K types on the union of the source and target vocabularies. We use the Moses toolkit (Koehn et al., 2007) to

filter out pairs where the number of tokens is more than 250 and pairs with a source/target length ratio higher than 1.5. For fair comparison, we add the Val data used in the AIW-based approach to the training set of the competing baselines.

- English-Vietnamese: we use the preprocessed version of IWSLT 2015 corpus (Cettolo et al., 2015) provided by (Luong and Manning, 2015). It consists of about 133K training pairs from the subtitles of TED and TEDx talks and their translations. We use "tst2013" as the test set and "tst2012" is divided and used as validation and meta-validation sets (with the ratio 2 to 1).

- English-Turkish: we use WMT parallel corpus (Bojar et al., 2016) with about 200K training pairs gathered from news articles. "newstest2016", "newstest2017" and "newstest2018" parts are used as validation, meta-validation and test set.

- English-Spanish: we have used the first 150K training pairs of Europarl corpus (Koehn, 2005). "newstest2011", "newstest2012" and "newstest2013" parts are used as validation, meta-validation and test set, respectively.

3.2 Auxiliary tasks

Following (Zaremoodi and Haffari, 2018), we have chosen following auxiliary tasks to inject the syntactic and semantic knowledge to improve NMT:

- Named-Entity Recognition (NER): we use CONLL shared task[1] data. This dataset is

---

[1] https://www.clips.uantwerpen.be/conll2003/ner

	En→Vi		En→Tr		En→Es			
	BLEU		BLEU		BLEU		METEOR	
	Dev	Test	Dev	Test	Dev	Test	Dev	Test
MT only	22.83	24.15	8.55	8.5	14.49	13.44	31.3	31.1
MTL with Fixed Schedule								
+ Uniform	23.10	24.81	9.14	8.94	12.81	12.12	29.6	29.5
+ Biased (Constant)[†‡]	23.42	25.22	10.06	9.53	15.14	14.11	31.8	31.3
+ Exponential[‡]	23.45	25.65	9.62	9.12	12.25	11.62	28.0	28.1
+ Sigmoid[‡]	23.35	25.36	9.55	9.01	11.55	11.34	26.6	26.9
MTL with Adaptive Schedule								
+ Biased + **AIW**	23.95	25.75	10.67	10.25	11.23	10.66	27.5	27.4
+ Uniform + **AIW**	24.38	**26.68**	11.03	**10.81**	16.05	**14.95**	33.0	**32.5**

Table 1: Results for three language pairs. "+ AIW" indicates Adaptive Importance Weighting is used in training. [†]: Proposed in (Zaremoodi and Haffari, 2018), [‡]: Proposed in (Kiperwasser and Ballesteros, 2018).

consists of a collection of newswire articles from the Reuters Corpus.

- Syntactic Parsing: we use Penn TreeBank parsing with the standard split (Marcheggiani and Titov, 2017). This task is casted to SEQ2SEQ transduction by linearising constituency trees (Vinyals et al., 2015)

- Semantic Parsing: we use Abstract Meaning Representation (AMR) corpus Release 2.0[2] linearised by the method proposed in (Konstas et al., 2017). This corpus is gathered from from newswire, weblogs, web discussion forums and broadcast conversations.

3.3 MTL architecture and training schedule

Since partial-sharing has been shown to be more effective than full sharing (Liu et al., 2017; Guo et al., 2018a; Zaremoodi and Haffari, 2018), we use the MTL architecture proposed in (Zaremoodi and Haffari, 2018). We use three stacked LSTM layers in encoders and decoders. For En→Vi and En→Tr, one/two layer(s) are shared among encoders/decoders while for En→Es, two/one layer(s) are shared among encoders/decoders. The LSTM dimensions, batch size and dropout are set to 512, 32 and 0.3, respectively. We use Adam optimiser (Kingma and Ba, 2014) with the learning rate of 0.001. We train models for 25 epochs and save the best model based on the perplexity on the validation (Val) set. We have implemented the methods using PyTorch on top of OpenNMT (Klein et al., 2017).

Fixed hand-engineered schedule baselines. We use different MTL scheduling strategies where at each update iteration:

- **Uniform**: Selects a random mini-batch from all of the tasks;

- **Biased** (Zaremoodi and Haffari, 2018): Selects a random mini-batch from the translation task (bias towards the main task) and another one for a randomly selected task.

We also use schedules proposed in (Kiperwasser and Ballesteros, 2018). They consider a slope parameter[3] α and the fraction of training epochs done so far $t = sents/\|corpus\|$. The schedules determine the probability of selecting each of the tasks as the source of the next training pair. In each of these schedules the probability of selecting the *main task* is:

- **Constant:** $P_m(t) = \alpha$; When α is set to 0.5, it is similar to the Biased schedule we have seen before.

- **Exponential:** $P_m(t) = 1 - e^{-\alpha t}$; In this schedule the probability of selecting the main task increases exponentially throughout the training.

- **Sigmoid:** $P_m(t) = \dfrac{1}{1 + e^{-\alpha t}}$; Similar to the previous schedule, the probability of selecting the main task increases, following a sigmoid function.

In each of these schedules, the rest of the probability is uniformly divided among the *remaining*

---

[2]https://catalog.ldc.upenn.edu/LDC2017T10

[3]Following their experiments, we set α to 0.5.

tasks. By using them, a mini-batch can have training pairs from different tasks which makes it inefficient for partially shared MTL models. Hence, we modified these schedules to select the source of the next training mini-batch.

Combination of Adaptive and Fixed schedules
As mentioned in Section 2, we assign an AIW to each training instance inside mini-batches of *all* tasks, i.e. applying AIWs on top of Uniform schedule. Additionally, we also apply it on top of Biased schedule to analyse the effect of the combination of AIWs (for instances) and a *hand-engineered* heuristic (for mini-batch selection).

3.4 Results and Analysis

Table 1 reports the results for baselines and the proposed method[4]. As seen, our method has made better use of the auxiliary tasks and achieved the highest performance (see Section 3.4 for an analysis of the generated translations). It shows that while some of the *heuristic*-based schedules are beneficial, our proposed Adaptive Importance Weighting approach outperforms them. There reasons are likely that the *hand-engineered* strategies do not consider the state of the model, and they do not distinguish among the auxiliary tasks.

It is interesting to see that the Biased schedule is beneficial for standard MTL, while it is harmful when combined with the AIWs. The standard MTL is not able to select training signals on-demand, and using a biased heuristic strategy improves it. However, our weighting method can selectively filter out training signals; hence, it is better to provide all of the training signals and leave the selection to the AIWs.

Analysis on how/when auxiliary tasks have been used? This analysis aims to shed light on how AIWs control the contribution of each task through the training. As seen, our method has the best result when it is combined with the Uniform MTL schedule. In this schedule, at each update iteration, we have one mini-batch from each of the tasks, and AIWs are determined for all of the training pairs in these mini-batches. For this analysis, we divided the training into 200 update iteration chunks. In each chunk, we compute the average weights assigned to the training pairs of each task.

---

[4]METEOR score (Denkowski and Lavie, 2014) is reported only for Spanish as it is the only target languages in our experiments which is supported by it.

Figure 1 shows the results of this analysis for the MTL model trained with En→Vi as the main task. and Figure 4 shows the results of this analysis for En→Es and En→Tr. Also, it can be seen that at the beginning of the training the Adaptive Importance Weighting mechanism gradually increases the training signals which come from the auxiliary tasks. However, after reaching a certain point in the training, it will gradually reduce the auxiliary training signals to concentrate more on the adaptation to the main task. It can be seen that the weighting mechanism distinguishes the importance of auxiliary tasks. More interestingly, it can be seen that for the English→Turkish, the contribution of NER task is more than the syntactic parsing while for the other languages we have seen the reverse. It shows that our method can *adaptively* determine the contribution of the tasks by considering the demand of the main translation task.

As seen, it gives more weight to the syntactic tasks at the beginning of the training while it gradually reduces their contribution and increases the involvement of the semantics-related task. We speculate the reason is that at the beginning of the training, the model requires more lower-level linguistic knowledge (e.g. syntactic parsing and NER) while over time, the needs of model gradually change to higher-level linguistic knowledge (e.g. semantic parsing).

Analysis of The Effect of Auxiliary Tasks on The Generated Translations In this analysis, we want to take a deeper look at the generated translations and see how the proposed method improved the quality of the translations. More specifically, we want to compare the number of words in the gold translations which are missed in the generated translations produced by the following systems: (i) MT only; (ii) MTL-Biased; (iii) MTL-Uniform + AIW. To find out what kind of knowledge is missed in the process of generating the translations, we categorised words by their Part-of-Speech tags and named-entities types. We have done this analysis on En→Es language pair as there are accurate annotators for the Spanish language. We use Stanford POS tagger (Toutanova et al., 2003) and named-entity recogniser (Finkel et al., 2005) to annotate Spanish gold translations. Then, we categorised the missed words in the generated translations concerning these tags, and count the number of missed words in each category. Figure 5 depicts the result. As seen in

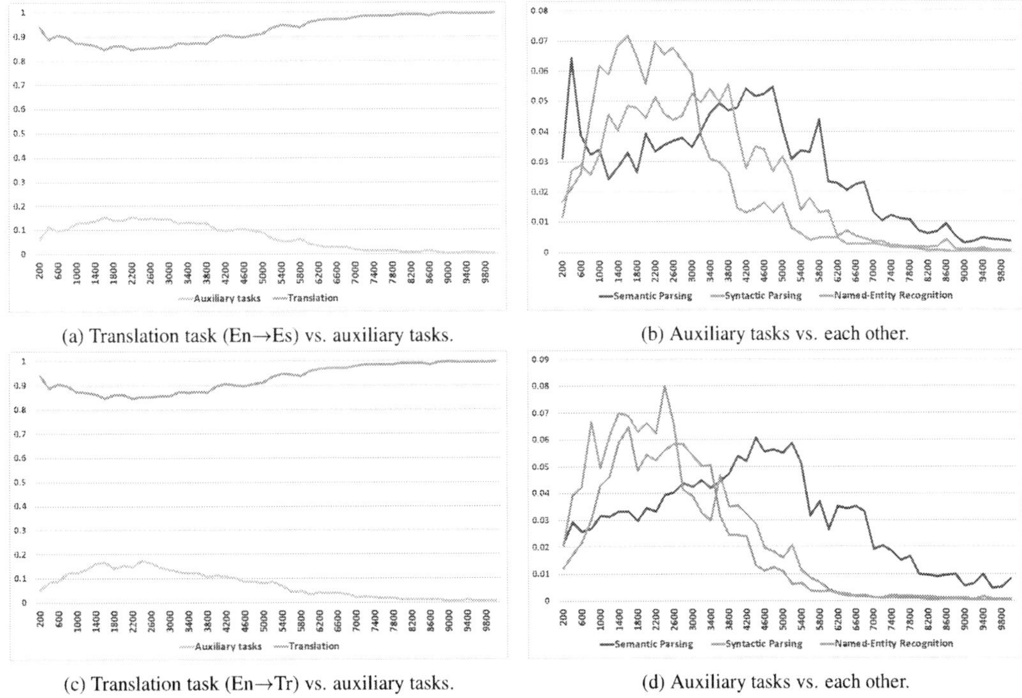

(a) Translation task (En→Es) vs. auxiliary tasks.

(b) Auxiliary tasks vs. each other.

(c) Translation task (En→Tr) vs. auxiliary tasks.

(d) Auxiliary tasks vs. each other.

Figure 4: Weights assigned to the training pairs of different tasks (averaged over 200 update iteration chunks). Y-axis shows the average weight and X-axis shows the number of update iteration. In the top figures, the main translation task is English→Spanish while in the bottom ones it is English→Turkish.

Figure 5a, the knowledge learned from auxiliary tasks helps the MTL model to miss less number of named-entities during translation. Moreover, AIWs help the MTL model further by making better use of the knowledge conveyed in the auxiliary tasks. We can see the same pattern for the POS of missed words. As seen, for most POS categories, the standard MTL has missed less number of words in comparison with the MT only baseline. Furthermore, our method helps the MTL model to miss even less amount of words in every of the POS categories (specifically in Noun and Preposition categories). We speculate the reason is that the AIWs makes it possible to control the contribution of each of the auxiliary tasks separately and taking into account the demand of the model at each stage of the training procedure.

4 Related Work

Multitask learning (Caruana, 1997) has been used for various NLP problems, e.g. machine translation (Dong et al., 2015), dependency parsing (Peng et al., 2017), key-phrase boundary classification (Augenstein and Søgaard, 2017), video captioning (Pasunuru and Bansal, 2017), Chinese word segmentation, and text classification problem (Liu et al., 2017). For the case of low-resource NMT, (Niehues and Cho, 2017) has explored the use of part-of-speech and named-entity recognition in improving NMT. (Kiperwasser and Ballesteros, 2018) has investigated part-of-speech tagging and dependency parsing tasks, and (Zaremoodi et al., 2018; Zaremoodi and Haffari, 2018) have tried syntactic parsing, semantic parsing, and named-entity recognition tasks.

The current research on MTL is focused on encouraging positive transfer and preventing the negative transfer phenomena in two lines of research: (1) Architecture design: works in this area try to learn effective parameter sharing among tasks (Ruder et al., 2017; Zaremoodi et al., 2018); (2) Training schedule: works in this area, including ours, focus on setting the importance of tasks.

Training schedule is the beating heart of MTL, and has a critical role in the *performance* of the resulted model. Since there are more than one task involved in MTL, the performance is measured differently in different MTL flavours: (1)

183

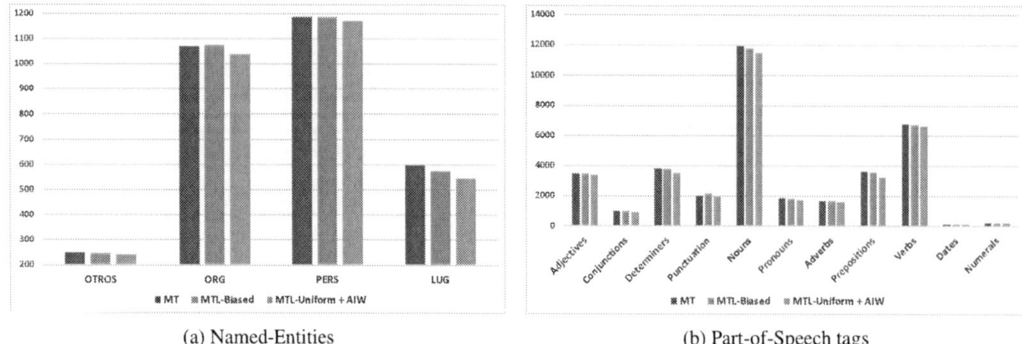

(a) Named-Entities   (b) Part-of-Speech tags

Figure 5: The number of words in the gold English→Spanish translation which are missed in the generated translations (lower is better). Missed words are categorised by their tags (Part-of-Speech and named-entity types).

general-MTL aims to improve performance of *all* tasks; (2) *biased-MTL* aims to improve *one* (or a subset) of tasks the most. Training schedules designed for the global-MTL are focused on co-evolving easy and difficult tasks uniformly. These methods are designed to achieve competitive performance with existing single-task models of each task (Chen et al., 2018; Guo et al., 2018b). On the other hand, training schedules for biased-MTL focus on achieving higher improvements on the main task, and our method belongs to this category.

Training schedules can be fixed/dynamic throughout the training and be hand-engineered/adaptive. (Zaremoodi and Haffari, 2018) has made use of a fixed hand-engineered schedule for improving low-resource NMT with auxiliary linguistic tasks. Recently, (Guo et al., 2019) has proposed an adaptive way to compute the importance weights of tasks. Instead of manual tuning of importance weights via a large grid search, they model the performance of each set of weights as a sample from a Gaussian Process (GP), and search for optimal values. In fact, their method is not completely adaptive as a strong prior needs to be set for the main task. This method can be seen as a guided yet computationally exhaustive trial-and-error where in each trial, MTL models need to be re-trained (from scratch) with the sampled weights. Moreover, the weight of tasks are fixed throughout the training. At least, for the case of low-resource NMT, it has been shown that *dynamically* changing the weights throughout the training is essential to make better use of auxiliary tasks (Kiperwasser and Ballesteros, 2018). (Kiperwasser and Ballesteros, 2018) has proposed *hand-engineered* training schedules

for MTL in NMT, where they dynamically change the importance of the main task vs the auxiliary tasks throughout the training process. While their method relies on *hand-engineered* schedules which should be tuned by trial-and-error, our proposed method *adaptively* and *dynamically* sets the importance of the tasks and learn the MTL model in the course of a single training run.

5 Conclusions

This paper presents a rigorous approach for adaptively and dynamically changing the training schedule in biased-MTL to make the best use of auxiliary tasks. To balance the importance of the auxiliary tasks vs. the main task, we re-weight training data of tasks to adjust their contributions to the generalisation capabilities of the resulted model on the main task. In this paper, we consider low-resource translation as the main task along with syntactic and semantic auxiliary tasks. Our experimental results on English to Vietnamese/Turkish/Spanish show up to +1.2 BLEU score improvement compared to strong baselines. Additionally, the analyses show that the proposed method *automatically* finds a schedule which puts more importance to the auxiliary syntactic tasks at the beginning while gradually it alters the importance toward the auxiliary semantic task. As this method does not rely on hand-engineered heuristics, as a future work, we want to apply it for effective learning of multitask architectures beyond NMT.

Acknowledgement

This work is supported by CSIRO Data61 through a PhD Fellowship to P. Z., and by an Amazon Research Award to G. H. This work is partly sponsored by DARPA through the contract no FA8750-19-2-0501. The views and conclusions contained herein are those of the authors and should not be interpreted as necessarily representing the official policies or endorsements, either expressed or implied, of DARPA or the US government. This work was supported by the Multi-modal Australian ScienceS Imaging and Visualisation Environment (MASSIVE) (www.massive.org.au) through computational infrastructure. We would like to thank anonymous reviewers for their insightful comments.

References

Isabelle Augenstein and Anders Søgaard. 2017. Multi-task learning of keyphrase boundary classification. In *Proceedings of the Annual Meeting of the Association for Computational Linguistics*, pages 341–346.

Ondrej Bojar, Rajen Chatterjee, Christian Federmann, Yvette Graham, Barry Haddow, Matthias Huck, Antonio Jimeno Yepes, Philipp Koehn, Varvara Logacheva, Christof Monz, et al. 2016. Findings of the 2016 conference on machine translation. In *ACL 2016 First Conference On Machine Translation (WMT16)*, pages 131–198. The Association for Computational Linguistics.

Rich Caruana. 1997. Multitask learning. *Machine learning*, 28(1):41–75.

Mauro Cettolo, Jan Niehues, Sebastian Stüker, Luisa Bentivogli, Roldano Cattoni, and Marcello Federico. 2015. The iwslt 2015 evaluation campaign. In *IWSLT 2015, International Workshop on Spoken Language Translation*.

Zhao Chen, Vijay Badrinarayanan, Chen-Yu Lee, and Andrew Rabinovich. 2018. Gradnorm: Gradient normalization for adaptive loss balancing in deep multitask networks. In *International Conference on Machine Learning*, pages 793–802.

R Dennis Cook and Sanford Weisberg. 1980. Characterizations of an empirical influence function for detecting influential cases in regression. *Technometrics*, 22(4):495–508.

Michael Denkowski and Alon Lavie. 2014. Meteor universal: Language specific translation evaluation for any target language. In *Proceedings of the EACL 2014 Workshop on Statistical Machine Translation*.

Daxiang Dong, Hua Wu, Wei He, Dianhai Yu, and Haifeng Wang. 2015. Multi-task learning for multiple language translation. In *Proceedings of the 53rd Annual Meeting of the Association for Computational Linguistics and the 7th International Joint Conference on Natural Language Processing (Volume 1: Long Papers)*, pages 1723–1732.

Jenny Rose Finkel, Trond Grenager, and Christopher Manning. 2005. Incorporating non-local information into information extraction systems by gibbs sampling. In *Proceedings of the 43rd annual meeting on association for computational linguistics*, pages 363–370.

Han Guo, Ramakanth Pasunuru, and Mohit Bansal. 2018a. Soft layer-specific multi-task summarization with entailment and question generation. In *Proceedings of the 56th Annual Meeting of the Association for Computational Linguistics*, pages 687–697.

Han Guo, Ramakanth Pasunuru, and Mohit Bansal. 2019. Autosem: Automatic task selection and mixing in multi-task learning. *CoRR*, abs/1904.04153.

Michelle Guo, Albert Haque, De-An Huang, Serena Yeung, and Li Fei-Fei. 2018b. Dynamic task prioritization for multitask learning. In *Proceedings of the European Conference on Computer Vision (ECCV)*, pages 270–287.

Diederik Kingma and Jimmy Ba. 2014. Adam: A method for stochastic optimization. *arXiv preprint arXiv:1412.6980*.

Eliyahu Kiperwasser and Miguel Ballesteros. 2018. Scheduled multi-task learning: From syntax to translation. *Transactions of the Association for Computational Linguistics*, 6:225–240.

Guillaume Klein, Yoon Kim, Yuntian Deng, Jean Senellart, and Alexander Rush. 2017. Opennmt: Open-source toolkit for neural machine translation. In *Proceedings of ACL 2017, System Demonstrations*, pages 67–72.

Philipp Koehn. 2005. Europarl: A parallel corpus for statistical machine translation. In *MT summit*, volume 5, pages 79–86.

Philipp Koehn, Hieu Hoang, Alexandra Birch, Chris Callison-Burch, Marcello Federico, Nicola Bertoldi, Brooke Cowan, Wade Shen, Christine Moran, Richard Zens, Chris Dyer, Ondřej Bojar, Alexandra Constantin, and Evan Herbst. 2007. Moses: Open source toolkit for statistical machine translation. In *Proceedings of the 45th Annual Meeting of the Association for Computational Linguistics on Interactive Poster and Demonstration Sessions*, pages 177–180.

Philipp Koehn and Rebecca Knowles. 2017. Six challenges for neural machine translation. In *Proceedings of the First Workshop on Neural Machine Translation*, pages 28–39.

Pang Wei Koh and Percy Liang. 2017. Understanding black-box predictions via influence functions. In *Proceedings of the 34th International Conference on Machine Learning-Volume 70*, pages 1885–1894. JMLR. org.

Ioannis Konstas, Srinivasan Iyer, Mark Yatskar, Yejin Choi, and Luke Zettlemoyer. 2017. Neural amr: Sequence-to-sequence models for parsing and generation. In *Proceedings of the Annual Meeting of the Association for Computational Linguistics*, pages 146–157.

Pengfei Liu, Xipeng Qiu, and Xuanjing Huang. 2017. Adversarial multi-task learning for text classification. In *Proceedings of the 55th Annual Meeting of the Association for Computational Linguistics*, pages 1–10.

Minh-Thang Luong and Christopher D. Manning. 2015. Stanford neural machine translation systems for spoken language domain. In *International Workshop on Spoken Language Translation*, Da Nang, Vietnam.

Diego Marcheggiani and Ivan Titov. 2017. Encoding sentences with graph convolutional networks for semantic role labeling. *arXiv preprint arXiv:1703.04826*.

Jan Niehues and Eunah Cho. 2017. Exploiting linguistic resources for neural machine translation using multi-task learning. In *Proceedings of the Second Conference on Machine Translation*, pages 80–89.

Ramakanth Pasunuru and Mohit Bansal. 2017. Multitask video captioning with video and entailment generation. In *Proceedings of ACL*.

Hao Peng, Sam Thomson, and Noah A. Smith. 2017. Deep multitask learning for semantic dependency parsing. In *Proceedings of the 55th Annual Meeting of the Association for Computational Linguistics (Volume 1: Long Papers)*, pages 2037–2048.

Mengye Ren, Wenyuan Zeng, Bin Yang, and Raquel Urtasun. 2018. Learning to reweight examples for robust deep learning. In *International Conference on Machine Learning*, pages 4331–4340.

Sebastian Ruder, Joachim Bingel, Isabelle Augenstein, and Anders Søgaard. 2017. Sluice networks: Learning what to share between loosely related tasks. *arXiv preprint arXiv:1705.08142*.

Rico Sennrich, Barry Haddow, and Alexandra Birch. 2016. Neural Machine Translation of Rare Words with Subword Units. In *Proceedings of the Annual Meeting of the Association for Computational Linguistics*, pages 1715–1725.

Kristina Toutanova, Dan Klein, Christopher D Manning, and Yoram Singer. 2003. Feature-rich part-of-speech tagging with a cyclic dependency network. In *Proceedings of the 2003 conference of the North American chapter of the association for computational linguistics on human language technology-volume 1*, pages 173–180.

Oriol Vinyals, Ł ukasz Kaiser, Terry Koo, Slav Petrov, Ilya Sutskever, and Geoffrey Hinton. 2015. Grammar as a foreign language. In *Advances in Neural Information Processing Systems*, pages 2773–2781.

Poorya Zaremoodi, Wray L. Buntine, and Gholamreza Haffari. 2018. Adaptive knowledge sharing in multi-task learning: Improving low-resource neural machine translation. In *Proceedings of the 56th Annual Meeting of the Association for Computational Linguistics,*, pages 656–661.

Poorya Zaremoodi and Gholamreza Haffari. 2018. Neural machine translation for bilingually scarce scenarios: a deep multi-task learning approach. In *Proceedings of the 2018 Conference of the North American Chapter of the Association for Computational Linguistics: Human Language Technologies*, pages 1356–1365.

On the Importance of Word Boundaries
in Character-level Neural Machine Translation

Duygu Ataman*
University of Trento
Fondazione Bruno Kessler
ataman@fbk.eu

Orhan Fırat
Google AI
orhanf@google.com

Mattia A. Di Gangi
University of Trento
Fondazione Bruno Kessler
digangi@fbk.eu

Marcello Federico
Amazon AI
marcfede@amazon.com

Alexandra Birch
University of Edinburgh
a.birch@ed.ac.uk

Abstract

Neural Machine Translation (NMT) models
generally perform translation using a fixed-
size lexical vocabulary, which is an important
bottleneck on their generalization capability
and overall translation quality. The standard
approach to overcome this limitation is to segment words into subword units, typically using
some external tools with arbitrary heuristics,
resulting in vocabulary units not optimized
for the translation task. Recent studies
have shown that the same approach can be
extended to perform NMT directly at the level
of characters, which can deliver translation
accuracy on-par with subword-based models,
on the other hand, this requires relatively
deeper networks. In this paper, we propose
a more computationally-efficient solution
for character-level NMT which implements
a hierarchical decoding architecture where
translations are subsequently generated at the
level of words and characters. We evaluate
different methods for open-vocabulary NMT
in the machine translation task from English
into five languages with distinct morphological typology, and show that the hierarchical
decoding model can reach higher translation
accuracy than the subword-level NMT model
using significantly fewer parameters, while
demonstrating better capacity in learning
longer-distance contextual and grammatical
dependencies than the standard character-level
NMT model.

1 Introduction

Neural Machine Translation (NMT) models are typically
trained using a fixed-size lexical vocabulary. In addition to
controlling the computational load, this limitation also serves
to maintain better distributed representations for the most frequent set of words included in the vocabulary. On the other
hand, rare words in the long tail of the lexical distribution are
often discarded during translation since they are not found
in the vocabulary. The prominent approach to overcome this
limitation is to segment words into subword units (Sennrich
et al., 2016) and perform translation based on a vocabulary
composed of these units. However, subword segmentation
methods generally rely on statistical heuristics that lack any
linguistic notion. Moreover, they are typically deployed as a
pre-processing step before training the NMT model, hence,
the predicted set of subword units are essentially not optimized for the translation task. Recently, (Cherry et al.,
2018) extended the approach of NMT based on subword units
to implement the translation model directly at the level of
characters, which could reach comparable performance to
the subword-based model, although this would require much
larger networks which may be more difficult to train. The
major reason to this requirement may lie behind the fact that
treating the characters as individual tokens at the same level
and processing the input sequences in linear time increases
the difficulty of the learning task, where translation would
then be modeled as a mapping between the characters in two
languages. The increased sequence lengths due to processing sentences as sequences of characters also augments the
computational cost, and a possible limitation, since sequence
models typically have limited capacity in remembering long-
distance context.

In many languages, words are the core atomic units of
semantic and syntactic structure, and their explicit modeling should be beneficial in learning distributed representations for translation. There have been early studies in NMT
which proposed to perform translation at the level of characters while also regarding the word boundaries in the translation model through a hierarchical decoding procedure, although these approaches were generally deployed through
hybrid systems, either as a back-off solution to translate unknown words (Luong and Manning, 2016), or as pre-trained
components (Ling et al., 2015). In this paper, we explore
the benefit of achieving character-level NMT by processing
sentences at multi-level dynamic time steps defined by the
word boundaries, integrating a notion of explicit hierarchy
into the decoder. In our model, all word representations are
learned compositionally from character embeddings using bi-

---

*Work done while the first author was a visiting post-
graduate research student at the University of Edinburgh and
prior to joining Amazon.

187

directional recurrent neural networks (bi-RNNs) (Schuster and Paliwal, 1997), and decoding is performed by generating each word character by character based on the predicted word representation through a hierarchical beam search algorithm which takes advantage of the hierarchical architecture while generating translations.

We present the results of an extensive evaluation comparing conventional approaches for open-vocabulary NMT in the machine translation task from English into five morphologically-rich languages, where each language belongs to a different language family and has a distinct morphological typology. Our findings show that using the hierarchical decoding approach, the NMT models are able to obtain higher translation accuracy than the subword-based NMT models in many languages while using significantly fewer parameters, where the character-based models implemented with the same computational complexity may still struggle to reach comparable performance. Our analysis also shows that explicit modeling of word boundaries in character-level NMT is advantageous for capturing longer-term contextual dependencies and generalizing to morphological variations in the target language.

2 Neural Machine Translation

In this paper, we use recurrent NMT architectures based on the model developed by Bahdanau et al. (Bahdanau et al., 2014). The model essentially estimates the conditional probability of translating a source sequence $x = (x_1, x_2, \ldots x_m)$ into a target sequence $y = (y_1, y_2, \ldots y_n)$, using the decomposition

$$p(y|x) = \prod_{j=1}^{n} p(y_j|y_{<j}, x_m, .., x_1) \qquad (1)$$

where $y_{<j}$ is the target sentence history defined by the sequence $\{y_1 \ldots y_{j-1}\}$.

The inputs of the network are *one-hot* vectors representing the tokens in the source sentence, which are binary vectors with a single bit set to 1 to identify a specific token in the vocabulary. Each one-hot vector is then mapped to a dense continuous representation, *i.e.* an embedding, of the source tokens via a look-up table. The representation of the source sequence is computed using a multi-layer bi-RNN, also referred as the *encoder*, which maps x into m dense vectors corresponding to the hidden states of the last bi-RNN layer updated in response to the input token embeddings.

The generation of the translation of the source sentence is called *decoding*, and it is conventionally implemented in an auto-regressive mode, where each token in the target sentence is generated based on an sequential classification procedure defined over the target token vocabulary. In this decoding architecture, a unidirectional recurrent neural network (RNN) predicts the most likely output token y_i in the target sequence using an approximate search algorithm based on the previous target token y_{i-1}, represented with the embedding of the previous token in the target sequence, the previous decoder hidden state, representing the sequence history, and the current attention context in the source sequence, represented by the *context vector* c_t. The latter is a linear combination of the encoder hidden states, whose weights are dynamically computed by a dot product based similarity metric called the *attention model* (Luong et al., 2015).

The probability of generating each target word y_i is estimated via a softmax function

$$p(y_i = z_j|x; \theta) = \frac{e^{z_j^T o_i}}{\sum_{k=1}^{K} e^{z_k^T o_i}} \qquad (2)$$

where z_j is the jth one-hot vector of the target vocabulary of size K, and o_i is the decoder output vector for the ith target word y_i. The model is trained by maximizing the log-likelihood of a parallel training set via stochastic gradient-descent (Bottou, 2010), where the gradients are computed with the back propagation through time (Werbos, 1990) algorithm.

Due to the softmax function in Equation 2, the size of the target vocabulary plays an important role in defining the computational complexity of the model. In the standard architecture, the embedding matrices account for the vast majority of the network parameters, thus, the amount of embeddings that could be learned and stored efficiently needs to be limited. Moreover, for many words corresponding to the long tail of the lexical distribution, the model fails in learning accurate embeddings, as they are rarely observed in varying context, leading the model vocabulary to typically include the most frequent set of words in the target language. This creates an important bottleneck over the vocabulary coverage of the model, which is especially crucial when translating into low-resource and morphologically-rich languages, which often have a high level of sparsity in the lexical distribution.

The standard approach to overcome this limitation has now become applying a statistical segmentation algorithm on the training corpus which splits words into smaller and more frequent *subword* units, and building the model vocabulary composed of these units. The translation problem is then modeled as a mapping between sequences of subword units in the source and target languages (Sennrich et al., 2016; **?**; Ataman et al., 2017). The most popular statistical segmentation method is Byte-Pair Encoding (BPE) (Sennrich et al., 2016), which finds the optimal description of a corpus vocabulary by iteratively merging the most frequent character sequences. One problem related to the subword-based NMT approach is that segmentation methods are typically implemented as pre-processing steps to NMT, thus, they are not optimized simultaneously with the translation task in an end-to-end fashion. This can lead to morphological errors at different levels, and cause loss of semantic or syntactic information (Ataman et al., 2017), due to the ambiguity in subword embeddings. In fact, recent studies have shown that the same approach can be extended to implement the NMT model directly at the level of characters, which could alleviate potential morphological errors due to subword segmentation. Although character-level NMT models have shown the potential to obtain comparable performance with subword-based NMT models, this would require increasing the computational cost of the model, defined by the network parameters (Kreutzer and Sokolov, 2018; Cherry et al., 2018). As given in Figure 1a implementing the NMT decoder directly at the level of characters leads to repetitive passes over the attention mechanism and the RNNs modeling the target language for each character in the sentence. Since the distributed representations of characters are shared among different word and sentence-level context, the translation task requires a network with high capacity to learn this vastly dynamic context.

3 Hierarchical Decoding

In this paper, we explore the benefit of integrating a notion of hierarchy into the decoding architecture which could increase the computational efficiency in character-level NMT, following the work of (Luong and Manning, 2016). In this architecture, the input embedding layer of the decoder is augmented with a character-level bi-RNN, which estimates a composition function over the embeddings of the characters in each word in order to compute the distributed representations of target words.

Given a bi-RNN with a forward (f) and backward (b) layer, the word representation **w** of a token of t characters

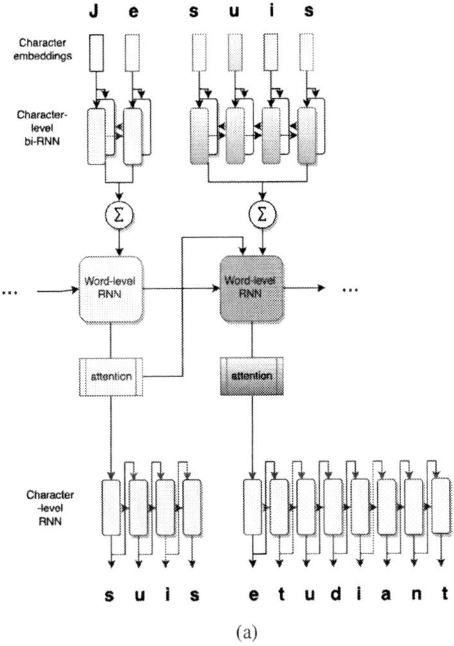 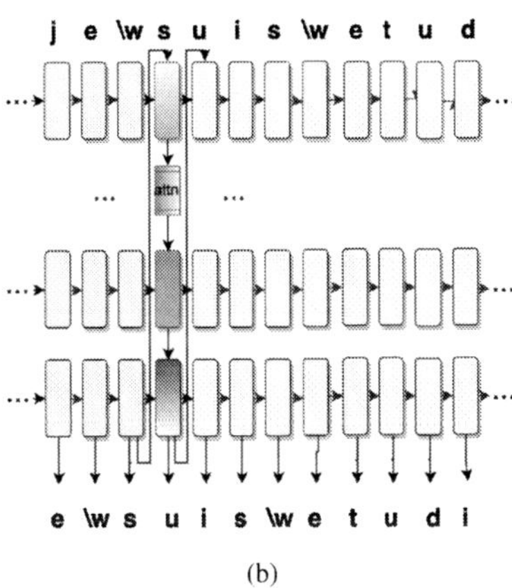

(b)

(a)

Figure 1: (a) Hierarchical NMT decoder: input words are encoded as character sequences and the translation is predicted at the level of words. The output words are generated as character sequences. (b) Character-level NMT decoder: the next token in the sentence is predicted by computing the attention weights and the target context repetitively for each character in the sentence.

is computed from the hidden states $\mathbf{h}_f^t$ and $\mathbf{h}_b^0$, *i.e.* the final outputs of the forward and backward RNNs, as follows:

$$\mathbf{w} = \mathbf{W}_f\mathbf{h}_f^t + \mathbf{W}_b\mathbf{h}_b^0 + \mathbf{b} \tag{3}$$

where $\mathbf{W}_f$ and $\mathbf{W}_b$ are weight matrices associated to each RNN and $\mathbf{b}$ is a bias vector. The embeddings of characters and the parameters of the word composition layer are jointly learned while training the NMT model. Since all target word representations are computed compositionally, the hierarchical decoding approach eliminates the necessity of storing word embeddings, significantly reducing the number of parameters.

Each word in the target sentence is predicted by an RNN operating at the level of words, using the compositional target word representations, target sentence history and the context vector computed by the attention mechanism only in the beginning of a new word generation. Instead of classifying the predicted target word in the vocabulary, its distributed representation is fed to a character-level RNN to generate the surface form of the word one character at a time by modeling the probability of observing the k_{th} character of the j_{th} word with length l, $p(y_{j,k}|y_{<j}, y_{j,<k})$, given the previous words in the sequence and the previous characters in the word.

The translation probability is then decomposed as:

$$p(y|x) = \prod_{j=1}^{n} \prod_{k=1}^{l} p(y_{j,k}|y_{j,<k}, y_{<j}, x_{<m}) \tag{4}$$

Similar to (Luong and Manning, 2016), the information necessary to generate the surface form is encoded into the attentional vector $\hat{h}_t$:

$$\hat{h}_t = \tanh(W[c_t; h_t]) \tag{5}$$

where h_t is the hidden state of the word-level RNN representing the current target context. The attentional vector is used to initialize the character RNN, and after the generation of the first character in the word, character decoding continues in an auto-regressive mode, where the embedding of the each character is fed to the RNN to predict the next character in the word. The decoder consecutively iterates over the words and characters in the target sentence, where each RNN is updated at dynamic time steps based on the word boundaries.

4   Hierarchical Beam Search

```
function HierarhicalBeamSearch(Hyp,Best,t)
NewHyp ← ()
for all (seq,score,state) in Hyp do:
    (chars,logpr,state) ← CharRNN_Fwd(tail(seq), state)
    for all (c,lp) in (characters,logpr) do:
        hyp=[append(seq,c),score+lp,state]
        if (IsSolution(hyp) and
        hyp.score > Best.score)
        then Best=hyp
        else Push(NewHyp,hyp)
        NewHyp ← Prune(NewHyp,Best)
        NewHyp ← TopB(NewHyp)
        NewHyp.state ← WordRNN_Fwd(NewHyp)
    if (NewHyp)
        return BeamSearch(NewHyp,Best,t+1)
    else return Best
```

Algorithm 1: Hierarchical beam search algorithm.

189

Model	BLEU					Avg. Num.
	AR	CS	DE	IT	TR	Params
Subwords	14.27	16.60	**24.29**	26.23	8.52	22M
Characters	12.72	**16.94**	22.23	24.33	**10.63**	7.3M
Hierarchical	**15.55**	16.79	23.91	**26.64**	9.74	7.3M

Table 1: Results of the evaluation of models in translating languages with different morphological typology using the IWSLT data sets. The average number of parameters are calculated only for the decoders of the NMT models at a resolution of millions (M). The best scores for each translation direction are in bold font. All improvements over the baselines are statistically significant (p-value < 0.01).

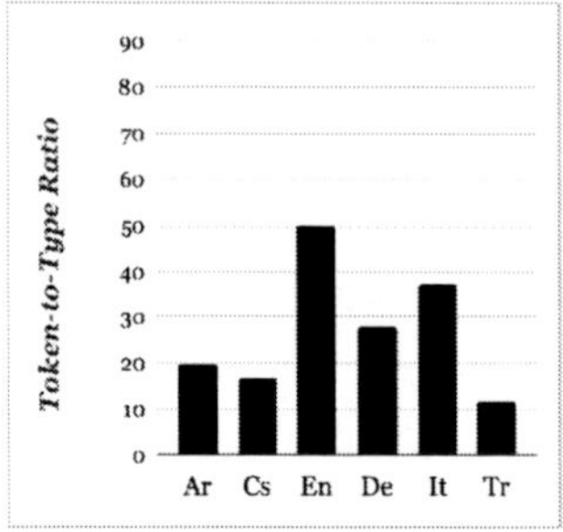
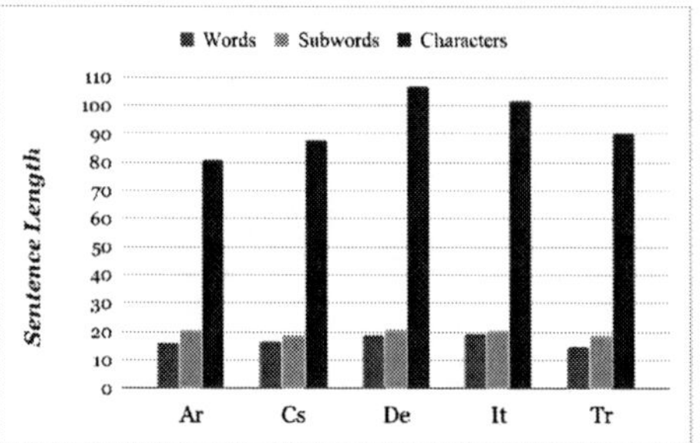

Figure 2: Lexical sparsity and average sentence lengths in different languages.

In order to achieve efficient decoding with the hierarchical NMT decoder, we implement a *hierarchical beam search* algorithm. Similar to the standard algorithm, the beam search starts by predicting the B most likely characters and storing them in a character beam along with their probabilities. The beams are reset each time the generation of a word is complete and the B most likely words are used to update the hidden states of the word-level RNN, which are fed to the character RNN to continue the beam search. When the beam search is complete, the most likely character sequence is generated as the best hypothesis.

5 Experiments

We evaluate decoding architectures using different levels of granularity in the vocabulary units and the attention mechanism, including the standard decoding architecture implemented either with subword (Sennrich et al., 2016) or fully character-level (Cherry et al., 2018) units, which constitute the baseline approaches, and the hierarchical decoding architecture, by implementing all in Pytorch (Paszke et al., 2017) within the OpenNMT-py framework (Klein et al., 2017). In order to evaluate how each generative method performs in languages with different morphological typology, we model the machine translation task from English into five languages from different language families and exhibiting distinct morphological typology: Arabic (*templatic*), Czech (*mostly fusional, partially agglutinative*), German (*fusional*), Italian (*fusional*) and Turkish (*agglutinative*). We use the TED Talks corpora (Cettolo, 2012) for training the NMT models, which range from 110K to 240K sentences, and the official development and test sets from IWSLT[1] (Cettolo et al., 2017). The low-resource settings for the training data allows us to examine the quality of the internal representations learned by each decoder under high data sparseness. In order to evaluate how the performance of each method scales with increasing data size, we evaluate the models also by training with a multi-domain training data using the public data sets from WMT[2] (Bojar et al., 2016) in the English-to-German direction, followed by an analysis on each model's capability in generalizing to morphological variations in the target language, using the Morpheval (Burlot et al., 2018) evaluation sets.

All models are implemented using gated recurrent units (GRU) (Cho et al., 2014) with the same number of parameters. The hierarchical decoding model implements a 3-layer GRU architecture, which is compared with a character-level decoder which also uses a 3-layer stacked GRU architecture. The subword-level decoder has a 2-layer stacked GRU architecture, to account also for the larger number of embedding parameters. The models using the standard architecture have the attention mechanism after the first GRU layer, and have residual connections after the second layer (Barone et al., 2017). The hierarchical decoder implements the attention mechanism after the second layer and has a residual connection between the first and second layers.

The source sides of the data used for training character-level NMT models are segmented using BPE with 16,000 merge rules on the IWSLT data, and 32,000 on WMT. For subword-based models we learn shared merging rules for BPE for 16,000 (in IWSLT) and 32,000 (in WMT) units. The models use an embedding and hidden unit size of 512 under low-resource (IWSLT) and 1024 under high-resource (WMT) settings, and are trained using the Adam (Kinga and Ba, 2015) optimizer with a learning rate of 0.0003 and decay of 0.5, batch size of 100 and a dropout of 0.2. Decoding in all models is performed with a beam size of 5. The accuracy of each output is measured in terms of the BLEU metric (Papineni et al., 2002) and the significance of the improvements are measured using bootstrap hypothesis testing (Clark et al., 2011).

---

[1] The International Workshop on Spoken Language Translation.

[2] The Conference on Machine Translation, with shared task organized for news translation.

Variation	Chars	Subwords	Hier.
Paradigm contrast features			
Positive vs. comparative adjective	**71.4**	68.4	70.1
Present vs. future tense	85.7	**92.0**	90.6
Negation	**97.8**	97.0	94.8
Singular vs. plural noun	88.2	**88.8**	88.6
Present vs. past tense	92.0	93.3	**95.4**
Compound generation	60.2	**65.4**	57.8
Indicative vs. conditional mode	86.4	88.2	**92.3**
Average	83.1	**84.7**	84.2
Agreement features			
Pronoun vs. Nouns (gender)	96.5	97.4	**98.8**
Pronoun vs. Nouns (number)	95.4	**96.0**	93.4
Pronoun (plural)	88.6	**94.3**	92.2
Pronoun (relative-gender)	74.2	76.4	**78.9**
Pronoun (relative-number)	84.2	**90.2**	87.0
Positive vs. superlative adjective	76.2	68.2	**80.4**
Simple vs. coordinated verbs (number)	**96.4**	93.4	97.2
Simple vs. coordinated verbs (person)	92.3	92.8	**93.5**
Simple vs. coordinated verbs (tense)	82.4	86.0	**90.2**
Average	87.4	88.3	**90.17**

Table 2: Results of the evaluation of models in capturing morphological variations in the output using the Morpheval English-German test set. The accuracy is measured with the percentage of correctly captured morphological contrasts. The best scores for each translation direction are in bold font.

6 Results

The results of the experiments given in Table 1 show that the hierarchical decoder can reach performance comparable to or better than the NMT model based on subword units in all languages while using almost three times less number of parameters. The improvements are especially evident in Arabic and Turkish, languages with the most complex morphology, where the accuracy with the hierarchical decoder is **1.28** and **1.22** BLEU points higher, respectively, and comparable in Czech, Italian and German, which represent the fusional languages. In Czech, the hierarchical model outperforms the subword-based model by **0.19** BLEU and in Italian by **0.41** BLEU points. The subword-based NMT model achieves the best performance in German, a language that is rich in compounding, where explicit subword segmentation might allow learning better representations for translation units.

The fully character-level NMT model, on the other hand, obtains higher translation accuracy than the hierarchical model in Turkish, with an improvement of **0.91** BLEU, and in Czech with **0.15** BLEU points. As can be seen in the statistical characteristics of the training sets illustrated by plotting the token-to-type ratios in each language (Figure 2), these two directions constitute the most sparse settings, where Turkish has the highest amount of sparsity in the benchmark, followed by Czech, and the improvements seem to be proportional to the amount of sparsity in the language. This suggests that in case of high lexical sparsity, learning to translate based on representations of characters might aid in reducing contextual sparsity, allowing to learn better distributed representations. As the training data size increases, one would expect the likelihood of observing rare words to decrease, especially in languages with low morphological complexity, along with the significance of representing rare and unseen words (Cherry

Model	newstest15
Subwords	**22.71**
Characters	20.34
Hierarchical	22.19

Table 3: Experiment results in the English-to-German direction with WMT data sets. Translation accuracy is measured with BLEU. Best scores are in bold font.

et al., 2018). Our results support this hypothesis, where decreasing lexical sparsity, either in the form of the training data size, or the morphological complexity of the target language, eliminates the advantage of character-level translation. In Arabic and Italian, where the training data is almost twice as large as the other languages, using the hierarchical model provides improvements of **2.83** and **2.31** BLEU points over the character-level NMT model. In German, the fully character-level NMT model still achieves the lowest accuracy, with **2.06** BLEU points below the subword-based model. This might be due to the increased level of contextual ambiguity leading to difficulty in learning reliable character embeddings when the model is trained over larger corpora. Another factor which might affect the lower performance of character-level models is the average sentence lengths, which are much longer compared to the sentence lengths resulting from with subword segmentation (Figure 2).

In the experiments conducted in the English-to-German translation direction, the results of which are given in Table 3, accuracy obtained with the hierarchical and subword-based NMT decoders significantly increase with the extension of

Input	when a friend of mine told me that I needed to see this great video about a guy protesting bicycle fines in New York City, I admit I wasn't very interested.
Output *Subword-based* *Decoder*	**bir arkadaşım New York'ta bisiklet protestosunu** protesto etmek **için bu filmi izlemeye** **ihtiyacım olduğunu söylemişti.**
Output *Character-based* *Decoder*	**bana bir arkadaşım** bana **New York'ta bir adam ile ilgili** bir adam hakkında **görmem gereken bir** adam hakkında görmem gerektiğini **söyledi.**
Output *Hierarchical* *Decoder*	**bir arkadaşım New York'ta bisiklet yapmaya** **ihtiyacım olduğunu söylediği zaman,** **kabul ettim.**
Reference	bir arkadaşım New York şehrindeki bisiklet cezalarını protesto eden bir adamın bu harika videosunu izlemem gerektiğini söylediğinde, kabul etmeliyim ki çok da ilgilenmemiştim.

Table 4: Example translations with different approaches in Turkish

the training data, where the subword-based model obtains the best accuracy, followed by the hierarchical model, and the character-level NMT model obtains significantly lower accuracy compared to both approaches. Studies have shown that character-level NMT models could potentially reach the same performance with the subword-based NMT models (Cherry et al., 2018), although this might require increasing the capacity of the network. On the other hand, the consistency in the accuracy obtained using the hierarchical decoding model from low to mid resource settings suggests that explicit modeling of word boundaries aids in achieving a more efficient solution to character-level translation.

Since solely relying on BLEU scores may not be sufficient in understanding the generative properties of different NMT models, we perform an additional evaluation in order to assess the capacity of models in learning syntactic or morphological dependencies using the Morpheval test suites, which consist of sentence pairs that differ by one morphological contrast, and each output accuracy is measured in terms of the percentage of translations that could convey the morphological contrast in the target language. Table 2 lists the performance of different NMT models implementing decoding at the level of subwords, characters, or hierarchical word-character units in capturing variances in each individual morphological paradigm and preserving the agreement between inflected words and their dependent lexical items. The results of our analysis support the benefit of using BPE in German as a subword segmentation algorithm, which obtains the highest accuracy in most of the morphological paradigm generation tasks, although the character-level model shows to be promising in capturing some morphological features better than the former, such as negation or comparative adjectives. In capturing syntactic agreement features, the hierarchical decoding model performs much better than the subword and character-level models, which is likely due to processing the sentence context at the word level, inducing a better notion of syntactic ordering during generation.

In order to better illustrate the differences in the outputs of each NMT model, we also present some sample translations in Table 4, obtained by translating English into Turkish using the NMT models trained on the TED Talks corpus. The input sentences are selected such that they are sufficiently long so that one can see the ability of each model in capturing long-distance dependencies in context. The input sentence is from a typical conversation, which requires remembering a long context with many references. We highlight the words in each output that is generated for the first time. Most of the models fail to generate a complete translation, starting to forget the sentence history after the generation of a few words, indicated by the start of generation of repetitions of the previously generated words. The character-level decoder seems to have the shortest memory span, followed by the subword-based decoder, which completely omits the second half of the sentence. Despite omitting the translations of the last four words in the input and some lexical errors, the hierarchical decoder is the only model which can generate a meaningful and grammatically-correct sentence, suggesting that modeling translation based on a context defined at the lexical level might help to learn better grammatical and contextual dependencies, and remembering longer history.

Although current methodology in NMT allows more efficient processing by implementing feed-forward architectures (Vaswani et al., 2017), our approach can conceptually be applied within these frameworks. In this paper, we limit the evaluation to recurrent architectures for comparison to previous work, including (Luong and Manning, 2016), (Sennrich et al., 2016) and (Cherry et al., 2018), and leave implementation of hierarchical decoding with feed-forward architectures to future work.

7 Conclusion

In this paper, we explored the idea of performing the decoding procedure in NMT in a multi-dimensional search space defined by word and character level units via a hierarchical decoding structure and beam search algorithm. Our model obtained comparable to better performance than conventional open-vocabulary NMT solutions, including subword and character-level NMT methods, in many languages while using a significantly smaller number of parameters, showing promising application under high-resource settings.Our software is available for public usage [3].

8 Acknowledgments

This project received funding from the European Unions Horizon 2020 research and innovation programme under grant agreements 825299 (GoURMET) and 688139 (SUMMA).

---

[3]https://github.com/d-ataman/Char-NMT

References

Duygu Ataman, Matteo Negri, Marco Turchi, and Marcello Federico. 2017. Linguistically motivated vocabulary reduction for neural machine translation from Turkish to English. *The Prague Bulletin of Mathematical Linguistics*, 108(1):331–342.

Dzmitry Bahdanau, Kyunghyun Cho, and Yoshua Bengio. 2014. Neural machine translation by jointly learning to align and translate. *Computing Research Repository*, arXiv:1409.0473.

Antonio Valerio Miceli Barone, Jindřich Helcl, Rico Sennrich, Barry Haddow, and Alexandra Birch. 2017. Deep architectures for neural machine translation. In *Proceedings of the 2nd Conference on Machine Translation*, pages 99–107.

Ondřej Bojar, Rajen Chatterjee, Christian Federmann, Yvette Graham, Barry Haddow, Matthias Huck, Antonio Jimeno Yepes, Philipp Koehn, Varvara Logacheva, Christof Monz, et al. 2016. Findings of the 2016 Conference on Machine Translation. In *Proceedings of the 1st Conference on Machine Translation*, volume 2, pages 131–198.

Léon Bottou. 2010. Large-Scale Machine Learning with Stochastic Gradient Descent. In *Proceedings of 19th International Conference on Computational Statistics (COMPSTAT)*, pages 177–186. Springer.

Franck Burlot, Yves Scherrer, Vinit Ravishankar, Ondřej Bojar, Stig-Arne Grönroos, Maarit Koponen, Tommi Nieminen, and François Yvon. 2018. The WMT'18 Morpheval test suites for English-Czech, English-German, English-Finnish and Turkish-English. In *Proceedings of the 3rd Conference on Machine Translation*, volume 2, pages 550–564.

Mauro Cettolo. 2012. WIT3: Web inventory of transcribed and translated talks. In *Conference of European Association for Machine Translation*, pages 261–268.

Mauro Cettolo, Marcello Federico, Luisa Bentivogli, Jan Niehues, Sebastian Stüker, Katsuitho Sudoh, Koichiro Yoshino, and Christian Federmann. 2017. Overview of the iwslt 2017 evaluation campaign. In *Proceedings of the 14th International Workshop on Spoken Language Translation*, pages 2–14.

Colin Cherry, George Foster, Ankur Bapna, Orhan Firat, and Wolfgang Macherey. 2018. Revisiting character-based neural machine translation with capacity and compression. In *Proceedings of the 2018 Conference on Empirical Methods in Natural Language Processing*, pages 4295–4305.

Kyunghyun Cho, Bart van Merrienboer, Dzmitry Bahdanau, and Yoshua Bengio. 2014. On the properties of neural machine translation: Encoder–decoder approaches. In *Proceedings of 8th Workshop on Syntax, Semantics and Structure in Statistical Translation (SSST)*, pages 103–111.

Jonathan H Clark, Chris Dyer, Alon Lavie, and Noah A Smith. 2011. Better hypothesis testing for statistical machine translation: Controlling for optimizer instability. In *Proceedings of the 49th Annual Meeting of the Association for Computational Linguistics*, volume 2, pages 176–181.

D Kinga and J Ba. 2015. Adam: A method for stochastic optimization. In *International Conference on Learning Representations (ICLR)*, volume 5.

Guillaume Klein, Yoon Kim, Yuntian Deng, Jean Senellart, and Alexander Rush. 2017. OpenNMT: Open-source toolkit for neural machine translation. *Proceedings of ACL 2017, System Demonstrations*, pages 67–72.

Julia Kreutzer and Artem Sokolov. 2018. Learning to segment inputs for nmt favors character-level processing. In *Proceedings of the 15th International Workshop on Spoken Language Translation*, pages 166–172.

Wang Ling, Isabel Trancoso, Chris Dyer, and Alan W. Black. 2015. Character-based neural machine translation. *Computing Research Repository*, arxiv:1511.04586.

Minh-Thang Luong and Christopher D. Manning. 2016. Achieving open vocabulary neural machine translation with hybrid word-character models. In *Proceedings of the 54th Annual Meeting of the Association for Computational Linguistics*, volume 1, pages 1054–1063.

Minh-Thang Luong, Hieu Pham, and Christopher D. Manning. 2015. Effective approaches to attention-based neural machine translation. In *Proceedings of the 2015 Conference on Empirical Methods in Natural Language Processing*, pages 1412–1421.

Kishore Papineni, Salim Roukos, Todd Ward, and Wei-Jing Zhu. 2002. BLEU: a Method for Automatic Evaluation of Machine Translation. In *Proceedings of the 40th Annual Meeting of the Association for Computational Linguistics*, pages 311–318.

Adam Paszke, Sam Gross, Soumith Chintala, Gregory Chanan, Edward Yang, Zachary DeVito, Zeming Lin, Alban Desmaison, Luca Antiga, and Adam Lerer. 2017. Automatic differentiation in Pytorch.

Mike Schuster and Kuldip K Paliwal. 1997. Bidirectional recurrent neural networks. *IEEE Transactions on Signal Processing*, 45(11):2673–2681.

Rico Sennrich, Barry Haddow, and Alexandra Birch. 2016. Neural machine translation of rare words with subword units. In *Proceedings of the 54th Annual Meeting of the Association for Computational Linguistics*, volume 1, pages 1715–1725.

Ashish Vaswani, Noam Shazeer, Niki Parmar, Jakob Uszkoreit, Llion Jones, Aidan N Gomez, Łukasz Kaiser, and Illia Polosukhin. 2017. Attention is all you need. In *Advances in Neural Information Processing Systems*, pages 5998–6008.

Paul J Werbos. 1990. Backpropagation Through Time: What it does and how to do it. In *Proceedings of the Institute of Electrical and Electronics Engineers (IEEE)*, volume 78, pages 1550–1560.

Big Bidirectional Insertion Representations for Documents

Lala Li
Google Research, Brain Team
`lala@google.com`

William Chan
Google Research, Brain Team
`williamchan@google.com`

Abstract

The Insertion Transformer is well suited for long form text generation due to its parallel generation capabilities, requiring $O(\log_2 n)$ generation steps to generate n tokens. However, modeling long sequences is difficult, as there is more ambiguity captured in the attention mechanism. This work proposes the Big Bidirectional Insertion Representations for Documents (Big BIRD), an insertion-based model for document-level translation tasks. We scale up the insertion-based models to long form documents. Our key contribution is introducing sentence alignment via sentence-positional embeddings between the source and target document. We show an improvement of +4.3 BLEU on the WMT'19 English→German document-level translation task compared with the Insertion Transformer baseline.

1 Introduction

Recently, insertion-based models (Stern et al., 2019; Welleck et al., 2019; Gu et al., 2019; Chan et al., 2019) have been introduced for text generation. Unlike traditional autoregressive left-to-right models (Cho et al., 2014; Sutskever et al., 2014; Vaswani et al., 2017), insertion-based models are not restricted to generating text sequences in a serial left-to-right manner, but these models are endowed with the capabilities of parallel generation. More specifically, Stern et al. (2019); Chan et al. (2019) showed that we can teach neural nets to generate text to follow a balanced binary tree order. An autoregressive left-to-right model would require $O(n)$ generation steps to generate n tokens, whereas the Insertion Transformer (Stern et al., 2019) and KERMIT (Chan et al., 2019) following a balanced binary tree policy requires only $O(\log_2 n)$ generation steps to generate n tokens. This is especially important for long-

form text generation, for example, Document-Level Machine Translation.

Document-Level Machine Translation is becoming an increasingly important task. Recent research suggests we are nearing human-level parity for sentence-level translation in certain domains (Hassan et al., 2018), however, we lag significantly behind in document-level translation (Lubli et al., 2018). Various papers have proposed incorporating context for document-level translation (Junczys-Dowmunt, 2019), which has been shown to improve translation quality. There are two primary methods to include context in a document-level machine translation model compared to a sentence-level translation model.

1. **Source Contextualization.** We can include source context, wherein when we generate the target sentence, we can condition on the corresponding source sentence and its neighbours, or even the whole source document. This allows the target sentence to be contextualized to the source document.

2. **Target Contextualization.** We can include target context, wherein when we generate the target sentence, we can condition on all the target tokens generated thus far in the whole document. This allows the target sentence to be contextualized to other target sentences.

Target contextualization is especially difficult in an autoregressive left-to-right model (i.e., Transformer (Vaswani et al., 2017)), the model must generate the whole document in linear fashion, which would be prohibitively expensive costing $O(n)$ iterations to generate n tokens. Additionally, the model is unable to model bidirectional context, since the text is always generated in a left-to-right manner. Some prior work have focused on utilizing block coordinate descent like algorithms during inference (Maruf and Haffari, 2018), however

Proceedings of the 3rd Workshop on Neural Generation and Translation (WNGT 2019), pages 194–198
Hong Kong, China, November 4, 2019. ©2019 Association for Computational Linguistics
www.aclweb.org/anthology/D19-56%2d

this adds complexity and additional runtime cost during inference.

Insertion-based models, for example, the Insertion Transformer (Stern et al., 2019) is one potential solution. The Insertion Transformer can generate text following a balanced binary tree order. It requires $O(\log_2 n)$ iterations to generate n tokens, offering significant inference time advantages over a serial generation model. The source document is naturally fully conditioned on, which provides full source contextualization. Additionally, the generation order offers bidirectional contextualization, permitting target contextualization that is not solely on a left-to-right basis.

In this paper, we present Big Bidirectional Insertion Representations for Documents (Big BIRD). We address the limitations of scaling up the Insertion Transformer to document-level machine translation. We present a model that can model long-form documents with thousands of tokens in a fully contextualized manner.

2 Big BIRD

In this section, we present Big Bidirectional Representations for Documents (Big BIRD). Big BIRD is an extension of the Insertion Transformer (Stern et al., 2019), scaling up from sentences to documents. The key contributions are 1) extending the context window size to cover a document, and 2) informing the model of sentence positional information, which are aligned between source and target sentences.

Insertion Transformer. In the Insertion Transformer (Stern et al., 2019), sequences are generated via insertion operations. In the context of Machine Translation, there is a source canvas x and a target canvas y, where the target canvas is updated at each iteration via inserting one token at each plausible location. At time t during training, a hypothesis target canvas $\hat{y}_t$ must be a subsequence of the final output. For example, if the final output is $[A, B, C, D, E]$, then $\hat{y}_t = [B, D]$ would be a valid intermediate canvas, in which case the model would be taught to predict $[A, C, E]$. The model is taught to insert multiple tokens at incomplete slots, or predict end-of-slot for completed slots. The intermediate canvases are uniformly sampled from the ground truth target sequence. During inference, the target canvas starts empty, and tokens will be inserted iteratively until the model predicts to insert empty tokens everywhere,

or the sequence has exceeded the specified maximum length.

Larger Context and Sentence-Positional Embeddings. Longer sequences lead to more uncertainties for the Insertion Transformer. For example, if a token in $\hat{y}_t$ appears in multiple sentences in the final output, there is ambiguity to the model which sentence it belongs to (and therefore where to attend to on both the source and target canvases). While there is location information endowed in the Transformer model, we hypothesize that token level positional information is insufficient (especially since we have limited training data). We believe that endowing the model with sentence-level positional information (i.e., which sentence each token belongs to) may help significantly disambiguate in such situations and help the model build a more robust attention mechanism.

Based on this motivation and assuming that the datasets have not only parallel documents, but also sentence alignment between source and target documents (which is true for WMT'19 document-level translation), we use sentence-positional embeddings on both the source and target sequences as shown in Figure 1. The intention is to endow the model with this prior knowledge on sentence alignment between the source and target, and thus more easily attend to the appropriate sentences based on sentence locality. More specifically, on the source side, we do not use any sentence separator tokens; on the target side, we start each sentence with a sentence separator. During inference we initialize the output hypothesis with empty $\langle s \rangle$ sentence separator tokens, where the number of $\langle s \rangle$ equals to the number of source sentences, which is equal to the number of target sentences to be generated. These $\langle s \rangle$ tokens serve as sentence anchor points, and have sentence-positional information. Figure 1 visualizes the model.

In this work we increased the context window size to cover multiple sentences or a short document. Note that there is only a limit on the maximum number of tokens in the entire sequence; there is no limit on the length of a single sentence, or the total number of sentences in the sequence.

3 Experiments

We experiment with the WMT'19 English→German document-level translation task (Barrault et al., 2019). The training dataset consists of parallel document-level data (Eu-

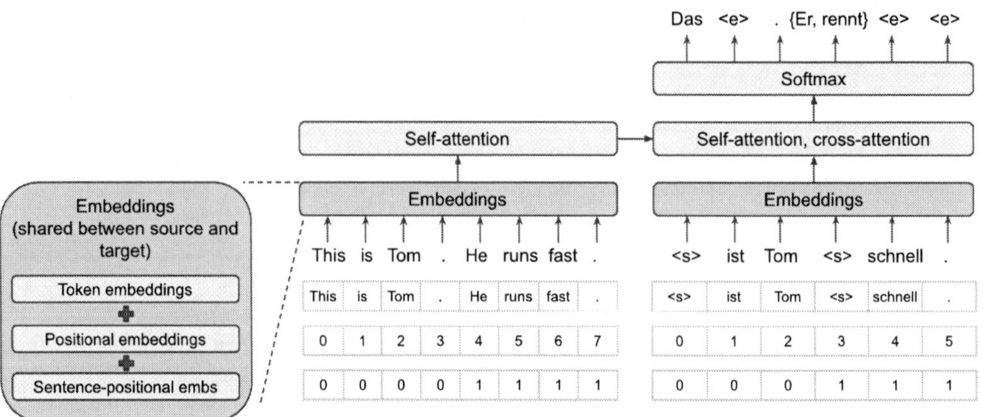

Figure 1: Big Bidirectional Insertion Representations for Documents

roparl, Rapid, News-Commentary) and parallel sentence-level data (WikiTitles, Common Crawl, Paracrawl). The test set is newstest2019. The document-level portion contains 68.4k parallel documents, or a total of 7.7M parallel sentences; while the sentence-level portion has 19.9M parallel sentences. We generated a vocabulary of 32k subwords from the training data using the SentencePiece tokenizer (Kudo and Richardson, 2018).

The Big BIRD model is as described in Section 2, and the baseline Insertion Transformer model has exactly the same configurations except without sentence-positional embeddings. To be explicit, our baseline Insertion Transformer model is also given the prior knowledge of number of source sentences in the document. The target canvas is initialized target with $\langle s \rangle$ sentence separator tokens, where the number of $\langle s \rangle$ tokens is equal to the number of sentences in the document. All our models follow the same architecture as the Transformer Base model in (Vaswani et al., 2017), and a context window of 1536 tokens during training (determined based on the longest document in the test set). All models were trained with the SM3 optimizer (Anil et al., 2019) with momentum 0.9, learning rate 0.1, and a quadratic learning rate warm-up schedule with 10k warm-up steps. The learning rate were chosen after some preliminary comparison runs between Adam and SM3. We opted to use the SM3 optimizer over Adam due to its more memory efficient properties, thus allowing us to use larger minibatches. Training was around 800k steps at batch size 512.

During training, each batch consists of 256 sub-

Model	BLEU
Insertion Transformer	25.3
Big BIRD	29.6

Table 1: WMT19 English→German Document-Level Translation.

documents and 256 sentences. Sub-documents are continuous sentences dynamically sampled from a document. The lengths of sub-documents are uniformly sampled in (0, 1536] tokens. The number of sampled sub-documents from each document is 1/10 of the number of sentences in the full document. Sentences directly come from sentence-level data. This 1:1 mixing of sub-documents and sentences results in training examples of vastly different lengths and therefore many masked positions, and we plan to improve it in the future by packing multiple sentences into one example.

We report sacreBLEU (Post, 2018) scores of the two models in Table 1. Our Big BIRD model outperforms the Insertion Transformer model by +4.3 BLEU.

When we inspected the outputs more closely for the two models, we uncovered an interesting phenomenon. The Insertion Transformer, even though its target canvas is also initialized with the correct number of sentence $\langle s \rangle$ separators, struggles to align source and target sentences. For example, it can map two sources sentences into one sentence in the target, or vice versa. This is not always bad, as long as it captures the semantics accurately. However, there are cases when misalignment causes loss of coherency. Table 2 shows such an example where Big BIRD captures alignment

Source:
(...) Chelsea faces Videoton in the UEFA Europa Leaguge at 3 p.m. on Thursday in London.

Target:
(...) Chelsea trifft in der UEFA Europa League am Donnerstag um 15 Uhr in London auf Videoton.

Insertion Transformer:
(...) Chelsea Gesichter am Donnerstag um 15.00 Uhr in London. Chelsea Gesichter Videoton in der UEFA Europa Leaguge.
Translation: (Google Translate)
Chelsea faces on Thursday at 15.00 in London. Chelsea faces Videoton in UEFA Europa Leaguge.

Big BIRD:
(...) Chelsea sieht am Donnerstag um 15.00 Uhr in London Videoton in der UEFA Europa Leaguge.
Translation: (Google Translate)
Chelsea sees Videoton in UEFA Europa League on Thursday at 15.00 in London.

Table 2: An example where the Insertion Transformer gets confused with sentence alignment: it maps one sentence from the source into two sentences in the translation and loses semantic accuracy. When given sentence alignment explicitly, i.e. Big BIRD, it translates the sentence coherently.

better than the Insertion Transformer, and therefore its translation is more accurate and coherent.

4 Conclusion

In this paper, we presented Big BIRD, an adaptation of the Insertion Transformer to document-level translation. In addition to a large context window, Big BIRD also uses sentence-positional embeddings to directly capture sentence alignment between source and target documents. We show both quantitatively and qualitatively the promise of Big BIRD, with a +4.3 BLEU improvement over the baseline model and examples where Big BIRD achieves better translation quality via sentence alignment. We believe Big BIRD is a promising direction for document level understanding and generation.

References

Rohan Anil, Vineet Gupta, Tomer Koren, and Yoram Singer. 2019. Memory-Efficient Adaptive Optimization for Large-Scale Learning. In *arXiv*.

Loc Barrault, Ondej Bojar, Marta R. Costa-juss, Christian Federmann, Mark Fishel, Yvette Graham, Barry Haddow, Matthias Huck, Philipp Koehn, Shervin Malmasi, Christof Monz, Mathias Mller, Santanu Pal, Matt Post, and Marcos Zampieri. 2019. Findings of the 2019 Conference on Machine Translation. In *ACL*.

William Chan, Nikita Kitaev, Kelvin Guu, Mitchell Stern, and Jakob Uszkoreit. 2019. KERMIT: Generative Insertion-Based Modeling for Sequences. In *arXiv*.

Kyunghyun Cho, Bart van Merrienboer, Caglar Gulcehre, Dzmitry Bahdanau, Fethi Bougares, Holger Schwenk, and Yoshua Bengio. 2014. Learning Phrase Representations using RNN Encoder-Decoder for Statistical Machine Translation. In *EMNLP*.

Jiatao Gu, Qi Liu, and Kyunghyun Cho. 2019. Insertion-based Decoding with Automatically Inferred Generation Order. In *arXiv*.

Hany Hassan, Anthony Aue andChang Chen, Vishal Chowdhary, Jonathan Clark, Christian Federmann, Xuedong Huang, Marcin Junczys-Dowmunt, William Lewis, Mu Li, Shujie Liu, Tie-Yan Liu, Renqian Luo, Arul Menezes, Tao Qin, Frank Seide, Xu Tan, Fei Tian, Lijun Wu, Shuangzhi Wu, Yingce Xia, Dongdong Zhang, Zhirui Zhang, and Ming Zhou. 2018. Achieving Human Parity on Automatic Chinese to English News Translation. In *arXiv*.

Marcin Junczys-Dowmunt. 2019. Microsoft Translator at WMT 2019: Towards Large-Scale Document-Level Neural Machine Translation. In *WMT*.

Taku Kudo and John Richardson. 2018. Sentencepiece: A simple and language independent subword tokenizer and detokenizer for neural text processing. In *Proceedings of the 2018 Conference on Empirical Methods in Natural Language Processing: System Demonstrations*, pages 66–71.

Samuel Lubli, Rico Sennrich, and Martin Volk. 2018. Has Machine Translation Achieved Human Parity? A Case for Document-level Evaluation. In *EMNLP*.

Sameen Maruf and Gholamreza Haffari. 2018. Document Context Neural Machine Translation with Memory Networks. In *ACL*.

Matt Post. 2018. A Call for Clarity in Reporting BLEU Scores. In *WMT*.

Mitchell Stern, William Chan, Jamie Kiros, and Jakob Uszkoreit. 2019. Insertion Transformer: Flexible Sequence Generation via Insertion Operations. In *ICML*.

Ilya Sutskever, Oriol Vinyals, and Quoc Le. 2014. Sequence to Sequence Learning with Neural Networks. In *NIPS*.

Ashish Vaswani, Noam Shazeer, Niki Parmar, Jakob Uszkoreit, Llion Jones, Aidan N. Gomez, Lukasz Kaiser, and Illia Polosukhin. 2017. Attention Is All You Need. In *NIPS*.

Sean Welleck, Kiante Brantley, Hal Daume, and Kyunghyun Cho. 2019. Non-Monotonic Sequential Text Generation. In *ICML*.

A Margin-based Loss with Synthetic Negative Samples for Continuous-output Machine Translation

Gayatri Bhat   **Sachin Kumar**   **Yulia Tsvetkov**

Language Technologies Institute
Carnegie Mellon University
`{gbhat,sachink,ytsvetko}@cs.cmu.edu`

Abstract

Neural models that eliminate the softmax bottleneck by generating word embeddings (rather than multinomial distributions over a vocabulary) attain faster training with fewer learnable parameters. These models are currently trained by maximizing densities of pretrained target embeddings under von Mises-Fisher distributions parameterized by corresponding model-predicted embeddings. This work explores the utility of margin-based loss functions in optimizing such models. We present **syn-margin** loss, a novel margin-based loss that uses a *synthetic* negative sample constructed from only the predicted and target embeddings at every step. The loss is efficient to compute, and we use a geometric analysis to argue that it is more consistent and interpretable than other margin-based losses. Empirically, we find that syn-margin provides small but significant improvements over both vMF and standard margin-based losses in continuous-output neural machine translation.

1 Introduction

A new approach to conditional language modeling (Kumar and Tsvetkov, 2019) generates continuous-valued embeddings in place of discrete tokens (such as words or subwords). These embeddings are trained to lie in a pretrained word embedding space by maximizing, at each step of training, the von Mises-Fisher (vMF) probability density of the target pretrained embedding given the model-predicted embedding (§2). This eliminates the softmax bottleneck to ensure time- and memory-efficient training.

We investigate alternative loss functions for this new class of models, specifically *margin-based* formulations. These have been used to train embeddings for a range of tasks (Bojanowski et al.,

2017; Bredin, 2017; Wu et al., 2018), and standard margin-based losses yield slight but inconsistent improvements over vMF on continuous-output neural machine translation (NMT). We propose **syn-margin**, a novel margin-based loss for which negative samples are *synthesized* using only the predicted and target embeddings, without sampling from or searching through the large pretrained embedding space (§3). These samples are constructed by extracting the portion of the predicted embedding that is not along the target embedding; intuitively, suppressing this component will increase the predicted embedding's similarity to the target. We use a geometric analysis to argue that this principled construction renders syn-margin loss more consistent and interpretable than standard margin-based losses that select negative samples randomly or heuristically (Collobert et al., 2011; Hadsell et al., 2006; Schroff et al., 2015; Mikolov et al., 2013a). Empirically, we find that syn-margin attains small but statistically significant improvements over vMF (§4) on continuous-output neural machine translation (NMT).

The key contributions of this work are: (1) the formulation of syn-margin loss, which is applicable across natural language processing and computer vision tasks for which the targets lie in pretrained embedding spaces (2) a geometric analysis of the functionality of syn-margin loss, which provides insights into the mechanism of margin-based losses in general and (3) the empirical result of improved performance on continuous-output NMT.

2 Continuous-output models

Conditional language models generate text conditioned on some input, e.g., produce translations of input sentences (Sutskever et al., 2014; Bahdanau et al., 2015; Luong et al., 2015). State-of-the-art

Proceedings of the 3rd Workshop on Neural Generation and Translation (WNGT 2019), pages 199–205
Hong Kong, China, November 4, 2019. ©2019 Association for Computational Linguistics
www.aclweb.org/anthology/D19-56%2d

neural models generate the text as a sequence of discrete tokens such as words.[1]

A traditional model, at every step of generation, produces a context vector $\mathbf{c}$ that encodes both the conditioning input and the output from previous generation steps. It then transforms $\mathbf{c}$ into a *discrete* distribution over the target vocabulary V using a softmax-activated linear transformation of size $|\mathbf{c}| \times |V|$. These models are typically trained using cross-entropy loss, and inference uses either greedy or beam decoding.

Instead of the multinomial distribution over V, continuous-output conditional language models generate a d-dimensional word embedding $\hat{\mathbf{u}}$ (Kumar and Tsvetkov, 2019). For this purpose, the $|\mathbf{c}| \times |V|$ transformation is replaced by a linear layer of size $|\mathbf{c}| \times d$. This design enables the model to have far fewer parameters than the original ($d \ll V$).

The model is trained and decoded in conjunction with a table of pretrained embeddings for words in V. Proposing that the *predicted embedding* $\hat{\mathbf{u}}$ parametrizes a von Mises-Fisher distribution over all d-dimensional vectors, Kumar and Tsvetkov (2019) train the model by maximizing the probability density at the target word's pretrained embedding $\mathbf{u}$ under this distribution centered at $\hat{\mathbf{u}}$:

$$p(\mathbf{u}; \hat{\mathbf{u}}) = C_m(\|\hat{\mathbf{u}}\|)e^{\hat{\mathbf{u}}^T \mathbf{u}}$$

where

$$C_m(\|\hat{\mathbf{u}}\|) = \frac{\|\hat{\mathbf{u}}\|^{d/2-1}}{(2\pi)^{d/2}I_{d/2-1}(\|\hat{\mathbf{u}}\|)}$$

with I_v being the modified Bessel function of the first kind of order v.

Thus, every predicted embedding is driven towards its *target embedding* $\mathbf{u}$, which can be identified since target words are available during training. This is much faster than training in the discrete-output case, since vMF densities are implicitly normalized. During inference, choosing the most likely word reduces to finding the predicted embedding's nearest neighbour (by cosine similarity) in the L_2-normalized pretrained embedding space.[2]

---

[1]The discrete units may be words, sub-word units (Sennrich et al., 2016), characters (Ling et al., 2015; Kim et al., 2016) or tokens of any other granularity. We focus on the generation of words, since pretrained embeddings spaces at this granularity are interpretable and semantically coherent across languages.

[2]In line with the inference mechanism, all references we

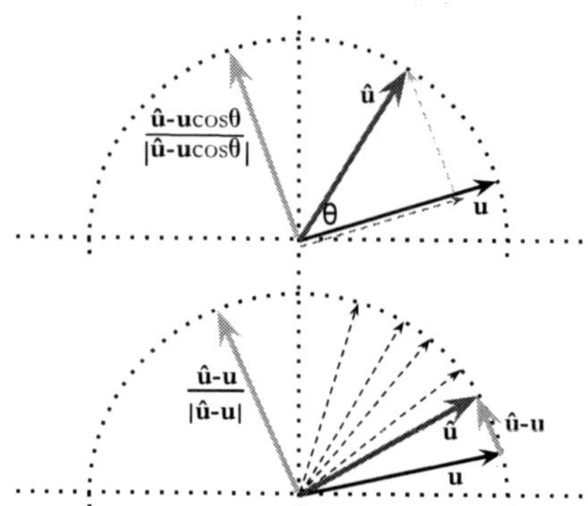

Figure 1: **Synthesizing negative samples.** Consider predicted and target embeddings $\hat{\mathbf{u}}$ (blue) and $\mathbf{u}$ (solid black), respectively. To synthesize a negative example for the margin-based loss by **projection** (top), we project $\hat{\mathbf{u}}$ onto $\mathbf{u}$ (dotted blue), use this to find component of $\hat{\mathbf{u}}$ that is orthogonal to $\mathbf{u}$ (dotted orange) and normalize it to obtain $\mathbf{u}_{\text{orth}}$ (solid orange). To synthesize by **difference** (bottom), we normalize $\hat{\mathbf{u}} - \mathbf{u}$ to obtain $\mathbf{u}_{\text{diff}}$ (long orange).

3 Margin-based loss formulations

To explore the space of additional loss functions for continuous-output models, we study margin-based losses commonly used to compare embeddings in both natural language and image processing (Collobert et al., 2011; Schroff et al., 2015) tasks:

$$\mathcal{L} = \max\{0, \lambda + \mathbf{u}'^T \hat{\mathbf{u}} - \mathbf{u}^T \hat{\mathbf{u}}\} \quad (1)$$

This requires $\hat{\mathbf{u}}$ to be closer to $\mathbf{u}$ than to some *negative sample* $\mathbf{u}'$ by a margin of λ. (Since the embeddings are normalized, inner product corresponds to cosine similarity.) Here λ is a hyperparameter that, along with $\mathbf{u}'$, decides whether $\hat{\mathbf{u}}$ is 'close enough' to $\mathbf{u}$.

The negative sample $\mathbf{u}'$ is usually chosen by (1) stochastic processes such as **negative sampling**: randomly choosing an embedding from the pretrained embedding table, and averaging loss over k random draws or (2) heuristic selections such as the **most informative negative sample** introduced by Lazaridou et al. (2015): the embedding in the table that is closest to $\hat{\mathbf{u}} - \mathbf{u}$.

3.1 The role of negative samples

What is the role of the negative sample in this margin-based loss? We investigate with a geomet-

---

make to 'similarity' or 'closeness' will be in the cosine, not Euclidean sense. In a slight change of notation, we will henceforth use $\hat{\mathbf{u}}$ to refer to the *unit vector* along a predicted embedding rather than the predicted embedding itself.

ric analysis.

At the outset, consider predicted and target embeddings $\hat{\mathbf{u}}$ and $\mathbf{u}$, both of unit length. The predicted embedding's components *parallel* and *orthogonal* to $\mathbf{u}$ are $(\hat{\mathbf{u}}^T\mathbf{u})\mathbf{u}$ and $\hat{\mathbf{u}}-(\hat{\mathbf{u}}^T\mathbf{u})\mathbf{u}$ (dotted blue and dotted orange lines respectively in Figure 1, which illustrates this decomposition). Let the unit vector along this orthogonal component be $\mathbf{u}_{\mathrm{orth}}$ (solid orange line). It follows that (1) $\mathbf{u}_{\mathrm{orth}} \perp \mathbf{u}$ and (2) $\hat{\mathbf{u}}$ is a linear combination of these orthogonal vectors, say, $\lambda_1\mathbf{u} + \lambda_2\mathbf{u}_{\mathrm{orth}}$.

Now, choose any embedding $\mathbf{x}$ of unit length from the d-dimensional space (not necessarily the pretrained embedding of any word) to use as the negative sample in a margin-based loss. Let its projections along $\mathbf{u}$ and $\mathbf{u}_{\mathrm{orth}}$ be $\lambda_3\mathbf{u}$ and $\lambda_4\mathbf{u}_{\mathrm{orth}}$ Since these are orthogonal, $\mathbf{x}$ decomposes as $\lambda_3\mathbf{u} + \lambda_4\mathbf{u}_{\mathrm{orth}} + \mathbf{y}$ where $\mathbf{y}$ is some vector orthogonal to both $\mathbf{u}$ and $\mathbf{u}_{\mathrm{orth}}$ ($\mathbf{y} = \mathbf{0}$ when $d = 2$).

Using the decomposed forms of $\hat{\mathbf{u}}$ and $\mathbf{u}_{\mathrm{orth}}$ in the margin-based loss, the second argument of equation 1 becomes

$$\lambda + \lambda_4\mathbf{u}_{\mathrm{orth}}{}^T\hat{\mathbf{u}} - (1-\lambda_3)\mathbf{u}^T\hat{\mathbf{u}} + \mathbf{y}^T(\lambda_1\mathbf{u}+\lambda_2\mathbf{u}_{\mathrm{orth}})$$

Applying orthogonality to set the final term to zero gives

$$\mathcal{L} = \max\{0, \lambda + \lambda_4\mathbf{u}_{\mathrm{orth}}{}^T\hat{\mathbf{u}} - (1-\lambda_3)\mathbf{u}^T\hat{\mathbf{u}}\}$$

Thus, *regardless of the actual negative sample chosen*, the loss reduces to a form wherein some scalar multiples of $\mathbf{u}$ and $\mathbf{u}_{\mathrm{orth}}$ are the positive and negative samples respectively. The loss essentially penalizes the component of $\hat{\mathbf{u}}$ that is orthogonal to $\mathbf{u}$.

3.2 Synthesized negative samples

Drawing on this insight, we propose to use the *synthesized* vector $\mathbf{u}_{\mathrm{orth}}$ as the negative sample in a margin-based loss. This sets λ_4 and λ_3 at 1 and 0 respectively, providing a steady training signal. In contrast, these coefficients fluctuate during training if heuristic or stochastic methods are used to select negative samples. We also propose a second closely related negative sample $\mathbf{u}_{\mathrm{diff}}$, synthesized by subtraction rather than projection: the unit vector along the difference $\hat{\mathbf{u}} - \mathbf{u}$ (see Figure 1 for a visualization). Synthesizing $\mathbf{u}_{\mathrm{orth}}$ and $\mathbf{u}_{\mathrm{diff}}$ is efficient since it does not require any sampling from or searching through the pretrained embedding space. We refer to the loss formulations using $\mathbf{u}_{\mathrm{orth}}$ and $\mathbf{u}_{\mathrm{diff}}$ as **syn-margin** by projection (SMP) and difference (SMD) respectively.

Although $\mathbf{u}_{\mathrm{orth}}$ and $\mathbf{u}_{\mathrm{diff}}$ are functions of $\hat{\mathbf{u}}$, they are plugged into $\mathcal{L}$ as *constant* vectors detached from the computational graph; this prevents them from being optimized to minimize $\mathcal{L}$. We highlight that using these synthesized negative samples cannot lead to a degenerate state in which all the word embeddings collapse to a single point. This is because the target embeddings are, unlike in some previous work that uses margin-based losses, pretrained and fixed.

4 Experimental Setup

We follow Kumar and Tsvetkov (2019) to conduct experiments on neural machine translation.

Datasets We evaluate our models on IWSLT'16 (Cettolo et al., 2015) French→English and German→English datasets. We pretrain target embeddings on a large English-language corpus (4B+ tokens) using FastText on default settings (Bojanowski et al., 2017) and L_2-normalize the embeddings. Vocabulary sizes are limited to 50000. We follow Kumar and Tsvetkov (2019) in using the standard development (tst2013 and tst2014) and test (tst2015 and tst2016) sets associated with the parallel corpora and in processing the data; train, development and test splits contain roughly 200K, 2300 and 2200 parallel sentences each.

Setup We use a neural machine translation system with attention (Bahdanau et al., 2015), set up to match that described in Kumar and Tsvetkov (2019). The encoder and decoder are 1-layer bidirectional and 2-layer LSTMs with 1024-dimensional hidden and output states. Word embeddings are 512-dimensional on the encoder side and 300-dimensional on the decoder side. Decoder input and target embeddings are tied to the same parameter matrix, these embeddings are transformed to the correct dimensions with a linear layer when used as inputs to the decoder. Generated embeddings are normalized before computing margin-based losses (vMF loss accounts separately for embedding norm). We train for up to 20 epochs with Adam (Kingma and Ba, 2015), an initial learning rate of 0.0005 and no dropout. During inference, vMF density is used to choose an output word given an embedding predicted by the vMF system, and the predicted embedding's nearest neighbour is chosen as the output for margin-trained systems. Hyperparameters are selected using performance on the development set and we report means and standard deviations of BLEU

Output Type	Loss Function	IWSLT Fr→En	IWSLT De→En
Discrete	**Cross-entropy: untied embeddings**	31.3 ± 0.4	25.1 ± 0.2
	Cross-entropy: tied embeddings	31.3 ± 0.9	24.8 ± 0.2
Continuous	**von Mises-Fisher**	31.8 ± 0.3	25.0 ± 0.2
	Most informative negative sample	32.0 ± 0.2	$25.1^{\ddagger} \pm 0.1$
	Negative sampling	$32.2^{*} \pm 0.4$	24.8 ± 0.2
	Syn-margin by difference (SMD)	$32.0^{*} \pm 0.3$	$\mathbf{25.4}^{*\dagger\ddagger} \pm 0.3$
	Syn-margin by projection (SMP)	$\mathbf{32.3}^{*\dagger} \pm 0.2$	$25.3^{*\ddagger} \pm 0.5$

Table 1: **Experimental results.** Means and standard deviations of BLEU scores across 4 runs of each experiment, for the (1) discrete-output baseline, (2) continuous-output models trained using vMF, most informative negative example (Lazaridou et al., 2015) and negative sampling, and (3) proposed syn-margin losses constructed using vector projection and vector difference, on IWSLT'16 Fr→En and De→En datasets. Asterisks, daggers and double daggers indicate significant gains over vMF, most informative negative sample and negative sampling respectively ($p = 0.05$).

scores (Papineni et al., 2002) over 4 runs of each experiment.

Baselines and benchmarks We compare syn-margin losses constructed using projection (SMP) and difference (SMD) techniques against: (1) vMF loss (specifically, the negative log-likelihood formulation in the original paper), (2) margin-based loss averaged over 5 negative samples drawn uniformly at random from the pretrained word embeddings and (3) margin-based loss using the most informative negative sample (Lazaridou et al., 2015). We also report results on a softmax-based system with identical architecture except in the last layer, initializing the softmax parameters with pretrained embeddings, with and without tied embeddings.

5 Results and Analysis

Syn-margin methods show small (+0.4 and +0.5 BLEU) and statistically significant gains over vMF on both datasets, although there is no consistent winner among the two syn-margin variants (Table 1). The improvement over most informative negative sample and negative sampling is less prominent, and significant only in some cases. Syn-margin's computational efficiency matches that of vMF (Figure 2).

Comparing translations produced by vMF and syn-margin models in the Fr→En task, we find SMP translations to be more grammatical. They better preserve grammatical information such as gender (SMP correctly predicts the fragment 'her personality' while vMF generates 'his personality') and tense (SMP generates 'does it predict' while vMF produces 'does it predicted'), and are better-formed without cascading errors.

Next, to develop a qualitative understanding of the synthesized negative samples, we identify predicted embeddings' and SMP negative samples' nearest neighbours (NN) among the pretrained target embeddings. Either both embeddings share a common NN, or in a weak pattern, the SMP's NN captures $\hat{u}$'s semantic or grammatical divergence from u. For instance, where the target is 'means' and the prediction's NN is 'meant', the negative sample's NN 'held' penalizes past-tense information in the predicted embedding. Similarly, target 'Hollywood' and prediction 'movies' are associated with negative sample 'concerts'. This confirms our intuition about the functionality of

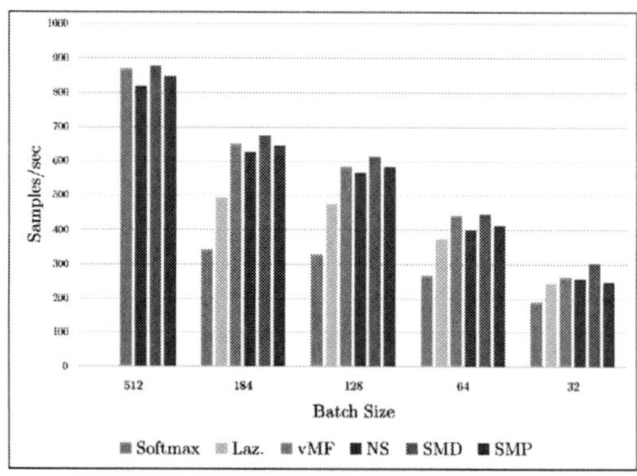

Figure 2: **Speed comparisons.** We compare the number of training instances that can processed per second for each loss formulation. Syn-margin is found to be faster than other margin-based methods, and comparable in speed to vMF.

	vMF	Laz	Random	SMD	SMP
Correct prediction: similarity to nearest neighbour	**0.96**	0.87	0.88	0.91	0.88
Wrong prediction: similarity to nearest neighbour	**0.91**	0.80	0.83	0.88	0.86
Wrong prediction: similarity to target embedding	0.39	0.28	0.21	0.41	**0.42**
Accuracy (%)	23.55	23.18	23.39	23.89	**24**
Accuracy @2 (%)	28.91	28.04	28.28	29.59	**29.89**
Accuracy @5 (%)	32.23	31.45	31.16	32.96	**33.22**
Accuracy @10 (%)	34.77	33.85	33.42	35.49	**35.6**

Table 2: **Error margins and accuracies.** The average similarity of predicted embeddings to their nearest neighbours is lower in SMP/SMD-trained models than in vMF-trained models. Among predicted embeddings whose nearest neighbours are not the targets, similarity to the targets increases when we switch from vMF to syn-margin loss. This is potentially linked to the increase in accuracies @2, 5 and 10 that results from the switch to syn-margin loss.

margin-based losses in general and syn-margin in particular.

We briefly analyze the properties of embeddings predicted by vMF and SMP Fr→En systems. Among incorrect predictions (cases in which the pretrained embedding closest to $\hat{\mathbf{u}}$ is not $\mathbf{u}$), the average cosine similarity between predicted embeddings and their nearest pretrained embeddings falls from vMF to SMP (0.91 to 0.86), while that between the predicted and target embeddings rises (0.39 to 0.42). This is accompanied by increases in accuracy @2, @5 and @10 (Table 2).

6 Related Work

Pretrained embeddings trained in an unsupervised manner (Mikolov et al., 2013a) are used as input and intermediate representations of data for natural language processing tasks such as part-of-speech tagging and named entity recognition (Ma and Hovy, 2016), sentiment analysis (Tang et al., 2016) and dependency parsing (He et al., 2018).

We build on (Kumar and Tsvetkov, 2019), one of the first instances of using pretrained embeddings as model *outputs* for complex sequence-generation tasks. Closely related work on embedding prediction includes zero-shot learning for word translation (Nakashole, 2018; Conneau et al., 2018) and image labeling (Lazaridou et al., 2015), as well as rare word prediction (Pinter et al., 2018) and classification (Card et al., 2019).

Margin-based losses are commonly used to train neural networks that predict dense vectors for classification tasks, and have long been used in computer vision. Standard formulations include contrastive (Hadsell et al., 2006) and triplet (Schroff et al., 2015) losses; triplet loss is identical to the max-margin framework we use. Other closely related approaches are the imposition of an angular margin constraint and the minimization of distance to the farthest intra-class example coupled with maximization of distance to the nearest inter-class example (Liu et al., 2016; Deng et al., 2017). In contrast to syn-margin, many of these losses pertain to *trainable* target embedding spaces.

The triplet loss has also been used in various NLP applications (Collobert et al., 2011). Techniques used to pick negative samples include perturbing training data (Smith and Eisner, 2005), sampling according to word frequency (Mikolov et al., 2013b), sampling until a non-zero loss is obtained (Weston et al., 2011) and searching for the negative sample that gives the largest (Rao et al., 2016) or most informative (Lazaridou et al., 2015) loss. These techniques also correspond to trainable target embedding spaces, and are all equally or less efficient than syn-margin.

7 Conclusion

We explore the use of margin-based loss functions to train continuous-output neural models, providing a geometric analysis of their functionality in this framework. Through this analysis, we develop a principled method to synthesize negative samples for margin-based losses, efficiently and on the fly. We argue that these negative samples are more consistent and interpretable than those picked using stochastic or heuristic techniques. Experiments on neural machine translation show that the proposed syn-margin loss improves over vMF and is either comparable or preferable to other margin-based losses. The analysis and loss function we propose are more generally applicable to neural models whose outputs lie in pretrained embedding spaces.

Acknowledgments

We gratefully acknowledge Anjalie Field, Aditi Chaudhury, Elizabeth Salesky, Shruti Rijhwani and our anonymous reviewers for the helpful feedback and discussions. This material is based upon work supported by NSF grant IIS1812327 and an Amazon MLRA award.

References

Dzmitry Bahdanau, Kyunghyun Cho, and Yoshua Bengio. 2015. Neural machine translation by jointly learning to align and translate. In *Proc. ICLR*.

Piotr Bojanowski, Edouard Grave, Armand Joulin, and Tomas Mikolov. 2017. Enriching word vectors with subword information. *TACL*.

Hervé Bredin. 2017. Tristounet: Triplet loss for speaker turn embedding. In *Proc. ICASSP*.

Dallas Card, Michael Zhang, and Noah A. Smith. 2019. Deep weighted averaging classifiers. In *Proc. FAT**.

Mauro Cettolo, Jan Niehues, Sebastian Stüker, Luisa Bentivogli, Roldano Cattoni, and Marcello Federico. 2015. The IWSLT 2015 evaluation campaign. In *Proc. IWSLT*.

Ronan Collobert, Jason Weston, Léon Bottou, Michael Karlen, Koray Kavukcuoglu, and Pavel Kuksa. 2011. Natural language processing (almost) from scratch. *JMLR*.

Alexis Conneau, Guillaume Lample, Marc'Aurelio Ranzato, Ludovic Denoyer, and Hervé Jégou. 2018. Word translation without parallel data. In *Proc. ICLR*.

Jiankang Deng, Yuxiang Zhou, and Stefanos Zafeiriou. 2017. Marginal loss for deep face recognition. In *Proc. CVPR, Faces in-the-wild Workshop/Challenge*.

Raia Hadsell, Sumit Chopra, and Yann LeCun. 2006. Dimensionality reduction by learning an invariant mapping. In *Proc. CVPR*.

Junxian He, Graham Neubig, and Taylor Berg-Kirkpatrick. 2018. Unsupervised learning of syntactic structure with invertible neural projections. In *Proc. EMNLP*.

Yoon Kim, Yacine Jernite, David Sontag, and Alexander M Rush. 2016. Character-aware neural language models. In *Proc. AAAI*.

Diederik P Kingma and Jimmy Ba. 2015. Adam: A method for stochastic optimization. In *Proc. ICLR*.

Sachin Kumar and Yulia Tsvetkov. 2019. Von Mises-Fisher loss for training sequence to sequence models with continuous outputs. In *Proc. ICLR*.

Angeliki Lazaridou, Georgiana Dinu, and Marco Baroni. 2015. Hubness and pollution: Delving into cross-space mapping for zero-shot learning. In *Proc. ACL*.

Wang Ling, Tiago Luís, Luís Marujo, Ramón Fernandez Astudillo, Silvio Amir, Chris Dyer, Alan W Black, and Isabel Trancoso. 2015. Finding function in form: Compositional character models for open vocabulary word representation. In *Proc. EMNLP*.

Weiyang Liu, Yandong Wen, Zhiding Yu, and Meng Yang. 2016. Large-margin softmax loss for convolutional neural networks. In *Proc. ICML*.

Minh-Thang Luong, Hieu Pham, and Christopher D. Manning. 2015. Effective approaches to attention-based neural machine translation. In *Proc. EMNLP*.

Xuezhe Ma and Eduard Hovy. 2016. End-to-end sequence labeling via bi-directional LSTM-CNNS-CRF. In *Proc. ACL*.

Tomas Mikolov, Kai Chen, Greg Corrado, and Jeffrey Dean. 2013a. Efficient estimation of word representations in vector space. In *ICLR Workshop*.

Tomas Mikolov, Ilya Sutskever, Kai Chen, Greg S Corrado, and Jeff Dean. 2013b. Distributed representations of words and phrases and their compositionality. In *Proc. NeurIPS*.

Ndapa Nakashole. 2018. Norma: Neighborhood sensitive maps for multilingual word embeddings. In *Proc. EMNLP*.

Kishore Papineni, Salim Roukos, Todd Ward, and Wei-Jing Zhu. 2002. BLEU: A method for automatic evaluation of machine translation. In *Proc. ACL*.

Yuval Pinter, Robert Guthrie, and Jacob Eisenstein. 2018. Mimicking word embeddings using subword RNNs. In *Proc. ACL*.

Jinfeng Rao, Hua He, and Jimmy Lin. 2016. Noise-contrastive estimation for answer selection with deep neural networks. In *Proc. CIKM*.

Florian Schroff, Dmitry Kalenichenko, and James Philbin. 2015. Facenet: A unified embedding for face recognition and clustering. In *Proc. CVPR*.

Rico Sennrich, Barry Haddow, and Alexandra Birch. 2016. Neural machine translation of rare words with subword units. In *Proc. ACL*.

Noah A Smith and Jason Eisner. 2005. Contrastive estimation: Training log-linear models on unlabeled data. In *Proc. ACL*.

Ilya Sutskever, Oriol Vinyals, and Quoc V Le. 2014. Sequence to sequence learning with neural networks. In *Proc. NIPS*.

Duyu Tang, Furu Wei, Bing Qin, Nan Yang, Ting Liu, and Ming Zhou. 2016. Sentiment embeddings with applications to sentiment analysis. *IEEE Transactions on Knowledge and Data Engineering*

Jason Weston, Samy Bengio, and Nicolas Usunier.
2011. Wsabie: Scaling up to large vocabulary image annotation. In *Proc. IJCAI*.

Ledell Yu Wu, Adam Fisch, Sumit Chopra, Keith
Adams, Antoine Bordes, and Jason Weston. 2018.
Starspace: Embed all the things! In *Proc. AAAI*.

Mixed Multi-Head Self-Attention for Neural Machine Translation

Hongyi Cui[1], Shohei Iida[1], Po-Hsuan Hung[1], Takehito Utsuro[1], Masaaki Nagata[2]

[1]Graduate School of Systems and Information Engineering, University of Tsukuba, Japan
[2]NTT Communication Science Laboratories, NTT Corporation, Japan

Abstract

Recently, the Transformer becomes a state-of-the-art architecture in the filed of neural machine translation (NMT). A key point of its high-performance is the multi-head self-attention which is supposed to allow the model to independently attend to information from different representation subspaces. However, there is no explicit mechanism to ensure that different attention heads indeed capture different features, and in practice, redundancy has occurred in multiple heads. In this paper, we argue that using the same global attention in multiple heads limits multi-head self-attention's capacity for learning distinct features. In order to improve the expressiveness of multi-head self-attention, we propose a novel Mixed Multi-Head Self-Attention (MMA) which models not only global and local attention but also forward and backward attention in different attention heads. This enables the model to learn distinct representations explicitly among multiple heads. In our experiments on both WAT17 English-Japanese as well as IWSLT14 German-English translation task, we show that, without increasing the number of parameters, our models yield consistent and significant improvements (0.9 BLEU scores on average) over the strong Transformer baseline. [1]

1 Introduction

Neural machine translation (NMT) has made promising progress in recent years with different architectures, ranging from recurrent neural networks (Sutskever et al., 2014; Cho et al., 2014; Bahdanau et al., 2015; Luong et al., 2015), convolutional networks (Gehring et al., 2017) and most recently, self-attention networks (Transformer) (Vaswani et al., 2017).

Among the different architectures, the Transformer (Vaswani et al., 2017) has recently attracted most attention in neural machine translation, due to its high parallelization in computation and improvements in quality. A key point of its high-performance is the multi-head self-attention which allows the model to jointly attend to information from different representation subspaces at different positions. There is a huge gap (around 1 BLEU score) between the performance of the Transformer with only one head and eight heads (Vaswani et al., 2017; Chen et al., 2018).

However, all encoder self-attention heads fully take global information into account, there is no explicit mechanism to ensure that different attention heads indeed capture different features (Li et al., 2018). Concerning the results presented by some latest researches, the majority of the encoder self-attention heads, can even be pruned away without substantially hurting model's performance (Voita et al., 2019; Michel et al., 2019). Moreover, the ability of multi-head self-attention, in which lacking capacity to capture local information (Luong et al., 2015; Yang et al., 2018; Wu et al., 2019) and sequential information (Shaw et al., 2018; Dehghani et al., 2019), has recently come into question (Tang et al., 2018).

Motivated by above findings, we attribute the redundancy arising in encoder self-attention heads to the using of same global self-attention among all attention heads. Additionally, it is because of the redundancy, multi-head self-attention is unable to leverage its full capacity for learning distinct features in different heads. In response, in this paper, we propose a novel Mixed Multi-Head Self-Attention (MMA) which can capture distinct features in different heads explicitly by different attention function. Concretely, MMA is composed of four attention functions: Global Atten-

---

[1]Our code is available at:
`https://github.com/yokusama/transformer-mma`

Proceedings of the 3rd Workshop on Neural Generation and Translation (WNGT 2019), pages 206–214
Hong Kong, China, November 4, 2019. ©2019 Association for Computational Linguistics
www.aclweb.org/anthology/D19-56%2d

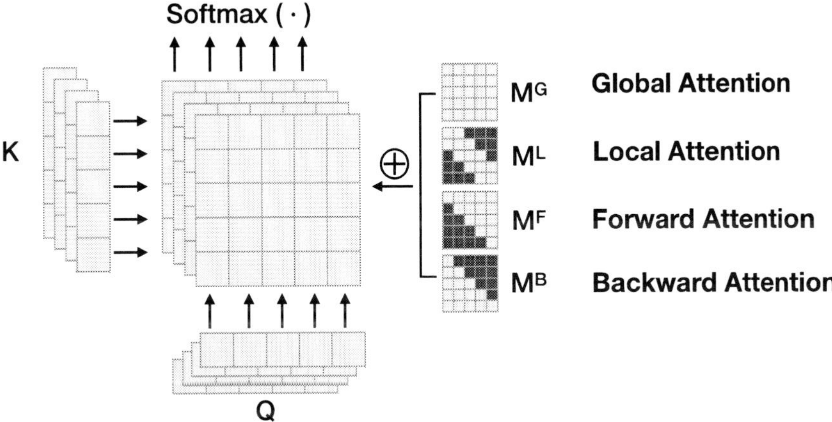

Figure 1: The architecture of Transformer with Mixed Multi-Head Self-Attention

tion which models dependency of arbitrary words directly. Local Attention, where attention scope is restricted for exploring local information. Forward and Backward Attention which attends to words from the future and from the past respectively, serving as a function to model sequence order. MMA enables the model to learn distinct representations explicitly in different heads and improves the expressive capacity of multi-head self-attention. Besides, our method is achieved simply by adding hard masks before calculating attention weights, the rest is the same as the original Transformer. Hence our method does not introduce additional parameters and does not affect the training efficiency.

The primary contributions of this work can be summarized as follows:

- We propose a novel Mixed Multi-Head Self-Attention (MMA) that extracts different aspects of features in different attention heads.

- Experimental results on two language pairs demonstrate that the proposed model consistently outperforms the vanilla Transformer in BLEU scores. Qualitative analysis shows our MMA can make better use of word order information and the improvement in translating relatively long sentence is especially significant.

2 Transformer Architecture

In this section, we briefly describe the Transformer architecture (Vaswani et al., 2017) which includes an encoder and a decoder. The Transformer aims to model a source sentence x to a target sentence y by minimizing the negative log likelihood of the target words.

The encoder consists of N identical layers, each layers has two sublayers with residual connection (He et al., 2016). The first is a multi-head self-attention layer and the second is a position wise fully connected feed-forward network layer:

$$\tilde{H}^l = \text{LN}(H^{l-1} + \text{MA}(Q^{l-1}, K^{l-1}, V^{l-1})) \quad (1)$$

$$H^l = \text{LN}(\tilde{H}^l + \text{FFN}(\tilde{H}^l)) \quad (2)$$

where Q^{l-1}, K^{l-1}, V^{l-1} come from the output of the previous encoder layer H^{l-1}. $\text{LN}(\cdot)$ and $\text{FFN}(\cdot)$ represent layer normalization (Ba et al., 2016) and feed-forward networks.

The multi-head attention $\text{MA}(\cdot)$ linearly project the queries, keys and values h times for different representation of Q, K, V, and computes scaled dot-product attention (Luong et al., 2015) $\text{ATT}(\cdot)$ for each representation. Then these are concatenated and once again projected, the final attentional context is calculated as follows:

$$head_h = \text{ATT}(QW_h^Q, KW_h^K, VW_h^V) \quad (3)$$

$$\text{MA} = \text{Concat}(head_h)W^O \quad (4)$$

where W_h^Q, W_h^K and W_h^V are parameter matrices to transform hidden state into different representation subspaces and W^O is output projection.

ATT($\cdot$) is computed by:

$$e_i = \frac{Q_i K^\top}{\sqrt{d}} \tag{5}$$

$$\mathrm{ATT}(Q, K, V) = \mathrm{Softmax}(e_i)V \tag{6}$$

where e_i is the i-th energy and d is the dimension of hidden state.

The decoder is also composed of N identical layers and it contains a third sublayer, which performs attention over the output of the encoder between the self-attention sublayer and feed-forward network sublayer.

3 Proposed Architecture

Our proposed approach is mainly motivated by the fact that redundancy has occurred in multi-heads (Voita et al., 2019; Michel et al., 2019), which limits the capacity of multi-head self-attention. As each self-attention layer has a same global receptive field, this can not guarantee that every head has learned useful features in different subspaces through the same attention function.

To tackle the problem mentioned above, besides global information, we also model local and sequential information for multi-head self-attention by applying local attention, forward attention and backward attention respectively. We refer to it as Mixed Multi-head Self-Attention (MMA), as shown in Figure 1. This is achieved by adding hard mask to each attention head. In this way, Eq.(3) is redefined as:

$$\mathrm{ATT}(Q, K, V) = \mathrm{Softmax}(e_i + M_i)V \tag{7}$$

Since attention weights are calculated by the softmax function, for i-th word, if a mask $M_{i,j} = -\infty$ is added to the j-th position, it means that $Softmax(e_{i,j} + M_{i,j}) = 0$ and there is no attention of Q_i to K_j. On the contrary, if a mask $M_{i,j} = 0$, it means no change in attention function and Q_i attends to and captures relevant information from K_j.

3.1 Global and Local Attention

Global attention and local attention differ in terms of whether the attention is placed on all positions or only a few positions. Global attention is the original attention function in Transformer (Vaswani et al., 2017), and it has a global receptive field which is used to connect with arbitrary words directly. Under our framework, we define the hard mask for global attention as follows:

$$M_{i,j}^G = 0 \tag{8}$$

But global attention may be less powerful and can potentially render it impractical for longer sequences (Luong et al., 2015). On the other hand, self-attention can be enhanced by local attention which focuses more on restricted scope rather than the entire context (Wu et al., 2019; Xu et al., 2019). Based on the above findings, we also define a local attention which simply employs a hard mask to restrict the attention scope by:

$$M_{i,j}^L = \begin{cases} 0, & i - w \le j \le i + w \\ -\infty, & otherwise \end{cases} \tag{9}$$

where w is the attention scope which means, for a given i-th word, it can only attends to the set of words within the window size $[i - w, i + w]$.

We aim to combine the strengths both of global attention and local attention. Towards this goal, we apply global attention and local attention to two distinct attention heads.

3.2 Forward and Backward Attention

As for RNN-based NMT, bidirectional recurrent encoder (Schuster and Paliwal, 1997) is the most commonly used encoder (Bahdanau et al., 2015). It consists of forward and backward recurrent encoding that receive information from both past and future words. However, the Transformer foregoes recurrence and completely relies on predefined position embedding to represent position information. Therefore, it has considerable difficulties in considering relative word order (Shaw et al., 2018).

In order to enhance the ability of position-awareness in self-attention, we present an straightforward way of modeling sequentiality in the self-attention by a forward attention which only attends to words from the future, and a backward attention which inversely only attends to words from the past. The masks in forward and backward attention can be formally defined as:

$$M_{i,j}^F = \begin{cases} 0, & i \le j \\ -\infty, & otherwise \end{cases} \tag{10}$$

$$M_{i,j}^B = \begin{cases} 0, & i \ge j \\ -\infty, & otherwise \end{cases} \tag{11}$$

| | En-Ja | | | Ja-En | | |
Model	#Params	BLEU	Δ	#Params	BLEU	Δ
Transformer	71M	33.58	–	71M	23.24	–
Transformer MMA	+ 0	34.39††	+ 0.81	+ 0	24.16††	+ 0.92

Table 1: Evaluation results on WAT17 English⇔Japanese translation task. #Params denotes the number of parameters and Δ denotes relative improvement over the Transformer baseline. † † ($p < 0.01$) indicates statistical significance different from the Transformer baseline.

Model	De-En
Variational Attention (Deng et al., 2018)	33.30
Pervasive Attention (Elbayad et al., 2018)	34.18
Multi-Hop Attention (Iida et al., 2019)	35.13
Dynamic Convolution (Wu et al., 2019)	35.20
RNMT Fine-tuned (Sennrich and Zhang, 2019)	35.27
Transformer (Vaswani et al., 2017)	34.46
Transformer MMA	35.41††

Table 2: Evaluation results on IWSLT14 De-En. Δ denotes relative improvement over the Transformer baseline. † † ($p < 0.01$) indicates statistical significance different from the Transformer baseline.

With the help of forward and backward attention, we assume that the Transformer can can make better use of word order information.

3.3 Mixed Multi-Head Self-Attention

With different heads applied different attention function and different receptive field, the model is able to learn different aspects of features. To fully utilize the different features, we concatenate all mixed attention heads as in Eq.(4):

$$\mathrm{MA} = \mathrm{Concat}(head_G, head_L, head_F, head_B)W^O$$

where $head_G$, $head_L$, $head_F$, $head_B$ represent head with global attention, local attention, forward attention and backward attention respectively.

Our method only adds hard masks before softmax function, the rest is the same as the original model. Hence our method brings increase the parameters of the Transformer and does not affect the training efficiency.

4 Experiments

4.1 Datasets

To test the proposed approach, we perform experiments on WAT17 English-Japanese and IWSLT14 German-English translation task with different amounts of training data.

WAT17 English-Japanese: We use the data from WAT17 English-Japanese translation task which created from ASPEC (Nakazawa et al., 2017).

Training, validation and test sets comprise 2M, 1.8K, 1.8K sentence pairs respectively. We adopt the official 16K vocabularies preprocessed by sentencepiece.[2]

IWSLT14 German-English: We use the TED data from the IWSLT14 German-English shared translation task (Cettolo et al., 2014) which contains 160K training sentences and 7K validation sentences randomly sampled from the training data. We test on the concatenation of tst2010, tst2011, tst2012, tst2013 and dev2010. For this benchmark, data is lowercased and tokenized with byte pair encoding (BPE) (Sennrich et al., 2016).

4.2 Setup

Our implementation is built upon open-source toolkit fairseq[3] (Ott et al., 2019). For WAT17 dataset and IWSLT14 dataset, we use the configurations of the Transformer *base* and *small* model respectively. Both of them consist of a 6-layer encoder and 6-layer decoder, the size of hidden state and word embedding are set to 512. The dimensionality of inner feed-forward layer is 2048 for *base* and 1024 for *small* model. The dropout probability is 0.1 and 0.3 for *base* and *small* model. Models are optimized with Adam (Kingma and Ba, 2014). We use the same warmup and decay strategy for learning rate as Vaswani et al. (2017) with 4000 warmup steps.

---

[2] https://github.com/google/sentencepiece
[3] https://github.com/pytorch/fairseq

Model	De-En	Δ	Ja-En	Δ
Transformer	34.46	–	23.24	–
- Position Embedding	16.55	–	12.83	–
Transformer MMA	35.41	+ 0.95	24.16	+ 0.92
- Position Embedding	34.66	+ 18.11	23.80	+10.97

Table 3: Results on IWSLT14 De-En and WAT17 Ja-En for effectiveness of learning word order. "- Position Embedding" indicates removing positional embedding from Transformer encoder or Transformer MMA encoder. Δ denotes relative improvement over the counterpart of the Transformer baseline.

During training, we employ label smoothing of value 0.1 (Szegedy et al., 2016). All models are trained on a single NVIDIA RTX2080Ti with a batch size of around 4096 tokens. The *base* model are trained for 20 epochs, the *small* model are trained for 45 epochs.

The number of heads are 8 for *base* model and 4 for *small* model. We replace multi-head self-attention in the encoder layers by our mixed multi-head self-attention. For a fair comparison, we apply each attention function twice in *base* model. By doing this, our Transformer MMA have the same number of parameters as the original Transformer.

For evaluation, we use a beam size of 5 for beam search, translation quality is reported via BLEU (Papineni et al., 2002) and statistical significance test is conducted by paired bootstrap resampling method (Koehn, 2004).

4.3 Results

In Table 1 and Table 2, we present the experiment results measured by BLEU on WAT17 and IWSLT14.

On WAT17 English⇒Japanese (En-Ja) and Japanese⇒English (Ja-En) translation task, without increasing the number of parameters, our Transformer MMA outperforms the corresponding baseline 0.81 BLEU score on En-Ja and 0.92 BLEU score on En-Ja.

On IWSLT14 German⇒English (De-En) translation task, our model achieves 35.41 in terms of BLEU score, with 0.95 improvement over the strong Transformer baseline. In order to compare with existing models, we list out some latest and related work and our model also achieves considerable improvements over these results.

Overall, our evaluation results show the introduction of MMA consistently improves the translation quality over the vanilla Transformer, and the proposed approach is stable across different languages pairs.

5 Analysis

5.1 Effectiveness of MMA

Neural machine translation must consider the correlated ordering of words, where order has a lot of influence on the meaning of a sentence (Khayrallah and Koehn, 2018). In vanilla Transformer, the position embedding is a deterministic function of position and it allows the model to be aware of the order of the sequence (Yang et al., 2019). As shown in Table 3, Transformer without position embedding fails on translation task, resulting in a decrease of 17.91 BLEU score. With the help of proposed MMA, the performance is only reduced by 0.75 BLEU score without position embedding, and 18.11 points higher than the Transformer baseline. The same result holds true for a distant language pair Japanese-English where word oder is completely different. When removing position embedding, the Transformer baseline drops to 12.83 BLEU score. However, our model still achieves 23.80 in terms of BLEU score, with 10.97 points improvement over the Transformer counterpart.

From the cognitive perspective, due to the character of local attention which only focuses on restricted scope, the local attention head's dependence on word order information is reduced. In the forward and backward head, directional information is explicitly learned by our forward and backward attention. The above experimental results confirm our hypothesis that, other than global information, Transformer MMA takes local and sequential information into account when performing self-attention function, revealing its effectiveness on utilizing word order information.

5.2 Effect on Sentence Length

Following Bahdanau et al. (2015), we group source sentences of similar lengths to evaluate the performance of the proposed Transformer MMA and vanilla Transformer. We divide our test set

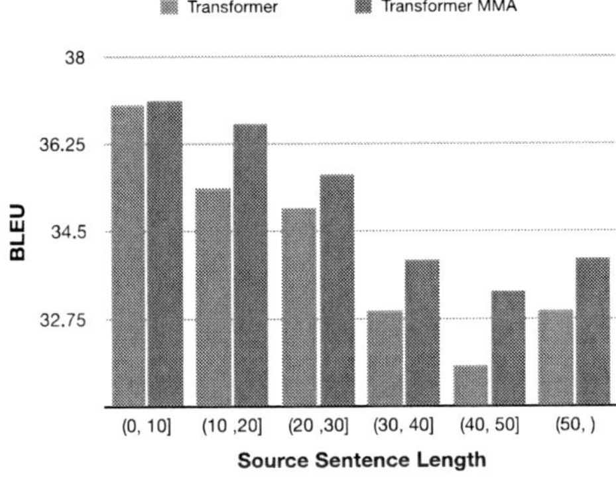

Figure 2: Translation results on test sets relative to source sentence length for IWSLT14 De-En.

Model	De-En	Δ
Transformer	34.46	–
+ Local Attention	35.05	+ 0.59
+ Forward Attention	34.83	+ 0.37
+ Backward Attention	35.13	+ 0.67
+ MMA	**35.41**	**+ 0.95**

Table 4: Results of ablation experiments on IWSLT14 De-En. Δ denotes relative improvement over baseline.

Model	De-En	Δ
Transformer	34.46	–
+ MMA (w = 1)	**35.41**	**+0.95**
+ MMA (w = 2)	35.31	+ 0.85
+ MMA (w = 3)	35.35	+ 0.89
+ MMA (w = 4)	35.22	+ 0.76

Table 5: Results of different attention scope on IWSLT14 De-En. Δ denotes relative improvement over baseline.

into six disjoint groups shown in Figure 2. The numbers on the X-axis represent source sentences that are not longer than the corresponding length, e.g., "(0, 10]" indicates that the length of source sentences is between 1 and 10.

In all length intervals, Transformer MMA consistently outperforms the Transformer baseline. Specifically, as the length of the source sentence increases, so does the increase in the improvement brought by MMA. One explanation is that when the length of the sentence is very short, four different attention functions are similar to each other. But as the length of the sentence increases, more distinct characteristics can be learned and the performance gap is becoming larger.

Moreover, encoding long sentences usually requires more long-range dependency. Concerning the ability to connect with distant words directly, global self-attention was speculated that it is better suited to capture long-range dependency. However, as noted in (Tang et al., 2018), aforesaid hypothesis is not empirically correct and self-attention does have trouble handling long sentences. In case of our Transformer MMA, with the exist of other attention functions served as auxiliary feature extractors, we think that the Transformer has more capacity for modeling longer sentences.

5.3 Ablation Study

For ablation study, the primary question is whether the Transformer benefits from the integration of different attention equally. To do evaluate the impact of various attention functions, we keep global self-attention head unchanged, and next we replace other heads with different attention function.

The results are listed in Table 4. Compared with the Transformer baseline, all integration methods that incorporate other attention function improve the performance of translation, from 0.37 to 0.67 BLEU score. And we can see that Transformer MMA performs best across all variants with the improvement of 0.95 BLEU score.

Furthermore, we investigate the effect of attention scope in our Transformer MMA, as illustrated in Table 5. As the number of attention scope progressively increases, there is no absolute trend in performance. However it is worth noting that when the attention scope is relatively small, the overall performance is better. Specifically, when the size of attention scope is 1, our Transformer MMA achieves the best result. One possible reason is that, in the case where there are already global features captured by global attention, the smaller the attention scope, the more local features can be learned by local attention.

5.4 Attention Visualization

To further explore the behavior of our Transformer MMA, we observe the distribution of encoder attention weights in our models and show an example of Japanese sentence as plotted in Figure 3.

The first discovery is that we find the word overlooks itself on the first layer in the global attention head. This contrasts with the results from Raganato and Tiedemann (2018). They find that, on the first layer of original Transformer, more en-

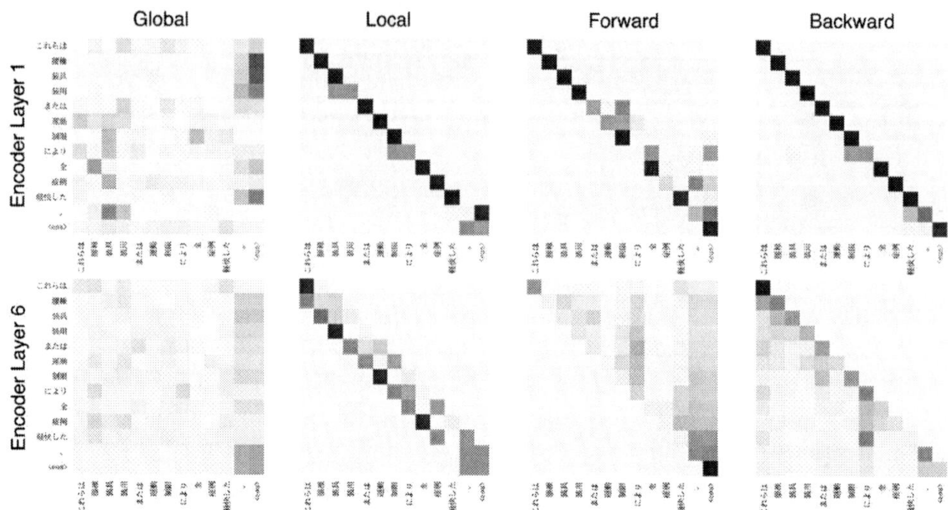

Figure 3: Visualization of the attention weights of Japanese sentence "これらは 腰椎 装具 装用 または 運動 制限 により 全 症例 軽快した 。" (meaning "These persons were improved in all cases by wearing lumbar braces or limiting exercises"). The deeper blue color refers to larger attention weights.

coder self-attention heads focus on the word itself. This change is in line with our assumption that, due to the existence of other attention heads, global attention head can focus more on capturing global information.

The second discovery is that, on the upper layers, forward and backward attention heads move the attention more on distant words. This suggests forward and backward attention is able to serve as a complement to capturing long-range dependency.

6 Related Work

In the field of neural machine translation, the two most used attention mechanisms are additive attention (Bahdanau et al., 2015) and dot attention (Luong et al., 2015). Based on the latter, Vaswani et al. (2017) proposed a multi-head self-attention, that is not only highly parallelizable but also with better performance.

However, self-attention, which employs neither recurrence nor convolution, has great difficulty in incorporating position information (Vaswani et al., 2017). To tackle this problem, Shaw et al. (2018) presented an extension that can be used to incorporate relative position information for sequence. And Shen et al. (2018) tried to encode the temporal order and introduced a directional self-attention which only composes of directional order. On the other hand, although

with a global receptive field, the ability of self-attention recently came into question (Tang et al., 2018). And modeling localness, either restricting context sizes (Yang et al., 2018; Wu et al., 2019; Child et al., 2019) or balancing the contribution of local and global information (Xu et al., 2019), has been shown to be able to improve the expressiveness of self-attention. In contrast to these studies, we aim to improve the self-attention in a systematic and multifaceted perspective, rather than just paying attention to one specific characteristic.

Compared to a conventional NMT model with only a single head, multi-head is assumed to have a stronger ability to extract different features in different subspaces. However, there are no explicit mechanism that make them distinct (Voita et al., 2019; Michel et al., 2019). Li et al. (2018) had shown that using a disagreement regularization to encourage different attention heads to have different behaviors can improve the performance of multi-head attention. Iida et al. (2019) proposed a multi-hop attention where the second-hop serves as a head gate function to normalize the attentional context of each head. Not only limited in the field of neural machine translation, Strubell et al. (2018) combined multi-head self-attention with multi-task learning, this led to a promising result for semantic role labeling. Similar to the above studies, we also attempt to model diversity for multi-head attention. In this work, we apply different attention function to capture different aspects of features in multiple heads directly, which is more intuitive and explicit.

7 Conclusion

In this work, we improve the self-attention networks by modeling multi-head attention to learn different aspects of feature through different attention function. Experimental results on WAT17 English-Japanese and IWSLT14 German-English translation tasks demonstrate that our proposed model outperforms the Transformer baseline as well as some latest and related models. Our analysis further shows our Transformer MMA can make better use of word order information and the improvement in translating longer sentences is especially significant. Moreover, we perform ablation study to compare different architectures. To explore the behavior of our proposed model, we visualize the attention distribution and confirm the diversity among multiple heads in MMA.

In the future, we plan to apply our method on other sequence to sequence learning tasks, such as text summarization.

References

Jimmy Ba, Jamie Ryan Kiros, and Geoffrey E. Hinton. 2016. Layer normalization. *ArXiv*.

Dzmitry Bahdanau, Kyunghyun Cho, and Yoshua Bengio. 2015. Neural machine translation by jointly learning to align and translate. In *ICLR*.

Mauro Cettolo, Jan Niehues, Sebastian Stüker, Luisa Bentivogli, and Marcello Federico. 2014. Report on the 11th IWSLT evaluation campaign, IWSLT 2014. In *IWSLT*.

Mia Xu Chen, Orhan Firat, Ankur Bapna, Melvin Johnson, Wolfgang Macherey, George Foster, Llion Jones, Mike Schuster, Noam Shazeer, Niki Parmar, Ashish Vaswani, Jakob Uszkoreit, Lukasz Kaiser, Zhifeng Chen, Yonghui Wu, and Macduff Hughes. 2018. The best of both worlds: Combining recent advances in neural machine translation. In *ACL*, pages 76–86.

Rewon Child, Scott Gray, Alec Radford, and Ilya Sutskever. 2019. Generating long sequences with sparse transformers. *ArXiv*.

Kyunghyun Cho, Bart van Merrienboer, Caglar Gulcehre, Dzmitry Bahdanau, Fethi Bougares, Holger Schwenk, and Yoshua Bengio. 2014. Learning phrase representations using rnn encoder–decoder for statistical machine translation. In *EMNLP*, pages 1724–1734.

Mostafa Dehghani, Stephan Gouws, Oriol Vinyals, Jakob Uszkoreit, and Lukasz Kaiser. 2019. Universal transformers.

Yuntian Deng, Yoon Kim, Justin Chiu, Demi Guo, and Alexander Rush. 2018. Latent alignment and variational attention. In *NIPS*.

Maha Elbayad, Laurent Besacier, and Jakob Verbeek. 2018. Pervasive attention: 2D convolutional neural networks for sequence-to-sequence prediction. In *CoNLL*, pages 97–107.

Jonas Gehring, Michael Auli, David Grangier, Denis Yarats, and Yann N Dauphin. 2017. Convolutional Sequence to Sequence Learning. In *ICML*.

Kaiming He, Xiangyu Zhang, Shaoqing Ren, and Jian Sun. 2016. Deep residual learning for image recognition. *CVPR*.

Shohei Iida, Ryuichiro Kimura, Hongyi Cui, Po-Hsuan Hung, Takehito Utsuro, and Masaaki Nagata. 2019. Attention over heads: A multi-hop attention for neural machine translation. In *ACL: Student Research Workshop*, pages 217–222.

Huda Khayrallah and Philipp Koehn. 2018. On the impact of various types of noise on neural machine translation. In *ACL: Workshop on Neural Machine Translation and Generation*, pages 74–83.

Diederik P. Kingma and Jimmy Ba. 2014. Adam: A method for stochastic optimization. In *ICLR*.

Philipp Koehn. 2004. Statistical significance tests for machine translation evaluation. In *EMNLP*, pages 388–395.

Jian Li, Zhaopeng Tu, Baosong Yang, Michael R. Lyu, and Tong Zhang. 2018. Multi-head attention with disagreement regularization. In *EMNLP*, pages 2897–2903.

Thang Luong, Hieu Pham, and Christopher D. Manning. 2015. Effective approaches to attention-based neural machine translation. In *EMNLP*, pages 1412–1421.

Paul Michel, Omer Levy, and Graham Neubig. 2019. Are sixteen heads really better than one? *ArXiv*.

Toshiaki Nakazawa, Shohei Higashiyama, Chenchen Ding, Hideya Mino, Isao Goto, Hideto Kazawa, Yusuke Oda, Graham Neubig, and Sadao Kurohashi. 2017. Overview of the 4th workshop on Asian translation. In *WAT*.

Myle Ott, Sergey Edunov, Alexei Baevski, Angela Fan, Sam Gross, Nathan Ng, David Grangier, and Michael Auli. 2019. fairseq: A fast, extensible toolkit for sequence modeling. In *NAACL*, pages 48–53.

Kishore Papineni, Salim Roukos, Todd Ward, and Wei-Jing Zhu. 2002. Bleu: a method for automatic evaluation of machine translation. In *ACL*, pages 311–318.

Alessandro Raganato and Jörg Tiedemann. 2018. An analysis of encoder representations in transformer-based machine translation. In *EMNLP Workshop BlackboxNLP: Analyzing and Interpreting Neural Networks for NLP*, pages 287–297.

Mike Schuster and Kuldip K Paliwal. 1997. Bidirectional recurrent neural networks. *IEEE Transactions on Signal Processing*.

Rico Sennrich, Barry Haddow, and Alexandra Birch. 2016. Neural machine translation of rare words with subword units. In *ACL*, pages 1715–1725.

Rico Sennrich and Biao Zhang. 2019. Revisiting low-resource neural machine translation: A case study. In *ACL*, pages 211–221.

Peter Shaw, Jakob Uszkoreit, and Ashish Vaswani. 2018. Self-attention with relative position representations. In *NAACL*, pages 464–468.

Tao Shen, Tianyi Zhou, Guodong Long, Jing Jiang, Shirui Pan, and Chengqi Zhang. 2018. Disan: Directional self-attention network for rnn/cnn-free language understanding. In *AAAI*.

Emma Strubell, Patrick Verga, Daniel Andor, David Weiss, and Andrew McCallum. 2018. Linguistically-informed self-attention for semantic role labeling. In *EMNLP*, pages 5027–5038.

Ilya Sutskever, Oriol Vinyals, and Quoc V. Le. 2014. Sequence to sequence learning with neural networks. In *NIPS*.

Christian Szegedy, Vincent Vanhoucke, Sergey Ioffe, Jonathon Shlens, and Zbigniew Wojna. 2016. Rethinking the inception architecture for computer vision. In *CVPR*.

Gongbo Tang, Mathias Müller, Annette Rios, and Rico Sennrich. 2018. Why self-attention? a targeted evaluation of neural machine translation architectures. In *EMNLP*, pages 4263–4272.

Ashish Vaswani, Noam Shazeer, Niki Parmar, Jakob Uszkoreit, Llion Jones, Aidan N Gomez, Ł ukasz Kaiser, and Illia Polosukhin. 2017. Attention is all you need. In *NIPS*.

Elena Voita, David Talbot, Fedor Moiseev, Rico Sennrich, and Ivan Titov. 2019. Analyzing multi-head self-attention: Specialized heads do the heavy lifting, the rest can be pruned. In *ACL*, pages 5797–5808.

Felix Wu, Angela Fan, Alexei Baevski, Yann Dauphin, and Michael Auli. 2019. Pay less attention with lightweight and dynamic convolutions. In *ICLR*.

Mingzhou Xu, Derek F. Wong, Baosong Yang, Yue Zhang, and Lidia S. Chao. 2019. Leveraging local and global patterns for self-attention networks. In *ACL*, pages 3069–3075.

Baosong Yang, Zhaopeng Tu, Derek F. Wong, Fandong Meng, Lidia S. Chao, and Tong Zhang. 2018. Modeling localness for self-attention networks. In *EMNLP*, pages 4449–4458.

Baosong Yang, Longyue Wang, Derek F. Wong, Lidia S. Chao, and Zhaopeng Tu. 2019. Assessing the ability of self-attention networks to learn word order. In *ACL*, pages 3635–3644.

Paraphrasing with Large Language Models

Sam Witteveen
Red Dragon AI
sam@reddragon.ai

Martin Andrews
Red Dragon AI
martin@reddragon.ai

Abstract

Recently, large language models such as GPT-2 have shown themselves to be extremely adept at text generation and have also been able to achieve high-quality results in many downstream NLP tasks such as text classification, sentiment analysis and question answering with the aid of fine-tuning. We present a useful technique for using a large language model to perform the task of paraphrasing on a variety of texts and subjects. Our approach is demonstrated to be capable of generating paraphrases not only at a sentence level but also for longer spans of text such as paragraphs without needing to break the text into smaller chunks.

1   Introduction

Paraphrase generation is an NLP task that has multiple uses in content creation, question answering, translation, and data augmentation. It is a task that has been attempted for many decades using statistical and rules-based approaches (McKeown, 1979; Meteer and Shaked, 1988).

We propose a system that generates paraphrased examples in an autoregressive fashion using a neural network, without the need for techniques such as top-k word selection or beam search.

We demonstrate that by using large language models we are able to produce not only paraphrases that are longer and of a higher quality than previous work, but can also paraphrase text beyond the individual sentence-level (i.e. full paragraphs at a time).

The large language models we use implement the encoder-decoder structure of the transformer architecture (Vaswani et al., 2017) which has been shown to learn different representations of language at each level of its encoding (Devlin et al., 2019). The power of language models like GPT-2 (Radford et al., 2019) and BERT allows them to

develop useful representations of language which can be used far beyond just generation of the next word (Rothe et al., 2019). In our experiments, we have observed that the models have representations of syntax and grammar, allowing them to be fine-tuned for the task of paraphrase generation.

2   Related Work

Paraphrase generation has attracted a number of different NLP approaches. These have included rule-based approaches (McKeown, 1979; Meteer and Shaked, 1988) and data-driven methods (Madnani and Dorr, 2010), with recently the most common approach being that the task is treated as a language translation task (Bannard and Callison-Burch, 2005; Barzilay and McKeown, 2001; Pang et al., 2003) - often performed using a bilingual corpus pivoting back and forth (Madnani and Dorr, 2010; Prakash et al., 2016; Mallinson et al., 2017). Other methods proposed include more recently the use of Deep Reinforcement Learning (Li et al., 2018) , supervised learning using sequence-to-sequence models (Gupta et al., 2018; Prakash et al., 2016) and unsupervised approaches (Bowman et al., 2016; Roy and Grangier, 2019).

3   Methodology

In this section, we define the task, present our implementation, describe our evaluation protocol and the paraphrase datasets used.

Paraphrase generation can be described as generating a phrase which is semantically as close as possible to the original while being rewritten in new words and phrases.

3.1   Large Language Model training

Training language models has become a popular way of creating models suited for Transfer Learning in the field of NLP. (Howard and Ruder, 2018;

		USE	ROUGE-L	BLEU
In:	A prisoner can asphyxiate himself in 90 seconds and, after eight minutes or so, he will be brain dead.			
Out:	In 90 seconds, a prisoner can asphyxiate himself and be brain dead after eight minutes or so.	0.9326	0.4706	0.4730
In:	The restaurant is a carved-off space up a couple of stairs to one side, dominated by faux bare-brick columns, faux-wood floors and an air of foetid despondency.			
Out:	It is a carved-off space, up a couple of flights of stairs, to the other side of the restaurant, dominated by fake bare-brick columns, fake wood floors and an air of foetid despondency.	0.8954	0.5000	0.5348
In:	I signed a bill that made the problem worse, and I want to admit it, he said.			
Out:	He signed a bill that made the problem worse and he wants to admit it.	0.8363	0.4667	0.5299
In:	It said the damage to the wing provided a pathway for hot gasses to penetrate the ship's thermal armor during Columbia's ill-fated reentry.			
Out:	The document says the damage to the wing provided a pathway for hot gases to penetrate Columbia's thermal armour during its fatal re-entry.	0.9190	0.4545	0.5445

Table 1: Examples of GPT-2 generated paraphrased sentences with scores for each pair

Peters et al., 2018; Radford et al., 2018; Dong et al., 2019). While these models are initially trained in a semi-supervised manner to predict the next word or words in a sequence, they can be fine-tuned and used for a variety of downstream NLP tasks such as text classification, sentiment analysis, tagging, and entity extraction.

More recently, large language models using transformer architectures are achieving state of the art results for many of these tasks while using less supervised data than previously needed.

One example of these large language models that has proven to be very good at text generation is GPT-2. It makes use of a transformer architecture and comes in various sizes up to 1.5 billion parameters. In these experiments, we have taken a pre-trained version of the GPT-2 model trained in a semi-supervised fashion on the WebText dataset (Radford et al., 2019) of over 8 million documents with 40 GB of text in total.

3.2 Fine-tuning for Task

We take the GPT-2 model and fine-tune it on a supervised dataset of pre-made paraphrase examples. These examples are fed into the model as original phrase / paraphrase pairs, separated by a specific identifying sequence (such as ">>>>").

This training is done for a small number of epochs to give the model just enough examples of what the task is asking from the model : The goal being to avoid overfitting the model on the new data, while giving it sufficient exposure to the task to enable it to learn the general pattern expected.

While we experimented with TPUs for the fine-tuning, in the end we were able to reproduce the same results on a single K-80 GPU with around 90 minutes of training.

Once the model is fine-tuned, we find that it can also produce similar paraphrase training examples if sampled from with no conditional input. To give an indication of training progress, these 'naive' paraphrases are sampled on a periodic basis during the training.

After fine-tuning on this dataset, we are then able to feed in any original phrase followed by the unique token and have the model generate paraphrases on demand.

3.3 Candidate Generation and Selection

After the model is trained, we then sample from the model using previously unseen sentences as conditional input. This conditional input allows us to generate multiple candidate sentences for the single original sentence.

While the quality of the paraphrases is somewhat variable, by generating multiple outputs and then scoring them, we can select just the best quality paraphrases based on a number of criteria that serve to filter our output down to a set of satisfactory results.

First, we obtain a similarity score between the generated paraphrase and the original sentence by using the Universal Sentence Encoder (USE) (Cer et al., 2018) to make a 512 dimensional sentence embedding for each output sentence and then compare them to the embedding of the original sentence via the cosine similarity measure.

As a second step, we measure the ROUGE-L (Lin, 2004) score of the candidate paraphrases against the original sentence and eliminate candidates with a ROUGE-L score of above 0.7 . This prevents candidates that are too close to the original sentence being chosen. After testing both cutoff scores for ROUGE-L and BLEU (Papineni et al., 2002), ROUGE-L has shown to be more useful at finding candidates that are more unique in comparison to the original sentence.

By choosing samples with sufficiently low ROUGE-L scores but as high a similarity as possible, we end up with an output that is semantically similar to the original phrase but has a unique word order when compared to the original phrase.

3.4 Datasets

We fine-tuned multiple versions of the model on several different datasets : 2 datasets of sentences and their matching paraphrases; and 1 dataset of paragraphs with matching paraphrases :

1. The MSR Paraphrase Identification dataset (Dolan et al., 2004) which consists of just over 4,000 examples of original sentences with a matching paraphrased sentence in its train set.

2. An original dataset of 10,000 sentences from online news articles along with matching paraphrases that were human-generated.

3. A further original dataset of paragraphs with corresponding paraphrased paragraphs from various entertainment, news, and food articles found online, where the paraphrases were human-generated.

We fine-tuned 3 versions of the GPT-2 model, one corresponding to each dataset, and then made predictions using the same system outlined above.

By calculating USE, ROUGE-L and BLEU scores for each dataset we are able to quantify the quality of human-generated paraphrases and then use that as a comparison for the models generated sentences (see Table 2).

Dataset	USE	R-L	BLEU
MSR_train	0.8462	0.4315	0.4593
MSR_test	0.8415	0.4202	0.4966
News dataset	0.8948	0.4686	0.5648
Paragraphs dataset	0.9208	0.4966	0.5762

Table 2: Average USE, ROUGE-L, BLEU Scores of the datasets

4   Experiments

We implemented the system described above using GPT-2 and trained it on the different datasets for various lengths of training.

To evaluate the output of the model, we randomly selected sentences from sources such as Wikipedia, news sites and entertainment sites with no matching paraphrase to use as the conditional input to the model.

5   Results and Scoring

When comparing our generated sentences with the average scores of the original datasets, we can see that that they compare favorably.

As discussed earlier, we assessed the semantic similarity of the sentence meanings using Universal Sentence Encoder (Cer et al., 2018) and compared them to the average USE score from the datasets that were trained on. This showed that the system can generate paraphrases which are semantically on par with the human-generated ones in each of the datasets.

We also compared the ROUGE-L (Lin, 2004) scores of the generated samples with the average values for the datasets which were human-generated. This again shows that our phrases are coherent and on par with human-generated paraphrases.

When we further compared the results of unfiltered examples generated by the model (Table 3) we observe that when the USE score is below 0.85 we see clear deterioration in the semantic similarity quality of the paraphrased versions.

We also observe that if the USE score is too close to 1.0 then the ROUGE-L score also rises and the generated examples are too similar in word

		USE	R-L
In:	A prisoner can asphyxiate himself in 90 seconds and, after eight minutes or so, he will be brain dead.		
Out 1:	After 8 minutes, a brain fart will subdue the sufferer.	0.524	0.0
Out 2:	After 8 minutes, he will be brain-dead and his heart will stop.	0.565	0.138
Out 3:	A brain aneurysm can asphyxiate itself in 90 seconds and, after eight minutes, it will be dead.	0.721	0.412
Out 4:	After eight minutes, a brain anesthetist can asphyxiate a prisoner in 90 seconds and for several minutes after that.	0.758	0.167
Out 5:	A brain-dead prisoner canasphyxiate himself in 90 seconds and then out loud after eight minutes.	0.809	0.312
Out 6:	At asphyxiation, the prisoner canasphyxiate himself in 90 seconds and, after 8 minutes, he will be brain dead.	0.884	0.514
Out 7:	After eight minutes, a prisoner can asphyxiate himself in 90 seconds and, after that, he will be brain dead.	0.884	0.514
Out 8*:	**In 90 seconds, a prisoner can asphyxiate himself and be brain dead after eight minutes or so**	**0.932**	**0.473**
Out 9:	A prisoner can asphyxiate himself in 90 seconds and, after eight minutes, he will be brain dead.	0.972	0.824

Table 3: Showing Candidates Selection and Scoring - *Selected Sentence

and phrase selection to the original sentence to be useful paraphrases.

This technique can be performed not only at sentence-level but also to generate paragraph-level paraphrases. Comparing USE and ROUGE-L scores of the generated paragraphs we see they are again on par with the human generated examples from our paragraph dataset (samples are given in the Supplemental Materials).

Due to the pre-training of the Language Model, the model is able to generalize to and generate paraphrases for types of content it has never seen during the fine-tuning phase.

6 Discussion

The technique outlined in this paper shows the applicability of large language models to the paraphrasing task. It also highlights that there is still much to be learnt about further applications of large language models, and also the approaches used to fine-tune and use them for applications.

Most of the results from models such as GPT-2 have focused on the quality of text generation rather than quantitative methods for measuring and improving the quality of text created, to make it more consistent and usable. We propose the scoring and filtering of candidates using techniques such as we have shown with USE and ROUGE-L, may be a useful technique not just for paraphrasing but other text generation tasks.

The ability of our technique to work with long spans of text also gives it an advantage over prior work which used rule-based and other statistical approaches which performed best on shorter spans of text.

Our experiments show that pre-training of GPT-2 on such a large amount of data in the WebText dataset allows it to 'understand' the syntax and to a degree the grammar of English allowing it to be able to quickly learn the task of paraphrasing through fine-tuning training on a small set of paraphrasing examples.

7 Future Work

Extrapolating from the paraphrasing results into more generalizable ideas, we hope to investigate the extent by which the representations learned in the different layers of the transformer network correspond to different parts of the linguistic hierarchy. One possible approach to doing this would be to trace a set of 'markers' through the transformer networks existing attention mechanism, in parallel to the text which gives rise to that structure.

In addition, the ability of the networks to learn tasks within the span of a single context frame indicates the possibility of an inherent bias towards meta-(or one-shot) learning. These will be the subject of further work.

Acknowledgments

We would like to thank Google for access to the TFRC TPU program which was used in training and fine-tuning models for this paper.

References

Colin J. Bannard and Chris Callison-Burch. 2005. Paraphrasing with bilingual parallel corpora. In *Proceedings of the 43rd Annual Meeting of the Association for Computational Linguistics (ACL05)*, pages 597–604, Ann Arbor, Michigan. Association for Computational Linguistics.

Regina Barzilay and Kathleen McKeown. 2001. Extracting paraphrases from a parallel corpus. In *Proceedings of the 39th Annual Meeting on Association for Computational Linguistics*, ACL '01, pages 50–57, Stroudsburg, PA, USA. Association for Computational Linguistics.

Samuel R. Bowman, Luke Vilnis, Oriol Vinyals, Andrew M. Dai, Rafal Józefowicz, and Samy Bengio. 2016. Generating sentences from a continuous space. In *Proceedings of The 20th SIGNLL Conference on Computational Natural Language Learning*, pages 10–21, Berlin, Germany. Association for Computational Linguistics.

Daniel Cer, Yinfei Yang, Sheng yi Kong, Nan Hua, Nicole Limtiaco, Rhomni St. John, Noah Constant, Mario Guajardo-Cespedes, Steve Yuan, Chris Tar, Yun-Hsuan Sung, Brian Strope, and Ray Kurzweil. 2018. Universal sentence encoder. *ArXiv*, abs/1803.11175.

Jacob Devlin, Ming-Wei Chang, Kenton Lee, and Kristina Toutanova. 2019. Bert: Pre-training of deep bidirectional transformers for language understanding. In *Proceedings of the 2019 Conference of the North American Chapter of the Association for Computational Linguistics: Human Language Technologies, Volume 1 (Long and Short Papers)*, pages 4171–4186, Minneapolis, Minnesota. Association for Computational Linguistics.

William B. Dolan, Chris Quirk, and Chris Brockett. 2004. Unsupervised construction of large paraphrase corpora: Exploiting massively parallel news sources. In *COLING*.

Li Dong, Nan Yang, Wenhui Wang, Furu Wei, Xiaodong Liu, Yu Wang, Jianfeng Gao, Ming Zhou, and Hsiao-Wuen Hon. 2019. Unified language model pre-training for natural language understanding and generation. *CoRR*, abs/1905.03197.

Ankush Gupta, Arvind Agarwal, Prawaan Singh, and Piyush Rai. 2018. A deep generative framework for paraphrase generation. In *Thirty-Second AAAI Conference on Artificial Intelligence*.

Jeremy Howard and Sebastian Ruder. 2018. Universal language model fine-tuning for text classification. In *Proceedings of the 56th Annual Meeting of the Association for Computational Linguistics (Volume 1: Long Papers)*, pages 328–339, Melbourne, Australia. Association for Computational Linguistics.

Zichao Li, Xin Jiang, Lifeng Shang, and Hang Li. 2018. Paraphrase generation with deep reinforcement learning. In *Proceedings of the 2018 Conference on Empirical Methods in Natural Language Processing*, pages 3865–3878.

Chin-Yew Lin. 2004. Rouge: A package for automatic evaluation of summaries. In *ACL 2004*, pages 74–81, Barcelona, Spain. Association for Computational Linguistics.

Nitin Madnani and Bonnie J. Dorr. 2010. Generating phrasal and sentential paraphrases: A survey of data-driven methods. *Computational Linguistics*, 36:341–387.

Jonathan Mallinson, Rico Sennrich, and Mirella Lapata. 2017. Paraphrasing revisited with neural machine translation. In *Proceedings of the 15th Conference of the European Chapter of the Association for Computational Linguistics: Volume 1, Long Papers*, pages 881–893.

Kathleen McKeown. 1979. Paraphrasing using given and new information in a question-answer system. In *17th Annual Meeting of the Association for Computational Linguistics*, pages 67–72.

Marie Meteer and Varda Shaked. 1988. Strategies for effective paraphrasing. In *Coling Budapest 1988 Volume 2: International Conference on Computational Linguistics*.

Bo Pang, Kevin Knight, and Daniel Marcu. 2003. Syntax-based alignment of multiple translations: Extracting paraphrases and generating new sentences. In *Proceedings of the 2003 Human Language Technology Conference of the North American Chapter of the Association for Computational Linguistics*, pages 181–188.

Kishore Papineni, Salim Roukos, Todd Ward, and Wei-Jing Zhu. 2002. Bleu: a method for automatic evaluation of machine translation. In *Proceedings of the 40th Annual Meeting of the Association for Computational Linguistics*, pages 311–318, Philadelphia, Pennsylvania, USA. Association for Computational Linguistics.

Matthew E. Peters, Mark Neumann, Mohit Iyyer, Matt Gardner, Christopher Clark, Kenton Lee, and Luke Zettlemoyer. 2018. Deep contextualized word representations. pages 2227–2237, New Orleans, Louisiana. Association for Computational Linguistics.

Aaditya Prakash, Sadid A. Hasan, Kathy Lee, Vivek V. Datla, Ashequl Qadir, Joey Liu, and Oladimeji Farri. 2016. Neural paraphrase generation with stacked residual LSTM networks. *CoRR*, abs/1610.03098.

Alec Radford, Karthik Narasimhan, Tim Salimans, and Ilya Sutskever. 2018. Improving language understanding by generative pre-training.

Alec Radford, Jeff Wu, Rewon Child, David Luan, Dario Amodei, and Ilya Sutskever. 2019. Language models are unsupervised multitask learners.

Sascha Rothe, Shashi Narayan, and Aliaksei Severyn. 2019. Leveraging pre-trained checkpoints for sequence generation tasks. *CoRR*, abs/1907.12461.

Aurko Roy and David Grangier. 2019. Unsupervised paraphrasing without translation. *ArXiv*, abs/1905.12752.

Ashish Vaswani, Noam Shazeer, Niki Parmar, Jakob Uszkoreit, Llion Jones, Aidan N Gomez, Łukasz Kaiser, and Illia Polosukhin. 2017. Attention is all you need. In *Advances in neural information processing systems*, pages 5998–6008.

Interrogating the Explanatory Power of Attention in Neural Machine Translation

Pooya Moradi, Nishant Kambhatla, and Anoop Sarkar

Simon Fraser University
8888 University Drive
Burnaby, BC, Canada
{pooya_moradi, nkambhat, anoop}@sfu.ca

Abstract

Attention models have become a crucial component in neural machine translation (NMT). They are often implicitly or explicitly used to justify the model's decision in generating a specific token but it has not yet been rigorously established to what extent attention is a reliable source of information in NMT. To evaluate the explanatory power of attention for NMT, we examine the possibility of yielding the same prediction but with counterfactual attention models that modify crucial aspects of the trained attention model. Using these counterfactual attention mechanisms we assess the extent to which they still preserve the generation of function and content words in the translation process. Compared to a state of the art attention model, our counterfactual attention models produce 68% of function words and 21% of content words in our German-English dataset. Our experiments demonstrate that attention models by themselves cannot reliably explain the decisions made by a NMT model.[1]

1 Introduction

One shortcoming of neural machine translation (NMT), and neural models in general, is that it is often difficult for humans to comprehend the reasons why the model is making predictions (Feng et al., 2018; Ghorbani et al., 2019). The main cause of such a difficulty is that in neural models, information is implicitly represented by real-valued vectors, and conceptual interpretation of these vectors remains a challenge. Why do we want neural models to be interpretable? In order to debug a neural model during the error analysis process in research experiments, it is necessary to know how much each part of the model is

contributing to the error in the prediction. Being able to interpret the deficiencies of a model is also crucial to further improve upon it. This requires an explainable understanding of the internals of the model, including how certain concepts are being modeled or represented. Therefore developing methods to interpret and understand neural models is an important research goal.

Visualizing and interpreting neural models has been extensively studied in computer vision (Simonyan et al., 2013; Bach et al., 2015; Zeiler and Fergus, 2014; Montavon et al., 2017), and more recently in natural language processing (NLP) (Karpathy et al., 2015; Li et al., 2016a; Strobelt et al., 2017, 2018). Recently, the integration of attention mechanism (Bahdanau et al., 2014) with an NMT sequence to sequence model (Sutskever et al., 2014) has led to significant improvements in translation quality especially for longer sentence lengths. The attention mechanism provides a weighted average over the information from the source encodings to be used at each translation step. These weights are often regarded as a measure of importance, and are implicitly or explicitly used as an explanation for the model's decision. However it has not yet been established to what extent such explanations are reliable.

The example in Figure 1 shows a model translating the German sentence "und wir wollen dieses material für alle verfügbar machen." (*and we want to make this material accessible to everyone.*). At the time that the model is translating "verfügbar" to "accessible", it is mostly attending to "verfügbar" (left heatmap). It is tempting to conclude that "verfügbar" having the most attention is why the model is generating the token "accessible". However, we manipulate the attention weights such that the "verfügbar" receives no attention and "alle" is given the most attention (right heatmap). We observe that in the second case, the

---

[1]The source code to reproduce the experiments is available at https://github.com/sfu-natlang/attention_explanation

Proceedings of the 3rd Workshop on Neural Generation and Translation (WNGT 2019), pages 221–230
Hong Kong, China, November 4, 2019. ©2019 Association for Computational Linguistics
www.aclweb.org/anthology/D19-56%2d

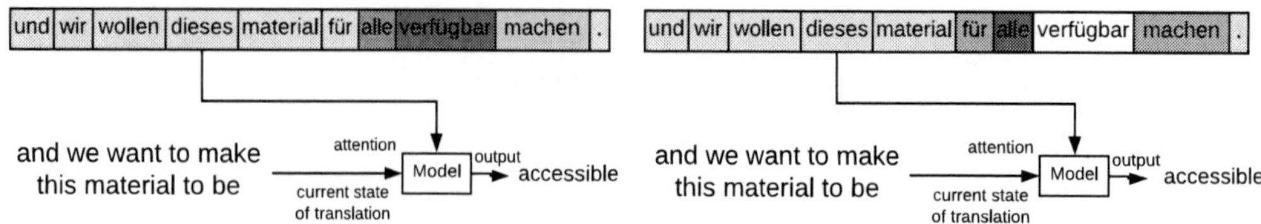

Figure 1: Two distinct attention weights yielding the same prediction. The model is translating the source word "verfügbar" to "accessible". In the left attention heatmap, the focus of the attention is on the word "verfügbar". However, in the right heatmap, "verfügbar" is not attended to at all and "alle" has received the most attention.

model makes the same decision again and outputs "accessible". This example shows that using attention weights to reason about the model's predictions can be misleading, as these two heatmaps convey different explanations.

There are relatively few previous studies on investigating the power of attention mechanism in rationalizing a model's predictions in NLP (Jain and Wallace, 2019; Serrano and Smith, 2019) and they all target text classification tasks where attention is over the input document. Their findings do not generalize easily to NMT due to the difference in how the decoder works in the translation task which produces a sequence rather than a class label. NMT is a sequence-to-sequence (Seq2Seq) task, which is different from text classification. Also, the size of the output space is quite limited in text classification, whereas in NMT, it is equal to the vocabulary size of the target language that can be very large. Furthermore, different neural architectures (e.g., presence of an encoder and decoder in NMT), require different analysis and interpretations. To the best of our knowledge there is no existing work on addressing the question of interpretability of attention models for the machine translation task.

To investigate if the explanation implied by attention weights faithfully justifies why a model produced its output, we study to what extent it is possible to yield the same prediction by using counterfactual attention weights that suggest a contradictory explanation. The intuition behind this approach is that multiple contradictory justifications should not exist for a decision. To be specific, in the setting of an encoder-decoder model (Sec 2), we propose several counterfactual attention weighting methods that suggest different explanations compared to the original attention weights (Sec 3) and analyze their performance in

preserving the generation of function[2] and content words (Sec 4). Function words (e.g., *a*, *the*, *is*) have little lexical meaning in contrast to content words and thus we are curious whether explanatory power of the attention mechanism differs for generation of these two groups of words.

2 Encoder-Decoder Model with Attention Mechanism

Given a training sentence pair $(\mathbf{x}, \mathbf{y})$ where $\mathbf{x} = [x_1, x_2, ..., x_m]$ is a sentence in the source language and $\mathbf{y} = [y_1, y_2, ..., y_n]$ is its corresponding translation in the target language, the encoder, which is a recurrent neural network (RNN), runs over the source sentence to calculate the contextualized representation of the source words. Here, we use a bidirectional encoder, and concatenate the forward and backward hidden states to build the final representation.

$$\overrightarrow{h_t} = \overrightarrow{f_{enc}}(x_t, \overrightarrow{h_{t-1}})$$
$$\overleftarrow{h_t} = \overleftarrow{f_{enc}}(x_t, \overleftarrow{h_{t+1}}) \quad (1)$$
$$h_t = [\overrightarrow{h_t}, \overleftarrow{h_t}]$$

Then the decoder starts to generate output tokens using the following probability distribution:

$$p(y_t|y_{<t}, x) = \mathit{softmax}(g_{dec}(s_t, c_t))$$

with g_{dec} being a transformation function that produces a vocabulary-sized vector, and s_t is the hidden unit of the decoder's RNN updated as:

$$s_t = f_{dec}(y_{t-1}, s_{t-1}, c_{t-1})$$

---

[2]The reference for function words (we added new function words including the EOS token to this) can be found at: semanticsimilarity.files.wordpress.com/ 2013/08/jim-oshea-fwlist-277.pdf

where f_{dec} is a RNN. Here c_t is the context vector calculated by attention mechanisms:

$$c_t = \sum_{i=1}^{m} \alpha_{ti} h_i$$

where α_t is the normalized attention weights over the source context:

$$\alpha_{ti} = \frac{e^{a(s_t, h_i)}}{\sum_j e^{a(s_t, h_j)}}$$

Here, a is a scoring function that determines the contribution of each source context vector to the final context vector. Implementation of a depends on the choice of the attention method. In this work, we use general attention (Luong et al., 2015) as the scoring function:

$$a(s_t, h_i) = s_t^\top W_a h_i$$

3 Approach

Given a trained NMT model M, a test sentence $\mathbf{x}$ with $\mathbf{y}$ being its translation generated by M at the decoding step t in which α_t is the attention vector, attending to the source word at position $m_t = \operatorname{argmax}_i \alpha_t[i]$ or k-best attended-to words in the source are often implicitly or explicitly regarded as a justification for the model's prediction at the time step t.

A vital criteria for such a justification is that one should not be able to find a contradictory explanation for the model's decision. More precisely, if at the time of inference, it is possible to manipulate the original attention weights to constitute an alternative attention vector α_t', such that $\operatorname{argmax}_i \alpha_t'[i] \neq m_t$ and the decision of the model is preserved, then these weights cannot be used for justification as they are contradictory. Thus, we are interested in assessing for what percentage of the words in the translation, counterfactual attention weights exist. These percentages can shed light on the reliability of the attention weights as a potential explanation. Note that at the inference time we manipulate attention vector for each output token separately and in isolation to make sure the output tokens at time steps $t + 1$ and after will not be affected by the change at time step t. This means that our output translations are unaffected by our counterfactual attention models which are purely for the examination of how attention might explain the model's decision.

The main task here is to find a counterfactual attention vector if it exists at all. An exhaustive search approach in which every possible attention vector is examined is computationally intractable and unlikely to provide much insight. Instead we experiment with a few specific counterfactual attention weighting methods that we think provide the most insight. It is important to note that in this case, the calculated percentage of the preserved words will be a lower-bound estimation for the true percentage. As a result, the explanation offered by attention weights are more unreliable than what we'll find. We experiment with the following attention methods to create counterfactual attention weights:

- `RandomPermute` (Jain and Wallace, 2019): We set $\alpha_t' = random\_permute(\alpha_t)$ such that $\operatorname{argmax}_i \alpha_t'[i] \neq m_t$.

- `Uniform`: In this method, $\alpha_t' = \frac{1}{m}\vec{1}$. Here, m is the length of the source sentence.

- `ZeroOutMax`: A simple approach to create a counterfactual attention vector is to remove the maximum attention weight. So we set $a(s_t, h_{m_t}) = -\infty$.

We also experiment with four additional attention methods where our motivation is not finding counterfactual attention weights, but to improve our understanding of how attention weights influence the model's prediction:

- `ZeroOut`: In what conditions does the decoder overlook the information provided by attention mechanism? To answer this question, we set all attention weights to zero at inference time (attention is still used while training the model).

- `LastEncoderState`: Here, we only use the final hidden state of the encoder as the context vector to be used in the decoder. Note that this is different from seq2seq without attention in which final hidden state of the encoder is used to initialize the decoder. When the focus is on the final hidden state of the encoder in the original attention weights, this method does not produce a counterfactual attention vector, which is why we don't intend to use this method to create a contradictory explanation, but rather to gain more insight into the sensitivity of the model to attention weights.

- `OnlyMax`: In this and the following method, the source hidden state with the maximum attention still receives the highest attention, and so these two methods do not output counterfactual attention vectors. However we are curious to what extent other attention weights are required to preserve the model's output. Note that the weights produced by these methods can be counted as contradictory when multiple attention weights are used for justifying predictions. Because although the most attended source context is not changed, the relative ranking of the rest of the source context in terms of attention weights is changed. However, these kinds of justifications are mostly discussed in text classification. In this specific method we only keep the most attended source hidden state: $\alpha_t'[m_t]=1$.

- `KeepMaxUniformOthers`: Here, we set $\alpha_t'[m_t] = \alpha_t[m_t]$, but for all other positions $\alpha_t'[i] = (1 - \alpha_t'[m_t])/m$. This is to investigate if using other source hidden states uniformly has any added benefit.

4 Experiments

4.1 Data

In this work we use the German-English dataset from IWSLT2014[3]. We concatenate dev2010, dev2012, tst2010, tst2011 and tst2012 to be used as the test data. Data is tokenized using Moses (Koehn et al., 2007).

4.2 Model Details

OpenNMT (Klein et al., 2017) is used for our Seq2Seq implementation. We use Long Short-Term Memory (LSTM) as RNN units. Each LSTM unit has 2 layers, and the dimension size for LSTM units and word embeddings is set to 500. The model is trained using Adam trainer with learning rate 0.001 for 50000 steps using early stopping. Vocabulary size for both the source and target language is set to 50000. Sentences longer that 50 tokens are pruned.

5 Results

Table 1 shows the percentage of function and content words generated by the trained model. As expected, the majority of the generated tokens are

[3]https://sites.google.com/site/iwsltevaluation2014/

function words. We discuss our findings in more detail in the subsequent subsections.

Number of tokens (+EOS)	139465
Percentage of function words	68%
Percentage of content words	32%

Table 1: Percentage of function and content words in the generated translation.

	Method	% for FWs	% for CWs
1	RandomPermute	33%	6%
2	Uniform	53%	11%
3	ZeroOutMax	52%	15%
4	Aggregate(1+2+3)	**68%**	**21%**
5	ZeroOut	9%	0%
6	LastEncoderState	20%	2%
7	OnlyMax	71%	83%
8	KeepMaxUniformOthers	86%	86%

Table 2: Percentage of the preserved function and content words in the proposed attention methods: Trying out all the methods to find a counterfactual attention vector maximizes the chance of success. We use methods in row 5-8 only to shed light on the sensitivity of the model's output to perturbation in attention weight. They are not necessarily counted as counterfactual attention methods. Higher preservation rate stands for better performance.

5.1 Effectiveness of the proposed counterfactual attention methods

Table 2 shows the percentage of function and content words for which counterfactual attention weights were found using the proposed attention methods. The `Uniform` method (row 2) is the most effective method to create counterfactual attention weights for function words. However, for content words, the `ZeroOutMax` method (row 3) is the most successful method.

From Table 2, we also derive that `RandomPermute` is not as effective as the `Uniform` and `ZeroOutMax` methods. Our justification is that in the `RandomPermute` method, it is highly probable that the context vector is biased toward a random source hidden state. Such bias can lead to misleading noise in the context vector. However, there isn't such a bias in the `Uniform` or `ZeroOutMax` methods.

To maximize the chance of finding a counterfactual attention, for each output token, we try out all the proposed methods to check if we can find a counterfactual attention (row 4). As evident from Table 2, this approach greatly increases the chance of finding a counterfactual attention. Note that as previously stated, these percentages are a lower-bound for the true percentage.

5.2 Function words are more easily generated compared to content words

An important observation in Table 2 is that the proposed methods are considerably more effective in preserving function words compared to content words. The production of function words rely more on the target context, in contrast to content words which rely more on the source context. Accordingly, perturbation in the original attention weights likely has significantly more impact on diminishing content words compared to function words.

This ties well with the main idea behind context gates in which the influence of source context and target context is controlled dynamically (Tu et al., 2017). Since the generation of function words relies more on the target context, one may wonder to what extent attention is needed for preserving function words? To answer this question, we completely zero out the attention using `ZeroOut`. Row 5 shows that only 9% of function words were preserved in this method.

Moreover it can be seen that the model could not preserve any content word when this method is employed. Interestingly, we found that the preserved function words in this method were all occurrences of ",". Apparently the decoder's language model is so strong in predicting "," without attention. This finding suggests that a basic representation of the source context is still necessary to preserve function words.

5.3 Highlighting top preserved tokens

An important question that may arise is whether each attention method tends to preserve a specific group of words. To address this question, we listed the top preserved function words and content words for all the proposed methods. We observed that they mostly preserve the same group of words but with different percentages. As a result, we only list the top preserved tokens for the aggregate method.

Table 3 contains the top 20 content words sorted by the number of times they were preserved. It is interesting to note that for many of these frequent tokens, more than half of their total occurrences are preserved without focusing on their corresponding translation in the source sentence (e.g., "going", "know", "thing", etc).

In Table 4, we sort such tokens based on their coverage, which is the percentage of their total

Token	# preserved	Coverage
going	310	70%
people	237	46%
know	219	62%
world	215	67%
like	189	47%
think	176	50%
way	162	68%
get	160	53%
thing	147	79%
things	142	56%
time	139	54%
see	137	51%
years	136	64%
make	126	49%
little	113	55%
just	109	29%
really	93	37%
bit	92	88%
said	89	59%
got	86	59%

Table 3: Top 20 content words preserved by the aggregate method sorted by the number of times they were preserved.

Token	Coverage	Total
bit	88%	105
course	87%	91
thank	83%	89
thing	79%	186
fact	78%	74
half	78%	27
own	75%	75
ones	73%	30
states	73%	30
difference	71%	21
going	70%	444
turns	69%	26
way	68%	237
able	67%	85
world	67%	323
doing	66%	103
planet	65%	37
years	64%	212
know	62%	353
united	62%	21

Table 4: Top 20 content words preserved by the aggregate method sorted by percentage of their total occurrences that are preserved (*coverage*).

occurrences that are not affected when a counter-facual attention is applied[4]. We repeat the same process for function words (Table 5 and Table 6).

As evident from Table 5, we have successfully yielded the same token in 94% of the occurrences of the EOS token but with a contradictory explanation. This can be explained by the previous findings suggesting special hidden units keep track of translation length (Shi et al., 2016). As a result, EOS token is generated upon receiving signal from these units rather than using attention. This indicates that attention weights are highly unreliable for explaining the generation of EOS tokens. This is worth noting because early generation of the EOS token is often a major reason of the under-translation problem in NMT (Kuang et al., 2018). Thus, attention weights should not be used to debug early generation of EOS, and that some other underlying influence in the network (Ding et al., 2017) might be responsible for the model's decision in this case.

5.4 Last encoder hidden state is a poor representation of the source context in the attentional model

The last encoder state in a non-attentional model is passed to the decoder as the representation of the source context (Cho et al., 2014) although the accuracy of this representation has been shown to degrade as sentence length increases (Bahdanau et al., 2014). We experiment with the `LastEncoderState` method to investigate how well the last encoder state can be representative of the source context in the attentional setting, and if exclusively attending to it can be used as a counterfactual attention.

Row 6 in Table 2 shows that there is a significant gap between the `LastEncoderState` and the counterfactual methods proposed in Table 2. A possible explanation for this result is that in the presence of attention mechanism, the model is trained to distribute the source-side information among the encoder states to be easier to select the relevant parts of the information with respect to the decoding state. Consequently, the last encoder state does no longer capture the whole information.

---

[4]We consider only the tokens that have appeared more than 20 times. The reason is that there are many preserved words that have appeared only once (coverage=1) and it is not clear if the coverage remains the same when frequency increases

Token	# preserved	Coverage
,	7329	85%
EOS	6364	94%
the	5210	82%
.	3947	60%
of	3003	87%
to	2923	86%
and	2639	67%
a	2187	65%
that	1936	69%
i	1737	76%
's	1732	95%
you	1501	72%
it	1497	72%
is	1496	88%
in	1364	64%
we	1246	64%
they	624	69%
"	620	81%
have	613	70%
be	582	91%
't	580	96%
're	542	86%
this	541	42%
so	531	57%
are	526	77%
was	514	66%
do	433	77%
about	417	65%
what	415	61%
can	400	54%

Table 5: Top 30 function words preserved by the aggregate method sorted by the number of times they were preserved.

If we look at Table 7, we can see that the most covered functions words, are the words that usually appear at the end of the sentence (e.g., "EOS", ".", "?", "!"). This is because most of the context captured by the last encoder state is centered around the last part of the sentence in which these tokens appear.

5.5 Attention of non-maximum source hidden states

Row 7 shows that a majority of output tokens can be preserved even when the model attends to a single source hidden state. Row 8 shows that when other source hidden states are uniformly combined, although the ratio of unaffected content words has increased by 3%, ratio of unaffected

Token	Coverage	Total
't	96%	602
's	95%	1819
EOS	94%	6748
be	91%	641
is	88%	1707
of	87%	3450
to	86%	3383
're	86%	631
,	85%	8582
'm	84%	311
been	82%	233
lot	82%	148
the	82%	6386
"	81%	770
are	77%	679
do	77%	565
i	76%	2290
who	73%	300
it	72%	2089
you	72%	2099
have	70%	876
up	70%	235
they	69%	904
that	69%	2812
well	67%	153
and	67%	3922
was	66%	774
were	65%	240
same	65%	154
a	65%	3369

Table 6: Top 30 function words preserved by the aggregate method sorted by coverage.

Token	Coverage	Total
EOS	99%	6748
.	98%	6526
?	88%	589
't	86%	602
!	68%	22
"	60%	770
's	24%	1819
;	24%	63
are	18%	679
is	18%	1707

Table 7: Top 10 unaffected function words in the `LastEncoderState` method.

function words has increased by 15%. This again underlines the importance of the basic representation of the source context for generation of function words.

5.6 Summary

Our findings can be summarized as follows:

- It is possible to generate 68% of function words and 21% of content words with a counterfactual attention indicating unreliability of using attention weights as explanation.

- The generation of function words relies more on the target context, whereas the generation of content words relies more on the source context. This results in a higher likelihood of generation of preserved function words compared to that of preserved content words.

- Generation of EOS tokens cannot be reliably explained by using attention weights. Instead, this depends on the length of the target translation which is implicitly pursued by special hidden units. As a result, EOS token is emitted upon receiving a signal from these units rather than information from attention.

- The last encoder state is a poor representation of the source sentence and cannot be effectively used as the source context vector.

- It is possible to generate 86% of tokens by only using the source hidden state with the maximum attention and using other source hidden states uniformly suggesting that it may not be necessary to assign highly tuned weights to each source hidden state.

6 Related Work

Relevance-based interpretation is a common technique in analyzing predictions in neural models. In this method, inputs of a predictor are assigned a scalar value quantifying the importance of that particular input on the final decision. Saliency methods use the gradient of the inputs to define importance (Li et al., 2016a; Ghaeini et al., 2018; Ding et al., 2019). Layer-wise relevance propagation that assigns relevance to neurons based on their contribution to activation of higher-layer neurons is also investigated in NLP (Arras et al., 2016; Ding et al., 2017; Arras et al., 2017). Another method to measure relevance is by removing the input, and tracking the difference in in network's output (Li et al., 2016b). While these methods focus on explaining a model's decision, Shi et al. (2016); Kádár et al. (2017); Calvillo and Crocker (2018) investigate how a particular concept is represented in the network.

Analyzing and interpreting the attention mechanism in NLP (Koehn and Knowles, 2017; Ghader and Monz, 2017; Tang and Nivre, 2018; Clark et al., 2019; Vig and Belinkov, 2019) is another direction that has drawn major interest. Although attention weights have been implicitly or explicitly used to explain a model's decisions, the reliability of this approach is not proven. Several attempts have been made to investigate the reliability of this approach for explaining a models' decision in NLP (Serrano and Smith, 2019; Baan et al., 2019; Jain et al., 2019; Jain and Wallace, 2019), and also in information retrieval (Jain and Madhyastha, 2019).

Our work was inspired by Jain and Wallace (2019). However, in this work we have focused on similar issues in neural machine translation which is has different challenges compared to text classification in terms of objective and architecture. Moreover, our paper studies the effect of different counterfactual attention methods.

7 Conclusion

Using attention weights to justify a model's prediction is tempting and seems intuitive at the first glance. It is, however, not clear whether attention can be employed for such purposes. There might exist alternative attention weights resulting in the same decision by the model but promoting different contradictory explanation.

We propose several attention methods to create counterfactual attention weights from the original weights, and we measure to what extent these new contradictory weights can yield the same output as the original one. We find that in many cases, an output token can be generated even though a counterfactual attention is fed to the decoder. This implies that using attention weights to rationalize a model's decision is not a reliable approach.

8 Future Work

In the future, we intend to study the extent to which attention weights correlate with importance measured by gradient-based methods. While we have separated function and content words in this work, we would like to extend our findings to other categories such as parts of speech (POS) or out-of-vocabulary (OOV) words. Another logical investigation for future would be to address interpretability of copy mechanism in NMT (Gu et al., 2016). Proving the correlation between attention and the model predictions in more sophisticated attention models such as Transformer (Vaswani et al., 2017) is also worth exploring.

Acknowledgments

We would like to thank the anonymous reviewers for their helpful comments. The research was also partially supported by the Natural Sciences and Engineering Research Council of Canada grants NSERC RGPIN-2018-06437 and RGPAS-2018-522574 and a Department of National Defence (DND) and NSERC grant DGDND-2018-00025 to the second author.

References

Leila Arras, Franziska Horn, Grégoire Montavon, Klaus-Robert Müller, and Wojciech Samek. 2016. Explaining predictions of non-linear classifiers in NLP. In Proceedings of the 1st Workshop on Representation Learning for NLP, pages 1–7, Berlin, Germany. Association for Computational Linguistics.

Leila Arras, Grégoire Montavon, Klaus-Robert Müller, and Wojciech Samek. 2017. Explaining recurrent neural network predictions in sentiment analysis. In Proceedings of the 8th Workshop on Computational Approaches to Subjectivity, Sentiment and Social Media Analysis, pages 159–168, Copenhagen, Denmark. Association for Computational Linguistics.

Joris Baan, Maartje ter Hoeve, Marlies van der Wees, Anne Schuth, and Maarten de Rijke. 2019. Do transformer attention heads provide transparency in abstractive summarization? arXiv preprint arXiv:1907.00570.

Sebastian Bach, Alexander Binder, Grégoire Montavon, Frederick Klauschen, Klaus-Robert Müller, and Wojciech Samek. 2015. On pixel-wise explanations for non-linear classifier decisions by layer-wise relevance propagation. PLOS ONE, 10(7):1–46.

Dzmitry Bahdanau, Kyunghyun Cho, and Yoshua Bengio. 2014. Neural machine translation by jointly learning to align and translate. arXiv preprint arXiv:1409.0473.

Jesús Calvillo and Matthew Crocker. 2018. Language production dynamics with recurrent neural networks. In Proceedings of the Eight Workshop on Cognitive Aspects of Computational Language Learning and Processing, pages 17–26, Melbourne. Association for Computational Linguistics.

Kyunghyun Cho, Bart van Merriënboer, Caglar Gulcehre, Dzmitry Bahdanau, Fethi Bougares, Holger Schwenk, and Yoshua Bengio. 2014. Learning phrase representations using RNN encoder–decoder for statistical machine translation. In Proceedings of the 2014 Conference on Empirical Methods in Natural Language Processing (EMNLP), pages 1724–1734, Doha, Qatar. Association for Computational Linguistics.

Kevin Clark, Urvashi Khandelwal, Omer Levy, and Christopher D. Manning. 2019. What does BERT look at? an analysis of BERT's attention. In Proceedings of the 2019 ACL Workshop BlackboxNLP: Analyzing and Interpreting Neural Networks for NLP, pages 276–286, Florence, Italy. Association for Computational Linguistics.

Shuoyang Ding, Hainan Xu, and Philipp Koehn. 2019. Saliency-driven word alignment interpretation for neural machine translation. In Proceedings of the Fourth Conference on Machine Translation, pages 1–12, Florence, Italy. Association for Computational Linguistics.

Yanzhuo Ding, Yang Liu, Huanbo Luan, and Maosong Sun. 2017. Visualizing and understanding neural machine translation. In Proceedings of the 55th Annual Meeting of the Association for Computational Linguistics (Volume 1: Long Papers), pages 1150–1159, Vancouver, Canada. Association for Computational Linguistics.

Shi Feng, Eric Wallace, Alvin Grissom II, Mohit Iyyer, Pedro Rodriguez, and Jordan Boyd-Graber. 2018. Pathologies of neural models make interpretations difficult. In Proceedings of the 2018 Conference on Empirical Methods in Natural Language Processing, pages 3719–3728, Brussels, Belgium. Association for Computational Linguistics.

Hamidreza Ghader and Christof Monz. 2017. What does attention in neural machine translation pay attention to? In Proceedings of the Eighth International Joint Conference on Natural Language Processing (Volume 1: Long Papers), pages 30–39, Taipei, Taiwan. Asian Federation of Natural Language Processing.

Reza Ghaeini, Xiaoli Fern, and Prasad Tadepalli. 2018. Interpreting recurrent and attention-based neural models: a case study on natural language inference. In Proceedings of the 2018 Conference on Empirical Methods in Natural Language Processing, pages 4952–4957, Brussels, Belgium. Association for Computational Linguistics.

Amirata Ghorbani, Abubakar Abid, and James Zou. 2019. Interpretation of neural networks is fragile. In Proceedings of the AAAI Conference on Artificial Intelligence, volume 33, pages 3681–3688.

Jiatao Gu, Zhengdong Lu, Hang Li, and Victor O.K. Li. 2016. Incorporating copying mechanism in sequence-to-sequence learning. In Proceedings

of the 54th Annual Meeting of the Association for Computational Linguistics (Volume 1: Long Papers), pages 1631–1640, Berlin, Germany. Association for Computational Linguistics.

Rishabh Jain and Pranava Madhyastha. 2019. Model explanations under calibration. arXiv preprint arXiv:1906.07622.

Sarthak Jain, Ramin Mohammadi, and Byron C. Wallace. 2019. An analysis of attention over clinical notes for predictive tasks. In Proceedings of the 2nd Clinical Natural Language Processing Workshop, pages 15–21, Minneapolis, Minnesota, USA. Association for Computational Linguistics.

Sarthak Jain and Byron C. Wallace. 2019. Attention is not explanation. In Proceedings of the 2019 Conference of the North American Chapter of the Association for Computational Linguistics: Human Language Technologies, Volume 1 (Long and Short Papers), pages 3543–3556, Minneapolis, Minnesota. Association for Computational Linguistics.

Akos Kádár, Grzegorz Chrupała, and Afra Alishahi. 2017. Representation of linguistic form and function in recurrent neural networks. Computational Linguistics, 43(4):761–780.

Andrej Karpathy, Justin Johnson, and Li Fei-Fei. 2015. Visualizing and understanding recurrent networks. arXiv preprint arXiv:1506.02078.

Guillaume Klein, Yoon Kim, Yuntian Deng, Jean Senellart, and Alexander Rush. 2017. OpenNMT: Open-source toolkit for neural machine translation. In Proceedings of ACL 2017, System Demonstrations, pages 67–72, Vancouver, Canada. Association for Computational Linguistics.

Philipp Koehn, Hieu Hoang, Alexandra Birch, Chris Callison-Burch, Marcello Federico, Nicola Bertoldi, Brooke Cowan, Wade Shen, Christine Moran, Richard Zens, Chris Dyer, Ondřej Bojar, Alexandra Constantin, and Evan Herbst. 2007. Moses: Open source toolkit for statistical machine translation. In Proceedings of the 45th Annual Meeting of the Association for Computational Linguistics Companion Volume Proceedings of the Demo and Poster Sessions, pages 177–180, Prague, Czech Republic. Association for Computational Linguistics.

Philipp Koehn and Rebecca Knowles. 2017. Six challenges for neural machine translation. In Proceedings of the First Workshop on Neural Machine Translation, pages 28–39, Vancouver. Association for Computational Linguistics.

Shaohui Kuang, Junhui Li, António Branco, Weihua Luo, and Deyi Xiong. 2018. Attention focusing for neural machine translation by bridging source and target embeddings. In Proceedings of the 56th Annual Meeting of the Association for Computational Linguistics (Volume 1: Long Papers), pages 1767–1776, Melbourne, Australia. Association for Computational Linguistics.

Jiwei Li, Xinlei Chen, Eduard Hovy, and Dan Jurafsky. 2016a. Visualizing and understanding neural models in NLP. In Proceedings of the 2016 Conference of the North American Chapter of the Association for Computational Linguistics: Human Language Technologies, pages 681–691, San Diego, California. Association for Computational Linguistics.

Jiwei Li, Will Monroe, and Dan Jurafsky. 2016b. Understanding neural networks through representation erasure. arXiv preprint arXiv:1612.08220.

Thang Luong, Hieu Pham, and Christopher D. Manning. 2015. Effective approaches to attention-based neural machine translation. In Proceedings of the 2015 Conference on Empirical Methods in Natural Language Processing, pages 1412–1421, Lisbon, Portugal. Association for Computational Linguistics.

Grégoire Montavon, Sebastian Lapuschkin, Alexander Binder, Wojciech Samek, and Klaus-Robert Müller. 2017. Explaining nonlinear classification decisions with deep taylor decomposition. Pattern Recognition, 65:211–222.

Sofia Serrano and Noah A. Smith. 2019. Is attention interpretable? In Proceedings of the 57th Annual Meeting of the Association for Computational Linguistics, pages 2931–2951, Florence, Italy. Association for Computational Linguistics.

Xing Shi, Kevin Knight, and Deniz Yuret. 2016. Why neural translations are the right length. In Proceedings of the 2016 Conference on Empirical Methods in Natural Language Processing, pages 2278–2282, Austin, Texas. Association for Computational Linguistics.

Karen Simonyan, Andrea Vedaldi, and Andrew Zisserman. 2013. Deep inside convolutional networks: Visualising image classification models and saliency maps. arXiv preprint arXiv:1312.6034.

Hendrik Strobelt, Sebastian Gehrmann, Michael Behrisch, Adam Perer, Hanspeter Pfister, and Alexander M Rush. 2018. S eq 2s eq-v is: A visual debugging tool for sequence-to-sequence models. IEEE transactions on visualization and computer graphics, 25(1):353–363.

Hendrik Strobelt, Sebastian Gehrmann, Hanspeter Pfister, and Alexander M Rush. 2017. Lstmvis: A tool for visual analysis of hidden state dynamics in recurrent neural networks. IEEE transactions on visualization and computer graphics, 24(1):667–676.

Ilya Sutskever, Oriol Vinyals, and Quoc V Le. 2014. Sequence to sequence learning with neural networks. In Advances in neural information processing systems, pages 3104–3112.

Rico Tang, Gongbo andSennrich and Joakim Nivre. 2018. An analysis of attention mechanisms: The case of word sense disambiguation in neural machine translation. In Proceedings of the Third Conference on Machine Translation: Research Papers, pages 26–35, Belgium, Brussels. Association for Computational Linguistics.

Zhaopeng Tu, Yang Liu, Zhengdong Lu, Xiaohua Liu, and Hang Li. 2017. Context gates for neural machine translation. Transactions of the Association for Computational Linguistics, 5:87–99.

Ashish Vaswani, Noam Shazeer, Niki Parmar, Jakob Uszkoreit, Llion Jones, Aidan N Gomez, Łukasz Kaiser, and Illia Polosukhin. 2017. Attention is all you need. In Advances in neural information processing systems, pages 5998–6008.

Jesse Vig and Yonatan Belinkov. 2019. Analyzing the structure of attention in a transformer language model. In Proceedings of the 2019 ACL Workshop BlackboxNLP: Analyzing and Interpreting Neural Networks for NLP, pages 63–76, Florence, Italy. Association for Computational Linguistics.

Matthew D Zeiler and Rob Fergus. 2014. Visualizing and understanding convolutional networks. In European conference on computer vision, pages 818–833. Springer.

Auto-Sizing the Transformer Network:
Improving Speed, Efficiency, and Performance
for Low-Resource Machine Translation

Kenton Murray   Jeffery Kinnison   Toan Q. Nguyen   Walter Scheirer   David Chiang
Department of Computer Science and Engineering
University of Notre Dame
{kmurray4, jkinniso, tnguye28, walter.scheirer, dchiang}@nd.edu

Abstract

Neural sequence-to-sequence models, particularly the Transformer, are the state of the art in machine translation. Yet these neural networks are very sensitive to architecture and hyperparameter settings. Optimizing these settings by grid or random search is computationally expensive because it requires many training runs. In this paper, we incorporate architecture search into a single training run through *auto-sizing*, which uses regularization to delete neurons in a network over the course of training. On very low-resource language pairs, we show that auto-sizing can improve BLEU scores by up to 3.9 points while removing one-third of the parameters from the model.

1   Introduction

Encoder-decoder based neural network models are the state-of-the-art in machine translation. However, these models are very dependent on selecting optimal hyperparameters and architectures. This problem is exacerbated in very low-resource data settings where the potential to overfit is high. Unfortunately, these searches are computationally expensive. For instance, Britz et al. (2017) used over 250,000 GPU hours to compare various recurrent neural network based encoders and decoders for machine translation. Strubell et al. (2019) demonstrated the neural architecture search for a large NLP model emits over four times the carbon dioxide relative to a car over its entire lifetime.

Unfortunately, optimal settings are highly dependent on both the model and the task, which means that this process must be repeated often. As a case in point, the Transformer architecture has become the best performing encoder-decoder model for machine translation (Vaswani et al., 2017), displacing RNN-based models (Bahdanau et al., 2015) along with much conventional wisdom about how to train such models. Vaswani

et al. ran experiments varying numerous hyperparameters of the Transformer, but only on high-resource datasets among linguistically similar languages. Popel and Bojar (2018) explored ways to train Transformer networks, but only on a high-resource dataset in one language pair. Less work has been devoted to finding best practices for smaller datasets and linguistically divergent language pairs.

In this paper, we apply *auto-sizing* (Murray and Chiang, 2015), which is a type of architecture search conducted during training, to the Transformer. We show that it is effective on very low-resource datasets and can reduce model size significantly, while being substantially faster than other architecture search methods. We make three main contributions.

1. We demonstrate the effectiveness of auto-sizing on the Transformer network by significantly reducing model size, even though the number of parameters in the Transformer is orders of magnitude larger than previous natural language processing applications of auto-sizing.

2. We demonstrate the effectiveness of auto-sizing on translation quality in very low-resource settings. On four out of five language pairs, we obtain improvements in BLEU over a recommended low-resource baseline architecture. Furthermore, we are able to do so an order of magnitude faster than random search.

3. We release GPU-enabled implementations of proximal operators used for auto-sizing. Previous authors (Boyd et al., 2010; Duchi et al., 2008) have given efficient algorithms, but they don't necessarily parallelize well on GPUs. Our variations are optimized for GPUs and are implemented as a general toolkit and are released as open-source software.[1]

---

[1] https://github.com/KentonMurray/ProxGradPytorch

Proceedings of the 3rd Workshop on Neural Generation and Translation (WNGT 2019), pages 231–240
Hong Kong, China, November 4, 2019. ©2019 Association for Computational Linguistics
www.aclweb.org/anthology/D19-56%2d

2 Hyperparameter Search

While the parameters of a neural network are optimized by gradient-based training methods, hyperparameters are values that are typically fixed before training begins, such as layer sizes and learning rates, and can strongly influence the outcome of training. Hyperparameter optimization is a search over the possible choices of hyperparameters for a neural network, with the objective of minimizing some cost function (e.g., error, time to convergence, etc.). Hyperparameters may be selected using a variety of methods, most often manual tuning, grid search (Duan and Keerthi, 2005), or random search (Bergstra and Bengio, 2012). Other methods, such as Bayesian optimization (Bergstra et al., 2011; Snoek et al., 2012), genetic algorithms (Benardos and Vosniakos, 2007; Friedrichs and Igel, 2005; Vose et al., 2019), and hypergradient updates (Maclaurin et al., 2015), attempt to direct the selection process based on the objective function. All of these methods require training a large number of networks with different hyperparameter settings.

In this work, we focus on a type of hyperparameter optimization called auto-sizing introduced by Murray and Chiang (2015) which only requires training one network once. Auto-sizing focuses on driving groups of weights in a parameter tensor to zero through regularization. Murray and Chiang (2015) focused on the narrow case of two hidden layers in a feed-forward neural network with a rectified linear unit activation. In this work, we look at the broader case of all of the non-embedding parameter matrices in the encoder and decoder of the Transformer network.

3 GPU Optimized Proximal Gradient Descent

Murray and Chiang (2015) train a neural network while using a regularizer to prune units from the network, minimizing:

$$\mathcal{L} = -\sum_{f,e \text{ in data}} \log P(e \mid f; W) + \lambda R(\|W\|),$$

where W are the parameters of the model and R is a regularizer. For simplicity, assume that the parameters form a single matrix W of weights. Murray

---

Algorithm 1 Parallel ℓ_∞ proximal step

Require: Vector $\mathbf{v}$ with n elements
Ensure: Decrease the largest absolute value in $\mathbf{v}$ until the total decrease is $\eta\lambda$

1: $v_i \leftarrow |v_i|$
2: sort $\mathbf{v}$ in decreasing order
3: $\delta_i \leftarrow v_i - v_{i+1}, \delta_n \leftarrow v_n$
4: $c_i \leftarrow \sum_{i'=1}^{i} i'\delta_{i'}$ ▷ prefix sum
5: $b_i = \frac{1}{i}(\text{clip}_{[c_{i-1},c_i]}(\eta\lambda) - c_{i-1})$
6: $p_i = \sum_{i'=i}^{n} b_{i'}$ ▷ suffix sum
7: $\mathbf{v} \leftarrow \mathbf{v} - \mathbf{p}$
8: restore order and signs of $\mathbf{v}$

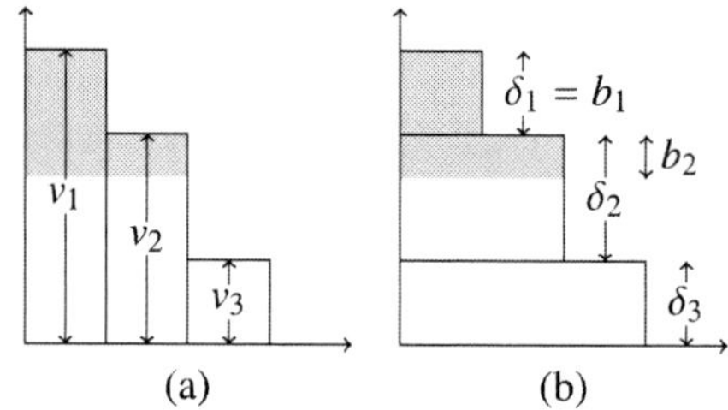

Figure 1: Illustration of Algorithm 1. The shaded area, here with value $\eta\lambda = 2$, represents how much the ℓ_∞ proximal step will remove from a sorted vector.

and Chiang (2015) try two regularizers:

$$R(W) = \sum_i \left(\sum_j W_{ij}^2 \right)^{\frac{1}{2}} \qquad (\ell_{2,1})$$

$$R(W) = \sum_i \max_j |W_{ij}| \qquad (\ell_{\infty,1})$$

The optimization is done using proximal gradient descent (Parikh and Boyd, 2014), which alternates between stochastic gradient descent steps and proximal steps:

$$W \leftarrow W - \eta\nabla \log P(e \mid f; w)$$

$$W \leftarrow \underset{W'}{\arg\min} \left(\frac{1}{2\eta}\|W - W'\|^2 + R(W') \right)$$

To perform the proximal step for the $\ell_{\infty,1}$ norm, they rely on a quickselect-like algorithm that runs in $O(n)$ time (Duchi et al., 2008). However, this algorithm does not parallelize well. Instead, we use Algorithm 1, which is similar to that of Quattoni et al. (2009), on each row of W.

The algorithm starts by taking the absolute value of each entry and sorting the entries in decreasing order. Figure 1a shows a histogram of sorted absolute values of an example $\mathbf{v}$. Intuitively, the goal of the algorithm is to cut a piece off the top with area $\eta\lambda$ (in the figure, shaded gray).

We can also imagine the same shape as a stack of horizontal layers (Figure 1b), each i wide and δ_i high, with area $i\delta_i$; then c_i is the cumulative area of the top i layers. This view makes it easier to compute where the cutoff should be. Let k be the index such that $\eta\lambda$ lies between c_{k-1} and c_k. Then $b_i = \delta_i$ for $i < k$; $b_k = \frac{1}{k}(\eta\lambda - c_{k-1})$; and $b_i = 0$ for $i > k$. In other words, b_i is how much height of the ith layer should be cut off.

Finally, returning to Figure 1b, p_i is the amount by which v_i should be decreased (the height of the gray bars). (The vector $\mathbf{p}$ also happens to be the projection of $\mathbf{v}$ onto the ℓ_1 ball of radius $\eta\lambda$.)

Although this algorithm is less efficient than the quickselect-like algorithm when run in serial, the sort in line 2 and the cumulative sums in lines 4 and 6 (Ladner and Fischer, 1980) can be parallelized to run in $O(\log n)$ passes each.

4   Transformer

The Transformer network, introduced by Vaswani et al. (2017), is a sequence-to-sequence model in which both the encoder and the decoder consist of stacked self-attention layers. Each layer of the decoder can attend to the previous layer of the decoder and the output of the encoder. The multi-head attention uses two affine transformations, followed by a softmax. Additionally, each layer has a position-wise feed-forward neural network (FFN) with a hidden layer of rectified linear units:

$$\text{FFN}(x) = W_2(\max(0, W_1 x + b_1)) + b_2.$$

The hidden layer size (number of columns of W_1) is typically four times the size of the model dimension. Both the multi-head attention and the feed-forward neural network have residual connections that allow information to bypass those layers.

4.1   Auto-sizing Transformer

Though the Transformer has demonstrated remarkable success on a variety of datasets, it is highly over-parameterized. For example, the English-German WMT '14 Transformer-base model proposed in Vaswani et al. (2017) has more

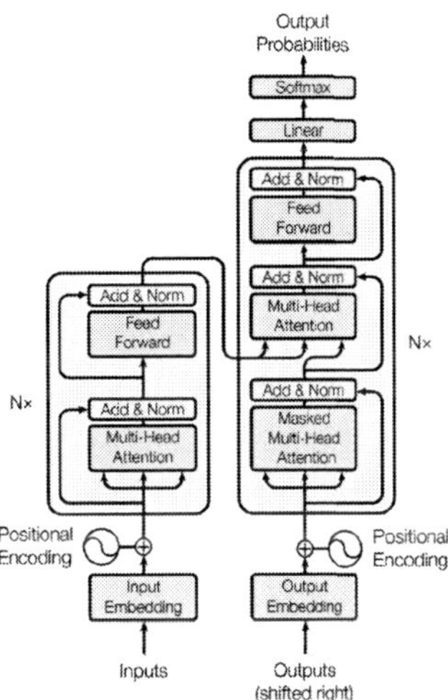

Figure 2: Architecture of the Transformer (Vaswani et al., 2017). We apply the auto-sizing method to the feed-forward (blue rectangles) and multi-head attention (orange rectangles) in all n layers of the encoder and decoder. Note that there are residual connections that can allow information and gradients to bypass any layer we are auto-sizing.

than 60M parameters. Whereas early NMT models such as Sutskever et al. (2014) have most of their parameters in the embedding layers, the added complexity of the Transformer, plus parallel developments reducing vocabulary size (Sennrich et al., 2016) and sharing embeddings (Press and Wolf, 2017) has shifted the balance. Nearly 31% of the English-German Transformer's parameters are in the attention layers and 41% in the position-wise feed-forward layers.

Accordingly, we apply the auto-sizing method to the Transformer network, and in particular to the two largest components, the feed-forward layers and the multi-head attentions (blue and orange rectangles in Figure 2). A difference from the work of Murray and Chiang (2015) is that there are residual connections that allow information to bypass the layers we are auto-sizing. If the regularizer drives all the neurons in a layer to zero, information can still pass through. Thus, auto-sizing can effectively prune out an entire layer.

4.2   Random Search

As an alternative to grid-based searches, random hyperparameter search has been demonstrated to be a strong baseline for neural network architecture searches as it can search between grid points to increase the size of the search space (Bergstra

Dataset	Size
Ara–Eng	234k
Fra–Eng	235k
Hau–Eng	45k
Tir–Eng	15k

Table 1: Number of parallel sentences in training bitexts. The French-English and Arabic-English data is from the 2017 IWSLT campaign (Mauro et al., 2012). The much smaller Hausa-English and Tigrinya-English data is from the LORELEI project.

and Bengio, 2012). In fact, Li and Talwalkar (2019) recently demonstrated that many architecture search methods do not beat a random baseline. In practice, randomly searching hyperparameter domains allows for an intuitive mixture of continuous and categorical hyperparameters with no constraints on differentiability (Maclaurin et al., 2015) or need to cast hyperparameter values into a single high-dimensional space to predict new values (Bergstra et al., 2011).

5 Experiments

All of our models are trained using the fairseq implementation of the Transformer (Gehring et al., 2017).[2] Our GPU-optimized, proximal gradient algorithms are implemented in PyTorch and are publicly available.[3] For the random hyperparameter search experiments, we use SHADHO,[4] which defines the hyperparameter tree, generates from it, and manages distributed resources (Kinnison et al., 2018). Our SHADHO driver file and modifications to fairseq are also publicly available.[5]

5.1 Settings

We looked at four different low-resource language pairs, running experiments in five directions: Arabic-English, English-Arabic, French-English, Hausa-English, and Tigrinya-English. The Arabic and French data comes from the IWSLT 2017 Evaluation Campaign (Mauro et al., 2012). The Hausa and Tigrinya data were provided by the LORELEI project with custom train/dev/test splits. For all languages, we tokenized and truecased the data using scripts from Moses (Koehn et al., 2007). For the Arabic systems, we translit-

erated the data using the Buckwalter transliteration scheme. All of our systems were run using subword units (BPE) with 16,000 merge operations on concatenated source and target training data (Sennrich and Haddow, 2016). We clip norms at 0.1, use label smoothed cross-entropy with value 0.1, and an early stopping criterion when the learning rate is smaller than 10^{-5}. All of our experiments were done using the Adam optimizer (Kingma and Ba, 2015), a learning rate of 10^{-4}, and dropout of 0.1. At test time, we decoded using a beam of 5 with length normalization (Boulanger-Lewandowski et al., 2013) and evaluate using case-sensitive, detokenized BLEU (Papineni et al., 2002).

5.1.1 Baseline

The originally proposed Transformer model is too large for our data size – the model will overfit the training data. Instead, we use the recommended settings in fairseq for IWSLT German-English as a baseline since two out of our four language pairs are also from IWSLT. This architecture has 6 layers in both the encoder and decoder, each with 4 attention heads. Our model dimension is $d_{model} = 512$, and our FFN dimension is 1024.

5.1.2 Auto-sizing parameters

Auto-sizing is implemented as two different types of group regularizers, $\ell_{2,1}$ and $\ell_{\infty,1}$. We apply the regularizers to the feed-forward network and multi-head attention in each layer of the encoder and decoder. We experiment across a range of regularization coefficient values, λ, that control how large the regularization proximal gradient step will be. We note that different regularization coefficient values are suited for different types or regularizers. Additionally, all of our experiments use the same batch size, which is also related to λ.

5.1.3 Random search parameters

As originally proposed, the Transformer network has 6 encoder layers, all identical, and 6 decoder layers, also identical. For our random search experiments, we sample the number of attention heads from $\{4, 8, 16\}$ and the model dimension (d_{model}) from $\{128, 256, 512, 1024, 2048\}$. Diverging from most implementations of the Transformer, we do not require the same number of encoder and decoder layers, but instead sample each from $\{2, 4, 6, 8\}$. Within a layer, we also sample the size of the feed-forward network (FFN), vary-

---

[2]https://github.com/pytorch/fairseq
[3]https://github.com/KentonMurray/ProxGradPytorch
[4]https://github.com/jeffkinnison/shadho
[5]https://bitbucket.org/KentonMurray/fairseq_autosizing

ing our samples over {512, 1024, 2048}. This too differs from most Transformer implementations, which have identical layer hyperparameters.

5.2 Auto-sizing vs. Random Search

Table 2 compares the performance of random search with auto-sizing across, BLEU scores, model size, and training times. The baseline system, the recommended IWSLT setting in fairseq, has almost 40 million parameters. Auto-sizing the feed-forward network sub-components in each layer of this baseline model with $\ell_{2,1} = 10.0$ or $\ell_{\infty,1} = 100.0$ removes almost one-third of the total parameters from the model. For Hausa-English and Tigrinya-English, this also results in substantial BLEU score gains, while only slightly hurting performance for French-English. The BLEU scores for random search beats the baseline for all language pairs, but auto-sizing still performs best on Tigrinya-English – even with 72 different, random hyperparameter configurations.

Auto-sizing trains in a similar amount of time to the baseline system, whereas the cumulative training time for all of the models in random search is substantially slower. Furthermore, for Tigrinya-English and French-English, random search found models that were almost 10 and 5 times larger respectively than the auto-sized models.

5.3 Training times

One of the biggest downsides of searching over architectures using a random search process is that it is very time and resource expensive. Contrary to that, auto-sizing relies on only training *one* model.

Auto-sizing relies on a proximal gradient step after a standard gradient descent step. However, the addition of these steps for our two group regularizers does not significantly impact training times. Table 3 shows the total training time for both $\ell_{2,1} = 0.1$ and $\ell_{\infty,1} = 0.5$. Even with the extra proximal step, auto-sizing using $\ell_{2,1}$ actually converges faster on two of the five language pairs. Note that these times are for smaller regularization coefficients. Larger coefficients will cause more values to go to zero, which will make the model converge faster.

5.4 Auto-sizing Sub-Components

As seen above, on very low-resource data, auto-sizing is able to quickly learn smaller, yet better, models than the recommended low-resource transformer architecture. Here, we look at the impact of applying auto-sizing to various sub-components of the Transformer network. In section 3, following the work of Murray and Chiang (2015), auto-sizing is described as intelligently applying a group regularizer to our objective function. The relative weight, or regularization coefficient, is a hyperparameter defined as λ. In this section, we also look at the impact of varying the strength of this regularization coefficient.

Tables 4 and 5 demonstrate the impact of varying the regularization coefficient strength has on BLEU scores and model size across various model sub-components. Recall that each layer of the Transformer network has multi-head attention sub-components and a feed-forward network sub-component. We denote experiments only applying auto-sizing to feed-forward network as "FFN". We also experiment with auto-sizing the multi-head attention in conjunction with the FFN, which we denote "All". A regularization coefficient of 0.0 refers to the baseline model without any auto-sizing. Columns which contain percentages refer to the number of rows in a PyTorch parameter that auto-sizing was applied to, that were entirely driven to zero. In effect, neurons deleted from the model. Note that individual values in a row may be zero, but if even a single value remains, information can continue to flow through this and it is not counted as deleted. Furthermore, percentages refer only to the parameters that auto-sizing was applied to, not the entire model. As such, with the prevalence of residual connections, a value of 100% does not mean the entire model was deleted, but merely specific parameter matrices. More specific experimental conditions are described below.

5.4.1 FFN matrices and multi-head attention

Rows corresponding to "All" in tables 4 and 5 look at the impact of varying the strength of both the $\ell_{\infty,1}$ and $\ell_{2,1}$ regularizers across all learned parameters in the encoder and decoders (multi-head and feed-forward network parameters). Using $\ell_{\infty,1}$ regularization (table 5), auto-sizing beats the baseline BLEU scores on three language pairs: Hau–Eng, Tir–Eng, Fra–Eng. However, BLEU score improvements only occur on smaller regularization coefficients that do not delete model portions.

Looking at $\ell_{2,1}$ regularization across all learned parameters of both the encoder and decoder ("Enc+Dec All" in table 4), auto-sizing beats the baseline on four of the five language pairs (all except Eng–Ara). Again, BLEU gains are on smaller

Language Pair	Search Strategy	BLEU	Model Size	Training Time
Tir–Eng	Standard Baseline	3.6	39.6M	1.2k
	Random Search	6.7	240.4M	43.7k
	Auto-sizing $\ell_{\infty,1}$	7.5	27.1M	2.1k
	Auto-sizing $\ell_{2,1}$	7.4	27.1M	1.2k
Hau–Eng	Standard Baseline	13.9	39.6M	4.2k
	Random Search	17.2	15.4M	87.0k
	Auto-sizing $\ell_{\infty,1}$	15.0	27.1M	7.6k
	Auto-sizing $\ell_{2,1}$	14.8	27.1M	3.5k
Fra–Eng	Standard Baseline	35.0	39.6M	11.3k
	Random Search	35.3	121.2M	116.0k
	Auto-sizing $\ell_{\infty,1}$	34.3	27.1M	28.8k
	Auto-sizing $\ell_{2,1}$	33.5	27.1M	11.5k

Table 2: Comparison of BLEU scores, model size, and training time on Tigrinya-English, Hausa-English, and French-English. Model size is the total number of parameters. Training time is measured in seconds. Baseline is the recommended low-resource architecture in fairseq. Random search represents the best model found from 72 (Tigrinya), 40 (Hausa), and 10 (French) different randomly generated architecture hyperparameters. Both auto-sizing methods, on both languages, start with the exact same initialization and number of parameters as the baseline, but converge to much smaller models across all language pairs. On the very low-resource languages of Hausa and Tigrinya auto-sizing finds models with better BLEU scores. Random search is eventually able to find better models on French and Hausa, but is an order of magnitude slower.

Language Pair	Baseline	$\ell_{2,1}$	$\ell_{\infty,1}$
Fra–Eng	11.3k	11.5k	28.8k
Ara–Eng	15.1k	16.6k	40.8k
Eng–Ara	16.6k	11.0k	21.9k
Hau–Eng	4.2k	3.5k	7.6k
Tir–Eng	1.2k	1.2k	2.1k

Table 3: Overall training times in seconds on a Nvidia GeForce GTX 1080Ti GPU for small regularization values. Note that high regularization values will delete too many values and cause training to end sooner. In general, $\ell_{2,1}$ regularization does not appreciably slow down training, but $\ell_{\infty,1}$ can be twice as slow. Per epoch, roughly the same ratios in training times hold.

regularization coefficients, and stronger regularizers that delete parts of the model hurt translation quality. Multi-head attention is an integral portion of the Transformer model and auto-sizing this generally leads to performance hits.

5.4.2 FFN matrices

As the multi-head attention is a key part of the Transformer, we also looked at auto-sizing just the feed-forward sub-component in each layer of the encoder and decoder. Rows deonted by "FFN" in tables 4 and 5 look at applying auto-sizing to all of the feed-forward network sub-components of the Transformer, but not to the multi-head attention. With $\ell_{\infty,1}$ regularization, we see BLEU improvements on four of the five language pairs. For both Hausa-English and Tigrinya-English, we see improvements even after deleting all of the feed-forward networks in all layers. Again, the residual connections allow information to flow around these sub-components. Using $\ell_{2,1}$ regularization, we see BLEU improvements on three of the language pairs. Hausa-English and Tigrinya-English maintain a BLEU gain even when deleting all of the feed-forward networks.

Auto-sizing only the feed-forward sub-component, and not the multi-head attention part, results in better BLEU scores, even when deleting all of the feed-forward network components. Impressively, this is with a model that has fully *one-third* fewer parameters in the encoder and decoder layers. This is beneficial for faster inference times and smaller disk space.

5.4.3 Encoder vs. Decoder

In table 4, experiments on Hau-Eng look at the impact of auto-sizing either the encoder or the decoder separately. Applying a strong enough regularizer to delete portions of the model ($\ell_{2,1} \geq 1.0$) only to the decoder ("Decoder All" and "Decoder

	Model Portion	0.0	0.1	0.25		0.5		1.0		10.0	
										$\ell_{2,1}$ coefficient	
Hau–Eng	Encoder All	13.9	16.0	17.1		17.4		15.3	89%	16.4	100%
	Encoder FFN		15.4	15.1		16.3		15.9	100%	16.7	100%
	Decoder All		12.6	16.1		16.2		13.0	3%	0.0	63%
	Decoder FFN		11.8	14.7		14.4		11.7	79%	13.1	100%
	Enc+Dec All		15.8	17.4		17.8		12.5	61%	0.0	100%
	Enc+Dec FFN		14.7	15.3		14.2		12.8	86%	14.8	100%
Tir–Eng	Encoder All	3.6	3.3	4.7		5.3		7.2		8.4	100%
	Enc+Dec All		3.8	4.0		6.5		7.0		0.0	100%
	Enc+Dec FFN		4.0	4.2		3.3		5.1		7.4	100%
Fra–Eng	Encoder All	35.0	35.7	34.5		34.1		33.6	97%	32.8	100%
	Enc+Dec All		35.2	33.1		29.8	23%	24.2	73%	0.3	100%
	Enc+Dec FFN		35.6	35.0		34.2	15%	34.2	98%	33.5	100%
Ara–Eng	Enc+Dec All	27.9	28.0	24.7	1%	20.9	20%	14.3	72%	0.3	100%
	Enc+Dec FFN		26.9	26.7	1%	25.5	23%	25.9	97%	25.7	100%
Eng–Ara	Enc+Dec All	9.4	8.7	7.5		5.8	23%	3.7	73%	0.0	100%
	Enc+Dec FFN		8.6	8.3	3%	8.3	22%	7.9	93%	8.0	100%

Table 4: BLEU scores and percentage of parameter rows deleted by auto-sizing on various sub-components of the model, across varying strengths of $\ell_{2,1}$ regularization. 0.0 refers to the baseline without any regularizer. Blank spaces mean less than 1% of parameters were deleted. In the two very low-resource language pairs (Hausa-English and Tigrinya-English), deleting large portions of the encoder can actually help performance. However, deleting the decoder hurts performance.

		0.0	0.1	0.25	0.5	1.0	10.0		100.0	
						$\ell_{\infty,1}$				
Hau–Eng	Enc+Dec All	13.9	15.5	14.7	16.0	16.7	14.9	4%	1.5	100%
	Enc+Dec FFN		13.4	14.3	14.1	12.9	15.3	0%	15.0	100%
Tir–Eng	Enc+Dec All	3.6	4.6	3.4	3.4	3.7	7.4	0%	2.4	100%
	Enc+Dec FFN		3.6	3.8	3.9	3.6	4.7	0%	7.5	100%
Fra–Eng	Enc+Dec All	35.0	35.2	35.4	34.9	35.3	26.3	13%	1.7	100%
	Enc+Dec FFN		34.8	35.5	35.4	35.0	34.1	0%	34.3	100%
Ara–Eng	Enc+Dec All	27.9	27.3	27.5	27.6	26.9	18.5	22%	0.6	100%
	Enc+Dec FFN		27.8	27.2	28.3	27.6	25.4	0%	25.4	100%
Eng–Ara	Enc+Dec All	9.4	9.1	8.3	8.4	8.7	5.2	25%	0.6	100%
	Enc+Dec FFN		8.8	9.2	9.0	8.9	8.2	0%	8.3	100%

Table 5: BLEU scores and percentage of model deleted using auto-sizing with various $l_{\infty,1}$ regularization strengths. On the very low-resource language pairs of Hausa-English and Tigrinya-English, auto-sizing the feed-forward networks of the encoder and decoder can improve BLEU scores.

FFN") results in a BLEU score drop. However, applying auto-sizing to only the encoder ("Encoder All" and "Encoder FFN") yields a BLEU gain while creating a smaller model. Intuitively, this makes sense as the decoder is closer to the output of the network and requires more modeling expressivity.

In addition to Hau–Eng, table 4 also contains experiments looking at auto-sizing all sub-components of all encoder layers of Tir–Eng and Fra–Eng. For all three language pairs, a small regularization coefficient for the $\ell_{2,1}$ regularizer applied to the encoder increases BLEU scores. However, no rows are driven to zero and the model size remains the same. Consistent with Hau–Eng, using a larger regularization coefficient drives all of the encoder's weights to all zeros. For the smaller Hau–Eng and Tir–Eng datasets, this actually results in BLEU gains over the baseline system. Surprisingly, even on the Fra–Eng dataset, which has more than 15x as much data as Tir–Eng, the performance hit of deleting the *entire* encoder was only 2 BLEU points.

Recall from Figure 2 that there are residual connections that allow information and gradients to flow around both the multi-head attention and feed-forward portions of the model. Here, we have the case that all layers of the encoder have been completely deleted. However, the decoder still attends over the source word and positional embeddings due to the residual connections. We hypothesize that for these smaller datasets that there are too many parameters in the baseline model and over-fitting is an issue.

5.5 Random Search plus Auto-sizing

Above, we have demonstrated that auto-sizing is able to learn smaller models, faster than random search, often with higher BLEU scores. To compare whether the two architecture search algorithms (random and auto-sizing) can be used in conjunction, we also looked at applying both $\ell_{2,1}$ and $\ell_{\infty,1}$ regularization techniques to the FFN networks in all encoder and decoder layers *during* random search. In addition, this looks at how robust the auto-sizing method is to different initial conditions.

For a given set of hyperparameters generated by the random search process, we initialize three *identical* models and train a baseline as well as one with each regularizer ($\ell_{2,1} = 1.0$ and $\ell_{\infty,1} = 10.0$).

	none	$\ell_{2,1}$	$\ell_{\infty,1}$
Hau–Eng	17.2	16.6	17.8
Tir–Eng	6.7	7.9	7.6
Fra–Eng	35.4	34.7	34.1
Ara–Eng	27.6	25.6	25.9
Eng–Ara	9.0	7.6	8.4

Table 6: Test BLEU scores for the models with the best dev perplexity found using random search over number of layers and size of layers. Regularization values of $\ell_{2,1} = 1.0$ and $\ell_{\infty,1} = 10.0$ were chosen based on tables 4 and 5 as they encouraged neurons to be deleted. For the very low-resource language pairs, auto-sizing helped in conjunction with random search.

We trained 216 Tir–Eng models ($3 \cdot 72$ hyperparameter config.), 120 Hau–Eng, 45 Ara–Eng, 45 Eng–Ara, and 30 Fra–Eng models. Using the model with the best dev perplexity found during training, table 6 shows the test BLEU scores for each of the five language pairs. For the very low-resource language pairs of Hau–Eng and Tir–Eng, auto-sizing is able to find the best BLEU scores.

6 Conclusion

In this paper, we have demonstrated the effectiveness of auto-sizing on the Transformer network. On very low-resource datasets, auto-sizing was able to improve BLEU scores by up to 3.9 points while simultaneously deleting one-third of the parameters in the encoder and decoder layers. This was accomplished while being significantly faster than other search methods.

Additionally, we demonstrated how to apply proximal gradient methods efficiently using a GPU. Previous work on optimizing proximal gradient algorithms serious impacts speed performance when the computations are moved off of a CPU and parallelized. Leveraging sorting and prefix summation, we reformulated these methods to be GPU efficient.

Overall, this paper has demonstrated the efficacy of auto-sizing on a natural language processing application with orders of magnitude more parameters than previous work. With a focus on speedy architecture search and an emphasis on optimized GPU algorithms, auto-sizing is able to improve machine translation on very low-resource language pairs without being resource or time-consuming.

Acknowledgements

This research was supported in part by University of Southern California, subcontract 67108176 under DARPA contract HR0011-15-C-0115. We would like to thank Justin DeBenedetto for helpful comments.

References

Dzmitry Bahdanau, Kyunghyun Cho, and Yoshua Bengio. 2015. Neural machine translation by jointly learning to align and translate. In *Proc. ICLR*.

P. G. Benardos and G.-C. Vosniakos. 2007. Optimizing feedforward artificial neural network architecture. *Engineering Applications of Artificial Intelligence*, 20:365–382.

James Bergstra and Yoshua Bengio. 2012. Random search for hyper-parameter optimization. *Journal of Machine Learning Research*, 13:281–305.

James S. Bergstra, Rémi Bardenet, Yoshua Bengio, and Balázs Kégl. 2011. Algorithms for hyper-parameter optimization. In *Advances in Neural Information Processing Systems*, pages 2546–2554.

Nicolas Boulanger-Lewandowski, Yoshua Bengio, and Pascal Vincent. 2013. Audio chord recognition with recurrent neural networks. In *Proc. International Society for Music Information Retrieval*, pages 335–340.

Stephen Boyd, Neal Parikh, Eric Chu, Borja Peleato, and Jonathan Eckstein. 2010. Distributed optimization and statistical learning via the alternating direction method of multipliers. *Foundations and Trends in Machine learning*, 3(1):1–122.

Denny Britz, Anna Goldie, Minh-Thang Luong, and Quoc Le. 2017. Massive exploration of neural machine translation architectures. In *Proc. EMNLP*, pages 1442–1451.

Kai-Bo Duan and S. Sathiya Keerthi. 2005. Which is the best multiclass SVM method? An empirical study. In *International Workshop on Multiple Classifier Systems*, pages 278–285.

John Duchi, Shai Shalev-Shwartz, Yoram Singer, and Tushar Chandra. 2008. Efficient projections onto the ℓ_1-ball for learning in high dimensions. In *Proc. ICML*, pages 272–279.

Frauke Friedrichs and Christian Igel. 2005. Evolutionary tuning of multiple SVM parameters. *Neurocomputing*, 64:107–117.

Jonas Gehring, Michael Auli, David Grangier, Denis Yarats, and Yann N. Dauphin. 2017. Convolutional Sequence to Sequence Learning. In *Proc. ICML*.

Diederik P. Kingma and Jimmy Lei Ba. 2015. Adam: A method for stochastic optimization. In *Proc. ICLR*.

Jeffery Kinnison, Nathaniel Kremer-Herman, Douglas Thain, and Walter Scheirer. 2018. Shadho: Massively scalable hardware-aware distributed hyperparameter optimization. In *Proc. IEEE Winter Conference on Applications of Computer Vision (WACV)*, pages 738–747.

Philipp Koehn, Hieu Hoang, Alexandra Birch, Chris Callison-Burch, Marcello Federico, Nicola Bertoldi, Brooke Cowan, Wade Shen, Christine Moran, Richard Zens, et al. 2007. Moses: Open source toolkit for statistical machine translation. In *Proc. ACL: Demos*, pages 177–180.

Richard E. Ladner and Michael J. Fischer. 1980. Parallel prefix computation. *J. ACM*, 27(4):831–838.

Liam Li and Ameet Talwalkar. 2019. Random search and reproducibility for neural architecture search.

Dougal Maclaurin, David Duvenaud, and Ryan Adams. 2015. Gradient-based hyperparameter optimization through reversible learning. In *Proc. ICML*, pages 2113–2122.

Cettolo Mauro, Girardi Christian, and Federico Marcello. 2012. Wit3: Web inventory of transcribed and translated talks. In *Proc. EAMT*, pages 261–268.

Kenton Murray and David Chiang. 2015. Auto-sizing neural networks: With applications to n-gram language models. In *Proc. EMNLP*.

Kishore Papineni, Salim Roukos, Todd Ward, and Wei-Jing Zhu. 2002. BLEU: a method for automatic evaluation of machine translation. In *Proc. ACL*, pages 311–318.

Neal Parikh and Stephen Boyd. 2014. Proximal algorithms. *Foundations and Trends in Optimization*, 1(3):123–231.

Martin Popel and Ondřej Bojar. 2018. Training tips for the Transformer model. *The Prague Bulletin of Mathematical Linguistics*, 110(1):43–70.

Ofir Press and Lior Wolf. 2017. Using the output embedding to improve language models. In *Proc. EACL: Volume 2, Short Papers*, pages 157–163.

Ariadna Quattoni, Xavier Carreras, Michael Collins, and Trevor Darrell. 2009. An efficient projection for $l_{1,\infty}$ regularization. In *Proc. ICML*, pages 857–864.

Rico Sennrich and Barry Haddow. 2016. Linguistic input features improve neural machine translation. In *Proc. First Conference on Machine Translation: Volume 1, Research Papers*, volume 1, pages 83–91.

Rico Sennrich, Barry Haddow, and Alexandra Birch. 2016. Neural machine translation of rare words with subword units. In *Proc. ACL*, pages 1715–1725.

Jasper Snoek, Hugo Larochelle, and Ryan P. Adams. 2012. Practical Bayesian optimization of machine learning algorithms. In *Advances in Neural Information Processing Systems*, pages 2951–2959.

Emma Strubell, Ananya Ganesh, and Andrew McCallum. 2019. Energy and policy considerations for deep learning in NLP. In *Proc. ACL*.

Ilya Sutskever, Oriol Vinyals, and Quoc V Le. 2014. Sequence to sequence learning with neural networks. In *Advances in Neural Information Processing Systems*, pages 3104–3112.

Ashish Vaswani, Noam Shazeer, Niki Parmar, Jakob Uszkoreit, Llion Jones, Aidan N. Gomez, Łukasz Kaiser, and Illia Polosukhin. 2017. Attention is all you need. In *Advances in Neural Information Processing Systems*, pages 5998–6008.

Aaron Vose, Jacob Balma, Alex Heye, Alessandro Rigazzi, Charles Siegel, Diana Moise, Benjamin Robbins, and Rangan Sukumar. 2019. Recombination of artificial neural networks. arXiv:1901.03900.

Learning to Generate Word- and Phrase-Embeddings for Efficient Phrase-Based Neural Machine Translation

Chan Young Park   Yulia Tsvetkov
Language Technologies Institute
Carnegie Mellon University
{chanyoun,ytsvetko}@cs.cmu.edu

Abstract

Neural machine translation (NMT) often fails in one-to-many translation, e.g., in the translation of multi-word expressions, compounds, and collocations. To improve the translation of phrases, phrase-based NMT systems have been proposed; these typically combine word-based NMT with external phrase dictionaries or with phrase tables from phrase-based statistical MT systems. These solutions introduce a significant overhead of additional resources and computational costs. In this paper, we introduce a phrase-based NMT model built upon continuous-output NMT, in which the decoder generates embeddings of words or phrases. The model uses a fertility module, which guides the decoder to generate embeddings of sequences of varying lengths. We show that our model learns to translate phrases better, performing on par with state of the art phrase-based NMT. Since our model does not resort to softmax computation over a huge vocabulary of phrases, its training time is about 112x faster than the baseline.

1 Introduction

Despite the successes of neural machine translation (Wu et al., 2016; Vaswani et al., 2017; Ahmed et al., 2018), state of the art NMT systems are still challenged by translation of typologically divergent language pairs, especially when languages are morphologically rich (Burlot and Yvon, 2017). One of the reasons lies in increased sparsity of word types, which leads to the demand for (often unavailable) significantly larger training corpora (Koehn and Knowles, 2017). Another reason is an implicit assumption of sequence to sequence (seq2seq) models that input sequences are translated into a target language word-by-word or subword-by-subword (Sennrich et al., 2016).

This is not the case for typologically divergent language pairs, for example when translating into English from agglutinative languages with high rates of morphemes per word (e.g., Turkish and Quechua) or languages with productive compounding processes like German or Finnish (Matthews et al., 2016). Another ubiquitous source of one-to-many correspondences is a translation of idiomatic phrases and multi-word expressions (Rikters and Bojar, 2017).

While outperformed by NMT overall, translation models in traditional statistical phrase-based approaches (Koehn, 2009, SMT) provide an inventory of phrase translations, which can be used to address the above challenges. To combine the benefits of NMT and phrase-based SMT, phrase-based NMT systems have been proposed (Huang et al., 2017; Lample et al., 2018) which combine word-based NMT with external phrase memories (Tang et al., 2016; Dahlmann et al., 2017). However, prior approaches to phrase-based NMT introduced a significant overhead of additional resources and computation.

We introduce a phrase-based continuous-output NMT (PCoNMT) model built upon continuous-output NMT (Kumar and Tsvetkov, 2019), in which the decoder generates embeddings of words or phrases (§2). The model extracts phrases in the target language from one-to-many word alignments and pre-computes word and phrase embeddings which constitute the output space of our model (§2.2). A fertility module guides the decoder, providing the probability of generating a word or a phrase at each time step (§2.3). Experimental results show that the proposed model outperforms the conventional attention-based NMT systems (Bahdanau et al., 2014) by up to 4.8 BLEU, and the baseline continuous-output models by up to 1.6 BLEU, and beat the state-of-the-art phrase-based NMT system in translation from German and Turkish into English.

Since our model does not resort to softmax

Proceedings of the 3rd Workshop on Neural Generation and Translation (WNGT 2019), pages 241–248
Hong Kong, China, November 4, 2019. ©2019 Association for Computational Linguistics
www.aclweb.org/anthology/D19-56%2d

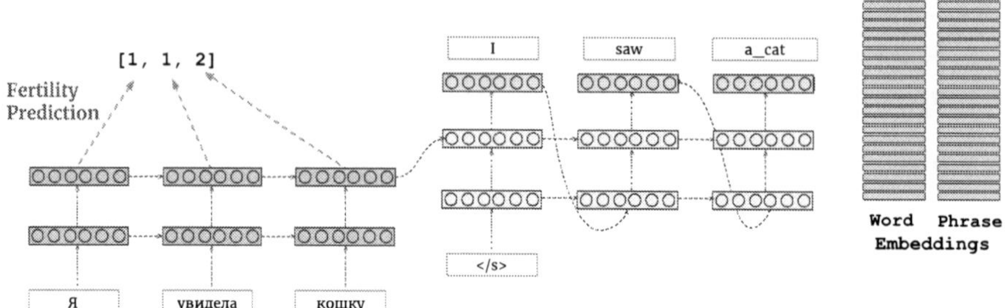

Figure 1: Phrase-based neural machine translation architectures generate word- and phrase embeddings at each step of decoding. The PCoNMT models are guided by on the fertility prediction and the attention.

computation over a huge vocabulary, it also maintains the computational efficiency of continuous-output NMT, even with additional ngram embedding tables, and is faster than the state-of-the-art baseline by 112x (§3), making our models energy-efficient (Strubell et al., 2019).

The key contributions of our work are twofold: (1) we develop a phrase-based NMT model that outperforms existing baselines and better translates phrases, while (2) maintaining the computational efficiency of NMT end-to-end approaches.[1]

2 Phrase-based Continuous-output NMT

2.1 Embedding output layer

Kumar and Tsvetkov (2019) introduced continuous-output machine translation (CoNMT) which replaces the softmax layer in the conventional seq2seq models with a continuous embeddings layer. The model predicts the embedding of the target word instead of its probability. It is trained to maximize the von Mises-Fisher (vMF) probability density of the pretrained target-language embeddings given the embeddings predicted by the model at every step; at inference time, predicted embedding is compared to the embeddings in the pre-trained embedding table, and the closest embedding is selected as an output word. While maintaining the translation quality of traditional seq2seq approaches, CoNMT approach alleviates the computational bottleneck of the softmax layer: it is substantially more efficient to train and the models are more compact, without limiting the output vocabulary size.

Extending the CoNMT approach, we propose phrase-based continuous-output NMT (PCoNMT). As depicted in Figure 1, we augment the original model with (1) additional embedding tables for phrases, and (2) a fertility module that guides the choice of embedding table to look-up in (described in §2.3). Having additional large embedding tables, which significantly increase the vocabulary size, could be a considerable overhead to a word-based model with the softmax layer. However, since we generate embeddings in the final layer and do not resort to the softmax computation, our models maintain the computational efficiency of continuous-output models (§3) during the training time. At inference time, the only overhead incurred by our model is getting another set of vMF scores for the phrase embedding table for each output step. This is almost negligible compared to the computation of the entire network.

In addition to efficiency benefits, since the PCoNMT approach enables us to pre-compute embeddings of less frequent phrases and phrases that do not have a literal translation, e.g., multi-word expressions, it facilitates better translations specifically where the translation is notoriously challenging for NMT.

2.2 Output embedding tables

To construct embedding tables for target-language phrases, we first extract the list of output phrases from parallel corpora. Following Tang et al. (2016), in this work, we focus on one-to-many word alignments in the training corpus. Consider as an example translation of German com-

---

[1] Our code and data are available at `https://github.com/chan0park/PCoNMT`

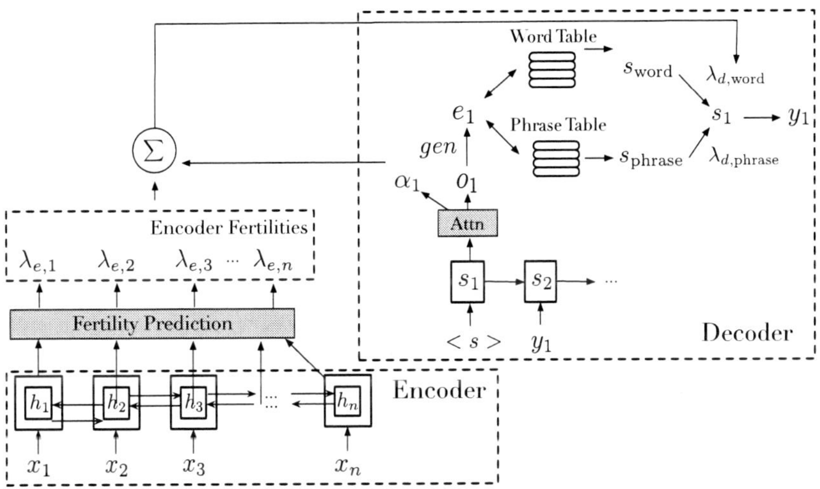

Figure 2: The detailed architecture of our model which consist of three components (encoder, fertility module, and decoder), described in §2. Given an input sentence $\{x_1, x_2 \ldots x_n\}$, our model generates the output sentence $\{y_1, y_2 \ldots y_m\}$, where y_i corresponds to words or phrases, e.g. *quality_of_life*. At each step, the decoder generates an embedding e_i, then the fertility module guides it to generate a word or a phrase, via the word- or phrase-embedding table, respectively.

pounds to English, e.g., *Lebensqualität* in German is translated as *quality of life*. We extract all such one-to-many word alignments from the parallel corpora using Fastalign (Dyer et al., 2013). There are several standard approaches to extract meaningful phrases from a monolingual corpus, such as using scores like pointwise mutual information (PMI) (Mikolov et al., 2013). However, for our model, we utilize word-alignment results to construct a phrase list since we are particularly interested in multi-word translation cases. Note that with this approach, phrases in target-side embedding tables can be different depending on which language pair and which corpus are being used.

After extracting all noisy one-to-many alignments from the parallel corpus, we filter our phrase list in order to keep only the useful phrases and to remove potential erroneous phrases coming from alignment errors. We filter according to the following heuristics: (1) a phrase should appear at least twice in the parallel corpus; (2) it should not contain any punctuation; (3) PMI of the phrase should be positive; (4) a bigram phrase should not repeat the same word; and (5) the phrase should not contain only stopwords.

We train embeddings for the resulting list of words and phrases as follows. First, we preprocess the target language's large monolingual corpus to concatenate words to match the longest phrase in the extracted phrase list. For example, the sen-

tence 'I went to a graduate school' will be converted into 'I went_to a graduate_school' if we have *went_to* and *graduate_school* in our phrase list. This concatenated corpus is then used to train fastText (Peters et al., 2018) embeddings for both phrases and words simultaneously. We use fastText because it encodes subword-level information which may provide a signal about each word in a phrase. From this training, we obtain both the word- and phrase-tables, which are of the same dimension.

2.3 Fertility module

We introduce a fertility module, similar to the fertility concept in SMT (Brown et al., 1993). The fertility indicates how many target words each source word should produce in the output. The SMT models keep the fertility probabilities over fertility count, typically from zero to four, and use it to produce probability over words. We integrate this fertility concept into our PCoNMT model.

Our fertility module predicts the fertility probability $\phi_e = [\phi_{e0}, ..., \phi_{eN}]$, where ϕ_{ei} indicates the scalar probability of the source word at position e being translated into i words. This is predicted based on the word embedding and encoder's output of the word: $\phi_e = \mathrm{FFNN}(x_e; h_e)$. FFNN is the feed-forward neural network, and $(x_e; h_e)$ denotes the concatenation of x_e and h_e, which are embedding and encoder's hidden state of eth source word, respectively. The dimension of fertility vector ϕ, N, can be arbitrarily large, but in this paper we explore two different variants; the first one is Fertility$_4$ where each dimension corresponds to zero to three words to produce respectively ($N \in \{0, 1, 2, 3\}$), and the second one is Fertility$_2$ which simplifies the fertility prediction into binary classification by setting $N=1$ as a cut-off point, i.e., whether the model should generate a word ($N \leq 1$) or a phrase ($N > 1$). Therefore, ϕ_e becomes a four-dimensional vector of $[\phi_{e0}, \phi_{e1}, \phi_{e2}, \phi_{e3}]$ for Fertility$_4$, and two-dimensional vector of $[\sum_{n=0}^{1} \phi_{en}, \sum_{n=2}^{\infty} \phi_{en}]$ for Fertility$_2$.

At decoding time, we combine this fertility probability of each source word and the attention to guide the decoder to generate a phrase or a word. To get the probability of producing a word $\lambda_{d,\text{word}}$ for timestep d, we use attention given to each source word as a weight to its fertility probability and sum over the entire source sentence:

$$\lambda_{d,\text{word}} = \begin{cases} \sum_e \mathbf{a}_{d,e} \left(\phi_{e0} + \phi_{e1}\right) & (\dim = 4) \\ \sum_e \mathbf{a}_{d,e} \left[\phi_e\right]_0 & (\dim = 2) \end{cases}$$
$$\lambda_{d,\text{phrase}} = 1 - \lambda_{d,\text{word}},$$

where $\mathbf{a}_{d,e}$ is a scalar value of attention assigned for source word e at timestep d and $[\phi_e]_0$ is the 0th element of ϕ_e, which basically is the same as $(\phi_{e0} + \phi_{e1})$ in Fertility$_4$. We use this $\lambda_{d,\text{word}}$ and $\lambda_{d,\text{phrase}}$ to weight the scores in word table and in phrase table, respectively:

$$s_{\text{word}} = \lambda_{d,\text{word}} \cdot \text{Score}(e_d, T_{\text{word}})$$
$$s_{\text{phrase}} = \lambda_{d,\text{phrase}} \cdot \text{Score}(e_d, T_{\text{phrase}})$$
$$y_d = \arg\max(s_{\text{word}}; s_{\text{phrase}}),$$

where s_{word} is a vector of scores for word in the word embedding table T_{word}, and Score is a score function to measure how similar the predicted embedding e_d and the embeddings in T. For the Score function, we use vMF as proposed in Kumar and Tsvetkov (2019). Finally, we get an output, y_d for the timestep d by doing $\arg\max$ over weighted scores from both word and phrase tables.

2.4 Model Training

The training of PCoNMT model is achieved by two separate steps. First, we only train the seq2seq modules as CoNMT does. We use vMF loss to optimize the embedding prediction. Once we find the optimal parameters for the CoNMT components,

	IWSLT	IWSLT$_{\text{MWT}}$
Attn	23.83	-
NPMT	27.27	-
CoNMT	27.07	24.98
PCoNMT	**28.69**	**28.89**
+Fertility$_4$	28.04	24.93
+Fertility$_2$	28.29	25.12

Table 1: Evaluation results (BLEU) on IWSLT 2014 De–En task.

	WMT	WMT$_{\text{MWT}}$
NPMT	3.58	-
CoNMT	7.44	7.67
PCoNMT	**8.87**	7.70
+Fertility$_4$	8.12	8.53
+Fertility$_2$	8.39	**8.61**

Table 2: Evaluation results (BLEU) on WMT 2017 Tr–En task.

we freeze those parameters, and separately train parameters of the fertility module.[2] During the preprocessing, we extract the actual fertility value for each source word using the word-alignment model and the filtered phrase list, then set it as a gold label for the fertility prediction training.

3 Experiments

In this section, we evaluate our model in terms of translation quality and training efficiency. We used IWSLT 2014 dataset for De–En machine translation task, following the same preprocessing and splits as in Ranzato et al. (2016). For the Tr–En task, we used WMT 17 train and test dataset (Bojar et al., 2018). The training corpora size for IWSLT 2014 and WMT 17 is about 153K and 200K sentences, respectively. All results are reported with case-sensitive BLEU-4 (Papineni et al., 2002). In addition to the two official datasets, we subset the given test sets to sentences that actually contain multi-word translation (MWT) cases by running the word-alignment model. The size of extracted MWT subsets for IWSLT 2014 and WMT 17 are 335 (5%) and 116

---

[2] Although we have omitted the results due to space, we also have tried jointly training the fertility prediction and translation in a multi-task learning setting. However, the joint-learning has consistently hurt the translation quality.

	speed ↓ (samples/sec)	convergence ↑ (epochs)	total time ↑ (hours)
NPMT	15.4	40	110
CoNMT	256.0	6	1.00
PCoNMT	261.0	6	0.98

Table 3: Training efficiency results on IWSLT 2014 De–En dataset.

(4%), respectively. Also note that following Kumar and Tsvetkov (2019), in this paper, we only used greedy decoding.

We compared our proposed model with three baselines: (1) Attn: Standard attention-based NMT model as in Wiseman and Rush (2016); (2) CoNMT: RNN-based Continuous-output NMT systems (Kumar and Tsvetkov, 2019); (3) NPMT: The state of the art phrase-based NMT model proposed by Huang et al. (2017). For NPMT, we ran its released code with the same pre-processed data we are using without changing any hyperparameters they set.[3] For both De–En and Tr–En CoNMT models, we used the best hyperparameter settings reported by Kumar and Tsvetkov (2019) for De–En. For our model, PCoNMT, we only changed the batch size from the original setting in CoNMT and chose other additional parameters based on the performance on the validation set.

Although we use recurrent architectures in this paper to make our findings comparable to prior work that uses the same setting, we believe using multi-layer self-attention mechanism (Vaswani et al., 2017) as a base of our model has further potential to improve the performance. Even with Transformers, the conventional token-by-token generation scheme will be still prone to mistakes in multi-word generations. Therefore, explicitly handling the phrase generation as we propose is likely to be helpful, which we leave it as future work.

Translation quality De–En and Tr–En translation results are summarized in Tables 1 and 2. PCoNMT significantly outperforms both the conventional attention-based model (by >4 BLEU) and its base CoNMT model (by 1.6 BLEU), and also performs better than NPMT (by 1.4 BLEU). The fertility module is shown to be relatively

---

[3] The number we got from the experiment is different from the one reported in the original paper, which possibly is rooting from slightly different preprocessing steps.

Class	De–En				Tr–En			
	Tot.	P	R	F-1	Tot.	P	R	F-1
$N \leq 1$	97%	0.97	0.96	0.97	97%	0.97	0.95	0.96
$N > 1$	3%	0.33	0.28	0.31	3%	0.17	0.1	0.13

Table 4: The Precision, Recall, and F1 evaluation results on the fertility prediction of Fertility$_2$. "Tot." is the percentage for the number of occurrences of each label in the gold label.

Class	De–En				Tr–En			
	Total	P	R	F-1	Total	P	R	F-1
$N = 0$	10%	0.59	0.09	0.15	14%	0.56	0.30	0.39
$N = 1$	86%	0.88	0.95	0.91	83%	0.86	0.91	0.89
$N = 2$	4%	0.27	0.35	0.31	3%	0.12	0.19	0.14
$N = 3$	0%	0.16	0.14	0.15	0%	0	0	0

Table 5: The Precision, Recall, and F1 evaluation results on the fertility prediction of Fertility$_4$. "Tot." is the percentage for the number of occurrences of each label in the gold label.

more helpful in Tr–En task, while showing less impact in De–En task. We also observed that Fertility$_2$ consistently generates better translations than Fertility$_4$. On the more difficult MWT subset containing multi-word phrases, PCoNMT obtains large absolute gains in BLEU, confirming their effectiveness in phrase translations. Examples of translations are shown in Table 7.

Computational efficiency We report the training efficiency of models in three metrics: speed, number of training epochs till convergence, and total training time. All results were measured on the same machine with the same batch size. The machine was a single-node local machine with NVIDIA GTX 1080 Ti. During the training, no other process was executed except for the training for the fair comparison.

Table 3 shows that CoNMT and PCoNMT can process 28 times faster than NPMT, and converge six times faster, i.e., reducing the entire training time by 112x. Somewhat surprisingly, PCoNMT further accelerates the CoNMT as it can reduce the timestep needed for a sample by generating phrases. This result proves that additional phrase embeddings of PCoNMT has little impact on computational efficiency while training.

Fertility Prediction Evaluation The fertility prediction can have a significant impact on the translation as it guides the decoder to decide when to generate phrases and when to generate words. We evaluate the prediction results on the test set with the gold label obtained from the word alignment model in Table 5 and Table 4.

In both datasets, we observe that the data is highly skewed toward word-level classes as most translations are word-to-word generation. This results in Fertility$_4$ not to predict $N = 3$ classes at all in the Tr–En dataset. The comparison between Table 5 and Table 4 shows that the Fertility$_2$ has slighly higher F-1 score than Fertility$_4$ in both datasets. It implies that aggregating the classes into two made the prediction task easier for the model, which thus led to the improved translation quality shown in the previous results.

Analysis on Generated Phrases Table 6 presents further analysis of the generated phrases. We first see in which category of phrases our model performs well compared to the baseline, CoNMT, to know from where the improvement of our model is coming. As for the phrase categories, we consider three categories, compound nouns (CNs, e.g., *thought_experiment*), verb phrases (VPs, e.g., *grow_apart*), and collocations (COs, e.g., *at_risk*). We randomly sampled a hundred generated phrases from the De–En test set, and manually annotate the category of phrases and whether it is the correct translation. We also look at the output of CoNMT baseline for the same test samples, and also annotate if the sampled phrases are well translated in the CoNMT output.

The results in Table 6 show that the most frequently generated phrases are collocations (56%) followed by verb phrases (28%) and compound nouns (16%). Among the entire sampled phrases, 64 percent of phrases were correct in PCoNMT output while CoNMT had 50 percent of them correct. Specifically, our model significantly outperformed the baseline in compound word generation cases while performs worse in verb phrases generation. By looking into the instances of wrong verb phrase generation, we found that a significant amount of those errors are related to the tense of the verb.

4   Related Work

Multi-word Expressions for NMT There have been several studies that incorporate multi-word phrases into supervised NMT (Tang et al., 2016; Wang et al., 2017; Dahlmann et al., 2017). Most approaches rely on pre-defined phrase dictionaries obtained from methods such as phrase-based Stastitical MT (Koehn et al., 2003) or word-

Category	Total	PCoNMT	CoNMT
CNs	16%	0.63	0.25
VPs	28%	0.5	0.57
COs	56%	0.71	0.54
Sum	100%	0.64	0.50

Table 6: Percentages of categories of randomly sampled 100 phrases generated by PCoNMT on IWSLT 2014 De–En test set and the accuracy of PCoNMT and CoNMT phrase translations, respectively.

alignment. Tang et al. (2016) use a method that combines phrase probability and word probability obtained from a softmax layer enabling the decoder to decide to switch between phrase generation and word generation based on context. Dahlmann et al. (2017) use a separate SMT model to generate phrases along with an NMT model. Wang et al. (2017) proposed a similar approach to have an SMT model run in parallel, where an additional module decide whether to use a phrase generator from the SMT model or the neural decoder.

Recent works have also explored using an additional RNN to compute phrase generation probabilities. Huang et al. (2017) proposed Neural Phrase MT (NPMT) that is built upon Sleep-WAke Network (SWAN), a segmentation-based sequence modeling technique, which automatically discovers phrases given the data and appends the special symbol $ to the source and target data. The model gets these segmented word/phrase sequences as input and keeps two levels of RNNs to encode and decode phrases. NPMT established state of the art results for phrase-based NMT, but at a price of significant computational overhead.

The main differences between previous studies and our work are: (1) we do not rely on SMT model and adapt in an end-to-end manner only requiring some preprocessing using word-alignment models; and (2) we use phrase embedding tables to represent phrases instead of keeping external phrase memory and its generation probability. By using the phrase embeddings along with the continuous-output layer, we significantly reduce the computational complexity and propose an approach to overcome the phrase generation bottleneck.

Fertility in MT Fertility (Brown et al., 1993) has been a core component in phrase-based SMT

German src	und Sie sollten auch an Dinge wie **Lebensqualität** denken
English ref	and you also want to think about things like **quality of life**
Baseline CoNMT	and you should think of things like **life**
PCoNMT	and you should think of things like **quality_of_life** .
German src	wer ein Gehirn hat , ist **gefährdet** .
English ref	everyone with a brain is **at risk** .
Baseline CoNMT	who has a brain is **risk** .
PCoNMT	who has a brain is **at_risk** .
German src	ich stecke **voller** Widersprüche .
English ref	I am **full of** contradictions .
Baseline CoNMT	I 'm put .
PCoNMT	I 'm **full_of** contradictions

Table 7: Translation output examples from CoNMT and PCoNMT systems.

models (Koehn et al., 2003). Fertility gives the likelihood of each source word of being translated into n words. Fertility helps in deciding which phrases should be stored in the phrase tables. Tu et al. (2016) revisited fertility to model coverage in NMT to address the issue of under-translation. They used a fertility vector to express how many words should be generated per source word and a coverage vector to keep track of words translated so far. We use a very similar concept in this work but the fertility module is introduced with a purpose to guide the decoder to switch over generating phrases and words.

5 Conclusion

We proposed PCoNMT, a phrase-based NMT system built upon continuous-output NMT models. We also introduced a fertility module that guides the decoder by providing the probabilities of generating a phrase and a word by leveraging the attention mechanism. Our experimental results showed that our model outperforms the state of the art phrase NMT systems, and also speeds up the computation by 112x.

Acknowledgments

We gratefully acknowledge Sachin Kumar and our anonymous reviewers for the helpful feedback. This material is based upon work supported by NSF grant IIS1812327 and an Amazon MLRA award.

References

Karim Ahmed, Nitish Shirish Keskar, and Richard Socher. 2018. Weighted transformer network for machine translation. In *Proc. ICLR*.

Dzmitry Bahdanau, Kyunghyun Cho, and Yoshua Bengio. 2014. Neural machine translation by jointly learning to align and translate. In *Proc. of ICLR*.

Ondřej Bojar, Christian Federmann, Mark Fishel, Yvette Graham, Barry Haddow, Philipp Koehn, and Christof Monz. 2018. Findings of the 2018 conference on machine translation (wmt18). In *Proceedings of the Third Conference on Machine Translation: Shared Task Papers*, pages 272–303.

Peter F Brown, Vincent J Della Pietra, Stephen A Della Pietra, and Robert L Mercer. 1993. The mathematics of statistical machine translation: Parameter estimation. *Computational linguistics*, 19(2):263–311.

Franck Burlot and François Yvon. 2017. Evaluating the morphological competence of machine translation systems. In *Proc. of WMT*, pages 43–55.

Leonard Dahlmann, Evgeny Matusov, Pavel Petrushkov, and Shahram Khadivi. 2017. Neural machine translation leveraging phrase-based models in a hybrid search. In *Proc. of EMNLP*.

Chris Dyer, Victor Chahuneau, and Noah A. Smith. 2013. A simple, fast, and effective reparameterization of IBM Model 2. In *Proc. of NAACL*.

Po-Sen Huang, Chong Wang, Sitao Huang, Dengyong Zhou, and Li Deng. 2017. Towards neural phrase-based machine translation. In *Proc. of ICLR*.

Philipp Koehn. 2009. *Statistical machine translation*. Cambridge University Press.

Philipp Koehn and Rebecca Knowles. 2017. Six challenges for neural machine translation. In *Proc. of WNGT*.

Philipp Koehn, Franz Josef Och, and Daniel Marcu. 2003. Statistical phrase-based translation. In *Proceedings of the 2003 Conference of the North American Chapter of the Association for Computational Linguistics on Human Language Technology - Volume 1*, NAACL '03, pages 48–54, Stroudsburg, PA, USA. Association for Computational Linguistics.

Sachin Kumar and Yulia Tsvetkov. 2019. Von mises-fisher loss for training sequence to sequence models with continuous outputs. In *Proc. of ICLR*.

Guillaume Lample, Myle Ott, Alexis Conneau, and Ludovic Denoyer. 2018. Phrase-based & neural unsupervised machine translation. In *Proc. of EMNLP*, pages 5039–5049.

Austin Matthews, Eva Schlinger, Alon Lavie, and Chris Dyer. 2016. Synthesizing compound words for machine translation. In *Proc. of ACL*, pages 1085–1094.

Tomas Mikolov, Ilya Sutskever, Kai Chen, Greg S Corrado, and Jeff Dean. 2013. Distributed representations of words and phrases and their compositionality. In *Advances in neural information processing systems*, pages 3111–3119.

Kishore Papineni, Salim Roukos, Todd Ward, and Wei-Jing Zhu. 2002. BLEU: a method for automatic evaluation of machine translation. In *Proc. of ACL*, pages 311–318.

Matthew Peters, Mark Neumann, Mohit Iyyer, Matt Gardner, Christopher Clark, Kenton Lee, and Luke Zettlemoyer. 2018. Deep contextualized word representations. In *Proceedings of the 2018 Conference of the North American Chapter of the Association for Computational Linguistics: Human Language Technologies, Volume 1 (Long Papers)*, pages 2227–2237.

Marc'Aurelio Ranzato, Sumit Chopra, Michael Auli, and Wojciech Zaremba. 2016. Sequence level training with recurrent neural networks.

Matss Rikters and Ondej Bojar. 2017. Paying attention to multi-word expressions in neural machine translation. In *Proc. of Machine Translation Summit*.

Rico Sennrich, Barry Haddow, and Alexandra Birch. 2016. Neural machine translation of rare words with subword units. In *Proc. of ACL*.

Emma Strubell, Ananya Ganesh, and Andrew McCallum. 2019. Energy and policy considerations for deep learning in nlp. In *Proc. of ACL*.

Yaohua Tang, Fandong Meng, Zhengdong Lu, Hang Li, and Philip LH Yu. 2016. Neural machine translation with external phrase memory. *arXiv preprint arXiv:1606.01792*.

Zhaopeng Tu, Zhengdong Lu, Yang Liu, Xiaohua Liu, and Hang Li. 2016. Modeling coverage for neural machine translation. In *Proceedings of the 54th Annual Meeting of the Association for Computational Linguistics (Volume 1: Long Papers)*, volume 1, pages 76–85.

Ashish Vaswani, Noam Shazeer, Niki Parmar, Jakob Uszkoreit, Llion Jones, Aidan N Gomez, Łukasz Kaiser, and Illia Polosukhin. 2017. Attention is all you need. In *Advances in neural information processing systems*, pages 5998–6008.

Xing Wang, Zhaopeng Tu, Deyi Xiong, and Min Zhang. 2017. Translating phrases in neural machine translation. In *Proc. of EMNLP*, pages 1421–1431.

Sam Wiseman and Alexander M Rush. 2016. Sequence-to-sequence learning as beam-search optimization. In *Proceedings of the 2016 Conference on Empirical Methods in Natural Language Processing*, pages 1296–1306.

Yonghui Wu, Mike Schuster, Zhifeng Chen, Quoc V Le, Mohammad Norouzi, Wolfgang Macherey, Maxim Krikun, Yuan Cao, Qin Gao, Klaus Macherey, et al. 2016. Google's neural machine translation system: Bridging the gap between human and machine translation. *arXiv preprint arXiv:1609.08144*.

Transformer and seq2seq model for Paraphrase Generation

Elozino Egonmwan and **Yllias Chali**
University of Lethbridge
Lethbridge, AB, Canada
{elozino.egonmwan, yllias.chali}@uleth.ca

Abstract

Paraphrase generation aims to improve the clarity of a sentence by using different wording that convey similar meaning. For better quality of generated paraphrases, we propose a framework that combines the effectiveness of two models – transformer and sequence-to-sequence (seq2seq). We design a two-layer stack of encoders. The first layer is a transformer model containing 6 stacked identical layers with multi-head self-attention, while the second-layer is a seq2seq model with gated recurrent units (GRU-RNN). The transformer encoder layer learns to capture long-term dependencies, together with syntactic and semantic properties of the input sentence. This rich vector representation learned by the transformer serves as input to the GRU-RNN encoder responsible for producing the state vector for decoding. Experimental results on two datasets- QUORA and MSCOCO using our framework, produces a new benchmark for paraphrase generation.

1 Introduction

Paraphrasing is a key abstraction technique used in Natural Language Processing (NLP). While capable of generating novel words, it also learns to compress or remove unnecessary words along the way. Thus, gainfully lending itself to abstractive summarization (Chen and Bansal, 2018; Gehrmann et al., 2018) and question generation (Song et al., 2018) for machine reading comprehension (MRC) (Dong et al., 2017). Paraphrases can also be used as simpler alternatives to input sentences for machine translation (MT) (Callison-Burch et al., 2006) as well as evaluation of natural language generation (NLG) texts (Apidianaki et al., 2018).

Existing methods for generating paraphrases, fall in one of these broad categories – rule-based (McKeown, 1983), seq2seq (Prakash et al., 2016),

reinforcement learning (Li et al., 2018), deep generative models (Iyyer et al., 2018) and a varied combination (Gupta et al., 2018; Mallinson et al., 2017) of the later three.

In this paper, we propose a novel framework for paraphrase generation that utilizes the transformer model of Vaswani et al. (2017) and seq2seq model of Sutskever et al. (2014) specifically GRU (Cho et al., 2014). The multi-head self attention of the transformer complements the seq2seq model with its ability to learn long-range dependencies in the input sequence. Also the individual attention heads in the transformer model mimics behavior related to the syntactic and semantic structure of the sentence (Vaswani et al., 2017, 2018) which is key in paraphrase generation. Furthermore, we use GRU to obtain a fixed-size state vector for decoding into variable length sequences, given the more qualitative learned vector representations from the transformer.

The main contributions of this work are:

- We propose a novel framework for the task of paraphrase generation that produces quality paraphrases of its source sentence.

- For in-depth analysis of our results, in addition to using BLEU (Papineni et al., 2002) and ROUGE (Lin, 2004) which are word-overlap based, we further evaluate our model using qualitative metrics such as Embedding Average Cosine Similarity (EACS), Greedy Matching Score (GMS) from Sharma et al. (2017) and METEOR (Banerjee and Lavie, 2005), with stronger correlation with human reference.

2 Task Definition

Given an input sentence $S = (s_1, ..., s_n)$ with n words, the task is to generate an alternative output

Proceedings of the 3rd Workshop on Neural Generation and Translation (WNGT 2019), pages 249–255
Hong Kong, China, November 4, 2019. ©2019 Association for Computational Linguistics
www.aclweb.org/anthology/D19-56%2d

S: What are the dumbest questions ever asked on Quora? **G:** what is the stupidest question on quora? **R:** What is the most stupid question asked on Quora?	**S:** Three dimensional rendering of a kitchen area with various appliances. **G:** a series of photographs of a kitchen **R:** A series of photographs of a tiny model kitchen
S: How can I lose fat without doing any aerobic physical activity **G:** how can i lose weight without exercise? **R:** How can I lose weight in a month without doing exercise?	**S:** a young boy in a soccer uniform kicking a ball **G:** a young boy kicking a soccer ball **R:** A young boy kicking a soccer ball on a green field.
S: How did Donald Trump won the 2016 USA presidential election? **G:** how did donald trump win the 2016 presidential **R:** How did Donald Trump become president?	**S:** The dog is wearing a Santa Claus hat. **G:** a dog poses with santa hat **R:** A dog poses while wearing a santa hat.
	S: the people are sampling wine at a wine tasting. **G:** a group of people wine tasting. **R:** Group of people tasting wine next to some barrels.

Table 1: Examples of our generated paraphrases on the QUORA sampled test set, where **S**, **G**, **R** represents Source, Generated and Reference sentences respectively.

Table 2: Examples of our generated paraphrases on the MSCOCO sampled test set, where **S**, **G**, **R** represents Source, Generated and Reference sentences respectively.

sentence $Y = (y_1, ..., y_m) \mid \exists y_m \notin S$ with m words that conveys similar semantics as S, where preferably, $m < n$ but not necessarily.

3 Method

In this section, we present our framework for paraphrase generation. It follows the popular encode-decode paradigm, but with two stacked layers of encoders. The first encoding layer is a transformer encoder, while the second encoding layer is a GRU-RNN encoder. The paraphrase of a given sentence is generated by a GRU-RNN decoder.

3.1 Stacked Encoders

3.1.1 Encoder – TRANSFORMER

We use the transformer-encoder as sort of a pre-training module of our input sentence. The goal is to learn richer representation of the input vector that better handles long-term dependencies as well as captures syntactic and semantic properties before obtaining a fixed-state representation for decoding into the desired output sentence. The transformer contains 6 stacked identical layers mainly driven by self-attention implemented by Vaswani et al. (2017, 2018).

3.1.2 Encoder – GRU-RNN

Our architecture uses a single layer uni-directional GRU-RNN whose input is the output of the trans-

former. The GRU-RNN encoder (Chung et al., 2014; Cho et al., 2014) produces fixed-state vector representation of the transformed input sequence using the following equations:

$$z = \sigma(x_t U^z + s_{t-1} W^z) \tag{1}$$

$$r = \sigma(x_t U^r + s_{t-1} W^r) \tag{2}$$

$$h = tanh(x_t U^h + (s_{t-1} \odot r) W^h) \tag{3}$$

$$s_t = (1 - z) \odot h + z \odot s_{t-1} \tag{4}$$

where r and z are the reset and update gates respectively, W and U are the network's parameters, s_t is the hidden state vector at timestep t, x_t is the input vector and $\odot$ represents the Hadamard product.

3.2 Decoder – GRU-RNN

The fixed-state vector representation produced by the GRU-RNN encoder is used as initial state for the decoder. At each time step, the decoder receives the previously generated word, y_{t-1} and hidden state s_{t-1} at time step t_{-1}. The output word, y_t at each time step, is a softmax probability of the vector in equation 3 over the set of vocabulary words, V.

50K					
MODEL	**BLEU**	**METEOR**	**R-L**	**EACS**	**GMS**
VAE-SVG-EQ (Gupta et al., 2018)	17.4	22.2	-	-	-
RbM-SL (Li et al., 2018)	35.81	28.12	-	-	-
TRANS (ours)	35.56	**33.89**	27.53	79.72	62.91
SEQ (ours)	34.88	32.10	29.91	78.66	61.45
TRANSEQ (ours)	37.06	33.73	**30.89**	80.81	**63.63**
TRANSEQ + beam (size=6) (ours)	**37.12**	33.68	30.72	**81.03**	63.50
100K					
MODEL	**BLEU**	**METEOR**	**R-L**	**EACS**	**GMS**
VAE-SVG-EQ (Gupta et al., 2018)	22.90	25.50	-	-	-
RbM-SL (Li et al., 2018)	**43.54**	32.84	-	-	-
TRANS (ours)	37.46	**36.04**	29.73	80.61	64.81
SEQ (ours)	36.98	34.71	32.06	79.65	63.49
TRANSEQ (ours)	38.75	35.84	**33.23**	81.50	**65.52**
TRANSEQ + beam (size=6) (ours)	38.77	35.86	33.07	**81.64**	65.42
150K					
MODEL	**BLEU**	**METEOR**	**R-L**	**EACS**	**GMS**
VAE-SVG-EQ (Gupta et al., 2018)	38.30	33.60	-	-	-
TRANS (ours)	39.00	**38.68**	32.05	81.90	65.27
SEQ (ours)	38.50	36.89	34.35	80.95	64.13
TRANSEQ (ours)	**40.36**	38.49	**35.84**	**82.84**	**65.99**
TRANSEQ + beam (size=6) (ours)	39.82	38.48	35.40	82.48	65.54

Table 3: Performance of our model against various models on the **QUORA** dataset with **50k,100k,150k** training examples. R-L refers to the ROUGE-L F1 score with 95% confidence interval

4 Experiments

We describe baselines, our implementation settings, datasets and evaluation of our proposed model.

4.1 Baselines

We compare our model with very recent models (Gupta et al., 2018; Li et al., 2018; Prakash et al., 2016) including the current state-of-the-art (Gupta et al., 2018) in the field. To further highlight the gain of stacking 2 encoders we use each component – Transformer (TRANS) and seq2seq (SEQ) as baselines.

- VAE-SVG-EQ (Gupta et al., 2018): This is the current state-of-the-art in the field, with a variational autoencoder as its main component.

- RbM-SL (Li et al., 2018): Different from the encoder-decoder framework, this is a generator-evaluator framework, with the evaluator trained by reinforcement learning.

- Residual LSTM (Prakash et al., 2016): This implements stacked residual long short term memory networks (LSTM).

- TRANS: Encoder-decoder framework as described in Section 3 but with a single transformer encoder layer.

- SEQ: Encoder-decoder framework as described in Section 3 but with a single GRU-RNN encoder layer.

4.2 Implementation

We used pre-trained 300-dimensional $gloVe$[1] word-embeddings (Pennington et al., 2014) as the distributed representation of our input sentences. We set the maximum sentence length to 15 and 10 respectively for our input and target sentences following the statistics of our dataset.

For the transformer encoder, we used the $transformer\_base$ hyperparameter setting from

[1] https://nlp.stanford.edu/projects/glove/

MODEL	BLEU	METEOR	R-L	EACS	GMS
Residual LSTM (Prakash et al., 2016)	37.0	27.0	-	-	-
VAE-SVG-EQ (Gupta et al., 2018)	41.7	31.0	-	-	-
TRANS (ours)	41.8	38.5	33.4	79.6	70.3
SEQ (ours)	40.7	36.9	35.8	78.9	70.0
TRANSEQ (ours)	43.4	38.3	37.4	80.5	71.1
TRANSEQ + beam (size=10) (ours)	**44.5**	**40.0**	**38.4**	**81.9**	**71.3**

Table 4: Performance of our model against various models on the MSCOCO dataset. R-L refers to the ROUGE-L F1 score with 95% confidence interval

the tensor2tensor library (Vaswani et al., 2018)[2], but set the hidden size to 300. We set dropout to 0.0 and 0.7 for MSCOCO and QUORA datasets respectively. We used a large dropout for QUORA because the model tends to over-fit to the training set. Both the GRU-RNN encoder and decoder contain 300 hidden units.

We pre-process our datasets, and do not use the pre-processed/tokenized versions of the datasets from tensor2tensor library. Our target vocabulary is a set of approximately 15,000 words. It contains words in our target training and test sets that occur at least twice. Using this subset of vocabulary words as opposed to over 320,000 vocabulary words contained in $gloVe$ improves both training time and performance of the model.

We train and evaluate our model after each epoch with a fixed learning rate of 0.0005, and stop training when the validation loss does not decrease after 5 epochs. The model learns to minimize the seq2seq loss implemented in `tensorflow API`[3] with `AdamOptimizer`. We use greedy-decoding during training and validation and set the maximum number of iterations to 5 times the target sentence length. For testing/inference we use beam-search decoding.

4.3 Datasets

We evaluate our model on two standard datasets for paraphrase generation – **QUORA**[4] and **MSCOCO** (Lin et al., 2014) as described in Gupta et al. (2018) and used similar settings. The **QUORA** dataset contains over 120k examples with a 80k and 40k split on the training and test sets respectively. As seen in Tables 1 and 2, while the QUORA dataset contains question pairs, MSCOCO contains free form texts which are human annotations of images. Subjective observation of the MSCOCO dataset reveals that most of its paraphrase pairs contain more novel words as well as syntactic manipulations than the QUORA pairs making it a more interesting paraphrase generation corpora. We split the QUORA dataset to 50k, 100k and 150k training samples and 4k testing samples in order to align with baseline models for comparative purposes.

4.4 Evaluation

For quantitative analysis of our model, we use popular automatic metrics such as BLEU, ROUGE, METEOR. Since BLEU and ROUGE both measure $n - gram$ word-overlap with difference in brevity penalty, we report just the ROUGE-L value. We also use 2 additional recent metrics – GMS and EACS by (Sharma et al., 2017)[5] that measure the similarity between the reference and generated paraphrases based on the cosine similarity of their embeddings on word and sentence levels respectively.

4.5 Result Analysis

Tables 3 and 4 report scores of our model on both datasets. Our model pushes the benchmark on all evaluation metrics compared against current published top models evaluated on the same datasets. Since several words could connote similar meaning, it is more logical to evaluate with metrics that match with embedding vectors capable of measuring this similarity. Hence we also report GMS and EACS scores as a basis of comparison for future work in this direction.

Besides quantitative values, Tables 1 and 2 show that our paraphrases are well formed, abstractive (*e.g dumbest – stupidest, dog is wearing*

[2]https://github.com/tensorflow/tensor2tensor

[3]https://www.tensorflow.org/api_docs/python/tf/contrib/seq2seq/sequence_loss

[4]https://data.quora.com/First-Quora-Dataset-Release-Question-Pairs

[5]https://github.com/Maluuba/nlg-eval

– dog poses), capable of performing syntactic manipulations (*e.g in a soccer uniform kicking a ball – kicking a soccer ball*) and compression. Some of our paraphrased sentences even have more brevity than the reference, and still remain very meaningful.

5   Related Work

Our baseline models – VAE-SVG-EQ (Gupta et al., 2018) and RbM-SL (Li et al., 2018) are both deep learning models. While the former uses a variational-autoencoder and is capable of generating multiple paraphrases of a given sentence, the later uses deep reinforcement learning. In tune, with part of our approach, ie, seq2seq, there exists ample models with interesting variants – residual LSTM (Prakash et al., 2016), bi-directional GRU with attention and special decoding tweaks (Cao et al., 2017), attention from the perspective of semantic parsing (Su and Yan, 2017).

MT has been greatly used to generate paraphrases (Quirk et al., 2004; Zhao et al., 2008) due to the availability of large corpora. While much earlier works have explored the use of manually drafted rules (Hassan et al., 2007; Kozlowski et al., 2003).

Similar to our model architecture, Chen et al. (2018) combined transformers and RNN-based encoders for MT. Zhao et al. (2018) recently used the transformer model for paraphrasing on different datasets. We experimented using solely a transformer but got better results with TRANSEQ. To the best of our knowledge, our work is the first to cross-breed the transformer and seq2seq for the task of paraphrase generation.

6   Conclusions

We proposed a novel framework, TRANSEQ that combines the efficiency of a transformer and seq2seq model and improves the current state-of-the-art on the QUORA and MSCOCO paraphrasing datasets. Besides quantitative results, we presented examples that highlight the syntactic and semantic quality of our generated paraphrases.

In the future, it will be interesting to apply this framework for the task of abstractive text summarization and other NLG-related problems.

Acknowledgments

We would like to thank the anonymous reviewers for their useful comments. The research reported in this paper was conducted at the University of Lethbridge and supported by Alberta Innovates and Alberta Education.

References

Marianna Apidianaki, Guillaume Wisniewski, Anne Cocos, and Chris Callison-Burch. 2018. Automated paraphrase lattice creation for hyter machine translation evaluation. In *Proceedings of the 2018 Conference of the North American Chapter of the Association for Computational Linguistics: Human Language Technologies, Volume 2 (Short Papers)*, pages 480–485.

Satanjeev Banerjee and Alon Lavie. 2005. Meteor: An automatic metric for mt evaluation with improved correlation with human judgments. In *Proceedings of the acl workshop on intrinsic and extrinsic evaluation measures for machine translation and/or summarization*, pages 65–72.

Chris Callison-Burch, Philipp Koehn, and Miles Osborne. 2006. Improved statistical machine translation using paraphrases. In *Proceedings of the main conference on Human Language Technology Conference of the North American Chapter of the Association of Computational Linguistics*, pages 17–24. Association for Computational Linguistics.

Ziqiang Cao, Chuwei Luo, Wenjie Li, and Sujian Li. 2017. Joint copying and restricted generation for paraphrase. In *Thirty-First AAAI Conference on Artificial Intelligence*.

Mia Xu Chen, Orhan Firat, Ankur Bapna, Melvin Johnson, Wolfgang Macherey, George Foster, Llion Jones, Mike Schuster, Noam Shazeer, Niki Parmar, et al. 2018. The best of both worlds: Combining recent advances in neural machine translation. In *Proceedings of the 56th Annual Meeting of the Association for Computational Linguistics (Volume 1: Long Papers)*, pages 76–86.

Yen-Chun Chen and Mohit Bansal. 2018. Fast abstractive summarization with reinforce-selected sentence rewriting. In *Proceedings of the 56th Annual Meeting of the Association for Computational Linguistics (Volume 1: Long Papers)*, volume 1, pages 675–686.

Kyunghyun Cho, Bart Van Merriënboer, Caglar Gulcehre, Dzmitry Bahdanau, Fethi Bougares, Holger Schwenk, and Yoshua Bengio. 2014. Learning phrase representations using rnn encoder-decoder for statistical machine translation. *arXiv preprint arXiv:1406.1078*.

Junyoung Chung, Caglar Gulcehre, KyungHyun Cho, and Yoshua Bengio. 2014. Empirical evaluation of gated recurrent neural networks on sequence modeling. *arXiv preprint arXiv:1412.3555*.

Li Dong, Jonathan Mallinson, Siva Reddy, and Mirella Lapata. 2017. Learning to paraphrase for question answering. In *Proceedings of the 2017 Conference on Empirical Methods in Natural Language Processing*, pages 875–886.

Sebastian Gehrmann, Yuntian Deng, and Alexander Rush. 2018. Bottom-up abstractive summarization. In *Proceedings of the 2018 Conference on Empirical Methods in Natural Language Processing*, pages 4098–4109.

Ankush Gupta, Arvind Agarwal, Prawaan Singh, and Piyush Rai. 2018. A deep generative framework for paraphrase generation. In *Thirty-Second AAAI Conference on Artificial Intelligence*.

Samer Hassan, Andras Csomai, Carmen Banea, Ravi Sinha, and Rada Mihalcea. 2007. Unt: Subfinder: Combining knowledge sources for automatic lexical substitution. In *Proceedings of the Fourth International Workshop on Semantic Evaluations (SemEval-2007)*, pages 410–413.

Mohit Iyyer, John Wieting, Kevin Gimpel, and Luke Zettlemoyer. 2018. Adversarial example generation with syntactically controlled paraphrase networks. In *Proceedings of the 2018 Conference of the North American Chapter of the Association for Computational Linguistics: Human Language Technologies, Volume 1 (Long Papers)*, pages 1875–1885.

Raymond Kozlowski, Kathleen F McCoy, and K Vijay-Shanker. 2003. Generation of single-sentence paraphrases from predicate/argument structure using lexico-grammatical resources. In *Proceedings of the second international workshop on Paraphrasing-Volume 16*, pages 1–8. Association for Computational Linguistics.

Zichao Li, Xin Jiang, Lifeng Shang, and Hang Li. 2018. Paraphrase generation with deep reinforcement learning. In *Proceedings of the 2018 Conference on Empirical Methods in Natural Language Processing*, pages 3865–3878.

Chin-Yew Lin. 2004. Rouge: A package for automatic evaluation of summaries. *Text Summarization Branches Out*.

Tsung-Yi Lin, Michael Maire, Serge Belongie, James Hays, Pietro Perona, Deva Ramanan, Piotr Dollár, and C Lawrence Zitnick. 2014. Microsoft coco: Common objects in context. In *European conference on computer vision*, pages 740–755. Springer.

Jonathan Mallinson, Rico Sennrich, and Mirella Lapata. 2017. Paraphrasing revisited with neural machine translation. In *Proceedings of the 15th Conference of the European Chapter of the Association for Computational Linguistics: Volume 1, Long Papers*, pages 881–893.

Kathleen R McKeown. 1983. Paraphrasing questions using given and new information. *Computational Linguistics*, 9(1):1–10.

Kishore Papineni, Salim Roukos, Todd Ward, and Wei-Jing Zhu. 2002. Bleu: a method for automatic evaluation of machine translation. In *Proceedings of the 40th annual meeting on association for computational linguistics*, pages 311–318. Association for Computational Linguistics.

Jeffrey Pennington, Richard Socher, and Christopher Manning. 2014. Glove: Global vectors for word representation. In *Proceedings of the 2014 conference on empirical methods in natural language processing (EMNLP)*, pages 1532–1543.

Aaditya Prakash, Sadid A Hasan, Kathy Lee, Vivek Datla, Ashequl Qadir, Joey Liu, and Oladimeji Farri. 2016. Neural paraphrase generation with stacked residual lstm networks. *arXiv preprint arXiv:1610.03098*.

Chris Quirk, Chris Brockett, and William Dolan. 2004. Monolingual machine translation for paraphrase generation. In *Proceedings of the 2004 conference on empirical methods in natural language processing*, pages 142–149.

Shikhar Sharma, Layla El Asri, Hannes Schulz, and Jeremie Zumer. 2017. Relevance of unsupervised metrics in task-oriented dialogue for evaluating natural language generation. *arXiv preprint arXiv:1706.09799*.

Linfeng Song, Zhiguo Wang, Wael Hamza, Yue Zhang, and Daniel Gildea. 2018. Leveraging context information for natural question generation. In *Proceedings of the 2018 Conference of the North American Chapter of the Association for Computational Linguistics: Human Language Technologies, Volume 2 (Short Papers)*, pages 569–574.

Yu Su and Xifeng Yan. 2017. Cross-domain semantic parsing via paraphrasing. In *Proceedings of the 2017 Conference on Empirical Methods in Natural Language Processing*, pages 1235–1246.

Ilya Sutskever, Oriol Vinyals, and Quoc V Le. 2014. Sequence to sequence learning with neural networks. In *Advances in neural information processing systems*, pages 3104–3112.

Ashish Vaswani, Samy Bengio, Eugene Brevdo, Francois Chollet, Aidan Gomez, Stephan Gouws, Llion Jones, Łukasz Kaiser, Nal Kalchbrenner, Niki Parmar, et al. 2018. Tensor2tensor for neural machine translation. In *Proceedings of the 13th Conference of the Association for Machine Translation in the Americas (Volume 1: Research Papers)*, volume 1, pages 193–199.

Ashish Vaswani, Noam Shazeer, Niki Parmar, Jakob Uszkoreit, Llion Jones, Aidan N Gomez, Łukasz Kaiser, and Illia Polosukhin. 2017. Attention is all you need. In *Advances in neural information processing systems*, pages 5998–6008.

Sanqiang Zhao, Rui Meng, Daqing He, Andi Saptono, and Bambang Parmanto. 2018. Integrating transformer and paraphrase rules for sentence simplification. In *Proceedings of the 2018 Conference on Empirical Methods in Natural Language Processing*, pages 3164–3173, Brussels, Belgium. Association for Computational Linguistics.

Shiqi Zhao, Cheng Niu, Ming Zhou, Ting Liu, and Sheng Li. 2008. Combining multiple resources to improve smt-based paraphrasing model. In *Proceedings of ACL-08: HLT*, pages 1021–1029.

Monash University's Submissions to the WNGT 2019 Document Translation Task

Sameen Maruf and **Gholamreza Haffari**
Faculty of Information Technology, Monash University, Australia
`{firstname.lastname}@monash.edu`

Abstract

We describe the work of Monash University for the shared task of Rotowire document translation organised by the 3rd Workshop on Neural Generation and Translation (WNGT 2019). We submitted systems for both directions of the English-German language pair. Our main focus is on employing an established document-level neural machine translation model for this task. We achieve a BLEU score of 39.83 (41.46 BLEU per WNGT evaluation) for En-De and 45.06 (47.39 BLEU per WNGT evaluation) for De-En translation directions on the Rotowire test set. All experiments conducted in the process are also described.

1 Introduction

This paper describes the work of Monash University for the shared task of Rotowire document translation organised by the 3rd Workshop on Neural Generation and Translation (WNGT 2019). Despite the boom of work on document-level machine translation in the past two years, we have witnessed a lack of the application of the proposed approaches to MT shared tasks. Thus, our main focus in this work is on employing an established document-level neural machine translation model for this task.

We first explore a strong sentence-level baseline, trained on large-scale parallel data made available by WMT 2019 for their news translation task.[1] We use this system as the initialisation of the document-level models, first proposed by Maruf et al. (2019), making use of the complete document (both past and future sentences) as the conditioning context when translating a sentence. Given the task of translating Rotowire basketball articles, we leverage the document-delimited data

provided by the organisers of WMT 2019 to train the document-level models. Due to resource constraints, we do not use any monolingual data nor any sort of pre-trained embeddings for training the baseline or our document-level models. We ensemble 3 independent runs of all models using two strategies of ensemble decoding. We have conducted experiments for both directions of the English-German language pair. Our submissions achieve a BLEU score of 39.83 (41.46 BLEU per WNGT evaluation) for En→De and 45.06 (47.39 BLEU per WNGT evaluation) for De→En translation directions on the Rotowire test set (Hayashi et al., 2019).

2 Sentence-level Model

As in the original paper, our document-level models are based on the state-of-the-art Transformer architecture (Vaswani et al., 2017). In the remainder of this section, we will describe how we prepare the data to train our sentence-level model and the training setup.

2.1 Data Preparation

To train our sentence-level model, we want to use the maximum allowable high-quality data from the English-German news task in WMT 2019. This would produce a fair baseline for comparing with our document-level models. Upon considering the task of translating basketball-related articles, we have decided to utilise parallel data from Europarl v9, Common Crawl, News Commentary v14 and the Rapid corpus.[2]

Before proceeding to the pre-processing, we remove repetitive sentences[3] from Rapid corpus occurring at the start and end of the documents.

---

[1] `http://www.statmt.org/wmt19/translation-task.html`

[2] Given the limited time and resources at our disposal, we did not use the ParaCrawl corpus.

[3] "European Commission - Announcement", "Related Links", "Audiovisual material", etc.

Proceedings of the 3rd Workshop on Neural Generation and Translation (WNGT 2019), pages 256–261
Hong Kong, China, November 4, 2019. ©2019 Association for Computational Linguistics
www.aclweb.org/anthology/D19-56%2d

Corpus	#Sentence-Pairs
Europarl v9	1.79M
Common Crawl	2.37M
News Commentary v14	0.33M
Rapid	1.46M
Rotowire	3247

Table 1: Sentence-parallel training corpora statistics.

From all corpora, we also remove sentences with length greater than 75 tokens after tokenisation.[4],[5] Table 1 summarises the number of sentences of each corpus in the pre-processed sentence-parallel dataset. We further apply truecasing using Moses (Koehn et al., 2007) followed by joint byte-pair encoding (BPE) with 50K merge operations (Sennrich et al., 2016).

2.2 Model and Training

We use the DyNet toolkit (Neubig et al., 2017) for all of our experiments; the implementation of the sentence-level system is in DyNet, namely *Transformer-DyNet*.[6] Our experiments are run on a single V100 GPU, so we use a rather small minibatch size of 900 tokens. Furthermore, we have filtered sentences with length greater than 85 tokens to fit the computation graph in GPU memory. The hyper-parameter settings are the same as in the Transformer-base model except the number of layers which is set to 4. We also employ all four types of dropouts as in the original Transformer with a rate of 0.1. We use the default Adam optimiser (Kingma and Ba, 2014) with an initial learning rate of 0.0001 and employ early stopping.

3 Document-level Models

The motivation behind our participation in the shared task is to test the document-level MT models (Maruf et al., 2019) on real world tasks. Here we will briefly describe the models, data pre-processing and training/decoding setup.

3.1 Model Description

There are two ways to incorporate context into the sentence-level model: (i) integrate monolingual context into the encoder, or (ii) integrate the bilingual context into the decoder. For both,

the document-level context representation is combined with the deep representation of either the source or target word (output from the last layer of the Transformer) using a gating mechanism (Tu et al., 2018).

The document-level context representation is itself computed in two ways: (i) a single-level flat attention over all sentences in the document-context, or (ii) a hierarchical attention which has the ability to identify the key sentences in the document-context and then attend to the key words within those sentences. For the former, we use a soft attention over the sentences, while for the latter we use a sparse attention over the sentences and a soft or sparse attention over the words in the sentences. For more details of how the document-level context representations are computed, we refer the reader to the original paper (Maruf et al., 2019).

3.2 Data Preparation

Since our document-level model requires document boundaries, we are unable to use the sentence-parallel corpus as is. Out of all the WMT19 corpora, News Commentary and Rapid corpus are document delimited.[7] The Rotowire dataset also has document boundaries provided. Thus, we decided to combine these three corpora to construct the document-parallel training corpus.[8] Furthermore, we remove documents from this document-parallel corpus which have sentence lengths greater than 75 (after tokenisation). We also remove short documents with number of sentences less than 5, and long documents with number of sentences greater than 145. The filtered document-parallel corpus comprises 49K documents making up approximately 1.36M sentence-pairs. The corpus is then truecased using the truecaser model trained on the sentence-level corpus followed by BPE. Since we filtered out sentences with lengths greater than 85 while training the baseline, we also filter those from the document-level corpus. However, removing individual sentences from documents could introduce noise in the training process, hence we remove entire such documents. Finally, we use 48K doc-

---

[4]The threshold was carefully chosen based upon the maximum length of sentences in the Rotowire training set so that we do not remove any of the sentences from the shared task corpus.

[5]Tokenisation script was provided by WNGT organisers.

[6]`https://github.com/duyvuleo/Transformer-DyNet`

[7]Europarl v9 also had document boundaries but these resulted in very long documents and thus we decided against using it for the document-level training.

[8]The training corpus used for training the document-level models is a subset of the training corpus used for training the baseline sentence-level model.

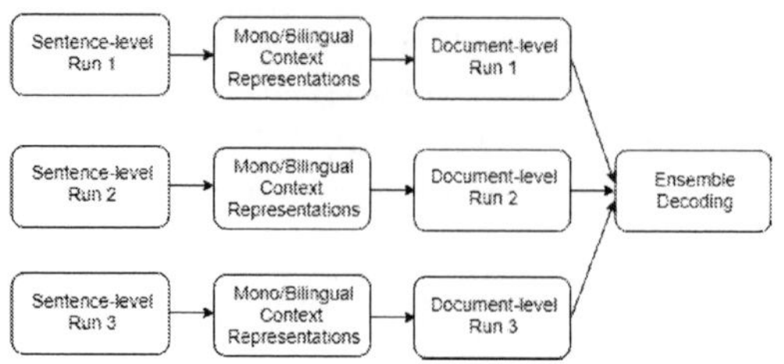

Figure 1: Ensemble decoding.

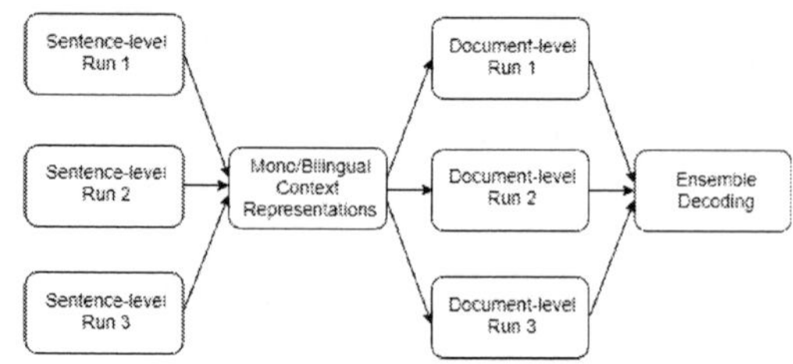

Figure 2: Ensemble-Avg decoding.

uments comprising 1.21M sentences for training our document-level models.

3.3 Training

We use a stage-wise method to train the variants of the document-context NMT model. We pre-train the sentence-level model described in the previous section and then use it to compute the monolingual and the bilingual context representations. These are then used to compute the document-level context representation in our models. The pre-trained sentence-level model is also used to initialise our document-level model and is further fine-tuned alongwith training the document-level model in the second stage. Here we also employ all four types of dropouts[9] but with a higher rate of 0.2 to avoid overfitting. Since the documents on average have lengths much shorter than 900 tokens, we update the model parameters after processing 5 documents instead of a single document.

3.4 Decoding

For the models using the source monolingual context, we do an initial pass over the source documents to compute the initial context representations, which are then used by the document-level model to perform a greedy decoding to obtain the target translations. For the models using the bilingual context, we need an initial bilingual context which is computed by generating initial translations from the sentence-level NMT model. This is followed by a second pass of decoding, where the translation for each sentence is updated using the document-context NMT model while fixing the translations of the other sentences. This is what we refer to as two-pass iterative decoding

(Maruf and Haffari, 2018). It should also be mentioned that since decoding is a computationally expensive process, we perform greedy decoding in both passes.

4 Experimental Evaluation

4.1 Setup

We have 3 independent runs of the sentence-level Transformer architecture. For each of these runs, we train the variants of the document-level models: (i) the flat attention over sentences in the context, and (ii) the hierarchical attention with sparse attention over sentences and soft/sparse attention over words in the sentences, using the two types of context. Results are reported on the Rotowire test set for the single best model obtained through early stopping on the Rotowire development set.

We also decode the test set with an ensemble of the systems for the 3 independent runs. This is done in two ways:

- *Ensemble*. This is the traditional way of ensembling where the different models are combined by averaging the target probability distributions when computing the softmax (Figure 1).

- *Ensemble-Avg*. Apart from combining the probability distributions at the softmax level, we also average the context representations from each run, i.e., we use the same initial context representations for the different runs of a document-level model (Figure 2).

For evaluation, BLEU (Papineni et al., 2002) is reported on the detruecased translations (with original tokenisation) and is calculated using the MultEval toolkit (Clark et al., 2011).

4.2 English→German

It can be seen from Table 2 that for all runs, the document-level models outperform the sentence-level baseline trained with 4 times the data. The

---

[9] *input dropout* - dropout applied to the sum of token embeddings and position encodings, *residual dropout* - dropout applied to the output of each sublayer before adding to the sublayer input, *relu dropout* - dropout applied to the inner layer output after ReLU activation in each feed-forward sublayer, and *attentiondropout* - dropout applied to attention weight in each attention sublayer

System	Transformer	Integration into Encoder			Integration into Decoder		
		Attention	H-Attention	H-Attention	Attention	H-Attention	H-Attention
		soft	*sparse-soft*	*sparse-sparse*	*soft*	*sparse-soft*	*sparse-sparse*
Run 1	34.70	37.93	**38.28**	37.07	38.23	38.13	**38.43**
Run 2	34.45	38.40	**38.72**	38.27	37.42	38.20	**39.02**
Run 3	33.15	37.43	**38.64**	38.25	38.64	**38.65**	37.97
Ensemble	36.10	39.36	**39.83**	39.28	39.33	39.51	**39.71**
Ensemble-Avg	36.10	39.25	**39.79**	39.22	39.42	39.54	**39.71**

Table 2: BLEU scores for the Transformer vs. variants of our document-level NMT model for English→German. **bold**: Best performance.

System	Transformer	Integration into Encoder			Integration into Decoder		
		Attention	H-Attention	H-Attention	Attention	H-Attention	H-Attention
		soft	*sparse-soft*	*sparse-sparse*	*soft*	*sparse-soft*	*sparse-sparse*
Run 1	37.75	42.58	**43.47**	42.58	**44.42**	44.30	42.96
Run 2	37.86	43.27	42.37	**43.81**	43.47	43.42	**44.05**
Run 3	37.35	43.75	44.08	**44.11**	43.53	**44.16**	43.81
Ensemble	39.33	44.23	44.52	**44.56**	44.94	**45.06**	44.66
Ensemble-Avg	39.33	43.66	43.85	**43.96**	44.83	**44.99**	44.62

Table 3: BLEU scores for the Transformer vs. variants of our document-level NMT model for German→English. **bold**: Best performance.

hierarchical attention model with soft attention over words is the best when using monolingual context (atleast +3.58 BLEU for all runs), while the hierarchical attention model with sparse attention over the words is the best in majority cases when using the bilingual context (atleast +3.73 BLEU for all runs). Among the two types of context, the bilingual context yields better BLEU scores in majority cases.

For traditional ensemble decoding, we get upto +3.73 BLEU improvement for our best hierarchical attention model over the sentence-level model. For ensemble-avg decoding, we see improvements almost equivalent to ensemble decoding. When it comes to speed, there is negligible difference between the two approaches.

4.3 German→English

From Table 3, we see that the document-level models again outperform the sentence-level Transformer baseline for all runs by a wider margin than for English→German. For the monolingual context, the hierarchical attention model with sparse attention over words is the best in majority cases (atleast +5.95 BLEU), while for the bilingual context, there does not seem to be a clear winner (atleast +6.19 BLEU). Again, using the bilin-

gual context yields better performance than using monolingual context in terms of BLEU.

For ensemble decoding, we get upto +5.73 BLEU improvement for our best hierarchical attention model when using the bilingual context over the sentence-level baseline. However, for the ensemble-avg decoding, we see the performance decrease in comparison to simple ensemble counterparts when using the monolingual context. The context representations that we averaged for the ensemble-avg decoding were coming from independent models (not checkpoints from the same model) and we believe this to be the reason we observe either deteriorating performance or no improvements for the ensemble-avg decoding in comparison to the ensemble decoding.

4.4 Analysis

Figure 3 illustrates the attention matrices[10] for an example German sentence as inferred by the flat and hierarchical attention models. The sentence-level attention component of the hierarchical attention model (Figure 3b) appears to be more distributed than its counterpart in the flat attention model (Figure 3a). For the word 'Sie' in the Ger-

---

[10]For this analysis, the attention weights are an average over heads of per-head attention weights.

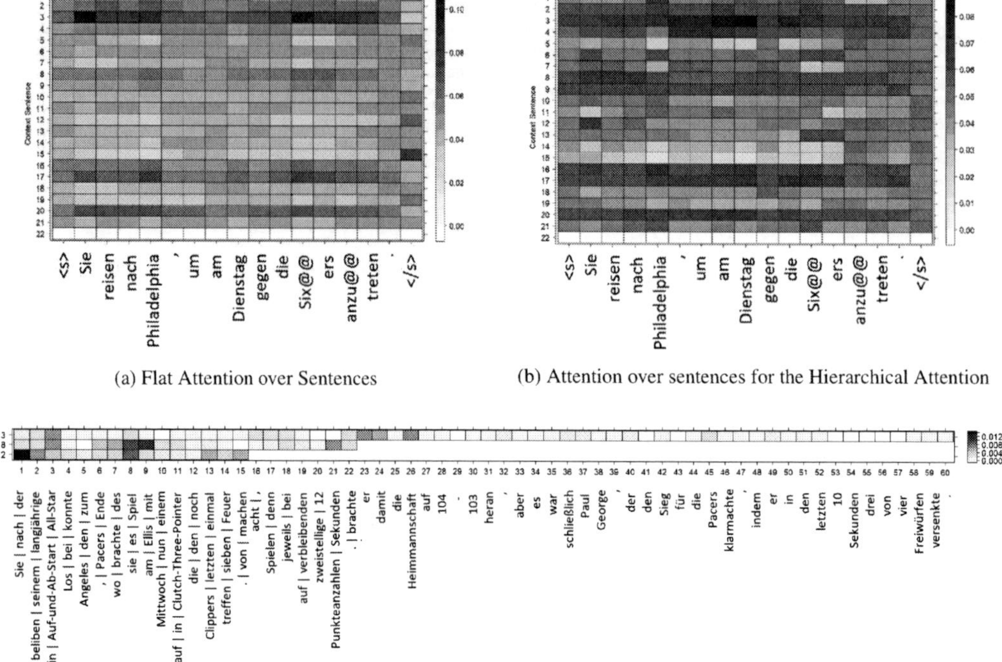

(a) Flat Attention over Sentences

(b) Attention over sentences for the Hierarchical Attention

(c) Scaled Attention over words for the Hierarchical Attention

Figure 3: Attention maps for the Flat Attention and Hierarchical Attention (sparse-sparse) models for a source sentence and source-side context (all in German). The current German sentence (position 22) has been masked.

man sentence, Figure 3c shows the scaled word-level attention map (scaled with the sentence-level attention weights) for the top three sentences, as observed in Figure 3b. *Sie* is an ambiguous pronoun in German and can be translated to *she, they* (sie) and even *you* in the polite form (Sie). It is even more ambiguous when used at the start of the sentence since the capitalisation removes this distinction. It can be seen from Figure 3c that the words given the highest attention weights while encoding this word are mostly other mentions of the same pronoun (Sie, sie). It should also be mentioned that in the 12-th sentence, both occurrences of the pronoun 'sie' also translate to 'they' as in the current sentence.

4.5 Submissions

We have submitted our best ensemble models, one for each translation direction, as reported in Tables 2 and 3, for the official evaluation. As mentioned before, we computed BLEU scores via MultEval toolkit on tokenised and cased Rotowire test set. Table 4 shows the scores as provided by the WNGT organisers. Surprisingly, the scores

Lang. Pair	Our Scores	WNGT Scores
En→De	39.83	41.46
De→En	45.06	47.39

Table 4: BLEU scores for submitted systems.

have increased further. We have been interested in exploring the effectiveness of NMT under constrained resource conditions, i.e., without back-translation on large monolingual data and pre-trained contextualised embeddings. We believe these enhancements could further improve upon the reported results.

Acknowledgments

The authors are grateful to the anonymous reviewers for their helpful comments and to Philip Arthur for discussion. This work was supported by the Multi-modal Australian ScienceS Imaging and Visualisation Environment (MASSIVE) (www.massive.org.au). G. H. is supported by a Google Faculty Research Award.

References

Jonathan H. Clark, Chris Dyer, Alon Lavie, and Noah A. Smith. 2011. Better hypothesis testing for statistical machine translation: Controlling for optimizer instability. In *Proceedings of the 49th Annual Meeting of the Association for Computational Linguistics: Human Language Technologies (Short Papers)*, pages 176–181. Association for Computational Linguistics.

Hiroaki Hayashi, Yusuke Oda, Alexandra Birch, Ioannis Constas, Andrew Finch, Minh-Thang Luong, Graham Neubig, and Katsuhito Sudoh. 2019. Findings of the third workshop on neural generation and translation. In *Proceedings of the Third Workshop on Neural Generation and Translation*.

Diederik P. Kingma and Jimmy Ba. 2014. Adam: A method for stochastic optimization. *CoRR*, abs/1412.6980.

Philipp Koehn, Hieu Hoang, Alexandra Birch, Chris Callison-Burch, Marcello Federico, Nicola Bertoldi, Brooke Cowan, Wade Shen, Christine Moran, Richard Zens, Chris Dyer, Ondřej Bojar, Alexandra Constantin, and Evan Herbst. 2007. Moses: Open source toolkit for statistical machine translation. In *Proceedings of the 45th Annual Meeting of the ACL on Interactive Poster and Demonstration Sessions*, pages 177–180. Association for Computational Linguistics.

Sameen Maruf and Gholamreza Haffari. 2018. Document context neural machine translation with memory networks. In *Proceedings of the 56th Annual Meeting of the Association for Computational Linguistics*. Association for Computational Linguistics.

Sameen Maruf, André F. T. Martins, and Gholamreza Haffari. 2019. Selective attention for context-aware neural machine translation. In *Proceedings of the 2019 Conference of the North American Chapter of the Association for Computational Linguistics: Human Language Technologies, Volume 1 (Long and Short Papers)*, pages 3092–3102, Minneapolis, Minnesota. Association for Computational Linguistics.

Graham Neubig, Chris Dyer, Yoav Goldberg, Austin Matthews, Waleed Ammar, Antonios Anastasopoulos, Miguel Ballesteros, David Chiang, Daniel Clothiaux, Trevor Cohn, Kevin Duh, Manaal Faruqui, Cynthia Gan, Dan Garrette, Yangfeng Ji, Lingpeng Kong, Adhiguna Kuncoro, Gaurav Kumar, Chaitanya Malaviya, Paul Michel, Yusuke Oda, Matthew Richardson, Naomi Saphra, Swabha Swayamdipta, and Pengcheng Yin. 2017. Dynet: The dynamic neural network toolkit. *arXiv preprint arXiv:1701.03980*.

Kishore Papineni, Salim Roukos, Todd Ward, and Wei-Jing Zhu. 2002. BLEU: A method for automatic evaluation of machine translation. In *Proceedings of the 40th Annual Meeting on Association for Computational Linguistics*, pages 311–318. Association for Computational Linguistics.

Rico Sennrich, Barry Haddow, and Alexandra Birch. 2016. Neural machine translation of rare words with subword units. In *Proceedings of the 54th Annual Meeting of the Association for Computational Linguistics*, pages 1715–1725.

Zhaopeng Tu, Yang Liu, Shuming Shi, and Tong Zhang. 2018. Learning to remember translation history with a continuous cache. *Transactions of the Association for Computational Linguistics (TACL)*, 6:407–420.

Ashish Vaswani, Noam Shazeer, Niki Parmar, Jakob Uszkoreit, Llion Jones, Aidan N Gomez, Łukasz Kaiser, and Illia Polosukhin. 2017. Attention is all you need. In *Advances in Neural Information Processing Systems 30*, pages 5998–6008. Curran Associates, Inc.

SYSTRAN @ WNGT 2019: DGT Task

Li Gong, Josep Crego, Jean Senellart
SYSTRAN / 5 rue Feydeau, 75002 Paris, France
`firstname.lastname@systrangroup.com`

Abstract

This paper describes SYSTRAN participation to the Document-level Generation and Translation (DGT) Shared Task of the 3rd Workshop on Neural Generation and Translation (WNGT 2019). We participate for the first time using a Transformer network enhanced with modified input embeddings and optimising an additional objective function that considers content selection. The network takes in structured data of basketball games and outputs a summary of the game in natural language.

1 Introduction

Data-to-text generation is an important task in natural language generation (NLG). It refers to the task of automatically producing a descriptive text from non-linguistic structured data (tables, database records, spreadsheets, *etc.*). Table 1 illustrates an example of data-to-text NLG, with statistics of a NBA basketball game (top) and the corresponding game summary (bottom).

Different from other NLG tasks (e.g., machine translation), data-to-text generation faces several additional challenges: First, data-to-text generation models have to select the content before generating text. In machine translation, the source and target sentences are semantically equivalent to each other, whereas in data-to-text generation, the model initially selects appropriate content from the input data to secondly generate fluent sentences that incorporate the selected content; Second, the training data in data-to-text generation task is often very limited. Unlike machine translation, where training data consist of translated sentence pairs, data-to-text generation models are trained from examples composed of structured data and its corresponding descriptive summary, which are much harder to produce.

In this paper, we tackle both challenges previously discussed. We introduce a new data-to-text generation model which jointly learns content selection and text generation. In addition, we present two data augmentation methods that further boost performance of the NLG system.

2 Data Resources

We use the official data set made available for the WNGT 2019 DGT task (Hayashi et al., 2019). It consists of the the ROTOWIRE dataset (Wiseman et al., 2017), a dataset of NBA basketball game summaries, paired with their corresponding box- and line-score tables. Table 1 illustrates an example of the dataset. In the box-score table, each team has at most 13 players and each player is described by 23 types of values. In the line-score table, each team has 15 different types of values. As for the associate summaries, the average length is 337 tokens, and the vocabulary size is $11.3K$. The ROTOWIRE dataset contains $4,853$ summaries in total, in which $3,398$ summaries are for training, 727 for validation and 728 for test. In addition, the next monolingual resources were considered usable in all tracks:

- Any monolingual data allowable by the WMT 2019 English-German news task,

- Pre-trained word/subword/character embeddings (e.g., GloVe, fastText),

- Pre-trained contextualized embeddings (e.g., ELMo, BERT),

- Pre-trained language models (e.g., GPT-2).

3 Data-to-Text Transformer Model

In this section, we present how we adapt the Transformer model for the data-to-text generation tasks. First, the input embedding of Transformer encoder is replaced by our record embedding to better incorporate the record information. Second, a new

Proceedings of the 3rd Workshop on Neural Generation and Translation (WNGT 2019), pages 262–267
Hong Kong, China, November 4, 2019. ©2019 Association for Computational Linguistics
www.aclweb.org/anthology/D19-56%2d

TEAM-NAME	WIN	LOSS	PTS	AST	...
Cavaliers	51	28	90	25	...
Celtics	37	42	99	30	...

NAME	POS	PTS	FGM	FGA	CITY	...
LeBron James	F	14	5	14	Cleveland	...
Kevin Love	F	19	6	12	Cleveland	...
Kyrie Irving	N/A	N/A	N/A	N/A	Cleveland	...
Brandon Bass	F	12	6	8	Boston	...
Avery Bradley	G	15	7	12	Boston	...
Marcus Smart	G	19	7	10	Boston	...
...	...	...	...	...	...	...

POS: position, PTS: points, FGM: Player field goals made; FGA: Player field goals attempted; AST: assists; CITY: player team city.

The **Boston Celtics (37-42)** defeated the **Cleveland Cavaliers (51-28) 99-90** on Friday in **Cleveland**. With the **Cavaliers** solidified as the No.2 seed for the Eastern Conference playoffs , they did not try particularly hard to win this game, starting with sitting **Kyrie Irving** (hip) to make sure he stays healthy. Regardless, the **Celtics** took advantage, picking up a huge victory as they fight to stay in the playoffs. **Marcus Smart** led the way scoring for **Boston**, posting **19** points on 7-of-10 shooting in **34** minutes. **Avery Bradley** was close behind, scoring **15** points (7-12 FG) in **31** minutes. The **Celtics** starting frontcourt of **Tyler Zeller** and **Brandon Bass** combined to score 25 points and grab 11 rebounds. **Boston**'s final starter, **Evan Turner**, struggled shooting the ball and only scored **four** points, but still managed to dish out **13** assists and grab **six** rebounds. **Isaiah Thomas**, as he has done so well since joining the **Celtics**, provided solid production off the bench, scoring **17** points (4-12 FG, 2-6 3Pt) in **23** minutes. ...

Table 1: Example of data-records (left) and document summary (right) from the RotoWire dataset. Entities and values corresponding to data-records are boldfaced.

learning objective is added into our model to improve its content-oriented performance.

3.1 Record Embedding

The input of data-to-text model encoder is a sequence of records. Each record is a tuple of four features (*Entity, Type, Value, Info*). Inspired by previous work (Yang et al., 2016; Wiseman et al., 2017; Puduppully et al., 2019), we embed features into vectors, and use the concatenation of feature embeddings as the embedding of record.

$$\mathbf{r}_i = [\mathbf{r}_{i,1}; \mathbf{r}_{i,2}; \mathbf{r}_{i,3}; \mathbf{r}_{i,4}] \tag{1}$$

where $\mathbf{r}_i \in \mathbb{R}^{dim}$ is the ith record embedding in the input sequence and $\mathbf{r}_{i,j} \in \mathbb{R}^{\frac{dim}{4}}$ is the jth feature embedding in $\mathbf{r}_i$.

Since there is no order relationship within the records, the positional embedding of the Transformer encoder is removed.

3.2 Content Selection Modeling

Besides record embedding, we also add a new learning objective into the Transformer model.

As presented before, we need to select the content from the input records before generating the output summary. Some records are generally important no mater the game context, such as the team name record and team score record, whereas the importance of some other records depend on the game context. For example, a player having the highest points in the game is more likely to be mentioned in the game summary. Within the Transformer architecture, the self-attention mechanism can generate the latent representation for each record by jointly conditioning on all other records in the input dataset. A binary prediction

layer is added on top of the Transformer encoder output (as shown in Figure 1) to predict whether or not one record will be mentioned in the target summary.

The architecture of our data-to-text Transformer model is shown in Figure 1. As presented before, the encoder takes the record embedding as input and generates the latent representation for each record in the input sequence. The output of encoder is then used to predict the importance of each record and also serves as the context of the decoder. The decoder of our model is the same as the original Transformer model in machine translation. It predicts the next word conditioned on the encoder output and the previous tokens in the summary sequence.

In content selection modeling, the input record sequences together with its label sequences are used to optimize the encoder by minimizing the cross-entorpy loss. In language generation training, the encoder and decoder are trained together to maximize the log-likelihood of the training data. The two learning objectives are trained alternatively.

4 Data Augmentation Methods

In data-to-text generation task, the model needs to not only generate fluent text, but also generate text which is coherent with the input records. Several content-oriented evaluation metrics are proposed in (Wiseman et al., 2017) to evaluate such cohesion, including the precision of record generation and the recall rate with respect to the records in gold summary.

In this section, we present two data augmentation methods: *synthetic data generation* and *train-*

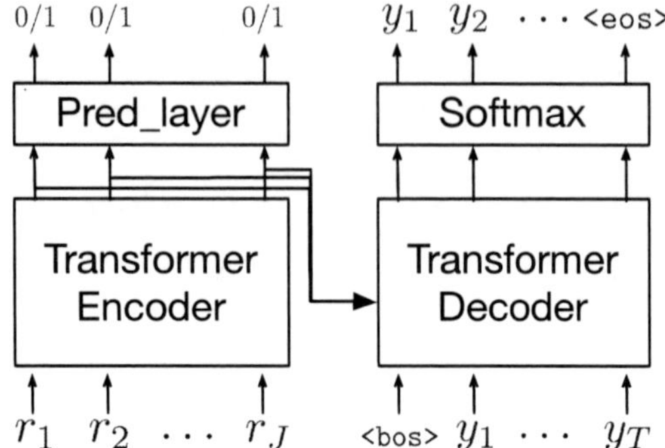

Figure 1: Model Architecture

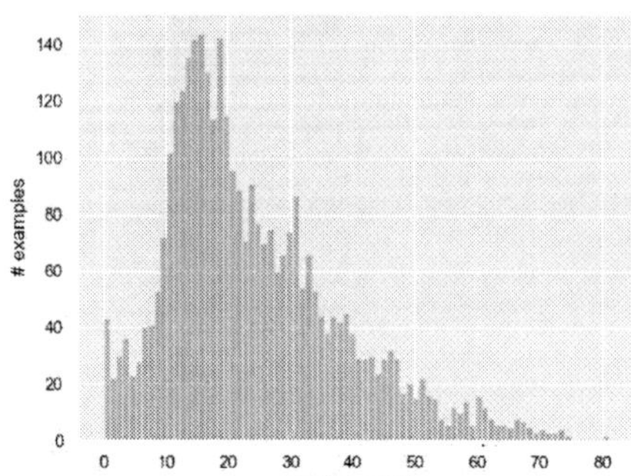

Figure 2: relation count distribution in training data.

ing data selection. Each of them has different impacts on the content-oriented evaluation results.

4.1 Synthetic Data Generation

In order to improve the cohesion between the input records and output summary, we need more data to enhance the encoder-decoder attention of the decoder. Here we introduce a method to generate synthetic training data.

We first randomly change the values of records and the changed record set ($\mathbf{s}'$) is then used to generate automatic summary ($\mathbf{t}'$) by a trained data-to-text system. The synthetic data pairs ($\mathbf{s}'$, $\mathbf{t}'$) are then used to improve such system.

In order to keep the data cohesion in the table, the change is constrained with the following rules:

- only numeric values are changed. Non-numeric values such as the position of a player or the city name of a team are kept the same.

- after the change, the team scores should not violate the win/loss relation

- the changed values should stay in the normal range of its value type. It should not bigger than its maximum value or smaller than its minimum value through all games.

Our data generation technique doubles the amount of training data available for learning.

4.2 Training Data Selection

A deficiency of data-to-text NLG systems is the poor coverage of relations produced in the generated summaries. In order to increase the coverage, a simple solution consists of learning to produce a larger number of relations. Here, we present a straightforward method to bias our model to output more relations by means of fine-tuning on the training examples containing a greater number of relations.

We use an information extraction (IE) system to extract the number of relations of each training summary. Then, we select for fine-tuning our baseline model the subset of training data in which each summary contains at least N relations. In this work, we take advantage of the IE system[1] provided by (Puduppully et al., 2019), and the distribution of the number of relations in the training summary is illustrated in Figure 2.

5 Experimental Setup

5.1 Data and Preprocessing

We run the experiments with the ROTOWIRE dataset (Wiseman et al., 2017), a dataset of NBA basketball game summaries, paired with their corresponding box- and line-score tables. Table 1 illustrates an example of the dataset. In the box-score table, each team has at most 13 players and each player is described by 23 types of values. In the line-score table, each team has 15 different types of values. In addition, the date of each game is converted into the day of the week (such as "*Saturday*") as an additional record. In the preprocessing step, the input box- and line-score tables are converted into a fix-length sequence of records. Each sequence contains 629 records.[2] As for the associate summaries, the average length is 337 tokens, and the vocabulary size is 11.3K. The

---

[1]The model is publicly available at `https://github.com/ratishsp/data2text-plan-py`

[2]In the 629 records, 598 records are for players, 30 records for teams and 1 record for the date.

ROTOWIRE dataset contains 4853 summaries in total, in which 3398 summaries are for training, 727 for validation and 728 for test.

In content selection modelling, we need the labels of input records to indicate which records in the input will be mentioned in the output summary. Here we use a very simple method to generate such labels. First, we label the entity records[3]. An entity record is labeled as 1 if its value is mentioned in the associated summary, otherwise it is labeled as 0. Second, for each player or team mentioned in the summary, the rest of its values in the table are labeled as 1 if they occur in the same sentence in the summary.

5.2 Evaluation metrics

The model output is evaluated with BLEU (Papineni et al., 2002) as well as several content-oriented metrics proposed by (Wiseman et al., 2017) including three following aspects:

- Relation Generation (RG) evaluates the number of extracted relations in automatic summaries and their correctness (precision) w.r.t the input record dataset;

- Content Selection (CS) evaluates the precision and recall rate of extracted relations in automatic summaries w.r.t that in the gold summaries;

- Content Ordering (CO) evaluates the normalized Damerau-Levenshtein Distance (Brill and Moore, 2000) between the sequence of extracted relations in automatic summaries and that in the gold summaries.

All these content-oriented metrics are based on an IE system which extracts record relations from summaries. For the purpose of comparison, we directly use the publicly available IE system of (Puduppully et al., 2019) to evaluate our models.

5.3 Training Details

In all experiments, we use our model with 1 encoder layer and 6 decoder layers, 512 hidden units (hence, the record feature embedding size is 128, see Section 3), 8 heads, GELU activations (Hendrycks and Gimpel, 2016), a dropout rate of 0.1 and learned positional embedding for

| Model | RG | | CS | | CO | BLEU |
	#	P%	P%	R%	DLD%	
GOLD	23.32	94.77	100	100	100	100
TEMPL	54.29	99.92	26.61	59.16	14.42	8.51
WS-2017	23.95	75.10	28.11	35.86	15.33	14.57
NCP-2019	33.88	87.51	33.52	51.21	18.57	16.19
DATA-TRANS	23.31	79.81	36.90	43.06	22.75	20.60
+DATA_GEN	22.59	**82.49**	**39.48**	42.84	23.32	19.76
+DATA_SEL	**26.94**	79.54	35.27	**47.49**	22.22	19.97
+BOTH	24.24	80.52	37.33	44.66	23.04	20.22

Table 2: Automatic evaluation on ROTOWIRE development set using relation generation (RG) count (#) and precision (P%), content selection (CS) precision (P%) and recall (R%), content ordering (CO) in normalized Damerau-Levenshtein distance (DLD%), and BLEU.

the decoder. The model is trained with the Adam optimizer (Kingma and Ba, 2014), learning rate is fixed to 10^{-4} and batch size is 6. As for inference, we use beam size 4 for all experiments, and the maximum decoding length is 600.

We implement all our models in Pytorch, and train them on 1 GTX 1080 GPU.

6 Results

The results of our model on the development set are summarized in Table 2. GOLD represents the evaluation result on the gold summary. The RG precision rate is 94.77%, indicating that the IE system for evaluation is not perfect but has very high precision. After that, results of three contrast systems are reported, where TEMPL and WS-2017 are the updated results[4] of Wiseman et al. (2017) models. TEMPL is template-based generator model which generates a summary consisting of 8 sentences: a general description sentence about the teams playing in the game, 6 player-specific sentences and a conclusion sentence. WS-2017 reports an encoder-decoder model with conditional copy mechanism. NCP-2019 is the best system configuration (NCP+CC) reported in (Puduppully et al., 2019) which is a neural content planning model enhanced with conditional copy mechanism. As for our model, results with four configurations are reported.

DATA-TRANS represents our data-to-text Transformer model (as illustrated in Figure 1) without any data augmentation. Comparing to NCP-2019, our model performs 3.4% higher on content selection precision, 4.2% higher on

---

[3]Record whose *Value* feature is an entity (see Section **??**), for example: "LeBron_James|NAME|LeBron_James|H/W". The labeling is according to the *Value* feature

[4]Here we all use the IE system of (Puduppully et al., 2019) which is improved from the original IE system of (Wiseman et al., 2017)

content ordering metric and 4.4 points higher on BLEU. Our model performs better on the CO metric, we attribute this improvement to that our model generates nearly the same number of relations as the gold summary which reduces the edit distance between the two sequences of relations. However, our model is 7.7% lower on RG precision. And on the CS recall rate, our model is 8.2% lower than NCP-2019. This is probably due to the fact that NCP-2019 generates much more records than our model (33.88 vs. 23.31) which could result higher coverage on the relations in gold summary.

Comparing to TEMPL and WS-2017, our model is much better on BLEU and CS precision. Our model generates nearly the same number of relations as WS-2017, but with 7.2% higher on recall rate and 7.4% higher on CO metric.

By synthetic data generation (+DATA_GEN), we generate synthetic table records as described in secion 4.1. These synthetic table records are then used as input to the DATA-TRANS model to generate summaries. All training table records are used to generate synthetic data. The synthetic data is then combined with the original training data to fine-tune the DATA-TRANS model. From Table 2, we can see that the RG and CS precisions are both improved by 2.7% and 2.6% respectively. There is no significant change on others metrics. The CO metric is slightly improved due to higher RG and CS precisions. The CS recall rate is slightly degraded with the number of extracted relations.

By training data selection (+DATA_SEL), we select the data whose summary contains the number of relations $N >= 16$ as the new training data. The result training data size is 2242 (original size: 3398). It is then used to fine-tune the DATA-TRANS model. As shown in Table 2, as expected, the model after fine-tuning generates more relations in the output summaries. The average number of relations in the output summaries increases from 23.31 to 26.94. Respectively, the CS recall is increased from 43.06% to 47.49%. However, the CS precision is slightly degraded by 1.6%.

Finally, we combine both of the data augmentation methods (+BOTH). Synthetic data generation improves the RG and CS precisions. Training data selection improves the CS recall rate by making the model generate more relations. To combine the two methods, we choose to fine-tune the +DATA_GEN model with the selected train-

Model	RG		CS		CO	BLEU
	#	P%	P%	R%	DLD%	
TEMPL	54.23	99.94	26.99	58.16	14.92	8.46
WS-2017	23.72	74.80	29.49	36.18	15.42	14.19
NCP-2019	34.28	87.47	34.18	51.22	18.58	16.50
DATA-TRANS	24.12	79.17	36.48	42.74	22.40	20.16
+DATA_GEN	24.01	**83.89**	**38.98**	42.85	23.02	19.48
+DATA_SEL	**27.47**	80.70	35.33	**46.25**	21.87	20.03
+BOTH	24.80	81.08	37.10	43.78	22.51	20.14

Table 3: Automatic evaluation on ROTOWIRE test set.

ing data of +DATA_SEL (so this configuration is actually +DATA_GEN+DATA_SEL). As shown in Table 2, all content-oriented evaluation metrics are improved compared to DATA-TRANS but not as much as each single of the data augmentation method. This configuration is like a trade-off between the two data augmentation configurations.

Results on the test set are reported in Table 3. They follow the same pattern as those found on the development set. Our DATA-TRANS model outperforms all other contrast systems on BLEU, CS precision and content ordering metrics. The synthetic data generation method helps to improve the RG and CS precisions. The training data selection method improves the CS recall by making the model generate more relations. Combining these two data augmentation methods, all content-oriented evaluation results are improved compared to DATA-TRANS. However, there is no significant change on BLEU.

7 Conclusions

We present an enhanced Transformer-based data-to-text generation model for the WNGT2019 English NLG task. Experimental results have shown that our enhanced transformer model outperforms current state-of-the-art system on BLEU, content selection precision and content ordering metics. In addition, we proposed two data augmentation methods, each of them improves different content-oriented evaluation metrics.

References

Eric Brill and Robert C Moore. 2000. An improved error model for noisy channel spelling correction. In *Proceedings of the 38th Annual Meeting on Association for Computational Linguistics*, pages 286–293. Association for Computational Linguistics.

Hiroaki Hayashi, Yusuke Oda, Alexandra Birch, Ioannis Constas, Andrew Finch, Minh-Thang Luong, Graham Neubig, and Katsuhito Sudoh. 2019. Findings of the third workshop on neural generation and translation. In *Proceedings of the Third Workshop on Neural Generation and Translation*.

Dan Hendrycks and Kevin Gimpel. 2016. Bridging nonlinearities and stochastic regularizers with gaussian error linear units.

Diederik P Kingma and Jimmy Ba. 2014. Adam: A method for stochastic optimization. *arXiv preprint arXiv:1412.6980*.

Kishore Papineni, Salim Roukos, Todd Ward, and Wei-Jing Zhu. 2002. Bleu: a method for automatic evaluation of machine translation. In *Proceedings of the 40th annual meeting on association for computational linguistics*, pages 311–318. Association for Computational Linguistics.

Ratish Puduppully, Li Dong, and Mirella Lapata. 2019. Data-to-text generation with content selection and planning. In *Proceedings of the AAAI Conference on Artificial Intelligence*, volume 33, pages 6908–6915.

Sam Wiseman, Stuart M Shieber, and Alexander M Rush. 2017. Challenges in data-to-document generation. *arXiv preprint arXiv:1707.08052*.

Zichao Yang, Phil Blunsom, Chris Dyer, and Wang Ling. 2016. Reference-aware language models. *arXiv preprint arXiv:1611.01628*.

University of Edinburgh's Submission to the Document-level Generation and Translation Shared Task

Ratish Puduppully [*] and **Jonathan Mallinson** [*] and **Mirella Lapata**
Institute for Language, Cognition and Computation
School of Informatics, University of Edinburgh
10 Crichton Street, Edinburgh EH8 9AB
r.puduppully@sms.ed.ac.uk J.Mallinson@ed.ac.uk mlap@inf.ed.ac.uk

Abstract

The University of Edinburgh participated in all six tracks: NLG, MT, and MT+NLG with both English and German as targeted languages. For the NLG track, we submitted a multilingual system based on the Content Selection and Planning model of Puduppully et al. (2019). For the MT track, we submitted Transformer-based Neural Machine Translation models, where out-of-domain parallel data was augmented with in-domain data extracted from monolingual corpora. Our MT+NLG systems disregard the structured input data and instead rely exclusively on the source summaries.

1 Track 1/2: Natural Language Generation

The Natural Language Generation (NLG) track revolved around systems that take structured data in the form of tabular data from a basketball game as input, and generate a summary of this game in the target language. We entered one multilingual system which outputs summaries in both English and German. A multilingual model allows us to overcome the limited amount of German training data.

We adopted the content selection and planning approach of Puduppully et al. (2019), made extensions to the model and parameterized the decoder with a language tag, indicating the target language. The training was done using the full ROTOWIRE English dataset and the ROTOWIRE English-German dataset. We first explain the approach of Puduppully et al. (2019), describe the

---

[*]Ratish worked on Tracks 1/2 and Jonathan on Tracks 3/4/5/6.

extensions to their model and show how language tags can be added to the decoder to indicate the target language.

1.1 The Content Selection and Planning Approach of Puduppully et al. (2019)

Puduppully et al. (2019) model $p(y|r)$ as the joint probability of text y and content plan z, given input r. They further decompose $p(y, z|r)$ into $p(z|r)$, a content selection and planning phase, and $p(y|r, z)$, a text generation phase:

$$p(y|r) = \sum_z p(y, z|r) = \sum_z p(z|r)p(y|r, z)$$

Given input records, probability $p(z|r)$ is modeled using Pointer Networks (Vinyals et al., 2015). The probability of output text y conditioned on previously generated content plan z and input table r is modeled as follows:

$$p(y|r, z) = \prod_{t=1}^{|y|} p(y_t|y_{<t}, z, r)$$

where $y_{<t} = y_1 \ldots y_{t-1}$. They use an encoder-decoder architecture with an attention mechanism to compute $p(y|r, z)$. The architecture is shown in Figure 1.

The content plan z is encoded into $\{e_k\}_{k=1}^{|z|}$ using a bidirectional LSTM. Because the content plan is a sequence of input records, they directly feed the corresponding content selected record vectors $\{r_j^{cs}\}_{j=1}^{|r|}$ as input to the LSTM units, which share the record encoder with the first stage. For details of the content selection stage, please refer Puduppully et al. (2019).

The text decoder is also based on a recurrent neural network with LSTM units. The decoder is initialized with the hidden states of the final step in the encoder. At decoding step t, the input of the LSTM unit is the embedding of the previously

Proceedings of the 3rd Workshop on Neural Generation and Translation (WNGT 2019), pages 268–272
Hong Kong, China, November 4, 2019. ©2019 Association for Computational Linguistics
www.aclweb.org/anthology/D19-56%2d

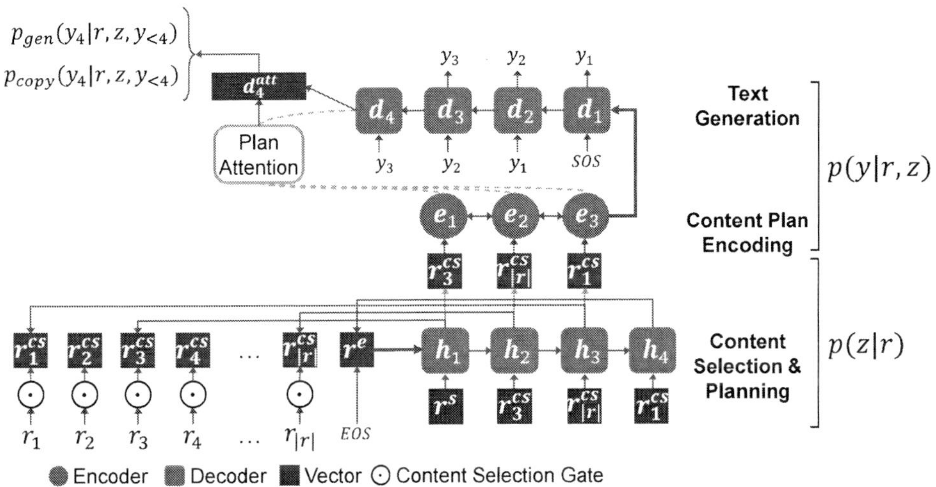

Figure 1: Generation model with content selection and planning. The text is generated conditioned on the input content plan. At any time step, output token is generated from vocabulary or copied from the content plan.

predicted word y_{t-1}. Let $\mathbf{d}_t$ be the hidden state of the t-th LSTM unit. The probability of predicting y_t from the output vocabulary is computed via:

$$\beta_{t,k} \propto \exp(\mathbf{d}_t^\mathsf{T}\mathbf{W}_b\mathbf{e}_k) \tag{1}$$

$$\mathbf{q}_t = \sum_k \beta_{t,k}\mathbf{e}_k$$

$$\mathbf{d}_t^{att} = \tanh(\mathbf{W}_d[\mathbf{d}_t; \mathbf{q}_t])$$

$$p_{gen}(y_t|y_{<t}, z, r) = \mathrm{softmax}_{y_t}(\mathbf{W}_y\mathbf{d}_t^{att} + \mathbf{b}_y) \tag{2}$$

where $\sum_k \beta_{t,k} = 1$, $\mathbf{W}_b \in \mathbb{R}^{n \times n}, \mathbf{W}_d \in \mathbb{R}^{n \times 2n}, \mathbf{W}_y \in \mathbb{R}^{n \times |\mathcal{V}_y|}, \mathbf{b}_y \in \mathbb{R}^{|\mathcal{V}_y|}$ are parameters, and $|\mathcal{V}_y|$ is the output vocabulary size.

They further augment the decoder with a copy mechanism, allowing the ability to copy words directly from the *value* portions of records in the content plan (i.e., $\{z_k\}_{k=1}^{|z|}$). They experimented with joint (Gu et al., 2016) and conditional copy methods (Gulcehre et al., 2016). Specifically, they introduce a variable $u_t \in \{0, 1\}$ for each time step to indicate whether the predicted token y_t is copied ($u_t = 1$) or not ($u_t = 0$). The probability of generating y_t is computed by:

$$p(y_t|y_{<t}, z, r) = \sum_{u_t \in \{0,1\}} p(y_t, u_t|y_{<t}, z, r)$$

where u_t is marginalized out.

1.2 Copying from Table and Plan

We extended the copy mechanism further such that u_t can take three values: y_t is generated from the vocabulary ($u_t = 0$), y_t is copied from the content plan ($u_t = 1$) and y_t is copied from the table ($u_t = 2$).

Conditional Copy The variable u_t is first computed as a switch gate, and then is used to obtain the output probability:

$$p(u_t|y_{<t}, z, r) = \mathrm{softmax}(\mathbf{w}_u \cdot \mathbf{d}_t^{att} + b_u)$$

$$\alpha_{t,j} \propto \exp(\mathbf{d}_t^\mathsf{T}\mathbf{W}_c\mathbf{r}_j^{cs}) \tag{3}$$

$$p(y_t, u_t|y_{<t}, z, r) =$$

$$\begin{cases} p(u_t|y_{<t}, z, r) \sum_{y_t \leftarrow z_k} \beta_{t,k} & u_t = 1 \\ p(u_t|y_{<t}, z, r) \sum_k \beta_{t,k} \sum_{\substack{y_t \leftarrow r_j \\ j \in \gamma_k}} \alpha_{t,j} & u_t = 2 \\ p(u_t|y_{<t}, z, r) p_{gen}(y_t|y_{<t}, z, r) & u_t = 0 \end{cases}$$

where $\sum_{j \in \gamma_k} \alpha_{t,j} = 1$. $y_t \leftarrow z_k$ indicates that y_t can be copied from z_k, $y_t \leftarrow r_j$ indicates that y_t can be copied from r_j. γ_k indicates records in table corresponding to the kth record in plan, for example: if k is 'PTS' value of player *Jeff Teague*, then γ_k corresponds to all the records for the entity *Jeff Teague* in the table including 'PTS', 'REB', 'NAME1', 'NAME2' etc. $\beta_{t,k}$ and $p_{gen}(y_t|y_{<t}, z, r)$ are computed as in Equations (1)–(2), and $\mathbf{w}_u \in \mathbb{R}^{3 \times n}, b_u \in \mathbb{R}^3$ are parameters.

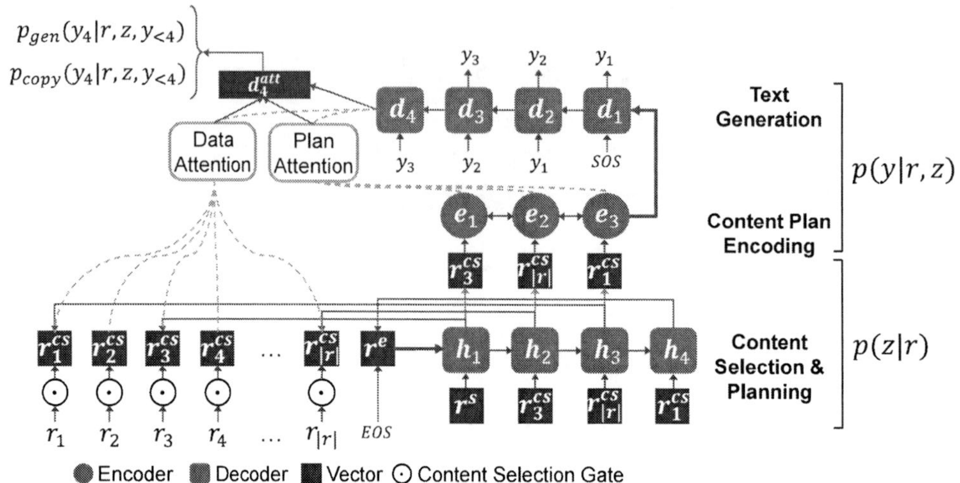

Figure 2: Generation model with content selection and planning and attention over table and content plan. The text is generated conditioned on the content plan and the table. At any time step, output token is generated from vocabulary, copied from the content plan or copied from input table.

1.3 Attending to the Table and Content Plan

The output text is generated by attending to both the content plan and the input table (See Figure 2.)

$$\delta_{t,j} \propto \exp(\mathbf{d}_t^\intercal \mathbf{W}_c \mathbf{r}_j^{CS}) \quad (4)$$

$$\mathbf{s}_t = \sum_j \delta_{t,j} \mathbf{r}_j^{CS}$$

$$\mathbf{d}_t^{att} = \tanh(\mathbf{W}_d[\mathbf{d}_t; \mathbf{q}_t; \mathbf{s}_t])$$

$$p_{gen}(y_t|y_{<t}, z, r) = \text{softmax}_{y_t}(\mathbf{W}_y \mathbf{d}_t^{att} + \mathbf{b}_y) \quad (5)$$

where $\sum_j \delta_{t,j} = 1$, $\mathbf{W}_c \in \mathbb{R}^{n \times n}$, $\mathbf{W}_d \in \mathbb{R}^{n \times 3n}$, $\mathbf{W}_y \in \mathbb{R}^{n \times |\mathcal{V}_y|}$, $\mathbf{b}_y \in \mathbb{R}^{|\mathcal{V}_y|}$ are parameters, and $|\mathcal{V}_y|$ is the output vocabulary size.

1.4 Feature for Team Points and Ranking of Player Points

Upon inspection of the RotoWire game summaries in the development set, we observed that the summaries often describe the statistics of the winning team followed by the statistics of the losing team. The highest ranked players of either team are also often described in sequence in the summaries. Currently, we rely on the word embeddings of the team and player points to help the model disambiguate the winning from the losing team and to learn the relative performances of the players. We hypothesize that explicitly providing information about the relative performance of players and teams should make the learning easier.

We thus experimented with a feature for the winning/losing team and the ranking of player points within a team. Specifically, we added a binary feature for team records: win for each record in the winning team, $loss$ for each record in the losing team. We further rank players in a team on the basis of their points and we add a feature indicating their rank in the team. For instance, *Kyle Lowry* scored the highest number of points in the home team and we add feature *hometeam-0* to each of his records. Player *Jahlil Okafor* was the second highest scorer in the visiting team and we add the feature *visteam-1* to each of his records and so on.

1.5 Training a Single Multilingual Model

We trained a single model for English and German data-to-text with a common BPE (Sennrich et al., 2015b) vocabulary of 2000 symbols for the output summaries. Player names and values of records in summaries were not BPEd. The target text was prefixed with token indicating the language of output 'EN' or 'DE'. During inference, we forced the model to generate output in the desired language.

1.6 Dataset

We made use of the full RotoWire English dataset of Wiseman et al. (2017) and the German dataset provided as part of the shared task. The statistics of the dataset are given in Table 1.

	Train	Dev	Test
English	3398	727	728
German	242	240	241

Table 1: Count of examples in Training, Development and Test sections of English and German dataset.

Model	RG P%	CS P%	CS R%	CO DLD%	BLEU
EN	91.41	30.91	64.13	21.72	17.01
DE	70.23	23.40	41.83	16.08	10.95

Table 2: Automatic evaluation for track 1/2 on the ROTOWIRE test set using record generation (RG) precision, content selection (CS) precision and recall, content ordering (CO) in normalized Damerau-Levenshtein distance, and BLEU.

1.7 Results

Table 2 shows our results for English and German datasets on the Test set as provided by the shared task organizers.

2 Track 3/4 : Machine Translation

The Machine Translation (MT) track revolves arround systems that translate source summaries to the target language. Our submission takes advantage of existing state-of-the-art techniques in machine translation, including (1) transformer networks (Vaswani et al., 2017). (2) subword units (Sennrich et al., 2015b) and (3) the inclusion of in-domain monolingual data used via back-translation (Sennrich et al., 2015a).

For our submission, we focus on finding in-domain basketball summary data from within general-purpose monolingual datasets. We develop several heuristics allowing us to extract millions of in-domain monolingual sentences, which are then back-translated and included within the training data. This additional monolingual data improves bleu scores between 5 and 7 points.

2.1 Data

The translation models were trained on both the ROTOWIRE English-German and all WMT19 parallel training data. A summary of the training data can be found in table 3. For ease of comparison to the NLG task, tokenization was done using the tokenizer provided by the shared task organizers. BPE was employed with a joint BPE subword vocabulary of 50k.

Dataset	Size
Europarl v9	18.39
Common Crawl corpus	24.00
News Commentary v14	3.38
Document-split Rapid corpus	14.01
Wikititles	13.05
ParaCrawl	162.64
ROTOWIRE EN-DE	0.033
Total	235.47

Table 3: Size (number of parallel training sentences) in 100,000 of the EN-DE training data.

2.1.1 In-Domain Parallel Data

Table 3 highlights the extremely limited amount of in-domain parallel training data used; ROTOWIRE English-German makes up only 0.001% the parallel training data. To ensure our translation system produces in-domain translation, we supplemented the parallel data with in-domain monolingual data. We used back-translation to translate clean monolingual data from the target language to the source language.

Finding in-domain data for basketball is not trivial, as there are no explicit basketball WMT19 monolingual training sets. Therefore, we extracted in-domain basketball data from the available general-purpose monolingual datasets.

We considered all documents within the News Crawl 2007-2018 dataset and included all sentences which appeared within a document where any of the following conditions were met: (1) Contains a player's name, as taken from the ROTOWIRE English-German training data; (2) Contains two team names; (3) the title contains the word *NBA*. For German, 1.1 million monolingual target sentences were collected, and for English, 4.32 million monolingual target sentences. These sentences were then back-translated via sampling (Edunov et al., 2018) and used to augment the parallel training data.

2.2 Model Description

For our submissions, we used the Transformer model as implemented within OpenNMT-py (Klein et al., 2017). Transformers are state-of-the-art NMT approaches which rely on multi-headed attention applied to both the source and target sentences. All experiments are performed with 6 encoder-decoder layers, with an embedding layer of size 512, a feed-forward layer size of 2048, and

	EN-DE	DE-EN
Monolingual	34.44	40.72
Parallel	28.65	33.48

Table 4: Track 3-6: ROTOWIRE dev set results, showing BLEU without monolingual data *Parallel* and with monolingual data *Monolingual*.

Model	RG P%	CS P%	CS R%	CO DLD%	BLEU
EN-DE	81.01	77.32	78.49	62.21	36.85
DE-EN	91.40	78.99	63.04	51.73	41.15

Table 5: Automatic evaluation for track 3-6 on the ROTOWIRE test set using record generation (RG) precision, content selection (CS) precision and recall, content ordering (CO) in normalized Damerau-Levenshtein distance, and BLEU.

8 attentional heads. We set the batch size to 4096 tokens and maximum sentence length to 100 BPE subwords. Dropout and label smoothing were also both set to 0.1. All other settings were set their default values as specified in OpenNMT-py. Decoding was performed with a beam size of ~15, length penalty averaging, and the decoder was constrained to block repeating 4-grams. Model selection was done using the BLEU score on the development set.

2.3 Results

Results on the development set in Table 4 show that the inclusion of monolingual data leads to a significant increase in bleu (between 5 and 7 points). Table 5 shows test set results for both English and German target languages. The results were provided by the shared task organizers.

3 Track 5/6: MT + NLG

The MT + NLG track combines the previous tracks, models take in as input both the structured data and the summary in the source language and produce a summary in the target language as output. We chose to disregard the structured data and instead exclusively use the source summary, translating it to the target language. As such this submission to this track is a replication of our MT submission with results shown in Table 5.

References

Sergey Edunov, Myle Ott, Michael Auli, and David Grangier. 2018. Understanding back-translation at scale. *arXiv preprint arXiv:1808.09381*.

Jiatao Gu, Zhengdong Lu, Hang Li, and Victor O.K. Li. 2016. Incorporating copying mechanism in sequence-to-sequence learning. In *Proceedings of the 54th Annual Meeting of the Association for Computational Linguistics (Volume 1: Long Papers)*, pages 1631–1640.

Caglar Gulcehre, Sungjin Ahn, Ramesh Nallapati, Bowen Zhou, and Yoshua Bengio. 2016. Pointing the unknown words. In *Proceedings of the 54th Annual Meeting of the Association for Computational Linguistics (Volume 1: Long Papers)*, pages 140–149.

Guillaume Klein, Yoon Kim, Yuntian Deng, Jean Senellart, and Alexander M. Rush. 2017. OpenNMT: Open-source toolkit for neural machine translation. In *Proc. ACL*.

Ratish Puduppully, Li Dong, and Mirella Lapata. 2019. Data-to-text generation with content selection and planning. In *Proceedings of the AAAI Conference on Artificial Intelligence*, volume 33, pages 6908–6915.

Rico Sennrich, Barry Haddow, and Alexandra Birch. 2015a. Improving neural machine translation models with monolingual data. *arXiv preprint arXiv:1511.06709*.

Rico Sennrich, Barry Haddow, and Alexandra Birch. 2015b. Neural machine translation of rare words with subword units. *arXiv preprint arXiv:1508.07909*.

Ashish Vaswani, Noam Shazeer, Niki Parmar, Jakob Uszkoreit, Llion Jones, Aidan N Gomez, Łukasz Kaiser, and Illia Polosukhin. 2017. Attention is all you need. In *Advances in neural information processing systems*, pages 5998–6008.

Oriol Vinyals, Meire Fortunato, and Navdeep Jaitly. 2015. Pointer networks. In C. Cortes, N. D. Lawrence, D. D. Lee, M. Sugiyama, and R. Garnett, editors, *Advances in Neural Information Processing Systems 28*, pages 2692–2700. Curran Associates, Inc.

Sam Wiseman, Stuart Shieber, and Alexander Rush. 2017. Challenges in data-to-document generation. In *Proceedings of the 2017 Conference on Empirical Methods in Natural Language Processing*, pages 2253–2263.

Naver Labs Europe's Systems for the Document-Level Generation and Translation Task at WNGT 2019

Fahimeh Saleh[*]
Monash University
fahimeh.saleh@monash.edu

Alexandre Bérard
Naver Labs Europe
first.last@naverlabs.com

Ioan Calapodescu

Laurent Besacier
Université Grenoble-Alpes
laurent.besacier@univ-grenoble-alpes.fr

Abstract

Recently, neural models led to significant improvements in both machine translation (MT) and natural language generation tasks (NLG). However, generation of long descriptive summaries conditioned on structured data remains an open challenge. Likewise, MT that goes beyond sentence-level context is still an open issue (e.g., document-level MT or MT with metadata). To address these challenges, we propose to leverage data from both tasks and do transfer learning between MT, NLG, and MT with source-side metadata (MT+NLG). First, we train document-based MT systems with large amounts of parallel data. Then, we adapt these models to pure NLG and MT+NLG tasks by fine-tuning with smaller amounts of domain-specific data. This end-to-end NLG approach, without data selection and planning, outperforms the previous state of the art on the Rotowire NLG task. We participated to the "Document Generation and Translation" task at WNGT 2019, and ranked first in all tracks.

1 Introduction

Neural Machine Translation (NMT) and Neural Language Generation (NLG) are the top lines of the recent advances in Natural Language Processing. Although state-of-the-art NMT systems have reported impressive performance on several languages, there are still many challenges in this field especially when context is considered. Currently, the majority of NMT models translate sentences independently, without access to a larger context (e.g., other sentences from the same document or structured information). Additionally, despite improvements in text generation, generating long descriptive summaries conditioned on structured data is still an open challenge (e.g., table records). Ex-

isting models lack accuracy, coherence, or adequacy to source material (Wiseman et al., 2017).

The two aspects which are mostly addressed in data-to-text generation techniques are identifying the most important information from input data, and verbalizing data as a coherent document: *"What to talk about and how?"* (Mei et al., 2016). These two challenges have been addressed separately as different modules in pipeline systems (McKeown, 1985; Reiter and Dale, 2000) or in an end-to-end manner with PCFGs or SMT-like approaches (Mooney and Wong, 2007; Angeli et al., 2010; Konstas and Lapata, 2013), or more recently, with neural generation models (Wiseman et al., 2017; Lebret et al., 2016; Mei et al., 2016). In spite of generating fluent text, end-to-end neural generation models perform weakly in terms of best content selection (Wiseman et al., 2017). Recently, Puduppully et al. (2019) trained an end-to-end data-to-document generation model on the Rotowire dataset (English summaries of basketball games with structured data).[1] They aimed to overcome the shortcomings of end-to-end neural NLG models by explicitly modeling content selection and planning in their architecture.

We suggest in this paper to leverage the data from both MT and NLG tasks with transfer learning. As both tasks have the same target (e.g., English-language stories), they can share the same decoder. The same encoder can also be used for NLG and MT if the NLG metadata is encoded as a text sequence. We first train domain-adapted document-level NMT models on large amounts of parallel data. Then we fine-tune these models on small amounts of NLG data, transitioning from MT to NLG. We show that separate data selection and ordering steps are not necessary if NLG model is trained at document level and is given

---

[*]This work was done while the author was visiting at Naver Labs Europe.

[1]https://github.com/harvardnlp/boxscore-data

Proceedings of the 3rd Workshop on Neural Generation and Translation (WNGT 2019), pages 273–279
Hong Kong, China, November 4, 2019. ©2019 Association for Computational Linguistics
www.aclweb.org/anthology/D19-56%2d

Corpus	Lang(s)	Split	Docs	Sents
DGT	EN-DE	train	242	3247
		valid	240	3321
		test	241	3248
Rotowire	EN	train	3398	45.5k
		valid	727	9.9k
		test	728	10.0k
WMT19-sent	EN-DE	train	–	28.5M
WMT19-doc			68.4k	3.63M
News-crawl	EN	train	14.6M	420M
	DE		25.1M	534M

Table 1: Statistics of the allowed resources. The English sides of DGT-train, valid and test are respectively subsets of Rotowire-train, valid and test. More monolingual data is available, but we only used Rotowire and News-crawl.

enough information. We propose a compact way to encode the data available in the original database, and enrich it with some extra facts that can be easily inferred with a minimal knowledge of the task. We also show that NLG models trained with this data capture document-level structure and can select and order information by themselves.

2 Document-Level Generation and Translation Task

The goal of the Document-Level Generation and Translation (DGT) task is to generate summaries of basketball games, in two languages (English and German), by using either structured data about the game, a game summary in the other language, or a combination of both. The task features 3 tracks, times 2 target languages (English or German): **NLG** (Data to Text), **MT** (Text to Text) and **MT+NLG** (Text + Data to Text). The data and evaluation are document-level, encouraging participants to generate full documents, rather than sentence-based outputs. Table 1 describes the allowed parallel and monolingual corpora.

3 Our MT and NLG Approaches

All our models (MT, NLG, MT+NLG) are based on Transformer Big (Vaswani et al., 2017). Details for each track are given in the following sections.

3.1 Machine Translation Track

For the MT track, we followed these steps:

1. Train sent-level MT models on all the WMT19 parallel data (doc and sent) plus DGT-train.

2. Back-translate (BT) the German and English News-crawl by sampling (Edunov et al., 2018),

3. Re-train sentence-level MT models on a concatenation of the WMT19 parallel data, DGT-train and BT. The later was split into 20 parts, one part for each training epoch. This is almost equivalent to oversampling the non-BT data by 20 and doing a single epoch of training.

4. Fine-tune the best sentence-level checkpoint (according to valid perplexity) on document-level data. Like Junczys-Dowmunt (2019), we truncated the WMT documents into sequences of maximum 1100 BPE tokens. We also aggregated random sentences from WMT-sent into documents, and upsampled the DGT-train data. Contrary to Junczys-Dowmunt (2019), we do not use any sentence separator or document boundary tags.

5. Fine-tune the best doc-level checkpoint on DGT-train plus back-translated Rotowire-train and Rotowire-valid.

We describe the pre-processing and hyperparameters in Section 4. In steps (1) and (3), we train for at most 20 epochs, with early stopping based on newstest2014 perplexity. In step (4), we train for at most 5 additional epochs, with early stopping according to DGT-valid perplexity (doc-level). In the last step, we train for 100 epochs, with BLEU evaluation on DGT-valid every 10 epochs. We also compute the BLEU score of the best checkpoint according to DGT-valid perplexity, and keep the checkpoint with highest BLEU.

The models in step (5) overfit very quickly, reaching their best valid perplexity after only 1 or 2 epochs. For DE-EN, we found that the best DGT-valid BLEU was achieved anywhere between 10 and 100 epochs (sometimes with a high valid perplexity). For EN-DE, perplexity and BLEU correlated better, and the best checkpoint according to both scores was generally the same. The same observations apply when fine-tuning on NLG or MT+NLG data in the next sections.

Like Berard et al. (2019), all our MT models use corpus tags: each source sentence starts with a special token which identifies the corpus it comes from (e.g., Paracrawl, Rotowire, News-crawl). At test time, we use the DGT tag.

One thing to note, is that document-level decoding is much slower than its sentence-level counterpart.[2] The goal of this document-level fine-tuning

---

[2] On a single V100, sent-level DGT-valid takes 1 minute to translate, while doc-level DGT-valid takes 6 minutes.

was not to increase translation quality, but to allow us to use the same model for MT and NLG, which is easier to do at the document level.

3.2 Natural Language Generation Track

Original metadata consists of one JSON document per game, containing information about teams and their players. We first generate compact representations of this metadata as text sequences. Then, we fine-tune our doc-level MT models (from step 4) on the NLG task by using this representation on the source side and full stories on the target side. We train on a concatenation of DGT-train, Rotowire-train and Rotowire valid. We filter the later to remove games that are also in DGT-valid. Our metadata has the following structure:

1. Date of the game as text.

2. Home team information (winner/loser tag, team name and city, points in the game, season wins and losses and team-level scores) and information about its next game (date, home/visitor tag, other team's name), inferred from the other JSON documents in Rotowire-train.

3. Visiting team information and details on its next game.

4. N best players of the home team (player name, followed by all his non-zero scores in a fixed order and his starting position). Players are sorted by points first, then by rebounds and assists.

5. N best players of the visiting team.

To help the models identify useful information, we use a combination of special tokens and positional information. For instance, the home team is always first, but a <WINNER> tag precedes the winning team and its players. We ignore all-zero statistics, but always use the same position for each type of score (e.g., points, then rebounds, then assists) and special tokens to help identify them (e.g., <PTS> 16 and <REB> 8). We try to limit the number of tags to keep the sequences short (e.g., made and attempted free throws and percentage: <FT> 3 5 60). An example of metadata representation is shown in Table 2.

3.3 MT+NLG Track

For the MT+NLG track, we concatenate the MT source with the NLG data. We use the same metadata encoding method as in the NLG track and we fine-tune our doc-level MT models (from step 4). We also randomly mask tokens in the MT source (by replacing them with a <MASK> token), with 20% or 50% chance (with one different sampling per epoch). The goal is to force the model to use the metadata because of missing information in the source. At test time, we do not mask any token.

4 Experiments

4.1 Data Pre-processing

We filter the WMT19-sent parallel corpus with `langid.py` (Lui and Baldwin, 2012) and remove sentences of more than 175 tokens or with a length ratio greater than 1.5. Then, we apply the official DGT tokenizer (based on NLTK's `word_tokenize`) to the non-tokenized text (everything but DGT and Rotowire).

We apply BPE segmentation (Sennrich et al., 2016) with a joined SentencePiece-like model (Kudo and Richardson, 2018), with 32k merge operations, obtained on WMT + DGT-train (English + German). The vocabulary threshold is set to 100 and inline casing is applied (Berard et al., 2019). We employ the same joined BPE model and Fairseq dictionary for all models. The metadata is translated into the source language of the MT model used for initialization,[3] and segmented into BPE (except for the special tokens) to allow transfer between MT and NLG. Then, we add a corpus tag to each source sequence, which specifies its origin (Rotowire, News-crawl, etc.)

Like Junczys-Dowmunt (2019), we split WMT19 documents that are too long into shorter documents (maximum 1100 BPE tokens). We also transform the sent-level WMT19 data into doc-level data by shuffling the corpus and grouping consecutive sentences into documents of random length. Finally, we upsample the doc-level data (WMT19 and DGT) by 8 times its original size (in terms of sent count). We do so by sampling random spans of consecutive sentences until reaching the desired size.

The DGT and Rotowire data is already tokenized and does not need filtering nor truncating. We segment it into BPE units and add corpus tags.

4.2 Settings

All the models are Transformer Big (Vaswani et al., 2017), implemented in Fairseq (Ott et al., 2018). We use the same hyper-parameters as Ott et al. (2018), with Adam and an inverse square root schedule with warmup (maximum LR 0.0005). We apply dropout and label smoothing with a rate of 0.1. The source and target embeddings are shared and tied with the last layer. We train with half-precision floats on 8 V100 GPUs, with at most 3500 tokens per batch and delayed updates of 10

---

[3] Only week days, months and player positions need to be translated.

Metadata	<DATE> Freitag Februar 2017 <WINNER> Oklahoma City Thunder <PTS> 114 <WINS> 29 <LOSSES> 22 <REB> 47 <AST> 21 <TO> 20 <FG> 38 80 48 <FG3> 13 26 50 <FT> 25 33 76 <NEXT> Sonntag Februar 2017 <HOME> Portland Trail Blazers <LOSER> Memphis Grizzlies <PTS> 102 <WINS> 30 <LOSSES> 22 <REB> 29 <AST> 21 <TO> 12 <FG> 40 83 48 <FG3> 3 19 16 <FT> 19 22 86 <NEXT> Samstag Februar 2017 <VIS> Minnesota Timberwolves <WINNER> <PLAYER> Russell Westbrook <PTS> 38 <REB> 13 <AST> 12 <STL> 3 <PF> 2 <FG> 8 20 40 <FG3> 5 7 71 <FT> 17 17 100 <POS> Guard <PLAYER> Steven Adams <PTS> 16 <REB> 12 <AST> 2 <STL> 1 <BLK> 2 <PF> 4 <FG> 7 13 54 <FT> 2 6 33 <POS> Center <PLAYER> Joffrey Lauvergne <PTS> 16 <REB> 8 <AST> 2 <PF> 3 <FG> 6 7 86 <FG3> 3 4 75 <FT> 1 2 50 <POS> Bank <LOSER> <PLAYER> Marc Gasol <PTS> 31 <REB> 4 <AST> 8 <STL> 2 <BLK> 1 <PF> 4 <FG> 14 24 58 <FG3> 0 4 0 <FT> 3 3 100 <POS> Center <PLAYER> Mike Conley <PTS> 18 <REB> 1 <AST> 2 <STL> 3 <FG> 7 16 44 <FG3> 1 5 20 <FT> 3 5 60 <POS> Guard <PLAYER> Zach Randolph <PTS> 16 <REB> 10 <AST> 3 <STL> 1 <PF> 4 <FG> 6 14 43 <FG3> 0 1 0 <FT> 4 4 100 <POS> Bank
Reference story	The Oklahoma City Thunder defeated the visiting Memphis Grizzlies 114 - 102 , at Chesapeake Energy Arena on Friday evening . The Grizzlies led by four after three quarters , but then Russell Westbrook went absolutely ballistic in the fourth quarter , scoring 19 points in the quarter , including 15 points straight and unanswered , to take his team from down 102 - 99 to the final score of 114 - 102 . This snaps the Grizzlies three-game win streak , while Westbrook added to his ridiculous triple-double count , as he notched his 25th of the season . The Thunder (29 - 22) only scored 21 points in the first quarter , before outscoring the Grizz by 12 in the second , to take an eight-point lead into half time . They were then outscored by 12 in the third , and entered the fourth down by four . The Thunder outscored the Grizz by 14 in the fourth , behind Russell Westbrook and his takeover .Westbrook finished with 38 points , 13 rebounds , 12 assists and three steals to lead his squad to a big win . Westbrook also matched a career-best as he went 17-of-17 from the foul line . Three other players scored in double digits for the Thunder , including Steven Adams and Joffrey Lauvergne , who pitched in 16 points each . The Thunder go on to visit Portland on Sunday Meanwhile , the Grizzlies (30 - 22) saw their win streak come to an end as they went scoreless in the last 2:50 as they were stifled by an overwhelming push of energy and intensity from the Thunder and their home crowd . Marc Gasol finished with a team-high 31 points , to go along with eight assists , four rebounds , two steals and one block , in 42 minutes . Zach Randolph came up big in 29 minutes off the bench , with 16 points and 10 rebounds , while Mike Conley chipped in 18 points , three steals and two assists . Chandler Parsons added 12 points on 3-of-6 shooting , in 25 minutes . The Grizzlies will have to put this one in the past , as they go right back in action on Saturday , when they visit Minnesota to take on the Timberwolves .
Generated story	The Oklahoma City Thunder defeated the Memphis Grizzlies , 114 - 102 , at Chesapeake Energy Arena on Friday . Despite there being just five ties and six lead changes in this game , it was close throughout . In fact , neither team led by more than 12 points , as the nine-point final margin was one of the largest leads of the game . Oklahoma City actually won this game , despite being out shot from the field , from three-point range and from the free-throw line . Rebounding was the decisive statistic , with the Thunder winning that battle , 47 - 29 . They also dominated the assist-to-turnover ratio , recording 10 more assists and committing three less turn-overs . The Grizzlies (30 - 22) have now lost three of their last four games , as they continue to fall down the standings . Marc Gasol did all he could for Memphis , as he led the team with 31 points , four rebounds , eight assists and two steals . Mike Conley finished second on the team , amassing 18 points and three steals . Zach Randolph was huge off the bench , providing 16 points , 10 rebounds and three assists . The Grizzlies will be off until Saturday , when they play the Minnesota Timberwolves on the road for their next game . The Thunder (29 - 22) have rode Russell Westbrook 's triple-double train all year and they got another one here . Westbrook collected 38 points , 13 rebounds , 12 assists and three steals . Steven Adams recorded a double-double , amassing 16 points and 12 rebounds . Joffrey Lauvergne was a nice spark off the bench , providing 16 points and eight rebounds . The Thunder will look to keep rolling on Sunday against the Portland Trail Blazers

Table 2: **Metadata:** our metadata encoding. **Reference story:** story #48 from DGT-valid. **Generated story:** output of the English NLG model (3-player). **Green:** text based on facts from the metadata. **Blue:** correct facts which are not explicitly in the metadata. **Red:** hallucinations or incorrect facts. **Orange:** repetitions.

Track	Target	Constrained	Valid	Test
NLG		no	23.5	20.5
MT	EN	yes	60.2	58.2
MT		no	64.2	62.2
MT+NLG		yes	64.4	62.2
NLG		no	16.9	16.1
MT	DE	yes	49.8	48.0
MT+NLG		yes	49.4	48.2

Table 3: Doc-level BLEU scores on the DGT valid and test sets of our submitted models in all tracks.

batches. When fine-tuning on DGT-train or Rotowire + DGT-train (Step 5 of the MT track, or NLG/MT+NLG fine-tuning), we use a fixed learning rate schedule (Adam with 0.00005 LR) and a much smaller batch size (1500 tokens on a single GPU without delayed updates). We train for 100 epochs, compute DGT-valid perplexity at each epoch, and DGT-valid BLEU every 10 epochs.

4.3 BLEU evaluation

Submitted models. For each track, we selected the best models according to their BLEU score on DGT-valid. The scores are shown in Table 3, and a description of the submitted models is given in Table 4. We compute BLEU using SacreBLEU with its tokenization set to *none*,[4] as the model outputs and references are already tokenized with NLTK. Hayashi et al. (2019) give the full results of

the task: the scores of the other participants, and values of other metrics (e.g., ROUGE). Our NLG models are "unconstrained" because the WMT19 parallel data, which we used for pre-training, was not allowed in this track. Similarly, we do two submissions for DE-EN MT: one constrained, where we fine-tuned the doc-level MT model on DGT-train only, and one unconstrained, where we also used back-translated Rotowire-train and valid. All the MT and MT+NLG models are ensembles of 5 fine-tuning runs. Cascading the English NLG model with the ensemble of EN-DE MT models gives a BLEU score of 14.9 on DGT-test, slightly lower than the end-to-end German NLG model (16.1). We see that in the same data conditions (unconstrained mode), the MT+NLG models are not better than the pure MT models. Furthermore, we evaluated the MT+NLG models with MT-only source, and found only a slight decrease of ≈ 0.3 BLEU, which confirms our suspicion that the NLG information is mostly ignored.

NMT analysis. Table 5 shows the BLEU scores of our MT models at different stages of training (sent-level, doc-level, fine-tuned), and compares them against one of the top contestants of the WMT19 news translation task (Ng et al., 2019).

English NLG analysis. Table 6 shows a 5.7 BLEU improvement on Rotowire-test by our English NLG model compared to the previous state

---

[4] SacreBLEU signature: *BLEU+case.mixed+numrefs.1+ smooth.exp+tok.none+version.1.3.1*

Track	N best players	Details
NLG (EN)	4	Rotowire BT + DGT-train + tags
NLG (DE)	6	Rotowire BT + DGT-train + tags
MT (DE-EN)	N/A	*Unconstrained:* Rotowire BT + DGT-train + tags + ensemble *Constrained:* DGT-train only + ensemble
MT (EN-DE)	N/A	DGT-train only + ensemble
MT+NLG (EN)	3	Rotowire BT + DGT-train + 20% text masking + tags + ensemble
MT+NLG (DE)	3	Rotowire BT + DGT-train + tags + ensemble

Table 4: Description of our submissions.

Model	Target	Valid	Test	News 2019
FAIR 2019		48.5	47.7	**41.0**
Sent-level	EN	55.6	54.2	40.9
Doc-level		56.5	55.0	38.5
Fine-tuned		**61.7**	**59.6**	21.7
FAIR 2019		37.5	37.0	40.8
Sent-level	DE	47.3	46.7	**42.9**
Doc-level		**48.2**	**47.5**	41.6
Fine-tuned		48.0	46.7	41.3

Table 5: BLEU scores of the MT models at different stages of training, and comparison with the state of the art. Scores on DGT-valid and DGT-test are doc-level, while News 2019 is sent-level (and so is decoding). On the latter, we used the DGT corpus tag for DE-EN, and the Paracrawl tag for EN-DE (we chose the tags with best BLEU on newstest2014). Scores by the "fine-tuned" models are averaged over 5 runs.

of the art. Figure 1 shows the DGT-valid BLEU scores of our English NLG models when varying the number of players selected in the metadata. We see that there is a sweet spot at 4, but surprisingly, increasing the number of players up to 8 does not degrade BLEU significantly. We hypothesize that because the players are sorted from best to worst, the models learn to ignore the last players.

From Table 7, we see that sorting players helps, but only slightly. Using only team-level information, and no information about players gives worse but still decent BLEU scores.

Week day, player position or team-level aggregated scores can be removed without hurting BLEU. However, information about next games

Model	Rotowire test
Wiseman et al. (2017)	14.5
Puduppully et al. (2019)	16.5
Ours (4-player)	22.2

Table 6: English NLG comparison against state-of-the-art on Rotowire-test. BLEU of submitted NLG (EN) model, averaged over 3 runs. Because Rotowire tokenization is slightly different, we apply a set of fixes to the model outputs (e.g., 1-of-3 → 1 - of - 3).

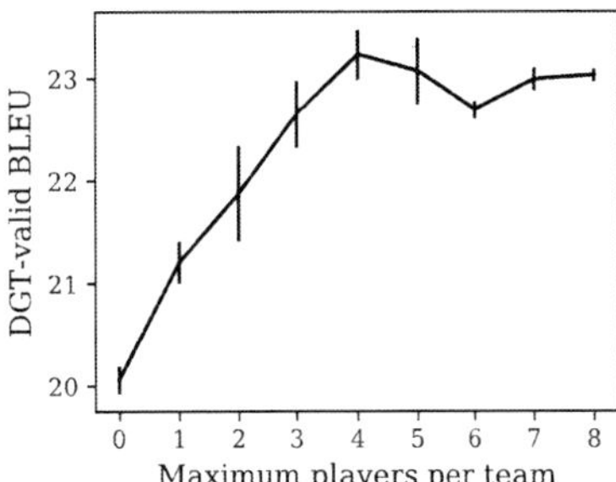

Figure 1: DGT-valid BLEU (by the best checkpoint) depending on the maximum number of selected players for the English NLG track.

Model	Valid	Test
Baseline (3 players, sorted)	**22.7**	20.4
No player	20.1	18.8
All players, sorted	**22.7**	20.9
All players, shuffled	22.0	20.0
(1) No next game	22.0	19.9
(2) No week day	22.2	20.5
(3) No player position	22.6	20.5
(4) No team-level sums	22.5	20.5
(5) Remove most tags	22.6	20.8
(1) to (5)	21.3	19.7

Table 7: English NLG ablation study, starting from a 3 best player baseline (the submitted NLG model has 4 players). BLEU averages over 3 runs. Standard deviation ranges between 0.1 and 0.4.

seems useful. Interestingly, relying on position only and removing most tags (e.g., <PTS>, <FT>) seems to be fine. In this case, we also print all-zero stats, for the position of each statistic to be consistent across players and games.

Train-test overlap on Rotowire. We found a significant overlap between Rotowire train and test: 222 out of 728 Rotowire-test games are also in Rotowire-train (68/241 for DGT-test). The corresponding stories are always different but bear many similarities (some sentences are completely identical). Rotowire-train gets 24.2 BLEU when evaluated against Rotowire-test (subset of 222 stories). This gives us an estimate of human-level performance on this task. Our submitted NLG model gets 21.8 on the same subset. This overlap may cause an artificial increase in BLEU, that would unfairly favor overfitted models. Indeed, when filtering Rotowire-train to remove games that were also in DGT test, we found a slight decrease in BLEU (19.8 instead of 20.4).

Stadium name (+)	REF: The Golden State Warriors (56 - 6) defeated the Orlando Magic (27 - 35) 119 - 113 at **Oracle Arena** on Monday . NLG: The Golden State Warriors (56 - 6) defeated the Orlando Magic (27 - 35) 119 - 113 on Monday at **Oracle Arena** .
Team alias (+)	REF: The Heat held the **Sixers** to 38 percent shooting and blocked 14 shots in the win . NLG: The **Sixers** shot just 38 percent from the field and 32 percent from the three-point line , while the Heat shot 44 percent from the floor and a meager 28 percent from deep .
Double-doubles or triple-doubles (+)	REF: **Kevin Love 's 29-point , 13-rebound double-double** led the way for the Cavs , who 'd rested Kyrie Irving on Tuesday . NLG: **Love** led the way for Cleveland with a **29-point , 13-rebound double-double** that also included three assists and two steals .
Player injuries (-)	NLG: The Timberwolves (28 - 44) checked in to Saturday 's contest with an injury-riddled frontcourt , as Ricky Rubio (**knee**) and Karl-Anthony Towns (**ankle**) were sidelined .
Ranking (-)	NLG: The Heat (10 - 22) fell to 10 - 22 and **remain in last place** in the Eastern Conference 's Southeast Division .
Season-level player stats (-)	NLG: It was a season-high in points for Thomas , **who 's now averaging 17 points per game on the season**

Table 8: Correctly predicted information that is not explicitly in the metadata (+), or hallucinations (-).

4.4 Qualitative evaluation

As shown in Table 2, the NLG model (3-player) has several good properties besides coherent document-level generation and the ability to "copy" metadata. It has learned generic information about the teams and players. As such, it can generate relevant information which is absent from metadata (see Table 8). For example, the model correctly predicts the name of the stadium where the game was played. This implies that it knows which team is hosting (this information is encoded implicitly by the position of the team in the data), and what is the stadium of this team's city (not in the metadata). Other facts that are absent from the metadata, and predicted correctly nonetheless, are team aliases (e.g., the *Sixers*) and player nicknames (e.g., *the Greek Freak*). The model can also generate other surface forms for the team names (e.g., *the other Cavalier*).

The NLG model can infer some information from the structured data, like double-digit scores, "double-doubles" (e.g., when a player has more than 10 points and 10 assists) and "triple-doubles". On the other hand, some numerical facts are inaccurate (e.g., score differences or comparisons). Some facts which are not present in the structured data, like player injuries, season-level player statistics, current ranking of a team, or timing information are hallucinated. We believe that most of these hallucinations could be avoided by adding the missing facts to the structured data. More rarely, model duplicates a piece of information.

Another of its flaws is a poor generalization to new names (team, city or player). This can quickly be observed by replacing a team name by a fictional one in the metadata. In this case, the model almost always reverts to an existing team. This may be due to overfitting, as earlier checkpoints seem to handle unknown team names better, even though they give lower BLEU. This generalization property could be assessed by doing a new train/test split, that does not share the same teams.

5 Conclusion

We participated in the 3 tracks of the DGT task: MT, NLG and MT+NLG. Our systems rely heavily on transfer learning, from document-level MT (high-resource task) to document-level NLG (low-resource task). Our submitted systems ranked first in all tracks.

For the MT task, the usual domain adaptation techniques performed well. The MT+NLG models did not show any significant improvement over pure MT. The MT models are already very good and probably do not need the extra context (which is generally encoded in the source-language summary already). Finally, our NLG models, bootstrapped from the MT models, do fluent and coherent text generation and are even able to infer some facts that are not explicitly encoded in the structured data. Some of their current limitations (mostly hallucinations) could be solved by adding extra information (e.g., injured players, current team rank, number of consecutive wins, etc.)

Our aggressive fine-tuning allowed us to specialize MT models into NLG models, but it will be interesting to study whether a single model can solve both tasks at once (i.e., with multi-task learning), possibly in both languages.

References

Gabor Angeli, Percy Liang, and Dan Klein. 2010. A Simple Domain-Independent Probabilistic Approach to Generation. In *EMNLP*.

Alexandre Berard, Calapodescu Ioan, and Claude Roux. 2019. NAVER LABS Europe's Systems for the WMT19 Machine Translation Robustness Task. In *WMT - Shared Task Paper*.

Sergey Edunov, Myle Ott, Michael Auli, and David Grangier. 2018. Understanding Back-Translation at Scale. In *EMNLP*.

Hiroaki Hayashi, Yusuke Oda, Alexandra Birch, Ioannis Constas, Andrew Finch, Minh-Thang Luong, Graham Neubig, and Katsuhito Sudoh. 2019. Findings of the Third Workshop on Neural Generation and Translation. In *Proceedings of the Third Workshop on Neural Generation and Translation (WNGT)*.

Marcin Junczys-Dowmunt. 2019. Microsoft Translator at WMT 2019: Towards Large-Scale Document-Level Neural Machine Translation. In *WMT - Shared Task Papers*.

Ioannis Konstas and Mirella Lapata. 2013. A Global Model for Concept-to-Text Generation.

Taku Kudo and John Richardson. 2018. SentencePiece: A simple and language independent subword tokenizer and detokenizer for Neural Text Processing. In *EMNLP*.

Rémi Lebret, David Grangier, and Michael Auli. 2016. Neural Text Generation from Structured Data with Application to the Biography Domain. In *EMNLP*.

Marco Lui and Timothy Baldwin. 2012. Langid.Py: An Off-the-shelf Language Identification Tool. In *Proceedings of the ACL 2012 System Demonstrations*, ACL.

Kathleen R. McKeown. 1985. *Text Generation: Using Discourse Strategies and Focus Constraints to Generate Natural Language Text*. Cambridge University Press.

Hongyuan Mei, Mohit Bansal, and Matthew R Walter. 2016. What to talk about and how? Selective Generation using LSTMs with Coarse-to-Fine Alignment. In *NAACL-HLT*.

Raymond J Mooney and Yuk Wah Wong. 2007. Generation by Inverting a Semantic Parser that Uses Statistical Machine Translation. In *NAACL-HLT*.

Nathan Ng, Kyra Yee, Alexei Baevski, Myle Ott, Michael Auli, and Sergey Edunov. 2019. Facebook FAIR's WMT19 News Translation Task Submission. In *WMT - Shared Task Papers*.

Myle Ott, Sergey Edunov, David Grangier, and Michael Auli. 2018. Scaling Neural Machine Translation. In *WMT*.

Ratish Puduppully, Li Dong, and Mirella Lapata. 2019. Data-to-Text Generation with Content Selection and Planning. In *Proceedings of the AAAI Conference on Artificial Intelligence*.

Ehud Reiter and Robert Dale. 2000. *Building Natural Language Generation Systems*. Cambridge University Press.

Rico Sennrich, Barry Haddow, and Alexandra Birch. 2016. Neural Machine Translation of Rare Words with Subword Units. In *ACL*.

Ashish Vaswani, Noam Shazeer, Niki Parmar, Jakob Uszkoreit, Llion Jones, Aidan N. Gomez, Łukasz Kaiser, and Illia Polosukhin. 2017. Attention Is All You Need. In *NIPS*.

Sam Wiseman, Stuart Shieber, and Alexander Rush. 2017. Challenges in Data-to-Document Generation. In *EMNLP*.

From Research to Production and Back:
Ludicrously Fast Neural Machine Translation

Young Jin Kim[†*] Marcin Junczys-Dowmunt[†*]
Hany Hassan[†] Alham Fikri Aji[‡] Kenneth Heafield[†‡]
Roman Grundkiewicz[†‡] Nikolay Bogoychev[‡]

[†]Microsoft, 1 Microsoft Way, Redmond, WA 98121, USA
{youki,marcinjd,hanyh}@microsoft.com

[‡]University of Edinburgh, Edinburgh, Scotland, EU
{a.fikri,kheafiel,rgrundkie,n.bogoych}@ed.ac.uk

Abstract

This paper describes the submissions of the "Marian" team to the WNGT 2019 efficiency shared task. Taking our dominating submissions to the previous edition of the shared task as a starting point, we develop improved teacher-student training via multi-agent dual-learning and noisy backward-forward translation for Transformer-based student models. For efficient CPU-based decoding, we propose pre-packed 8-bit matrix products, improved batched decoding, cache-friendly student architectures with parameter sharing and light-weight RNN-based decoder architectures. GPU-based decoding benefits from the same architecture changes, from pervasive 16-bit inference and concurrent streams. These modifications together with profiler-based C++ code optimization allow us to push the Pareto frontier established during the 2018 edition towards 24x (CPU) and 14x (GPU) faster models at comparable or higher BLEU values. Our fastest CPU model is more than 4x faster than last year's fastest submission at more than 3 points higher BLEU. Our fastest GPU model at 1.5 seconds translation time is slightly faster than last year's fastest RNN-based submissions, but outperforms them by more than 4 BLEU and 10 BLEU points respectively.

1 Introduction

This paper describes the submissions of the "Marian" team to the Workshop on Neural Generation and Translation (WNGT 2019) efficiency shared task (Hayashi et al., 2019). The goal of the task is to build NMT systems on CPUs and GPUs placed on the Pareto Frontier of efficiency and accuracy.

Marian (Junczys-Dowmunt et al., 2018a) is an efficient neural machine translation (NMT) toolkit written in pure C++ based on dynamic computational graphs.[1] Marian is a research tool which can

be used to define state-of-the-art systems that at the same time can produce truly deployment-ready models across different devices. This is accomplished within a single execution engine that does not require specialized, inference-only decoders. Our submissions to last year's edition of the same shared task defined the Pareto frontiers for translation quality versus CPU-based and GPU-based decoding speed (Junczys-Dowmunt et al., 2018b).

The title of this paper refers to beneficial co-development of our shared task submissions and our in-productions systems at Microsoft. The improvements from our submission to last year's edition of the shared task (Junczys-Dowmunt et al., 2018b) enabled fast CPU-based decoding with light-weight Transformer models and were a first step towards deploying them in Microsoft's online translation services. Subsequent improvements resulted in a successful launch of Marian as the Microsoft Translator training and inference tool (Microsoft-Translator). Our submissions to this year's edition start out with the currently deployed student model architectures as they are used for Microsoft online-translation systems and explore better teacher-student training and faster CPU-bound inference for the needs of the shared task. These innovations are finding their way back into our production systems at the time of writing.

We improve all aspects of our submissions from last year. Better teachers trained via multi-agent dual learning provide higher quality training data for student models. Better teacher-student training via noisy backward-forward translation minimizes the gap between teacher and student and allows to strongly reduce student size via parameter sharing and fewer decoder layers. At the same time, we are able to shift the need for smaller architectures to decoding with low-precision inference (8-bit on the CPU, 16-bit on the GPU). Similar to last year, we do not let the BLEU score drop below 26 points.

---

[*]First authors with equal contribution.

[1]https://github.com/marian-nmt/marian

Proceedings of the 3rd Workshop on Neural Generation and Translation (WNGT 2019), pages 280–288
Hong Kong, China, November 4, 2019. ©2019 Association for Computational Linguistics
www.aclweb.org/anthology/D19-56%2d

2 Better teacher-student training

Extending our submission from last year (Junczys-Dowmunt et al., 2018b), we train four forward (en-de) and four inverse (de-en) teacher models according to the Transformer-big configuration (model size 1024, filter size 4096, 6 blocks, file size 813 MiB) from Vaswani et al. (2017). We think of a teacher as the set of all models that have been used to create the artificial training data.

Unless stated differently, our student is a single model that follows the Transformer-base configuration (model size 512, filter size 2048, 6 blocks) with modifications. See Section 3 for details. For all models, we use the same vocabulary of 32,000 subwords, computed with SentencePiece (Kudo and Richardson, 2018). The training data is provided by the shared task organizers and restricted to about 4 Million sentences from the WMT news translation task for English-German. Use of other data is not permitted.

We again implement the interpolated sequence-level knowledge distillation method proposed by Kim and Rush (2016): The teacher ensemble is used to forward-translate the training data and collect 8-best lists for each sentence. Choosing the best translation for each sentence based on sentence-level BLEU compared to the original target, we create a synthetic target data. The student is trained on the original source and this synthetic forward translated target.

Table 1 contains BLEU scores of the teacher ensemble (T) and a student model distilled from this teacher (Student ← T). The gap is 2.4 BLEU.

2.1 Knowledge distillation with noisy backward-forward translation

In our experience, student training benefits from forward-translated data that was not seen during teacher training. Since we do not have access to additional monolingual source data, we generate noisy back-translated sentences (Edunov et al., 2018), one set per inverse teacher model. Noisy sentences are generated by sampling from the output softmax distribution via added Gumbel noise. We then use the forward (en-de) teacher ensemble to translate the sampled English sentences into German and choose the best output from the 8-best list measured against the original target. This increases the training corpus 5-fold. Training on this new data reduces the gap to the teacher to 1.3 BLEU; a single teacher model is only 0.4 BLEU better.

System	BLEU
Teacher (T)	28.9
Single teacher model	28.0
Student without teacher	25.9
Student ← T	26.5
Student ← T with 4×NBFT	27.6
Teacher with MADL (T-MADL)	29.8
Single teacher model	29.2
Student ← T-MADL	26.9
Student ← T-MADL with 4×NBFT	28.3

Table 1: Effects of noisy backward-forward translation (NBFT) and Multi-Agent Dual Learning on teacher-student training (newstest2014)

It seems unusual to feed our student with degraded training data, but the goal is to closely mimic the teacher. Since the forward translations are correct outputs of the teacher over noised inputs, the space of probed translations that would not be available to the student otherwise is increased. The role of choosing the best translation from the 8-best list should be investigated in the future.

2.2 Multi-Agent Dual Learning

Apart from closing the gap between teacher and student, we can try to improve the teacher and hope the student follows. We adapt Multi-Agent Dual Learning (MADL) by Wang et al. (2019) for this purpose. MADL requires additional monolingual data which we cannot supply. Instead, using the teacher-ensembles for each direction, we generate synthetic German and English corpora from the training data (without noise). We again select the best translations from the generated 8-best lists and join (original English - original German), (original English - synthetic German) and (synthetic English - original German) data sets into new training data for four new teacher models.

Individual teacher models improve by about 1.2 BLEU and an ensemble of four new teachers by 0.9 BLEU (Table 1). We repeat the interpolated knowledge-distillation procedure with the new teacher. The student model (T ← T-MADL) improves only slightly when trained without the noisy input data (+0.4 BLEU), but by a large margin with noisy forward-backward translation. The gap between the new teacher and its student remains at 1.5 BLEU, but a student outperforms a single teacher without MADL (28.3 vs 28.0).

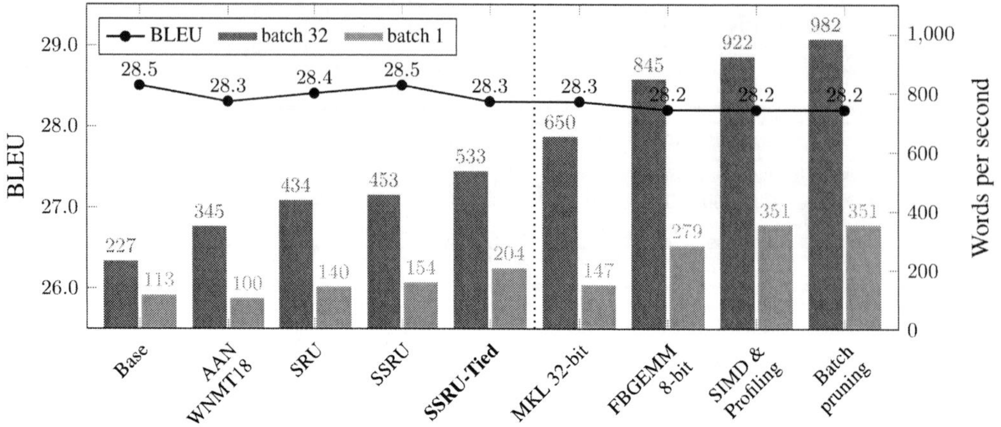

(a) Performance on a single CPU core and thread for newstest2014 on AWS m5.large, dedicated instance

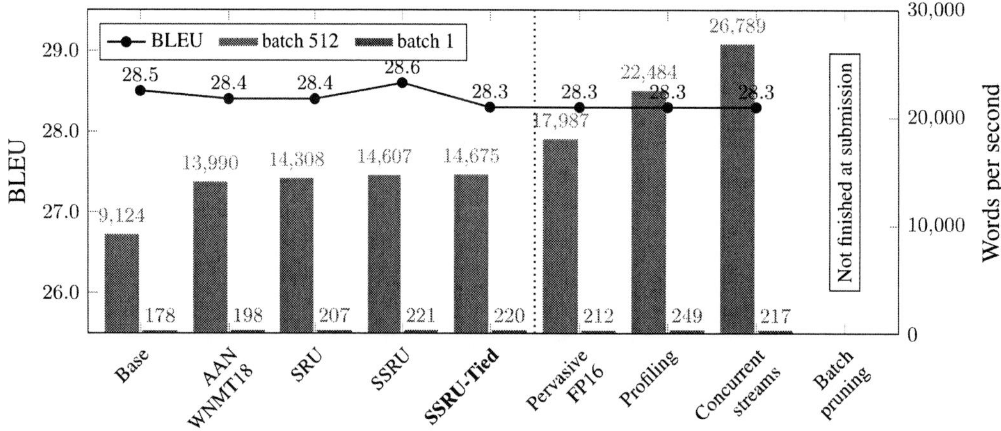

(b) Performance on a NVidia Volta 100 GPU for newstest2014 on AWS p3.x2large

Figure 1: BLEU scores versus words per second with different student architectures and optimizations on CPU and GPU. Results left of the dotted black line are for different architectures with Marian v1.7 as it was released before the shared task. Results right of the dotted black line are recently implemented runtime optimizations applied to "SSRU-Tied". These optimizations will be available with Marian v1.9.

3   Faster student architectures

As mentioned before, our student architecture is a variant of the Transformer-base configuration from Vaswani et al. (2017) with a model size of 512, filter size of 2048 and six blocks of layers in encoder and decoder. Our encoder is always a Transformer encoder with self-attention, our decoder differs in choice of auto-regression mechanisms and parameter tying. In this section, we do not change dimensions or number of blocks. Other dimensions and model depths are discussed in Section 6.

Figure 1 provides an overview about the evolution of student architectures explored for the previous shared task, as Microsoft in-production models

and as candidate submissions for the current edition of the shared task. All student variants have been trained with the best teacher-student procedure from the previous section; the example model used there was SSRU-Tied (bold in Figure. 1) which is also the Microsoft Translator in-production model.

We discuss the influence of self-regression mechanisms in Section 3.1 and parameter tying in Section 3.2. Architecture-indepedent but device-specific optimizations for the CPU are detailed in Section 4 and for the GPU in Section 5. More general optimizations are outlined in Section 4.2. Performance has been measured with Marian v1.7, measurements are self-reported by Marian.

3.1 SSRU instead of self-attention or AAN

In previous work (Junczys-Dowmunt et al., 2018b) and later experiments, we found that replacing the self-attention mechanims in Transformer decoders with an Average Attention Network (Zhang et al., 2018) or modern RNN variants does not affect student quality while resulting in faster decoding on GPU and CPU. This is mainly caused by reducing the decoder complexity from $O(n^2)$ to $O(n)$ over the number of output tokens n. In Figure 1 we see how switching from a vanilla Transformer-base variant to a student with AAN improves speed on both devices, but more so on the GPU.

While we had good results for AANs in Junczys-Dowmunt et al. (2018b), we feel somewhat uneasy about the flat element-wise average used to accumulate over inputs. RNNs share the linear computational complexity of the AAN over input size during decoding[2], but can learn a more complex accumulation function. A particularly interesting RNN variant is the SRU (Simple Recurrent Unit) proposed earlier than AANs by Lei et al. (2017)[3]. This RNN variant has no matrix multiplication in its recurrent step and is (at decode-time) surprisingly similar to the AAN if we think of the forget-gate as an adaptive exponential average:

$$
\begin{aligned}
\mathbf{f}_t &= \sigma(\mathbf{W}_t\mathbf{x}_t + \mathbf{b}_f) \\
\mathbf{r}_t &= \sigma(\mathbf{W}_r\mathbf{x}_t + \mathbf{b}_r) \\
\mathbf{c}_t &= \mathbf{f}_t \odot \mathbf{c}_{t-1} + (1 - \mathbf{f}_t) \odot \mathbf{W}\mathbf{x}_t \\
\mathbf{h}_t &= \mathbf{r}_t \odot \tanh(\mathbf{c}_t) + (1 - \mathbf{r}_t) \odot \mathbf{x}_t
\end{aligned}
$$

where the cell-state $\mathbf{c}_{t-1}$ is elementwise-interpolated via forget-gate $\mathbf{f}_t$ with its transformed input $\tilde{\mathbf{x}}_t$ to form the new cell-state $\mathbf{c}_t$. The original formulation adds an output reset-gate $\mathbf{r}_t$ to act as a learnable skip connection for the input $\mathbf{x}_t$ and $\tanh(\mathbf{c}_t)$.

In the Transformer, every block $g(\cdot)$ is followed by an additive skip connection and a layer-normalization operation (Ba et al., 2016):

$$
\mathbf{h}_t = \boldsymbol{\alpha} \odot \mathrm{LN}(g(\mathbf{x}_t) + \mathbf{x}_t) + \boldsymbol{\beta}
$$

where $\boldsymbol{\alpha}$ and $\boldsymbol{\beta}$ are trainable scale and bias vectors.

Given that this construction fulfills a similar role to the reset-gate in the original SRU formulation, we drop the reset-gate $\mathbf{r}_t$ and replace the tanh non-linearity with a ReLU operation[4] to arrive at our Simpler Simple Recurrent Unit (SSRU):

$$
\begin{aligned}
\mathbf{f}_t &= \sigma(\mathbf{W}_t\mathbf{x}_t + \mathbf{b}_f) \\
\mathbf{c}_t &= \mathbf{f}_t \odot \mathbf{c}_{t-1} + (1 - \mathbf{f}_t) \odot \mathbf{W}\mathbf{x}_t \\
\mathbf{h}_t &= \boldsymbol{\alpha} \odot \mathrm{LN}(\mathrm{ReLU}(\mathbf{c}_t) + \mathbf{x}_t) + \boldsymbol{\beta}
\end{aligned}
$$

which replaces the self-attention block in the transformer decoder. This variant saves another matrix multiplication and does not seem to suffer from any performance degradation for student models[5] compared to self-attention, AANs, traditional RNN variants, or the original SRU. In Figure 1a we can see how switching from Base to AAN to SRU and finally to SSRU does not affect BLEU much (within 0.2 per cent) and is actually highest for the SSRU. Speed on CPU increases significantly, both for batch size 32 and 1. On the GPU (Figure 1b) there are small improvements.

3.2 Tied decoder layers

Work on the Universal Transformer (Dehghani et al., 2019) has shown the effectiveness of depth-wise recurrence in Transformer models — i.e. the same parameters are being reused for every corresponding layer across Transformer blocks without quality loss. This is remarkable by itself, but there is also a potential for efficient CPU-bound computations. Although the repeated application of the same parameter set across different layers does not reduce the total number of floating point operations[6] that need to be performed compared to using different parameters per layer, it reduces the parameter size of the decoder layers six-fold and improves CPU cache-locality.

We tie all layers in the decoder (not the encoder) and probably manage to keep the entire set of decoder parameters in L2-cache during translation. Moving from SSRU to SSRU-Tied in Figure 1a, we see a 1.39x speed up and a small drop of 0.2 BLEU. The GPU is largely unaffected since cache-locality is less of an issue here.

---

[2] AANs parallelize better during training since the average can be computed non-recurrently, however for the small student models the increase in training time is negligible.

[3] We are describing the SRU based on V1 of the preprint on Arxiv from September 2017. Subsequent updates and publications seem to have changed the implementation, resulting in more complex variants, e.g. Lei et al. (2018). We implemented the SRU at time of publication of V1 and missed the updates, but our variant seems to work just fine.

[4] The transformer uses ReLU non-linearities everywhere.

[5] It seems however that student-sized models trained from scratch behave worse when using either SRU or SSRU compared to all the alternatives. There is however no difference between the SRU and SSRU which seems to confirm that the reset-gate $\mathbf{r}_t$ can be dropped when the additive skip-connection is already present.

[6] It does when projections of the encoder into decoder space for purpose of applying cross-attention can be cached.

Optimization	Batch 1	Batch 32
mixed 32/16-bit	1.38 (1.00)	0.82 (1.00)
8-bit FBGEMM	1.89 (1.36)	1.30 (1.58)
SIMD & Profiling	2.39 (1.72)	1.42 (1.73)
Batch pruning	2.39 (1.72)	1.51 (1.84)

Table 2: Relative speed-up for new CPU-bound optimizations compared to float32 MKL baseline and WNMT2018 mixed precision inference (in parentheses) for same SSRU-Tied student model.

4 Optimizing for the CPU

All CPU-bound results in Figure 1a have been computed with a setup from our WNMT2018 submission (Junczys-Dowmunt et al., 2018b). On batch-level, a shortlist selects the 75 most common target words and up to 75 most probable translations per input-batch word. This set of words is used to create an output vocabulary matrix over a couple of hundred words instead of 32,000 which reduces the computational load with no loss in quality (compare with GPU-bound BLEU scores in Figure 1b).

For systems left of the dotted black line, matrix multiplication is executed with mixed 32-bit (Intel's MKL library) and 16-bit (own implementation based on Devlin (2017)) kernels. All systems right of the dotted line, are the same model as "SSRU-Tied" without re-training, but executed with different runtime optimizations. In this section we discuss new runtime optimizations which will be available in Marian v1.9.

4.1 8-bit matrix multiplication with packing

The AWS m5.large target platform for CPU-bound decoding is equipped with an Intel Xeon Platinum 8175 CPU. This CPU supports 8-bit integer instructions with AVX-512 (Advanced Vector eXtensions-512) which can be used to accelerate deep neural network models (Wu et al., 2016; Rodriguez et al., 2018; Bhandare et al., 2019). With the open source FBGEMM library, we integrated 8-bit quantization and matrix multiplication routines with AVX-512 SIMD instructions into our code.

To fully benefit from the faster computation of matrix products in 8-bit, we chose to pre-quantize and pre-pack all parameter matrices offline, except for the embeddings matrix, then save them to a model file. Activations computed during inference are quantized on-the-fly. Matrix products with the short-listed output layer or with non-parameter matrices are executed in 32-bit with MKL.

Quantization. Among the quantization methods offered by FBGEMM, we see the best results when quantizing each column of the weight matrix separately with different scales and offsets per column which have to be provided to the FBGEMM API.

As reported by Lin et al. (2016); Bhandare et al. (2019) and confirmed by our own observations, the distribution of floating point values per column in a weight matrix seems to follow a normal distribution. We compute the average $\bar{x}_j$ and standard deviation σ_j per column j and quantize with saturation into the range $(\bar{x}_j - 7\sigma_j, \bar{x}_j + 7\sigma_j)$. We determined the factor 7 empirically, testing BLEU for values from 1 to 10. This prevents outliers in the weight matrix from distorting the resolution of the quantized values. We seem to lose no more than 0.3 BLEU due to quantization for some models, and only 0.1 BLEU for SSRU-Tied in a base configuration. By comparison, when quantizing to minimum-maximum values in columns, we lose up to 4.0 BLEU for certain models. See the FBGEMM blog (FBGEMM) for more details on quantization.

Packing. We mentioned in Section 3.2 how the repeated application of the same parameters across layers helps L2-cache locality. Packing allows us to also benefit from the CPU's L1-cache and vector registers by changing the layout of the input matrices for a GEMM operation. The FBGEMM API explicitly exposes the packing operation as well as matrix multiplication on pre-quantized and pre-packed matrices.

In Table 2 we see a respectable speed-up against a pure MKL float32 version and our mixed 32/16-bit inference (in parentheses). The speed-up is more impressive in the case of batch-size 1 which is our deployment scenario, but the large batch which we use for the shared task benefits as well.

4.2 Other optimizations

Speed improvements in one part of the code often expose bottlenecks in other places, as these now take up a larger fraction of the time during profiling. We found that element-wise kernels did not vectorize properly and fixed that; we replaced expensive C++ shared-pointers with light-weight non-locking smart-pointers for all small objects and changed the access pattern to model configuration options; we improved our beam-search algorithm to remove finished batch-entries dynamically. The combined speed-up (Table 2) from these optimizations further improves on top of the "fancier" methods.

5 Optimizing for the GPU

We use the same models for our GPU-bound experiments as for CPU decoding. Different than for our experiments on the CPU, we see in Figure 1b that the most influential architecture change is the replacement of decoder self-attention with complexity $O(n^2)$ with any other auto-regressive layer with complexity $O(n)$. There are small speed improvements as we move to layers with smaller amounts of FLOPS, but the parallelization inside the GPU nearly hides these changes. As mentioned before, layer-tying barely affects the speed while there was significant improvement on the CPU. We gain a lot more from the model-independent runtime optimizations described next.

Pervasive FP16 inference. On NVidia Volta 100 GPUs with at least CUDA 9.2 it is straightforward to activate FP16 matrix multiplication with very small modifications to the code. All other operations are executed in 32-bit floating point while inputs to the matrix product are rounded on-the-fly. Outputs are accumulated in 32-bit floats. We used this for our GPU submissions last year.

This year we extended Marian to perform pervasive FP16 inference, i.e. parameters are directly stored in 16-bit floats and all operations stay in 16-bit. The matrix product does not need to convert to 16-bit before or to 32-bit after execution. Improvements in speed stem from operations other than the matrix product and from faster memory access and copying. In Figure 1b, we see a respectable speed improvement for large batches and no loss in BLEU. Interestingly, there is no speed-up for batch-size 1.

Profiling. GPU decoding also benefits strongly from the profiler-based optimizations mentioned in Section 4.2. In a situation where the translation of a full WMT test sets can be performed in one or two second, the time spent during the construction or destruction of millions of book-keeper objects like hypotheses or beams starts to matter a lot. The gain here is larger than for the pervasive FP16 inference. Unfortunately we did not finish the GPU version of the batch-pruning algorithm in time for the shared-task or this description.[7] With the large batches we could expect additional improvements.

---

[7] The beam search algorithm in the FP16 branch had diverged from the CPU branch and there was no good way to quickly apply the new beam search version to GPU decoding. This will be done in Marian v1.9.

Concurrent streams. We found that the powerful Volta 100 GPU was not fully saturated even when decoding with large batch sizes. Hence, we send multiple batches at once to the same GPU using two CPU threads. The CUDA scheduler assigns different default streams to each CPU thread and we get similar benefits from streams as if these were assigned explicitly. Going beyond two threads does not seem to help. In the case of decoding with batch size 1 it's actually detrimental. We hypothesize that our GPU decoding is not as efficient as it could be and unnecessarily exchanges information between GPU and CPU. This happens in shorter and more frequent intervals for batch-size 1.

6 Submissions and discussion

6.1 Submissions

We submit four CPU students and three GPU systems, summarized in Table 3. We report model configurations, architectures, dimensions, depth, number of parameters, file sizes in MiB for CPU and GPU, translation speed in words per second and BLEU for newstest2014, omitting newstest2015. Time has been measured by the shared-task organizers on AWS m5.large (CPU) and p3.x2large (GPU) instances.

Until this moment, we kept model dimensions and decoder depth constant while optimizing a configuration that corresponds to the Microsoft in-production models (bold row in Table 3). For the final shared task submissions, we vary model dimensions and — similar to Senellart et al. (2018) — decoder depth in order to explore the trade-offs between quality and speed on the Pareto frontier.

We train a shallower base-configuration "(1) Base" with two tied decoder layers and small loss in BLEU compared to the 6-layer version. The speed-up is significant on both device types. To cover higher-quality models, we add a "(2) Large" configuration with improved BLEU but slower translation speed. As in the previous year, we do not submit models below 26 BLEU, but due to the improved teacher-student training, we can cut down model size drastically before that threshold is reached. We are seeing respectable BLEU scores for our "(3) Small" and "(4) Tiny" configurations at impressive word-per-second rates, 2,668 and 3,597 respectively. Compared to last year's fastest CPU-bound submission (Senellart et al., 2018), these are more than three and four times faster at over 3 points higher BLEU.

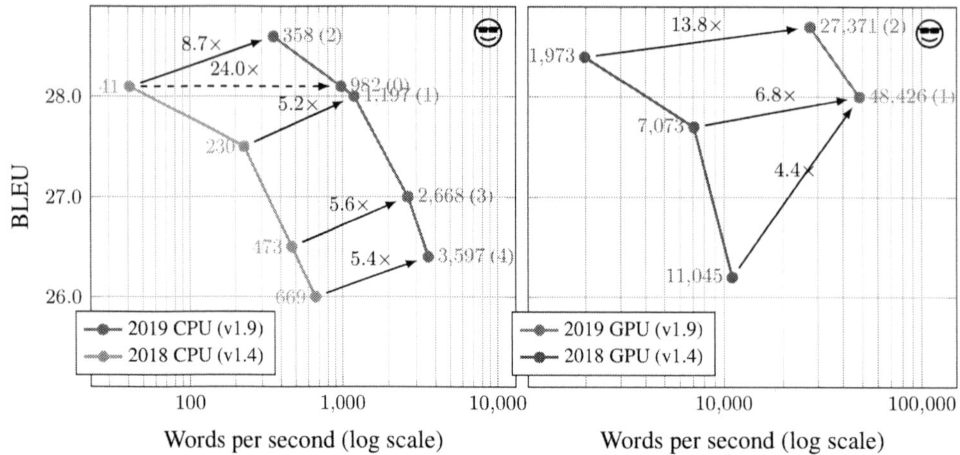

Figure 2: Relative speed improvements for fastest Marian models of comparable or better quality than submissions to WNMT2018 on newstest2014. Numbers in parentheses next to words-per-second values correspond to numbered submissions in Table 3. We also include our unsubmitted in-production model (0).

Configuration	Auto-reg.	Emb.	FFN	Depth	Params.	File size [MiB] CPU	GPU	Words per second CPU	GPU	BLEU
Teacher×8	Self-Att.	1024	4096	6	1673.3 M	–		–		29.8
Base	Self-Att.	512	2048	6	60.6 M	–		–		28.5
Base	SSRU	512	2048	6	57.4 M	–		–		28.5
(0) Base	**SSRU**	**512**	**2048**	**6 tied**	**39.0 M**	–		**982**	**26,789**	**28.2**
(1) Base[†‡]	SSRU	512	2048	2 tied	39.0 M	85	75	1,197	48,246	28.0
(2) Large[†‡]	SSRU	1024	3072	6 tied	108.4 M	199	207	358	27,371	28.6
(3) Small[†]	SSRU	256	2048	3 tied	17.6 M	41	34	2,668	–	27.0
(4) Tiny[†]	SSRU	256	1536	1	15.7 M	39	31	3,597	–	26.4
(5) Base 4-bit[‡]	SSRU	512	2048	2 tied	39.0 M	–	19	–	23,532	27.5

Table 3: Configuration of student models and submissions. Models marked with † were submitted to the CPU track, with ‡ to the GPU track. Speed and BLEU for submissions as reported by the shared-task organizers.

The file sizes reported in Table 3 refer to pre-packed 8-bit models with 32-bit embeddings for the CPU, and to models stored in FP16 for the GPU. As a separate experiment, we also applied 4-bit logarithmic quantization to further reduce the model size (Aji and Heafield, 2019) for a GPU model: "(5) Base 4-bit". This model is quantized in the form of $s \cdot 2^k$ where s is an optimized scale factor. We do not quantize biases. After initial quantization, we finetune the model to recover from the loss of quality. However, compression is only done on the model level. Therefore in this experiment, we only aim to improve the efficiency in terms of model size. We compressed the model size 8x smaller compared to 32-bit floating-point model, with a 0.5 drop to 27.5 BLEU. By quantizing the base model, we gained smaller model size (19 MiB) and better BLEU compared to the Tiny model (31 MiB).

6.2 Results and discussion

Unfortunately, in this edition of the efficiency shared task, we competed mostly against ourselves; one other team participated in the GPU track (see Figure 3), no other in the CPU track. Hence, we concentrate on improvements against our own historic results. Based on Figure 2, we can claim that the Marian 2019 team has left the Marian 2018 team in the dust. We connected each of our past submissions with one of our current submissions via a speed-up arrow if the current submission is the fastest model to have at least equal BLEU. The connected models are not necessarily similar in terms of size or architecture. By combining improved knowledge distillation methods with more efficient models and more optimized code, we were able to push the Pareto frontier towards 4.4 to 24.0 times faster translation systems at improved BLEU.

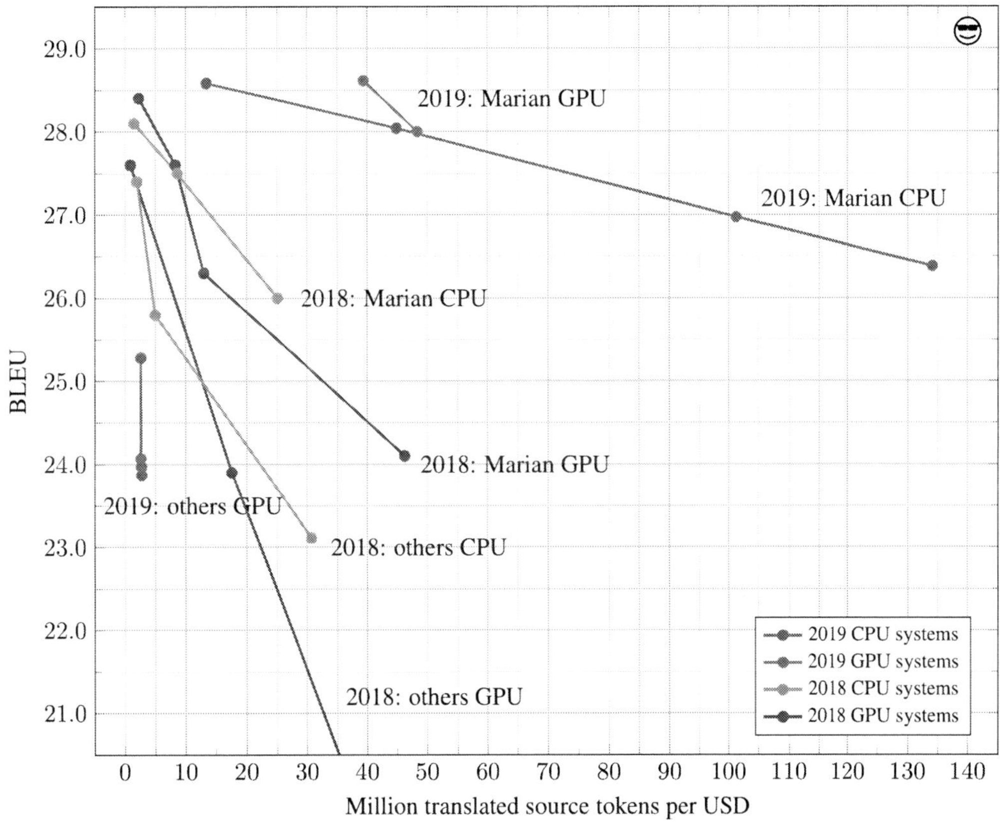

Figure 3: Pareto frontier for cost-effectiveness vs BLEU for all submissions (ours and other participants) from 2018 and 2019 on newstest2014 as reported by the organizers. We omit the weak baselines.

In Junczys-Dowmunt et al. (2018b), we compared the cost-effectiveness of GPU and CPU decoding in terms of millions of words translated per USD based on AWS instance costs. We updated the costs to reflect current prices, 0.096 USD and 3.06 USD per hour for CPU and GPU instances respectively, and visualized the results for all participants from both shared tasks — WNMT2018 and WNGT2019 — in Figure 3. Compared to last year where CPU and GPU decoding were similarly cost-effective at similar BLEU, we are starting to see a trend that highly-efficient CPU decoding is about to out-compete GPU-bound decoding in terms of cost-effectiveness according to the AWS price model.

If run on the GPU, the smaller models from our fastest CPU-track submissions would not improve speed-wise over our fastest GPU-track submissions; they would just achieve lower BLEU scores at similar speed. Our mid-sized student model already translates a WMT test set in ca. 1.5 seconds, the smaller models cannot improve over that for

these short test sets. Furthermore, these are cost-effectiveness scores reported within settings of the shared task which favors (maybe unrealistically) bulk and batched translation. At Microsoft Translator, our preferred scenario is translation with batch-size 1 for low latency.

Going back to Figure 1 and comparing speed for batch-size 1 alone, we are seeing that a single CPU core with our highly optimized CPU models is faster than a Volta 100 GPU with the same models. This may of course be an artifact of under-optimized GPU performance in Marian, but on the other hand, we do not see any other participant in the shared task with more efficient GPU decoding algorithms. There is also the unexplored question of multi-core CPU decoding, where the current shared-task setup — again somewhat unrealistically — allows only single-thread CPU-bound submissions. Improvements here might go a long way in term of better cost-effectiveness on the CPU compared to the GPU.

Acknowledgments

The authors would like to thank Shufang Xie from Microsoft Research Asia for his help with the MADL training procedure. Co-authors from the University of Edinburgh would like to acknowledge:

This work was supported by funding from the European Union's Horizon 2020 research and innovation programme under grant agreements No 825303 (Bergamot).

It was performed using resources provided by the Cambridge Service for Data Driven Discovery (CSD3) operated by the University of Cambridge Research Computing Service (http://www.csd3.cam.ac.uk/), provided by Dell EMC and Intel using Tier-2 funding from the Engineering and Physical Sciences Research Council (capital grant EP/P020259/1), and DiRAC funding from the Science and Technology Facilities Council (www.dirac.ac.uk).

References

Alham Fikri Aji and Kenneth Heafield. 2019. Neural machine translation with 4-bit precision and beyond.

Jimmy Lei Ba, Jamie Ryan Kiros, and Geoffrey E. Hinton. 2016. Layer Normalization. In NIPS 2016 Deep Learning Symposium, Barcelona, Spain.

Aishwarya Bhandare, Vamsi Sripathi, Deepthi Karkada, Vivek Menon, Sun Choi, Kushal Datta, and Vikram Saletore. 2019. Efficient 8-bit quantization of transformer neural machine language translation model. arXiv preprint arXiv:1906.00532.

Mostafa Dehghani, Stephan Gouws, Oriol Vinyals, Jakob Uszkoreit, and Lukasz Kaiser. 2019. Universal transformers. In 7th International Conference on Learning Representations, ICLR 2019, New Orleans, LA, USA, May 6-9, 2019.

Jacob Devlin. 2017. Sharp models on dull hardware: Fast and accurate neural machine translation decoding on the CPU. In Proceedings of the 2017 Conference on Empirical Methods in Natural Language Processing, pages 2820–2825, Copenhagen, Denmark. Association for Computational Linguistics.

Sergey Edunov, Myle Ott, Michael Auli, and David Grangier. 2018. Understanding back-translation at scale. In Proceedings of the 2018 Conference on Empirical Methods in Natural Language Processing, pages 489–500, Brussels, Belgium. Association for Computational Linguistics.

FBGEMM. Open-sourcing FBGEMM for state-of-the-art server-side inference [online].

Hiroaki Hayashi, Yusuke Oda, Alexandra Birch, Ioannis Constas, Andrew Finch, Minh-Thang Luong, Graham Neubig, and Katsuhito Sudoh. 2019. Findings of the third workshop on neural generation and translation. In Proceedings of the Third Workshop on Neural Generation and Translation.

Marcin Junczys-Dowmunt, Roman Grundkiewicz, Tomasz Dwojak, Hieu Hoang, Kenneth Heafield, Tom Neckermann, Frank Seide, Ulrich Germann, Alham Fikri Aji, Nikolay Bogoychev, et al. 2018a. Marian: Fast neural machine translation in C++. In Proceedings of ACL 2018, System Demonstrations, pages 116–121.

Marcin Junczys-Dowmunt, Kenneth Heafield, Hieu Hoang, Roman Grundkiewicz, and Anthony Aue. 2018b. Marian: Cost-effective high-quality neural machine translation in C++. In Proceedings of the 2nd Workshop on Neural Machine Translation and Generation, pages 129–135.

Yoon Kim and Alexander M Rush. 2016. Sequence-level knowledge distillation. In Proceedings of the 2016 Conference on Empirical Methods in Natural Language Processing, pages 1317–1327.

Taku Kudo and John Richardson. 2018. Sentencepiece: A simple and language independent subword tokenizer and detokenizer for neural text processing. In Proceedings of the 2018 Conference on Empirical Methods in Natural Language Processing: System Demonstrations, pages 66–71.

Tao Lei, Yu Zhang, and Yoav Artzi. 2017. Training RNNs as fast as CNNs. CoRR, abs/1709.02755.

Tao Lei, Yu Zhang, Sida I. Wang, Hui Dai, and Yoav Artzi. 2018. Simple recurrent units for highly parallelizable recurrence. In Proceedings of the 2018 Conference on Empirical Methods in Natural Language Processing, pages 4470–4481, Brussels, Belgium. Association for Computational Linguistics.

Darryl Lin, Sachin Talathi, and Sreekanth Annapureddy. 2016. Fixed point quantization of deep convolutional networks. In International Conference on Machine Learning, pages 2849–2858.

Microsoft-Translator. Neural machine translation enabling human parity innovations in the cloud [online].

Andres Rodriguez, Eden Segal, Etay Meiri, Evarist Fomenko, Young Jin Kim, Haihao Shen, and Barukh Ziv. 2018. Lower numerical precision deep learning inference and training. Intel White Paper.

Jean Senellart, Dakun Zhang, Bo Wang, Guillaume Klein, Jean-Pierre Ramatchandirin, Josep Crego, and Alexander Rush. 2018. OpenNMT system description for WNMT 2018: 800 words/sec on a single-core CPU. In Proceedings of the 2nd Workshop on Neural Machine Translation and Generation, pages 122–128, Melbourne, Australia. Association for Computational Linguistics.

Ashish Vaswani, Noam Shazeer, Niki Parmar, Jakob Uszkoreit, Llion Jones, Aidan N Gomez, Łukasz Kaiser, and Illia Polosukhin. 2017. Attention is all you need. In Advances in neural information processing systems, pages 5998–6008.

Yiren Wang, Yingce Xia, Tianyu He, Fei Tian, Tao Qin, ChengXiang Zhai, and Tie-Yan Liu. 2019. Multi-agent dual learning. In International Conference on Learning Representations.

Yonghui Wu, Mike Schuster, Zhifeng Chen, Quoc V Le, Mohammad Norouzi, Wolfgang Macherey, Maxim Krikun, Yuan Cao, Qin Gao, Klaus Macherey, et al. 2016. Google's neural machine translation system: Bridging the gap between human and machine translation. arXiv preprint arXiv:1609.08144.

Biao Zhang, Deyi Xiong, and Jinsong Su. 2018. Accelerating neural transformer via an average attention network. In Proceedings of the 56th Annual Meeting of the Association for Computational Linguistics (Volume 1: Long Papers), pages 1789–1798, Melbourne, Australia. Association for Computational Linguistics.

Selecting, Planning, and Rewriting: A Modular Approach for Data-to-Document Generation and Translation

Lesly Miculicich[*†]   Marc Marone [*‡]
Hany Hassan[‡]

[†] Idiap Research Institute, Ecole Polytechnique Federale de Lausanne (EPFL), Switzerland
`lmiculicich@idiap.ch`

[‡]Microsoft, 1 Microsoft Way, Redmond, WA 98121, USA
`{v-mamaro,hanyh}microsoft.com`

Abstract

In this paper, we report our system submissions to all 6 tracks of the WNGT 2019 shared task on Document-Level Generation and Translation. The objective is to generate a textual document from either structured data: *generation task*, or a document in a different language: *translation task*. For the translation task, we focused on adapting a large scale system trained on WMT data by fine tuning it on the RotoWire data. For the generation task, we participated with two systems based on a selection and planning model followed by (a) a simple language model generation, and (b) a GPT-2 pre-trained language model approach. The selection and planning module chooses a subset of table records in order, and the language models produce text given such a subset.

1 Introduction

Data-to-text generation focuses on generating natural text from structured inputs such as table records. Traditional data-to-text systems used a pipelined approach for data selection followed by planning and text generation. Recently, End-to-End neural generation systems have been proposed such as (Wiseman et al., 2017). While such systems generate more fluent output, they are not faithful to the facts in the structured data.

One of the difficulties of the generation task is that the models have to learn two different aspects: "what to say" (i.e. selecting relevant information) and "how to say it" (i.e. generating the actual text based on these facts). We believe that available data-sets are too small for allowing current neural network models, based on encoder-decoder architectures, to capture the complexity of the problem. Recently, (Puduppully et al., 2019) proposed an end-to-end system that explicitly models a content selection and planning module separated from

the text generation, showing improvements with respect to previous end-to-end systems (Wiseman et al., 2017). We adopt this approach and divide our model into two parts noted as: content selection and planning, and text generation. This division helps the system to produce more coherent document structure. One drawback of this approach is the limitation of the language model generation coverage. We tackle this limitation by adopting pre-trained language models such as OpenAI's GPT-2 (Radford et al., 2019). Following the shared task guidelines (Hayashi et al., 2019), we evaluate our models using an information extraction (IE) system.

2 Translation Tasks

We submitted translation results for both directions: English-to-German and German-to-English. Our models are based on the transformer architecture trained with multi-agent dual learning (MADL) (Xia et al., 2019). This system uses the *transformer_big* configuration (modelsize 1024, filter size 4096, 6 blocks for each encoder and decoder) from (Vaswani et al., 2017), using dropout of 0.2. It is trained with 3 primary translations models and 3 dual translation models (for details refer to (Xia et al., 2019)). The base models were trained with 20M filtered sentence-pairs from WMT 2019 shared translation task (Bojar et al., 2019), plus 120M English, and 120M German monolingual sentences from *Newscrawl* (Bojar et al., 2019). The vocabulary is shared and composed of word segments obtained by applying the BPE algorithm with 35K merge operations.

We fine-tuned the base models with 3K sentence-pairs of the Rotowire English-German parallel data. We use batches of 4096 tokens and optimize with different learning rates. The best result was obtained with learning rate of 10^{-5} for both directions. Additionally, for the German-to-English translation task, we back-translate the

---

*Equal contribution. Work done while interning at Microsoft

Proceedings of the 3rd Workshop on Neural Generation and Translation (WNGT 2019), pages 289–296
Hong Kong, China, November 4, 2019. ©2019 Association for Computational Linguistics
www.aclweb.org/anthology/D19-56%2d

monolingual Rotowire English corpus. For this purpose, the documents were split into sentences[1] to obtain 45K English sentences in total, then we use the MADL model which was fine-tuned with parallel Rotowire data to obtain their respective German translations. Finally, we fine-tune the MADL system again using the concatenation of original parallel sentences and the back-translated corpus. Since we do not have an in-domain monolingual German corpus, we ensemble 3 replicas of the fine-tuned MADL models trained with 10, 20, and 30% dropout for the English-German task. Additionally, we back-translate 1M monolingual sentences from *Newscrawl* which were selected based on their similarity to Rotowire data following (Moore and Lewis, 2010). However, this did not lead to any further improvements in the systems.

All translation systems used text summaries only. We did not use the additional data tables in the submitted results for the MT + NLG track. In our experiments, we find that adding the structured data did not lead to improvements over the baseline systems.

2.1 Results

Table 1 shows the results of our systems for both directions measured with sacre-BLEU. Fine tuning with Rotowire parallel data brings an improvement of 7.9 BLEU points for English-to-German and 9.3 for German-to-English in the test set. Further improvement of 1.9 BLEU points is obtained with back-translation of monolingual Rotowire data for the latter direction. The dropout ensemble adds a very small gain of 0.2 BLEU. We found that selected data from *Newscrawl* does not add any significant improvement.

We also evaluate our German-to-English system with the content oriented metrics provided by the organizers of the shared-task. Table 2 shows the values for development and test sets. We show the results measured with the ground-truth translation for comparison. The content generation (RG) of the best system reaches two percentage points higher than the ground-truth. The translation model produces fewer referring expressions, and morphological variations than the ground-truth to refer to entities, which makes it easier for the information extraction tools to recognize them. The Content selection (CS) reaches high

	EN → DE	DE → EN
MADL	39.99	48.71
+ RW parallel	47.90	57.99
+ RW monolingual *	–	59.94
+ Ensemble *	48.09	–

Table 1: Machine translation results measured with sacre-BLEU and task-specific tokenization[1]. * denotes a late entry, not in the official evaluation.

precision (92%) and recall (93%), and the content order (CO) score is 89. Further manual analysis indicates that the main issues are the translation of textual numbers, and the morphological variation of entities.

3   Generation Task

One of the difficulties of the data-to-document generation task, as formulated by (Wiseman et al., 2017), is that the models have to learn to select a relatively small portion of table records and their order for generating text. We argue that the size of available data-sets for training (i.e. Rotowire with 3.4K samples) is too small for allowing the network to capture the complexity of the task. In consequence, following (Puduppully et al., 2019; Moryossef et al., 2019), we divide the work in two parts : (a) content selection and planning, and (b) text generation. The idea is to introduce a direct signal to the system i.e. adding a loss function that guides an orderly selection of records, alleviating the work of the text generator.

Our system is based on (Puduppully et al., 2019) with two main differences. First, we use a transformer network for encoding each record in relation to other records, instead of a more complex gated approach as previous work. Second, we share the vocabularies of record *values* and summary text, thus the final estimated distribution for prediction over the whole vocabulary is summed instead of concatenated. Figure 1 shows the architecture of the model. In the following, we describe each component in detail:

3.1   Content selection and Planning

Given a set of records $r = r_1, r_2, ..., r_M$, the objective is to select a subset of them in the correct order $\tilde{r} \in r$. We use an encoder-decoder architecture to model this problem. Similar to (Wiseman et al., 2017), we create embeddings of each feature record (e.g. value, key, etc.) and concatenate

---

[1]https://github.com/neulab/DGT

	Dev			Test		
	RG (P%/#)	CS (P%/R%)	CO	RG (P%/#)	CS (P%/R%)	CO
Ground truth	92.0 (23.1)	100 / 100	100	92.3 (22.6)	100 / 100	100
MADL	90.4 (19.2)	90.6 / 78.8	74.4	91.7 (19.3)	89.6 / 77.1	75.1
+ RW parallel + RW mono.	94.4 (24.2)	93.6 / 93.8	89.9	94.1 (23.3)	92.6 / 93.1	89.1

Table 2: Content evaluation of the German-to-English translation models on test and dev-sets from parallel Rotowire using the IE models of (Puduppully et al., 2019). RG:Content generation, CS: Content selection, CO: Content order.

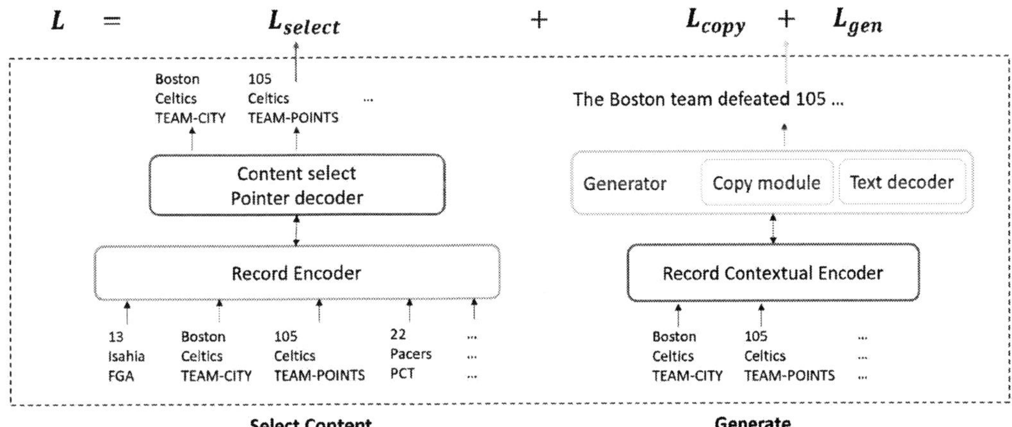

Figure 1: Content selection and generation

them. Then, we encode them using a transformer network. The transformer self-attention allows the network to capture the relationships among records and estimate their relative salience. However, we do not use positional embeddings as the records do not have a sequential nature. The decoder is a recurrent pointer network which predicts one record $\tilde{r}_t$ at each time-step based on previous predictions as follows:

$$\tilde{r}_t = softmax(\hat{h}_1, ..., \hat{h}_M) \quad (1)$$

$$\hat{h}_i = f(h_i, s_t) \quad (2)$$

$$s_t = g(s_{t-1}, \tilde{r}_{t-1}) \quad (3)$$

where f is a non-linear function, g is an auto-regressive network (i.e. LSTM, transformer) and h_i is the encoded state of the record r_i using the transformer. When using LSTM, the initial state is the average of the encoder output h. We optimize this sub-network with a cross-entropy loss L_{select}, and the ground truth targets are extracted following (Puduppully et al., 2019).

3.2 Text Generation

The text generator is also an encoder-decoder network. The encoder is a bi-directional LSTM or

transformer that receives a set of record as input. During training the input are the ground truth targets $\tilde{r}_{gold}$, and during decoding the predictions of the *content selection and planning* $\tilde{r}$.

The decoder has two parts: a *text decoder* and a *copy module* that uses a copy mechanism to directly predict encoded records. We share the vocabulary of the copy-decoder and the record feature *value* of the encoder so the probability distributions of generating and copying are summed for each shared word, similar to (See et al., 2017). The embeddings of all record features are shared for both content selection, and text generation. The optimization is performed with a cross-entropy loss L_{gen} for the generation, and a binary cross-entropy loss L_{copy} for the copy module.

3.3 Joint regularized training (End-to-end)

We train the *content selector* and *text generator* in a joint manner by adding their losses $L = L_{select} + L_{gen} + L_{copy}$. This can be seen as a regularization process where the loss of one network regularizes the other. We observe that the performance of the separately trained networks are worse than the jointly trained ones. The input

	P	R	F1	DL
Single Baseline	41	68	51	0.76
Single CSP	43	67	52	0.75
Joint Baseline + TG	45	62	52	0.75
Joint CSP + TG	46	71	56	0.70

Table 3: Evaluation of Content Selection and Planning (CSP) module, with and without joint training with the Text Generator (TG). Baseline: (Puduppully et al., 2019). P: precision, R: recall, DL: Damerau-Levenshtein distance.

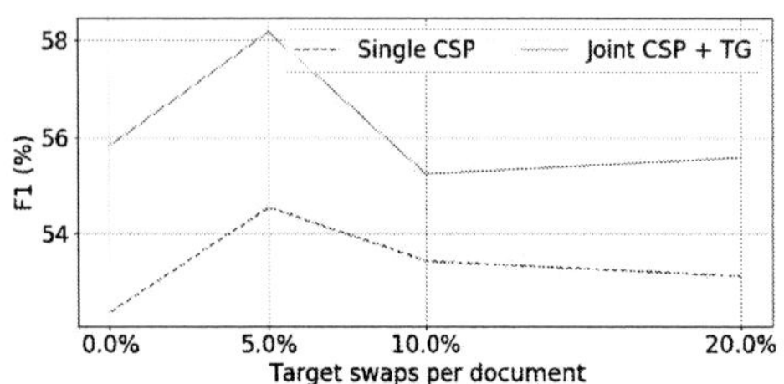

Figure 2: Augmenting data by swapping the target values of each document at different percentage rates. In each case, we doubled the training set.

for the text generator is ground truth during training. At decoding time, we perform 2 consecutive beam search of 5 beams, the first one for the content selection, and the second for generating text. We tuned the architecture using the development set. We evaluated different configurations of transformers and LSTMs, from 1 to 2 layers, with dimensions of 252 and 512, and dropout from 0.1 to 0.3. The best results are obtained using LSTMs decoders with 512 size dimension for all hidden layers and embeddings, each encoder and decoder has 2 layers, and we use dropout of 0.3. We also used data augmentations by swapping values in of the target at a range of 10, 20, and 30 percent of the values in each sample. Finally, we train the network with batches of 5 document samples, and updated the parameters each 20 batches. We use Adam optimizer at an initial learning rate of 10^{-3}.

3.4 Results

We test the *content selection and planning* module by comparing the output subset of records with the ground-truth records (i.e. the records extracted from the summary text with the IE tools). We use F1 and Damerau-Levenshtein (DL), the later to evaluate the correct order of records. The workshop metrics are not used here because the independently trained models do not output text. Re-

sults in Table 3 show that our model outperforms the baseline (Puduppully et al., 2019), and the joint training helps to further improve over the single models. Figure 2 shows the F1 scores while augmenting data by varying the percentage of swaps in the target training set. Adding samples with 5% of random swaps in each sample document helps both single and jointly trained models. Finally, Table 4 shows the evaluation results of the final joint system with the workshop metrics.

During a qualitative evaluation, we noticed that the *content selection and planning* module learns to output the most common sequence of records in the training data. In general, the sequence of records depends on the style of the commentator (e.g. describing first match results and then important player's scores). Our system mismatches less common styles, which affects the scoring of testing and development that contain different distribution of record sequences.

4 Generation with Pretrained LM

We experiment with using pretrained language models to enhance coverage and fluency of the text generation, since the amount of training data available for the generation the task is relatively small. In particular, we use a pretrained PyTorch implementation[2] of the GPT-2 (Radford et al., 2019) language model. The original GPT-2 description showed that this large scale language model additionally learned to complete other tasks such as summarization and translation. For example, the language model can be used for summarization, by providing an input document concatenated with the string `TL;DR:` and the output is the generated summary. Inspired by these results, we propose our summary *rewrite model*. Our model is a two phases approach: the first is the content selection model proposed in 3.1, the second is a GPT2-based generation module. Based on the output of the content selection module, our model provides a rough summary as input to GPT-2 model which generates the desired summary.

The baseline results in (Wiseman et al., 2017) show that simple templates are very effective at conveying information from the data tables. We use similar templates to generate a rough summary that is used as input in our *rewrite model*. The model takes input

---

[2]`https://github.com/huggingface/pytorch-transformers`

		Data to EN				Data to DE		
	BLEU	RG	CS (P/R)	CO	BLEU	RG	CS (P/R)	CO
End-to-end	15.03	93.38	32.34 / 58.04	18.52	11.66	80.30	27.89 / 48.96	16.43
GPT-50	15.17	94.35	33.84 / 53.82	19.26	11.84	82.79	34.23 / 42.32	16.93
GPT-90	13.03	88.70	32.81 / 50.64	17.34	10.43	75.05	30.97 / 41.48	16.27

Table 4: Generation results of our submitted systems as reported by the shared task organizers (Hayashi et al., 2019). RG: Relation Generation precision, CS: Content Selection (precision/recall), CO: Content Ordering.

of the form `template summary <R> gold summary`, which is used to fine-tune the pre-trained GPT-2 model. The templates consist of simple sentences involving a single record from the dataset, such as the number of points scored by a player. At training time we generate templates from the ground truth records following (Puduppully et al., 2019). At test time, we use the content selection module to select appropriate records. This effectively replaces the original generator network with the GPT-2 model, using text as an intermediate encoding. See Appendix sections A.1 and A.2 for a full example.

4.1 Decoding

Recently, (Holtzman et al., 2019) suggested that top-k token sampling (as used in the original GPT-2 results) is not ideal for generating realistic text from likelihood trained language models. They instead propose *Nucleus Sampling* or top-p sampling, which samples tokens from the top p portion of the output distribution. We experiment with several values of p and find that this provides an effective way to control generation quality. Our submitted models (GPT-50 and GPT-90) sample from the top 50% and 90% of the output distribution when decoding.

4.2 Results

We find that the template rewriting approach is competitive with the end-to-end trained models in terms of content metrics (Table 4), and subjectively appears to create natural sounding generations.

For lower values of p in top-p sampling, we find that the model remains more true to the templates, tending to create short summaries that do not deviate much from the input facts. For larger values of p, where decoding is allowed to sample from more of the distribution, the output tends be longer but may deviate from the facts. We also note that when regenerating summaries for high values of p (with a different random seed), there are signif-

icant changes to the text but not to the facts reflected in the summary. See Appendix sections A.4 and A.5 for examples of generations at various p values. For both settings we observe occasional mistakes such as repetitions, suggesting that our values for p should have been tuned more carefully.

For the German generation track, we apply our model described in 2 to the English generations, since we did not have a GPT-2 scale language model for German.

5 Discussion and Conclusion

For the translation task we experimented with a simple fine tuning approach for a large scale system trained on general domain data. It proved very effective to fine tune a pre-trained system using RotoWire data. Our analysis indicates that the remaining problems are more related to number formatting which is a more generic issue for NMT systems and not a domain specific problem.

The generation task proved to be more challenging. Mainly generating faithful, accurate and fluent summaries can be a quite challenging task given the discrepancies between the provided data and the desired summaries. Our analysis indicates that there is a mismatch between the gold selection plan and the system output. The system outputs the most common sequence of facts whereas the gold presents more variety of fact sequences due to different writing styles. This issue should be further studied in future.

Utilizing large scale pre-trained LMs (such as GPT-2) is a very promising direction, since it decouples the dependency of selection and generation resources. Our current approach of feeding the template-based input to GPT2 is quite simple and efficient. We would like to investigate more principled methods of doing this in the future.

6 Acknowledgment

We would like to thank Tao Qin and his team at MSRA for providing the MADL translation baseline systems.

References

Ondřej Bojar, Rajen Chatterjee, Christian Federmann, Mark Fishel, Yvette Graham, Barry Haddow, Matthias Huck, Antonio Jimeno Yepes, Philipp Koehn, André Martins, Christof Monz, Matteo Negri, Aurélie Névéol, Mariana Neves, Matt Post, Marco Turchi, and Karin Verspoor. 2019. Proceedings of the fourth conference on machine translation (volume 2: Shared task papers, day 1). Florence, Italy. Association for Computational Linguistics.

Hiroaki Hayashi, Yusuke Oda, Alexandra Birch, Ioannis Constas, Andrew Finch, Minh-Thang Luong, Graham Neubig, and Katsuhito Sudoh. 2019. Findings of the third workshop on neural generation and translation. In *Proceedings of the Third Workshop on Neural Generation and Translation*.

Ari Holtzman, Jan Buys, Maxwell Forbes, and Yejin Choi. 2019. The curious case of neural text degeneration. *arXiv preprint arXiv:1904.09751*.

Robert C. Moore and William Lewis. 2010. Intelligent selection of language model training data. In *Proceedings of the ACL 2010 Conference Short Papers*, pages 220–224, Uppsala, Sweden. Association for Computational Linguistics.

Amit Moryossef, Yoav Goldberg, and Ido Dagan. 2019. Step-by-step: Separating planning from realization in neural data-to-text generation. In *Proceedings of the 2019 Conference of the North American Chapter of the Association for Computational Linguistics: Human Language Technologies, Volume 1 (Long and Short Papers)*, pages 2267–2277, Minneapolis, Minnesota. Association for Computational Linguistics.

Ratish Puduppully, Li Dong, and Mirella Lapata. 2019. Data-to-text generation with content selection and planning. In *Proceedings of the AAAI Conference on Artificial Intelligence*, volume 33, pages 6908–6915.

Alec Radford, Jeff Wu, Rewon Child, David Luan, Dario Amodei, and Ilya Sutskever. 2019. Language models are unsupervised multitask learners.

Abigail See, Peter J. Liu, and Christopher D. Manning. 2017. Get to the point: Summarization with pointer-generator networks. In *Proceedings of the 55th Annual Meeting of the Association for Computational Linguistics (Volume 1: Long Papers)*, pages 1073–1083, Vancouver, Canada. Association for Computational Linguistics.

Ashish Vaswani, Noam Shazeer, Niki Parmar, Jakob Uszkoreit, Llion Jones, Aidan N Gomez, Łukasz Kaiser, and Illia Polosukhin. 2017. Attention is all you need. In *Advances in neural information processing systems*, pages 5998–6008.

Sam Wiseman, Stuart Shieber, and Alexander Rush. 2017. Challenges in data-to-document generation. In *Proceedings of the 2017 Conference on Empirical Methods in Natural Language Processing*, pages 2253–2263, Copenhagen, Denmark. Association for Computational Linguistics.

Yingce Xia, Xu Tan, Fei Tian, Fei Gao, Di He, Weicong Chen, Yang Fan, Linyuan Gong, Yichong Leng, Renqian Luo, Yiren Wang, Lijun Wu, Jinhua Zhu, Tao Qin, and Tie-Yan Liu. 2019. Microsoft research asia's systems for WMT19. In *Proceedings of the Fourth Conference on Machine Translation (Volume 2: Shared Task Papers, Day 1)*, Florence, Italy. Association for Computational Linguistics.

A Rewrite Model

Below are example generations from our models, with some highlighted comparisons. "..." indicates text omitted for brevity.

Each configuration correctly introduces the teams. However, note that the stadium differs. The End-to-end model claims that the game took place at the United Center. The GPT models claim that the game took place at the Air Canada Cent(er|re), the correct stadium for the home team (the Toronto Raptors). In fact, the GPT model uses what may be a more correct spelling (centre).

All models report player statistics (some example sentences are **bolded**) and game statistics. There are some occasional mistakes. . Some are logical (the Raptors won), and others seems to be related to decoding.

A.1 Gold Template Input

```
The Raptors are from Toronto.  The
Raptors were HOME. The Raptors scored
122 points.  The 76ers are from
Philadelphia.  The 76ers were AWAY.
The 76ers scored 95 points.  ... Robert
Covington scored 20 points.  Robert
Covington had 5 rebounds.  Robert
Covington had 2 assists.  Robert
Covington had 2 steals.  Robert
Covington made 7 shots.  Robert
Covington had 11 attempts.  Jahlil
Okafor scored 15 points.  ...
```

A.2 Gold Summary

The host Toronto Raptors defeated the Philadelphia 76ers, 122 – 95, at Air Canada Center on Monday. ... The Raptors were lights – out shooting, as they went 55 percent from the field and 68 percent from three – point range. They also held the Sixers to just 42 percent from the field and dominated the defensive rebounding, 34 – 26. Fastbreak points was a huge difference as well, with Toronto winning that battle, 21 – 6. ... **Robert Covington had one of his best games of the season though, tallying 20 points, five rebounds, two assists and two steals on 7 – of – 11 shooting. Jahlil Okafor got the start for Embiid and finished with 15 points and five rebounds.** ...

A.3 End-to-End Summary

The Toronto Raptors defeated the visiting Philadelphia 76ers 122 – 95 , at United Center on Saturday evening. The Raptors (11 – 6) came in to Friday's contest having lost four of their last six games, and have now lost five of their last seven games. **They were led by Terrence Ross, who scored a game – high 22 points on 8 – of – 11 shooting from the field and 3 – of – 5 from three – point range. Kyle Lowry followed up with 24 points, eight assists and four rebounds, in 32 minutes. Jonas Valanciunas recorded a double – double with 12 points and 11 rebounds, in 22 minutes off the bench.** The Raptors shot 55 percent from the field and 68 percent from long range , while the 76ers shot 55 percent from the field and 68 percent from behind the arc . **Robert Covington was the high – point man for the 76ers, with 20 points , including 6 – of – 9 from three – point range.** ... The Sixers will look to bounce back when they visit the New York Knicks on Monday.

A.4 Top-0.5 Sampling (GPT-50)

The Toronto Raptors defeated the Philadelphia 76ers, 122 – 95, at Air Canada Centre on Saturday. The Raptors (11 – 6) were able to prevail despite being outshot, out rebounded and out – rebounded by the Sixers (7 – 15) in the contest. ... **The Raptors were led by Terrence Ross, who posted a game – high 22 points on 8 – of – 11 shooting, including 3 – of – 5 from long range. Kyle Lowry followed up with 24 points, eight assists and four rebounds, in 32 minutes. Jonas Valanciunas chipped in 12 points and 11 rebounds, in 22 minutes off the bench.** The Raptors shot a respectable 55 percent from the field and 68 percent from long range, but were out – rebounded by the Sixers by a 52 – 40 margin. Philadelphia had five players in double figures, **led by Robert Covington, who scored 20 points on 6 – of – 9 shooting from**

A.5 Top-0.9 Sampling (GPT-90)

We show summaries from two different seeds for
the least restrictive sampling setting, $p = 0.9$.
Some details change but most of the content
supported by the data remains the same. Aggregated across the entire set, the information metrics
remain nearly identical. This less restricted model
more frequently outputs hallucinations and surrounding details not supported by the tabular data.

Sample One:

Sample Two:

Efficiency through Auto-Sizing:
Notre Dame NLP's Submission to the WNGT 2019 Efficiency Task

Kenton Murray   **Brian DuSell**   **David Chiang**
Department of Computer Science and Engineering
University of Notre Dame
{kmurray4,bdusell1,dchiang}@nd.edu

Abstract

This paper describes the Notre Dame Natural Language Processing Group's (NDNLP) submission to the WNGT 2019 shared task (Hayashi et al., 2019). We investigated the impact of auto-sizing (Murray and Chiang, 2015; Murray et al., 2019) to the Transformer network (Vaswani et al., 2017) with the goal of substantially reducing the number of parameters in the model. Our method was able to eliminate more than 25% of the model's parameters while suffering a decrease of only 1.1 BLEU.

1 Introduction

The Transformer network (Vaswani et al., 2017) is a neural sequence-to-sequence model that has achieved state-of-the-art results in machine translation. However, Transformer models tend to be very large, typically consisting of hundreds of millions of parameters. As the number of parameters directly corresponds to secondary storage requirements and memory consumption during inference, using Transformer networks may be prohibitively expensive in scenarios with constrained resources. For the 2019 Workshop on Neural Generation of Text (WNGT) Efficiency shared task (Hayashi et al., 2019), the Notre Dame Natural Language Processing (NDNLP) group looked at a method of inducing sparsity in parameters called auto-sizing in order to reduce the number of parameters in the Transformer at the cost of a relatively minimal drop in performance.

Auto-sizing, first introduced by Murray and Chiang (2015), uses group regularizers to encourage parameter sparsity. When applied over neurons, it can delete neurons in a network and shrink the total number of parameters. A nice advantage of auto-sizing is that it is independent of model architecture; although we apply it to the Transformer

network in this task, it can easily be applied to any other neural architecture.

NDNLP's submission to the 2019 WNGT Efficiency shared task uses a standard, recommended baseline Transformer network. Following Murray et al. (2019), we investigate the application of auto-sizing to various portions of the network. Differing from their work, the shared task used a significantly larger training dataset from WMT 2014 (Bojar et al., 2014), as well as the goal of reducing model size even if it impacted translation performance. Our best system was able to prune over 25% of the parameters, yet had a BLEU drop of only 1.1 points. This translates to over 25 million parameters pruned and saves almost 100 megabytes of disk space to store the model.

2 Auto-sizing

Auto-sizing is a method that encourages sparsity through use of a group regularizer. Whereas the most common applications of regularization will act over parameters individually, a group regularizer works over groupings of parameters. For instance, applying a sparsity inducing regularizer to a two-dimensional parameter tensor will encourage individual values to be driven to 0.0. A sparsity-inducing group regularizer will act over defined sub-structures, such as entire rows or columns, driving the entire groups to zero. Depending on model specifications, one row or column of a tensor in a neural network can correspond to one neuron in the model.

Following the discussion of Murray and Chiang (2015) and Murray et al. (2019), auto-sizing works by training a neural network while using a regularizer to prune units from the network, minimizing:

$$\mathcal{L} = - \sum_{f, e \text{ in data}} \log P(e \mid f; W) + \lambda R(\|W\|).$$

W are the parameters of the model and R is a reg-

Proceedings of the 3rd Workshop on Neural Generation and Translation (WNGT 2019), pages 297–301
Hong Kong, China, November 4, 2019. ©2019 Association for Computational Linguistics
www.aclweb.org/anthology/D19-56%2d

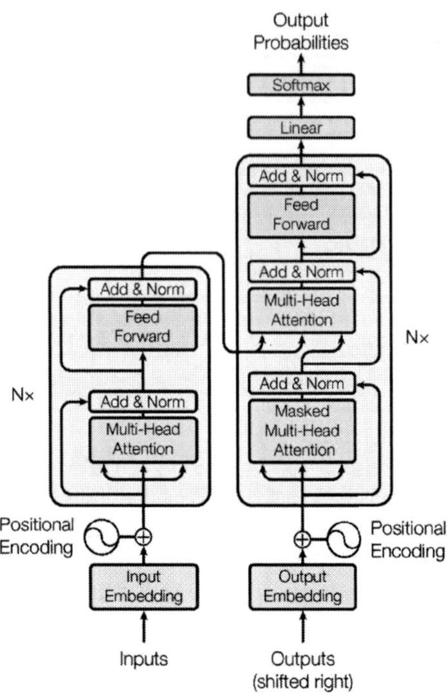

Figure 1: Architecture of the Transformer (Vaswani et al., 2017). We apply the auto-sizing method to the feed-forward (blue rectangles) and multi-head attention (orange rectangles) in all N layers of the encoder and decoder. Note that there are residual connections that can allow information and gradients to bypass any layer we are auto-sizing. Following the robustness recommendations, we instead layer norm before.

ularizer. Here, as with the previous work, we experiment with two regularizers:

$$R(W) = \sum_i \left(\sum_j W_{ij}^2 \right)^{\frac{1}{2}} \qquad (\ell_{2,1})$$

$$R(W) = \sum_i \max_j |W_{ij}| \qquad (\ell_{\infty,1})$$

The optimization is done using proximal gradient descent (Parikh and Boyd, 2014), which alternates between stochastic gradient descent steps and proximal steps:

$$W \leftarrow W - \eta \nabla \log P(e \mid f; w)$$

$$W \leftarrow \arg\min_{W'} \left(\frac{1}{2\eta} \|W - W'\|^2 + R(W') \right)$$

3 Auto-sizing the Transformer

The Transformer network (Vaswani et al., 2017) is a sequence-to-sequence model in which both the

encoder and the decoder consist of stacked self-attention layers. The multi-head attention uses two affine transformations, followed by a softmax layer. Each layer has a position-wise feed-forward neural network (FFN) with a hidden layer of rectified linear units. Both the multi-head attention and the feed-forward neural network have residual connections that allow information to bypass those layers. In addition, there are also word and position embeddings. Figure 1, taken from the original paper, shows the architecture. NDNLP's submission focuses on the N stacked encoder and decoder layers.

The Transformer has demonstrated remarkable success on a variety of datasets, but it is highly over-parameterized. For example, the baseline Transformer model has more than 98 million parameters, but the English portion of the training data in this shared task has only 116 million tokens and 816 thousand types. Early NMT models such as Sutskever et al. (2014) have most of their parameters in the embedding layers, but the transformer has a larger percentage of the model in the actual encoder and decoder layers. Though the group regularizers of auto-sizing can be applied to any parameter matrix, here we focus on the parameter matrices within the encoder and decoder layers.

We note that there has been some work recently on shrinking networks through pruning. However, these differ from auto-sizing as they frequently require an arbitrary threshold and are not included during the training process. For instance, See et al. (2016) prunes networks based off a variety of thresholds and then retrains a model. Voita et al. (2019) also look at pruning, but of attention heads specifically. They do this through a relaxation of an ℓ_0 regularizer in order to make it differentiable. This allows them to not need to use a proximal step. This method too starts with pre-trained model and then continues training. Michel et al. (2019) also look at pruning attention heads in the transformer. However, they too use thresholding, but only apply it at test time. Auto-sizing does not require a thresholding value, nor does it require a pre-trained model.

Of particular interest are the large, position-wise feed-forward networks in each encoder and decoder layer:

$$\text{FFN}(x) = W_2(\max(0, W_1 x + b_1)) + b_2.$$

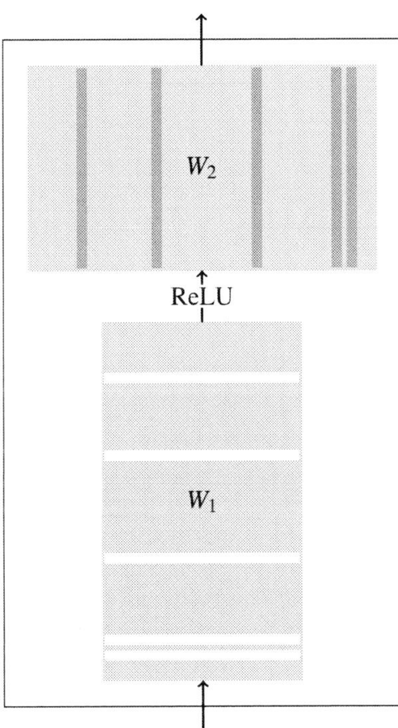

Figure 2: Auto-sizing FFN network. For a row in the parameter matrix W_1 that has been driven completely to 0.0 (shown in white), the corresponding column in W_2 (shown in blue) no longer has any impact on the model. Both the column and the row can be deleted, thereby shrinking the model.

W_1 and W_2 are two large affine transformations that take inputs from D dimensions to $4D$, then project them back to D again. These layers make use of rectified linear unit activations, which were the focus of auto-sizing in the work of Murray and Chiang (2015). No theory or intuition is given as to why this value of $4D$ should be used.

Following (Murray et al., 2019), we apply the auto-sizing method to the Transformer network, focusing on the two largest components, the feed-forward layers and the multi-head attentions (blue and orange rectangles in Figure 1). Remember that since there are residual connections allowing information to bypass the layers we are auto-sizing, information can still flow through the network even if the regularizer drives all the neurons in a layer to zero – effectively pruning out an entire layer.

4 Experiments

All of our models are trained using the fairseq implementation of the Transformer (Gehring et al., 2017).[1] For the regularizers used in auto-sizing, we make use of an open-source, proximal gradient toolkit implemented in PyTorch[2] (Murray et al., 2019). For each mini-batch update, the stochastic gradient descent step is handled with a standard PyTorch forward-backward call. Then the proximal step is applied to parameter matrices.

4.1 Settings

We used the originally proposed transformer architecture – with six encoder and six decoder layers. Our model dimension was 512 and we used 8 attention heads. The feed-forward network sub-components were of size 2048. All of our systems were run using subword units (BPE) with 32,000 merge operations on concatenated source and target training data (Sennrich and Haddow, 2016). We clip norms at 0.1, use label smoothed cross-entropy with value 0.1, and an early stopping criterion when the learning rate is smaller than 10^{-5}. We used the Adam optimizer (Kingma and Ba, 2015), a learning rate of 10^{-4}, and dropout of 0.1. Following recommendations in the fairseq and tensor2tensor (Vaswani et al., 2018) code bases, we apply layer normalization before a sub-component as opposed to after. At test time, we decoded using a beam of 5 with length normalization (Boulanger-Lewandowski et al., 2013) and evaluate using case-sensitive, tokenized BLEU (Papineni et al., 2002).

For the auto-sizing experiments, we looked at both $\ell_{2,1}$ and $\ell_{\infty,1}$ regularizers. We experimented over a range of regularizer coefficient strengths, λ, that control how large the proximal gradient step will be. Similar to Murray and Chiang (2015), but differing from Alvarez and Salzmann (2016), we use one value of λ for all parameter matrices in the network. We note that different regularization coefficient values are suited for different types or regularizers. Additionally, all of our experiments use the same batch size, which is also related to λ.

4.2 Auto-sizing sub-components

We applied auto-sizing to the sub-components of the encoder and decoder layers, without touching the word or positional embeddings. Recall from

---

[1] https://github.com/pytorch/fairseq
[2] https://github.com/KentonMurray/ProxGradPytorch

System	Disk Size	Number of Parameters	newstest2014	newstest2015
Baseline	375M	98.2M	25.3	27.9
All $\ell_{2,1} = 0.1$	345M	90.2M	21.6	24.1
Encoder $\ell_{2,1} = 0.1$	341M	89.4M	23.2	25.5
Encoder $\ell_{2,1} = 1.0$	327M	85.7M	22.1	24.5
FFN $\ell_{2,1} = 0.1$	326M	85.2M	24.1	26.4
FFN $\ell_{2,1} = 1.0$	279M	73.1M	24.0	26.8
FFN $\ell_{2,1} = 10.0$	279M	73.1M	23.9	26.5
FFN $\ell_{\infty,1} = 100.0$	327M	73.1M	23.8	26.0

Table 1: Comparison of BLEU scores and model sizes on newstest2014 and newstest2015. Applying auto-sizing to the feed-forward neural network sub-components of the transformer resulted in the most amount of pruning while still maintaining good BLEU scores.

Figure 1, that each layer has multi-head attention and feed-forward network sub-components. In turn, each multi-head attention sub-component is comprised of two parameter matrices. Similarly, each feed-forward network has two parameter matrices, W_1 and W_2. We looked at three main experimental configurations:

- All: Auto-sizing is applied to every multi-head attention and feed-forward network sub-component in every layer of the encoder and decoder.

- Encoder: As with All, auto-sizing is applied to both multi-head attention and feed-forward network sub-components, but only in the encoder layers. The decoder remains the same.

- FFN: Auto-sizing applied only to the feed-forward network sub-components W_1 and W_2, but not to the multi-head portions. This too is applied to both the encoder and decoder.

4.3 Results

Our results are presented in Table 1. The baseline system has 98.2 million parameters and a BLEU score of 29.7. It takes up 375 megabytes on disk. Our systems that applied auto-sizing only to the feed-forward network sub-components of the transformer network maintained the best BLEU scores while also pruning out the most parameters of the model. Overall, our best system used $\ell_{2,1} = 1.0$ regularization for auto-sizing and left 73.1 million parameters remaining. On disk, the model takes 279 megabytes to store – roughly 100 megabytes less than the baseline. The performance drop compared to the baseline is 1.1 BLEU points, but the model is over 25% smaller.

Applying auto-sizing to the multi-head attention and feed-forward network sub-components of *only* the encoder also pruned a substantial amount of parameters. Though this too resulted in a smaller model on disk, the BLEU scores were worse than auto-sizing just the feed-forward sub-components. Auto-sizing the multi-head attention and feed-forward network sub-components of both the encoder *and* decoder actually resulted in a larger model than the encoder only, but with a lower BLEU score. Overall, our results suggest that the attention portion of the transformer network is more important for model performance than the feed-forward networks in each layer.

5 Conclusion

In this paper, we have investigated the impact of using auto-sizing on the transformer network of the 2019 WNGT efficiency task. We were able to delete more than 25% of the parameters in the model while only suffering a modest BLEU drop. In particular, focusing on the parameter matrices of the feed-forward networks in every layer of the encoder and decoder yielded the smallest models that still performed well.

A nice aspect of our proposed method is that the proximal gradient step of auto-sizing can be applied to a wide variety of parameter matrices. Whereas for the transformer, the largest impact was on feed-forward networks within a layer, should a new architecture emerge in the future, auto-sizing can be easily adapted to the trainable parameters.

Overall, NDNLP's submission has shown that auto-sizing is a flexible framework for pruning parameters in a large NMT system. With an aggressive regularization scheme, large portions of the model can be deleted with only a modest impact on BLEU scores. This in turn yields a much smaller model on disk and at run-time.

Acknowledgements

This research was supported in part by University of Southern California, subcontract 67108176 under DARPA contract HR0011-15-C-0115.

References

Jose M Alvarez and Mathieu Salzmann. 2016. Learning the number of neurons in deep networks. In *Advances in Neural Information Processing Systems*, pages 2270–2278.

Ondrej Bojar, Christian Buck, Christian Federmann, Barry Haddow, Philipp Koehn, Johannes Leveling, Christof Monz, Pavel Pecina, Matt Post, Herve Saint-Amand, et al. 2014. Findings of the 2014 workshop on statistical machine translation. In *Proceedings of the ninth workshop on statistical machine translation*, pages 12–58.

Nicolas Boulanger-Lewandowski, Yoshua Bengio, and Pascal Vincent. 2013. Audio chord recognition with recurrent neural networks. In *Proc. International Society for Music Information Retrieval*, pages 335–340.

Jonas Gehring, Michael Auli, David Grangier, Denis Yarats, and Yann N. Dauphin. 2017. Convolutional Sequence to Sequence Learning. In *Proc. ICML*.

Hiroaki Hayashi, Yusuke Oda, Alexandra Birch, Ioannis Constas, Andrew Finch, Minh-Thang Luong, Graham Neubig, and Katsuhito Sudoh. 2019. Findings of the third workshop on neural generation and translation. In *Proceedings of the Third Workshop on Neural Generation and Translation*.

Diederik P. Kingma and Jimmy Lei Ba. 2015. Adam: A method for stochastic optimization. In *Proc. ICLR*.

Paul Michel, Omer Levy, and Graham Neubig. 2019. Are sixteen heads really better than one? *Advances in Neural Information Processing Systems*.

Kenton Murray and David Chiang. 2015. Auto-sizing neural networks: With applications to n-gram language models. In *Proc. EMNLP*.

Kenton Murray, Jeffery Kinnison, Toan Q. Nguyen, Walter Scheirer, and David Chiang. 2019. Auto-sizing the transformer network: Improving speed, efficiency, and performance for low-resource machine translation. In *Proceedings of the Third Workshop on Neural Generation and Translation*.

Kishore Papineni, Salim Roukos, Todd Ward, and Wei-Jing Zhu. 2002. BLEU: a method for automatic evaluation of machine translation. In *Proc. ACL*, pages 311–318.

Neal Parikh and Stephen Boyd. 2014. Proximal algorithms. *Foundations and Trends in Optimization*, 1(3):123–231.

Abigail See, Minh-Thang Luong, and Christopher D Manning. 2016. Compression of neural machine translation models via pruning. In *Proceedings of The 20th SIGNLL Conference on Computational Natural Language Learning*, pages 291–301.

Rico Sennrich and Barry Haddow. 2016. Linguistic input features improve neural machine translation. In *Proc. First Conference on Machine Translation: Volume 1, Research Papers*, volume 1, pages 83–91.

Ilya Sutskever, Oriol Vinyals, and Quoc V Le. 2014. Sequence to sequence learning with neural networks. In *Advances in Neural Information Processing Systems*, pages 3104–3112.

Ashish Vaswani, Samy Bengio, Eugene Brevdo, Francois Chollet, Aidan N. Gomez, Stephan Gouws, Llion Jones, Łukasz Kaiser, Nal Kalchbrenner, Niki Parmar, Ryan Sepassi, Noam Shazeer, and Jakob Uszkoreit. 2018. Tensor2tensor for neural machine translation. *CoRR*, abs/1803.07416.

Ashish Vaswani, Noam Shazeer, Niki Parmar, Jakob Uszkoreit, Llion Jones, Aidan N. Gomez, Łukasz Kaiser, and Illia Polosukhin. 2017. Attention is all you need. In *Advances in Neural Information Processing Systems*, pages 5998–6008.

Elena Voita, David Talbot, Fedor Moiseev, Rico Sennrich, and Ivan Titov. 2019. Analyzing multi-head self-attention: Specialized heads do the heavy lifting, the rest can be pruned. In *Proceedings of the 57th Annual Meeting of the Association for Computational Linguistics*, pages 5797–5808, Florence, Italy. Association for Computational Linguistics.

Author Index

Association for Computational Linguistics
209 N. Eighth Street
Stroudsburg, Pennsylvania 18360

ISBN 978-1-7138-0072-9